Europe in figures

Eurostat yearbook 2009

(with CD-ROM)

Europe Direct is a service to help you find answers
to your questions about the European Union

Freephone number (*):

00 800 6 7 8 9 10 11

(*) Certain mobile telephone operators do not allow access
to 00 800 numbers or these calls may be billed.

More information on the European Union is available on the Internet (http://europa.eu).

Luxembourg: Office for Official Publications of the European Communities, 2009

ISBN 978-92-79-11625-4
ISSN 1681-4789
DOI 10.2785/29733
Cat. No. KS-CD-09-001-EN-C

Theme: General and regional statistics
Collection: Statistical books

Printed in Belgium

Acknowledgements

The editor-in-chief and the editorial team of the Eurostat yearbook would like to thank all those who were involved in its preparation. The yearbook could only be published thanks to the support of the following colleagues:

Eurostat, the Statistical Office of the European Communities

Directorate C: National and European accounts

C1 National accounts – methodology and analysis: Paul Konijn, Lars Svennebye

C2 National accounts – production: Jukka Jalava, Andreas Krüger, Jenny Runesson

C3 Public finance: Lena Frej-Ohlsson

C4 Balance of payments: Franca Faes-Cannito, Merja Hult, Mushtaq Hussain, Maria Isabel Lazaro, Luca Pappalardo

C5 Validation of public accounts: Peter Parlasca, Gilles Thouvenin, John Verrinder, Monika Wozowczyk

Directorate D: Economic and regional statistics

D1 Key indicators for European policies: Graham Lock, Gian Luigi Mazzi, Rosa Ruggeri Cannata, Andrea Scheller, Vincent Tronet

D2 Regional indicators and geographical information: Teodóra Brandmüller, Berthold Feldmann, Pedro Jorge Martins Ferreira, Baudouin Quennery, Åsa Önnerfors

D3 Short-term statistics: Digna Amil, Anastassios Giannoplidis, Liselott Öhman

D4 Price statistics: Tatiana Mrlianova, Christine Wirtz

Directorate E: Agriculture and environment statistics; statistical cooperation

E1 Farms, agro-environment and rural development: Catherine Coyette, Johan Selenius

E2 Agricultural and fisheries statistics: Steffie Bos, Céline Ollier, Ole Olsen, Iulia Paula Pop, Franco Zampogna

E3 Environmental statistics and accounts: Julio Cabeça, Jürgen Förster, Julie Hass, Christian Heidorn, Jean Klein, Wilhelmus Kloek, Daniel Rase, Ute Roewer, Marilise Wolf-Crowther

Directorate F: Social statistics and information society

F1 Demographic and migration statistics: **Anthony Albertinelli, Veronica Corsini, Piotr Juchno, Anne Herm, Gregor Kyi, Rosemarie Olsson, Giampaolo Lanzieri**

F2 Labour market statistics: **Luis Biedma, Simone Casali, Didier Dupré, Arturo de la Fuente Nuño, Sabine Gagel, Ingo Kuhnert, Fabrice Romans**

F3 Living conditions and social protection statistics: **Teresa Bento, Peter Borg, Antonella Puglia, Laura Wahrig, Pascal Wolff**

F4 Education, science and culture statistics: **Bernard Felix, Sylvain Jouhette, Agnieszka Litwińska, Lene Mejer, Tomas Meri, Reni Petkova, Sergiu Pârvan, Fernando Reis, Veijo Ritola, Tomas Uhlar, Håkan Wilen**

F5 Health and food safety statistics: **Lucian Agafiţei, Hartmut Buchow, Bart De Norre, Elodie Cayotte**

F6 Information society and tourism statistics: **Christophe Demunter, Giuseppe di Giacomo, Heidi Seybert, Ulrich Spörel, Albrecht Wirthmann**

Directorate G: Business statistics

G1 Structural business statistics: **Aleksandra Stawińska, Brian Williams**

G2 International trade statistics – methodology and classifications: **Aleš Čapek**

G3 International trade statistics – production: **Gilberto Gambini**

G4 Energy statistics: **Antigone Gikas**

G5 Transport statistics: **Giuliano Amerini, Anna Białas-Motyl, Luis Antonio De La Fuente, Yves Mahieu, Jonas Noreland, Simo Pasi, Hans Strelow**

European Free Trade Association (EFTA)

Richard Ragnarson

Directorate-General for Translation of the European Commission

Office for official publications of the European Communities

Contents

Contents

The Eurostat yearbook

Europe in figures – Eurostat yearbook 2009 provides users of official statistics with an overview of the wealth of information that is available on Eurostat's website and within its online databases. It belongs to a set of general compendium publications and, of these, it provides the most extensive set of analyses and detailed data. Europe in figures has been conceived as a publication that provides a balanced set of indicators, with a broad cross-section of information.

EUROSTAT DATA CODES – EASY ON-LINE ACCESS TO THE FRESHEST DATA

Eurostat data codes (such as 'tps00001' and 'nama_gdp_c') (*) allow the reader to easily access the most recent data on the Eurostat website. In this yearbook they are given below the tables and graphs (figures) in the source field whenever Eurostat data is presented.

Note that the data on the website is frequently updated and may also be more detailed or be available in a variety of different measurement units. Please note also that this description presents the situation in February 2009 and that the browsing tools described underneath are evolving. The latest information concerning the data code can be found on the Eurostat website at http://epp.eurostat.ec.europa.eu/portal/page/portal/publications/datacode.

In the PDF version of this yearbook the reader is led directly to the relevant table when clicking on a hyper-link formed by the data code in the source of each table or figure. The browsing tool for a collection of main tables is called TGM (Tables, Graphs and Maps), where data can be visualised with graphs and maps in addition to a standard, tabular presentation. For the other type of code, complete data sets can be viewed using a browsing tool called the Data Explorer.

Readers of the paper version can access the tables either:

- directly with the default browsing tool (TGM or Data Explorer depending on the type (*) of data code) by using the link, http://ec.europa.eu/eurostat/product?code=<data_code>&mode=view (where <data_code> is to be replaced by the data code in question), or;
- by choosing a browsing tool (TGM, Data Explorer, EVA, EVA Java) and then selecting which tools to use to filter and download information in various formats (HTML, TAB, TXT, XML, DFT and TSV)) by using the link, http://ec.europa.eu/eurostat/product?code=<data_code> (where <data_code> is to be replaced by the data code in question).

(*) There are two types of data codes:

Main tables have 8-character data codes which consist of 3 or 5 letters – the first of which is 't' – followed by 5 or 3 digits, e.g. 'tps00001' and 'tsdph220'.

Other data sets are stored as complete databases and have data codes that use an underscore '_' within the syntax of the code, e.g. 'nama_gdp_c' and 'proj_08c2150p'.

Structure of the publication

Europe in figures is divided into an introduction, 16 main chapters and a set of annexes. The main chapters contain data and/or background information relating to particular topics, starting with a spotlight chapter on creativity and innovation – the theme of the European year 2009.

Each subchapter starts with an introduction containing background information and policy relevance, followed by some details regarding definitions and data availability and then a commentary on the main findings. The main focus of each subchapter is a set of tables and graphs that have been selected to show the wide variety of data available for that particular topic; often these include information on how important benchmark indicators have developed during recent years within the EU, its Member States and the euro area. Users will find a great deal more information when consulting the Eurostat website, which contains subject-specific publications and online databases. The annexes at the end of the publication contain details of classifications, a list of statistical symbols, abbreviations and acronyms, and a subject index.

CD-ROM and web files on the Eurostat website

The paper version of the yearbook is accompanied by a CD-ROM which contains the full yearbook content in PDF format, as well as all tables and graphs in Excel spreadsheet format. In addition, the Eurostat website dedicates a specific section to the yearbook, which contains the PDF version of the publication as well as all tables and graphs in Excel format. The PDF version of the publication allows direct access to all databases used in the production of tables and graphs (http://epp.eurostat.ec.europa.eu/portal/page/portal/publications/eurostat_yearbook).

Data extraction, coverage and presentation

The statistical data presented in the yearbook were extracted during September 2008 and represent data availability at that time. The accompanying text was drafted during September and October 2008.

In time-series, the data are generally presented for the latest 11 years for which information is available. Longer time-series will usually be available when consulting Eurostat's online databases. Please note that the Eurostat website is constantly updated, therefore new data becomes available during the production of this publication. Often, due to its complex nature, the data production or collection might require longer periods between the reference period of the data and the data availability. Please consult the Eurostat website for more information on the production calendar (normally varying by data set).

The tables and graphs generally show all of the country information that has been collected for each particular indicator. This publication generally presents information for the 27 Member States of the EU (EU-27), the euro area (based on 15 members), as well as the individual Member States. The EU-27 and euro area aggregates are only provided when information for all of the countries is available, or if an estimate has been made for missing information. Any partial totals that are created are systematically footnoted with respect to the missing components of the geographical aggregate in question.

Time-series for geographical aggregates are based on a consistent set of countries for the whole of the time period shown (unless otherwise indicated). In other words, although the EU has only had 25 Member States since the start of 2004 and 27 Member States since the start of 2007, the time-series for EU-27 refer to a sum or an average for all 27 countries for the whole of the period presented, as if all 27 Member States had been part of the EU in earlier periods. In a similar vein, the data for the euro area are consistently presented for all 15 members, despite the later accessions of Greece, Slovenia, Cyprus and Malta to the euro area, or the future (at time of writing) euro area enlargement (Slovakia joins the euro area on 1 January 2009). As such, unless otherwise stated, the data for the euro area covers the 15 Member States that share the euro as a common currency (Belgium, Germany, Greece, Spain, France, Ireland, Italy, Cyprus, Luxembourg, Malta, the Netherlands, Austria, Portugal, Slovenia and Finland) for each reference year.

The order of the EU Member States used in the Eurostat yearbook generally follows their order of protocol; in other words, the alphabetical order of the countries' names in their respective native languages; in most graphs the data are ranked according to the values of a particular indicator.

When available, information is also presented for the (at time of writing) candidate countries of Croatia, the former Yugoslav Republic of Macedonia and Turkey, for EFTA countries, as well as for Japan and the United States. In the event that any of these non-member countries did not provide data, then these have been excluded from the tables and graphs in an attempt to save space; however, the full set of 27 Member States is maintained in tables, with footnotes being added in graphs for those countries for which information is missing. In the event that a reference year is not available for a particular country, then efforts have been made to fill tables and graphs with previous reference years (again these exceptions are footnoted); generally, an effort has been made to go back two years to fill any gaps.

Eurostat online databases contain a large amount of meta-data that provides information on the status of particular values or series. In order to improve readability, the majority of this meta-data has been omitted when constructing the tables and graphs. Nevertheless, individual data cells that are forecasts, provisional or estimates are shown in an italic font – note that these values are likely to change in the future. Equally, when important breaks in series are present, these have been footnoted appropriately. A colon (:) is used to represent data that is not available, either because the value was not provided by the statistical authority or because the value is confidential. In graphs, missing information is footnoted as being not available. The dash (-) is used to indicate values that are not relevant or not applicable in tables.

Information on EU policies and other activities

The yearbook aims at providing statistical information on the European Union, its Member States and some other countries. It also provides information on related EU policies and activities. Such information does not necessarily reflect the official views of Eurostat or the European Commission. Further information about such policies and activities may be found on the website of the European Commission at http://ec.europa.eu.

Statistical symbols

Statistical data are often accompanied by additional information in the form of statistical symbols (also called 'flags') to indicate missing information or some other meta-data. In this yearbook, the use of statistical symbols has been restricted to a minimum. The following symbols are included where necessary:

Italic Value is a forecast, provisional or an estimate and is therefore likely to change

: Not available, confidential or unreliable value

– Not applicable or zero by default

0 Less than half the final digit shown and greater than real zero

Breaks in series are indicated in the footnotes provided with each table and graph.

In the case of the EU Member States, even when data are not available, all countries have been included in tables (use has been made of the colon (:) to indicate that data are not available), while in graphs footnotes are used to indicate those countries for which data are not available. For non-member countries outside of the EU, when data are not available for a particular indicator the country has been removed from the table or graph in question.

Eurostat – the Statistical Office of the European Communities

Eurostat is the Statistical Office of the European Communities, situated in Luxembourg. Its task is to provide the European Union (EU) with statistics at a European level that enable comparisons between countries and regions. Eurostat's mission is 'to provide the European Union with a high-quality statistical information service'. To meet this challenge, Eurostat aims:

- to implement a set of standards, methods and organisational structures which allow comparable, reliable and relevant statistics to be produced throughout the Community, in line with the principles of the European statistics code of practice;
- to provide the European institutions and the governments of the Member States with the information needed to implement, monitor and evaluate Community policies;
- to disseminate statistics to the European public and enterprises and to all economic and social agents involved in decision-making, and;
- to facilitate the improvement of the statistical systems of the Member States and support developing countries, as well as the countries moving towards a market economy.

As one of the Directorate-Generals of the European Commission, Eurostat is headed by a Director-General. Under him are seven Directors responsible for different areas of activity (Directorates as of November 2008):

- A. Resources;
- B. Statistical methods and tools; dissemination;
- C. National and European accounts;
- D. Economic and regional statistics;
- E. Agriculture and environment statistics; statistical cooperation;
- F. Social statistics and information society;
- G. Business statistics.

In 2008, Eurostat had around 890 posts; of these some 75 % were civil servants, 8 % were seconded national experts, and 17 % had other types of contract. Eurostat's executed budget was around EUR 66 million in 2008 (excluding costs of statutory staff and administrative expenses) of which EUR 48 million were budgeted for the implementation of the statistical programme. In addition, a budget of EUR 18 million was sub-delegated to Eurostat by other Directorates-General.

Since the early days of the European Communities, there was a realisation that the planning and implementation of Community policies must be based on reliable and comparable statistics. As a result, the European statistical system (ESS) was built-up gradually to provide comparable statistics at an EU level. For this purpose, Eurostat does not work alone. The ESS comprises Eurostat and the statistical offices, ministries, agencies and central banks that collect official statistics in the EU Member States, Iceland, Liechtenstein, Norway and Switzerland (you can find the contact details and Internet addresses of all members of the ESS by choosing the link to the 'European Statistical System (ESS)' from the list of activities presented on the right-hand menu of the Eurostat homepage and then selecting the link to 'National Statistical Institutes').

The ESS functions as a network in which Eurostat's role is to lead the way in the harmonisation of statistics in close co-operation with the national statistical authorities. At the heart of the ESS is the Statistical Programme Committee (SPC), which brings together the heads of Member States' national statistical offices and is chaired by Eurostat. The SPC discusses joint actions and programmes to be carried out to meet EU information requirements. It agrees a five-year programme, which is implemented by the national authorities and monitored by Eurostat.

Information for a modern society – impartiality and objectivity

To actively participate in a democratic Europe, public administrations, researchers, trade unions, businesses and political parties, among others, need high-quality, impartial, reliable and comparable statistical data. These actors need to be able to access data without exclusion: in other words, no key information should be withheld from particular citizens, enterprises or public bodies. Rather, each of these should have equal access to the data available. Eurostat and its partners in the ESS provide equal opportunities to access a wide range of comprehensive information on social, economic and environmental developments in Europe, through providing free access to data on the Eurostat website.

Today's information society is characterised by the rapid transfer and sheer scale of data flows. While access to and the transfer of information has grown exponentially, the reliability of information cannot always be guaranteed. Access to reliable and high-quality statistics and Eurostat's obligation for trustworthiness is enshrined in law, as Article 285(2) of the EC Treaty says: 'The production of Community statistics shall conform to impartiality, reliability, objectivity, scientific independence, cost-effectiveness and statistical confidentiality; it shall not entail excessive burdens on economic operators'. These are principles upon which Eurostat's day-to-day work is based.

A practical guide to accessing European statistics

It is easier for people to understand each other if they know about each other's conditions of life and work, and they have information on trends that are developing within society as a whole. Comparisons, however, require comparable statistics that, in turn, demand the use of a common 'statistical language'. This common language has to embrace concepts, methods and definitions, as well as technical standards and infrastructures, often referred to by statisticians as harmonisation. This is Eurostat's raison d'être – and sums up what the ESS is all about.

The data that are collected, harmonised and reported upon by Eurostat have been agreed through a well-defined political process at the European level in which the Member States are deeply involved. Most surveys and data collection exercises are based on European regulations or directives that are legally binding.

The simplest way of accessing Eurostat's broad range of statistical information is through the Eurostat website (http://ec.europa.eu).

Eurostat provides users with free access to its Internet databases and all of its publications in PDF format. The website is updated twice daily and provides direct access to the latest and most comprehensive statistical information available on the EU, its Member States, its candidate countries and EFTA countries. The information published on the website is available in German, English and French. Eurostat is continuously working on improvements to the website in terms of functionality and design.

For full access to all of the services available through the website, it is recommended that users should take a few moments to register from the homepage. Registration is free of charge and allows access to:

- tailor-made e-mail alerts informing you of new publications as soon as they are online;
- access enhanced functionalities of the databases (save queries and make bulk downloads).

The information on the website is structured according to a set of 'themes', which may be accessed from the menu bar of the homepage, providing access to:

- general and regional statistics;
- economy and finance;
- population and social conditions;
- industry, trade and services;
- agriculture and fisheries;
- external trade;
- transport;
- environment and energy;
- science and technology.

Within each of these themes the user is initially presented with the possibility of accessing information relating to tables, data(bases), methodology or publications, by means of a series of tabbed pages. Those users who are not able to limit their search by statistical theme can enter the website through a series of tabs on the homepage which provide access to the full range of tables, data, methodology and publications.

Tables, graphs and maps (TGM)

The most important indicators may be found in the form of tables, graphs and maps. They can be accessed through the Eurostat database or from the homepage for each of the nine statistical themes detailed above. Main tables are generally presented for a single indicator, with European aggregates and data for the Member States on the y-axis and time on the x-axis (they can be accessed by clicking on this icon, ▦). The data are selected from key EU policy indicators, including short-term economic data, long-term indicators, structural indicators, and sustainable development indicators. The new tables, graphs and maps interface (TGM)

allows, in addition to tables, for customisable graphs and maps of the same indicators (the interface can be accessed by clicking on this icon, ▦).

Some of the most important indicators that are produced in this format are listed below. Chapter 16 'Linking statistics to European policies' gives more information on some of these indicators.

Euro-Indicators – this is a collection of the freshest, monthly and quarterly data, used to evaluate the economic situation within the euro area and the EU. Euro-Indicators are updated daily and the publication of key figures is announced as part of Eurostat's release calendar [1] and is available on the Eurostat website at: http://ec.europa.eu/eurostat/euroindicators.

Structural indicators – these are used to assess the longer-term progress being made within the EU in the domains of employment, innovation and research, economic reform, social cohesion, and the environment, as well as the general economic background; they are most relevant for political debate with respect to the revised Lisbon objectives.

Sustainable development indicators – a sustainable development strategy was adopted by the European Council in Gothenburg in June 2001, and renewed in June 2006; it aims to reconcile economic development, social cohesion and protection of the environment. Monitoring progress towards this goal is an essential part of the strategy, while a parallel objective is to inform the general public about progress in attaining the commonly agreed objectives of sustainable development.

(1) http://epp.eurostat.ec.europa.eu/portal/pls/portal/ddis.release_calendar.xml.

The business cycle clock – the business cycle clock (BCC) is a new interactive IT tool that shows how many economic indicators evolve in close proximity to one another. Moving as a 'cloud' of indicators, some have a clear lead in development – e.g. economic sentiment – whereas others lag behind. These and other dynamic patterns can be visually observed, and can help the user to understand today's and yesterday's economics. The BCC tool can be consulted via the following link: http://epp.eurostat.ec.europa.eu/cache/BCC2.

Country profiles interface – this offers the possibility to visualise major statistical indicators, of different countries and/or EU aggregates, in a user-friendly map-based presentation (regional data should be available after the summer of 2009). The interface can be accessed via the following link: http://epp.eurostat.ec.europa.eu/cache/BCC2.

Data

More detailed statistics and larger volumes of data can be downloaded from databases. The easiest way to access these is to use the new data explorer (🖳) that provides an intuitive way to select and organise data. Alternatively, users can click on the following icon (🖳) to select information of interest through a number of selection screens for each dimension of the data set; the data can be extracted in a variety of formats (text files, HTML, Excel, etc.). Databases can be accessed via the following link on the Eurostat homepage: http://epp.eurostat.ec.europa.eu/portal/page/portal/statistics/search_database.

Reference metadata

From December 2008 onwards, the ESMS (Euro SDMX Metadata Structure) is progressively being used to replace the SDDS format. This new format is based on a Statistical Data and Metadata eXchange initiative (SDMX), carried out by seven international organisations at a worldwide level, which was adopted in January 2009. The ESMS uses a subset of 21 cross domain concepts (plus sub-concepts) and will become the new standard for reference metadata in the European Statistical System. It also puts more emphasis on quality-related information (containing concepts such as accuracy, comparability, coherence and timeliness).

Reference Metadata may be accessed either from the heading 'Reference Metadata' or directly from the data navigation tree, where an icon (🖽) is used to signify the availability of additional metadata information.

For more information on SDMX, please refer to: http://www.sdmx.org/.

Publications

Eurostat produces a variety of publications, both for non-experts and specialists. All of these are available on the Eurostat website in PDF format, free of charge. As with the data, the publications are organised under Eurostat's nine statistical themes. There are a variety of different types of publication, ranging from news and data releases to more in-depth analyses in the form of the statistical books collection. Among the most interesting collections are:

* **News releases** – rapid updates providing information about the release of new key data on the EU;
* **Statistics in focus and Data in focus** – these are relatively short publications which present up-to-date summaries of the main results of statistical surveys, studies and analyses;
* **Pocketbooks** – these handy, pocket-sized publications present main indicators for a particular theme in a concise format;
* **Statistical books** – a collection of comprehensive studies; these publications are usually quite lengthy and provide analyses, tables and graphs for one or more statistical domains;
* **Methodologies and working papers** – intended for specialists who want to consult methodologies, nomenclatures, or specific studies for a particular data set.

All PDF versions of these products are available for consultation and download via the Eurostat website. Alternatively, some Eurostat publications are also printed or made available on CD-ROM or DVD; these can be ordered from the website of the EU bookshop (http://bookshop.europa.eu) or through sales agents in the Member States. The bookshop is managed by the Office for Official Publications of the European Communities (http://publications.europa.eu).

Support for users

Eurostat and the other members of the European statistical system, have set-up a system of user support centres for Internet users. These exist in 22 of the Member States, Croatia, Norway, Switzerland and Turkey. In order to offer the best possible and personalised support, requests should, whenever possible, be addressed to the relevant national support centre. The mission of each centre is to provide additional help and guidance to users who are having difficulty in finding the statistical data they require. More information (requires users to be logged in) is available on the Eurostat website at: https://ec.europa.eu/eurostat/xtnetassist/login.htm.

Eurostat's service for journalists

Statistics make news and they are essential to many stories, features and in-depth analyses. Printed media, as well as radio and TV, use Eurostat data intensively. Eurostat's press office puts out user-friendly news releases on a key selection of data covering the EU, the euro area, the Member States and their partners. All Eurostat news releases are available free of charge on the Eurostat website at 11 a.m. (C.E.T.) on the day they are released. Just under 200 press releases were published in the last year, of which three quarters were based on monthly or quarterly Euro-Indicators. Other releases covered major international events and important Eurostat publications.

Eurostat's media support centre helps professional journalists find data on all kinds of topics. Journalists can contact media support for further information on news releases and other data (tel. (352) 4301-33408; e-mail: Eurostat-mediasupport@ec.europa.eu).

ABSTRACT

Europe in figures – Eurostat yearbook 2009 – presents a comprehensive selection of statistical data on Europe. The yearbook may be viewed as an introduction to European statistics and provides guidance to the vast range of data freely available from the Eurostat website at http://ec.europa.eu/eurostat.

Most data cover the period 1997-2007 for the European Union and some indicators are provided for other countries such as candidate countries to the European Union, members of EFTA, Japan or the United States (subject to availability). With just over 500 statistical tables, graphs and maps, the yearbook treats the following areas: the economy, population, education, health, living conditions and welfare, the labour market, industry and services, agriculture, forestry and fisheries, external trade, transport, the environment, energy, science and technology and Europe's regions. This edition's spotlight chapter covers creativity and innovation – the theme of the European year 2009.

Editor-in-chief

Gunter Schäfer

Eurostat, Head of Dissemination unit

Editors

Diana Ivan, Annika Johansson Augier, Jukka Piirto, Ulrich Wieland

Eurostat, Dissemination unit

Contact details

Eurostat,

Statistical Office of the European Communities,

Bâtiment Joseph Bech,

5, rue Alphonse Weicker

2721 Luxembourg

E-mail: estat-user-support@ec.europa.eu

Production, desktop publishing

Informa sàrl

Giovanni Albertone, Simon Allen, Edward Cook, Sabine Joham Allen, Séverine Gautron, Andrew Redpath

For more information please consult

Internet: http://ec.europa.eu/eurostat

Data extracted

September 2008

Foreword

Official statistics play a fundamental role in today's society. Public administrations, policy-makers, economic operators, markets, researchers and citizens rely on high quality statistics to describe developments in the economic, social, environmental and cultural spheres as accurately as possible. Statistical authorities respond to the needs of these users who require easy and timely access to such high quality information.

Impartial and objective statistical information is essential in order to enable well informed decisions based on an accurate and relevant picture of society. Statistical information underpins transparency and openness of policy decisions; official statistics therefore are a public good and a basis for the smooth functioning of democracy.

At a European level, statistics are increasingly important for the definition, implementation, monitoring and evaluation of policies. Europe needs a plethora of statistical data which meet the highest possible standards in terms of quality. For example, reliable statistics are needed to assess macro-economic developments such as inflation, employment, government finances, economic growth and the business cycle in general: in order to facilitate economic policy coordination among Member States, which is especially important in the current economic situation; to keep Europe on the path to sustainable development; and finally, to reinforce a commitment to solidarity and social justice. European statistics thus constitute an essential information tool that may help monitor European Union strategic objectives, as well as sustaining underlying policies and supporting instruments.

Eurostat, the Statistical Office of the European Communities, ensures the development, production and dissemination of harmonised statistics at European level. Eurostat gets most of its data from the national statistical authorities in the Member States. It then processes, analyses and publishes that data at a European level, following common statistical concepts, methods and standards. Eurostat also supports and encourages the development of similar statistical systems within countries neighbouring the European Union, driving thereby a process of statistical harmonisation.

This year, 2009, is the European year of Creativity and Innovation; therefore, the spotlight (opening) chapter of this publication reflects this by focusing on statistics relevant to these topics. I hope this publication will encourage you to use Eurostat's data for your information needs and daily work. Please consult our website at http://ec.europa.eu/eurostat which offers you free access to nearly all Eurostat data and publications.

Walter Radermacher

Director-General, Eurostat

Science, technology, innovation and entrepreneurship: 2009, the year of creativity and innovation

Each year a subject is chosen to be the focus of attention for a campaign within the European Union: the year 2009 is the European Year of Creativity and Innovation. The aim for 2009 is to promote creativity and capacity for innovation as key competences for all, to help meet challenges by raising public awareness, disseminate information about good practices, stimulate education and research, creativity and innovation, and promote policy debate and change. By combining actions at Community, national, regional and local levels, it is hoped that this can 'generate synergies and help to focus policy debate on specific issues'.

The European Year of Innovation and Creativity is proposed as a cross-cutting initiative covering not only education and culture, but also other policy domains such as enterprise, media, research, social and regional policy and rural development. As such, the activities of the Year should focus on creating an environment favourable to creativity and innovation and become a strong impetus for long-term policy priorities. All forms of innovation including social and entrepreneurial innovation should be taken into account. Artistic creation and new approaches in culture should also receive due attention, as important means of communication between people in Europe and in the follow-up to the 2008 European Year of Intercultural Dialogue.

Modern economies place increasing emphasis on adding value by means of better use of knowledge and innovation. Most analysts agree that education and training can be a determining factor in enhancing creativity, innovation performance and competitiveness – the 'knowledge triangle' comprising education, research and innovation. However, creativity and innovation are also linked to personal attributes, based on cultural and interpersonal skills and values. Creativity is a human characteristic that manifests itself in many contexts, from works of art, design and craft, to scientific breakthroughs and entrepreneurship. Creativity and innovation have the potential to lead to new products, services, processes, strategies and organisations that arise from new ideas and associations, irrespective of whether the domain is economic, social or artistic. As such, creativity and innovation can be stimulated through a broad, creative, skills base, as well as the development of motivation and a sense of initiative.

In October 2006, the European Parliament and the Council adopted a decision (No 1639/2006/CE) establishing a competitiveness and innovation framework programme (CIP)[1]. The CIP runs from 2007 to 2013, and aims to promote the competitiveness of European enterprises. With small and medium-sized enterprises (SMEs) as its main target, the programme aims to support innovation activities (including eco-innovation), provide better access to finance and deliver business support services in the regions. It is hoped that it will encourage a better take-up and use of information and communications technologies (ICT) and help to develop the information society, while also promoting the increased use of renewable energies and energy efficiency.

In December 2006, the seventh framework programme of the European Community for research and technological development for the period 2007 to 2013 (FP7) was established[2]. FP7 will be implemented through specific programmes corresponding to the main themes of European research policy, with funding amounting to around EUR 53 billion. In April 2007, the European Commission adopted a Green paper titled 'The European Research Area: New Perspectives'[3]. This opens discussions on a number of issues, notably the mobility of researchers, developing research infrastructure and institutions, as well as improvements in the circulation and sharing of knowledge, research programmes, and global research cooperation. It aims to tackle underinvestment, and fragmentation. The principles of the overall governance of the European Research Area (ERA) are known as the 'Ljubljana Process' stemming from discussions in Ljubljana and Brdo (Slovenia) in April 2008. Five initiatives for the development of ERA have been foreseen, with several already adopted in 2008; these concern researchers, research infrastructure, knowledge sharing, joint programming, and international science and technology cooperation.

In a wider context, by placing competitiveness at the heart of the European political agenda, the reinvigorated Lisbon process aims to make Europe a more attractive place to invest, by boosting entrepreneurial initiative and creating a productive environment where innovation capacity can grow and develop. In October 2005 and September 2006 the European Commission adopted two Communications titled 'More Research and Innovation - Investing for Growth and Employment: A Common Approach' and 'Putting knowledge into practice: A broad-based innovation strategy for the EU'. These point the way forward to accompany industry-led and society-driven innovation with competitiveness and public policies at all levels. The second of these Communications singles out ten priority actions, notably to encourage the emergence of 'lead markets' where public authorities create conditions for a successful market uptake of innovative products and services in a focused way in areas such as e-health, internal security, eco-innovation and eco-construction.

(1) http://ec.europa.eu/cip/index_en.htm.
(2) http://cordis.europa.eu/fp7/home_en.html.
(3) http://ec.europa.eu/research/era/index_en.html.

In two recent Communications[4], the European Commission has set out its vision for improving the patent system in Europe. A strong industrial property rights system is seen as one driving force for innovation, stimulating R&D investment and facilitating the transfer of knowledge from the laboratory to the marketplace. The latest Communication includes initiatives on enforcement, innovation support for small and medium-sized enterprises, and the quality of industrial property rights. It complements a 2007 Communication on the patent system, which set out a way forward towards the adoption of a Community patent and an integrated EU-wide jurisdiction for patents.

The overall objective of the European Year of Creativity and Innovation is to promote creativity for all, as a driver for innovation and as a key factor for the development of personal, occupational, entrepreneurial and social competences through lifelong learning. This chapter looks at some of these specific areas through official statistics.

1.1 Education

Education is seen as a key to developing an innovation-orientated society, for the development of entrepreneurial skills, as well as literacy, scientific and mathematical competence, languages and digital literacy. Lifelong training and education offer an important opportunity for individuals to maintain or improve their skills situation. Education, vocational training and lifelong learning play a vital role in the economic and social strategy of Europe. More general information on education in Europe is available in Chapter 4.

Within the EU-27 education participation rates of persons aged 15 to 24 slipped back slightly to 59.3 % in 2006. Nevertheless, a sustained period of increase in earlier years meant that this rate was still 6.4 percentage points higher than in 1998. The participation rate for female pupils and students was higher than for their male counterparts within the EU-27 as a whole, and this situation was repeated in every Member State except the Netherlands and Germany, where the rates for females were slightly lower.

Public expenditure on tertiary level education averaged 1.15 % of GDP in the EU-27 in 2005, up from 1.05 % in 2001. The highest shares were recorded in the Nordic Member States, and the lowest in Romania, Slovakia, Bulgaria and Italy.

Maths, science and technology graduates made up more than one fifth (22.4 %) of all graduates in the EU-27 in 2006, with Austria recording a share closer to one third (32.3 %).

Around one third of employees in the EU-27 participated in continuing vocational training (CVT) courses during 2005. Among the Member States, the proportion ranged from 50 % or more in the Czech Republic and Slovenia to 15 % or less in Greece, Lithuania, Latvia and Bulgaria.

(4) 'Enhancing the patent system in Europe'; 'An Industrial Property Rights Strategy for Europe'; http://ec.europa.eu/internal_market/indprop/rights/index_en.htm.

Table 1.1: Students studying in secondary and post-secondary non-tertiary education, 2006 (1)
(1 000)

	Total	of which (%): Human-ities & arts	Social sciences, bus. & law	Science, maths & computing	Engin., manufac. & constr.	Agric. & veterinary	Health & welfare	Services
EU-27	3 282	3.7	20.1	2.9	29.1	3.4	9.1	12.4
Euro area	2 269	3.4	20.3	2.2	23.6	2.6	10.7	10.4
Belgium	95.7	12.3	16.5	1.3	19.0	1.6	18.4	10.6
Bulgaria	37.4	2.4	18.1	1.3	54.8	7.5	0.7	15.1
Czech Republic	114.9	8.1	26.6	:	38.8	3.3	5.4	16.9
Denmark	64.3	12.4	21.2	25.8	18.4	1.8	14.2	6.2
Germany	709.9	2.4	29.9	3.0	28.9	2.3	10.2	11.0
Estonia	7.2	3.3	14.6	4.8	44.0	5.1	4.2	24.1
Ireland (2)	77.1	2.8	13.2	4.0	30.5	2.4	8.7	13.6
Greece (2)	63.5	5.2	22.9	23.2	17.1	1.3	26.6	3.7
Spain	:	:	:	:	:	:	:	:
France	516.1	2.2	25.8	:	37.4	4.7	13.3	16.6
Italy	437.8	:	:	:	:	:	:	:
Cyprus	:	:	:	:	:	:	:	:
Latvia	9.8	5.4	15.0	5.5	42.9	1.9	4.2	25.1
Lithuania	10.9	3.3	29.1	:	41.0	1.2	2.4	22.5
Luxembourg	2.5	2.7	38.9	2.3	33.1	3.5	7.1	4.9
Hungary	55.5	4.5	21.8	8.8	32.0	3.0	7.9	21.1
Malta	1.7	8.5	12.4	18.1	32.7	1.2	7.0	19.0
Netherlands	132.0	2.2	21.0	5.1	21.0	4.1	26.1	17.4
Austria (2)	97.6	:	:	:	:	:	:	:
Poland	332.7	2.0	24.7	5.2	38.6	2.7	5.6	21.1
Portugal	:	:	:	:	:	:	:	:
Romania	260.9	:	11.2	:	55.4	11.5	:	12.9
Slovenia	20.8	0.4	35.9	1.8	31.7	4.4	9.4	13.2
Slovakia	63.1	3.2	23.2	4.2	36.4	3.6	4.9	23.4
Finland	60.2	5.5	19.8	3.4	29.6	5.0	15.7	21.0
Sweden	56.0	23.4	6.6	0.2	33.9	5.7	11.5	10.7
United Kingdom	:	:	:	:	:	:	:	:
FYR of Macedonia	16.7	2.6	20.4	1.0	44.5	6.6	12.2	12.1
Iceland	2.7	9.0	15.0	1.7	37.1	3.5	11.8	18.5
Liechtenstein	0.4	5.7	:	:	:	:	:	:
Norway	26.9	3.9	8.9	2.9	39.3	3.7	25.6	15.6
Switzerland	72.2	3.1	32.5	9.1	27.8	3.4	11.3	8.8

(1) ISCED levels 3 and 4.
(2) 2005.

Source: Eurostat (educ_grad5)

Figure 1.1: Participation in education among students aged 15-24 years, 2006 (1)

(% share of corresponding age population)

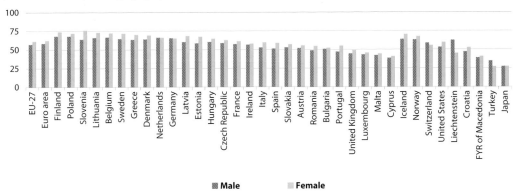

■ **Male**　　■ **Female**

(1) This indicator gives the percentage of all 15-24 year olds who are still in education (at any of the ISCED levels). It gives an indication of the number of young people who have not abandoned their efforts to improve their skills through education. The figure ranks countries based on the average of male and female.

Source: Eurostat (educ_thpar)

Figure 1.2: Public expenditure on tertiary level education, 2005 (1)

(% share of GDP)

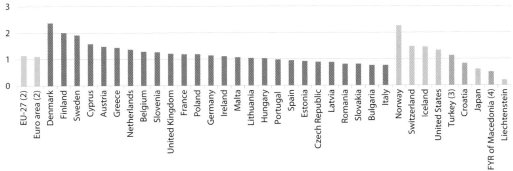

(1) Generally, the public sector funds education either by bearing directly the current and capital expenses of educational institutions or by supporting students and their families with scholarships and public loans as well as by transferring public subsidies for educational activities to private firms or non-profit organisations. Both types of transactions together are reported as total public expenditure on education. Luxembourg, not available.
(2) Estimate.
(3) 2004.
(4) 2003.

Source: Eurostat (educ_figdp)

Table 1.2: Students studying creative or innovative subjects in tertiary education, 2006 (1)
(1 000)

	Total	Arts	of which: (%) Journa- lism & info.	Life science	Phys. science	Maths & stats.	Com- puting	Engin. & engin. trades	Manuf. & pro- cessing	Archi- tecture & build.
EU-27	18 775	3.9	1.6	2.3	2.4	1.2	4.0	8.7	1.2	3.7
Euro area	11 191	4.3	1.7	2.3	2.6	1.2	3.9	9.4	0.8	4.2
Belgium	394	5.0	2.5	2.2	1.3	0.4	3.0	6.3	0.2	4.0
Bulgaria	243	2.3	1.5	0.7	1.6	0.5	2.2	16.8	1.8	2.4
Czech Republic	337	2.4	1.1	1.4	1.7	0.8	4.6	9.3	1.9	3.3
Denmark	229	3.5	1.2	1.6	1.5	1.1	3.8	5.9	0.7	3.5
Germany	2 289	3.7	1.1	2.6	4.4	2.4	5.9	11.0	0.8	3.9
Estonia	68	4.5	1.7	1.9	1.8	0.6	5.8	5.7	2.1	4.5
Ireland	186	8.5	0.3	3.5	2.3	0.8	5.0	4.8	0.8	4.9
Greece (2)	647	1.7	1.2	5.1	3.6	2.9	4.1	5.2	7.8	3.5
Spain	1 789	4.6	1.6	1.8	2.2	0.7	6.7	11.7	0.8	5.3
France	2 201	4.2	1.4	2.3	3.8	1.6	2.6	6.5	0.8	2.1
Italy	2 029	5.7	3.2	3.8	1.5	0.9	1.7	8.9	0.8	5.9
Cyprus	21	3.3	2.6	0.2	2.1	1.3	9.1	4.4	0.0	1.7
Latvia	131	2.6	1.2	0.4	0.8	0.3	3.6	5.6	1.0	3.5
Lithuania	199	2.8	0.8	0.6	1.1	0.9	3.5	11.2	2.2	4.6
Luxembourg	3	:	:	:	:	:	:	:	:	:
Hungary	439	1.4	2.6	0.7	1.1	0.4	3.1	8.5	1.2	2.7
Malta	9	5.9	2.9	1.1	0.5	2.8	4.0	4.8	0.0	2.8
Netherlands	572	4.4	0.8	0.7	0.7	0.2	5.0	4.4	0.4	3.4
Austria	253	4.2	2.5	3.2	2.6	1.1	5.6	6.5	1.3	4.1
Poland	2 146	1.1	0.9	1.9	1.7	0.8	5.0	6.9	2.7	2.8
Portugal	367	4.5	2.2	2.2	2.1	1.0	2.0	13.1	1.1	7.7
Romania	835	1.6	1.9	2.4	:	2.3	:	13.6	3.8	0.8
Slovenia	115	1.5	0.6	1.1	1.1	0.5	2.8	8.3	3.5	3.9
Slovakia	198	1.7	2.0	2.4	1.9	0.7	4.0	10.6	1.8	4.0
Finland	309	5.4	1.0	1.6	2.6	1.5	5.7	20.9	1.4	3.3
Sweden	423	3.6	2.0	2.4	1.9	1.7	3.7	13.0	0.5	2.8
United Kingdom	2 336	6.7	2.0	3.6	3.5	1.4	5.1	4.3	0.8	3.2
Croatia	137	2.5	6.2	1.0	1.7	1.6	3.1	9.5	2.7	4.1
FYR of Macedonia	48	1.3	1.2	1.3	2.8	0.7	2.4	10.1	4.9	3.3
Turkey	2 343	1.3	4.3	1.0	2.7	1.5	2.4	8.3	2.8	2.2
Iceland	16	2.7	1.3	2.4	2.0	0.5	3.1	4.6	0.2	2.5
Liechtenstein	1	0.0	0.0	0.0	0.0	0.0	0.0	0.0	0.0	25.0
Norway	215	3.2	1.9	1.4	1.3	0.9	4.2	4.4	0.3	1.9
Switzerland	205	4.0	1.9	3.1	3.4	0.8	3.4	8.7	0.5	4.2
Japan	4 085	3.8	:	:	:	:	:	:	:	:
United States	17 487	3.3	2.8	2.8	1.0	0.6	4.5	4.7	1.4	0.6

(1) ISCED levels 5 and 6.
(2) 2005.

Source: Eurostat (educ_enrl5)

Table 1.3: Graduates in creative or innovative subjects, 2006 (1)

(1 000)

	Total	Arts	of which: (%) Journa- lism & info.	Life science	Phys. science	Maths & stats.	Com- puting	Engin. & engin. trades	Manuf. & pro- cessing	Archi- tecture & build.
EU-27	3 846	3.9	1.9	2.4	2.1	1.1	3.9	7.8	1.2	2.9
Euro area	2 113	4.2	2.1	2.3	2.3	1.2	3.9	9.1	1.0	3.3
Belgium	82	4.0	1.8	2.2	1.5	0.5	3.5	6.2	0.3	2.8
Bulgaria	45	2.2	1.2	0.9	1.7	0.4	2.4	12.7	1.5	1.4
Czech Republic	69	2.7	1.0	1.4	1.8	0.8	3.6	10.3	1.8	2.9
Denmark	48	3.3	1.3	1.6	1.3	1.0	3.3	5.7	1.2	4.0
Germany	415	3.8	1.1	2.3	3.2	2.0	3.9	8.9	0.9	3.7
Estonia	12	4.6	1.7	2.1	1.8	0.6	4.9	5.3	2.1	2.5
Ireland (2)	60	4.3	0.3	1.6	1.1	0.5	2.9	2.6	0.5	1.9
Greece (2)	60	2.4	0.9	3.4	4.0	2.4	5.2	7.3	1.0	4.0
Spain	286	5.0	1.8	1.6	1.8	0.6	6.1	11.5	1.0	4.0
France	644	3.7	2.2	2.7	2.8	1.5	4.1	9.4	1.3	2.1
Italy	279	6.5	4.7	3.4	1.3	0.9	1.3	10.1	0.7	5.1
Cyprus	4	4.3	2.0	0.2	2.2	2.0	5.4	3.1	0.0	1.1
Latvia	26	2.2	1.1	0.5	0.7	0.3	3.1	4.3	0.6	1.9
Lithuania	43	2.8	0.8	0.7	1.1	0.9	3.3	9.9	1.9	4.1
Luxembourg	:	:	:	:	:	:	:	:	:	:
Hungary	70	1.3	2.8	0.5	0.8	0.3	4.2	3.9	1.4	1.4
Malta	3	4.2	0.8	0.9	0.8	0.0	4.5	2.3	0.0	2.5
Netherlands	117	4.1	0.6	0.9	0.9	0.3	4.3	4.2	0.4	3.2
Austria	35	4.0	3.3	3.5	2.0	0.6	6.4	13.0	2.0	4.8
Poland	504	0.9	0.9	2.0	1.3	0.8	4.0	4.7	1.9	1.7
Portugal	72	5.3	2.5	2.2	2.9	1.7	5.1	8.0	1.4	5.7
Romania	175	1.7	1.8	2.9	:	1.7	:	12.3	3.1	0.4
Slovenia	17	1.6	0.6	0.9	0.7	0.5	1.4	7.1	2.6	3.0
Slovakia	40	2.2	2.1	2.4	2.2	0.5	3.4	9.5	1.4	4.1
Finland	40	6.1	1.1	1.3	2.1	0.9	4.4	17.0	1.1	2.4
Sweden	61	2.7	1.9	2.4	1.5	0.6	3.6	14.8	0.7	3.0
United Kingdom	640	6.9	2.4	3.4	3.4	1.3	5.3	4.4	0.7	3.1
Croatia	21	2.6	2.2	1.6	1.6	0.8	2.3	6.8	1.7	3.0
FYR of Macedonia	7	2.7	0.9	1.5	3.5	1.0	1.4	7.7	3.6	2.5
Turkey	373	1.3	4.0	1.0	2.4	1.4	3.0	9.0	3.1	2.2
Iceland	3	3.6	1.1	2.8	1.9	0.0	3.2	3.5	0.2	2.9
Liechtenstein	0	0.0	0.0	0.0	0.0	0.0	0.0	0.0	0.0	34.8
Norway	34	3.4	2.1	1.7	1.0	0.4	5.0	4.7	0.3	2.5
Switzerland	69	3.1	1.3	2.1	2.4	0.5	5.3	8.2	0.7	3.1
Japan	1 068	4.3	:	:	:	:	:	:	:	:
United States	2 639	3.7	3.7	3.2	1.3	0.8	3.7	4.7	1.1	1.4

(1) Graduates from ISCED levels 5 and 6.
(2) 2005.

Source: Eurostat (educ_grad5)

Figure 1.3: Maths, science and technology graduates, 2006 (1)
(% share of all graduates)

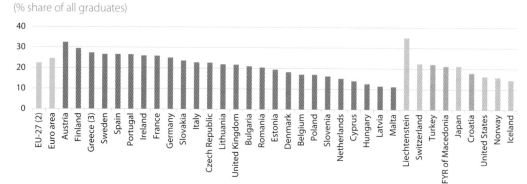

(1) This indicator shows the proportion of all graduates (ISCED levels 5 and 6) from both public and private institutions completing graduate and post-graduate studies in maths, science and technology fields compared with all graduates. Luxembourg, not available.
(2) Estimate.
(3) 2005.

Source: Eurostat (educ_grad5)

Figure 1.4: Continuing vocational training by type of activity received, 2005 (1)
(% of participants in CVT by type of activity)

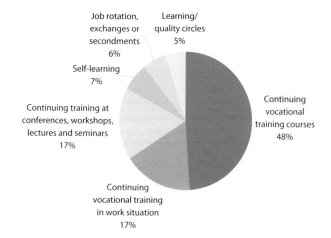

(1) Figures do not sum to 100 % due to rounding.

Source: Eurostat (trng_cvts3_01, trng_cvts3_03)

Table 1.4: Adult population aged 25 to 64 participating in education and training, 2005

(%)

	Proportion of employees participating in CVT courses	Proportion of enterprises providing CVT courses	Enterprises providing CVT courses by type of course	
			Internal courses	External courses
EU-27	33	49	54	89
Belgium	40	48	98	99
Bulgaria	15	21	58	80
Czech Republic	59	63	66	80
Denmark	35	81	64	96
Germany	30	54	72	90
Estonia	24	56	40	94
Ireland	:	:	:	:
Greece	14	19	38	82
Spain	33	38	44	88
France	46	71	44	92
Italy	29	27	48	86
Cyprus	30	47	31	94
Latvia	15	30	22	97
Lithuania	15	26	34	95
Luxembourg	49	61	63	87
Hungary	16	34	39	94
Malta	32	31	63	82
Netherlands	34	70	36	95
Austria	33	67	43	96
Poland	21	24	43	95
Portugal	28	32	50	82
Romania	17	28	49	74
Slovenia	50	61	49	94
Slovakia	38	38	37	88
Finland	39	70	43	94
Sweden	46	72	62	93
United Kingdom	33	67	67	81
Norway	29	55	66	79

Source: Eurostat (trng_cvts3_41, trng_cvts3_05)

1.2 Research and development

Increased levels of research and development (R & D) expenditure are seen as one means to achieve the goals set out in 2000 by the European Council in Lisbon: in 2002 a target that investment in R & D should reach 3 % of GDP by 2010 was set. Research and development is defined as comprising creative work undertaken on a systematic basis to increase the stock of knowledge (of man, culture and society) and the use of this stock to devise new applications. More information on the sources and methods concerning R & D expenditure data are available in Subchapter 14.2.

Government support for R & D represented 0.8 % of GDP in the EU-27 in 2006, with the highest shares (1.0 %) recorded in France, Spain and Finland: all of the Member States that joined the EU in 2004 or 2007 recorded shares below the EU-27 average, while Greece, Luxembourg and Ireland recorded the lowest shares among the EU-15 Member States. Around 30 % of government support for R & D was allocated to research financed from general university funds (GUF), an objective which covers R & D related to various fields of science: natural, engineering, medical, agricultural, social sciences and humanities. Defence related appropriations accounted for 13 % of all government appropriations, although this objective had a much higher share in a small number of Member States, notably the United Kingdom, France, Sweden and Spain.

Extending the coverage to include also private funding, total R & D expenditure in the EU-27 was EUR 213 100 million in 2006, equivalent to 1.84 % of GDP. The ratio to GDP is referred to as R & D intensity and this showed high values in the Nordic Member States, Germany and Austria, with only Sweden and Finland above the 3 % target set for 2010; the lowest levels of R & D intensity were recorded in Cyprus, Romania, Slovakia and Bulgaria.

Figure 1.5: Government budget appropriations or outlays for research and development, 2007 (1)
(% share of GDP)

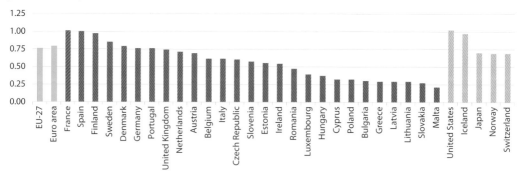

(1) Data on government budget appropriations or outlays on R & D (GBAORD) refer to budget provisions, not to actual expenditure, i.e. GBAORD measures government support for R & D using data collected from budgets. GBAORD are a way of measuring government support; Estonia, Romania and Iceland, 2008; EU-27, euro area, Belgium, Bulgaria, Spain, France, Italy, Cyprus, Latvia, Malta, Poland, Slovenia, Sweden, the United Kingdom, Switzerland and Japan, 2006; Hungary, 2005; EU-27, estimate.

Source: Eurostat (tsc00007)

Table 1.5: Government budget appropriations or outlays for research and development, 2007 (1)

	Total research and development		Civil research and development		
	(EUR per inhabitant)	(EUR million)	(EUR per inhabitant)	(EUR million)	(% of total research and development)
EU-27	178.2	87 840	154.7	76 255	86.8
Euro area	:	66 925	:	59 846	89.4
Belgium	185.1	1 946	184.6	1 940	99.7
Bulgaria	9.8	75	:	:	:
Czech Republic	75.3	774	73.4	755	97.5
Denmark	328.6	1 790	326.7	1 780	99.4
Germany	223.6	18 405	209.9	17 274	93.9
Estonia	58.8	79	58.2	78	99.0
Ireland	230.6	995	230.6	995	100.0
Greece	60.3	673	59.9	670	99.5
Spain	223.9	9 799	187.6	8 209	83.8
France	289.3	18 225	224.6	14 147	77.6
Italy	154.9	9 099	152.8	8 975	98.6
Cyprus	61.6	47	61.6	47	100.0
Latvia	20.1	46	20.0	46	99.7
Lithuania	24.2	82	24.0	81	99.2
Luxembourg	298.2	142	298.2	142	100.0
Hungary	32.6	329	32.5	329	99.9
Malta	26.0	11	26.0	11	100.0
Netherlands	243.9	3 990	239.0	3 910	98.0
Austria	225.3	1 870	225.3	1 870	100.0
Poland	22.5	858	22.3	850	99.1
Portugal	116.7	1 237	115.9	1 228	99.3
Romania	19.2	415	18.8	405	97.6
Slovenia	86.5	173	85.2	171	98.4
Slovakia	27.8	150	27.2	146	97.8
Finland	327.8	1 730	320.0	1 689	97.6
Sweden	295.7	2 675	245.9	2 225	83.2
United Kingdom	233.9	14 124	167.7	10 127	71.7
Iceland	401.8	124	401.8	124	100.0
Norway	423.2	1 981	399.6	1 871	94.4
Switzerland	284.7	2 123	283.0	2 111	99.4
Japan	:	24 478	:	23 221	94.9
United States	:	102 917	:	42 932	41.7

(1) EU-27, euro area, Belgium, Bulgaria, Spain, France, Italy, Cyprus, Latvia, Malta, Poland, Slovenia, Sweden, the United Kingdom, Switzerland and Japan, 2006; Hungary, 2005.

Source: Eurostat (gba_nabsfin)

Figure 1.6: Socio-economic objectives of government budget appropriations or outlays for research and development, EU-27, 2006 (1)

(% share of total)

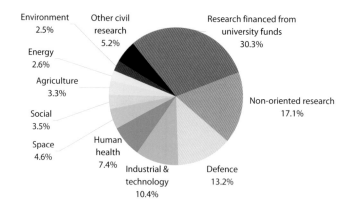

Environment 2.5%	Research financed from university funds 30.3%
Other civil research 5.2%	
Energy 2.6%	
Agriculture 3.3%	Non-oriented research 17.1%
Social 3.5%	
Space 4.6%	Human health 7.4%
Industrial & technology 10.4%	Defence 13.2%

(1) Figures do not sum to 100 % due to rounding.

Source: Eurostat (gba_nabsfin)

Figure 1.7: Gross domestic expenditure on research and development

(% share of GDP)

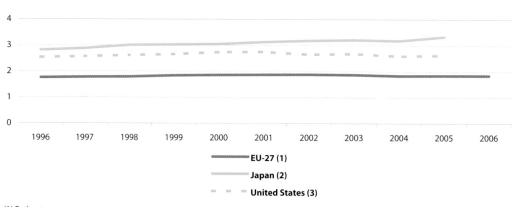

EU-27 (1)
Japan (2)
United States (3)

(1) Estimates.
(2) Break in series, 1996; not available, 2006.
(3) Break in series, 1998; excludes most or all capital expenditure.

Source: Eurostat (tsc00001)

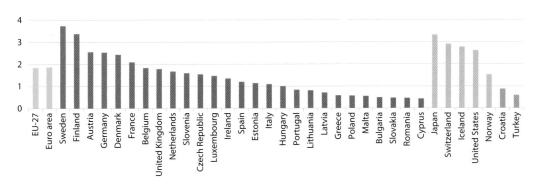

Figure 1.8: Gross domestic expenditure on research and development, 2006 (1)

(% share of GDP)

(1) Ireland, Austria, Slovakia and Finland, 2007; Italy, Iceland and Japan, 2005; Switzerland, 2004; EU-27, estimate.

Source: Eurostat (tsiir020)

Figure 1.9: Gross domestic expenditure on research and development, by source of funds, EU-27, 2005 (1)

(% share of total)

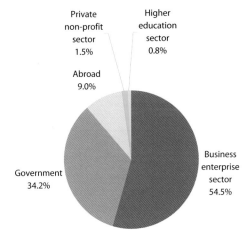

(1) Estimates.

Source: Eurostat (rd_e_gerdfund)

Table 1.6: Research and development expenditure, 2006 (1)

	Research and development expenditure		Expenditure by sector of performance (%)			
	(EUR per inhabitant)	(EUR million)	Business enterprise	Government	Higher education	Private non-profit
EU-27	432.3	213 127	63.7	13.5	21.9	0.9
Euro area	:	156 953	63.7	14.6	21.0	0.7
Belgium	551.5	5 798	67.9	8.6	22.3	1.2
Bulgaria	15.7	121	25.5	64.1	9.6	0.9
Czech Republic	171.8	1 761	66.2	17.5	15.9	0.4
Denmark	985.5	5 349	66.6	6.7	26.1	0.6
Germany	713.8	58 848	69.9	13.8	16.3	0.0
Estonia	112.3	151	44.4	13.1	40.6	1.8
Ireland	579.4	2 500	66.8	6.8	26.4	0.0
Greece	109.9	1 223	30.0	20.8	47.8	1.3
Spain	270.0	11 815	55.5	16.7	27.6	0.2
France	600.7	37 844	63.3	17.3	18.2	1.3
Italy (2)	266.8	15 599	50.4	17.3	30.2	2.1
Cyprus	80.7	62	22.3	28.4	41.7	7.6
Latvia	49.0	112	50.4	15.1	34.5	0.0
Lithuania	56.0	191	27.9	22.8	49.2	0.0
Luxembourg	1 059.1	497	84.9	12.6	2.4	0.0
Hungary	89.4	900	48.3	25.4	24.4	:
Malta	68.0	28	61.8	4.8	33.4	0.0
Netherlands	545.5	8 910	57.6	14.1	:	:
Austria	777.1	6 423	66.7	5.1	26.3	0.4
Poland	39.6	1 513	31.5	37.0	31.0	0.4
Portugal	122.4	1 294	41.7	:	:	:
Romania	20.6	444	48.5	32.3	17.7	1.5
Slovenia	241.5	484	60.2	24.5	15.1	0.2
Slovakia	40.2	217	43.1	32.8	24.1	0.1
Finland	1 140.0	6 016	71.5	9.7	18.7	0.0
Sweden	1 292.2	11 691	74.9	4.5	20.4	0.2
United Kingdom	563.6	34 037	61.7	10.0	26.1	2.2
Croatia	67.0	297	36.7	26.5	36.6	0.1
Turkey	33.5	2 432	37.0	11.7	51.3	0.0
Iceland	1 238.5	364	51.5	23.5	22.0	3.0
Norway	877.2	4 071	54.1	15.7	30.2	0.0
Japan	953.6	121 831	76.4	8.3	13.4	1.9
Russian Federation	59.3	8 466	66.6	27.0	6.1	0.3
United States	878.6	260 803	69.6	12.0	14.1	4.3

(1) Ireland and Finland, 2007; Italy, Iceland, Japan and the United States, 2005.
(2) Higher education, break in series.

Source: Eurostat (rd_e_gerdtot)

1.3 Science and technology personnel

The European Commission has placed renewed emphasis on the conversion of Europe's scientific expertise into marketable products and services, while also focusing on improving the mobility of European researchers, encouraging networks between researchers from different Member States. Researchers are professionals engaged in the conception or creation of new knowledge, products, processes, methods and systems, and in the management of the projects concerned. More information on the sources and methods concerning data on human resources in science and technology are available in Subchapter 14.1.

In total there were 3.1 million R & D personnel (head count) in the EU-27 in 2006, representing 1.3 % of the labour force. Generally Member States with a high R & D intensity recorded also a high share of R & D personnel in the labour force, with Finland and Sweden again leading the way.

Restricting the coverage, across the EU-27 there were 1.9 million researchers (head count) in 2006. Approximately half of all researchers were active in the business enterprise sector, with more than one third in higher education, and most of the remainder in the government sector. Within the business enterprise sector, manufacturing enterprises employed just over 70 % of all business enterprise researchers.

Human resources in science and technology (HRST) is a broader concept and includes individuals who have successfully completed tertiary-level education and/or work in a science and technology occupation as professionals or technicians. In total there were around 85 million such persons in the EU-27 in 2006, with an almost equal split between men and women. Around two fifths of these were considered to be core science and technology personnel, in other words they were classified as human resources in science and technology both in terms of their level of education and their occupation. In total there were around 10 million scientists and engineers in the EU-27 in 2006, of which more than two thirds were male.

Looking at international mobility, around 5 % of the human resources in science and technology in EU-27 Member States were not nationals of the Member State where they were resident: the share of non-nationals exceeded 10 % in Estonia, Cyprus and Ireland, and most notably in Luxembourg where the share was 45 %.

High and medium-high technology manufacturing concerns the manufacture of chemicals (NACE Rev. 1.1 Division 24), machinery and equipment (NACE Rev. 1.1 Subsection DK), electrical and optical equipment (NACE Rev. 1.1 Subsection DL) and transport equipment (NACE Rev. 1.1 Subsection DM), and these sectors combined contributed around 10 % of total employment in Germany, the Czech Republic and Slovakia, but less than 2 % in Cyprus, Luxembourg and Latvia, compared with an EU-27 average of 6.6 %. High-technology knowledge-intensive services include post and telecommunications (NACE Rev. 1.1 Division 64), computer and related activities (NACE Rev. 1.1 Division 72) and research and development (NACE Rev. 1.1 Division 73). These activities contributed 3.3 % of total employment in the EU-27, ranging from 4 % or more in the Nordic Member States and the United Kingdom, to 1.6 % in Romania.

Table 1.7: Research and development personnel, 2006

	Research and development personnel (1 000)		of which (%, based on fte) (2)			
	(head count) (1)	(full-time equivalent) (2)	Business enterprise	Govern-ment	Higher education	Private non-profit
EU-27	3 112.6	2 167.4	53.3	15.2	30.2	1.2
Euro area	2 233.9	1 563.2	54.3	15.3	29.2	1.2
Belgium	78.5	55.2	58.4	7.0	33.6	1.0
Bulgaria	18.6	16.3	15.1	62.8	21.2	0.9
Czech Republic	69.2	47.7	50.5	22.4	26.8	0.3
Denmark	67.3	45.2	64.8	7.3	27.3	0.6
Germany	678.9	489.1	63.8	15.7	20.4	0.0
Estonia	8.7	4.7	34.4	15.1	48.3	2.2
Ireland	30.6	17.6	61.2	7.1	31.7	0.0
Greece	61.5	35.1	32.4	13.0	53.9	0.6
Spain	309.9	189.0	43.9	18.3	37.5	0.3
France	432.6	353.6	56.2	14.0	27.9	1.8
Italy (3)	277.4	175.2	40.4	18.7	38.2	2.8
Cyprus	2.5	1.2	25.4	29.1	38.1	7.4
Latvia	10.7	6.5	28.7	17.9	53.4	0.0
Lithuania	16.3	11.4	11.2	25.6	63.2	0.0
Luxembourg	5.0	4.6	81.7	12.9	5.4	0.0
Hungary	50.4	26.0	35.7	31.5	32.8	0.0
Malta	1.4	0.8	53.5	5.7	40.8	0.0
Netherlands	113.6	94.7	55.8	13.5	:	:
Austria	:	50.3	67.9	4.7	26.8	0.5
Poland	121.3	73.6	19.3	24.0	56.5	0.3
Portugal	44.6	25.7	23.8	17.6	45.4	13.1
Romania	42.2	30.8	44.7	27.2	27.8	0.3
Slovenia	13.4	9.8	49.2	29.1	21.4	0.3
Slovakia	23.1	15.0	20.9	24.8	54.2	0.1
Finland	79.9	58.3	56.6	12.7	29.8	0.8
Sweden	117.7	78.7	73.2	4.6	21.8	0.4
United Kingdom	:	323.4	45.0	6.3	:	2.0
Croatia	:	8.5	26.1	31.9	41.9	0.2
Turkey	105.0	54.4	33.1	17.8	49.1	0.0
Iceland	5.7	3.2	47.4	26.3	23.0	3.3
Norway	54.3	31.7	52.1	16.8	31.1	0.0
China	:	1 502.5	65.7	18.1	16.1	0.0
Japan	:	921.2	66.2	6.8	25.4	1.6
Russian Federation (4)	807.1	916.5	56.2	32.5	11.0	0.3

(1) Belgium, Bulgaria, Denmark, Germany, Greece, Italy, Cyprus, Lithuania, Luxembourg, the Netherlands, Portugal, Sweden, Iceland and Norway, 2005.
(2) France, Italy, Portugal, the United Kingdom, Iceland and Japan, 2005.
(3) Higher education, break in series.
(4) Data in head counts are underestimated.

Source: Eurostat (rd_p_perssci)

Figure 1.10: Research and development personnel, 2006 (1)

(% share of total labour force)

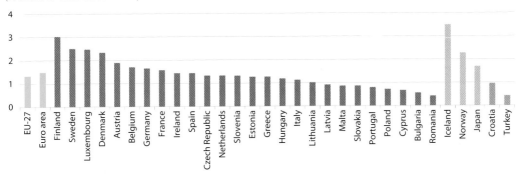

(1) R & D personnel include all persons employed directly on R & D, plus persons supplying direct services to R & D, such as managers, administrative staff and office staff. Head count (HC) data measure the total number of R & D personnel; EU-27, estimate; Belgium, Bulgaria, Denmark, Germany, Greece, France, Italy, Cyprus, Lithuania, Luxembourg, the Netherlands, Portugal, Sweden, Iceland, Norway and Japan, 2005; Austria and Croatia, 2004; the United Kingdom, not available.

Source: Eurostat (tsc00002)

Figure 1.11: Researchers, EU-27, 2006 (1)

(% breakdown by sector of performance, based on full-time equivalents)

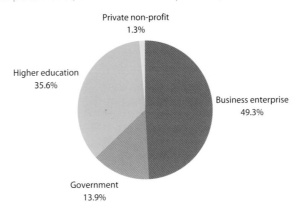

(1) Estimates; figures do not sum to 100 % due to rounding.

Source: Eurostat (rd_p_perssci)

Figure 1.12: Business enterprise researchers, EU, 2005 (1)

(% breakdown by activity, based on head counts)

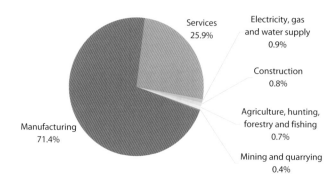

Services
25.9%

Electricity, gas
and water supply
0.9%

Construction
0.8%

Agriculture, hunting,
forestry and fishing
0.7%

Mining and quarrying
0.4%

Manufacturing
71.4%

(1) Average composed of those Member States for which data are available; Belgium and the Czech Republic 2006; France and Austria, 2004; Bulgaria, 2003; Denmark, Luxembourg, Malta, Slovakia and the United Kingdom, not available; figures do not sum to 100 % due to rounding.

Source: Eurostat (rd_p_bempocc)

Figure 1.13: Government and higher education researchers, EU, 2006 (1)

(% breakdown by field of science, based on full-time equivalents)

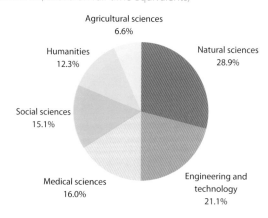

Agricultural sciences
6.6%

Humanities
12.3%

Natural sciences
28.9%

Social sciences
15.1%

Medical sciences
16.0%

Engineering and
technology
21.1%

(1) Average composed of those Member States for which data are available; the Czech Republic, Estonia, Ireland, Spain, Latvia, Hungary, Malta, Poland, Romania, Slovenia and Slovakia, 2006; Belgium, Bulgaria, Denmark, Germany, Italy, Cyprus, Lithuania, Luxembourg and Portugal, 2005; Greece, France, the Netherlands, Austria, Finland, Sweden and the United Kingdom, not available.

Source: Eurostat (rd_p_perssci)

Table 1.8: Researchers, 2006

	Researchers (1 000)		of which (%, based on fte) (2)			
	(head count) (1)	(full-time equivalent) (2)	Business enterprise	Govern- ment	Higher education	Private non-profit
EU-27	1 891.1	1 301.0	49.3	13.9	35.6	1.3
Euro area	1 298.0	895.3	50.3	13.9	34.5	1.3
Belgium	48.8	33.9	50.5	7.4	41.4	0.7
Bulgaria	11.9	10.3	12.6	59.5	26.7	1.2
Czech Republic	39.7	26.3	43.0	25.0	31.8	0.2
Denmark	43.5	28.7	60.6	7.6	31.0	0.7
Germany	411.8	282.1	60.6	14.2	25.2	:
Estonia	6.4	3.5	24.9	14.6	58.1	2.3
Ireland	18.6	12.2	57.5	4.1	38.4	:
Greece	33.4	19.9	27.1	11.3	60.8	0.7
Spain	193.0	115.8	34.5	17.3	47.9	0.3
France	253.0	204.5	53.2	12.7	32.4	1.7
Italy (3)	125.5	82.5	33.9	17.5	44.9	3.7
Cyprus	1.4	0.8	23.2	15.2	57.0	4.6
Latvia	7.2	4.0	19.3	14.9	65.8	0.0
Lithuania	11.9	8.0	10.9	21.2	67.8	:
Luxembourg	2.4	2.3	73.9	16.5	9.6	:
Hungary	32.8	17.5	35.6	29.8	34.6	:
Malta	1.0	0.5	46.3	3.6	50.1	0.0
Netherlands	49.8	45.9	60.6	15.6	:	:
Austria	:	30.5	63.6	4.0	31.9	0.5
Poland	96.4	59.6	15.7	20.9	63.2	0.2
Portugal	37.8	21.1	19.0	15.8	51.9	13.3
Romania	30.1	20.5	37.6	27.2	34.8	0.4
Slovenia	8.2	5.8	38.8	30.9	29.8	0.5
Slovakia	18.8	11.8	16.1	21.2	62.6	0.1
Finland	53.3	40.4	56.2	11.1	31.8	0.9
Sweden	82.5	55.7	67.6	5.5	26.4	0.4
United Kingdom	:	180.5	51.9	5.2	:	2.1
Croatia	:	5.2	13.8	31.2	54.9	0.1
Turkey	90.1	42.7	26.4	11.0	62.6	:
Iceland	3.8	2.2	47.0	23.2	27.1	2.6
Norway	37.0	21.7	49.4	15.9	34.7	:
China	:	1 223.8	63.5	17.2	19.3	:
Japan	861.9	704.9	68.3	4.8	25.6	1.3
Russian Federation (4)	388.9	464.4	51.0	33.1	15.6	0.4
United States	:	1 394.7	79.2	:	:	:

(1) Belgium, Bulgaria, Denmark, Germany, Greece, France, Italy, Cyprus, Lithuania, Luxembourg, the Netherlands, Portugal, Sweden, Iceland, Norway and Japan, 2005.
(2) France, Italy, Portugal, the United Kingdom, Iceland, Norway, Japan and the United States, 2005.
(3) Higher education, break in series.
(4) Data in head counts are underestimated.

Source: Eurostat (rd_p_perssci)

Figure 1.14: Human resources in science and technology with tertiary education, 2006 (1)

(% of human resources in science and technology aged 25-64 years with a tertiary education in the specified field)

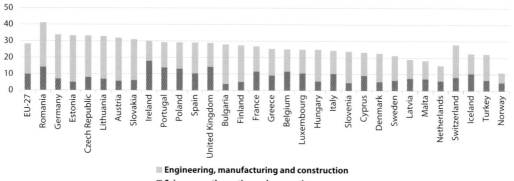

■ **Engineering, manufacturing and construction**
▨ **Science, mathematics and computing**

(1) Ireland and Norway, 2005; persons aged 25-64.

Source: Eurostat (hrst_st_nfiesex)

Figure 1.15: Human resources in science and technology, 2006 (1)

(% of total)

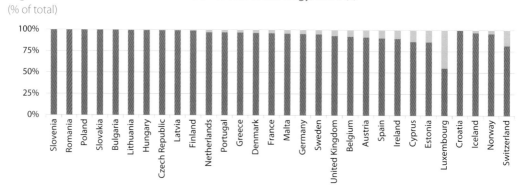

■ **Non-national**
▨ **National**

(1) Ireland, 2005; Italy, not available; persons aged 25-64.

Source: Eurostat (hrst_st_nnat)

Table 1.9: Human resources in science and technology, 2006 (1)

	Human resources in science and technology			Core			Scientists and engineers		
	(1 000)	**Male (%)**	**Female (%)**	**(1 000)**	**Male (%)**	**Female (%)**	**(1 000)**	**Male (%)**	**Female (%)**
EU-27	85 422	49.9	50.1	34 455	48.5	51.5	10 338	68.8	31.2
Belgium	2 183	50.5	49.6	919	47.4	52.6	335	51.3	48.7
Bulgaria	1 069	40.8	59.2	488	32.6	67.6	96	52.1	46.9
Czech Republic	1 736	48.4	51.6	537	54.4	45.6	164	70.1	29.9
Denmark	1 333	48.4	51.7	676	44.1	55.9	163	70.6	29.4
Germany	16 708	52.9	47.1	6 416	56.5	43.5	2 156	76.7	23.3
Estonia	281	37.7	61.9	106	29.2	71.7	26	53.8	46.2
Ireland	772	47.4	52.7	324	46.0	54.0	138	50.0	49.3
Greece	1 496	51.7	48.3	754	51.1	48.9	194	69.1	30.9
Spain	8 442	51.3	48.7	3 519	48.8	51.2	911	59.2	40.8
France	11 122	49.6	50.4	4 567	48.1	51.9	1 342	77.0	23.0
Italy	8 359	50.9	49.1	2 633	48.8	51.2	713	69.1	30.9
Cyprus	143	52.4	48.3	65	52.3	49.2	16	56.3	37.5
Latvia	365	37.5	62.7	142	31.7	68.3	37	45.9	54.1
Lithuania	588	37.2	62.8	245	28.6	71.4	65	44.6	55.4
Luxembourg	89	52.8	47.2	45	53.3	46.7	10	80.0	20.0
Hungary	1 402	41.7	58.3	569	43.1	56.9	161	67.7	32.3
Malta	44	59.1	40.9	17	52.9	47.1	5	60.0	40.0
Netherlands	3 716	51.6	48.4	1 640	52.3	47.7	453	68.4	31.6
Austria	1 432	55.0	45.0	443	53.3	46.7	118	76.3	23.7
Poland	5 051	41.6	58.4	2 194	39.6	60.4	782	46.7	53.3
Portugal	1 105	47.1	52.9	524	39.5	60.5	146	55.5	44.5
Romania	2 095	46.1	53.9	935	47.6	52.4	367	62.4	37.6
Slovenia	368	45.9	54.3	162	40.1	60.5	50	64.0	34.0
Slovakia	797	44.2	55.7	274	49.6	50.4	67	65.7	34.3
Finland	1 234	45.4	54.5	550	41.3	58.9	166	72.9	26.5
Sweden	2 098	48.4	51.6	1 005	40.7	59.2	292	62.0	38.0
United Kingdom	11 395	52.1	47.9	4 704	48.2	51.8	1 369	80.3	19.6
Turkey	4 216	66.6	33.4	1 488	62.8	37.2	317	73.2	26.8
Iceland	61	44.3	55.7	22	45.5	54.5	12	50.0	41.7
Norway	1 079	49.1	51.0	565	44.1	55.9	111	58.6	41.4
Switzerland	1 883	57.6	42.4	763	64.1	35.8	286	83.2	16.4

(1) Persons aged 25-64.

Source: Eurostat (hrst_st_ncat)

Figure 1.16: Persons employed in high- and medium high-technology manufacturing, 2006
(% of total employment)

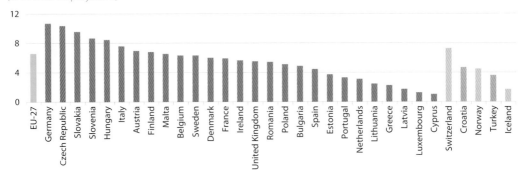

Source: Eurostat (htec_emp_nat)

Figure 1.17: Persons employed in high-technology knowledge intensive services, 2006
(% of total employment)

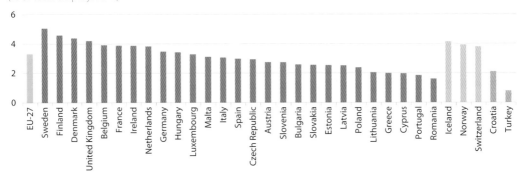

Source: Eurostat (htec_emp_nat)

1.4 Innovation

The fifth Community Innovation Survey (CIS5) collected information about both product and process innovation and organisational and marketing innovation. For the purpose of this survey, 'innovation' is defined as a new or significantly improved product (good or service) introduced to the market, or the introduction within an enterprise of a new or significantly improved process. Innovations are based on the results of new technological developments, new combinations of existing technology, or the utilisation of other knowledge acquired by the enterprise. Innovations may be developed by the innovating enterprise or by another enterprise. However, purely selling innovations wholly produced and developed by other enterprises is not included as an innovation activity, nor is introducing products with purely aesthetic changes. Innovations should be new to the enterprise concerned: for product innovations they do not necessarily have to be new to the market and for process innovations the enterprise does not necessarily have to be the first one to have introduced the process.

Enterprises with innovation activity include all types of innovator, namely product innovators, process innovators, as well as enterprises with only on-going and/or abandoned innovation activities. The proportion of enterprises with innovation activity may also be referred to as the propensity to innovate.

The EU's Summary Innovation Index (SII) provides an overall assessment of innovation performance. Based on performance in 2003 and 2007, four main groupings of Member States can be determined. The first group can be considered as 'innovation leaders': Sweden, Finland, Denmark, Germany and the United Kingdom all reported indices well above the EU-27 average. The second group can be thought of as 'innovation followers', including Luxembourg, Ireland, the Netherlands, Austria, Belgium and France (scores below those of the innovation leaders but equal to or above that of the EU-27). The third group can be termed 'moderate innovators', including Estonia, the Czech Republic, Slovenia, Italy, Cyprus and Spain (with scores below the EU-27 average). The last group represent those countries that are 'catching-up', including Malta, Lithuania, Greece, Hungary, Portugal, Slovakia, Poland, Bulgaria, Latvia and Romania (with scores significantly below the EU-27 average, but moving towards the EU-27 average over time).

In 2006 just under 40 % of the EU-27's enterprises were considered as innovative. Germany had the highest propensity to innovate with almost two thirds (62.6 %) of all enterprises having some form of innovation activity. Generally, the majority of core innovative enterprises operated within the industrial economy (56.9 % among the 21 Member States for which data are available), a share that rose to 72.4 % in Bulgaria. A breakdown by enterprise size class shows that large (250 and more employees) innovative enterprises were more inclined to introduce products new to the market: almost half (47.4 %) of all large innovative enterprises did so in the EU-27 in 2006. In many of the Member States, large innovative enterprises were also more likely to introduce processes innovations that they had developed.

In many of the Member States, a large majority of innovation expenditure was spent on the acquisition of machinery, equipment and software. Otherwise, the breakdown of innovation expenditure in 2006 shows that intramural R & D spending was generally the next most important category, followed by extramural R & D expenditure.

Using information from within the enterprise was the most widespread source of information for innovation among innovative enterprises in 2006 (44.0 % of enterprises among those countries for which data are available). Only a relatively small proportion of innovative enterprises used higher education institutes (4.3 %) or government and public research institutes (3.7 %) as a source of information for innovation.

The most important effect of innovation was the product-oriented effect of improving the quality of goods and services; across the EU (data for 20 Member States), 35.5 % of innovative enterprises noted improved quality, while 31.6 % of innovative enterprises cited a wider range of goods and services as an effect of innovation. In each of the Member States for which data are available (except Bulgaria), a majority of innovative enterprises introduced organisational or marketing innovations, the most common effects of which were reduced customer response time and/or the improved quality of goods and services.

Innovative enterprises across the EU protected their intellectual property by registering trademarks (16.3 % of innovative enterprises), applying for patents (8.0 %) and registering industrial designs (7.6 %). Claiming copyrights (3.6 %) was the least used protection method in 2006.

Among non-innovative enterprises in the EU in 2006 (data for 19 Member States), around one in six (16.7 %) stated that an important factor in not innovating was a perceived lack of demand to do so. A little under one in every ten (9.0 %) non-innovative enterprises across the EU stated that they no longer innovated due to prior innovations.

Figure 1.18: Summary Innovation Index (SII), 2003 and 2007 (1)

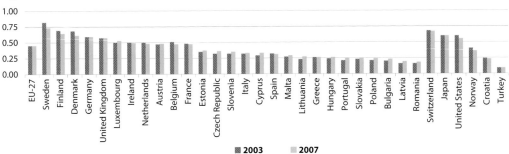

(1) The Summary Innovation Index gives an 'at a glance' overview of aggregate national innovation performance and is a composite indicator of 25 measures. The SII can range from 0 (worst performance) to 1 (best performance). Countries are categorised as either innovation leaders, innovation followers, moderate innovators or catching-up countries.

Source: European Commission, Directorate-General for Enterprise and Industry (European Innovation Scoreboard, 2007 - Comparative analysis of innovation performance)

Figure 1.19: Evolution of the Summary Innovation Index (SII)

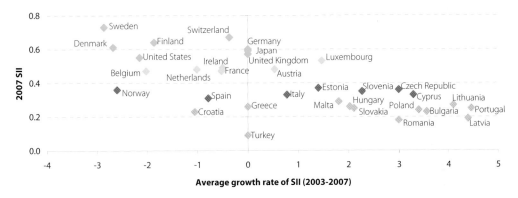

Source: European Commission, Directorate-General for Enterprise and Industry (European Innovation Scoreboard, 2007 - Comparative analysis of innovation performance)

Figure 1.20: Innovative enterprises, 2006 (1)

(% of all enterprises)

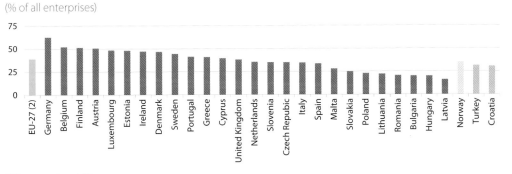

(1) France, not available.
(2) Excluding France.

Source: Eurostat (inn_cis5_prod)

Table 1.10: Proportion of innovative enterprises which introduced products new to the market or own-developed process innovations, 2006

(% of innovative enterprises within size class or total)

| | Process innovations: developed by the enterprise or group | | | | Product innovations: new to market | | | |
	Total	With 10 to 49 employees	With 50 to 249 employees	With > 250 employees	Total	With 10 to 49 employees	With 50 to 249 employees	With > 250 employees
EU-27 (1)	:	:	:	:	32.4	29.3	36.9	47.4
Belgium	40.0	38.2	43.3	49.8	41.4	38.6	44.1	65.3
Bulgaria	37.9	37.3	38.1	41.4	41.3	38.6	46.2	45.7
Czech Republic	39.0	37.6	41.8	39.7	38.9	32.5	48.3	51.2
Denmark	35.0	32.5	41.3	41.1	33.8	30.9	37.9	50.7
Germany	30.9	27.7	32.4	50.1	30.4	25.9	35.3	47.7
Estonia	41.3	40.0	41.8	58.5	32.9	32.9	32.1	36.4
Ireland	42.4	41.1	42.1	58.8	40.8	38.0	47.0	51.6
Greece	48.6	46.7	55.8	47.9	35.8	29.5	55.0	58.6
Spain	47.8	46.3	51.8	54.1	18.3	14.8	26.0	39.5
France	:	:	:	:	:	:	:	:
Italy	:	:	:	:	29.5	26.8	37.2	50.1
Cyprus	31.7	33.0	31.5	13.0	34.4	30.7	42.2	52.2
Latvia	:	:	:	:	44.7	49.8	34.0	41.9
Lithuania	35.2	33.2	40.7	36.9	36.0	36.8	32.4	38.5
Luxembourg	45.5	42.1	51.7	52.9	58.9	59.3	52.3	74.2
Hungary	28.5	28.7	25.6	33.8	30.9	30.1	29.6	38.2
Malta	46.7	41.3	52.1	66.7	59.0	57.1	60.4	66.7
Netherlands	23.0	22.1	22.4	35.4	48.1	46.1	50.8	59.5
Austria	37.2	35.7	37.8	48.0	45.4	42.1	48.8	65.0
Poland	47.0	48.1	46.1	46.0	32.7	33.1	30.6	37.5
Portugal	46.2	45.8	47.4	46.9	29.8	26.5	37.1	48.5
Romania	69.2	70.0	68.0	68.1	24.7	22.1	26.6	33.9
Slovenia	39.2	41.2	35.1	40.0	51.1	52.5	44.9	59.4
Slovakia	31.8	26.0	38.8	38.4	37.6	34.7	39.8	43.8
Finland	38.3	38.0	38.1	42.1	44.6	44.3	40.7	58.0
Sweden	36.6	36.8	:	:	51.3	49.3	55.8	58.3
United Kingdom	:	:	:	:	31.6	31.0	31.7	39.8
Croatia	36.0	36.7	34.4	35.8	31.7	28.5	33.1	47.5
Turkey	64.3	64.3	62.8	69.9	59.6	62.3	50.5	52.9
Norway	29.3	28.5	29.8	36.8	39.9	40.6	37.0	42.0

(1) Excluding France.

Source: Eurostat (inn_cis5_prod)

Figure 1.21: Enterprises engaged in innovation activities, by economic activities, 2006 (1)
(% share of innovative enterprises)

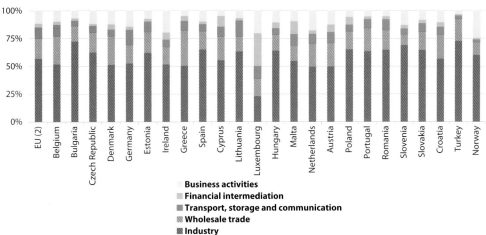

■ **Business activities**
■ **Financial intermediation**
■ **Transport, storage and communication**
▨ **Wholesale trade**
▨ **Industry**

(1) Data for France, Italy, Latvia, Finland and the United Kingdom, not available; data for Sweden, incomplete; the core aggregate covers enterprises in industry (NACE Sections C, D and E), wholesale trade (NACE Division 51), transport, storage and communication (NACE Section I), financial intermediation (NACE Section J) and business activities (NACE Division 72 and NACE Groups 74.2 and 74.3).
(2) Average based upon data for 21 Member States, excluding France, Italy, Latvia, Finland, Sweden and the United Kingdom.

Source: Eurostat (inn_cis5_exp)

Figure 1.22: Innovative enterprises having received any public funding, 2006 (1)
(% share of innovative enterprises)

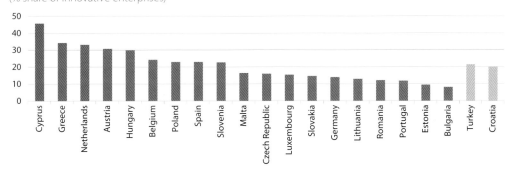

(1) Denmark, Ireland, France, Italy, Latvia, Finland, Sweden and the United Kingdom, not available.

Source: Eurostat (inn_cis5_pub)

Table 1.11: Breakdown of innovation expenditure by category, 2006
(% of total innovation expenditure)

	Expenditure in intramural R&D	Expenditure in extramural R&D	Expenditure for acquisition of machinery, equipment & software	Expenditure for acquisition of other external knowledge
Belgium	47.1	22.2	29.4	1.3
Bulgaria	5.8	1.2	91.3	1.7
Czech Republic	24.0	17.8	55.1	3.2
Denmark	59.0	17.2	18.9	5.0
Germany	:	:	:	:
Estonia	8.1	3.4	87.1	1.4
Ireland	37.8	6.1	40.7	15.3
Greece	35.4	8.4	54.9	1.3
Spain	35.6	14.2	33.9	6.3
France	:	:	:	:
Italy	:	:	:	:
Cyprus	2.4	8.1	84.9	4.7
Latvia	:	:	:	:
Lithuania	24.6	7.7	65.2	2.5
Luxembourg	38.9	14.3	36.8	10.0
Hungary	17.4	17.7	61.3	3.6
Malta	22.4	3.5	63.0	11.1
Netherlands	59.3	17.6	20.8	2.3
Austria	:	:	:	:
Poland	8.7	4.4	83.3	3.6
Portugal	27.2	7.1	58.9	6.9
Romania	14.0	1.9	81.6	2.6
Slovenia	32.6	7.4	58.0	2.1
Slovakia	7.6	3.9	86.2	2.4
Finland	:	:	:	:
Sweden	60.2	19.8	:	:
United Kingdom	:	:	:	:
Croatia	19.8	7.5	67.9	4.7
Turkey	30.2	3.0	62.5	3.9

Source: Eurostat (inn_cis5_exp)

Figure 1.23: Sources of information for innovation, average, 2006 (1)

(% of enterprises with innovation activities)

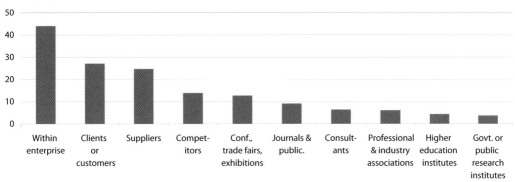

(1) Note that multiple answers could be given; average based upon data for 18 Member States, excluding Denmark, Germany, Ireland, France, Italy, Latvia, Finland, Sweden and the United Kingdom.

Source: Eurostat (inn_cis5_sou)

Figure 1.24: Effects of innovation, average, 2006 (1)

(% of enterprises with innovation activities)

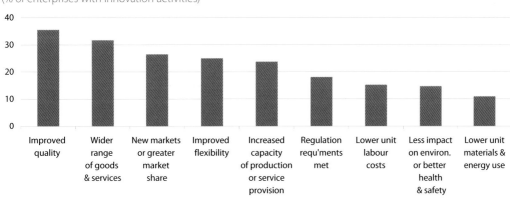

(1) Note that multiple answers could be given; average based upon data for 20 Member States, excluding Belgium, Germany, Ireland, France, Italy, Slovenia and the United Kingdom.

Source: Eurostat (inn_cis5_eff)

Table 1.12: Effects of innovation, 2006 (1)

(% of enterprises with innovation activities)

	Wider range of goods & services	New markets/ greater market share	Impr. quality	Impr. flexib.	Incr. cap. of prod./ service prov.	Lower unit labour costs	Lower unit materials & energy use	Less env. impact or better health & safety	Met regula- tions
Belgium	:	:	:	:	:	:	:	:	:
Bulgaria	38.2	30.1	38.9	21.0	21.7	15.9	13.2	20.9	25.3
Czech Republic	39.3	28.8	38.2	25.4	26.1	18.2	14.2	13.8	7.2
Denmark	18.6	15.8	16.6	15.3	18.8	11.5	7.3	5.3	9.2
Germany	:	:	:	:	:	:	:	:	:
Estonia	29.8	25.7	27.2	20.0	20.5	14.3	7.8	8.4	6.8
Ireland	:	:	:	:	:	:	:	:	:
Greece	9.1	11.6	5.8	8.3	9.2	26.2	20.7	12.9	11.3
Spain	25.2	18.6	33.5	22.6	27.4	12.9	8.5	13.4	19.8
France	:	:	:	:	:	:	:	:	:
Italy	:	:	:	:	:	:	:	:	:
Cyprus	45.3	37.9	57.5	69.8	62.5	29.2	19.9	38.0	56.0
Latvia	27.8	15.8	26.5	16.4	17.3	6.2	5.4	6.3	13.9
Lithuania	32.4	28.0	34.4	25.0	30.5	10.7	8.5	9.9	25.2
Luxembourg	57.7	45.1	62.1	35.2	33.6	13.0	6.8	12.9	28.5
Hungary	32.4	26.2	37.2	21.9	22.3	6.2	7.2	13.6	19.8
Malta	27.7	15.9	31.3	21.0	18.5	11.8	7.7	8.7	20.0
Netherlands	44.8	38.8	44.0	31.8	31.6	16.6	10.5	11.7	14.6
Austria	39.4	33.7	48.7	30.0	27.8	11.9	9.7	13.4	18.5
Poland	36.1	26.9	38.1	20.8	25.7	13.8	11.6	18.5	24.7
Portugal	34.1	25.4	44.3	31.2	36.5	22.4	15.0	24.1	25.6
Romania	37.0	29.4	41.7	28.2	34.1	18.3	14.8	23.7	20.9
Slovenia	:	:	:	:	:	:	:	:	:
Slovakia	38.1	23.1	41.6	28.5	27.2	8.0	10.8	13.8	13.4
Finland	16.5	15.5	16.9	14.4	15.3	10.7	5.2	7.2	9.6
Sweden	33.0	24.3	34.2	18.4	23.1	17.0	10.2	14.0	17.8
United Kingdom	:	:	:	:	:	:	:	:	:
Croatia	39.1	32.8	52.3	34.5	32.2	19.9	15.1	18.0	31.5
Turkey	38.3	32.6	49.5	39.4	39.4	18.0	10.2	21.6	28.8

(1) Note that multiple answers could be given.

Source: Eurostat (inn_cis5_eff)

Table 1.13: Enterprises that introduced organisational and/or marketing innovations, 2006 (1)
(% of enterprises with innovation activities)

	Total	Highly important effects of organisational innovation			
		Reduced customer response time	Improved quality of goods & services	Reduced costs per unit output	Improved employee satisfaction and/or reduced rates of employee turnover
Belgium	66.8	25.7	26.9	12.7	9.8
Bulgaria	46.2	12.9	23.1	10.9	9.9
Czech Republic	69.7	21.2	27.8	11.9	13.0
Denmark	76.0	22.1	17.0	12.6	12.1
Germany	84.6	:	:	:	:
Estonia	70.9	26.9	24.8	13.6	12.5
Ireland	65.7	38.6	39.7	29.6	16.6
Greece	86.2	8.3	1.5	23.6	21.3
Spain	:	:	:	:	:
France	:	:	:	:	:
Italy	:	:	:	:	:
Cyprus	80.1	42.1	45.4	22.3	27.7
Latvia	70.5	23.2	30.1	6.7	11.4
Lithuania	73.1	16.2	25.3	15.1	15.5
Luxembourg	83.4	34.4	46.9	14.2	18.8
Hungary	70.9	42.5	39.6	21.0	11.5
Malta	82.1	31.8	33.8	21.0	15.9
Netherlands	53.5	19.4	23.3	10.0	9.5
Austria	77.9	26.2	31.9	10.8	14.0
Poland	72.2	26.9	25.8	9.9	10.2
Portugal	82.4	37.9	43.3	20.9	18.5
Romania	73.9	34.9	39.2	16.2	16.0
Slovenia	76.6	51.4	56.3	37.6	24.7
Slovakia	:	:	:	:	:
Finland	:	:	:	:	:
Sweden	:	:	:	:	:
United Kingdom	:	:	:	:	:
Croatia	76.4	34.9	37.7	13.6	19.2
Turkey	76.6	25.4	37.6	15.6	14.8
Norway	64.0	13.0	17.5	14.5	9.8

(1) Note that multiple answers could be given.

Source: Eurostat (inn_cis5_mo and inn_cis5_oref)

Figure 1.25: Protection methods (copyright, registered designs, trademarks, patents) used by innovative and non-innovative enterprises, average, 2006 (1)

(% of enterprises with innovation activities)

(1) Note that multiple answers could be given; average based upon data for 18 Member States, excluding Denmark, Germany, France, Italy, Latvia, Slovenia, Finland, Sweden and the United Kingdom.

Source: Eurostat (inn_cis5_pat)

Figure 1.26: Enterprises citing various highly important hampering effects, average, 2006 (1)

(% of enterprises with innovation activities)

(1) Note that multiple answers could be given; average based upon data for 19 Member States, excluding Belgium, Denmark, Germany, France, Italy, Slovenia, Finland and the United Kingdom.

Source: Eurostat (inn_cis5_ham)

Figure 1.27: Reasons not to innovate, 2006 (1)

(% of non-innovative enterprises)

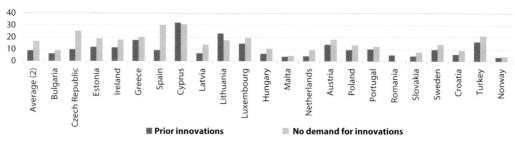

(1) Note that multiple answers could be given; Belgium, Denmark, Germany, Italy, Slovenia and Finland, not available.
(2) Average based upon data for 19 Member States, excluding Belgium, Denmark, Germany, France, Italy, Slovenia, Finland and the United Kingdom.

Source: Eurostat (inn_cis5_ham)

1.5 Patents

Intellectual property rights provide a link between innovation, inventions and the marketplace. Applying for a patent, for example, makes an invention public but at the same time gives it protection. A count of patents is one measure that reflects a country's inventive activity and also shows its capacity to exploit knowledge and translate it into potential economic gains. In this context, indicators based on patent statistics are widely used to assess the inventive and innovative performance. While patents are generally used to protect R & D results, they are also significant as a source of technical information, which may prevent re-inventing and re-developing ideas because of a lack of information. More information on the sources and methods concerning patent data are available in Subchapter 14.3 of this publication.

The falling trend in patent applications between 2000 and 2005 is linked to the length of patenting procedures and should not be understood as a real decline in patenting activity. For this reason the 2005 figures in Eurostat's reference database are flagged as provisional.

Among the Member States, Germany had by far the highest number of patent applications to the European Patent Office (EPO), some 11 500 in 2005 (which was almost half the total number made by enterprises from within the EU-27). In relative terms, the Member States with the highest number of patent applications per million inhabitants were Luxembourg (143) and Germany (139), followed some way behind by Austria (79).

About one third (32.5 %) of the high-technology patent applications made to the EPO in 2005 came from EU-27 Member States, a further one quarter (25.6 %) coming from Japan. A little over one half (52.4 %) of these high-technology applications concerned communications technology, and a further one third (32.1 %) related to computer and automated business equipment.

A little over one fifth (21.7 %) of the patent applications by EU-27 Member States to the EPO in 2005 concerned performing operations (such as printing and shaping) and transport (such as forms of transport or hoisting, lifting and hauling). Patents concerning electricity (such as basic elements, circuitry and power distribution) were the next most common (14.7 %), followed closely by patents in physics (such as optics, checking devices and information storage) and then human necessities (such as foodstuffs, personal or domestic articles and health articles).

Figure 1.28: Patent applications to the European Patent Office (EPO), 2005 (1)

(applications per million inhabitants)

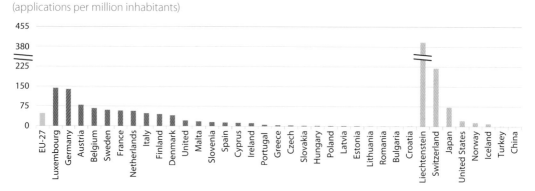

(1) Data refer to applications filed directly under the European Patent Convention or to applications filed under the Patent Co-operation Treaty and designated to the EPO (Euro-PCT). For patent applications to the EPO all direct applications (EPO-direct) are taken into account, but among the PCT applications (applications following the procedure laid down by the PCT) made to the EPO only those that have entered into the regional phase are counted. Patent applications are counted according to the year in which they were filed. Estimates.

Source: Eurostat (pat_ep_nipc)

Figure 1.29: High-technology patent applications made to the European Patent Office (EPO), 2005 (1)

(% of total)

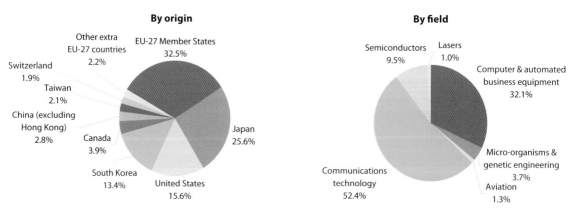

By origin

Other extra EU-27 countries 2.2%
EU-27 Member States 32.5%
Switzerland 1.9%
Taiwan 2.1%
China (excluding Hong Kong) 2.8%
Canada 3.9%
Japan 25.6%
South Korea 13.4%
United States 15.6%

By field

Semiconductors 9.5%
Lasers 1.0%
Computer & automated business equipment 32.1%
Micro-organisms & genetic engineering 3.7%
Aviation 1.3%
Communications technology 52.4%

(1) Provisional.

Source: Eurostat (pat_ep_ntec)

Table 1.14: Patent applications to the European Patent Office (EPO), 2005 (1)

	Total		of which (%):							
	(1 000)	(per million inhab.)	Human neces-sities	Perfor-ming oper.; transp.	Chem.; metall.	Textiles; paper	Fixed constr.	Mech. eng.; lighting; heating; weapons	Physics	Elec-tricity
EU-27	23.4	47.7	12.4	21.7	6.4	1.9	5.8	11.7	13.0	14.8
Belgium	0.7	66.6	13.8	17.9	11.5	1.9	3.8	5.4	14.9	19.6
Bulgaria	0.0	0.3	:	37.5	:	:	:	:	25.1	37.5
Czech Republic	0.0	3.5	8.9	32.5	14.6	5.6	3.7	:	11.5	13.3
Denmark	0.2	40.0	23.5	13.7	4.5	0.5	10.2	6.8	8.7	20.6
Germany	11.5	138.9	10.9	24.0	6.2	1.8	5.4	12.8	13.0	13.9
Estonia	0.0	1.5	25.0	:	:	:	:	:	50.0	25.0
Ireland	0.0	11.8	8.7	17.3	2.1	0.7	4.1	16.5	18.4	15.8
Greece	0.0	3.9	14.9	11.4	7.6	:	9.9	11.4	10.3	16.0
Spain	0.6	13.6	16.9	22.3	8.7	1.6	9.7	10.0	7.8	9.0
France	3.6	57.7	13.2	18.5	4.8	0.9	5.4	11.5	14.6	19.0
Italy	2.8	48.0	16.4	23.4	4.9	3.8	6.6	12.3	9.0	10.0
Cyprus	0.0	12.5	14.3	:	:	21.4	42.9	10.7	10.7	:
Latvia	0.0	1.6	:	53.3	:	:	:	:	26.7	20.0
Lithuania	0.0	0.6	:	:	25.0	:	:	:	50.0	:
Luxembourg	0.1	143.3	4.6	28.8	11.5	:	2.1	17.9	8.3	9.2
Hungary	0.0	2.1	17.9	10.4	15.8	:	2.4	:	12.6	17.3
Malta	0.0	17.6	84.7	:	:	:	:	:	3.5	11.7
Netherlands	0.9	56.5	14.2	22.0	12.7	1.2	7.1	4.7	16.6	10.0
Austria	0.6	79.1	11.0	19.7	8.1	3.9	9.9	12.0	11.4	10.3
Poland	0.1	1.7	2.1	11.6	7.3	1.5	5.4	18.8	12.5	26.0
Portugal	0.1	5.6	6.7	4.4	3.3	:	5.9	17.3	8.4	36.7
Romania	0.0	0.4	26.0	39.0	:	:	:	:	20.8	13.0
Slovenia	0.0	15.1	16.6	16.6	4.7	6.6	8.3	5.3	6.6	1.9
Slovakia	0.0	2.2	:	4.2	20.1	:	8.4	50.5	:	16.8
Finland	0.2	44.7	13.4	13.1	8.0	4.3	3.4	7.9	12.5	25.2
Sweden	0.5	60.2	7.3	19.0	7.1	0.6	5.2	10.8	17.1	20.7
United Kingdom	1.3	21.1	12.1	14.8	6.9	1.5	5.0	11.1	16.3	20.6
Croatia	0.0	1.0	31.4	:	:	:	:	11.8	:	33.1
Turkey	0.0	0.6	11.3	20.1	8.8	2.5	12.6	17.6	4.4	7.5
Iceland	0.0	10.2	66.7	:	:	:	:	33.3	:	:
Liechtenstein	0.0	391.6	35.2	27.1	11.1	:	3.7	10.5	8.9	:
Norway	0.1	14.5	8.0	23.6	6.8	2.0	1.9	9.9	7.0	14.4
Switzerland	1.6	219.0	14.2	18.7	6.9	2.2	4.7	5.7	21.5	12.3
China	0.5	0.4	8.3	10.5	2.3	0.2	0.9	2.0	11.9	56.4
Japan	9.2	71.8	5.0	19.5	6.5	0.8	0.5	7.8	26.9	24.5
Russian Federation	0.0	0.3	7.9	16.0	14.7	4.1	2.4	:	17.6	20.6
United States	6.4	21.7	14.2	13.6	7.3	0.7	1.1	9.7	21.0	21.3

(1) Provisional.

Source: Eurostat (pat_ep_nipc)

1.6 Business start-ups and entrepreneurship

The Entrepreneurship Action Plan adopted in 2004 established a mechanism to foster entrepreneurship. A 2006 final report on its implementation concluded that its underlying goals had been achieved, and that it had built the path to further actions to be carried out under the competitiveness and innovation framework programme (CIP). Furthermore, it provided the platform for stronger recognition of SME issues leading to the June 2008 proposal by the European Commission for a 'Small Business Act' [5]. This proposal aims to address the needs of Europe's small and medium-sized enterprises, to make Europe more entrepreneurial, and to help its enterprises thrive, by improving the conditions for SMEs while taking account of their diversity. The proposal focuses on promoting entrepreneurship, anchoring the 'Think Small First' principle in policy-making and supporting SMEs' growth.

A majority (57.7 %) of individuals in the EU-25 that launched or were launching their own businesses did so because they saw an opportunity to do so, rather than solely out of necessity (27.0 %). Among the Member States, Greece stood out as the only country where the single largest factor for business start-ups was out of necessity (42.4 % of individuals), which was in stark contrast to the four fifths (82.9 %) of entrepreneurs in Denmark who did so because they saw an opportunity.

A little over one half of the EU-25's entrepreneurs stated that having an appropriate business idea and receiving necessary financial support were very important in making their decision to set up their businesses. For a little over one quarter of entrepreneurs, dissatisfaction with their previous situation and/or changes in family circumstances were also very important reasons to start-up their businesses, with one third (35.5 %) also citing contact with an appropriate business partner as very important.

Among individuals who had never started a business and were not taking steps to start one, a little under two thirds (61.7 %) had never thought about it, this share rising to about three quarters in Belgium and Lithuania. A relatively high proportion of individuals (20.5 %) across the EU-25, who had not yet started a business, had at one time thought about doing so, and in cases taken steps to do so before giving up. In Germany, the United Kingdom and Austria, the proportion of those who did not follow through their interest was relatively high (about 25 %).

The employer enterprise birth rate for the business economy (NACE Rev. 1.1 Sections C to K, excluding holding companies) was 11.3 % among the 13 Member States for which data are available for 2005. This compared with a birth rate of 9.3 % for the same countries when considering all enterprises, not just those with employees. Employer enterprise birth rates were generally higher than birth rates for all enterprises in 2005, exceptions being in Bulgaria, Latvia and Romania.

(5) http://ec.europa.eu/enterprise/entrepreneurship/sba_en.htm.

There is considerable policy interest in the way in which enterprises grow and create employment. Across the 12 Member States for which data are available, the number of persons employed in newly born enterprises in 2005 was the equivalent of 3.5 % of the total number of persons employed in all employer enterprises; the corresponding share for employer enterprise deaths in 2004 was 2.9 % of the workforce. Newly born enterprises accounted for a particularly high share of the workforce in Slovakia (5.9 %), other high shares being in Spain (4.4 %) and Romania (4.1 %).

There is also interest in enterprises (new or established) that display particularly rapid rates of growth. This sub-group are likely to have behaved in an atypical fashion, in that they are likely to have done something different or new in terms of product or process development, in order to achieve such rapid growth. Across the 14 Member States for which data are available for 2005, high-growth enterprises accounted for an average 3.8 % of employment across active enterprises and 5.9 % of turnover. In many of the Member States that joined the EU in either 2004 or 2007, these rates were considerably higher.

Figure 1.30: Preference for being an employee or self-employed, 2007

(%)

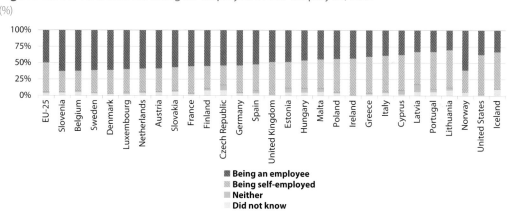

Being an employee
Being self-employed
Neither
Did not know

Source: European Commission, Flash Eurobarometer 192 (Entrepreneurship Survey of the EU (25 Member States), United States, Iceland and Norway)

Figure 1.31: Business start-up decision by entrepreneurs, 2007

(%)

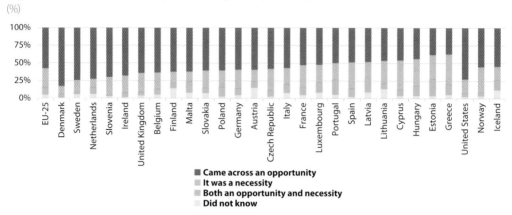

- ■ **Came across an opportunity**
- ▨ **It was a necessity**
- ▨ **Both an opportunity and necessity**
- ▨ **Did not know**

Source: European Commission, Flash Eurobarometer 192 (Entrepreneurship Survey of the EU (25 Member States), United States, Iceland and Norway)

Figure 1.32: Change in 'real' employer businesses, total economy (NACE Rev. 1.1 Sections A to Q),
1997-2007 (1)

(percentage points)

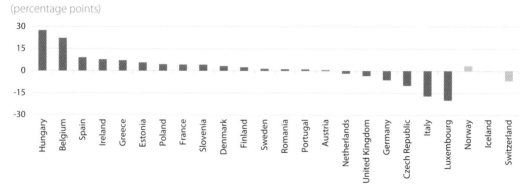

(1) Overall growth of the number of self-employed persons (aged 15 or more), who are not working alone and who are not family workers (in other words, who employ at least one other person); Bulgaria, Cyprus, Latvia, Lithuania, Malta and Slovakia, not available.

Source: Eurostat (lfsa_egaps)

Figure 1.33: Preference for self-employment status - main elements, EU-25, 2007
(% of those who have started a business or are taking steps to start one or who thought of it or had already taken steps to start a business but gave up)

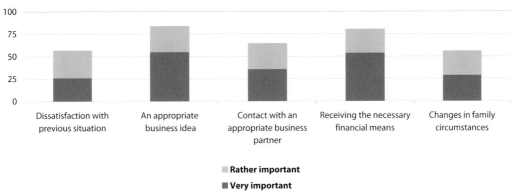

Source: European Commission, Flash Eurobarometer 192 (Entrepreneurship Survey of the EU (25 Member States), United States, Iceland and Norway)

Figure 1.34: Experience in setting up a business: among those who have not yet done this, EU-25, 2007
(%)

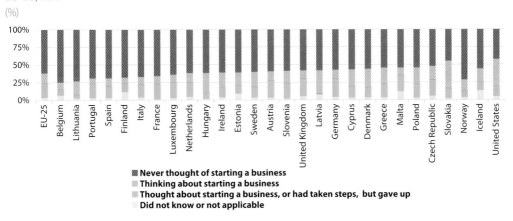

Source: European Commission, Flash Eurobarometer 192 (Entrepreneurship Survey of the EU (25 Member States), United States, Iceland and Norway)

Figure 1.35: Comparison of enterprise birth rates and employer enterprise birth rates, 2005 (1)

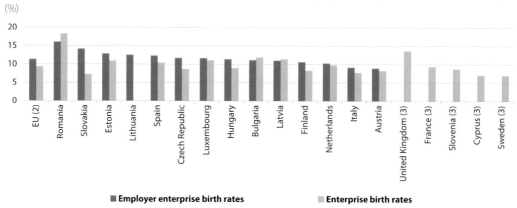

(1) Enterprise birth rates are defined as the number of enterprise births in the reference period (t), divided by the number of enterprises active in t; data for Belgium, Denmark, Germany, Ireland, Greece, Malta, Poland and Portugal, not available.
(2) EU average based on data available for Bulgaria, the Czech Republic, Estonia, Spain, Italy, Latvia, Luxembourg, Hungary, the Netherlands, Austria, Romania, Slovakia and Finland.
(3) Data for employer enterprise birth rates, not available.

Source: Eurostat (bd_9f_size_cl)

Figure 1.36: Proportion of employment among employer enterprise births and employer enterprise deaths, 2005 (1)

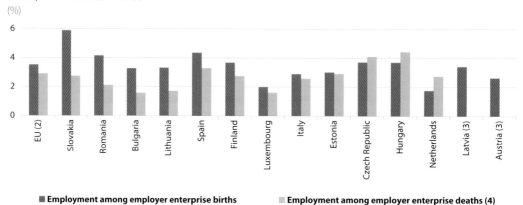

(1) Data for Belgium, Denmark, Germany, Ireland, Greece, France, Cyprus, Malta, Poland, Portugal, Slovenia, Sweden and the United Kingdom, not available.
(2) EU average based on data available for Bulgaria, the Czech Republic, Estonia, Spain, Italy, Lithuania, Luxembourg, Hungary, the Netherlands, Romania, Slovakia and Finland.
(3) Data for employment among employer enterprise deaths, not available.
(4) Numbers of persons employed in employer enterprise deaths, 2004.

Source: Eurostat (bd_9f_size_cl)

Figure 1.37: High-growth firm rate by employment/turnover, business economy (Sections C to K), 2005 (1)

(% of active enterprises)

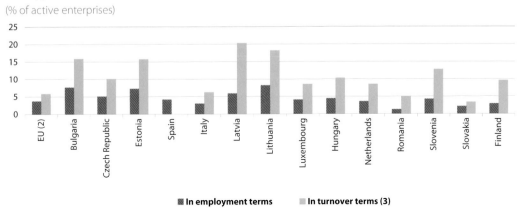

(1) Share of high growth enterprises in the population of active enterprises, measured in employment/turnover; all enterprises with average annualised growth greater than 20 % per annum, over a three year period should be considered as high-growth enterprises; enterprises with ten or more employees; data for Belgium, Denmark, Germany, Ireland, Greece, France, Cyprus, Malta, Austria, Poland, Portugal, Sweden and the United Kingdom, not available.
(2) EU average composed of available countries shown in graph.
(3) Spain, not available.

Source: Eurostat (bd_9n)

Figure 1.38: Employment/turnover growth rate of 'gazelles', business economy (Sections C to K), 2005 (1)

(% of active enterprises)

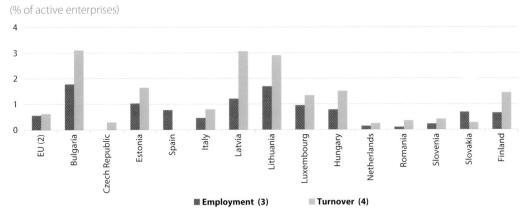

(1) Share of young high growth enterprises in the population of active enterprises, measured in employment/turnover; all enterprises up to 5 years old with average annualised growth greater than 20 % per annum, over a three year period, should be considered as gazelles; enterprises with ten or more employees; data for Belgium, Denmark, Germany, Ireland, Greece, France, Cyprus, Malta, Austria, Poland, Portugal, Sweden and the United Kingdom, not available.
(2) EU average composed of available countries shown in graph.
(3) Czech Republic, not available.
(4) Spain, not available.

Source: Eurostat (bd_9n)

1.7 Factors of business success

Averaging across the Member States for which data are available, the overwhelming majority (81.2 %) of enterprises born in 2002 had no employees when starting-up. At start-up in 2002, very few (1.5 %) enterprises had more than 10 employees, the rest (16.8 %) employing between 1 and 9 persons. Of those enterprises born in 2002 that had survived to 2005, however, many had grown in terms of employee numbers: on average, 29.4 % of enterprises had between 1 and 9 employees

and 4.1 % had more than 10 or more employees. There was particularly strong employment growth among surviving enterprises in Lithuania, where the number of enterprises without employees fell to almost none (0.3 %), whilst those employing over ten employees grew from 4.4 % at start-up in 2002 to 23.5 % of surviving enterprises in 2005. Strong employment growth in surviving start-ups was also noted in Bulgaria, Estonia and Romania.

Figure 1.39: Business units having been born in 2002 and surviving to 2005 (1)
(% share of total number of units having been born in 2002 and surviving to 2005)

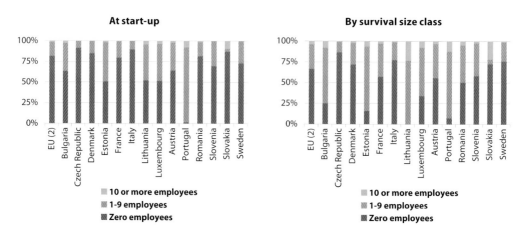

(1) Units within industry and services excluding public administration and management activities of holding companies (NACE Rev. 1.1 Sections C to K excluding Class 74.15); Slovenia, not available for
(2) Average of those Member States for which data are available.

Source: Eurostat (fobs_isc and fobs_ssc)

Table 1.15: Business units having survived from 2002 to 2005, according to status of the
founder (1)

(% share of total number of units having survived)

	By gender		By age			By education			
	Male	Female	Less than 30	30-39 years	40+ years	Primary & lower secondary	Upper secondary	Post-secondary non-tertiary	Tertiary
EU (2)	72.9	27.1	25.0	35.6	39.3	27.6	41.2	10.1	21.1
Bulgaria	59.2	40.8	15.3	28.7	55.9	5.0	45.1	18.7	31.2
Czech Republic	72.7	27.3	33.2	32.7	34.1	13.1	61.7	6.7	18.5
Denmark	79.6	20.4	15.9	35.9	48.2	20.5	24.2	15.7	39.6
Estonia	76.0	24.0	25.3	39.5	35.2	2.8	19.8	20.5	56.9
France	79.4	20.6	8.8	34.0	57.1	23.6	42.5	:	33.9
Italy	74.8	25.2	29.9	40.0	30.1	32.3	46.3	2.3	19.2
Latvia	64.7	35.3	18.1	34.6	47.3	2.3	37.4	10.1	50.2
Lithuania	74.1	25.9	6.6	33.8	59.5	1.2	13.3	17.1	68.4
Luxembourg	81.6	18.4	10.1	36.5	53.3	19.4	23.7	18.2	38.7
Austria	72.3	27.7	10.8	39.7	49.5	5.7	36.6	22.0	35.6
Portugal	85.8	14.2	13.0	31.3	55.7	51.2	26.4	6.7	15.7
Romania	64.4	35.6	23.2	32.3	44.6	52.1	10.0	32.5	5.4
Slovenia	73.4	26.6	24.7	33.2	42.0	4.0	41.3	25.4	29.3
Slovakia	70.0	30.0	31.1	31.4	37.5	28.5	45.3	4.6	21.6
Sweden	79.2	20.8	14.1	34.9	51.1	15.7	35.2	20.9	28.2

(1) Units within industry and services excluding public administration and management activities of holding companies (NACE Rev. 1.1
Sections C to K excluding Class 74.15).
(2) Average of those Member States for which data are available.

Source: Eurostat (fobs_gen, fobs_age and fobs_edu)

Economy

2

Economic and social progress and constant improvements in living and working conditions are fundamental objectives for the EU. Over the last five decades policy-makers have strived to improve economic integration (through removing barriers to the free movement of goods, services, money and people) with the goal of creating more jobs and economic growth. Much has been achieved: such as the customs union, then the single market and, more recently, economic and monetary union (EMU).

The chief objective of the Single European Act was to add new momentum to the process of the European construction so as to complete the internal market [1]. Since 1993 the European single market has strongly enhanced the possibility for people, goods, services and money to move around Europe as freely as within a single country. These freedoms, foreseen from the outset of the EC in the Treaty establishing the European Economic Community of 1957 have been designed: to allow individuals the right to live, work, study or retire in another Member State; to increase competition leading to lower prices, a wider choice of things to buy and higher levels of protection for consumers; and to make it easier and cheaper for businesses to interact across borders. It is now easier to travel across the EU's internal frontiers, in particular within the Schengen area, or to order a wide range of products that may be delivered from all over the EU. According to the European Commission, the single market has created 2.5 million new jobs since 1993 and generated more than EUR 800 000 million in extra wealth, through abolishing tariffs and quotas, as well as technical and administrative obstacles to free trade [2]. The creation of the single market has increased incentives to liberalise previously protected monopoly markets for utilities such as telecommunications, electricity, gas and water. As a result, many households and industries across Europe are increasingly able to choose who supplies them with related services. Nevertheless, there remain areas, for example in relation to financial services and transportation, where separate national markets still exist.

(1) http://europa.eu/scadplus/treaties/singleact_en.htm.
(2) http://europa.eu/pol/overview_en.htm.

The Council and Parliament of the EU adopted in 2005 the 'Integrated Guidelines Package'[3] which is a roadmap for spurring growth and creating jobs in a socially cohesive and environmentally responsible EU for the period 2005 to 2008. This package represents a comprehensive strategy of macro-economic, micro-economic and employment policies. Under the package, Member States draw up national reform programmes, using the tax and social welfare policy mix they think best suits national circumstances.

2.1 National accounts

Introduction

The most frequently used measure for the overall size of an economy is gross domestic product (GDP). It corresponds to the total monetary value of all production activity in a certain geographic area. GDP at market prices is the final result of the production activity of all producer units within a certain area (for example, a national territory), no matter whether the units are owned by nationals or foreigners. GDP, and in particular GDP per capita, is one of the main indicators used for economic analysis, as well as spatial and/or temporal comparisons, in particular as a measure of living standards.

Household saving rates vary considerably between countries because of institutional, demographic and socio-economic differences between countries. Government provisions for old-age pensions, the extent to which governments provide insurance against sickness and unemployment, and the demographic age structure of the population will all influence the rate at which a population saves – older persons tend to run down their financial assets during their retirement to the detriment of saving. Finally, the availability and price of credit, as well as attitudes towards debt may also influence choices made by individuals regarding whether to spend or save; something that became apparent with devastating effect during the autumn of 2008.

Aside from individuals' choices as to consumption and savings patterns, the Member States of the EU also need to have sound public finances, by balancing their choice of expenditure priorities in relation to the types and levels of taxes that they fix. The governments of the Member States retain responsibility for fixing their levels of direct taxation – i.e. tax on personal incomes and company profits, savings and capital gains. In the area of company tax, the EU has two goals: preventing harmful tax competition between Member States and supporting the principle of free movement of capital. Cross-border payments of interest, royalties and dividends to sister and parent companies have progressively been exempted from withholding tax in the country from which the payment is made and discussions are under way on having a common tax base for companies, i.e. the rules applying to each type of transaction would be the same across the EU in order to prevent unfair competition, while still leaving Member States free to set actual tax rates.

(3) http://eur-lex.europa.eu/LexUriServ/LexUriServ.do?uri=OJ:L:2005:205:0021:0027:EN:PDF.

Definitions and data availability

The European system of (integrated economic) accounts provides the methodology for national accounts in Europe. The current version, **ESA 95**, is fully consistent with the worldwide guidelines on the national accounts, the SNA 93.

Data within the national accounts domain encompasses information on GDP and its components, employment, final consumption aggregates, income, and savings. Many of these annual variables are also calculated on a quarterly basis. Breakdowns exist for certain variables by economic activity (industries, as defined by NACE), investment products, final consumption purpose (as defined by COICOP) and institutional sectors.

An analysis of the economy of different countries can be facilitated by studying GDP per capita, so removing the influence of the absolute size of the population. **GDP per capita** is a broad economic indicator of living standards, and a basic measure of the competitiveness of an economy. The volume index of **GDP per capita in purchasing power standards** (PPS) is expressed in relation to the EU average (set to equal 100). If the index of a country is higher/lower than 100, this country's level of GDP per head is above/below the EU-27 average. Such comparisons of the wealth and competitiveness of countries should ideally be made using a PPS based series. To do this, measures of GDP in national currencies are converted into a common currency using purchasing power parities (PPPs) that reflect the purchasing power of each currency, rather than using market exchange rates. GDP per capita in purchasing power standards (the common currency), therefore eliminates differences in price levels between countries and also allows a comparison between economies of different

absolute sizes. Note that the index, calculated from PPS figures is intended for cross-country comparisons rather than for temporal comparisons.

The calculation of the annual **growth rate of GDP at constant prices** is intended to allow comparisons of the dynamics of economic development both over time and between economies of different sizes, irrespective of price levels.

A further set of national accounts data is used within the context of competitiveness analyses, namely indicators relating to the productivity of the workforce, such as labour productivity measures. GDP in PPS per person employed is intended to give an overall impression of the productivity of national economies. It should be kept in mind, though, that this measure depends on the structure of total employment and may, for instance, be lowered by a shift from full-time to part-time work. **GDP in PPS per hour worked** therefore gives a clearer picture of productivity, through the use of a more consistent measure of labour input.

GDP can be defined and calculated in three ways:

- the output approach – as the sum of gross value added of the various institutional sectors or the various industries, plus taxes and less subsidies on products;
- the expenditure approach – as the sum of final uses of goods and services by resident institutional units (final consumption and gross capital formation), plus exports and minus imports of goods and services;
- the income approach – as the sum of the compensation of employees, net taxes on production and imports, gross operating surplus and mixed income.

The output approach

Gross value added is defined as the value of all newly generated goods and services less the value of all goods and services consumed in their creation; the depreciation of fixed assets is not included. When calculating value added, output is valued at basic prices and intermediate consumption at purchasers' prices. Taxes less subsidies on products have to be added to value added to obtain GDP at market prices.

Various measures of **labour productivity** are available, for example, based on GDP (or value added) in PPS either relative to the number of persons employed or to the number of hours worked.

The breakdown of the gross value added generated by particular industries is presented in terms of six NACE Rev. 1 headings, covering: agriculture, hunting and fishing; industry; construction; trade, transport and communication services; business activities and financial services, and other services.

In the system of national accounts, only households, non-profit institutions serving households (NPISH) and government have final consumption, whereas corporations have intermediate consumption. **Private final consumption expenditure**, or that performed by households and NPISH, is defined as expenditure on goods and services for the direct satisfaction of individual needs, whereas **government consumption expenditure** includes goods and services produced by government, as well as purchases of goods and services by government that are supplied to households as social transfers in kind.

The expenditure approach

National accounts aggregates from the expenditure approach are used by the European Central Bank (ECB) and European Commission services as important tools for economic analysis and policy decisions. The quarterly series are central to business-cycle analysis and subsequent policy decisions. These series are also widely employed for supporting business decisions in the private sector, in particular within financial markets.

The expenditure approach of GDP is defined as private final consumption expenditure + government final consumption expenditure + gross capital formation + exports - imports.

Private final consumption expenditure includes final expenditure of households and non-profit institutions serving households (NPISH), in other words, expenditure on goods or services that are used for the direct satisfaction of individual needs. **NPISHs** are private, non-market producers which are separate legal entities. Their principal resources, apart from those derived from occasional sales, are derived from voluntary contributions in cash or in kind from households in their capacity as consumers, from payments made by general governments and from property income. Examples of NPISHs include churches, trade unions or political parties.

Government final consumption expenditure includes two categories of expenditure; the value of goods and services produced by general government itself other than own-account capital formation and sales, and purchases by general government of goods and services produced by market producers that are supplied to households – without any transformation – as social transfers in kind.

Gross fixed capital formation consists of resident producers' acquisitions, less disposals, of fixed assets plus certain additions to the value of non-produced assets realised by productive activity. **Fixed assets** are tangible or intangible assets produced as outputs from processes of production that are themselves used repeatedly, or continuously, in processes of production for more than one year; such assets may be outputs from production processes or imports. Investment may be made by public or private institutions. **Gross capital formation** is the sum of gross fixed capital formation and the change in inventories. **Changes in inventories** are measured by the value of the entries into inventories less the value of withdrawals and the value of any recurrent losses of goods held in inventories.

The **external balance** is the difference between exports and imports of goods and services. Depending on the size of exports and imports, it can be positive (a surplus) or negative (a deficit).

The income approach

Eurostat data on income from input factors are crucial to economic analysis in a number of contexts inside and outside the European Commission. Typical examples are studies of competitiveness, of income distribution inequalities, or of long-term economic developments. Users outside the European Commission include, in particular, academia and financial institutions.

Production requires 'input factors' such as the work of employees and capital; these input factors have to be paid for. The income-side approach shows how GDP is distributed among different participants in the production process, as the sum of:

- **compensation of employees**: the total remuneration, in cash or in kind, payable by an employer to an employee in return for work done by the latter during the accounting period; the compensation of employees is broken down into: wages and salaries (in cash and in kind); employers' social contributions (employers' actual social contributions and employers' imputed social contributions);
- **gross operating surplus**: this is the surplus (or deficit) on production activities before account has been taken of the interest, rents or charges paid or received for the use of assets;
- **mixed income**: this is the remuneration for the work carried out by the owner (or by members of his/her family) of an unincorporated enterprise; this is referred to as 'mixed income' since it cannot be distinguished from the entrepreneurial profit of the owner;
- **taxes on production and imports less subsidies**: these consist of compulsory (in the case of taxes) unrequited payments to or from general government or institutions of the EU, in respect of the production or import of goods and services, the employment of labour, and the ownership or use of land, buildings or other assets used in production.

Household saving is the main domestic source of funds to finance capital investment. Savings rates can be measured on either a gross or net basis. **Net saving rates** are measured after deducting consumption of fixed capital (depreciation). The system of accounts also provides for both disposable income and saving to be shown on a gross basis, in other words, with both aggregates including the consumption of fixed capital. In this respect, household savings may be estimated by subtracting consumption expenditure and the adjustment for the change in net equity of households in pension funds reserves from disposable income. The latter consists essentially of income from employment and from the operation of unincorporated enterprises, plus receipts of interest, dividends and social benefits minus payments of income taxes, interest and social security contributions.

Main findings

The GDP of the EU-27 was EUR 12 303 961 million in 2007, with the countries of the euro area accounting for a little under three quarters (72.5 %) of this total. The sum of the four largest EU economies (Germany, the United Kingdom, France and Italy) accounted for almost two thirds (64.0 %) of the EU-27's GDP in 2007. Cross-country comparisons should be made with caution and it is necessary to consider the effect of exchange rate fluctuations when analysing data. For example, the apparent fluctuation of GDP in the United States is, to a large degree, a reflection of a strong dollar between 2001 and 2003 and a subsequent

reversal to a strong euro thereafter, rather than any inherent change in the level of GDP in dollar terms (which has continued to rise).

Having grown at an average rate of around 3 % per annum during the late 1990s, real GDP growth slowed considerably after the turn of the millennium, to just above 1 % per annum in both 2002 and 2003, before rebounding more strongly in 2006 and 2007 back to about 3.0 % per annum.

In order to look at standards of living, one of the most frequently cited statistics is that of GDP per capita. Across the EU-27 as a whole, GDP per capita was EUR 24 800 in 2007. Among Member States, by far the highest level was recorded for Luxembourg (EUR 75 200 per capita). Even after accounting for the relatively high cost of living in Luxembourg, GDP per capita in PPS terms remained almost twice as high as in any other Member State; these high values for Luxembourg are partly explained by the importance of cross-border workers from Belgium, France and Germany. The lowest levels of GDP per capita among the Member States were recorded in Bulgaria and Romania, where living standards (again in PPS terms) were approximately 40 % of the EU-27 average in 2007.

In recent years, labour productivity among those Member States that joined the EU since 2004, in particular the Czech Republic, Poland, Slovenia, Slovakia and the Baltic Member States has been converging quickly towards the EU-27 average.

There has been a considerable shift in the economic structure of the EU economy in the last few decades, with the proportion of gross value added accounted for by agriculture and industry falling, with that for most services rising. This change is, at least in part, a result of phenomena such as technological change, the evolution of relative prices, and globalisation, often resulting in manufacturing bases being moved to lower labour-cost regions. More than one quarter (28.2 %) of the EU-27's gross value added was accounted for by business activities and financial services in 2007. There were three other sectoral branches that also contributed significant shares of just over one fifth of total value added, namely other services (largely made up of public administrations, education and health systems, as well as other community, social and personal service activities (22.3 %)); trade, transport and communication services (21.2 %); and industry (20.2 %). The remainder of the economy was divided between construction (6.3 %) and agriculture, hunting and fishing (1.9 %).

As such, the three groups of services identified above accounted for 71.7 % of total gross value added in the EU-27 in 2007. The relative importance of services was particularly high in Luxembourg, France, the United Kingdom and Belgium, as well as the holiday destinations of Cyprus and Malta. Services accounted for more than three quarters of total value added in each of these six countries.

Final consumption expenditure across the EU-27 rose by 28.1 % between 1996 and 2007. This was very similar to the growth in GDP during the same period (31.2 %). Growth in gross capital formation outstripped both, increasing by 48.8 % during the same period. Final consumption expenditure of households and non-profit institutions serving households rose by 30.1 % between 1996 and 2007, and represented 57.5 % of the EU-27's GDP in 2007. This share has been relatively stable over time, although it has declined in recent years from a peak of 58.7 % in 2001.

The share of total GDP that is devoted to investment in fixed assets is an important indicator of future economic growth – especially the level of investment in machinery and equipment and ICT products. Gross fixed capital formation represented 20.6 % of the EU-27's GDP in 2007. This marked the fourth successive year that the relative importance of gross fixed capital formation had risen, from a low of 19.6 % of GDP at the bottom of the last economic slowdown in 2003. There was a wide variation in investment intensity that may, in part, reflect the different economic structures of the Member States. Gross fixed capital formation as a share of GDP ranged from more than 30 % in Estonia, Latvia, Spain and Romania, to less than 19 % of GDP in Sweden, Germany and the United Kingdom.

The external balance of goods and services has been in surplus during the last decade. Nonetheless, in the most recent years the relative size of the surplus has decreased, reaching 0.4 % of GDP in 2007.

The higher the output of an economy, the more income can be redistributed to the factors that have provided for its creation. Between 1998 and 2007, the GDP of the EU-27 (measured at current prices) rose by a total of 51.1 %. In comparison, the income of employees rose by 47.7 % in total over the same period. The fastest

growth in income factors was recorded for taxes on production and imports less subsidies, resulting largely from a marked acceleration during periods of economic expansion (the late 1990s and again from 2004 onwards).

Within the EU-27, the breakdown of GDP by input factors in 2007 was dominated by the compensation of employees (48.5 %), while gross operating surplus and mixed income accounted for 39.2 % of GDP and taxes on production and imports less subsidies the remaining 12.3 %.

In some countries, gross national saving as a proportion of national disposable income fell considerably between 1997 and 2007. This was particularly the case in Portugal (down 7.2 points), Slovakia (down 3.3 points), the United Kingdom (down 2.9 points), Ireland (down 2.8 points) and Italy (down 2.5 points). The

highest national savings rates (between 27.8 % and 28.6 %) were recorded in the Netherlands, Sweden and Finland.

In relation to gross household disposable income, gross household savings represented 10.7 % of GDP in 2007 for the EU-27. Belgium, Germany, France, Italy and Austria reported a savings rate of around 14-16 % of their gross household disposable income. In contrast, Finland, the United Kingdom and Denmark reported household savings rates of between 2.5 % and 5.5 % in 2006 and 2007, while rates in Greece and Lithuania fell to around 1 %. Romania and Estonia reported negative values between 2003 and 2006, indicating that households in these countries were spending more money than they earned, and funded some of their expenditure through credit, but Estonia reported a positive value in 2007.

Figure 2.1: GDP per capita at current market prices, 2007

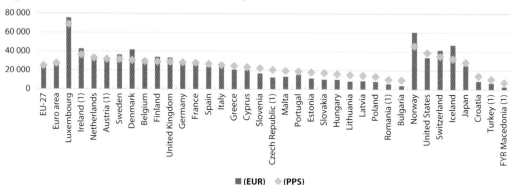

(1) Forecasts.

Source: Eurostat (nama_gdp_c and tec00001)

Table 2.1: GDP per capita at current market prices
(PPS, EU-27=100)

	1998	1999	2000	2001	2002	2003	2004	2005	2006	2007	GDP per capita, 2007 (PPS)	GDP per capita, 2007 (EUR)
EU-27	100	100	100	100	100	100	100	100	100	100	24 800	24 800
Euro area (1)	115	114	114	114	113	112	111	111	110	110	27 300	27 800
Belgium (2)	123	123	126	124	125	123	121	121	120	118	29 300	31 100
Bulgaria	27	27	28	29	31	33	34	35	37	38	9 500	3 800
Czech Republic	71	70	69	70	71	74	75	76	78	82	20 200	12 400
Denmark	132	131	132	128	129	125	126	127	126	123	30 500	41 700
Germany	123	123	119	117	116	117	117	115	114	113	28 100	29 500
Estonia	42	42	45	46	50	55	57	62	68	71	17 600	11 400
Ireland	122	127	131	133	138	141	142	144	145	146	36 200	42 600
Greece	84	83	84	87	91	92	94	96	97	98	24 300	20 500
Spain	96	97	98	98	101	101	101	103	105	107	26 500	23 400
France (2)	115	115	116	116	116	112	110	112	112	111	27 600	29 800
Italy	120	118	117	118	112	111	107	105	103	101	25 200	25 900
Cyprus	87	88	89	91	90	89	91	93	92	93	23 100	19 900
Latvia	36	36	37	39	41	43	46	50	54	58	14 400	8 800
Lithuania	40	39	39	42	44	49	51	53	56	60	15 000	8 300
Luxembourg	218	238	244	235	241	247	253	264	279	276	68 500	75 200
Hungary	53	54	56	59	62	64	63	64	65	64	15 700	10 100
Malta	81	81	84	78	80	79	77	78	77	77	19 200	13 200
Netherlands	129	131	135	134	134	130	130	132	132	133	32 900	34 600
Austria	132	132	132	125	127	127	127	128	127	127	31 600	32 600
Poland	48	49	48	48	48	49	51	51	52	54	13 300	8 100
Portugal	77	79	78	78	77	77	75	75	75	75	18 600	15 400
Romania	:	26	26	28	29	31	34	35	39	41	10 100	5 600
Slovenia	78	80	79	79	81	82	85	87	88	89	22 000	16 600
Slovakia	52	51	50	53	54	56	57	61	64	69	17 000	10 200
Finland	115	115	118	116	116	113	117	115	117	117	29 000	34 000
Sweden	123	126	127	122	121	123	125	124	124	126	31 300	36 300
United Kingdom	116	116	117	118	119	120	122	119	118	116	28 700	33 200
Croatia	44	43	43	44	46	48	49	50	52	56	13 900	8 600
FYR of Macedonia	27	27	27	25	25	26	27	28	28	29	7 300	2 700
Turkey	43	39	40	36	34	34	37	39	41	42	10 500	6 500
Iceland	141	140	132	133	130	126	131	135	130	129	32 000	46 900
Norway	139	145	165	162	155	157	165	180	186	184	45 700	60 400
Switzerland	150	147	146	141	142	138	136	135	137	140	34 700	41 500
Japan	121	118	117	114	112	112	113	114	114	114	28 200	25 000
United States	160	162	159	155	152	154	155	158	157	155	38 500	33 400

(1) EA-13 instead of EA-15 for 1998-2003.
(2) Break in series, 2004.

Source: Eurostat (tsieb010, tec00001 and nama_gdp_c)

Table 2.2: GDP at current market prices

(EUR 1 000 million)

	1998	1999	2000	2001	2002	2003	2004	2005	2006	2007	Share of EU-27, 2007 (%)
EU-27	8 142	8 558	9 173	9 549	9 911	10 077	10 577	11 035	11 641	12 304	100.0
Euro area	6 140	6 422	6 757	7 051	7 299	7 514	7 819	8 109	8 499	8 919	72.5
Belgium	228	238	252	259	268	275	290	302	317	331	2.7
Bulgaria	11	12	14	15	17	18	20	22	25	29	0.2
Czech Republic	55	56	61	69	80	81	88	100	113	127	1.0
Denmark	155	163	174	179	185	189	197	208	220	228	1.9
Germany	1 952	2 012	2 063	2 113	2 143	2 164	2 211	2 243	2 322	2 423	19.7
Estonia	5	5	6	7	8	9	10	11	13	15	0.1
Ireland	79	91	105	117	130	139	149	161	175	186	1.5
Greece	122	132	138	146	158	171	185	199	214	229	1.9
Spain	537	580	630	681	729	783	841	909	982	1 051	8.5
France	1 315	1 368	1 441	1 497	1 549	1 595	1 660	1 726	1 807	1 892	15.4
Italy	1 087	1 127	1 191	1 249	1 295	1 335	1 392	1 428	1 480	1 536	12.5
Cyprus	9	9	10	11	11	12	13	14	15	16	0.1
Latvia	6	7	8	9	10	10	11	13	16	20	0.2
Lithuania	10	10	12	14	15	16	18	21	24	28	0.2
Luxembourg	17	20	22	23	24	26	27	30	34	36	0.3
Hungary	42	· 45	52	60	71	75	82	89	90	101	0.8
Malta	3	4	4	4	4	4	5	5	5	5	0.0
Netherlands	360	386	418	448	465	477	491	513	540	567	4.6
Austria	190	198	208	212	219	223	233	244	257	271	2.2
Poland	153	157	186	212	210	192	204	244	272	309	2.5
Portugal	106	114	122	129	135	139	144	149	155	163	1.3
Romania	37	33	40	45	48	53	61	80	98	121	1.0
Slovenia	19	20	21	22	24	25	27	28	30	34	0.3
Slovakia	20	19	22	24	26	29	34	38	45	55	0.4
Finland	116	123	132	140	144	146	152	157	167	180	1.5
Sweden	226	241	266	251	264	276	288	295	313	332	2.7
United Kingdom	1 280	1 384	1 573	1 613	1 679	1 616	1 745	1 805	1 913	2 019	16.4
Croatia	19	19	20	22	24	26	29	31	34	37	0.3
FYR of Macedonia	3	3	4	4	4	4	4	5	5	5	0.0
Turkey	239	234	290	218	243	268	315	387	419	479	3.9
Iceland	7	8	9	9	9	10	11	13	13	15	0.1
Liechtenstein	:	3	3	3	3	3	3	3	:	:	:
Norway	135	149	183	191	204	199	208	243	269	284	2.3
Switzerland	244	252	271	285	296	288	292	299	310	312	2.5
Japan	3 448	4 102	5 057	4 580	4 162	3 744	3 707	3 666	3 485	3 197	26.0
United States	7 802	8 696	10 629	11 309	11 072	9 690	9 395	9 985	10 496	10 075	81.9

Source: Eurostat (tec00001), CH: Secrétariat de l'Etat à l'Economie / JP: Bureau of Economic Analysis / US: Economic and Social Research Institute

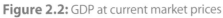
Figure 2.2: GDP at current market prices
(EUR 1 000 million)

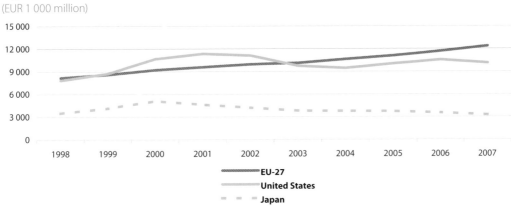

Source: Eurostat (tec00001)

Figure 2.3: Real GDP growth, EU-27
(% change compared with the previous year)

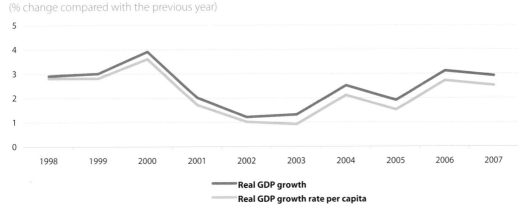

Source: Eurostat (tsieb020 and tsdec100)

Table 2.3: Labour productivity

	Labour productivity per person employed (EU-27=100, based on a PPS series)						Labour productivity per hour worked (EU-15=100, based on a PPS series)					
	2002	2003	2004	2005	2006	2007	2002	2003	2004	2005	2006	2007
EU-27	100.0	100.0	100.0	100.0	100.0	100.0	86.8	87.2	87.6	87.6	87.8	88.0
Euro area	:	:	110.3	110.6	110.2	110.2	:	:	101.1	101.8	101.7	101.8
Belgium (1)	136.6	134.8	132.2	132.0	131.3	130.2	127.9	126.4	126.8	125.2	124.1	123.7
Bulgaria	33.1	33.5	33.8	34.3	34.8	35.7	29.6	30.1	30.1	30.7	31.3	32.0
Czech Republic	63.1	66.7	68.1	68.9	70.4	73.6	48.0	50.6	51.8	52.1	53.3	:
Denmark	108.6	106.4	108.8	109.2	108.3	106.0	103.1	101.2	103.9	105.2	103.7	100.4
Germany	106.5	108.8	108.3	107.4	106.9	105.7	108.9	111.7	111.6	111.2	110.9	109.7
Estonia	49.3	53.0	55.3	59.0	61.7	64.7	37.9	40.6	42.6	45.1	47.2	49.8
Ireland	133.5	135.5	134.8	133.8	134.7	135.7	103.5	105.9	106.2	105.5	106.5	:
Greece	100.5	100.3	101.8	103.5	103.8	105.0	70.4	70.5	72.7	73.7	71.8	:
Spain	105.0	104.0	102.2	102.0	102.9	105.1	90.1	90.0	89.9	90.8	92.4	95.6
France (1)	125.7	121.8	120.8	123.7	124.0	124.3	120.8	117.4	114.9	117.8	119.5	:
Italy	117.8	115.7	112.3	111.1	108.9	108.0	95.1	93.6	91.3	90.7	89.1	88.0
Cyprus	84.6	82.7	82.9	84.2	85.0	86.1	65.1	63.8	65.6	67.7	67.7	68.9
Latvia	43.1	44.3	46.0	49.2	50.9	53.6	33.0	33.6	36.1	38.6	39.9	42.1
Lithuania	48.0	52.0	53.3	54.6	57.1	60.7	39.4	43.0	43.8	43.4	45.7	48.2
Luxembourg	163.5	166.8	169.8	175.6	183.9	180.3	147.9	151.2	159.0	166.1	170.3	174.0
Hungary	71.0	71.9	72.2	73.4	74.5	73.9	51.8	53.2	53.7	54.7	55.6	55.4
Malta	92.1	90.4	90.4	90.7	90.6	90.1	77.0	76.1	75.1	75.3	75.3	75.1
Netherlands	113.4	111.0	112.4	115.3	114.4	114.3	119.0	117.0	119.3	122.9	122.1	:
Austria	118.0	118.8	119.0	119.9	119.8	119.9	101.0	101.2	101.9	103.6	103.5	104.8
Poland	54.1	62.6	65.0	65.3	66.2	67.4	43.2	48.9	51.1	51.7	52.8	54.9
Portugal	68.0	68.5	67.2	68.6	68.5	69.9	56.8	58.1	56.6	58.1	57.7	59.3
Romania	29.2	31.2	34.4	36.3	39.2	41.0	23.1	25.1	27.7	29.1	:	:
Slovenia	76.7	78.1	80.9	82.7	83.9	84.3	64.4	65.3	69.5	71.1	72.1	72.6
Slovakia	62.6	63.4	65.6	68.8	71.7	76.8	53.3	55.9	56.5	58.0	60.8	64.2
Finland	111.6	109.6	112.8	110.8	112.3	111.9	95.5	94.1	97.2	95.7	97.3	97.3
Sweden	107.8	110.2	113.5	112.9	113.8	115.3	99.9	102.9	105.0	104.5	105.5	106.1
United Kingdom	110.3	110.6	112.3	109.7	109.5	108.8	89.1	90.3	92.5	89.9	90.3	89.8
Croatia	58.1	60.1	60.9	62.0	64.2	68.4	:	:	:	:	:	:
Turkey	49.0	49.7	54.0	56.1	59.7	62.4	:	:	:	:	:	:
Iceland	104.4	101.5	107.8	108.8	104.3	102.3	85.1	82.9	88.4	90.1	86.2	84.2
Norway	131.7	135.2	142.6	155.3	158.9	154.7	137.7	142.7	149.4	162.4	167.5	163.0
Switzerland	107.5	105.7	105.2	105.2	105.8	108.9	97.5	95.3	93.6	93.6	94.8	97.7
United States	138.0	139.8	140.8	143.2	142.8	142.7	112.6	115.5	117.0	119.3	:	:

(1) 2004, break in series.

Source: Eurostat (tsieb030 and tsieb040), OECD

Table 2.4: Gross value added at basic prices

(% share of total gross value added)

	Agriculture, hunting & fishing		Industry		Construction		Trade, transport & communication services		Business activities & financial services		Other services	
	1997	2007	1997	2007	1997	2007	1997	2007	1997	2007	1997	2007
EU-27	2.8	1.9	23.3	20.2	5.6	6.3	21.3	21.2	24.9	28.2	22.2	22.3
Euro area	2.8	1.9	22.7	20.4	5.7	6.5	21.0	20.7	25.3	28.0	22.4	22.4
Belgium	1.6	0.9	23.5	18.9	4.9	5.2	21.3	23.5	26.3	28.4	22.5	23.2
Bulgaria	26.2	6.2	26.4	24.1	2.7	8.2	17.5	24.4	18.8	22.0	8.4	15.1
Czech Republic (1)	4.2	2.6	33.0	32.0	7.5	6.2	24.7	25.3	14.8	16.6	15.8	17.3
Denmark	3.2	1.3	20.9	20.1	4.8	5.6	22.5	21.6	21.8	24.5	26.8	26.8
Germany	1.3	0.9	25.1	26.4	6.0	4.0	17.8	17.6	27.3	29.2	22.6	21.9
Estonia	5.2	2.8	24.9	21.3	6.1	9.1	26.7	26.9	20.2	23.3	16.9	16.6
Ireland (1)	5.2	1.7	33.1	25.0	5.6	9.9	18.6	16.8	18.7	26.4	18.9	20.2
Greece (2)	6.6	3.6	13.9	14.8	7.0	8.3	30.1	30.6	20.6	18.8	21.7	24.0
Spain	5.0	2.9	22.2	17.5	7.1	12.3	26.4	24.4	18.3	22.1	21.0	20.9
France	3.2	2.2	18.4	14.1	5.1	6.5	19.1	18.7	29.4	33.3	24.8	25.3
Italy	3.2	2.0	24.4	20.8	5.1	6.3	23.9	22.5	22.8	27.6	20.6	20.8
Cyprus	4.0	2.2	13.4	9.8	7.9	9.1	29.9	27.2	22.6	27.8	22.2	23.8
Latvia	5.1	3.3	25.3	13.6	4.2	8.4	31.5	33.0	14.0	23.5	19.9	18.2
Lithuania	11.4	5.3	23.5	23.3	7.6	10.0	27.7	31.5	11.5	14.7	18.3	15.1
Luxembourg	0.8	0.4	14.7	9.3	6.2	5.1	23.1	20.8	37.8	49.0	17.3	15.4
Hungary	5.9	4.2	28.1	25.2	4.6	4.2	23.2	21.3	19.1	23.0	19.1	22.2
Malta	2.8	2.3	22.3	17.7	4.3	3.8	31.6	27.0	17.4	20.9	21.5	28.3
Netherlands	3.5	2.0	20.6	18.8	5.3	5.6	22.3	21.9	26.0	28.3	22.4	23.4
Austria	2.3	1.8	23.0	23.5	7.9	7.1	24.7	23.1	20.3	24.2	21.7	20.4
Poland	6.6	4.3	26.1	23.2	7.2	7.9	26.4	27.9	15.3	18.4	18.2	18.3
Portugal	4.6	2.5	22.0	18.0	7.0	6.5	24.2	24.3	19.7	22.4	22.5	26.3
Romania (1, 3)	16.0	8.8	29.1	27.5	5.6	8.4	25.5	25.4	12.4	17.6	11.3	12.2
Slovenia	4.2	2.0	29.1	27.5	6.7	7.0	21.7	22.5	18.8	21.6	19.5	19.4
Slovakia	5.3	2.9	28.0	30.3	7.3	6.7	26.3	26.6	17.0	17.8	16.2	15.8
Finland	4.1	3.2	27.4	26.2	4.9	6.4	21.8	21.6	19.3	21.2	22.7	21.4
Sweden	2.5	1.5	25.1	23.7	4.0	5.0	19.0	19.4	24.2	24.0	25.1	26.3
United Kingdom	1.4	0.9	24.9	16.6	5.0	5.2	21.9	21.1	25.4	33.8	21.4	22.4
Croatia	8.7	6.8	24.2	23.3	7.1	6.8	25.6	26.0	17.1	18.8	17.2	18.2
FYR of Macedonia (1)	12.8	12.6	28.4	23.5	6.2	6.7	22.2	28.1	10.2	10.6	20.3	18.6
Turkey	14.3	7.6	24.9	19.3	6.0	4.9	34.2	27.6	8.0	17.6	12.7	10.1
Iceland (1)	10.2	6.1	20.8	15.5	8.3	10.5	22.0	18.4	17.0	27.6	21.8	21.9
Norway	2.4	1.4	32.5	37.8	4.7	5.2	21.4	16.7	16.8	18.3	22.2	20.5
Switzerland	1.8	1.2	23.0	22.5	5.5	5.5	22.0	21.8	21.8	23.6	26.0	25.4
Japan	1.5	:	25.5	:	7.6	:	17.6	:	17.2	:	26.8	:
United States (3)	1.3	:	20.0	:	4.6	:	19.9	:	30.7	:	23.5	:

(1) 2006 instead of 2007.
(2) 2000 instead of 1997.
(3) 1998 instead of 1997.

Source: Eurostat (tec00003, tec00004, tec00005, tec00006, tec00007 and tec00008)

Figure 2.4: Gross value added at basic prices, EU-27, 2007 (1)
(% share of total gross value added)

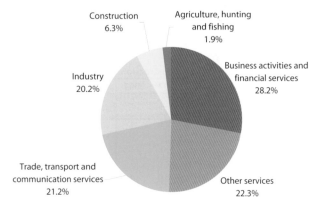

(1) Figures do not sum to 100 % due to rounding.

Source: Eurostat (tec00007, tec00008, tec00006, tec00004, tec00005 and tec00003)

Figure 2.5: Consumption expenditure and gross capital formation at constant prices, EU-27
(2000=100)

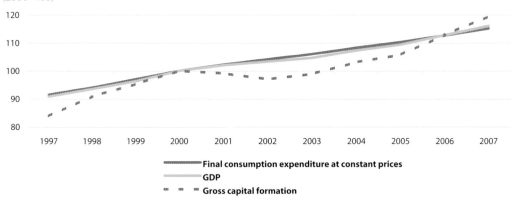

Source: Eurostat (nama_gdp_k)

Figure 2.6: Expenditure components of GDP, EU-27
(EUR 1 000 million)

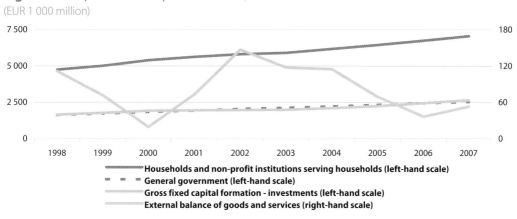

Households and non-profit institutions serving households (left-hand scale)
General government (left-hand scale)
Gross fixed capital formation - investments (left-hand scale)
External balance of goods and services (right-hand scale)

Source: Eurostat (tec00009, tec00010, tec00011 and tec00110)

Figure 2.7: Expenditure components of GDP, EU-27, 2007
(% share of GDP)

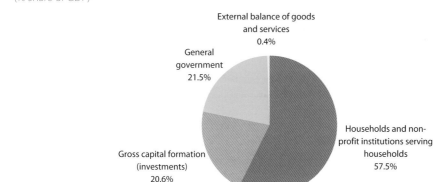

External balance of goods
and services
0.4%

General
government
21.5%

Households and non-
profit institutions serving
households
57.5%

Gross capital formation
(investments)
20.6%

Source: Eurostat (tec00009, tec00011, tec00010 and tec00110)

Figure 2.8: Gross fixed capital formation, 2007
(% share of GDP)

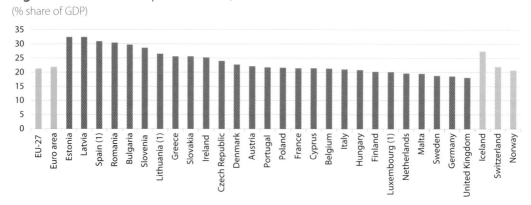

(1) Estimate.

Source: Eurostat (tec00011)

Figure 2.9: Distribution of income, EU-27
(1998=100)

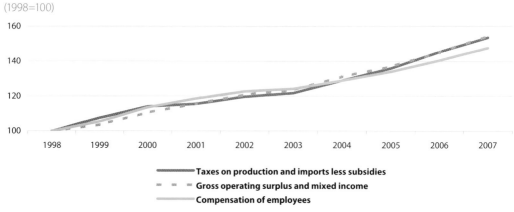

Taxes on production and imports less subsidies
Gross operating surplus and mixed income
Compensation of employees

Source: Eurostat (tec00016, tec00015 and tec00013)

Figure 2.10: Distribution of income, 2007
(% share of GDP)

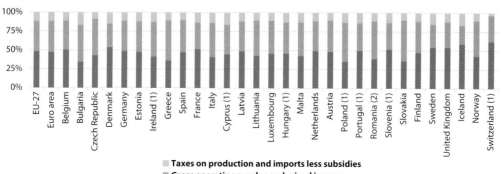

■ Taxes on production and imports less subsidies
▨ Gross operating surplus and mixed income
▨ Compensation of employees

(1) 2006.
(2) 2005.

Source: Eurostat (tec00016, tec00015 and tec00013)

Figure 2.11: Gross national savings (1)
(% of gross national disposable income)

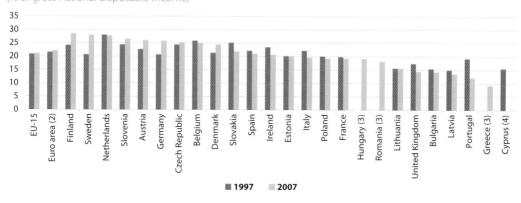

▨ 1997 ▨ 2007

(1) Luxembourg and Malta, not available.
(2) EA-13 instead of EA-15.
(3) 1997, not available.
(4) 2007, not available.

Source: Eurostat (nama_inc_c)

Table 2.5: Gross household savings (1)

(% of gross household disposable income)

	1997	1998	1999	2000	2001	2002	2003	2004	2005	2006	2007
EU-27	:	:	12.0	11.3	12.3	12.1	12.1	11.7	11.6	11.0	10.7
Belgium	17.7	17.0	17.2	15.4	16.4	15.8	14.7	13.3	12.6	12.9	13.7
Bulgaria	:	:	:	:	:	:	:	:	-22.7	:	:
Czech Republic	11.0	9.2	8.5	8.5	7.4	8.1	7.4	5.7	8.1	9.1	8.8
Denmark	5.0	6.3	3.8	4.9	8.8	8.8	9.4	6.3	2.6	4.0	:
Germany	15.9	15.9	15.3	15.1	15.2	15.7	16.0	16.1	16.3	16.2	16.7
Estonia	6.5	4.5	2.6	4.1	3.1	0.5	-1.6	-4.8	-3.8	-3.0	0.8
Ireland	:	:	:	:	:	10.3	10.6	13.7	11.6	10.3	9.2
Greece	:	:	:	2.5	1.7	1.1	1.6	1.5	0.7	1.2	:
Spain	:	:	:	11.1	11.1	11.4	12.0	11.3	11.3	11.2	10.2
France	15.8	15.4	15.1	14.9	15.6	16.7	15.6	15.6	14.6	14.9	15.6
Italy	20.2	16.8	15.8	14.2	16.0	16.8	16.0	16.0	15.9	15.1	14.2
Cyprus	:	:	:	:	:	:	:	:	:	:	:
Latvia	1.8	0.7	-0.7	2.9	-0.4	1.5	3.0	4.7	1.2	-3.6	:
Lithuania	3.4	7.2	7.8	7.2	6.2	6.1	3.7	1.9	1.6	0.7	:
Luxembourg	:	:	:	:	:	:	:	:	:	:	:
Hungary	:	:	:	13.9	13.7	11.4	9.2	11.6	11.4	12.0	:
Malta	:	:	:	:	:	:	:	:	:	:	:
Netherlands	17.6	16.6	13.8	11.9	14.5	13.7	13.0	13.0	12.2	11.5	13.4
Austria	12.6	13.3	14.5	13.9	12.9	12.9	14.0	14.1	14.5	15.4	16.3
Poland	14.1	14.4	12.9	10.7	12.1	8.4	7.8	7.2	7.2	6.6	:
Portugal	10.8	10.5	9.8	10.2	10.9	10.6	10.5	9.7	9.2	8.1	6.6
Romania	:	:	:	:	:	:	-7.5	-3.0	-10.9	-14.1	:
Slovenia	:	:	:	14.5	16.1	16.9	14.8	15.9	16.8	16.1	:
Slovakia	13.9	12.4	11.2	11.1	9.1	8.9	7.1	6.3	6.9	6.1	7.7
Finland	9.1	7.9	9.3	7.6	7.8	7.9	8.4	9.4	8.0	5.6	5.5
Sweden	7.2	6.4	6.0	7.4	11.8	11.6	11.4	10.3	9.5	9.8	11.0
United Kingdom	9.6	7.4	5.2	4.7	6.0	4.8	5.1	4.0	5.1	4.2	2.5
Norway	8.1	10.5	9.5	9.2	8.2	12.7	13.3	11.8	14.5	5.6	4.6
Switzerland	15.8	15.8	16.0	16.9	17.1	16.1	14.8	14.4	15.3	17.1	:

(1) Including net adjustment for the change in net equity of households in pension funds reserves.

Source: Eurostat (tsdec240)

2.2 Government finances

Introduction

The disciplines of the Stability and Growth Pact (SGP) keep economic developments in the EU, and in the euro area countries in particular, broadly synchronised[4]. They prevent Member States from taking policy measures which would unduly benefit their own economies at the expense of others. There are two key principles to the Pact: namely, that the deficit must not exceed 3 % of gross domestic product (GDP) and that the debt-to-GDP ratio should not be more than 60 %.

A revision in March 2005 based on the first five years of experience left these principles unchanged, but introduced greater flexibility in exceeding the deficit threshold in hard economic times or to finance investment in structural improvements. It also gave Member States a longer period to reverse their excessive deficits – although, if they do not bring their economies back into line, corrective measures, or even fines, can be imposed.

Each year, Member States provide the European Commission with detailed information on their economic policies and the state of their public finances. Euro area countries provide this information in the context of the 'stability programmes', while other Member States do so in the form of 'convergence programmes'. The European Commission assesses whether the policies are in line with agreed economic, social and environmental objectives and may choose to issue a warning if it believes a deficit is becoming abnormally high.

Definitions and data availability

Member States acknowledge the need for solid and sustainable government finances. Under the rules on budgetary discipline within the EU Stability and Growth Pact (Amsterdam, 1997), Member States are to avoid situations of 'excessive government deficits': their ratio of planned or actual government deficit to GDP should be no more than 3 %, and their ratio of government debt to GDP should be no more than 60 % (unless the excess over the reference value is only exceptional or temporary, or unless the ratios have declined substantially and continuously).

The Member States should, by law, notify their **government deficit and debt statistics** to the European Commission before 1 April and 1 October of each year under the 'excessive deficit procedure'. In addition, Eurostat collects the data and ensures that Member States comply with the relevant regulations. The main aggregates of general government are provided by the Member States to Eurostat twice a year, according to the ESA 95 transmission programme.

The data presented within this section correspond to the main revenue and expenditure items of the general government sector, which are compiled on a national accounts (ESA 95) basis. The difference between total revenue and total expenditure – including capital expenditure (in particular, gross fixed capital formation) – equals net lending/net borrowing, which is also the balancing item of the non-financial accounts.

---

(4) http://ec.europa.eu/economy_finance/sg_pact_fiscal_policy/fiscal_policy528_en.htm.

The **general government sector** includes all institutional units whose output is intended for individual and collective consumption, and mainly financed by compulsory payments made by units belonging to other sectors, and/or all institutional units principally engaged in the redistribution of national income and wealth. The general government sector is subdivided into four subsectors: central government, State government, local government, and social security funds:

- **Central government** covers all administrative departments of the State and other central agencies whose responsibilities extend over the whole economic territory, except for the administration of the social security funds.
- **State government** covers separate institutional units exercising some of the functions of government at a level below that of central government and above that of the governmental institutional units existing at local level, except for the administration of social security funds.
- **Local government** concerns all types of public administration whose competence extends to only a local part of the economic territory apart from local agencies of social security funds.
- **Social security funds** comprises all central, State and local institutional units whose principal activity is to provide social benefits, and which fulfil each of the two following criteria: (i) by law or regulation (except

regulations concerning government employees), certain groups of the population are obliged to participate in the scheme or to pay contributions, and (ii) general government is responsible for the management of the institution in respect of settlement or approval of the contributions and benefits independently of its role as a supervisory body or employer.

The main **revenue of general government** consists of taxes, social contributions, sales and property income. It is defined in ESA-95 by reference to a list of categories: market output, output for own final use, payments for the other non-market output, taxes on production and imports, other subsidies on production, receivable property income, current taxes on income, wealth, etc., social contributions, other current transfers and capital transfers.

The main expenditure items consist of the compensation of civil servants, social benefits, interest on the public debt, subsidies and gross fixed capital formation. **Total general government expenditure** is defined in ESA-95 by reference to a list of categories: intermediate consumption, gross capital formation, compensation of employees, other taxes on production, subsidies, payable property income, current taxes on income, wealth, etc., social benefits, some social transfers, other current transfers, some adjustments, capital transfers and transactions on non-produced assets.

The **public balance** is defined as general government net borrowing/net lending reported for the Excessive Deficit Procedure and is expressed in relation to GDP. General government comprises central, state and local government, as well as social security funds. Under the convergence criteria, the ratio of planned or actual government deficit (net borrowing) to GDP should be no more than 3 %.

General government consolidated gross debt is also expressed as a percentage of GDP. It refers to the consolidated stock of gross debt at nominal value at the end of the year. Under the convergence criteria, the ratio of general government consolidated gross debt to GDP should generally be no more than 60 % (unless the ratio is sufficiently diminishing and approaching the reference value at a satisfactory pace).

Compulsory levies correspond to revenues which are levied (in cash or in kind) by central, state and local governments, and social security funds. Compulsory levies (generally referred to as taxes) are organised into three main areas, covered by the following headings:

- **taxes on income and wealth**, including all compulsory payments levied periodically by general government on the income and wealth of enterprises and households;
- **taxes on production and imports**, including all compulsory payments levied by general government with respect to the production and importation of goods and services, the employment of labour, the ownership or use of land, buildings or other assets used in production;

- **social contributions**, including all employers and employees social contributions, as well as imputed social contributions that represent the counterpart to social benefits paid directly by employers.

Data on public procurement are based on information contained in the calls for competition and contract award notices submitted for publication in the Official Journal of the European Communities (the S series). The numerator is the value of public procurement, which is openly advertised. For each of the sectors – works, supplies and services – the number of calls for competition published is multiplied by an average based, in general, on all the prices provided in the contract award notices published in the Official Journal during the relevant year. The value of public procurement is then expressed relative to GDP.

State aid is made up of sectoral State aid (given to specific activities such as agriculture, fisheries, manufacturing, mining, services), ad-hoc State aid (given to individual enterprises), and State aid for horizontal objectives such as research and development, safeguarding the environment, support to small and medium-sized enterprises, employment creation or training, including aid for regional development. The first two of these (sectoral and ad-hoc State aid) are considered potentially more distortive to competition.

Main findings

The public (general government) deficit of the EU-27, measured in terms of a percentage share of GDP, fell to -0.9 % in 2007, its lowest rate since 2000. The trend was similar in the euro area, where the deficit was steadily reduced from 2.9 % of GDP recorded for 2004 to -0.6 % of GDP for 2007. The deficit ratios for all of the Member States, with the exception of Hungary (-5.5 %), were within the target reference value of -3 % in 2007, up from only fifteen of the Member States in 2004. Of the 26 Member States within the Maastricht target, ten reported a surplus, the highest of which were in Finland (5.3 %) and Denmark (4.4 %), while the public balance was in equilibrium for Germany and Latvia. In the period between 2004 and 2007, most of the deficit ratios in the Member States were reduced; this was also the case in Turkey and Croatia.

For the first time since the launch of the euro, average general government gross debt across the EU-27 fell below the target 60 % of GDP in 2007, reaching 58.7 %. The average rate across the euro area also fell to its lowest level in 2007 (66.4 %), but remained above the target. Some 19 of the Member States had a debt ratio below 60 % of GDP in 2007, the same number as in 2004. Throughout this period, Italy recorded the highest debt ratio, at over 100 %. Greece followed closely, but reduced its debt-to-GDP ratio from 98.6 % to 94.5 %. At the other end of the scale, Estonia and Luxembourg reported the lowest debt to GDP ratios, both below 7 % throughout the period considered. During the period from 2004 to 2007, the debt ratios in Bulgaria and Denmark fell at the most rapid pace.

General government expenditure may be identified by function using the classification of the functions of government – COFOG. In all of the Member States, social protection measures accounted for the highest proportion of government expenditure, albeit ranging in 2006 from a little less than 10 % of GDP in Estonia, Ireland and Latvia to over 21 % in Sweden, France (2005), Denmark and Germany. Average expenditure on general public services and health across the euro area was broadly similar (each being about 7 % in 2005), with both expenditure on education and economic affairs accounting for a slightly lower proportion (between 4 % and 5 % on average).

The importance of the general government sector in the economy may be measured in terms of total government revenue and expenditure as a percentage of GDP. In the EU-27, total government revenue in 2007 amounted to 44.9 % of GDP, and expenditure to 45.8 % of GDP; in the euro area, the equivalent figures were 45.7 % and 46.3 % respectively.

The level of general government expenditure and revenue varies considerably between the Members States. Those with the highest levels of combined government expenditure and revenue as a proportion of GDP in 2007 were Sweden, Denmark, France and Finland, for which the government sector represented over 100 % of GDP. Nine Member States reported relatively low combined revenue and expenditure to GDP ratios below 80 %. Out of these, the government sector was smallest for Slovakia, Romania, Estonia and Lithuania, where revenue plus expenditure accounted for less than 72 % of GDP in 2007.

The main types of government revenue are taxes on income and wealth, taxes on production and imports, and social contributions. These three sources of revenue accounted for over 90 % of EU-27 revenue in 2007. The structure of taxes within the EU-27 shows that receipts from these three main tax headings were roughly equal in 2007: social contributions accounted for 13.6 % of GDP, taxes on production and imports for 13.5 %, and current taxes on income and wealth for 13.4 %. In a similar way to the distribution of government expenditure, there was considerable variation in the structure of taxes across the Member States. As may be expected, those countries that reported relatively high levels of expenditure tended to be those that also raised more taxes (as a proportion of GDP). For example, the highest return from taxes was 49.4 % of GDP recorded in Denmark, with Sweden recording the next highest share. The proportion of GDP accounted for by taxes was about 30 % in Lithuania, Romania and Slovakia, with the relative importance of current taxes on income and wealth particularly low in the latter two countries.

The value of public procurement, which is openly advertised, expressed as a proportion of GDP, rose between 1996 and 2006 in each of the 15 Member States for which data are available, with the exception of Portugal. Public procurement accounted for 3.3 % of GDP in the EU-25 in 2006, with a high of 13.8 % recorded in Latvia.

In total, EU State aid amounted to 0.6 % of GDP in 2006, which marked a reduction compared with its peak value of 0.7 % in 2002. This average masks significant disparities between Member States: the ratio of total State aid to GDP ranged from 0.4 % or less in Estonia, Belgium, Italy, the Netherlands, Luxembourg, Greece, the United Kingdom and Bulgaria (2004) to 1.5 % or more in Finland, Hungary, Latvia, Romania (2004) and Malta. The relatively high importance of State aid in some of the Member States that joined the EU since 2004 may be largely attributed to pre-accession measures that are either being phased out under transitional arrangements or are limited in time. In absolute numbers, State aid by EU-25 Member States amounted to EUR 66 805 million in 2006.

Figure 2.12: Public balance
(net borrowing/lending of consolidated general government sector, % of GDP)

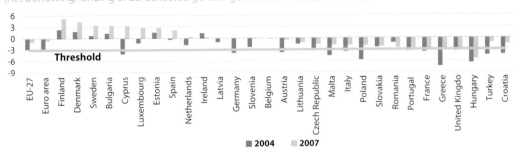

Source: Eurostat (tsieb080)

Table 2.6: Public balance, general government debt

	Public balance (net borrowing/lending of consolidated general government sector, % of GDP)				General government debt (general government consolidated gross debt, % of GDP)			
	2004	2005	2006	2007	2004	2005	2006	2007
EU-27	-2.8	-2.5	-1.4	-0.9	62.1	62.6	61.3	58.7
Euro area	-2.9	-2.5	-1.3	-0.6	69.6	70.2	68.5	66.4
Belgium	0.0	-2.3	0.3	-0.2	94.2	92.1	88.2	84.9
Bulgaria	1.4	1.8	3.0	3.4	37.9	29.2	22.7	18.2
Czech Republic	-3.0	-3.6	-2.7	-1.6	30.4	29.7	29.4	28.7
Denmark	1.9	5.0	4.8	4.4	43.8	36.4	30.4	26.0
Germany	-3.8	-3.4	-1.6	0.0	65.6	67.8	67.6	65.0
Estonia	1.6	1.8	3.4	2.8	5.1	4.5	4.2	3.4
Ireland	1.4	1.6	3.0	0.3	29.5	27.4	25.1	25.4
Greece	-7.4	-5.1	-2.6	-2.8	98.6	98.0	95.3	94.5
Spain	-0.3	1.0	1.8	2.2	46.2	43.0	39.7	36.2
France	-3.6	-2.9	-2.4	-2.7	64.9	66.4	63.6	64.2
Italy	-3.5	-4.2	-3.4	-1.9	103.8	105.8	106.5	104.0
Cyprus	-4.1	-2.4	-1.2	3.3	70.2	69.1	64.8	59.8
Latvia	-1.0	-0.4	-0.2	0.0	14.9	12.4	10.7	9.7
Lithuania	-1.5	-0.5	-0.5	-1.2	19.4	18.6	18.2	17.3
Luxembourg	-1.2	-0.1	1.3	2.9	6.3	6.1	6.6	6.8
Hungary	-6.5	-7.8	-9.2	-5.5	59.4	61.6	65.6	66.0
Malta	-4.6	-3.0	-2.6	-1.8	72.6	70.4	64.2	62.6
Netherlands	-1.7	-0.3	0.5	0.4	52.4	52.3	47.9	45.4
Austria	-3.7	-1.5	-1.5	-0.5	63.8	63.5	61.8	59.1
Poland	-5.7	-4.3	-3.8	-2.0	45.7	47.1	47.6	45.2
Portugal	-3.4	-6.1	-3.9	-2.6	58.3	63.6	64.7	63.6
Romania	-1.2	-1.2	-2.2	-2.5	18.8	15.8	12.4	13.0
Slovenia	-2.3	-1.5	-1.2	-0.1	27.6	27.5	27.2	24.1
Slovakia	-2.4	-2.8	-3.6	-2.2	41.4	34.2	30.4	29.4
Finland	2.4	2.9	4.1	5.3	44.1	41.3	39.2	35.4
Sweden	0.8	2.2	2.3	3.5	51.2	50.9	45.9	40.6
United Kingdom	-3.4	-3.4	-2.6	-2.9	40.4	42.1	43.1	43.8
Croatia	-4.3	-4.0	-2.4	-1.6	43.2	43.7	40.8	37.7
Turkey	-4.5	-0.6	-0.1	-1.2	59.2	52.3	46.1	38.8
Norway	11.1	15.2	19.3	:	45.6	43.8	48.9	:

Source: Eurostat (tsieb080 and tsieb090)

Figure 2.13: General government debt

(general government consolidated gross debt, % of GDP)

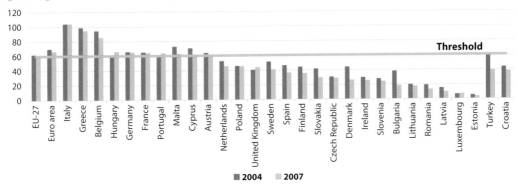

Source: Eurostat (tsieb090)

Figure 2.14: General government expenditure by COFOG function, 2006 (1)

(% of GDP)

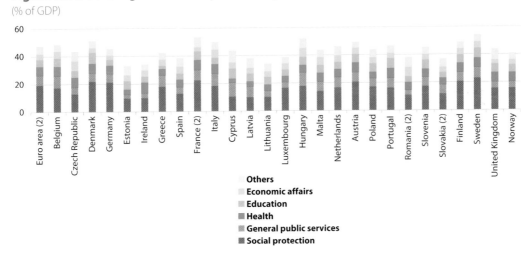

- Others
- Economic affairs
- Education
- Health
- General public services
- Social protection

(1) COFOG: classification of the functions of government; Bulgaria, not available.
(2) 2005.

Source: Eurostat (gov_a_exp)

Figure 2.15: Government revenue and expenditure, 2007 (1)
(% of GDP)

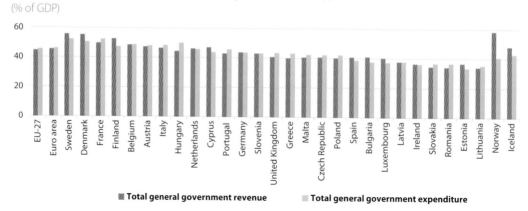

■ **Total general government revenue**   ■ **Total general government expenditure**

(1) The figure is ranked on the average of revenue and expenditure.

Source: Eurostat (tec00021 and tec00023)

Figure 2.16: Taxes and social contributions, 2007
(% of GDP)

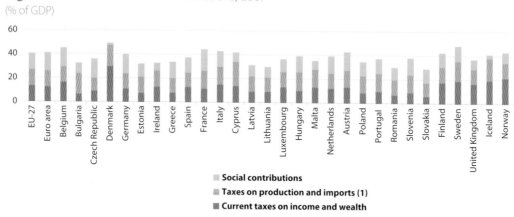

■ **Social contributions**
▨ **Taxes on production and imports (1)**
■ **Current taxes on income and wealth**

(1) For Denmark, includes taxes on production and imports collected on behalf of EU institutions.

Source: Eurostat (tec00019, tec00020 and tec00018)

Figure 2.17: Public procurement (1)

(value of public procurement which is openly advertised, as % of GDP)

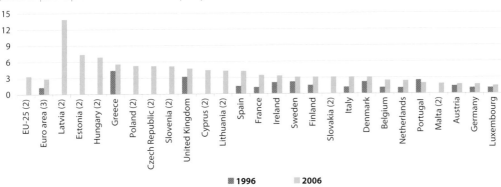

■ 1996   ■ 2006

(1) Bulgaria and Romania, not available.
(2) Not available for 1996.
(3) EA-12 instead of EA-15.

Source: Eurostat (tsier090), Commission services

Figure 2.18: State aid, 2006 (1)

(% of GDP)

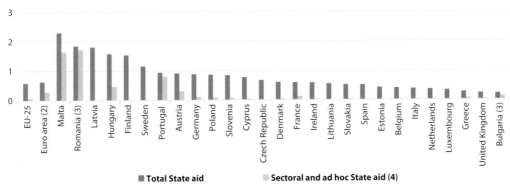

■ Total State aid   ■ Sectoral and ad hoc State aid (4)

(1) The figure is ranked on total State aid.
(2) EA-13 instead of EA-15, 2005.
(3) 2004.
(4) 2005.

Source: Eurostat (tsier100), Commission services

2.3 Exchange rates and interest rates

Introduction

On 1 January 2002, around 7 800 million notes and 40 400 million coins entered circulation, valued at EUR 144 000 million, as the euro became the common currency of 12 of the Member States; these were Belgium, Germany, Ireland, Greece, Spain, France, Italy, Luxembourg, the Netherlands, Austria, Portugal and Finland. Slovenia subsequently joined the euro area at the start of 2007 as did Cyprus and Malta on 1 January 2008, bringing the number of Member States using the euro to 15.

Economic and Monetary Union (EMU) consists of three stages coordinating economic policy and culminating with the adoption of the euro. All EMU members are eligible to adopt the euro. At the time of writing, it is expected that Slovakia will adopt the euro on 1 January 2009.

The entry criteria for the euro include two years of prior exchange rate stability via membership of the Exchange Rate Mechanism (ERM), as well as criteria relating to interest rates, budget deficits, inflation rates, and debt-to-GDP ratios.

Through using a common currency the countries of the euro area have removed exchange rates and therefore benefit from lower transaction costs. The size of the euro area market is also likely to promote investment and trade. Those countries joining the euro area have agreed to allow the European Central Bank (ECB) to be responsible for maintaining price stability, through the definition and implementation of monetary policy. When the euro was launched in 1999, the ECB took over full responsibility for monetary policy throughout the euro area, including setting benchmark interest rates and managing the euro area's foreign exchange reserves. The ECB has defined price stability as a year-on-year increase in the harmonised index of consumer prices (HICP) for the euro area close to but below 2 % over the medium term (see section 2.5 for more details in relation to consumer prices). Monetary policy decisions are taken by the ECB's governing council which meets every month to analyse and assess economic developments and the risks to price stability and to decide on the appropriate level of interest rates.

The ECB also has the job of ensuring that payments move smoothly across EU financial markets. The ECB and the European Commission are working jointly on a Single Euro Payments Area (SEPA) – a system that aims to make virtually all forms of cross-border euro payment faster and no more expensive than domestic payments by 2010.

Definitions and data availability

Exchange rates are the price or value of one country's currency in relation to another. Eurostat's database contains a number of different data sets concerning exchange rates. Three main areas are distinguished:

- data on bilateral exchange rates between currencies, including some special conversion factors for the countries that have adopted the euro;
- data on fluctuations in the exchange rate mechanism (ERM and ERM II) of the EU;
- data on effective exchange rate indices.

Bilateral exchange rates are available with reference to the euro; before 1999, exchange rates were given in relation to the ecu (European currency unit). The ecu ceased to exist on 1 January 1999, when it was replaced by the euro at an exchange rate of 1:1. From that date, the currencies of the euro area became subdivisions of the euro at irrevocably fixed rates of conversion. **Daily exchange rates** are available from 1974 onwards against a large number of currencies. These daily values are used to construct monthly and annual averages, which are based on business day rates. Alternatively, month-end and year-end rates are also provided for the daily rate of the last business day of the month/year.

An **interest rate** is defined as the cost or price of borrowing, or the gain from lending; interest rates are traditionally expressed in annual percentage terms. Interest rates are distinguished either by the period of lending/borrowing, or by the parties involved in the transaction (business, consumers, governments or interbank operations).

Central bank interest rates are key reference rates set by the ECB and national central banks (for those countries outside of the euro area). Central bank interest rates are also referred to as official interest rates; they are the main instrument of monetary policy for central banks.

Eurostat publish statistics on interest rates under several headings:

- **long-term interest rates**: government bond yields with a 10 years' maturity and interest rates used for the Maastricht criterion on long-term interest rates;

- **central bank interest rates**: different rates that central banks fix to conduct the monetary policy (reference rates);
- **short-term interest rates**: rates on money markets for different maturities (overnight, 1 to 12 months);
- **retail bank interest rates**: lending and deposit interest rates of commercial banks (non-harmonised and historical series), and harmonised MFI interest rates (monetary financial institutions interest rates);
- **convergence of interest rates**: the standard deviation and the coefficient of variation for: loans to households for house purchases; loans to non-financial corporations over one year; loans to non-financial corporations up to one year.

Main findings

It is important to note that nearly all of the information presented in this publication has been converted into euro (EUR). As such, when making comparisons between countries it is necessary to bear in mind the possible effect of currency fluctuations on the evolution of particular series. The value of the euro against the yen or the dollar depreciated considerably in 1999 and 2000. However, the following years saw a marked appreciation in the value of the euro, such that it reached record highs against the yen (EUR 1 = JPY 168.45) in July 2007 and against the dollar (EUR 1 =USD 1.59) in July 2008; afterwards the value of the euro fell.

At the end of the last period of rapid economic growth, global interest rates started to fall, with sizeable and successive reductions in 2001. This pattern continued within the euro area (and to a lesser degree the United States) during 2002 and 2003, such that official lending rates of central banks reached historic lows – nowhere was this more evident than in Japan (where deflationary pressures resulted in an interest rate close to zero).

With signs of an economic recovery, there were several rate rises in the United States during 2004, which were confirmed in 2005 and 2006. Subsequently, the federal funds rate remained unchanged between June 2006 and September 2007, when it fell to 4.75 % on the back of fears

for a slowdown in economic activity, in particular within the housing market with concerns over the subprime market. European interest rates followed this trend, and during the period from December 2005 to July 2007 there were nine individual increases in interest rates, as the ECB tightened monetary policy. In an abrupt turnabout, there was a co-ordinated interest rate reduction of a half-point (0.5 %) by the ECB, the US Federal Reserve, the Bank of England, and the central banks of Canada, Sweden and Switzerland in October 2008, in order to encourage inter-bank lending, which had dried up (the so-called credit crunch) as the full-exposure of some banks to sub-prime markets became clearer.

Figure 2.19: Exchange rates against the euro (1)
(1998=100)

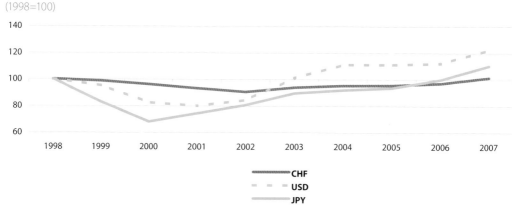

(1) CHF, Swiss franc; JPY, Japanese Yen; USD, United States Dollar; a reduction in the value of the index shows an appreciation in the value of the foreign currency and a depreciation in the value of the euro.

Source: Eurostat (tec00033), ECB

Table 2.7: Exchange rates against the euro (1)

(1 EUR =... national currency)

	1999	2000	2001	2002	2003	2004	2005	2006	2007
Bulgaria	1.9558	1.9522	1.9482	1.9492	1.9490	1.9533	1.9558	1.9558	1.9558
Czech Republic	36.884	35.599	34.068	30.804	31.846	31.891	29.782	28.342	27.766
Denmark	7.4355	7.4538	7.4521	7.4305	7.4307	7.4399	7.4518	7.4591	7.4506
Estonia	15.647	15.647	15.647	15.647	15.647	15.647	15.647	15.647	15.647
Latvia	0.6256	0.5592	0.5601	0.5810	0.6407	0.6652	0.6962	0.6962	0.7001
Lithuania	4.2641	3.6952	3.5823	3.4594	3.4527	3.4529	3.4528	3.4528	3.4528
Hungary	252.77	260.04	256.59	242.96	253.62	251.66	248.05	264.26	251.35
Poland	4.2274	4.0082	3.6721	3.8574	4.3996	4.5268	4.0230	3.8959	3.7837
Romania	1.6345	1.9922	2.6004	3.1270	3.7551	4.0510	3.6209	3.5258	3.3328
Slovakia	44.123	42.602	43.300	42.694	41.489	40.022	38.599	37.234	33.775
Sweden	8.8075	8.4452	9.2551	9.1611	9.1242	9.1243	9.2822	9.2544	9.2501
United Kingdom	0.65874	0.60948	0.62187	0.62883	0.69199	0.6787	0.68380	0.68173	0.68434
Croatia	7.5805	7.6432	7.4820	7.4130	7.5688	7.4967	7.4008	7.3247	7.3376
Turkey	0.4472	0.5748	1.1024	1.4397	1.6949	1.7771	1.6771	1.8090	1.7891
Iceland	77.180	72.580	87.420	86.180	86.650	87.140	78.230	87.760	87.630
Norway	8.3104	8.1129	8.0484	7.5086	8.0033	8.3697	8.0092	8.0472	8.0165
Switzerland	1.6003	1.5579	1.5105	1.4670	1.5212	1.5438	1.5483	1.5729	1.6427
Japan	121.32	99.47	108.68	118.06	130.97	134.44	136.85	146.02	161.25
United States	1.0658	0.9236	0.8956	0.9456	1.1312	1.2439	1.2441	1.2556	1.3705

(1) The euro replaced the ecu on 1 January 1999; on 1 January 2002, it also replaced the notes and coins of 12 Community currencies with the introduction of the euro to the euro area (EA-12) members; on 1 January 2007, the euro came into circulation in Slovenia; on 1 January 2008, the euro came into circulation in Cyprus and Malta.

Source: Eurostat (tec00033), ECB

Figure 2.20: Central bank interest rates: official lending rates for loans

(%)

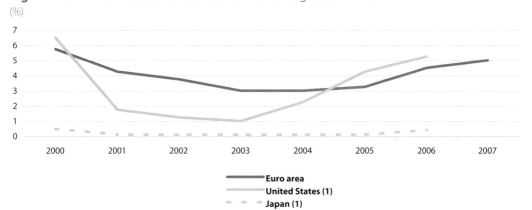

Euro area
United States (1)
Japan (1)

(1) 2007, not available.

Source: Eurostat (irt_cb_a), ECB, national central banks

Table 2.8: Interest rates

(%)

	Central bank interest rates: official lending rates for loans		EMU convergence criterion bond yields (Maastricht criterion) (1)		Short-term interest rates: three-month inter-bank rates (annual average)		Short-term interest rates: day-to-day money rates (annual average) (2)	
	2002	2007	2002	2007	2002	2007	2002	2007
EU-27	:	:	:	4.56	3.83	4.64	3.76	2.70
Euro area	3.75	5.00	4.91	:	3.32	4.28	3.29	3.87
Belgium	:	:	4.99	4.33	-	-	-	-
Bulgaria	:	:	:	4.54	4.91	4.90	2.39	4.03
Czech Republic	3.75	4.50	4.88	4.30	3.54	3.10	3.57	2.77
Denmark	2.95	4.25	5.06	4.29	3.54	4.44	3.49	2.68
Germany	:	:	4.78	4.22	-	-	-	-
Estonia	-	:	8.42	6.09	3.88	4.88	3.04	:
Ireland	:	:	5.01	4.31	-	-	-	-
Greece	:	:	5.12	4.50	-	-	-	-
Spain	:	:	4.96	4.31	-	-	-	-
France	:	:	4.86	4.30	-	-	-	-
Italy	:	:	5.03	4.49	-	-	-	-
Cyprus	5.00	5.00	5.70	4.48	4.40	4.15	3.53	3.81
Latvia	5.00	7.50	5.41	5.28	4.35	8.68	3.39	5.79
Lithuania	10.00	:	6.06	4.55	3.74	5.11	2.58	4.37
Luxembourg	:	:	4.70	4.56	-	-	-	-
Hungary	9.50	8.50	7.09	6.74	9.21	7.86	8.87	7.64
Malta	4.30	5.00	5.82	4.72	4.01	4.26	3.93	4.10
Netherlands	:	:	4.89	4.29	-	-	-	-
Austria	:	:	4.97	4.29	-	-	-	-
Poland	8.75	6.50	7.36	5.48	8.98	4.74	9.48	4.42
Portugal	:	:	5.01	4.42	-	-	-	-
Romania	20.40	7.50	:	7.13	27.31	7.24	23.35	6.89
Slovenia	10.50	:	8.71	4.53	8.03	:	4.88	3.37
Slovakia	8.00	5.75	6.94	4.49	7.77	4.34	7.18	3.83
Finland	:	:	4.98	4.29	-	-	-	-
Sweden	4.50	4.75	5.30	4.17	4.27	3.89	4.17	2.10
United Kingdom	4.00	5.50	4.91	5.06	4.06	6.00	3.95	5.64
Turkey	58.94	17.50	:	:	:	:	49.54	17.32
Japan	0.10	0.75	:	:	0.08	0.79	0.00	0.00
United States	1.25	4.25	:	:	1.79	5.30	1.67	3.22

(1) The indicator for Estonia represents interest rates on new EEK-denominated loans to non-financial corporations and households with maturity over 5 years; however, a large part of the underlying claims are linked to variable interest rates. The indicator for Luxembourg is based on a basket of long-term bonds, which have an average residual maturity close to ten years; the bonds are issued by a private credit institution.
(2) Denmark and Slovenia, 2006; EU-27, Japan and United States, 2005.

Source: Eurostat (irt_cb_a, irt_lt_mcby_a, tec00035 and tec00034), ECB, national central banks

2.4 Wages and labour costs

Introduction

Globalisation, the behaviour of firms, employment-related policies and changes in the structure of markets may influence the way in which labour markets develop. The level and structure of labour costs are among some of the key macro-economic indicators used by policy-makers, employers and trade unions in assessing labour market supply and demand conditions.

Within the context of the renewed Lisbon strategy, as highlighted in the Integrated Guidelines for Growth and Employment there are two key guidelines, namely to ensure:

- 'that wage developments contribute to macro-economic stability and growth, and;
- employment-friendly labour cost developments and wage-setting mechanisms by encouraging social partners within their own responsibilities to set the right framework for wage-bargaining in order to reflect productivity and labour market challenges at all relevant levels and to avoid gender pay gaps, by reviewing the impact on employment of non-wage labour costs and where appropriate adjust their structure and level, especially to reduce the tax burden on the low-paid' [5].

At the individual country level, nominal and real wage flexibility is considered key to rebalancing relative competitive positions.

Article 141(1) of the EC Treaty sets out the principle of equal pay for male and female workers for equal work or work of equal value, and Article 141(3) provides the legal basis for legislation on the equal treatment of men and women in employment matters. The European Commission Communication [6] of March 2006 on a roadmap for equality between women and men in the period between 2006-2010 is the latest review of this principle (among others), and was given further notice through the designation of 2007 as the European Year of Equal Opportunities. The gender pay gap is a multidimensional phenomenon that may be related to a number of effects, such as the composition of the labour force, remuneration and personnel selection effects. Gender differences are not restricted to pay, and the principle of equal treatment has been extended to cover a range of employment aspects, including equal access to self-employment, working conditions and vocational training. Policy measures within this area are designed to take account of differences in male and female labour market participation rates and career structures, wage structures, promotion policies, as well as the concentration of women in low pay sectors and occupations.

(5) http://europa.eu/scadplus/leg/en/cha/c11323.htm.

(6) COM(2006) 92 final; http://eur-lex.europa.eu/LexUriServ/LexUriServ.do?uri=COM:2006:0092:FIN:EN:PDF.

Definitions and data availability

Labour costs refer to the expenditure incurred by employers in order to employ personnel. They include employee compensation (including wages, salaries in cash and in kind, employers' social security contributions), vocational training costs, other expenditure such as recruitment costs, spending on working clothes and employment taxes regarded as labour costs minus any subsidies received. These labour cost components and their elements are defined in Commission Regulation (EC) 1737/2005 of 21 October 2005 amending Regulation (EC) No 1726/1999 as regards the definition and transmission of information on labour costs implementing Council Regulation (EC) No 530/1999 concerning structural statistics on earnings and labour costs. Data relate to three core indicators:

- **average monthly labour costs**, defined as total labour costs per month divided by the corresponding number of employees, expressed as full-time units;
- **average hourly labour costs**, defined as total labour costs divided by the corresponding number of hours worked;
- the **structure of labour costs** (wages and salaries; employers' social security contributions; other labour costs), expressed as a percentage of total labour costs.

Gross earnings are the most important part of labour costs – information is provided on average annual gross earnings. Main definitions on earnings are set up in Commission Regulation (EC) 1738/2005 of 21 October 2005 amending Regulation

(EC) No 1916/2000 as regards the definition and transmission of information on the structure of earnings implementing Council Regulation (EC) No 530/1999 concerning structural statistics on earnings and labour costs. Gross earnings cover remuneration in cash paid directly by the employer, before tax deductions and social security contributions payable by wage earners and retained by the employer. All bonuses, whether or not regularly paid, are included (13th or 14th month, holiday bonuses, profit-sharing, allowances for leave not taken, occasional commissions, etc.). The information is presented for full-time employees working in industry and services (as covered by NACE Sections C to K). The statistical unit is the enterprise or local unit. The population consists of all units having employees, although it is at present still confined to enterprises with at least 10 employees in most countries.

Net earnings are derived from gross earnings and represent the part of remuneration that employees can actually spend. Compared with gross earnings, net earnings do not include social security contributions and taxes, but do include family allowances.

The **gender pay gap** is given as the difference between average gross hourly earnings of male paid employees and of female paid employees, expressed as a percentage of average gross hourly earnings of male paid employees. The target population consists of all paid employees aged 16-64 that are at work for at least 15 hours per week. The values used were calculated before switching to a new methodology based on the harmonised structure of earnings survey.

Minimum wages are enforced by law and apply nationwide to the majority of full-time employees in each country. Minimum wages are expressed as gross amounts, that is, before the deduction of income tax and social security contributions. For most countries, the minimum wage is agreed in terms of an hourly or monthly rate, with the following exceptions for those countries where the minimum wage is fixed at an hourly rate:

- France: minimum wage per hour * 35 hours per week * 52/12;
- Ireland and the United Kingdom: minimum wage per hour * 39 hours per week * 52/12.
- In the case of Greece, Spain and Portugal, where 14 monthly minimum wages are paid per year, the minimum monthly wage is multiplied by 14/12.

The **tax wedge** on labour costs is defined as income tax on gross wage earnings plus the employee's and the employer's social security contributions, expressed as a percentage of the total labour costs of the earner. This indicator is available for single persons without children earning 67 % of the average earnings of an average worker in NACE Sections C to K (the business economy). The **unemployment trap** measures the proportion of gross earnings which is taxed away by higher tax and social security contributions and the withdrawal of unemployment and other benefits when an unemployed person returns to employment; it is defined as the difference between gross earnings and the increase of the net income when moving from unemployment to employment, expressed as percentage of the gross earnings. The indicator is available for single persons without children earning 67 % of the average earnings of an

average worker in NACE Sections C to K. The **low wage trap** measures the proportion of gross earnings which is taxed away through the combined effects of income taxes, social security contributions, and any withdrawal of benefits when gross earnings increase from 33 % to 67 % of the average earnings of an average worker in NACE Sections C to K. This indicator is available for single persons without children and for one-earner couples with two children between 6 and 11 years old.

Main findings

Gross annual earnings of full-time employees in enterprises with 10 or more employees averaged EUR 28 992 in the EU-27 in 2006. Among the Member States, average earnings were highest in Denmark (EUR 48 307), followed by the United Kingdom, Luxembourg, Germany and Ireland (2005) – all above EUR 40 000 – and lowest in Romania (EUR 3 713) and Bulgaria (EUR 2 195).

Despite some progress, there remains an important gap between the earnings of men and women in the EU. Women were paid, on average, 15 % less than their male counterparts within the EU-27 in 2006. The pay gap was below 10 % in Ireland, Italy (2005), Portugal, Slovenia, Belgium and Malta (where it was 3 %), but was wider than 20 % in Estonia, Cyprus, Germany, Slovakia, the United Kingdom, Austria and Finland. Various effects may contribute to these gender pay gaps, such as: differences in labour force participation rates, differences in the occupations and activities that tend to be male or female dominated, differences in the degrees to which men and women work on a part-time basis, as well as the attitudes of personnel departments within private and public bodies towards career development and unpaid/maternity leave.

2 Economy

Statutory minimum wages also vary considerably between Member States, and reflect to some degree the price levels in each economy, with the highest minimum wage in 2008 being recorded in Luxembourg (EUR 1 570 per month) and the lowest in Bulgaria and Romania (EUR 113 and EUR 141 respectively).

There were quite large differences in the structure of labour costs within the Member States in 2006; the relative importance of wages and salaries ranged from less than 70 % of total labour costs in Belgium, France, Italy (2002), Hungary and Sweden to more than 83 % in Denmark, Cyprus, Luxembourg and Malta. When social security and other non-salary costs account for a relatively high share of labour costs then this is likely to deter employers from hiring until they are absolutely sure that they require new labour.

Table 2.9: Earnings in industry and services (average gross annual earnings of full time employees in enterprises with 10 or more employees)
(EUR)

	1996	1997	1998	1999	2000	2001	2002	2003	2004	2005	2006
EU-27	:	:	:	:	:	27 948	30 142	30 349	28 226	28 992	:
Euro area (1)	:	:	:	:	28 786	29 588	30 379	31 089	32 471	33 164	:
Belgium	29 131	28 901	29 616	30 701	31 644	33 109	34 330	34 643	35 704	36 673	37 674
Bulgaria	795	896	1 216	1 330	1 436	1 518	1 588	1 678	1 784	1 978	2 195
Czech Republic	:	:	:	:	:	:	6 016	6 137	6 569	7 405	8 284
Denmark	36 376	36 235	37 209	39 515	40 962	41 661	43 577	44 692	46 122	47 529	48 307
Germany	35 254	35 093	35 432	36 228	37 319	38 204	39 153	40 056	40 954	41 694	42 382
Estonia	:	:	:	:	:	:	:	:	:	:	:
Ireland	:	:	:	:	:	:	:	:	:	40 462	:
Greece	11 917	12 605	13 210	13 926	14 721	15 431	16 278	16 739	:	:	:
Spain	16 043	16 192	16 528	17 038	17 432	17 768	18 462	19 220	19 828	20 439	21 150
France	25 089	25 545	25 777	26 339	26 712	27 418	28 185	28 847	29 608	30 521	:
Italy	:	:	:	:	:	:	:	:	:	:	:
Cyprus	12 980	14 021	14 709	15 161	16 335	16 948	17 740	18 406	19 290	20 549	21 310
Latvia	:	:	:	:	:	:	:	:	3 806	4 246	5 211
Lithuania	1 597	2 286	2 799	3 017	:	:	:	:	:	:	:
Luxembourg	:	32 600	33 337	34 462	35 875	37 745	38 442	39 587	40 575	42 135	43 621
Hungary	3 158	3 543	3 686	3 770	4 173	4 898	5 846	6 196	7 100	7 798	7 840
Malta (2)	9 322	10 144	10 745	11 608	11 658	11 974	12 096	11 886	11 926	11 180	11 669
Netherlands	28 140	28 061	29 189	30 426	31 901	33 900	35 200	36 600	37 900	38 700	:
Austria	:	:	:	:	:	:	:	:	34 995	36 032	36 673
Poland	3 076	:	4 156	5 310	:	7 510	:	:	6 230	6 270	:
Portugal	:	:	:	:	12 620	13 338	13 322	13 871	14 253	14 715	15 930
Romania	:	:	:	:	:	:	:	:	2 414	3 155	3 713
Slovenia	:	:	:	:	:	:	:	:	:	:	:
Slovakia	:	3 179	3 292	3 125	3 583	3 837	4 582	4 945	5 706	6 374	7 040
Finland	23 883	24 005	24 944	25 739	27 398	28 555	29 916	30 978	31 988	33 290	34 080
Sweden	:	:	:	:	31 621	30 467	31 164	32 177	33 620	34 049	35 084
United Kingdom	:	:	29 370	32 269	37 677	39 233	40 553	38 793	41 253	42 866	44 496
Croatia	:	:	:	:	:	:	:	8 491	9 036	9 634	:
Iceland	:	:	:	32 311	37 639	34 101	36 764	:	:	:	:
Norway	:	:	31 456	33 741	36 202	38 604	43 736	42 882	42 224	45 485	47 221
Switzerland	42 194	:	40 727	:	43 683	:	48 498	:	45 760	:	46 058

(1) EA-13 instead of EA-15.
(2) Break in series, 2000.

Source: Eurostat (tps00175)

Figure 2.21: Earnings in industry and services (average gross annual earnings of full-time employees in enterprises with 10 or more employees), 2006 (1)

(EUR)

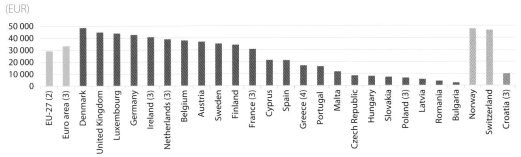

(1) Estonia, Italy, Lithuania and Slovenia, not available.
(2) EA-13 instead of EA-15, 2005.
(3) 2005.
(4) 2003.

Source: Eurostat (tps00175)

Table 2.10: Minimum wage

(EUR/month, as of 1 January)

	1998	1999	2000	2001	2002	2003	2004	2005	2006	2007	2008
Belgium	:	1 074	1 096	1 118	1 163	1 163	1 186	1 210	1 234	1 259	1 310
Bulgaria	:	33	38	44	51	56	61	77	82	92	113
Czech Republic	:	93	111	144	175	199	207	235	261	288	304
Denmark	:	:	:	:	:	:	:	:	:	:	:
Germany	:	:	:	:	:	:	:	:	:	:	:
Estonia	:	:	:	:	118	138	159	172	192	230	278
Ireland	:	:	945	945	1 009	1 073	1 073	1 183	1 293	1 403	1 462
Greece	:	505	526	544	552	605	631	668	668	658	681
Spain	:	416	425	433	516	526	537	599	631	666	700
France	:	1 036	1 049	1 083	1 126	1 154	1 173	1 197	1 218	1 254	1 280
Italy	:	:	:	:	:	:	:	:	:	:	:
Cyprus	:	:	:	:	:	:	:	:	:	:	:
Latvia	:	75	84	89	107	116	121	116	129	172	229
Lithuania	:	92	106	120	120	125	125	145	159	174	232
Luxembourg	:	1 162	1 191	1 259	1 290	1 369	1 403	1 467	1 503	1 570	1 570
Hungary	:	89	100	151	202	212	189	232	247	258	273
Malta	:	462	500	532	552	534	542	557	580	585	612
Netherlands	:	1 064	1 092	1 154	1 207	1 249	1 265	1 265	1 273	1 301	1 335
Austria	:	:	:	:	:	:	:	:	:	:	:
Poland	:	159	159	196	212	201	177	205	234	246	313
Portugal	:	357	371	390	406	416	426	437	450	470	497
Romania	:	28	25	44	62	73	69	72	90	114	141
Slovenia	335	351	359	387	419	451	471	490	512	522	539
Slovakia	:	:	:	:	114	133	148	167	183	217	243
Finland	:	:	:	:	:	:	:	:	:	:	:
Sweden	:	:	:	:	:	:	:	:	:	:	:
United Kingdom	:	866	970	1 130	1 118	1 106	1 083	1 197	1 269	1 361	1 223
Turkey	:	217	206	230	171	189	240	240	331	298	354
United States	:	762	883	995	1 001	877	727	666	753	676	696

Source: Eurostat (tps00155)

Figure 2.22: Gender pay gap - female earnings lower than male earnings, 2006
(% difference between average gross hourly earnings of male and female employees, as % of male gross earnings, unadjusted form)

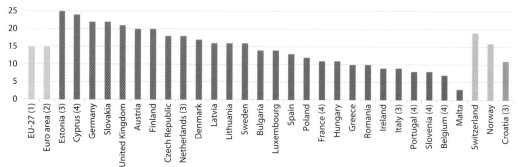

(1) Estimate.
(2) EA-13 instead of EA-15; estimate for 2005.
(3) 2005.
(4) Provisional.

Source: Eurostat (tsiem030)

Figure 2.23: Tax rate on low wage earners: tax wedge on labour cost, 2006
(%)

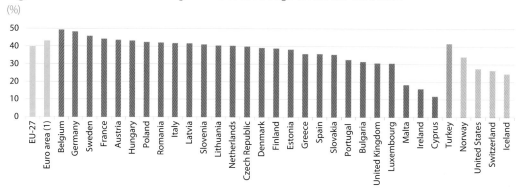

(1) EA-13 instead of EA-15.

Source: Eurostat (tsiem060), OECD, Commission services

Figure 2.24: Labour costs (average hourly labour costs in industry and services of full-time employees in enterprises with 10 or more employees), 2006 (1)

(EUR)

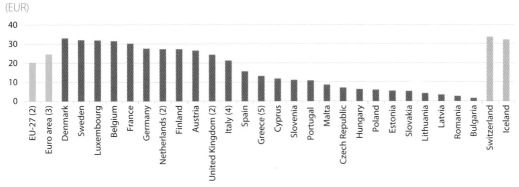

(1) Ireland, not available.
(2) 2005.
(3) EA-13 instead of EA-15, 2005.
(4) 2004.
(5) 2003.

Source: Eurostat (tps00173)

Figure 2.25: Breakdown of labour costs, business economy, 2006 (1)

(% share of total labour costs)

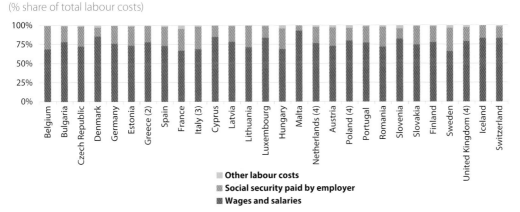

■ Other labour costs
▨ Social security paid by employer
▨ Wages and salaries

(1) Ireland, not available.
(2) 2003.
(3) 2002.
(4) 2005.

Source: Eurostat (tps00115, tps00114 and tps00113)

2.5 Consumer prices and comparative price levels

Introduction

Changes in the price of consumer goods and services are usually referred to as the inflation rate. They measure the loss of living standards due to price inflation and are some of the most well-known economic statistics.

Price stability is one of the main objectives of the European Central Bank (ECB), with the inflation rate used as a prime indicator for monetary policy management in the euro area. The ECB has defined price stability as an annual increase in the harmonised index of consumer prices (HICP) for the euro area of below, but close to, 2 % (over the medium-term).

HICPs are economic indicators constructed to measure, over time, the change in prices of consumer goods and services that are acquired by households. HICPs give comparable measures of inflation in the euro area, the European Union, the European Economic Area, as well as for individual countries. They are calculated according to a harmonised approach and a single set of definitions, providing an official measure of consumer price inflation for the purposes of monetary policy and assessing inflation convergence as required under the Maastricht criteria.

A comparison of price changes between countries depends not only on movements in price levels, but also exchange rates – together these two forces impact upon price and cost competitiveness of individual Member States.

With the introduction of the euro, prices within those Member States that share a common currency are said to be more transparent, as it is relatively simple for consumers to compare the price of items across borders. Such comparisons that provide an economic case for purchasing a good or service from another country have led to an increase in cross-border trade. From an economic point of view, the price of a given good within the single market should not differ significantly depending on geographic location, beyond differences that may be explained by transport costs or tax differences. However, not all goods and services converge at the same pace. For example, price convergence in housing does not necessarily follow the same pace as for tradable goods. Indeed, even within individual countries there are large (and perhaps growing) discrepancies in the price of housing for rent or for sale between regions.

Definitions and data availability

The **inflation rate** is calculated from harmonised indices of consumer prices – it equates to the all-items harmonised index of consumer prices. **Harmonised indices of consumer prices (HICPs)** are presented with a common reference year, which is currently 2005=100. Normally the indices are used to create percentage changes that show price increases/decreases for the period in question. Although the rates of change shown in this publication are annual averages, the basic indices are compiled on a monthly basis and are published at this frequency by Eurostat. Eurostat publishes HICPs some 14 to 16 days after the end of the reporting month, with these series starting in the mid-1990s.

HICPs cover practically every good and service that may be purchased by households in the form of final monetary consumption expenditure. Owner occupied housing is, however, not yet reflected in the HICPs. The different goods and services are classified according to an international classification of individual consumption by purpose, known as COICOP/HICP. At its most disaggregated level, Eurostat publishes around 100 sub-indices, which can be aggregated to broad categories of goods and services. In order to improve the comparability and reliability of HICPs, sampling, replacement and quality adjustment procedures are periodically reviewed, the latest changes being set out in Commission Regulation (EC) No 1334/2007 of 14 November 2007.

There are three key HICP aggregate indices: the **monetary union index of consumer prices (MUICP)** for the euro area; the **European index of consumer prices (EICP)** covering all Member States; and the **European Economic Area index of consumer prices (EEAICP)**, which additionally covers Iceland and Norway. Note that these aggregates reflect changes over time in their country composition through the use of a chain index formula – for example, the MUICP includes Slovenia only from 2007 onwards, while the EICP index only includes Bulgaria and Romania from 2007 onwards.

Purchasing power parities (PPPs) estimate price-level differences between countries. They make it possible to produce meaningful volume or price-level indicators required for cross-country comparisons. PPPs are aggregated price ratios calculated from price comparisons over a large number of goods and services. PPPs are employed either:

- as currency converters to generate volume measures with which to compare levels of economic performance, total consumption, investment, overall productivity and selected private household expenditures;
- or as price measures with which to compare relative price levels, price convergence and competitiveness.

Eurostat produces three sets of data using PPPs:

- levels and indices of real final expenditure – these are measures of volume; they indicate the relative magnitudes of the product groups or aggregates being compared; at the level of GDP, they are used to compare the economic size of countries;
- levels and indices of real final expenditure per head – these are standardised measures of volume; they indicate the relative levels of the product groups or aggregates being compared after adjusting for differences in the size of populations between countries; at the level of GDP, they are often used to compare the economic well-being of populations;
- **comparative price levels** – these are the ratios of PPPs to exchange rates; these indices provide a comparison of the countries' price levels with respect to the EU average – if the price level index is higher than 100, the country concerned is relatively expensive compared with the EU average and vice versa; at the level of GDP, they provide a measure of the differences in the general price levels of countries.

The coefficient of variation of comparative price levels is applied as an indicator of price convergence among EU Member States – if the coefficient of variation for comparative price levels for the EU decreases/increases over time, the national price levels in the Member States are converging/diverging.

The real effective exchange rate is deflated by nominal unit labour costs. This relative price and cost indicator aims to assess a country's competitiveness relative to its principal competitors in international markets, with changes in cost and price competitiveness depending not only on exchange rate movements but also on price trends. Double export weights are used to calculate the index, reflecting not only competition in the home markets of the various competitors, but also competition in export markets elsewhere. A rise in the index means a loss of competitiveness.

Main findings

Compared with historical trends, consumer price indices have risen only at a moderate pace during the last two decades. The EU inflation rate decreased during the 1990s, reaching 1.2 % by 1999, after which the pace of price increases settled at around 2 % per annum during the period 2000 to 2007. This pattern was quite similar to the evolution of inflation in the United States, while Japan has been characterised by exceptionally low inflation – often deflation (in other words falling prices) during the last decade.

In 2007, the highest rates of price inflation among the EU-27 Member States were recorded in Latvia (10.1 %), Hungary (7.9 %), Bulgaria (7.6 %) and Estonia (6.7 %). In general, inflation was often somewhat higher than the EU average among those Member States that joined the EU since 2004.

Among the constituent price indices for different goods and services, the average price of education rose sharpest (8.6 %) in the EU. There was also a relatively strong price rise for alcoholic drinks and tobacco (3.8 %), largely reflecting changes in duties. The continued rise in the price of oil and gas was often a factor behind higher prices, particularly for housing, water, electricity, gas and other fuels (3.3 %) and transport (2.5 %). Strong demand for staple foods (particularly from Asia) was a key factor behind the relatively strong price increases for food and non-alcoholic beverages (3.5 %). In contrast, the price of clothing and footwear, as well as recreation and culture remained almost unchanged, and the average price of communications declined

(-2.0 %), reflecting technology gains and increased competition.

The relative price levels of private household consumption vary significantly between the Member States. With the average for the EU-27 being defined as 100, comparative price levels within the Member States ranged in 2007 from 46.0 in Bulgaria to 136.9 in Denmark.

Nevertheless, over the decade between 1997 and 2007, there was a convergence of prices; the coefficient of variation of comparative price levels declined from 37.8 % in 1997 to 26.2 % by 2007. The pace at which price convergence took place slowed somewhat from 2000, but accelerated again after 2003.

Figure 2.26: HICP all-items, annual average inflation rates

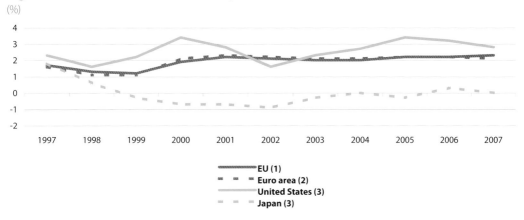

(1) The data refer to the official EU aggregate, its country coverage changes in line with the addition of new EU Member States and integrates them using a chain index formula; 1996, not available; 1997-1999, estimates.
(2) The data refer to the official euro area aggregate, its country coverage changes in line with the addition of new EU Member States and integrates them using a chain index formula.; 1996, not available; 1997, estimate.
(3) National CPI: not strictly comparable with the HICP.

Source: Eurostat (tsieb060)

Table 2.11: HICP all-items, annual average inflation rates

(%)

	1997	1998	1999	2000	2001	2002	2003	2004	2005	2006	2007
EU (1)	1.7	1.3	1.2	1.9	2.2	2.1	2.0	2.0	2.2	2.2	2.3
Euro area (2)	1.6	1.1	1.1	2.1	2.3	2.2	2.1	2.1	2.2	2.2	2.1
Belgium	1.5	0.9	1.1	2.7	2.4	1.6	1.5	1.9	2.5	2.3	1.8
Bulgaria	:	18.7	2.6	10.3	7.4	5.8	2.3	6.1	6.0	7.4	7.6
Czech Republic	8.0	9.7	1.8	3.9	4.5	1.4	-0.1	2.6	1.6	2.1	3.0
Denmark	2.0	1.3	2.1	2.7	2.3	2.4	2.0	0.9	1.7	1.9	1.7
Germany	1.5	0.6	0.6	1.4	1.9	1.4	1.0	1.8	1.9	1.8	2.3
Estonia	9.3	8.8	3.1	3.9	5.6	3.6	1.4	3.0	4.1	4.4	6.7
Ireland	1.3	2.1	2.5	5.3	4.0	4.7	4.0	2.3	2.2	2.7	2.9
Greece	5.4	4.5	2.1	2.9	3.7	3.9	3.4	3.0	3.5	3.3	3.0
Spain	1.9	1.8	2.2	3.5	2.8	3.6	3.1	3.1	3.4	3.6	2.8
France	1.3	0.7	0.6	1.8	1.8	1.9	2.2	2.3	1.9	1.9	1.6
Italy	1.9	2.0	1.7	2.6	2.3	2.6	2.8	2.3	2.2	2.2	2.0
Cyprus	3.3	2.3	1.1	4.9	2.0	2.8	4.0	1.9	2.0	2.2	2.2
Latvia	8.1	4.3	2.1	2.6	2.5	2.0	2.9	6.2	6.9	6.6	10.1
Lithuania	10.3	5.4	1.5	1.1	1.6	0.3	-1.1	1.2	2.7	3.8	5.8
Luxembourg	1.4	1.0	1.0	3.8	2.4	2.1	2.5	3.2	3.8	3.0	2.7
Hungary	18.5	14.2	10.0	10.0	9.1	5.2	4.7	6.8	3.5	4.0	7.9
Malta	3.9	3.7	2.3	3.0	2.5	2.6	1.9	2.7	2.5	2.6	0.7
Netherlands	1.9	1.8	2.0	2.3	5.1	3.9	2.2	1.4	1.5	1.7	1.6
Austria	1.2	0.8	0.5	2.0	2.3	1.7	1.3	2.0	2.1	1.7	2.2
Poland	15.0	11.8	7.2	10.1	5.3	1.9	0.7	3.6	2.2	1.3	2.6
Portugal	1.9	2.2	2.2	2.8	4.4	3.7	3.3	2.5	2.1	3.0	2.4
Romania	154.8	59.1	45.8	45.7	34.5	22.5	15.3	11.9	9.1	6.6	4.9
Slovenia	8.3	7.9	6.1	8.9	8.6	7.5	5.7	3.7	2.5	2.5	3.8
Slovakia	6.0	6.7	10.4	12.2	7.2	3.5	8.4	7.5	2.8	4.3	1.9
Finland	1.2	1.3	1.3	2.9	2.7	2.0	1.3	0.1	0.8	1.3	1.6
Sweden	1.8	1.0	0.5	1.3	2.7	1.9	2.3	1.0	0.8	1.5	1.7
United Kingdom	1.8	1.6	1.3	0.8	1.2	1.3	1.4	1.3	2.1	2.3	2.3
Turkey	85.6	82.1	61.4	53.2	56.8	47.0	25.3	10.1	8.1	9.3	8.8
Iceland	1.8	1.3	2.1	4.4	6.6	5.3	1.4	2.3	1.4	4.6	3.6
Norway	2.6	2.0	2.1	3.0	2.7	0.8	2.0	0.6	1.5	2.5	0.7
Switzerland	:	:	:	:	:	:	:	:	:	1.0	0.8
Japan (3)	1.8	0.6	-0.3	-0.7	-0.7	-0.9	-0.3	0.0	-0.3	0.3	0.0
United States (3)	2.3	1.6	2.2	3.4	2.8	1.6	2.3	2.7	3.4	3.2	2.8

(1) The data refer to the official EU aggregate, its country coverage changes in line with the addition of new EU Member States and integrates them using a chain index formula.
(2) The data refer to the official euro area aggregate, its country coverage changes in line with the addition of new EU Member States and integrates them using a chain index formula.
(3) National CPI: not strictly comparable with the HICP.

Source: Eurostat (tsieb060)

Table 2.12: Comparative price levels (1)

(final consumption by private households including indirect taxes, EU-27=100)

	1996	1997	1998	1999	2000	2001	2002	2003	2004	2005	2006
EU-27	100.0	100.0	100.0	100.0	100.0	100.0	100.0	100.0	100.0	100.0	100.0
Euro area (2)	104.0	102.8	102.2	100.5	101.0	101.1	103.5	103.6	102.5	102.5	102.0
Belgium	105.8	107.5	106.8	102.0	103.2	101.5	106.5	106.7	106.0	106.2	105.4
Bulgaria	34.0	37.5	37.9	38.7	41.0	40.8	40.7	42.0	43.1	44.8	46.0
Czech Republic	44.4	47.4	46.4	48.1	50.0	57.1	54.5	55.4	58.4	61.5	62.6
Denmark	131.6	129.4	131.5	130.3	135.2	133.8	141.1	139.6	139.6	139.2	136.9
Germany	109.6	108.7	107.3	106.6	107.0	106.6	106.1	104.7	103.7	103.3	103.2
Estonia	50.8	54.1	56.9	57.3	61.1	60.8	62.0	63.0	64.6	66.5	71.3
Ireland	113.0	108.1	111.6	114.9	119.3	125.2	126.4	125.9	124.8	124.9	126.0
Greece	87.6	85.7	88.3	84.8	82.3	80.2	85.9	87.6	88.4	89.1	88.6
Spain	86.9	85.5	86.0	85.0	85.4	84.6	88.3	91.0	92.0	93.3	93.0
France	112.0	110.7	109.3	105.9	104.1	103.5	110.0	109.9	107.4	107.3	106.7
Italy	99.7	97.9	98.2	97.5	99.7	102.7	103.6	104.9	104.0	104.1	102.9
Cyprus	86.6	87.1	87.4	88.1	88.9	89.1	90.9	91.2	89.7	90.1	87.7
Latvia	47.8	49.2	52.3	58.8	59.0	57.0	54.4	56.1	57.1	60.6	65.0
Lithuania	43.2	45.6	46.8	52.7	54.1	54.2	52.3	53.5	55.1	56.6	59.7
Luxembourg	106.6	104.2	102.9	101.5	103.5	102.1	103.2	103.0	102.7	103.2	105.1
Hungary	46.4	45.7	47.1	49.2	52.9	57.4	58.2	62.0	63.5	60.0	65.7
Malta	68.7	69.4	70.5	73.3	74.8	74.6	72.0	73.2	73.1	73.4	73.2
Netherlands	103.4	102.1	102.7	100.0	103.0	102.9	107.8	106.1	104.5	103.9	103.1
Austria	107.1	105.3	104.9	101.9	104.8	103.4	103.3	103.3	101.9	101.2	100.0
Poland	51.8	53.5	51.9	57.9	64.8	61.2	54.4	53.2	61.3	62.1	63.4
Portugal	82.5	84.0	83.4	83.0	84.4	86.3	86.0	87.4	85.3	85.7	84.6
Romania	34.7	43.2	37.9	42.5	41.7	43.0	43.4	43.3	54.3	57.0	64.7
Slovenia	72.4	74.1	74.1	72.9	73.9	74.4	76.2	75.5	75.8	75.3	76.9
Slovakia	41.6	41.9	40.5	44.4	43.4	44.8	50.7	54.9	55.8	58.3	63.0
Finland	125.0	123.0	122.3	120.9	124.8	123.9	126.6	123.8	123.3	121.7	121.4
Sweden	131.6	127.0	126.4	127.6	119.9	121.7	123.5	121.4	117.9	117.5	116.4
United Kingdom	107.6	112.2	115.6	120.0	116.8	117.1	107.8	108.5	110.2	110.8	112.3
Croatia	:	:	:	:	:	:	64.8	66.5	69.0	69.9	69.5
FYR of Macedonia	:	:	:	:	:	:	43.9	44.4	44.0	44.5	43.0
Turkey	:	:	56.0	62.5	47.7	51.6	57.2	59.1	68.4	68.4	72.2
Iceland	120.8	124.7	126.7	144.0	127.9	134.6	138.4	137.9	152.3	141.7	146.0
Norway	136.6	131.0	134.3	137.7	141.8	151.2	142.1	135.2	140.0	139.8	137.5
Switzerland	135.8	136.4	139.7	142.6	146.3	146.7	143.8	140.8	137.9	134.2	125.7
Japan	158.8	146.9	173.1	198.4	177.7	156.3	136.5	129.5	119.6	109.1	:
United States	100.0	100.6	105.6	121.0	126.1	119.7	101.4	92.8	92.0	91.6	:

(1) Belgium and France, break in the series for 2003.
(2) EA-13 instead of EA-15.

Source: Eurostat (tsier010)

Economy

Figure 2.27: HICP main headings, annual average inflation rates, EU, 2007
(%)

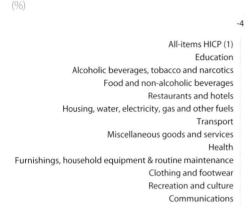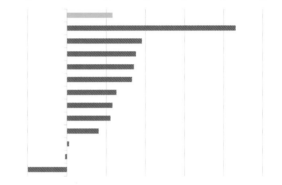

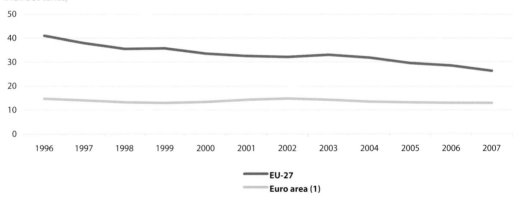

(1) More commonly referred to as the inflation rate.

Source: Eurostat (prc_hicp_aind)

Figure 2.28: Price convergence between EU Member States
(%, coefficient of variation of comparative price levels of final consumption by private households including indirect taxes)

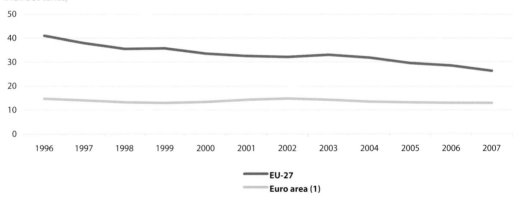

━━━ **EU-27**
━━━ **Euro area (1)**

(1) EA-13 instead of EA-15.

Source: Eurostat (tsier020)

EUROPE IN FIGURES — Eurostat yearbook 2009 ◼ **eurostat**

2.6 Balance of payments – current account

Introduction

The balance of payments is a statistical statement that summarises the transactions of an economy with the rest of the world. Transactions are organised in two different accounts, the current account and the capital and financial account, whose sum, in principle, should be zero, as for each credit transaction there is a corresponding one on the debit side. Thus, the current account balance determines the exposure of an economy vis-à-vis the rest of the world, whereas the capital and financial account explains how it is financed.

Definitions and data availability

The **current account** gauges a country's economic position in the world, covering all transactions that occur between resident and non-resident entities and refer to trade in goods and services, income and current transfers. More specifically, the four main components of the current account are defined as follows:

- **Trade in goods** covers general merchandise, goods for processing, repairs on goods, goods procured in ports by carriers, and non-monetary gold. Exports and imports of goods are recorded on a fob/fob basis, i.e. at market value at the customs frontiers of exporting economies, including charges for insurance and transport services up to the frontier of the exporting country.

- **Trade in services** consists of the following items: transportation services performed by EU residents for non-EU residents, or vice versa, involving the carriage of passengers, the movement of goods, rentals of carriers with crew and related supporting and auxiliary services; travel, which includes primarily the goods and services EU travellers acquire from non-EU residents, or vice versa; and other services, which include communication services, construction services, insurance services, financial services, computer and information services, royalties and licence fees, other business services (which comprise merchanting and other trade-related services, operational leasing services and miscellaneous business, professional and technical services), personal, cultural and recreational services and government services not included elsewhere.

- **Income** covers two types of transactions: compensation of employees paid to non-resident workers or received from non-resident employers, and investment income accrued on external financial assets and liabilities.

- **Current transfers** include general government current transfers, for example transfers related to international cooperation between governments, payments of current taxes on income and wealth, etc., and other current transfers, for example workers' remittances, insurance premiums (less service charges), and claims on non-life insurance companies.

Under the balance of payment conventions, transactions which represent an inflow of real resources, an increase in assets or a decrease in liabilities (such as, exports of goods) are recorded as credits, and transactions representing an outflow of real resources, a decrease in assets or an increase in liabilities (such as, imports of goods) are recorded as debits.

Main findings

The current account deficit of the EU-27 was EUR 72 400 million in 2007 (corresponding to 0.6 % of GDP), which although slightly less than the deficit of 2006, nevertheless confirmed the stark turnaround from relatively small surpluses recorded for the period between 2002 and 2004. The overall deficit for 2007 comprised deficits in the current account for goods (-1.2 % of GDP) and for current transfers (-0.5 %), as well as positive balances for the income account (0.4 %) and for services (0.7 %).

Most of the EU-27's current account transactions in 2007 took place with the United States (26.7 % of credits and 21.7 % of debits). All other partners recorded shares of less than 10 %; the next most significant partner was Switzerland (9.1 % credits, 8.4 % debits), and then China (3.9 % and 9.6 %), the Russian Federation (5.1 % and 6.4 %) and Japan (3.7 % and 4.7 %).

Accordingly, the EU-27 recorded a surplus of just over EUR 100 000 million vis-à-vis the United States in 2007, but deficits with China (EUR 143 100 million), the Russian Federation (EUR 37 000 million) and Japan (EUR 27 200 million).

Figure 2.29: Current account transactions, EU-27 (1)

(EUR 1 000 million)

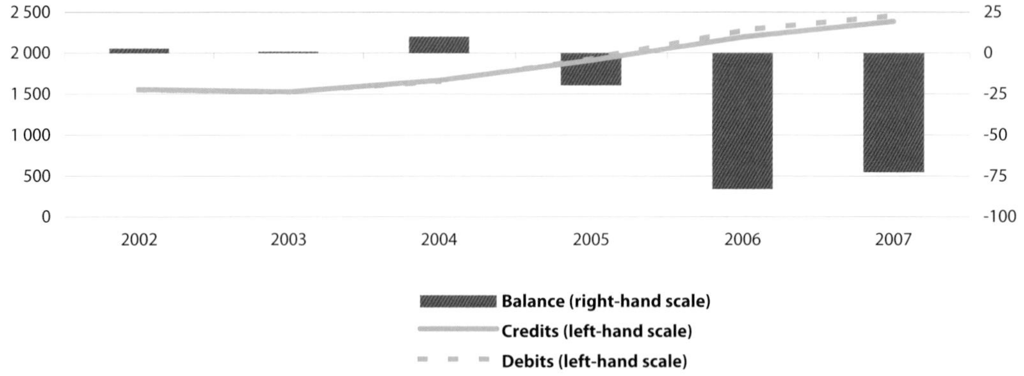

	Balance (right-hand scale)
	Credits (left-hand scale)
	Debits (left-hand scale)

(1) EU-25: for 2002-2003; 2007, provisional data.

Source: Eurostat (tec00038)

Table 2.13: Current account balance for EU Member States with the rest of the world

(EUR million)

	2003	2004	2005	2006	2007 (1)
EU-27 (2)	:	10 300	-19 600	-82 900	-72 400
Euro area (3)	33 200	62 000	17 100	-1 700	27 400
Belgium	5 600	10 200	7 900	8 400	6 400
Bulgaria	-1 500	-1 300	-2 700	-4 500	-6 200
Czech Republic	-5 000	-4 700	-1 800	-3 800	-3 500
Denmark	6 500	5 900	9 000	5 900	2 500
Germany	44 000	102 900	116 600	141 500	184 200
Estonia	-1 000	-1 200	-1 100	-2 100	-2 700
Ireland	0	-900	-5 700	-7 300	-9 300
Greece	-11 000	-10 500	-14 000	:	:
Spain	-27 500	-44 200	-66 900	-87 700	-105 800
France	7 000	8 500	-15 700	-22 500	-21 900
Italy	-17 300	-13 000	-23 400	-37 900	-37 900
Cyprus	-300	-600	-800	-900	-1 500
Latvia	-800	-1 400	-1 600	-3 600	-4 600
Lithuania	-1 100	-1 400	-1 500	-2 600	-3 800
Luxembourg	2 100	3 300	3 300	3 500	3 600
Hungary	-5 900	-6 900	-6 000	-5 400	-5 000
Malta	-100	-300	-400	-400	-300
Netherlands	26 200	36 900	36 600	44 500	36 800
Austria	-500	1 100	2 800	6 300	8 800
Poland	-4 100	-8 200	-3 000	-7 300	-11 500
Portugal	-8 500	-10 900	-14 100	-15 700	-15 900
Romania	-2 900	-5 100	-6 900	-10 200	-17 100
Slovenia	-200	-700	-600	-900	-1 600
Slovakia	-200	-1 200	-3 200	-3 600	-3 100
Finland	7 500	10 000	5 700	7 600	8 200
Sweden	19 800	19 200	20 500	26 500	27 900
United Kingdom	-21 300	-28 700	-45 300	-74 500	-85 100

(1) Provisional data.
(2) EU-25 for 2003; EU vis-à-vis extra-EU.
(3) EA-13 instead of EA-15; euro area vis-à-vis extra euro area.

Source: Eurostat (tec00038)

Table 2.14: Current account, balance by components, 2007
(% of GDP)

	Current account	Goods	Services	Income	Current transfers
EU-27	-0.6	-1.2	0.7	0.4	-0.5
Euro area (1)	0.3	0.7	0.5	0.0	-0.9
Belgium	1.9	0.2	1.5	2.0	-1.7
Bulgaria	-21.5	-25.6	3.8	-1.0	1.0
Czech Republic	-2.7	3.1	1.6	-7.2	-0.2
Denmark	1.1	-0.4	2.4	0.7	-1.6
Germany	7.6	8.4	-1.3	1.7	-1.3
Estonia	-17.7	-17.0	6.5	-7.2	0.0
Ireland	-5.0	12.3	-2.2	-14.5	-0.7
Greece	:	:	:	:	:
Spain	-10.1	-8.5	2.1	-3.0	-0.6
France	-1.2	-2.0	0.5	1.6	-1.2
Italy	-2.5	0.1	-0.4	-1.3	-0.9
Cyprus	-9.6	-29.4	23.7	-3.8	0.0
Latvia	-23.1	-24.6	3.5	-3.5	1.5
Lithuania	-13.6	-14.6	2.1	-4.3	2.9
Luxembourg	10.0	-9.4	53.7	-29.6	-4.7
Hungary	-4.9	1.4	1.1	-7.7	0.3
Malta	-5.5	-16.6	14.8	-1.8	-1.8
Netherlands	6.5	6.8	0.3	1.1	-1.6
Austria	3.2	0.5	4.5	-1.4	-0.4
Poland	-3.7	-3.7	0.9	-3.0	2.0
Portugal	-9.8	-10.7	3.8	-4.5	1.6
Romania	-14.1	-14.6	0.2	-3.8	4.0
Slovenia	-4.8	-5.1	3.0	-2.1	-0.9
Slovakia	-5.7	-1.5	0.7	-4.4	-0.5
Finland	4.6	4.8	-0.1	0.6	-0.8
Sweden	8.4	4.1	3.1	2.2	-1.1
United Kingdom	-4.2	-6.3	2.8	0.4	-1.0

(1) EA-13 instead of EA-15.

Source: Eurostat (tec00038, tec00039, tec00040, tec00041, tec00042 and tec00001)

Figure 2.30: Current account, credit by partner country, EU-27, 2007 (1)
(% of total credits)

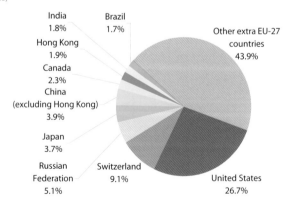

India 1.8%
Brazil 1.7%
Hong Kong 1.9%
Canada 2.3%
China (excluding Hong Kong) 3.9%
Japan 3.7%
Russian Federation 5.1%
Switzerland 9.1%
United States 26.7%
Other extra EU-27 countries 43.9%

(1) Figures do not sum to 100 % due to rounding.

Source: Eurostat (bop_q_eu)

Figure 2.31: Current account, debit by partner country, EU-27, 2007 (1)
(% of total debits)

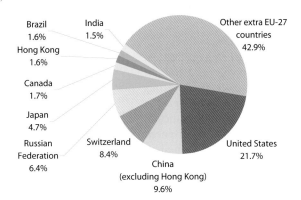

(1) Figures do not sum to 100 % due to rounding.

Source: Eurostat (bop_q_eu)

Figure 2.32: Current account balance with selected partners, EU-27, 2007
(EUR 1 000 million)

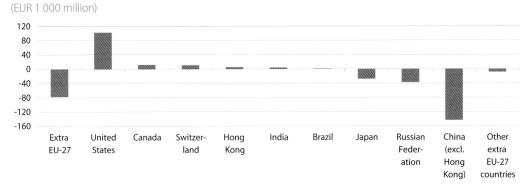

Source: Eurostat (bop_q_eu)

2.7 Balance of payments – foreign direct investment

Introduction

In a world of increasing globalisation, where political, economic and technological barriers are rapidly disappearing, the ability of a country to participate in global activity is an important indicator of its performance and competitiveness. In order to remain competitive, modern day business relationships extend well beyond the traditional foreign exchange of goods and services, as witnessed by the increasing reliance of firms on mergers, partnerships, joint ventures, licensing agreements, and other forms of business cooperation.

External trade may be complemented or substituted by producing (and often selling) goods and services in countries other than where an enterprise was first established: this approach is known as foreign direct investment (FDI), whereby the enterprise concerned either invests to establish a new plant/office, or alternatively, purchases existing assets of a foreign enterprise. FDI is a type of international investment where an entity that is resident in one economy (the direct investor) acquires a lasting interest (at least 10 % of the voting power) in an enterprise operating in another economy. The lasting interest implies the existence of a long-term relationship between the direct investor and the enterprise, and a significant degree of influence by the investor on the management of the enterprise.

Conventional trade is less important for services than for goods and while trade in services has been growing, the share

of services in total intra-EU trade has changed little during the last decade. However, FDI is expanding more rapidly for services than for goods, as FDI in services has increased at a more rapid pace than conventional trade in services. As a result, the share of services in total FDI flows and positions has increased substantially, with European services becoming increasingly international.

Definitions and data availability

Formally defined, a **direct investment enterprise** is an unincorporated or incorporated enterprise in which a direct investor owns 10 % or more of the ordinary shares or voting power (for an incorporated enterprise) or the equivalent (for an unincorporated enterprise).

FDI statistics for the EU give a detailed presentation of FDI flows and stocks, showing which Member States invest in which countries and sectors. Eurostat collects FDI statistics for quarterly and annual flows, as well as for stocks at the end of the year. FDI stocks (assets and liabilities) are part of the international investment position of an economy at the end of the year.

Outward flows and stocks of FDI (or FDI abroad) report investment by entities resident in the reporting economy in an affiliated enterprise abroad. **Inward flows and stocks** of FDI report investment by foreigners in enterprises resident in the reporting economy. FDI flows are new investment made during the reference period, whereas FDI stocks provide

information on the position, in terms of value, of all previous investments at the end of the reference period.

The **intensity of FDI** can be measured by averaging the value of inward and outward flows during a particular reference period and expressing this in relation to GDP.

The **financial account of the balance of payments** (BoP) records all financial transactions; it includes foreign direct investment, portfolio investment, other investment and reserve asset flows. There are two kinds of FDI:

- the creation of productive assets by foreigners (greenfield investment);
- the purchase of existing assets by foreigners (acquisitions, mergers, takeovers, etc.).

FDI differs from portfolio investments because it is made with the purpose of having control or an effective voice in management and a lasting interest in the enterprise. Direct investment not only includes the initial acquisition of equity capital, but also subsequent capital transactions between the foreign investor and domestic and affiliated enterprises.

The sign convention adopted for the data shown in this section, for both flows and stocks, is that investment is always recorded with a positive sign, and a disinvestment with a negative sign.

Main findings

Flows of FDI fluctuate considerably from one year to the next – partly as a function of economic fortunes, with FDI flows generally increasing during times of rapid growth, while disinvestment is more likely during periods of recession as companies focus on core activities in their domestic market. Inflows of FDI from non-Community countries into the EU-27 were valued at EUR 319 161 million in 2007, which was about double (90 %) the amount in 2006. Outward flows of FDI from the EU-27 to non-Community countries were valued at EUR 419 912 million. Despite the rapid increase in inward flows of FDI, the EU-27 remained a net investor abroad with net outflows of EUR 100 751 million in 2007 (only slightly lower than the value of EUR 106 074 recorded in 2006).

Stocks of FDI show the value of all previous investments at the end of the reference period. Inward FDI stocks for the EU-27 accounted for 17.7 % of GDP in 2006, while outward FDI stocks were valued at 23.2 % of GDP. A more detailed analysis by partner reveals that stocks of EU-27 FDI abroad were largely concentrated in North America (39.9 % of the total in 2006). North America was an even more important partner in terms of stocks of FDI within the EU-27, accounting for 49.6 % of all FDI made by non-member countries. The share of Asian countries in outward stocks fell from 15.0 % to 13.6 % while inward stocks of FDI rose from 8.9 % to 10.1 % between 2005 and 2006.

It should be noted that the relatively high importance of FDI in Luxembourg should be interpreted with caution, and results mainly from the role of Luxembourg-based holding companies.

Table 2.15: Foreign direct investment (1)

	FDI flows, 2007 (EUR million) (2)			FDI flows, 2007 (% of GDP) (3)			FDI stocks, 2006 (% of GDP) (4)		
	Inward	Outward	Net outflows	Inward	Outward	Net outflows	Inward	Outward	Net FDI assets
EU-27	319 161	419 912	100 751	2.6	3.4	0.8	17.7	23.2	-5.5
Euro area (5)	197 880	334 048	314 260	:	:	:	:	:	:
Belgium	28 537	37 881	9 344	8.6	11.5	2.9	:	:	:
Bulgaria	6 101	191	-5 910	21.1	0.7	-20.4	63.2	0.9	62.3
Czech Republic	6 710	979	-5 731	5.3	0.8	-4.5	54.2	3.0	51.2
Denmark	8 272	11 863	3 591	3.6	5.2	1.6	46.7	51.5	-4.8
Germany	37 205	122 325	85 120	1.5	5.0	3.5	24.5	33.5	-9.0
Estonia	1 815	1 123	-692	11.7	7.2	-4.5	72.7	20.7	52.0
Ireland	18 917	12 109	-6 808	10.2	6.5	-3.7	68.1	53.6	14.5
Greece	1 399	3 894	2 495	0.6	1.7	1.1	14.7	8.0	6.7
Spain	39 006	87 387	48 381	3.7	8.3	4.6	34.0	39.4	-5.4
France	109 487	159 306	49 819	5.8	8.4	2.6	35.3	49.1	-13.8
Italy	22 660	64 153	41 493	1.5	4.2	2.7	15.1	19.4	-4.3
Cyprus	1 518	777	-741	9.7	5.0	-4.7	75.4	25.6	49.8
Latvia	1 595	166	-1 429	8.0	0.8	-7.2	35.8	2.3	33.5
Lithuania	1 412	431	-981	5.0	1.5	-3.5	35.3	3.3	32.0
Luxembourg (6)	86 798	132 865	46 067	240.2	367.7	127.5	123.1	88.1	35.0
Hungary	26 831	25 800	-1 031	26.5	25.5	-1.0	98.9	40.2	58.7
Malta	696	14	-682	12.9	0.3	-12.6	93.6	16.4	77.2
Netherlands (7)	72 653	22 768	-49 885	12.8	4.0	-8.8	70.6	101.1	-30.5
Austria	22 605	23 154	549	8.3	8.5	0.2	24.1	22.7	1.4
Poland	12 831	2 392	-10 439	4.2	0.8	-3.4	34.7	4.5	30.2
Portugal	4 115	4 542	427	2.5	2.8	0.3	37.3	25.1	12.2
Romania	7 256	-49	-7 305	6.0	0.0	-6.0	35.3	0.7	34.6
Slovenia	1 073	1 154	81	3.2	3.4	0.2	22.2	11.4	10.8
Slovakia	2 157	150	-2 007	3.9	0.3	-3.6	65.7	2.1	63.6
Finland	6 193	6 300	107	3.4	3.5	0.1	30.3	42.7	-12.4
Sweden	13 728	26 831	13 103	4.1	8.1	4.0	49.4	59.8	-10.4
United Kingdom	135 670	165 416	29 746	6.7	8.2	1.5	44.9	57.2	-12.3
Croatia	2 714	164	-2 550	7.9	0.5	-7.4	60.6	5.3	55.3
Turkey	15 922	744	-15 178	3.8	0.2	-3.6	16.0	1.6	14.4
Switzerland	20 945	55 684	34 739	6.8	18.0	11.2	53.5	127.1	-73.6
Japan	-5 181	40 035	45 216	-0.1	1.1	1.2	2.3	9.8	-7.5
United States	139 689	172 518	32 829	1.3	1.6	0.3	12.9	17.2	-4.3

(1) EU-27, FDI with extra-EU-27 partners; EA-12: FDI with extra-EA-12 partners; all other countries, FDI with the rest of the world.
(2) Euro area, Croatia, Turkey, Switzerland, Japan and the United States, 2006.
(3) Croatia, Turkey, Switzerland, Japan and the United States, 2006.
(4) Austria, Portugal and Sweden, 2005.
(5) EA-12 instead of EA-15.
(6) Special purpose entities excluded from FDI stocks.
(7) Excluding special purpose entities.

Source: Eurostat (tec00049, tec00053, tec00046 and tec00047), Bank of Japan, Bureau of Economic Analysis

Figure 2.33: Stocks of foreign direct investment abroad, EU-27, 2006 (1)
(% of extra EU-27 FDI)

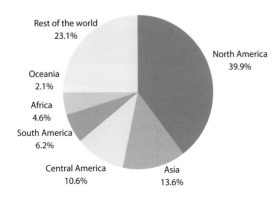

(1) Figures do not sum to 100 % due to rounding.

Source: Eurostat (tec00094)

Figure 2.34: Stocks of foreign direct investment in the EU-27, 2006
(% of extra EU-27 FDI)

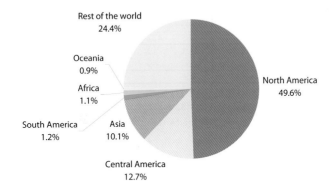

Source: Eurostat (tec00095)

Table 2.16: Foreign direct investment stocks for selected partner countries, 2006 (1)

(EUR 1 000 million)

	Outward				Inward				Net assets abroad (2)			
	Total	EU-27	JP	US	Total	EU-27	JP	US	Total	EU-27	JP	US
EU-27	2 706	–	76	934	2 057	–	99	954	649	–	-24	-19
Euro area (3)	3 074	–	70	613	2 615	–	72	631	459	–	-2	-18
Belgium	:	:	:	:	:	:	:	:	:	:	:	:
Bulgaria	0	0	:	0	16	7	0	0	-16	-7	:	0
Czech Republic	3	2	0	0	61	54	1	3	-58	-52	-1	-3
Denmark	113	69	1	12	103	74	0	8	10	-4	1	4
Germany	778	:	7	162	570	:	12	78	209	:	-5	84
Estonia	3	2	0	0	10	8	0	0	-7	-6	0	0
Ireland	94	63	:	11	119	91	3	9	-25	-29	:	2
Greece	17	:	0	1	31	:	0	2	-14	:	0	-1
Spain	387	235	2	27	334	249	2	56	53	-14	-1	-29
France	887	:	26	142	637	:	13	69	249	:	13	74
Italy	288	212	1	21	224	172	3	20	64	40	-2	1
Cyprus	4	2	0	0	11	7	0	0	-7	-4	0	0
Latvia	0	0	0	0	6	4	0	0	-5	-4	0	0
Lithuania	1	1	0	0	8	7	0	0	-8	-7	0	0
Luxembourg (4)	30	19	0	4	42	34	0	5	-12	-15	0	-1
Hungary	36	13	0	5	89	40	1	2	-53	-27	-1	3
Malta	1	0	0	:	5	3	0	0	-4	-2	0	:
Netherlands (4)	546	337	2	72	381	223	9	73	164	114	-7	-1
Austria (5)	55	39	0	2	59	41	1	7	-3	-2	-1	-5
Poland	12	9	0	0	94	80	1	7	-82	-71	-1	-7
Portugal (5)	37	25	0	0	56	40	0	1	-18	-15	0	-1
Romania	1	0	0	0	34	30	0	1	-34	-29	0	-1
Slovenia	3	1	0	0	7	5	0	0	-3	-4	0	0
Slovakia	1	1	0	0	29	27	0	1	-28	-26	0	-1
Finland	71	56	0	5	51	46	0	1	21	10	0	4
Sweden (5)	176	:	0	27	145	:	2	26	31	:	-1	1
United Kingdom	1 094	456	4	276	859	432	22	265	235	24	-18	11
Croatia	2	0	:	0	21	19	:	0	-19	-19	:	0
Turkey	7	4	0	0	67	49	1	4	-60	-45	-1	-4
Switzerland	393	:	6	82	166	:	1	38	228	:	6	45
Japan	341	:	–	119	82	:	–	32	259	:	–	87
United States	1 810	:	70	–	1 358	:	160	–	452	:	-91	–

(1) EU-27: FDI stocks in extra-EU-27 partners; EA-12: FDI stocks in extra-EA-12 partners; all other countries: FDI stocks in the rest of the world.
(2) Outward stocks - inward stocks.
(3) EA-12 instead of EA-15.
(4) Excluding special purpose entities.
(5) 2005.

Source: Eurostat (tec00052 and tec00051)

2.8 Development aid

Introduction

More than half the money spent throughout the world on helping developing countries comes from the EU and its Member States. The aims of this development aid were laid out in a December 2005 document agreed by the European Parliament, Council and Commission titled 'European Consensus on Development', which seeks, in particular, to reduce poverty, to develop democratic values, and to support national strategies and procedures. The ultimate objective of the EU is to enable disadvantaged people in the third world to take control of their own development, through attacking the main sources of their vulnerability, such as access to food, clean water, education, health, employment, land and social services.

The EU's development strategy focuses on financial and technical assistance to improve basic, physical and social infrastructures and the productive potential of poor nations, including their administrative and institutional capacities. This support has the potential to help third world countries benefit from international trade opportunities and secure more inward investment to broaden their economic bases.

The EU's activities also extend to external trade policy, which is used to drive development through the opening-up of markets. Since the 1970s, the EU has reduced or removed tariffs and eliminated quotas on imports from developing countries, a policy that was further extended in 2001 to cover the complete removal of tariffs on all imports (except arms) from the 49 least-developed countries (LDCs) of the world.

The EU promotes self-help and poverty eradication through policies that focus on consolidating the democratic process, expanding social programmes, strengthening institutional frameworks, and reinforcing the respect for human rights, including equality between men and women. Indeed, all trade or cooperation agreements with the third world include a human rights clause as a matter of routine, and failure to comply gives rise to automatic penalties, frozen or cancelled aid.

Aside from long-term, strategic, development aid, the EU also plays an important role in rapidly alleviating human suffering – as a result of natural disaster or military conflict. The EU's relief activities are global and have, since 1992, been handled by ECHO, its humanitarian aid office. ECHO considers its first duty to be towards the victims of disaster, through the emergency provision of supplies, such as tents, blankets, food, medicines, water purification systems and fuel. The annual budget of this office in 2007 was about EUR 750 million, a little over one half (55 %) of which was allocated to African, Caribbean and Pacific (ACP) countries. In the past, global relief operations have included the Asian tsunami in December 2004 and the effects of hurricane Katrina in August 2005. Key regions to which assistance has been provided in 2007 stretched from the Sudan and the Democratic Republic of Congo in Africa, to the Palestinian Territories in the Middle East, or the northern Caucasus (particularly Chechnya) to Afghanistan, Iran and Pakistan in Asia. Most of this EU aid is in the form of non-repayable grants.

Economy

Definitions and data availability

Official development assistance (ODA) consists of grants or loans that are undertaken by the official sector with the promotion of economic development and welfare in the recipient countries as the main objective. In addition to ODA, **total financing** for development refers to net disbursements, other official flows, and private flows. **Other official flows** are transactions which do not meet the conditions for eligibility as ODA (or official aid), either because they are not primarily aimed at development, or because they have a grant element of less than 25 %.

Private flows include private export credits, direct investment and financing to multilateral institutions. Foreign direct investment includes significant investments by foreign companies of production facilities or ownership stakes taken in the national companies.

Commitments include both bilateral commitments and commitments to regional banks. Bilateral commitments are recorded as the full amount of the expected transfer, irrespective of the time required for the completion of disbursements. **Disbursements** are the release of funds to, or the purchase of goods or services for a recipient. Disbursements record the actual international transfer of financial resources, or of goods or services valued at the cost of the donor.

Main findings

The EU-15 Member States paid almost EUR 47 000 million in official development assistance to DAC (Development Assistance Committee) countries in 2006, a further EUR 75 000 million coming in the form of private flows. DAC countries refer to 'developing countries and territories' within Part I of the OECD DAC List of Aid Recipients.

There is a long-standing United Nations target of reaching a level of aid equivalent to 0.7 % of donors' gross national income (GNI). While EU members, like other industrialised countries, have accepted this 0.7 % target for spending, currently only Denmark, Luxembourg, the Netherlands and Sweden have reached this goal. EU ministers agreed in May 2005 to set a collective target of 0.56 % of GNI by 2010, on the way to achieving the UN target of 0.7 % by 2015. The earlier commitment to reach an EU average of 0.39 % by 2006 was met.

Table 2.17: Official development assistance

	Official development assistance (% of gross national income)					Official development assistance per capita (EUR)				
	2003	2004	2005	2006	2007	2002	2003	2004	2005	2006
Belgium	0.60	0.41	0.53	0.50	0.43	109.80	158.00	113.10	151.30	149.40
Bulgaria	:	:	:	0.00	0.06	:	:	:	:	:
Czech Republic	0.11	0.11	0.11	0.12	0.11	4.70	7.80	8.50	10.60	12.50
Denmark	0.84	0.85	0.81	0.80	0.81	323.00	286.20	302.70	312.20	326.80
Germany	0.28	0.28	0.36	0.36	0.37	68.30	72.70	73.40	98.30	100.10
Estonia	:	:	:	0.09	0.12	:	:	:	:	:
Ireland	0.39	0.39	0.42	0.54	0.54	108.40	111.30	122.10	144.50	187.30
Greece	0.21	0.16	0.17	0.17	0.16	26.60	29.00	23.30	27.80	30.30
Spain	0.23	0.24	0.27	0.32	0.41	44.00	40.60	45.40	56.10	67.90
France	0.40	0.41	0.47	0.47	0.39	97.60	107.30	109.90	132.70	131.30
Italy	0.17	0.15	0.29	0.20	0.19	43.10	37.30	34.00	69.80	49.60
Cyprus	:	0.03	0.09	0.15	0.12	:	:	:	:	:
Latvia	:	0.06	0.07	0.06	0.06	:	:	:	:	:
Lithuania	:	0.04	0.06	0.08	0.11	:	:	:	:	:
Luxembourg	0.81	0.83	0.86	0.89	0.90	352.70	380.80	420.90	458.00	503.90
Hungary	0.03	0.07	0.11	0.13	0.07	:	1.90	5.60	8.00	11.80
Malta	:	0.18	0.18	0.15	0.15	:	:	:	:	:
Netherlands	0.80	0.73	0.82	0.81	0.81	218.70	216.10	207.50	251.60	265.40
Austria	0.20	0.23	0.52	0.47	0.49	68.50	55.40	66.90	153.70	144.10
Poland	0.01	0.05	0.07	0.09	0.09	0.40	0.60	2.50	4.30	6.20
Portugal	0.22	0.63	0.21	0.21	0.19	33.00	27.30	80.20	29.30	30.50
Romania	:	:	:	0.00	0.07	:	:	:	:	:
Slovenia	:	0.10	0.10	0.12	0.12	:	:	:	:	:
Slovakia	0.05	0.07	0.12	0.10	0.09	1.30	2.50	4.20	8.40	8.10
Finland	0.35	0.37	0.46	0.40	0.40	93.80	94.80	104.30	137.80	125.10
Sweden	0.79	0.78	0.94	1.02	0.93	238.00	236.30	242.90	298.60	346.80
United Kingdom	0.34	0.36	0.47	0.51	0.36	88.30	93.80	105.60	144.20	166.80
Turkey	0.04	0.11	0.17	0.18	:	1.10	0.80	3.80	6.70	:
Iceland	0.17	0.18	0.18	0.27	0.25	46.50	53.90	58.50	73.80	105.50
Norway	0.92	0.87	0.94	0.89	0.95	394.20	395.00	383.40	482.60	501.40
Switzerland	0.39	0.41	0.44	0.39	0.37	135.60	156.90	168.80	190.60	174.90

Source: Eurostat (tsdgp100 and tsdgp520), OECD (DAC database)

Economy

Figure 2.35: Total financing for developing countries, EU-15
(EUR million)

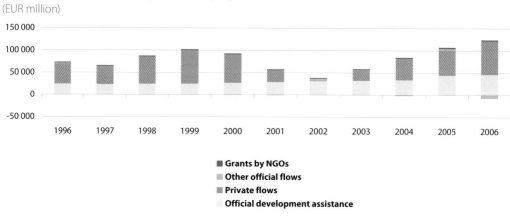

■ **Grants by NGOs**
■ **Other official flows**
▨ **Private flows**
□ **Official development assistance**

Source: Eurostat (tsdgp310), OECD (DAC database)

Figure 2.36: Official development assistance, EU-15
(% share of GNI)

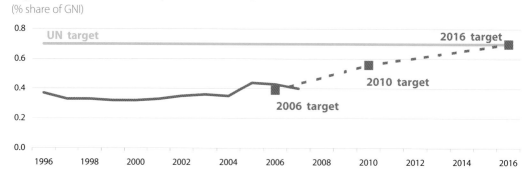

Source: Eurostat (tsdgp100), OECD (DAC database)

Population

3

This chapter focuses on Europe's population: it starts with a presentation of the current demographic situation, comparing the population structure in the EU and the rest of the world (Subchapter 3.1), followed by a more detailed description of the picture within the EU itself (Subchapter 3.2). The analysis then moves on to look at the different components that contribute to population change (Subchapter 3.3), in particular, births (Subchapter 3.4), life expectancy and death (Subchapter 3.5), and migratory flows (Subchapter 3.6).

Three factors are at the heart of Europe's ageing society: persistently low fertility rates, high life expectancy, and baby-boom generations that reach higher ages. Together with other factors, such as unemployment and changes in the span of the average working life, the age structure of the population impacts on the numerical balance of the population aged 65 years and over and the population aged between 15 and 64 years old, the latter conventionally considered as the working age population. Future demographic trends are likely to see a continuous increase in the proportion of the EU's population that is aged above the age of 65.

It is likely that the EU will, in the coming decades, face a number of significant challenges, which will need to be taken into account within a variety of different policy areas. In order to address these challenges, the European Commission released a Green Paper in March 2005 (COM(2005) 94) entitled 'Confronting demographic change: a new solidarity between the generations' [1], in which it was recognised that young adults are increasingly living with their parents for longer, while parents often have to support dependent elderly people. In a Communication from October 2006 on the demographic future of Europe [2], the Commission emphasised the need for the Member States to promote demographic renewal, linking action to the renewed Lisbon strategy and gender equality policy. These ideas were elaborated in a Communication of May 2007 [3] on promoting solidarity between the generations.

---

(1) http://ec.europa.eu/employment_social/news/2005/mar/comm2005-94_en.pdf.
(2) The demographic future of Europe – from challenge to opportunity – COM(2006) 571.
(3) COM(2007) 244 final.

3.1 EU population compared with other regions of the world

Definitions and data availability

The data in this subchapter is provided by the Population Division of the Department of Economic and Social Affairs of the United Nations (UN) Secretariat – for more information: http://esa.un.org/unpp.

Since the 1970s, the UN has been involved in several multi-national survey programmes whose results provide key information about fertility, mortality, maternal and child health. The UN data reflects demographic information produced by other UN agencies or bodies, such as, Economic and Social Commissions, the High Commissioner for Refugees (UNHCR), the United Nations Children's Fund (UNICEF), and the World Health Organization (WHO). Data from other organisations, such as Eurostat, is also consulted and used when elaborating forecasts. **UN population data** is often based on registers or estimates of population on a date close to 1 July (mid-year population), in comparison with Eurostat data that generally reflects the situation as of 1 January in each reference year. Note the data collection made by the UN is only revised every five years, and as such the UN data reported in this edition of the Eurostat yearbook is the same as that found in the last edition.

The preparation of **population estimates and projections** by the UN involves two distinct processes: the incorporation of new and relevant information regarding past demographic dynamics; and the formulation of assumptions about the future paths of fertility, mortality and international migration. In fact, population projections are what-if scenarios that aim to provide information about the likely future size and structure of the population for a specific set of assumptions. Because of the inherent uncertainty of demographic behaviour and in order to take into account alternative assumptions, projection variants are produced: low; medium; high; constant-fertility; instant-replacement-fertility; constant-mortality; no change (constant- fertility and constant-mortality); and zero-migration. For the purposes of this publication, the medium variant has been selected. Under this variant, total fertility in all countries is assumed to converge towards 1.85 children per woman, although not all countries reach this level during the projection period. Mortality is projected on the basis of models concerning changes in life expectancy. These models produce smaller gains the higher the life expectancy that has already been reached. The selection of a model for each country is based on recent trends in life expectancy by gender.

For countries highly affected by the HIV/AIDS epidemic, a model incorporating a slow pace of mortality decline has generally been used to project a certain slowdown in the reduction of general mortality risks not related to HIV/AIDS. Under the normal migration assumption, the future path of international migration is set on the basis of past international migration estimates and consideration of the policy stance of each country with regard to future international migration flows. Projected levels of net migration are generally kept constant over most of the projection period.

Main findings

In comparison to other regions, the EU's population is growing at a relatively slow pace. Between 1960 and 2005 the world's population more than doubled, rising from 3 032 million inhabitants to 6 515 million, while the corresponding rate of change in the EU-27 was an overall increase of 21.9 % to reach 491 million inhabitants. The fastest expansions in world population during the last 45 years were reported in particular for countries in Africa, Asia, and Latin America and the Caribbean.

The relative weight of the EU-27's population fell from 13.3 % of the world total in 1960 to 7.5 % by 2005. This trend is projected (medium variant) to continue, such that by 2050, the EU-27 will account for 5.4 % of the world's population. The proportion of the world's population that are Chinese is also expected to decline to around 15 % by 2050, almost 5 percentage points down on its share of 2005; although the total number of Chinese people is projected to increase by almost 100 million over the period considered. In contrast, population growth in India is more pronounced and the UN projects this pattern will continue, as India is likely to become the most populous nation on the planet before 2050, when its population is expected to be a little over 1 650 million persons.

The world's population growth peaked in the period 1985-1990, when the number of global inhabitants increased, on average, by 87.9 million persons per annum. By 2050, the rate of population growth is expected to have slowed considerably, such that each year will see an additional 33.1 million inhabitants on the planet. The world's population is projected (medium variant), nevertheless, to grow by 41.1 % overall between 2005 and 2050. The fastest growing population among the world's continents is projected to be that of Africa, where the UN foresees the number of inhabitants in 2050 being a little more than twice as high as in 2005. For means of comparison, the UN projects that the populations of Asia, Latin America and the Caribbean, North America, and Oceania will rise by between 34 % and 46 % overall between 2005 and 2050.

Table 3.1: World population

(million)

	1960	1965	1970	1975	1980	1985	1990	1995	2000	2005
World	3 032	3 343	3 699	4 076	4 451	4 855	5 295	5 719	6 124	6 515
Europe (1)	605	635	657	676	693	707	721	729	729	731
Africa	282	320	364	416	480	554	637	726	821	922
Asia	1 704	1 899	2 139	2 394	2 636	2 896	3 181	3 452	3 705	3 938
Latin America and the Caribbean	220	253	288	325	364	404	444	484	523	558
Northern America	204	219	232	243	256	269	284	300	316	332
Oceania	16	18	20	21	23	25	27	29	31	33
	1960	1965	1970	1975	1980	1985	1990	1995	2000	2005
EU-27	403	420	435	447	457	464	470	477	483	491
China	657	729	831	928	999	1 067	1 149	1 214	1 270	1 313
India	446	494	549	614	689	771	860	954	1 046	1 134
Japan	94	99	104	112	117	121	124	125	127	128
Russian Federation	120	127	130	134	139	143	149	149	147	144
United States	186	199	210	220	231	243	256	270	285	300

(1) EU-27, Albania, Andorra, Belarus, Bosnia and Herzegovina, Croatia, Faeroe Islands, Iceland, Liechtenstein, the former Yugoslav Republic of Macedonia, Republic of Moldova, Montenegro, Norway, the Russian Federation, Serbia, Switzerland and the Ukraine.

Source: Eurostat (demo_pjan), United Nations, Population Division of the Department of Economic and Social Affairs

Table 3.2: World population

(% share of world regions and some countries in total world population)

	1960	1965	1970	1975	1980	1985	1990	1995	2000	2005
Europe (1)	20.0	19.0	17.8	16.6	15.6	14.6	13.6	12.7	11.9	11.2
Africa	9.3	9.6	9.8	10.2	10.8	11.4	12.0	12.7	13.4	14.2
Asia	56.2	56.8	57.8	58.7	59.2	59.7	60.1	60.4	60.5	60.4
Latin America and the Caribbean	7.3	7.6	7.8	8.0	8.2	8.3	8.4	8.5	8.5	8.6
Northern America	6.7	6.6	6.3	6.0	5.7	5.5	5.4	5.2	5.2	5.1
Oceania	0.5	0.5	0.5	0.5	0.5	0.5	0.5	0.5	0.5	0.5
	1960	1965	1970	1975	1980	1985	1990	1995	2000	2005
EU-27	13.3	12.6	11.8	11.0	10.3	9.5	8.9	8.3	7.9	7.5
China	21.7	21.8	22.5	22.8	22.4	22.0	21.7	21.2	20.7	20.2
India	14.7	14.8	14.9	15.1	15.5	15.9	16.2	16.7	17.1	17.4
Japan	3.1	3.0	2.8	2.7	2.6	2.5	2.3	2.2	2.1	2.0
Russian Federation	4.0	3.8	3.5	3.3	3.1	3.0	2.8	2.6	2.4	2.2
United States	6.1	6.0	5.7	5.4	5.2	5.0	4.8	4.7	4.7	4.6

(1) EU-27, Albania, Andorra, Belarus, Bosnia and Herzegovina, Croatia, Faeroe Islands, Iceland, Liechtenstein, the former Yugoslav Republic of Macedonia, Republic of Moldova, Montenegro, Norway, the Russian Federation, Serbia, Switzerland and the Ukraine.

Source: Eurostat (demo_pjan), United Nations, Population Division of the Department of Economic and Social Affairs

Figure 3.1: World population
(% of total)

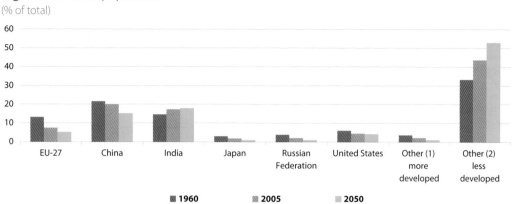

(1) Excluding EU-27, Japan, the Russian Federation and the United States.
(2) Excluding China and India.

Source: Eurostat (demo_pjan), United Nations, Population Division of the Department of Economic and Social Affairs

Figure 3.2: Population change
(average annual change, million)

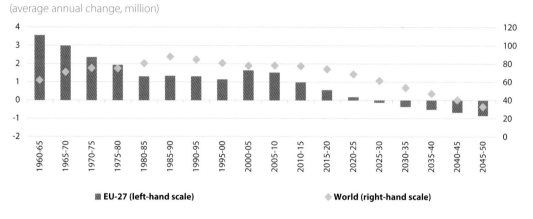

Source: Eurostat (demo_pjan), United Nations, Population Division of the Department of Economic and Social Affairs

Table 3.3: Population and population projections
(million)

	2005	2010	2015	2020	2025	2030	2035	2040	2045	2050
World	6 515	6 907	7 295	7 667	8 011	8 318	8 587	8 824	9 026	9 191
Europe (1)	731	730	727	722	715	707	698	687	676	664
Africa	922	1 032	1 149	1 271	1 394	1 518	1 643	1 765	1 884	1 998
Asia	3 938	4 166	4 389	4 596	4 779	4 931	5 052	5 148	5 220	5 266
Latin America and the Caribbean	558	594	628	660	688	713	733	750	762	769
Northern America	332	349	364	379	393	405	417	427	436	445
Oceania	33	35	37	39	41	43	45	46	48	49
	2005	**2010**	**2015**	**2020**	**2025**	**2030**	**2035**	**2040**	**2045**	**2050**
EU-27	491	498	502	505	506	506	504	501	498	494
China	1 313	1 352	1 389	1 421	1 446	1 458	1 458	1 448	1 431	1 409
India	1 134	1 220	1 303	1 379	1 447	1 506	1 554	1 597	1 632	1 658
Japan	128	128	127	124	122	118	115	111	107	103
Russian Federation	144	140	136	132	128	124	120	116	112	108
United States	300	315	329	343	355	366	376	386	394	402

(1) EU-27, Albania, Andorra, Belarus, Bosnia and Herzegovina, Croatia, Faeroe Islands, Iceland, Liechtenstein, the former Yugoslav Republic of Macedonia, Republic of Moldova, Montenegro, Norway, the Russian Federation, Serbia, Switzerland and the Ukraine.

Source: Eurostat (demo_pjan), United Nations, Population Division of the Department of Economic and Social Affairs

3.2 EU-27 population

Introduction

The data in this subchapter is provided by Eurostat, in contrast to that used in the opening subchapter from the United Nations. There are methodological differences in the projections made by Eurostat and the United Nations that explain the differences in the reported values

The EU-27's population age structure is the result of many years of high birth rates, followed by low birth rates, accompanied by a steady, gradual increase in life expectancy and migration flows.

Over the last 40 years much of the European labour force has been made-up of members of the baby-boom generations, who have formed a high proportion of the working age population. This demographic characteristic is projected to end during the coming decades, as the baby-boom generation take their retirement. Europe's fertility rates have been in decline since the 1970s, and the number of young people entering the labour market has become progressively smaller. As a result, the proportion of people of working age in the EU-27 is shrinking at the same time as those who are taking their retirement expands.

Old age dependency is likely to result in increased burdens for the working population to provide for the social expenditure that is related to population ageing, in the form of pensions, healthcare and institutional or private (health) care. Increasing labour force participation is one factor that helps to reconcile demographic developments and the social expenditure burden, while pension reforms have already been started in several Member States. In addition, policymakers have also considered ways of creating more flexible working opportunities that may be of interest to the elderly, or delaying the average age when this cohort exit the labour market.

The ability of the EU as a whole to increase productivity and to make full use of its human resources will play an important role in determining its ability to cope with the socio-economic transformations that are linked to demographic ageing. Much of the care required by the elderly is currently provided by their descendents. However, with an increasing share of older people likely to live away from their families, the need for professional care can be expected to increase. Moreover, the fastest growing age group in Europe will be those aged over 80. As a result, providing social and healthcare, as well as adapted housing, transport/mobility facilities and other public infrastructure for this population group will be a major challenge. The demand for services of this type will not only depend on the absolute number of elderly persons, but also on their future health.

In order to address the demographic challenge of an ageing population, the Stockholm European Council of 2001 agreed that half of the EU population in the 55-64 age group should be in employment by 2010. Employment guidelines and a report by the employment taskforce chaired by Wim Kok urged the adoption of a comprehensive active ageing policy centred on appropriate financial incentives to encourage longer working lives, lifelong learning strategies, and improved quality of work. A Commission Green Paper 'faced with demographic change, a new solidarity between the generations'[4] concluded that Europe should pursue three priorities:

(4) COM(2005) 94 final; http://ec.europa.eu/employment_social/news/2005/mar/comm2005-94_en.pdf.

- modernisation of social protection systems, increasing the rate of female employment and the employment of older workers, innovative measures to support the birth rate and appropriate management of immigration;
- ensuring a balance between the generations, in the sharing of time throughout life, in the distribution of the benefits of growth, and in that of funding needs stemming from pensions and health-related expenditure;
- finding new bridges between the stages of life as young people find it difficult to get into employment; An increasing number of 'young retirees' want to participate in social and economic life; study time is getting longer and young working people want to spend time with their children; these changes alter the frontiers and the bridges between activity and inactivity.

Definitions and data availability

Eurostat produces a large range of demographic data, including statistics on population, births and deaths, marriages and divorces. A number of important policies, notably in social and economic fields, use population data – such as, fertility rates and life expectancy when planning social policies for retirement schemes, or regional population data for calculating GDP per capita which is used as part of the decision-making criteria for the allocation of structural funds to economically less advantaged regions.

There has, until recently, been no comprehensive legal base for the collection of statistics on migration and international protection, with Eurostat generally compiling statistics in this area under specific arrangements with the Member States. However, the European Parliament and the Council recently adopted a Regulation on Community statistics on migration and international protection [5]. This new Regulation specifies the collection of statistics relating to international migration flows, foreign population stocks, acquisition of citizenship, asylum applications and decisions, measures taken against illegal entry and stay, returns of unauthorised migrants, and residence permits issued to third- country citizens. Its focus is to harmonise statistical outputs, based on a set of common definitions relating to immigration, border management, and asylum issues, and on established international standards (in particular, the UN recommendations for migration statistics). The Regulation provides a framework which needs to be completed through the adoption of implementing measures in the form of Commission regulations.

In July 2008, the European Parliament and the Council adopted a regulation on population and housing censuses [6]. This regulation will make data from censuses conducted in the EU Member States more comparable. During 2009, the European Commission will put forward implementing measures to complete the framework regulation.

Most European countries evaluate **population** data on the basis of gender and age breakdowns as of 1 January (although some countries adopt another date). Unless otherwise stipulated, the population data presented is based on this date.

(5) Regulation (EC) No 862/2007 of the European Parliament and of the Council of 11 July 2007 on Community statistics on migration and international protection and repealing Council Regulation (EEC) No 311/76 on the compilation of statistics on foreign workers (text with EEA relevance); http://eur-lex.europa.eu/ LexUriServ/LexUriServ.do?uri= OJ:L:2007:199:0023:01:EN:HTML.

(6) Regulation (EC) No 763/2008 of the European Parliament and of the Council of 9 July 2008 on population and housing censuses; http://eur-lex.europa.eu/LexUriServ/LexUriServ.do?uri=OJ:L:2008:218:0014:0020:EN:PDF.

Population figures are generally given in relation to data from the most recent census, adjusted by the components of population change produced since the last census, or alternatively population registers. Note that demographic statistics for the EU-27, euro area and France have a break in series in 1998, as prior to this date information for France was collected on the basis of metropolitan France (in other words excluding the French overseas departments), while from 1998 onwards these are included.

Every three to five years, Eurostat produces **demographic projections**. Those presented here relate to the EUROPOP2008 convergence scenario, national level, which is one of a set of 'what-if' scenarios. To this end, a projection is a conditional statement, whose numerical outcome is the result of explicit assumptions that are extended to the far future. The projections are made using the latest available figures for the population on 1 January, with assumptions made with respect to mortality, fertility and migration by sex and by age. In particular, for the EUROPOP2008 convergence scenario population projections, the assumptions have been developed in a conceptual framework of convergence of demographic values as a result of decreasing socio-economic and cultural differences between the Member States of the EU.

Age dependency ratios are important demographic indicators that relate the young and old age population (those generally inactive) to the population of working age. In this publication the following terminology is used:

- **young age dependency ratio**: the population aged up to 14 years related to the population aged between 15 and 64 years;

- **old age dependency ratio**: the population aged 65 years or older related to the population aged between 15 and 64 years;
- **total dependency ratio**: the population aged up to 14 years and aged 65 years or older related to the population aged between 15 and 64 years.

Main findings

The population of the 27 Member States of the EU grew from 403 million in 1960 to just over 495 million in 2007. Population growth in the EU-27 was strongest at the beginning of this period in the 1960s, when average annual increases were generally over 3 million persons per year, peaking at 4.2 million in 1963. The rate of population change slowed down significantly in the 1970s, and by the 1980s the average increase in population was around one and a quarter million persons each year. This level of population growth continued during much of the next 20 years, although there appears to have been a reversal in the trend observed during the period from 2003 to 2007, as the number of EU-27 inhabitants rose by approximately 2 million a year.

Germany had the largest population among the Member States in 2007, accounting for almost 17 % of the EU-27 total. Together with France, the United Kingdom and Italy, who had similar sized populations, these four countries together comprised almost 54 % of the total population of the EU-27. The twelve Member States that have joined the EU since 2004 had a combined population of 103.3 million persons in 2007, representing a little more than one fifth (almost 21 %) of the EU-27's total population.

In a majority of European countries, populations continued to grow through to 2007, although the situation varied between Member States. Most of the overall population growth in the EU-27 in the last decade may be attributed to an increased number of inhabitants in Ireland, Spain, France, Italy and the United Kingdom; in relative terms, Ireland, Spain and Cyprus recorded the highest population growth rates.

According to the latest population projections (EUROPOP2008 convergence scenario), Eurostat projects that the EU-27's population will rise to a high of 521 million persons in 2035, thereafter falling to about 506 million inhabitants by 2060. The changes expected in population levels within the EU-27 by 2060 will not be distributed equally across the Member States. At one end of the projections, the populations of Cyprus, Ireland and Luxembourg are projected to grow by over 50 % from 2008 to 2060, while the populations of Belgium, Spain, France, Sweden and the United Kingdom are projected to grow by between 15 % and 25 % by 2060. In contrast, the populations of Poland, Estonia, Hungary, Slovakia and Germany are projected to have shrunk by between 10 % and 20 % by 2060, with even stronger declines of between 20 % and 30 % in Bulgaria, Latvia, Lithuania and Romania.

The EU-27's population has aged in the decade through until 2007. Those aged less than 15 years accounted for 15.8 % of the EU-27's population in 2007, although this rate varied considerably among the Member States, from lows of 13.4 % in

Bulgaria and 13.9 % in Germany to a high of 20.3 % in Ireland. In contrast, the proportion of the EU-27 population aged more than 64 years grew to 16.9 % in 2007, the share rising to almost 20 % in Italy and Germany.

A little more than two thirds (67.2 %) of the EU-27's population were of working age (15 to 64 years old) in 2007. In a series of population pyramids, projections through until 2050 suggest, however, that this relatively large proportion of the population may shrink gradually to about 57 % of the total. This narrower working base will need to support a growing population of persons aged over 65 years or more (nearly 29 % of the population). The importance of the very old (80 years or more) will be considerable by 2060, when this age group is likely to account for 12.0 % of the EU-27's population, swelled by numbers from the so-called baby-boom generation.

These EU developments should also be viewed in a global context and over the longer-term.

Europe reported the lowest share of young persons (15.9 %) and the highest share of old persons (also 15.9 %) across any of the continents in 2005. For means of comparison, the overall share of young persons in the world population was 28.3 % in 2005, while older generations accounted for 7.3 % of the global population. Young age dependency ratios in Europe declined over the period 1960 to 2005 from 41.4 % to 23.3 %. Europe recorded the largest increase across the continents in relation to the old age dependency ratio during the period 1960 to 2005. The European old age dependency ratio rose from 13.7 % to 23.3 %, which was almost three times the pace of the next highest increase which was recorded in Oceania, where old age dependency increased from 12.2 % to 15.8 %. Combining these two sets of indicators, the total dependency ratio in 2005 ranged from 46.6 % in Europe to a high of 81.2 % in Africa, where the vast majority of dependents are children. The

fall in young age dependency in Europe was largely counterbalanced by an increase in old age dependency, resulting in a relatively small net change in total dependency in comparison to the most other continents. Nevertheless, this has necessitated a switch in social expenditure to more healthcare and pensions for the elderly.

Table 3.4: Total population and population projections (1)

(at 1 January, million)

	1960	1970	1980	1990	2000	2007	2010	2020	2030	2040	2050	2060
EU-27 (2)	402.6	435.5	457.1	470.4	482.8	495.1	499.4	513.8	519.9	520.1	515.3	505.7
Euro area (2)	:	274.1	287.6	295.6	307.3	319.6	322.9	334.1	339.1	340.4	337.3	330.6
Belgium	9.1	9.7	9.9	9.9	10.2	10.6	10.8	11.3	11.7	12.0	12.2	12.3
Bulgaria	7.8	8.5	8.8	8.8	8.2	7.7	7.6	7.2	6.8	6.3	5.9	5.5
Czech Republic	9.6	9.9	10.3	10.4	10.3	10.3	10.4	10.5	10.4	10.2	9.9	9.5
Denmark	4.6	4.9	5.1	5.1	5.3	5.4	5.5	5.7	5.8	5.9	5.9	5.9
Germany	72.5	78.3	78.2	79.1	82.2	82.3	82.1	81.5	80.2	77.8	74.5	70.8
Estonia	1.2	1.4	1.5	1.6	1.4	1.3	1.3	1.3	1.3	1.2	1.2	1.1
Ireland	2.8	2.9	3.4	3.5	3.8	4.3	4.6	5.4	5.9	6.2	6.5	6.8
Greece	8.3	8.8	9.6	10.1	10.9	11.2	11.3	11.6	11.6	11.6	11.4	11.1
Spain	30.3	33.6	37.2	38.8	40.0	44.5	46.7	51.1	52.7	53.3	53.2	51.9
France (3)	45.5	50.5	53.7	56.6	58.8	61.5	62.6	65.6	68.0	69.9	71.0	71.8
Italy	50.0	53.7	56.4	56.7	56.9	59.1	60.0	61.4	61.9	62.0	61.2	59.4
Cyprus	0.6	0.6	0.5	0.6	0.7	0.8	0.8	1.0	1.1	1.2	1.3	1.3
Latvia	2.1	2.4	2.5	2.7	2.4	2.3	2.2	2.2	2.0	1.9	1.8	1.7
Lithuania	2.8	3.1	3.4	3.7	3.5	3.4	3.3	3.2	3.1	2.9	2.7	2.5
Luxembourg	0.3	0.3	0.4	0.4	0.4	0.5	0.5	0.6	0.6	0.7	0.7	0.7
Hungary	10.0	10.3	10.7	10.4	10.2	10.1	10.0	9.9	9.7	9.4	9.1	8.7
Malta	0.3	0.3	0.3	0.4	0.4	0.4	0.4	0.4	0.4	0.4	0.4	0.4
Netherlands	11.4	13.0	14.1	14.9	15.9	16.4	16.5	16.9	17.2	17.2	16.9	16.6
Austria	7.0	7.5	7.5	7.6	8.0	8.3	8.4	8.7	9.0	9.1	9.1	9.0
Poland	29.5	32.7	35.4	38.0	38.7	38.1	38.1	38.0	37.0	35.2	33.3	31.1
Portugal	8.8	8.7	9.7	10.0	10.2	10.6	10.7	11.1	11.3	11.5	11.4	11.3
Romania	18.3	20.1	22.1	23.2	22.5	21.6	21.3	20.8	20.0	19.2	18.1	16.9
Slovenia	1.6	1.7	1.9	2.0	2.0	2.0	2.0	2.1	2.0	2.0	1.9	1.8
Slovakia	4.0	4.5	5.0	5.3	5.4	5.4	5.4	5.4	5.3	5.1	4.9	4.5
Finland	4.4	4.6	4.8	5.0	5.2	5.3	5.3	5.5	5.6	5.5	5.4	5.4
Sweden	7.5	8.0	8.3	8.5	8.9	9.1	9.3	9.9	10.3	10.5	10.7	10.9
United Kingdom	52.2	55.5	56.3	57.2	58.8	60.9	62.0	65.7	69.2	72.0	74.5	76.7
Croatia	4.1	4.4	4.6	4.8	4.4	4.4	:	:	:	:	:	:
FYR of Macedonia	1.4	1.6	1.9	1.9	2.0	2.0	:	:	:	:	:	:
Turkey	27.1	34.9	44.0	55.5	66.9	69.7	:	:	:	:	:	:
Iceland	0.2	0.2	0.2	0.3	0.3	0.3	:	:	:	:	:	:
Liechtenstein	0.0	0.0	0.0	0.0	0.0	0.0	:	:	:	:	:	:
Norway	3.6	3.9	4.1	4.2	4.5	4.7	4.8	5.2	5.5	5.7	5.9	6.0
Switzerland	5.3	6.2	6.3	6.7	7.2	7.5	7.7	8.2	8.6	8.9	9.1	9.2

(1) From 2010 onwards the data refer to projections (EUROPOP2008 convergence scenario).

(2) Break in series, 1998.

(3) Metropolitan France, excluding the four overseas departments (French Guyana, Guadeloupe, Martinique and Réunion).

Source: Eurostat (demo_pjan and proj_08c2150p)

Figure 3.3: Population by age class, EU-27
(1997=100)

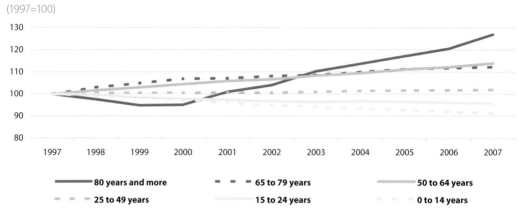

- 80 years and more
- 65 to 79 years
- 50 to 64 years
- 25 to 49 years
- 15 to 24 years
- 0 to 14 years

Source: Eurostat (tps00010)

Figure 3.4: Age pyramid, EU-27, 2007
(% of total population)

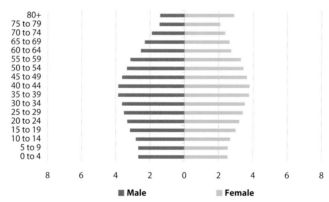

■ Male   ■ Female

Source: Eurostat (demo_pjan)

Figure 3.5: Moving age pyramids, EU-27 (1)

(% of total population)

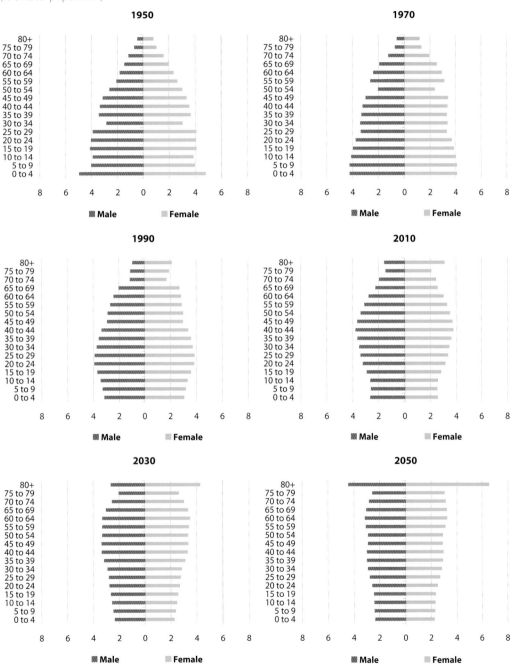

(1) Limited data availability for 1950 and 1970, based on those Member States for which data are available; from 2010 onwards the data refer to projections (EUROPOP2008 convergence scenario).

Source: Eurostat (demo_pjan and proj_08c2150p)

Table 3.5: Population by age class, 2007 (1)

(% of total population)

	0 to 14 years	15 to 24 years	25 to 49 years	50 to 64 years	65 to 79 years	80 years and more
EU-27	15.8	12.6	36.3	18.3	12.6	4.3
Euro area	15.6	11.9	36.8	18.0	13.2	4.5
Belgium	17.0	12.1	35.4	18.5	12.5	4.6
Bulgaria	13.4	13.3	35.6	20.4	13.8	3.5
Czech Republic	14.4	13.1	36.9	21.2	11.1	3.3
Denmark	18.6	11.4	34.7	20.0	11.2	4.1
Germany	13.9	11.7	36.3	18.4	15.2	4.6
Estonia	14.9	15.4	34.7	17.9	13.6	3.5
Ireland	20.3	14.8	38.3	15.5	8.4	2.7
Greece	14.3	11.6	37.6	18.0	14.7	3.9
Spain	14.5	11.5	40.5	16.8	12.1	4.5
France	18.6	12.8	34.2	18.2	11.4	4.8
Italy	14.1	10.2	37.3	18.4	14.6	5.3
Cyprus	17.9	15.5	37.3	16.9	9.5	2.8
Latvia	14.0	15.7	35.6	17.6	13.7	3.4
Lithuania	15.9	15.7	36.2	16.6	12.5	3.1
Luxembourg	18.3	11.8	38.8	17.1	10.7	3.3
Hungary	15.2	12.8	35.7	20.4	12.3	3.6
Malta	16.7	14.2	34.6	20.6	10.8	3.0
Netherlands	18.1	12.0	36.1	19.4	10.8	3.7
Austria	15.6	12.3	37.6	17.6	12.4	4.5
Poland	15.8	15.9	36.0	18.9	10.6	2.9
Portugal	15.5	11.9	37.4	18.0	13.2	4.1
Romania	15.4	14.9	37.0	17.8	12.2	2.7
Slovenia	14.0	12.7	37.8	19.6	12.5	3.4
Slovakia	16.1	15.6	38.0	18.4	9.3	2.5
Finland	17.1	12.5	32.9	21.1	12.3	4.2
Sweden	17.0	12.7	33.2	19.7	12.0	5.4
United Kingdom	17.6	13.4	35.1	17.9	11.5	4.5
Croatia	15.6	12.9	35.2	19.2	14.0	3.1
FYR of Macedonia	18.9	16.0	36.9	17.0	9.6	1.6
Turkey	27.9	17.4	37.5	11.1	:	:
Iceland	21.8	14.6	36.0	15.9	8.6	3.1
Liechtenstein	17.1	12.3	39.0	19.7	8.9	3.0
Norway	19.4	12.5	35.0	18.5	10.0	4.7
Switzerland	15.8	11.9	37.2	18.9	11.6	4.6

(1) Euro area and Iceland, 2006.

Source: Eurostat (tps00010)

Figure 3.6: Proportion of the population aged under 15
(% of total population)

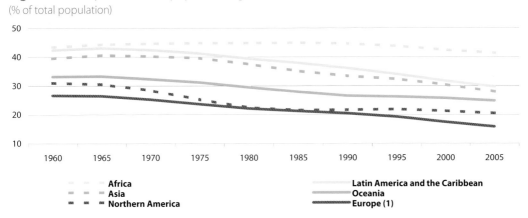

(1) EU-27, Albania, Andorra, Belarus, Bosnia and Herzegovina, Croatia, Faeroe Islands, Iceland, Liechtenstein, the former Yugoslav Republic of Macedonia, Republic of Moldova, Montenegro, Norway, the Russian Federation, Serbia, Switzerland and the Ukraine.

Source: United Nations, Population Division of the Department of Economic and Social Affairs

Figure 3.7: Proportion of the population aged 65 and over
(% of total population)

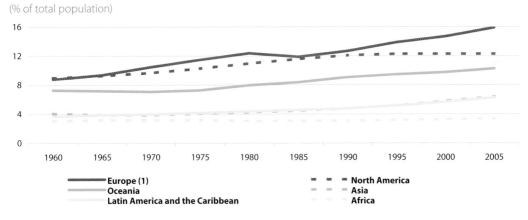

(1) EU-27, Albania, Andorra, Belarus, Bosnia and Herzegovina, Croatia, Faeroe Islands, Iceland, Liechtenstein, the former Yugoslav Republic of Macedonia, Republic of Moldova, Montenegro, Norway, the Russian Federation, Serbia, Switzerland and the Ukraine.

Source: United Nations, Population Division of the Department of Economic and Social Affairs

Table 3.6: Age related dependency ratios
(%)

	Young age dependency ratio						Old age dependency ratio					
	1960	1970	1980	1990	2000	2007	1960	1970	1980	1990	2000	2007
EU-27	:	:	:	29.2	25.7	23.5	:	:	:	20.6	23.2	25.2
Euro area (1)	:	:	:	27.0	24.4	23.4	:	:	:	21.0	24.2	26.5
Belgium	36.2	37.5	31.0	27.0	26.9	25.8	18.5	21.2	21.9	22.1	25.5	25.9
Bulgaria	39.4	33.9	33.5	30.9	23.4	19.4	11.2	14.0	17.8	19.5	23.8	24.9
Czech Republic	39.5	32.0	37.0	33.0	23.9	20.2	14.6	17.9	21.6	19.0	19.8	20.2
Denmark	39.8	36.4	32.7	25.5	27.6	28.2	16.4	18.9	22.2	23.2	22.2	23.2
Germany	31.1	36.8	28.6	23.1	23.1	21.0	17.0	21.4	23.9	21.6	23.9	29.9
Estonia	:	33.3	32.8	33.7	27.3	21.9	:	17.7	19.0	17.5	22.4	25.1
Ireland	53.2	54.2	51.8	44.7	32.8	29.7	19.2	19.3	18.2	18.6	16.8	16.2
Greece	37.6	37.5	36.2	29.3	22.9	21.3	14.2	17.2	20.6	20.4	24.2	27.6
Spain	42.6	44.2	41.2	30.5	21.8	21.1	12.7	15.2	17.1	20.2	24.5	24.2
France	42.2	40.0	35.4	30.5	29.0	28.1	18.7	20.6	22.1	21.1	24.6	25.2
Italy	37.4	38.1	35.1	24.5	21.2	21.3	14.0	16.7	20.3	21.5	26.8	30.2
Cyprus	:	:	:	41.2	34.5	25.7	:	:	:	17.2	17.0	17.6
Latvia	:	32.8	30.7	32.1	26.7	20.2	:	18.0	19.6	17.7	22.1	24.8
Lithuania	:	43.2	36.2	33.9	30.6	23.2	:	15.9	17.4	16.2	20.8	22.7
Luxembourg	31.5	33.8	28.1	24.9	28.3	27.1	15.9	19.1	20.3	19.3	21.4	20.7
Hungary	38.7	31.3	33.8	31.0	24.8	22.1	13.6	17.0	20.9	20.0	22.0	23.2
Malta	:	:	36.1	35.8	30.2	24.0	:	:	12.5	15.7	17.9	19.8
Netherlands	49.1	43.8	34.3	26.4	27.4	26.8	14.6	16.2	17.4	18.6	20.0	21.5
Austria	33.0	39.5	32.4	26.0	25.4	23.1	18.4	22.7	24.3	22.1	22.9	25.0
Poland	54.5	42.0	36.8	39.0	28.6	22.3	9.5	12.6	15.5	15.4	17.6	19.0
Portugal	46.8	46.8	41.6	31.6	24.0	23.0	12.4	14.9	17.8	20.0	23.7	25.6
Romania	:	39.8	42.1	36.0	27.7	22.1	:	13.0	16.3	15.6	19.7	21.3
Slovenia	:	37.7	34.6	30.6	23.0	19.9	:	14.8	16.4	15.5	19.8	22.7
Slovakia	51.1	43.4	41.2	39.6	28.8	22.4	11.1	14.4	16.7	16.0	16.6	16.5
Finland	49.4	37.7	30.2	28.7	27.2	25.7	11.6	13.6	17.6	19.8	22.2	24.8
Sweden	34.5	31.8	30.9	27.7	28.8	25.9	17.8	20.7	25.3	27.7	26.9	26.4
United Kingdom	35.9	38.2	33.2	29.0	29.4	26.5	18.0	20.5	23.3	24.1	24.3	24.1
Croatia	:	:	:	29.0	24.4	23.2	:	:	:	17.0	24.4	25.4
FYR of Macedonia	:	:	:	:	33.3	27.1	:	:	:	:	14.6	16.0
Turkey	74.7	77.7	69.7	57.6	46.6	42.2	6.4	8.2	8.4	7.1	8.3	10.1
Iceland (1)	60.9	56.4	44.3	38.8	35.8	32.8	14.0	15.0	15.7	16.4	17.8	17.6
Liechtenstein	44.7	43.5	33.1	27.4	26.3	24.0	12.3	12.3	12.9	14.2	14.8	16.8
Norway	41.3	39.1	35.5	29.2	30.8	29.3	17.3	20.4	23.3	25.2	23.5	22.2
Switzerland	36.8	36.5	30.2	24.9	25.9	23.1	15.5	17.3	20.9	21.3	22.7	23.8

(1) 2006 instead of 2007.

Source: Eurostat (demo_pjanind)

Figure 3.8: Young age dependency ratio

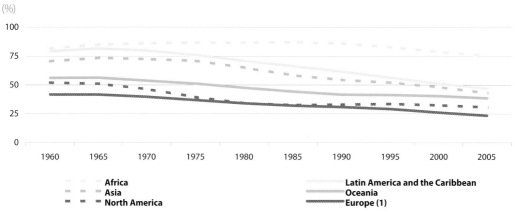

(1) EU-27, Albania, Andorra, Belarus, Bosnia and Herzegovina, Croatia, Faeroe Islands, Iceland, Liechtenstein, the former Yugoslav Republic of Macedonia, Republic of Moldova, Montenegro, Norway, the Russian Federation, Serbia, Switzerland and the Ukraine.

Source: United Nations, Population Division of the Department of Economic and Social Affairs

Figure 3.9: Old age dependency ratio

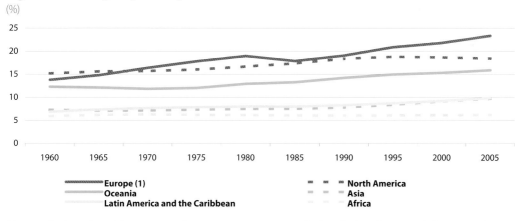

(1) EU-27, Albania, Andorra, Belarus, Bosnia and Herzegovina, Croatia, Faeroe Islands, Iceland, Liechtenstein, the former Yugoslav Republic of Macedonia, Republic of Moldova, Montenegro, Norway, the Russian Federation, Serbia, Switzerland and the Ukraine.

Source: United Nations, Population Division of the Department of Economic and Social Affairs

Figure 3.10: Proportion of the population aged 0-14 and 65 years and more, EU-27 (1)
(% of total population)

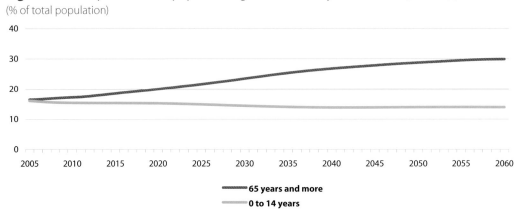

- 65 years and more
- 0 to 14 years

(1) From 2008 onwards the data refer to projections (EUROPOP2008 convergence scenario).

Source: Eurostat (tps00010 and proj_08c2150p)

Figure 3.11: Proportion of the population aged 80 years and more, EU-27 (1)
(% of total population)

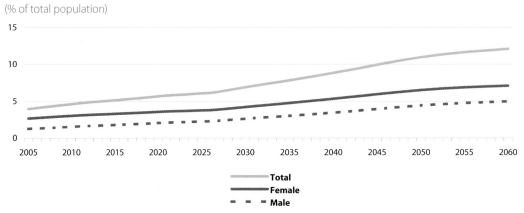

- Total
- Female
- Male

(1) From 2008 onwards the data refer to projections (EUROPOP2008 convergence scenario).

Source: Eurostat (demo_pjan and proj_08c2150p)

3.3 Components of population change

Introduction

This subchapter focuses on population change, which is made up of two distinct aspects: namely, natural population change and net migration. Natural population change is the difference between live births and deaths, or put in general terms, fertility and mortality. Births are covered in more detail within the next subchapter, while life expectancy and deaths are treated in Subchapter 3.5, and migration in Subchapter 3.6.

There are many countries within the EU-27 that currently report a higher number of deaths than births. In some of these, the negative evolution of natural population change is (at least) partly offset by positive net migration; this is a pattern that exists in western Germany, northern Italy, Slovenia or southern Sweden. The opposite pattern is much rarer, as there are only a handful of cases in the EU where positive natural change (more births than deaths) has been compensated by negative net migration; one example is northern Poland.

When the two components of population change do not compensate, but rather add to each other, they can lead to more significant swings in overall population change. In recent years this has been the case in Ireland and Denmark, most of the Benelux and France, as well as more specific regions in southern and eastern Spain, where natural population increases have been accompanied by positive net migration. In contrast, some regions in eastern Germany, north western Spain, southern Italy, the Baltic States, as well

as the Czech Republic, Hungary, Poland, Romania and Slovakia have witnessed both components of population change moving in a negative direction; it is in these areas of the EU where the largest declines in population have been recorded in the last decade. Often, their population is expected to continue falling in the coming years. More details concerning regional population density and the evolution of population change across EU regions can be found in Chapter 15, more specifically in Maps 15.3 and 15.4.

Definitions and data availability

Population change is defined as the difference between the size of the population at the end and the beginning of a period. It is equal to the algebraic sum of natural increase and net migration including corrections (see below for more details). There is negative change when both of these components are negative or when one is negative and has a higher absolute value than the other.

Natural population increase is defined as the difference between the number of live births and the number of deaths during the year. The natural increase is negative (in other words, a natural decrease) when the number of deaths exceeds the number of live births.

Net migration is defined as the difference between immigration into and emigration from the area considered during the reference year (net migration is therefore negative when the number of emigrants exceeds the number of immigrants). Since most countries either do not have accurate figures on immigration and emigration, or have no figures at all, net migration is generally estimated on the basis of the difference between population change and natural increase between two dates (in Eurostat's database, this concept is generally referred to as corrected net migration).

Main findings

During the ten years through until 2007, net migration was the main driver of population change in the EU-27. Population growth across the EU-27 of 2.4 million persons in 2007 comprised a positive net migration of 1.9 million persons and a natural population increase of 0.5 million persons.

The patterns of population change vary considerably across the Member States. In some Member States, there were steady declines in the natural population between 1997 and 2007 (and indeed longer in some cases); in Germany the decline was almost 1.2 million persons, and in Bulgaria, Latvia and Romania closer to 0.5 million. In contrast, there were relatively high natural increases in Ireland, Spain, France, the Netherlands and the United Kingdom.

Negative net migration (including corrections) is relatively rare among the Member States. Over the period 2002 to 2007, only six countries (Bulgaria, Latvia, Lithuania, the Netherlands, Poland and Romania) reported negative net migration. High negative values of net migration in Romania, Poland and Bulgaria, as well as in the Czech Republic and Slovakia at the beginning of the decade reflect differences between populations estimated before the last population census compared with census results. The highest positive values of net migration over the period 2002 to 2007 were recorded in Spain and Italy, followed by the United Kingdom, France and Germany.

As many European countries are currently at a point in the demographic cycle where natural population change is close to being balanced or negative, the relative importance of migration increases. However, as Europe's population ages, natural population change might become once again the principal component of population change – however, it will then be negative.

Table 3.7: Natural population change

(1 000)

	1997	1998	1999	2000	2001	2002	2003	2004	2005	2006	2007
EU-27 (1)	223.7	168.8	162.3	296.4	231.8	152.1	104.0	391.9	292.0	475.9	483.8
Euro area (1)	267.9	227.0	251.5	347.8	319.7	275.2	205.4	401.3	291.0	405.4	378.5
Belgium	12.4	9.7	9.3	10.0	10.7	5.6	5.1	13.7	14.7	19.8	20.0
Bulgaria	-57.7	-52.8	-39.5	-41.4	-44.2	-46.1	-44.6	-40.2	-42.3	-39.5	-37.7
Czech Republic	-22.1	-19.0	-20.3	-18.1	-17.0	-15.5	-17.6	-9.5	-5.7	1.4	10.0
Denmark	7.8	7.7	7.1	9.1	7.1	5.5	7.1	8.8	9.3	9.5	8.5
Germany	-48.2	-67.3	-75.6	-71.8	-94.1	-122.4	-147.2	-112.6	-144.4	-148.9	-140.9
Estonia	-6.0	-7.3	-6.0	-5.3	-5.9	-5.4	-5.1	-3.7	-3.0	-2.4	-1.6
Ireland	21.2	22.4	21.3	23.4	27.6	31.1	32.7	33.8	33.6	36.8	42.9
Greece	2.3	-1.8	-2.7	-2.0	-0.3	-0.3	-1.1	0.7	2.5	6.6	2.3
Spain	19.5	4.7	9.0	37.2	46.2	50.2	57.1	82.7	79.0	111.5	106.7
France	:	225.1	229.2	267.5	262.9	248.3	231.3	280.7	269.6	303.3	290.0
Italy	-22.4	-51.0	-20.5	-12.4	-16.8	-17.5	-44.8	17.5	-34.9	2.1	-7.5
Cyprus	4.1	3.4	3.4	3.1	3.3	2.7	2.9	3.1	2.8	3.6	3.1
Latvia	-14.7	-15.8	-13.4	-12.0	-13.3	-12.5	-11.4	-11.7	-11.3	-10.8	-9.8
Lithuania	-3.3	-3.7	-3.6	-4.8	-8.9	-11.1	-10.4	-10.9	-13.3	-13.5	-13.3
Luxembourg	1.6	1.5	1.8	2.0	1.7	1.6	1.3	1.9	1.8	1.7	1.6
Hungary	-39.1	-43.6	-48.6	-38.0	-35.1	-36.0	-41.2	-37.4	-38.2	-31.7	-35.2
Malta	2.0	1.7	1.3	1.5	1.1	0.9	0.9	0.9	0.7	0.7	0.8
Netherlands	56.7	61.9	60.0	66.1	62.2	59.7	58.4	57.5	51.5	49.7	47.9
Austria	4.6	2.9	-0.1	1.5	0.7	2.3	-0.3	4.7	3.0	3.6	1.6
Poland	32.4	20.3	0.6	10.3	5.0	-5.7	-14.2	-7.4	-3.9	4.6	10.6
Portugal	8.3	7.3	8.1	14.6	7.7	8.1	3.7	7.3	1.9	3.5	-1.0
Romania	-42.4	-31.9	-30.6	-21.3	-39.2	-59.1	-54.1	-42.6	-41.1	-38.6	-37.2
Slovenia	-0.8	-1.2	-1.4	-0.4	-1.0	-1.2	-2.1	-0.6	-0.7	0.8	1.4
Slovakia	7.0	4.4	3.8	2.4	-0.8	-0.7	-0.5	1.9	1.0	0.6	0.6
Finland	10.2	7.8	8.2	7.4	7.6	6.1	7.6	10.2	9.8	10.8	9.7
Sweden	-2.8	-4.2	-6.6	-3.0	-2.3	0.8	6.2	10.4	9.6	14.7	15.7
United Kingdom	96.9	87.7	67.9	70.7	66.9	62.6	84.4	132.9	139.9	176.3	194.7
Croatia	3.5	-5.2	-6.8	-6.5	-8.6	-10.5	-12.9	-9.4	-9.3	-8.9	-11.7
FYR of Macedonia	12.9	12.4	10.5	12.1	10.1	9.8	9.0	5.4	4.1	4.0	3.1
Turkey	1 056.0	1 046.0	1 024.0	948.0	940.0	933.0	925.0	917.0	911.0	906.0	897.0
Iceland	2.3	2.4	2.2	2.5	2.4	2.2	2.3	2.4	2.4	2.5	2.6
Liechtenstein	0.2	0.2	0.2	0.2	0.2	0.2	0.1	0.2	0.2	0.1	0.1
Norway	15.2	14.2	14.1	15.2	12.7	11.0	14.0	15.8	15.5	17.3	16.5
Switzerland	17.7	16.4	15.9	15.9	11.1	10.6	8.8	12.9	11.8	13.1	13.4

(1) Break in series, 1998.

Source: Eurostat (tps00007)

Figure 3.12: Population change, net migration (including corrections) and natural population change, EU-27

(million)

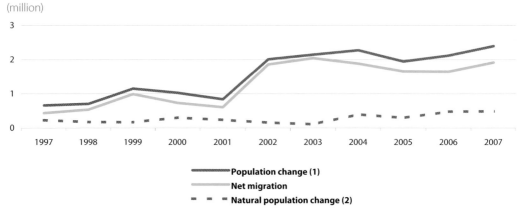

(1) Break in series, 1998; provisional data for 2007.
(2) Provisional data for 2007.

Source: Eurostat (tps00006, tsdde230 and tps00007)

Figure 3.13: Net migration (including corrections) and natural population change, 2002-2007

(average annual change, %)

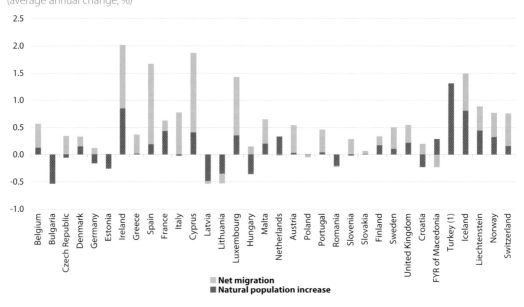

(1) Break in series, 2007.

Source: Eurostat (demo_gind)

3.4 Families and births

Introduction

Family structures differ from one Member State to another, reflecting different historical developments, social attitudes and traditions. However, there are a number of common demographic characteristics that are apparent across the whole of the EU, including: a reduction in the number of marriages; an increase in the average age at which people marry; and an increase in the number of divorces. These trends have resulted in more households and households of a smaller average size, as a higher proportion of people live alone. The changes observed in the age structure of the EU-27's population may also explain, to some degree, the growing proportion of people living alone. Indeed, the highest proportion of people living alone is found among the elderly.

The slowdown in the EU-27's population growth can be partly attributed to the fact that people are generally having fewer children. Fertility rates have fallen in the EU in recent decades. A total fertility rate of around 2.1 children per woman is considered to be the replacement level – in other words, the average number of children per woman required to keep the natural population stable in the long-run, under the theoretical assumption of no migration. The total fertility rate of the EU-27 declined from almost 2.6 in the first half of the 1960s to about 1.4 during the period 1995 to 2005.

While fertility rates of women aged less than 30 have declined since the 1970s, fertility rates of those aged 30 or more have risen since the 1980s. As such, part of the decline in fertility within the EU is likely to be a result of postponement of childbearing.

Relatively high fertility rates tend to be recorded in those Member States which have implemented a range of family-friendly policies, such as the introduction of accessible and affordable childcare and/or more flexible working patterns (France, the Nordic countries, or the Netherlands). Most commentators agree that fertility will increase if there are stimuli, such as higher economic growth and security, more childcare facilities, fiscal measures that support families, family benefit income, a stock of suitable housing, or a range of policies designed to reconcile work and family life, such as more flexible working arrangements (part-time or telework). While a conventional analysis of declining fertility rates might suggest that the decline in fertility rates could be related to increased female participation in the labour market, there is clear evidence of a positive relationship in many countries, for example, in the Nordic countries or Spain, where tertiary-educated women in employment tend to have more children than less educated women.

Definitions and data availability

Live births are defined as the birth of children that showed any sign of life; they refer to the number of births excluding stillbirths (total births include live births and stillbirths). **Stillbirths** are defined as the expulsion or extraction from the mother of a dead foetus after the time at which it would normally be presumed capable of independent extra-uterine existence (commonly taken to be after 24 or 28 weeks of gestation). **Live births outside marriage** are defined as births where the mother's marital status at the time of birth is other than married. The **crude birth rate** is the ratio of the number of births during the year to the average population in that year; the value is expressed per 1 000 inhabitants.

Total fertility rates are defined as the mean number of children that would be born alive to a woman during her lifetime if she were to pass through her childbearing years conforming to the fertility rates by age of a given year. The total fertility rate is therefore the completed fertility of a hypothetical generation, computed by adding the fertility rates by age for women in a given year (the number of women at each age is assumed to be the same). The **mean age of women at childbearing** is defined as the mean age of women when their children are born. For a given calendar year, the mean age of women at childbearing can be calculated using fertility rates by age (in general, the reproductive period is between 15 and 49 years of age).

The **crude marriage rate** is the ratio of the number of marriages during the year to the average population in that year; the value is expressed per 1 000 inhabitants. In a similar vein, the **crude divorce rate** is the ratio of the number of divorces during the year to the average population in that year; the value is expressed per 1 000 inhabitants. Divorce is possible in all EU Member States, except Malta; in almost all countries divorces are registered at a court.

Main findings

Since the 1960 and the beginning of the 21st century, the number of births in Europe declined sharply, through to a relative low of just under 5 million births in 2002. Since then, there has been a steady and moderate rebound. This broad trend was reflected in the developments for many of the Member States. However, the number of births has continued to decline relatively steadily in some countries, such as Germany and the Netherlands. In contrast, the number of births in Spain has risen strongly and steadily during the ten-year period through until 2007.

Crude birth rates express the number of births in relation to the whole population: the European crude birth rate (10.2 births per 1 000 inhabitants) was the lowest among the continents and approximately half the world average of 21.1 for the period 2000 to 2005. The EU-27 rate fluctuated during this five-year period between 10.3 and 10.6, which was slightly above the latest crude birth rates registered for Russia (9.9) or Japan (9.0), but lower than those recorded for China (13.6), the United States (14.1) or India (25.1).

The fertility rate of women in Europe fell at a relatively fast pace between the early 1960s and late 1990s, from an average of 2.58 children per woman to 1.40 children. This trend was reflected across most of the continents, with average rates for the world as a whole declining from 4.98 children to 2.65 children in the same period. Among the Member States, France had the highest fertility rate, reaching an average of two children per woman in 2006. In contrast, some of the lowest fertility rates in the EU-27 were registered in southern and eastern Europe, the lowest being in Slovakia (1.24 children per woman in 2006).

As well as having fewer children, women have tended to have their children later in life. The mean age for women giving birth rose to over 30 in seven of the Member States (Spain, Ireland, Italy, the Netherlands, Sweden, Denmark and Finland) by 2006, and was between 29 and 30 in a further nine of the Member States. The trend for postponing birth was, in the last decade, most prevalent in the Czech Republic, the Baltic States, Hungary and Slovenia, where the average age of women giving birth rose by at least two years in the period 1996 to 2006.

Across the EU-27 as a whole, the number of marriages per 1 000 persons decreased; the rate was about 5 % lower in the years after 2000 than during the late 1990s. In Cyprus, there was a strong decline in the marriage rate between 2001 and 2007 (almost halving to 7.5 marriages per 1 000 persons), and a more steady and prolonged decline in the Netherlands to 4.5 marriages per 1 000 persons in 2007.

Although marriage is a form of commitment of union between partners, irreparable differences can lead to divorce. The number of divorces in the EU-27 grew steadily to pass one million a year in 2005, the equivalent of about 42 per 100 marriages, or, in terms of an annual rate, two divorces per 1 000 persons each year. When marriage ends in divorce, the mean duration of each marriage exceeds ten years in every Member State, rising to nearly 17 years in Italy.

Table 3.8: Average number of live births per year
(1 000)

	1960-65	65-70	70-75	75-80	80-85	85-90	90-95	95-00	00-05
World	111 829	117 740	119 550	120 479	128 653	136 825	135 888	133 632	133 493
Europe (1)	11 873	10 838	10 453	10 128	10 080	9 806	8 366	7 431	7 419
Africa	14 449	16 066	18 151	20 550	23 311	25 728	27 850	30 062	32 816
Asia	70 704	76 143	75 917	74 190	78 945	84 627	82 844	79 547	76 623
Latin America and the Caribbean	9 691	10 233	10 804	11 389	11 769	11 790	11 757	11 683	11 601
Northern America	4 663	4 002	3 735	3 760	4 064	4 356	4 518	4 341	4 461
Oceania	449	459	491	463	484	518	554	567	573
	1960-65	65-70	70-75	75-80	80-85	85-90	90-95	95-00	00-05
EU-27 (2)	7 609	7 457	6 897	6 475	6 130	5 905	5 483	5 108	5 072
China	26 313	28 798	25 131	20 745	21 627	24 721	21 555	19 848	17 569
India	19 108	20 241	21 699	23 452	25 048	26 524	27 890	27 728	27 408
Japan	1 662	1 793	2 147	1 759	1 533	1 281	1 213	1 213	1 141
Russian Federation	2 585	1 854	2 027	2 163	2 371	2 363	1 620	1 326	1 441
United States	4 197	3 618	3 383	3 396	3 689	3 973	4 123	3 992	4 124

(1) EU-27, Albania, Andorra, Belarus, Bosnia and Herzegovina, Croatia, Faeroe Islands, Iceland, Liechtenstein, the former Yugoslav Republic of Macedonia, Republic of Moldova, Montenegro, Norway, the Russian Federation, Serbia, Switzerland and the Ukraine.
(2) Break in series, 1998.

Source: Eurostat (tps00111), United Nations, Population Division of the Department of Economic and Social Affairs

Table 3.9: Number of live births

(1 000)

	1997	1998	1999	2000	2001	2002	2003	2004	2005	2006	2007
EU-27 (1)	5 117.9	5 074.8	5 073.4	5 121.6	5 022.1	4 993.3	5 040.8	5 117.0	5 134.6	5 223.1	5 266.1
Euro area (1)	3 200.1	3 191.4	3 221.6	3 287.3	3 236.6	3 230.3	3 245.8	3 281.9	3 269.4	3 308.0	3 308.0
Belgium	116.2	114.2	114.2	114.9	114.2	111.2	112.1	115.6	118.0	121.4	120.7
Bulgaria	64.1	65.4	72.3	73.7	68.2	66.5	67.4	69.9	71.1	74.0	75.3
Czech Republic	90.7	90.5	89.5	90.9	90.7	92.8	93.7	97.7	102.2	105.8	114.6
Denmark	67.6	66.2	66.2	67.1	65.5	64.1	64.7	64.6	64.3	65.0	64.1
Germany	812.2	785.0	770.7	767.0	734.5	719.3	706.7	705.6	685.8	672.7	682.7
Estonia	12.6	12.2	12.4	13.1	12.6	13.0	13.0	14.0	14.4	14.9	15.8
Ireland	52.8	54.0	53.9	54.8	57.9	60.5	61.5	62.0	61.0	64.2	70.6
Greece	102.0	100.9	100.6	103.3	102.3	103.6	104.4	105.7	107.5	112.0	110.0
Spain	369.0	365.2	380.1	397.6	406.4	418.8	441.9	454.6	466.4	483.0	488.3
France	758.1	768.6	776.5	808.2	804.1	793.6	793.9	800.2	807.8	830.3	816.5
Italy	534.5	515.4	537.2	543.1	535.3	538.2	544.1	562.6	554.0	560.0	563.2
Cyprus	9.3	8.9	8.5	8.4	8.2	7.9	8.1	8.3	8.2	8.7	8.5
Latvia	18.8	18.4	19.4	20.2	19.7	20.0	21.0	20.3	21.5	22.3	23.3
Lithuania	37.8	37.0	36.4	34.1	31.5	30.0	30.6	30.4	30.5	31.3	32.3
Luxembourg	5.5	5.4	5.6	5.7	5.5	5.3	5.3	5.5	5.4	5.5	5.5
Hungary	100.4	97.3	94.6	97.6	97.0	96.8	94.6	95.1	97.5	99.9	97.6
Malta	4.8	4.7	4.4	4.4	4.0	3.9	4.1	3.9	3.9	3.9	3.9
Netherlands	192.4	199.4	200.4	206.6	202.6	202.1	200.3	194.0	187.9	185.1	180.9
Austria	84.0	81.2	78.1	78.3	75.5	78.4	76.9	79.0	78.2	77.9	76.3
Poland	412.6	395.6	382.0	378.3	368.2	353.8	351.1	356.1	364.4	374.2	387.9
Portugal	113.0	113.5	116.0	120.0	112.8	114.4	112.5	109.3	109.4	105.4	102.5
Romania	236.9	237.3	234.6	234.5	220.4	210.5	212.5	216.3	221.0	219.5	214.7
Slovenia	18.2	17.9	17.5	18.2	17.5	17.5	17.3	18.0	18.2	18.9	19.6
Slovakia	59.1	57.6	56.2	55.2	51.1	50.8	51.7	53.7	54.4	53.9	54.4
Finland	59.3	57.1	57.6	56.7	56.2	55.6	56.6	57.8	57.7	58.8	58.7
Sweden	90.5	89.0	88.2	90.4	91.5	95.8	99.2	100.9	101.3	105.9	107.4
United Kingdom	726.6	716.9	700.0	679.0	669.1	668.8	695.5	716.0	722.5	748.6	770.7
Croatia	55.5	47.1	45.2	43.7	41.0	40.1	39.7	40.3	42.5	41.4	42.0
FYR of Macedonia	29.5	29.2	27.3	29.3	27.0	27.8	27.0	23.4	22.5	22.6	22.7
Turkey	1 480.0	1 472.0	1 451.0	1 363.0	1 362.0	1 362.0	1 361.0	1 360.0	1 361.0	1 362.0	1 361.0
Iceland	4.2	4.2	4.1	4.3	4.1	4.0	4.1	4.2	4.3	4.4	4.5
Liechtenstein	0.4	0.4	0.4	0.4	0.4	0.4	0.3	0.4	0.4	0.4	0.4
Norway	59.8	58.4	59.3	59.2	56.7	55.4	56.5	57.0	56.8	58.5	58.5
Switzerland	80.6	78.9	78.4	78.5	72.3	72.4	71.8	73.1	72.9	73.4	74.4

(1) Break in series, 1998.

Source: Eurostat (tps00111)

Table 3.10: Crude birth rate

(‰)

	1960-65	65-70	70-75	75-80	80-85	85-90	90-95	95-00	00-05
World	35.1	33.4	30.8	28.3	27.6	27.0	24.7	22.6	21.1
Europe (1)	19.2	16.8	15.7	14.8	14.4	13.7	11.5	10.2	10.2
Africa	48.0	47.0	46.5	45.9	45.1	43.2	40.8	38.9	37.7
Asia	39.2	37.7	33.5	29.5	28.5	27.9	25.0	22.2	20.1
Latin America and the Caribbean	41.0	37.9	35.3	33.0	30.6	27.8	25.3	23.2	21.5
Northern America	22.0	17.7	15.7	15.1	15.5	15.8	15.5	14.1	13.8
Oceania	26.7	24.5	24.0	21.0	20.4	20.1	19.9	18.9	17.8
	1960-65	**65-70**	**70-75**	**75-80**	**80-85**	**85-90**	**90-95**	**95-00**	**00-05**
EU-27 (2)	18.3	17.4	15.6	14.3	13.3	12.6	11.6	10.6	10.4
China	38.0	36.9	28.6	21.5	20.9	22.3	18.2	16.0	13.6
India	40.7	38.8	37.3	36.0	34.3	32.5	30.7	27.7	25.1
Japan	17.2	17.6	19.9	15.4	12.9	10.5	9.7	9.6	9.0
Russian Federation	21.0	14.4	15.3	15.9	16.8	16.2	10.9	8.9	9.9
United States	21.8	17.7	15.7	15.1	15.6	15.9	15.7	14.4	14.1

(1) EU-27, Albania, Andorra, Belarus, Bosnia and Herzegovina, Croatia, Faeroe Islands, Iceland, Liechtenstein, the former Yugoslav Republic of Macedonia, Republic of Moldova, Montenegro, Norway, the Russian Federation, Serbia, Switzerland and the Ukraine.
(2) Break in series, 1998.

Source: Eurostat (tps00112), United Nations, Population Division of the Department of Economic and Social Affairs

Figure 3.14: Live births outside marriage and crude birth rate, EU-27

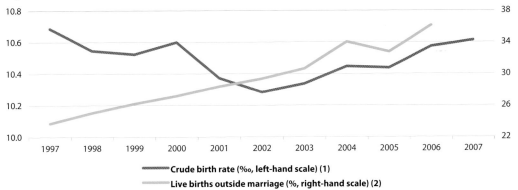

(1) Break in series, 1998; provisional data for 2007.
(2) Not available for 2007; excluding Belgium from 1998 onwards; excluding Italy for 2004 and 2006.

Source: Eurostat (tps00112 and demo_fagec)

Table 3.11: Total fertility rate

(mean number of children per woman)

	1996	1997	1998	1999	2000	2001	2002	2003	2004	2005	2006
Belgium	1.59	1.60	:	:	:	:	:	:	:	:	:
Bulgaria	1.23	1.09	1.11	1.23	1.26	1.20	1.21	1.23	1.29	1.31	1.37
Czech Republic	1.18	1.17	1.16	1.13	1.14	1.14	1.17	1.18	1.22	1.28	1.33
Denmark	1.75	1.76	1.73	1.75	1.78	1.76	1.72	1.76	1.78	1.80	1.83
Germany	1.32	1.37	1.36	1.36	1.38	1.35	1.34	1.34	1.36	1.34	1.32
Estonia	1.37	1.32	1.28	1.32	1.39	1.34	1.37	1.37	1.47	1.50	1.55
Ireland	1.88	1.93	1.93	1.89	1.88	1.93	1.96	1.95	1.93	1.86	1.90
Greece	1.28	1.28	1.26	1.24	1.26	1.25	1.27	1.28	1.30	1.33	1.39
Spain	1.16	1.17	1.16	1.19	1.23	1.24	1.26	1.31	1.33	1.35	1.38
France	:	:	1.78	1.81	1.89	1.90	1.88	1.89	1.92	1.94	2.00
Italy	1.20	1.21	:	1.23	1.26	1.25	1.27	1.29	:	1.32	:
Cyprus	1.95	1.86	1.76	1.67	1.64	1.57	1.49	1.50	1.49	1.42	1.47
Latvia	1.18	1.14	1.12	1.19	1.24	1.21	1.23	1.29	1.24	1.31	1.35
Lithuania	1.49	1.47	1.46	1.46	1.39	1.30	1.24	1.26	1.26	1.27	1.31
Luxembourg	1.77	1.72	1.68	1.74	1.76	1.65	1.63	1.62	1.66	1.66	1.65
Hungary	1.46	1.37	1.32	1.28	1.32	1.31	1.30	1.27	1.28	1.31	1.34
Malta	:	:	:	:	:	:	:	:	:	1.38	1.41
Netherlands	1.53	1.56	1.63	1.65	1.72	1.71	1.73	1.75	1.73	1.71	1.70
Austria	1.45	1.39	1.37	1.34	1.36	1.33	1.39	1.38	1.42	1.41	1.40
Poland	1.59	1.52	1.44	1.37	1.35	1.32	1.25	1.22	1.23	1.24	1.27
Portugal	1.44	1.47	1.47	1.50	1.55	1.45	1.47	1.44	1.40	1.40	1.35
Romania	1.37	1.40	1.40	1.39	1.39	1.31	1.26	1.27	1.29	1.32	1.31
Slovenia	1.28	1.25	1.23	1.21	1.26	1.21	1.21	1.20	1.25	1.26	1.31
Slovakia	1.47	1.43	1.37	1.33	1.29	1.20	1.18	1.20	1.24	1.25	1.24
Finland	1.76	1.75	1.70	1.74	1.73	1.73	1.72	1.77	1.80	1.80	1.84
Sweden	1.60	1.52	1.50	1.50	1.54	1.57	1.65	1.71	1.75	1.77	1.85
United Kingdom	1.73	1.72	1.71	1.68	1.64	1.63	1.64	1.71	1.77	1.78	1.84
Croatia	:	:	:	:	1.47	1.38	:	1.32	1.34	1.41	1.38
FYR of Macedonia	2.07	1.93	1.90	1.76	1.88	1.73	1.80	1.77	1.52	1.46	1.46
Iceland	2.12	2.04	2.05	1.99	2.08	1.95	1.93	1.99	2.04	2.05	2.08
Liechtenstein	:	:	:	:	1.57	1.52	1.47	1.37	1.44	1.49	1.42
Norway	1.89	1.86	1.81	1.84	1.85	1.78	1.75	1.80	1.83	1.84	1.90
Switzerland	1.50	1.48	1.47	1.48	1.50	1.38	1.39	1.39	1.42	1.42	1.43

Source: Eurostat (tsdde220)

Table 3.12: Average fertility rates

(mean number of children per woman)

	1960-65	65-70	70-75	75-80	80-85	85-90	90-95	95-00	00-05
World	4.98	4.90	4.47	3.92	3.58	3.38	3.05	2.80	2.65
Europe (1)	2.58	2.36	2.16	1.97	1.89	1.83	1.57	1.40	1.41
Africa	6.87	6.80	6.72	6.61	6.45	6.13	5.68	5.28	4.98
Asia	5.65	5.67	5.04	4.19	3.67	3.40	2.97	2.67	2.47
Latin America and the Caribbean	5.97	5.54	5.04	4.48	3.92	3.41	3.03	2.73	2.52
Northern America	3.35	2.55	2.01	1.78	1.81	1.89	1.99	1.95	1.99
Oceania	3.98	3.57	3.23	2.73	2.59	2.51	2.48	2.42	2.37
China	5.72	6.06	4.86	3.32	2.55	2.46	1.92	1.78	1.70
India	5.82	5.61	5.26	4.89	4.50	4.15	3.86	3.46	3.11
Japan	2.02	2.00	2.07	1.81	1.76	1.66	1.49	1.39	1.29
Russian Federation	2.55	2.02	2.03	1.94	2.04	2.12	1.55	1.25	1.30
United States	3.31	2.55	2.02	1.79	1.83	1.92	2.03	1.99	2.04

(1) EU-27, Albania, Andorra, Belarus, Bosnia and Herzegovina, Croatia, Faeroe Islands, Iceland, Liechtenstein, the former Yugoslav Republic of Macedonia, Republic of Moldova, Montenegro, Norway, the Russian Federation, Serbia, Switzerland and the Ukraine.

Source: United Nations, Population Division of the Department of Economic and Social Affairs

Figure 3.15: Mean age of women at childbearing (1)

(years)

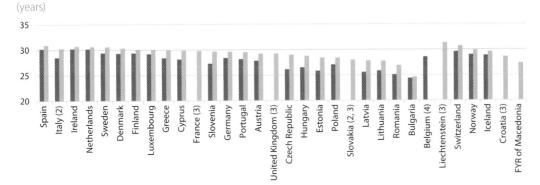

(1) Malta, not available.
(2) 2005 instead of 2006.
(3) Not available for 1996.
(4) Not available for 2006.

Source: Eurostat (tps00017)

Table 3.13: Marriages

(per 1 000 persons)

	1997	1998	1999	2000	2001	2002	2003	2004	2005	2006	2007
EU-27 (1)	5.15	5.11	5.2	5.18	4.87	4.89	4.85	4.86	4.88	:	:
Euro area	:	:	:	5.12	4.82	4.82	4.7	4.64	4.61	4.45	:
Belgium	4.69	4.35	4.32	4.40	4.09	3.91	4.03	4.15	4.12	4.25	4.28
Bulgaria	4.18	4.31	4.33	4.30	3.99	3.71	3.92	3.99	4.33	4.26	3.87
Czech Republic	5.61	5.35	5.20	5.39	5.12	5.17	4.79	5.04	5.06	5.15	5.53
Denmark	6.48	6.55	6.66	7.19	6.82	6.92	6.50	6.98	6.67	6.71	6.70
Germany	5.15	5.09	5.25	5.09	4.73	4.75	4.64	4.80	4.71	4.54	4.48
Estonia	3.99	3.92	4.06	4.01	4.14	4.31	4.21	4.45	4.55	5.18	5.23
Ireland	4.25	4.52	4.93	5.04	4.98	5.23	5.08	5.07	5.13	5.13	:
Greece	5.62	5.12	5.62	4.48	5.21	5.27	5.54	4.64	5.50	5.18	5.16
Spain	4.96	5.21	5.21	5.38	5.11	5.12	5.05	5.06	4.83	4.61	:
France	4.87	4.64	4.87	5.03	4.84	4.65	4.56	4.46	4.51	4.34	4.19
Italy	4.88	4.92	4.93	4.99	4.58	4.65	4.48	4.28	4.23	4.13	4.21
Cyprus	10.71	11.40	13.22	14.08	15.07	14.48	7.69	7.23	7.76	6.80	7.50
Latvia	3.98	4.00	3.93	3.88	3.93	4.16	4.30	4.48	5.45	6.39	6.80
Lithuania	5.26	5.21	5.07	4.83	4.53	4.66	4.91	5.57	5.84	6.26	6.83
Luxembourg	4.78	4.80	4.86	4.92	4.49	4.53	4.43	4.36	4.41	4.16	4.10
Hungary	4.56	4.37	4.44	4.71	4.28	4.53	4.48	4.33	4.39	4.42	4.06
Malta	6.43	6.51	6.35	6.60	5.58	5.66	5.90	5.99	5.88	6.25	6.06
Netherlands	5.45	5.54	5.66	5.53	4.97	5.20	4.86	4.51	4.52	4.35	4.49
Austria	5.20	4.91	4.94	4.90	4.25	4.52	4.58	4.71	4.75	4.46	4.33
Poland	5.30	5.42	5.68	5.49	5.10	5.02	5.12	5.02	5.42	5.93	6.52
Portugal	6.52	6.57	6.75	6.23	5.67	5.45	5.15	4.68	4.61	4.52	4.37
Romania	6.68	6.46	6.23	6.05	5.87	5.92	6.16	6.61	6.56	6.79	8.78
Slovenia	3.78	3.80	3.89	3.62	3.48	3.54	3.39	3.28	2.88	3.17	3.17
Slovakia	5.19	5.10	5.07	4.81	4.42	4.66	4.83	5.18	4.85	4.81	5.08
Finland	4.56	4.66	4.70	5.05	4.79	5.19	4.95	5.61	5.58	5.36	5.58
Sweden	3.65	3.57	4.03	4.50	4.02	4.26	4.36	4.79	4.92	5.02	5.24
United Kingdom	5.32	5.21	5.13	5.19	4.84	4.94	5.14	5.20	5.23	:	:
Croatia	5.40	5.35	5.27	4.93	4.97	5.13	5.03	5.11	4.98	4.97	:
FYR of Macedonia	7.05	6.97	7.03	7.03	:	7.15	7.11	6.92	7.12	7.31	7.58
Turkey	:	:	:	:	:	:	6.80	8.75	9.05	8.91	:
Iceland	5.46	5.58	5.62	6.32	5.21	5.75	5.29	5.19	5.42	5.53	:
Liechtenstein	12.55	:	:	7.23	5.99	5.19	4.37	4.76	5.38	4.31	5.10
Norway	5.41	5.27	5.26	5.65	5.09	5.30	4.90	4.06	4.84	4.66	4.98
Switzerland	5.52	5.44	5.69	5.53	4.98	5.51	5.46	5.34	5.40	5.32	5.34

(1) Break in series, 1998.

Source: Eurostat (tps00012)

Table 3.14: Divorces

(per 1 000 persons)

	1997	1998	1999	2000	2001	2002	2003	2004	2005	2006	2007
EU-27 (1)	1.8	1.8	1.8	1.8	1.9	1.9	2.0	2.0	2.0	:	:
Belgium	2.6	2.6	2.6	2.6	2.8	3.0	3.0	3.0	2.9	2.8	2.9
Bulgaria	1.1	1.3	1.2	1.3	1.3	1.3	1.5	1.9	1.9	1.9	2.1
Czech Republic	3.2	3.1	2.3	2.9	3.1	3.1	3.8	3.2	3.1	3.1	3.0
Denmark	2.4	2.5	2.5	2.7	2.7	2.8	2.9	2.9	2.8	2.6	2.6
Germany	2.3	2.3	2.3	2.4	2.4	2.5	2.6	2.6	2.4	2.3	:
Estonia	3.8	3.2	3.3	3.1	3.2	3.0	2.9	3.1	3.0	2.8	2.8
Ireland	0.0	0.4	0.6	0.7	0.7	0.7	0.7	0.8	0.8	:	:
Greece	0.9	0.7	0.9	1.0	1.1	1.0	1.1	1.1	1.2	1.3	1.2
Spain	0.9	0.9	0.9	0.9	1.0	1.0	1.1	1.2	1.7	:	:
France	2.0	2.0	2.0	1.9	1.9	1.9	2.1	2.2	2.5	2.2	:
Italy	0.6	0.6	0.6	0.7	0.7	0.7	0.8	0.8	0.8	:	0.8
Cyprus	1.3	1.3	1.7	1.7	1.7	1.9	2.0	2.2	2.0	2.3	2.1
Latvia	2.5	2.6	2.5	2.6	2.4	2.5	2.1	2.3	2.8	3.2	3.3
Lithuania	3.2	3.3	3.2	3.1	3.2	3.0	3.1	3.2	3.3	3.3	3.4
Luxembourg	2.4	2.4	2.4	2.4	2.3	2.4	2.3	2.3	2.3	2.5	2.3
Hungary	2.4	2.5	2.5	2.3	2.4	2.5	2.5	2.4	2.5	2.5	2.5
Malta	-	-	-	-	-	-	-	-	-	-	-
Netherlands	2.2	2.1	2.1	2.2	2.3	2.1	1.9	1.9	2.0	1.9	2.0
Austria	2.3	2.2	2.3	2.4	2.6	2.4	2.3	2.4	2.4	2.5	2.4
Poland	1.1	1.2	1.1	1.1	1.2	1.2	1.3	1.5	1.8	1.9	1.7
Portugal	1.4	1.5	1.7	1.9	1.8	2.7	2.2	2.2	2.2	2.3	2.4
Romania	1.6	1.8	1.6	1.4	1.4	1.5	1.5	1.6	1.5	1.5	1.7
Slovenia	1.0	1.0	1.0	1.1	1.1	1.2	1.2	1.2	1.3	1.2	1.4
Slovakia	1.7	1.7	1.8	1.7	1.8	2.0	2.0	2.0	2.1	2.4	2.3
Finland	2.6	2.7	2.7	2.7	2.6	2.6	2.6	2.5	2.6	2.5	2.5
Sweden	2.4	2.3	2.4	2.4	2.4	2.4	2.4	2.2	2.2	2.2	2.3
United Kingdom	2.8	2.7	2.7	2.6	2.7	2.7	2.8	2.8	2.6	:	:
Croatia	0.9	0.9	0.8	1.0	1.1	1.0	1.1	1.1	1.1	1.1	:
FYR of Macedonia	0.5	0.5	0.5	0.7	0.7	0.6	0.7	0.8	0.8	0.7	0.7
Turkey	:	:	:	:	:	:	0.7	1.3	1.3	1.3	:
Iceland	1.9	1.8	1.7	1.9	1.9	1.8	1.8	1.9	1.9	1.6	:
Liechtenstein	2.1	:	:	3.9	2.5	2.9	2.5	2.9	2.7	2.3	2.8
Norway	2.3	2.1	2.0	2.2	2.3	2.3	2.4	2.4	2.4	2.3	2.2
Switzerland	2.4	2.5	2.9	1.5	2.2	2.2	2.3	2.4	2.9	2.8	2.6

(1) Break in series, 1998.

Source: Eurostat (tps00013)

3

3.5 Life expectancy

Introduction

Another contributing factor to the ageing of the EU's population is a gradual increase in life expectancies. This may, at least in part, be attributed to higher standards of living, better healthcare, as well as more awareness of health issues.

A set of health expectancy indicators have been developed to extend the concept of life expectancy to cover morbidity and disability, so as to assess the quality of life; these indicators are included in the list of structural indicators on the basis of which the Commission draws up its annual synthesis report, thereby integrating public health into the Lisbon strategy.

The EC Treaty (Title XIII Public Health, Article 152) states that 'Community action, which shall complement national policies, shall be directed towards improving public health, preventing human illness and diseases, and obviating sources of danger to human health.' The ongoing programme of Community action in the field of public health (2003-2008) targets the following objectives:

- to improve information and knowledge for the development of public health;
- to enhance the capability of responding rapidly and in a co-ordinated fashion to threats in health;
- and to promote health and prevent disease through addressing health determinants across all policies and activities.

The European Commission report on 'Long-term care in the European Union' released in April 2008, analyses the main challenges Member States face in the field of long-term care, their strategies for tackling them and presents possible solutions[7].

Definitions and data availability

According to the United Nations (UN) definition, a death is the permanent disappearance of all evidence of life at any time after live birth has taken place (postnatal cessation of vital functions without capacity of resuscitation); this definition therefore excludes foetal deaths.

Life expectancy can be given for any age. It relates to the mean number of years still to be lived by a person who has reached a certain age, if subjected throughout the rest of his or her life to the current mortality conditions (age-specific probabilities of dying). The most common life expectancy figures relate to life expectancy at birth, measured as the mean number of years that a newborn child can expect to live if subjected throughout his/her life to the current mortality conditions; in this publication life expectancy is also presented at age 65.

Health expectancies extend the concept of life expectancy to morbidity and disability, in order to assess the quality of life. These are composite indicators that combine mortality data with data referring

(7) http://ec.europa.eu/employment_social/news/2008/apr/long_term_care_en.pdf.

to health. The **Healthy Life Years (HLY)** indicator measures the number of remaining years that a person of a specific age is still expected to live in a healthy condition. A healthy condition is defined by the absence of limitations in functioning/disability. Therefore, the indicator is also called disability-free life expectancy (DFLE). HLY indicators are calculated by gender, at birth, and at the age of 65.

Main findings

Increasing life expectancy is one of the many factors that contribute towards Europe's ageing population profile. This indicator has gradually risen for males and females in Europe, as in other world regions, and this trend is expected to continue. EU-27 life expectancy of a boy at birth was 75.2 years in 2004, while the life expectancy of a newborn girl was just over six years higher at 81.5 years. There remain quite large variations in life expectancies across the EU-27. For males, the lowest life expectancy in 2006 was recorded in Lithuania (65.3 years) and the highest in Sweden and Cyprus (both 78.8); for women, the range was narrower, from a low of 76.2 years in Romania to a high of 84.4 in both Spain and France.

Gender differences in life expectancy were, in the 1960s, associated with unfavourable male mortality. This pattern was reversed in the 1980s as the gender gap closed in north western Europe, followed by southern Europe in the 1990s. The difference in life expectancies has been further narrowed in recent years, as the growth in female life expectancy slowed somewhat. The convergence of life expectancy figures may be a consequence of more similar circumstances in terms of the lifestyles led by men and women in the EU – for example, fewer men are working in areas of the economy where high degrees of physical effort are required throughout the working day (agriculture, mining, or the manufacture of iron and steel). Nevertheless, persistently higher male mortality is recorded throughout the entire life cycle and with respect to all of the main causes of death.

Health expectancies can be used to measure the potential of the population to participate in society. There are many Member States that are in the process of implementing or considering changes to their statutory age for retirement, as well as the promotion of policies that actively encourage older persons to remain in work longer. In 2005, for most countries, healthy life years at birth for females were above those for men. The exceptions included Cyprus, the Netherlands, Portugal, Sweden, Iceland and Norway, where men at birth had 1 to 2 years of healthy life more (compared with women).

As people are living longer there has been a growing interest in the older generations – both as potential actors in the workforce, or as a specific market of consumers. This is borne out when looking at the life expectancy of those persons who are aged 65; in 2006, the average man of this age could be expected to live an additional 12.7 years in Latvia, rising to 18.2 additional years in France. The life expectancy of women at the age of 65 was higher, ranging from 16.3 years in Bulgaria to 22.7 years in France.

Table 3.15: Life expectancy at birth

(years)

	Male						Female					
	1996	1998	2000	2002	2004	2006	1996	1998	2000	2002	2004	2006
EU-27	:	:	:	74.5	75.2	:	:	:	:	80.9	81.5	:
Euro area	:	:	:	76.0	76.8	:	:	:	:	82.2	82.8	:
Belgium	73.9	74.4	74.6	75.1	76.0	76.6	80.7	80.7	81.0	81.2	81.8	82.3
Bulgaria	67.4	67.4	68.4	68.8	68.9	69.2	74.5	74.6	75.0	75.5	75.8	76.3
Czech Republic	70.4	71.2	71.7	72.1	72.6	73.5	77.5	78.2	78.5	78.7	79.2	79.9
Denmark	73.1	74.0	74.5	74.8	75.4	76.1	78.3	79.0	79.2	79.4	80.2	80.7
Germany	73.6	74.5	75.1	75.7	76.5	77.2	80.1	80.8	81.2	81.3	81.9	82.4
Estonia	64.3	64.1	65.5	65.3	66.4	67.4	75.6	75.4	76.2	77.0	77.8	78.6
Ireland	73.1	73.4	74.0	75.2	76.4	77.3	78.7	79.1	79.2	80.5	81.4	82.1
Greece	75.1	75.4	75.5	76.2	76.6	77.2	80.2	80.3	80.6	81.1	81.3	81.9
Spain	74.5	75.3	75.8	76.3	76.9	77.7	82.0	82.4	82.9	83.2	83.7	84.4
France	:	74.8	75.3	75.7	76.7	77.3	:	82.6	83.0	83.0	83.8	84.4
Italy	75.5	76.1	77.0	77.4	77.9	:	81.8	82.2	82.9	83.2	83.8	:
Cyprus	:	:	:	76.4	76.8	78.8	:	:	:	81.0	82.1	82.4
Latvia	:	:	:	64.7	65.9	65.4	:	:	:	76.0	76.2	76.3
Lithuania	64.6	66.0	66.8	66.2	66.3	65.3	75.9	76.6	77.5	77.5	77.7	77.0
Luxembourg	73.3	73.7	74.6	74.6	75.9	76.8	80.2	80.8	81.3	81.5	82.3	81.9
Hungary	66.3	66.5	67.6	68.3	68.7	69.2	75.0	75.6	76.2	76.7	77.2	77.8
Malta	74.8	74.9	76.2	76.3	77.4	77.0	79.6	80.0	80.3	81.3	81.2	81.9
Netherlands	74.7	75.2	:	76.0	76.9	77.7	80.5	80.8	:	80.7	81.5	82.0
Austria	73.7	74.5	75.2	75.8	76.4	77.2	80.2	81.0	81.2	81.7	82.1	82.8
Poland	68.1	68.9	69.6	70.3	70.6	70.9	76.6	77.4	78.0	78.8	79.2	79.7
Portugal	71.6	72.4	73.2	73.8	75.0	75.5	79.0	79.5	80.2	80.6	81.5	82.3
Romania	65.1	66.3	67.7	67.3	68.2	69.2	72.8	73.8	74.8	74.7	75.5	76.2
Slovenia	71.1	71.3	72.2	72.6	73.5	74.5	79.0	79.2	79.9	80.5	80.8	82.0
Slovakia	68.8	68.6	69.2	69.8	70.3	70.4	77.0	77.0	77.5	77.7	78.0	78.4
Finland	73.1	73.6	74.2	74.9	75.4	75.9	80.7	81.0	81.2	81.6	82.5	83.1
Sweden	76.6	76.9	77.4	77.7	78.4	78.8	81.7	82.1	82.0	82.1	82.8	83.1
United Kingdom	74.3	74.8	75.5	76.0	76.8	:	79.5	79.8	80.3	80.6	81.0	:
Croatia	:	:	70.7	:	71.9	72.5	:	:	77.7	:	78.8	79.3
FYR of Macedonia	70.3	70.2	70.8	70.6	71.5	71.7	74.8	74.4	75.2	75.6	75.8	76.2
Iceland	76.5	77.7	77.8	78.6	78.9	79.5	81.2	81.6	81.6	82.5	83.2	82.9
Liechtenstein	72.3	73.6	73.9	77.1	78.5	78.9	81.6	82.1	79.9	82.3	85.1	83.1
Norway	75.4	75.6	76.0	76.4	77.6	78.2	81.2	81.4	81.5	81.6	82.6	82.9
Switzerland	76.0	76.4	77.0	77.9	78.6	79.2	82.2	82.7	82.8	83.2	83.8	84.2

Source: Eurostat (tps00025)

Figure 3.16: Life expectancy at birth, 2006 (1)

(years)

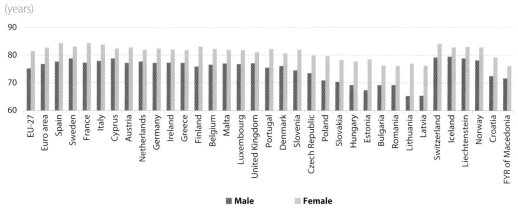

■ **Male**　　■ **Female**

(1) The United Kingdom, 2005; EU-27, euro area and Italy, 2004; the figure is ranked on the average of male and female.

Source: Eurostat (tps00025)

Figure 3.17: Life expectancy at 65, 2006 (1)

(years)

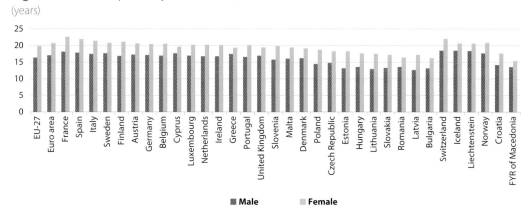

■ **Male**　　■ **Female**

(1) The United Kingdom, 2005; EU-27, euro area and Italy, 2004; the figure is ranked on the average of male and female.

Source: Eurostat (tsdde210)

3.6 Migration and asylum

Introduction

Migration is influenced by a combination of economic, political and social factors. These factors may act in a migrant's country of origin (push factors) or in the country of destination (pull factors). The relative economic prosperity and political stability of the EU are thought to exert a considerable pull effect on immigrants.

International migration may increasingly be used as a tool to solve specific labour market shortages, but alone will almost certainly not be enough to reverse the ongoing trend of population ageing.

Migration policies are increasingly concerned with attracting a particular migrant profile, often in an attempt to alleviate specific skills shortages. Selection can be carried out on the basis of language proficiency, work experience, education and/or age, or alternatively by employers so that migrants already have a job upon their arrival. Besides policies to encourage labour recruitment, immigration policy is often focused on two areas: preventing unauthorised migration[8] and the illegal employment of migrants who are not permitted to work, and promoting the integration of immigrants into society. Significant resources have been mobilised to fight people smuggling and trafficking networks in the EU.

Some of the most important legal texts adopted in the area of immigration include:

- Council Directive 2003/86/EC on the right to family reunification[9];
- Council Directive 2003/109/EC on a long-term resident status for third country nationals[10];
- Council Directive 2004/1 14/EC on the admission of students[11], and;
- Council Directive 2005/71/EC for the facilitation of the admission of researchers into the EU[12].

The Commission re-launched in 2005 the debate on the need for a common set of rules for the admission of economic migrants with a Green Paper on an EU approach to managing economic migration[13], which led to the adoption of a 'policy plan on legal migration' at the end of 2005[14]. In July 2006 the Commission adopted a communication on policy priorities in the fight against illegal immigration of third-country nationals[15] which aims to strike a balance between security and basic rights of individuals during all stages of the illegal immigration process. In June 2007, Council conclusions on the strengthening of integration policies in the EU by promoting unity in diversity were adopted, while in September 2007, the Commission presented its third annual report on migration and integration[16].

---

(8) In June 2008, the European Parliament approved at first reading a new Directive on the return of illegal immigrants, a key step towards a European immigration policy that aims to encourage the voluntary return of illegal immigrants but otherwise lay down minimum standards for their treatment.

(9) http://eur-lex.europa.eu/LexUriServ/site/en/oj/2003/l_251/l_25120031003en00120018.pdf.

(10) http://eur-lex.europa.eu/LexUriServ/site/en/oj/2004/l_016/l_01620040123en00440053.pdf.

(11) http://eur-lex.europa.eu/LexUriServ/site/en/oj/2004/l_375/l_37520041223en00120018.pdf.

(12) http://eur-lex.europa.eu/LexUriServ/site/en/oj/2005/l_289/l_28920051103en00150022.pdf.

(13) COM(2004) 811; http://ec.europa.eu/justice_home/doc_centre/immigration/work/doc/com_2004_811_en.pdf.

(14) COM(2005) 669; http://eur-lex.europa.eu/LexUriServ/site/en/com/2005/com2005_0669en01.pdf.

(15) COM(2006) 402; http://eur-lex.europa.eu/LexUriServ/site/en/com/2006/com2006_0402en01.pdf.

(16) COM(2007) 512; http://ec.europa.eu/justice_home/fsj/immigration/docs/com_2007_512_en.pdf.

The 1951 Geneva Convention relating to the Status of Refugees (as amended by the 1967 New York Protocol) has for more than 50 years defined who is a refugee, and laid down a common approach towards refugees that has been one of the cornerstones for the development of a common asylum system within the EU. Asylum is a form of protection given by a state on its territory. It is granted to a person who is unable to seek protection in his/her country of citizenship and/or residence, in particular for fear of being persecuted for reasons of race, religion, nationality, membership of a particular social group, or political opinion.

Since the beginning of 1990s, the flow of persons seeking international protection in the EU has been such that the Member States have decided to find common solutions to this challenge. The European Commission adopted on 17 February 2006 a communication on strengthened practical cooperation in the area of asylum presenting a vision of how Member States should further cooperate on asylum with a view to the establishment of a fully harmonised EU system. A number of directives in this area have been developed, the four main legal instruments on asylum including:

* the Reception Conditions Directive [17];
* the Asylum Procedures Directive [18];
* the Qualification Directive [19], and;
* the Dublin Regulation [20].

The EU is also focusing on the need for better coordination in partnership with third countries to deal more effectively with root causes and to provide for durable solutions to resolve refugee situations. In this context, the Council has invited the Commission to develop Regional Protection Programmes (RPP) to enhance protection capacity and develop resettlement programmes. A new financial instrument was adopted in March 2004 to establish a programme for financial and technical assistance to third countries in the area of migration and asylum (AENEAS); it is a multi-annual programme for the period 2004-2008.

Definitions and data availability

Eurostat produces statistics on a range of issues related to international migration and asylum. Data are supplied on a monthly, quarterly and annual basis by national statistical institutes and by ministries of justice and the interior. Whereas some Member States base their migration flow and migrant population stock statistics on population registers, others may use sample surveys or data extracted from administrative procedures such as the issuing of residence permits. Many statistics are currently sent to Eurostat as part of a joint migration data collection organised by Eurostat in cooperation with the United Nations Statistical Division, the United Nations Economic Commission for Europe and the International Labour Office.

(17) Council Directive 2003/9/EC of 27 January 2003; http://eur-lex.europa.eu/LexUriServ/LexUriServ.do?uri=OJ:L:2003:031:0018:0025:EN:PDF.

(18) Council Directive 2005/85/EC of 1 December 2005; http://eur-lex.europa.eu/LexUriServ/LexUriServ.do?uri=OJ:L:2005:326:0013:0034:EN:PDF.

(19) Council Directive 2004/83/EC of 29 April 2004 on minimum standards for the qualification and status of third country nationals or stateless persons as refugees or as persons who otherwise need international protection and the content of the protection granted; http://eur-lex.europa.eu/LexUriServ/LexUriServ.do?uri=CELEX:32004L0083:EN:HTML.

(20) Council Regulation (EC) No 343/2003 of 18 February 2003 establishing the criteria and mechanisms for determining the Member State responsible for examining an asylum application lodged in one of the Member States by a third-country national; http://eur-lex.europa.eu/LexUriServ/LexUriServ.do?uri=OJ:L:2003:050:0001:0010:EN:PDF.

Most important areas of Community statistics have a clear basis in European law, defining the responsibilities of Member States and of Eurostat in terms of the collection, transmission and publication of data. The **migration statistics** domain had been unusual in not having a legal base, being instead governed by a series of voluntary agreements between Eurostat and the data suppliers in Member States. While this may have been appropriate in the past, it became clear that the growing policy importance of this subject at both national and European level meant that a more formal approach was necessary. In the autumn of 2005 the Commission adopted a proposal for a regulation on statistics on migration and international protection, which was adopted by the European Parliament and the Council by the summer of 2007[21]. The adoption of the Regulation 862/2007 is designed as a step towards the provision of reliable and harmonised statistics on migration and asylum.

The focus of the Regulation is to provide harmonised statistical definitions based on existing international standards and on European legislation and policy on immigration, asylum and border control issues. Although these definitions must be applied, Member States remain free to use any appropriate data sources, according to national availability and practice. The Regulation allows for the use of scientifically sound estimates in cases where directly observed data are not available. To allow Member States time to make necessary amendments to their data collection systems, the proposed Regulation also allows for data to be supplied according to national definitions in the first year following its coming into force (2008), which will then be reported in the following year. The Regulation provides a framework which needs to be completed through the adoption of implementing measures in the form of Commission Regulations.

The Regulation covers most of Eurostat's existing statistics on migration related issues. Statistics on immigration and emigration flows, together with statistics on the citizenship and country of birth composition of the resident population, provide information on the impact of migration on the size and structure of the population. Statistics on asylum applications and the subsequent decisions to grant or refuse refugee status or other types of international protection will be adapted somewhat under the Regulation. For example, asylum applications statistics will be collected on a monthly basis as these are needed to allow a continuous monitoring of short-term variations in the origin and numbers of asylum seekers. In comparison, data on appeals against asylum decisions are relatively complex to collect and are not needed so frequently – and so will only be collected annually.

The only new area of statistics covered by the Regulation is that of residence permits issued to non-EU citizens. These statistics offer a useful insight into the reasons for immigration – as a distinction can be made between permits issued under different immigration rules regarding the reunification of families, economic migrants, and persons admitted as students. A further aspect of the Regulation is that most of the statistics to be collected will include a disaggregation by age and sex. This is of particular interest when trying to monitor policies aimed at preventing the trafficking of women and children.

---

(21) Regulation (EC) No 862/2007 of the European Parliament and of the Council of 11 July 2007; http://eur-lex.europa.eu/LexUriServ/site/en/oj/2007/l_199/l_19920070731en00230029.pdf.

A **national citizen** is defined as a person who is a citizen of the country in which he or she is currently resident. **Non-nationals** are persons who are not citizens of the country in which they are currently resident.

Net migration is the difference between immigration into and emigration from the country during the year (net migration is therefore negative when the number of emigrants exceeds the number of immigrants). Since several countries either do not have accurate figures on immigration and emigration or have no figures at all, net migration is sometimes estimated on the basis of the difference between population change and natural increase between two dates. These statistics on net migration (including corrections) are therefore affected by the statistical inaccuracies in the two components of the population change as well as administrative corrections. Net migration gives no indication of the relative scale of the separate immigration and emigration flows to and from a country; a country may report low net migration but experience very high immigration and emigration flows. **Immigrants** are those persons arriving or returning from abroad to take up residence in a country for a certain period, having previously been resident elsewhere. **Emigrants** are people leaving their country of usual residence and effectively taking up residence in another country.

The **acquisition of citizenship** refers to grants of citizenship of the reporting country to persons who have previously been citizens of another country or who have been stateless.

An **asylum applicant** is defined as a person who has requested protection under: either Article 1 of the 1951 Geneva (amended by the 1967 New York Protocol), or, within the remit of the United Nations

Convention Against Torture and other forms of cruel or inhuman treatment (UNCAT) or the European Convention on Human Rights or other relevant instruments of protection. This definition is intended to refer to all who apply for protection on an individual basis, irrespective of whether they lodge their application on arrival at an airport or land border, or from inside the country, and irrespective of whether they entered the territory legally (for example, as a tourist) or illegally. An **asylum seeker** is a person awaiting a decision on an application for refugee status or another form of international protection. A **refugee** (as defined by Article 1 of the 1951 UN Convention) is someone with a well-founded fear of being persecuted for reasons of race, religion, nationality, membership of a particular social group or political opinion. Data on **asylum decisions** refer to the date on which a decision was made, not to the date of the asylum application. Data is collected on decisions at 1st instance. **Total decisions** cover positive decisions, negative decisions and other non-status decisions. These figures only cover grants of refugee status as defined by Article 1 of the Geneva Convention of 28 July 1951 relating to the status of refugees, as amended by the New York Protocol of 31 January 1967; they therefore exclude grants of other types of protection status such as humanitarian protection.

Main findings

While net migration into the EU has been positive and generally rising since the end of the 1980s, there is a volatile nature to migratory patterns over time. After a rapid increase during the first years of the 21st century, with 2 million more immigrants than emigrants in 2003, net migration has decreased somewhat since in the EU-27. Net migration ranged between 1.64 and 2.03 million per annum between 2002 and 2007, while net migration was never over the threshold of a million before 2002. When expressed as a ratio in relation to the total population, immigration accounted for 0.39 % of the total number of inhabitants in the EU-27 in 2007.

The vast majority of the Member States reported positive net migration (including corrections) the only exceptions with negative net migration (including corrections) in 2007 were Poland (-20 500), Lithuania (-5 200), the Netherlands (-1 600), Bulgaria (-1 400) and Latvia (-600). In relative terms, positive net migration accounted for 1.64 % of the population in Cyprus in 2007, while Spain (1.58 %), Ireland (1.49 %) and Luxembourg (1.26 %) were the only other countries to record net migration above the threshold of 1 % of the total population. At the other end of the scale, the loss of population through net migration ranged from 0.01 % of the total population of the Netherlands to 0.15 % in Lithuania.

There are a number of different types of migration that may be identified: among them, economic migration (the search for work), family reunification, retirement, study, or asylum. In most of the Member States for which data are available for 2006, a majority of migrants were at the lower end of the working age range (between 15 and 34 years). Indeed, in the United Kingdom this age group accounted for more than three quarters of all immigrants (76.4 %).

Most Member States counted more non-EU nationals than citizens of EU-27 Member States among their foreign immigrants. The exceptions were Germany, Ireland, Luxembourg, Hungary, Austria and Slovakia, where more EU-27 citizens than non-EU citizens immigrated. Returning nationals accounted for a minority of immigrants in most countries. However, in Denmark, Lithuania, Poland (permanent stays only) and Finland there were more national immigrants returning home than either non-national EU-27 immigrants or immigrants from countries outside of the EU.

There are two different categories of person which should be taken into account when studying asylum statistics. The first includes persons who have lodged an asylum claim and whose claim is under consideration by a relevant authority. The second is composed of persons who have been recognised, after consideration, as refugees or have been granted another kind of international protection. Asylum-seekers generally remain within the territory of the Member State concerned during consideration of their claims. The number of asylum-seekers has decreased over the past few years in the EU, having peaked in 1992 (670 000 applications in the EU-15) and again in 2001 (424 000 applications in the EU-27). By 2007, there were an estimated 218 900 asylum applications received in the EU-27, a slight upturn on the figure for 2006. More applications for asylum were lodged in Sweden than any other Member State in 2007, with France, the United Kingdom, Greece and Germany being the other main recipients of applications. Only a minority of asylum applicants are recognised as refugees or are granted subsidiary protection. Over half (57.8 %) of all EU-27 asylum decisions in 2006 resulted in a rejection, while some 55 135 persons were granted refugee status or subsidiary protection the same year.

Table 3.16: Net migration (including corrections)
(1 000)

	1997	1998	1999	2000	2001	2002	2003	2004	2005	2006	2007
EU-27 (1)	430	529	980	725	600	1 852	2 035	1 875	1 660	1 639	1 908
Euro area (1)	:	434	835	975	1 235	1 658	1 806	1 606	1 404	1 319	1 579
Belgium	10	12	16	14	36	41	35	36	51	53	62
Bulgaria	0	0	0	0	-214	1	0	0	0	0	-1
Czech Republic	12	9	9	7	-43	12	26	19	36	35	84
Denmark	12	11	9	10	12	10	7	5	7	10	20
Germany	93	47	202	168	275	219	142	82	82	26	48
Estonia	-7	-7	-1	0	0	0	0	0	0	0	0
Ireland	17	16	24	32	39	33	31	48	66	67	64
Greece	61	55	45	29	38	38	35	41	40	40	41
Spain	94	159	238	390	441	649	625	610	641	605	702
France (1)	:	-1	150	158	173	184	189	105	92	90	71
Italy	50	56	35	50	50	345	612	557	324	377	494
Cyprus	5	4	4	4	5	7	12	16	14	9	13
Latvia	-9	-6	-4	-6	-5	-2	-1	-1	-1	-2	-1
Lithuania	-22	-22	-21	-20	-3	-2	-6	-10	-9	-5	-5
Luxembourg	4	4	4	3	3	3	5	4	6	5	6
Hungary	18	17	17	17	10	4	16	18	17	21	14
Malta	1	0	0	10	2	2	2	2	2	2	2
Netherlands	30	44	44	57	56	28	7	-10	-23	-26	-2
Austria	2	8	20	17	44	35	38	62	56	29	31
Poland	-12	-13	-14	-410	-17	-18	-14	-9	-13	-36	-20
Portugal	29	32	38	47	65	70	64	47	38	26	20
Romania	-13	-6	-3	-4	-558	-2	-7	-10	-7	-6	1
Slovenia	-1	-5	11	3	5	2	4	2	6	6	14
Slovakia	2	1	1	-22	1	1	1	3	3	4	7
Finland	5	4	3	2	6	5	6	7	9	11	14
Sweden	6	11	14	24	29	31	29	25	27	51	54
United Kingdom	58	97	138	144	151	158	178	227	193	247	175
Croatia	0	-4	-23	-52	14	9	12	12	8	7	6
FYR of Macedonia	-2	-2	-2	-3	-3	-25	-3	0	-1	-1	0
Turkey	101	99	79	58	2	-1	-3	1	-1	-3	0
Iceland	0	1	1	2	1	0	0	1	4	5	4
Liechtenstein	0	1	0	0	0	0	0	0	0	0	0
Norway	10	13	19	10	8	17	11	13	18	24	40
Switzerland	-3	11	25	24	41	48	42	38	32	37	69

(1) Break in series: for 1997 France includes metropolitan regions only.

Source: Eurostat (tsdde230)

Figure 3.18: Net migration (including corrections), EU-27 (1)
(1 000)

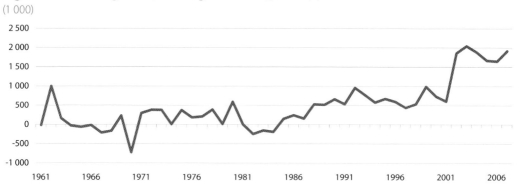

(1) Break in series: up to and including 1997 France includes metropolitan regions only; 2007 data are provisional.

Source: Eurostat (tsdde230)

Figure 3.19: Net migration rate (including corrections) (1)
(% of the total population)

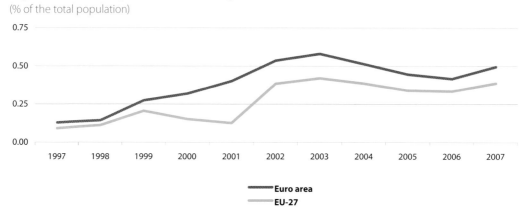

(1) Break in series: for 1997 France includes metropolitan regions only; 2007 data are provisional.

Source: Eurostat (tsdde230 and tps00001)

Figure 3.20: Net migration (including corrections), 2007 (1)

(% of the population)

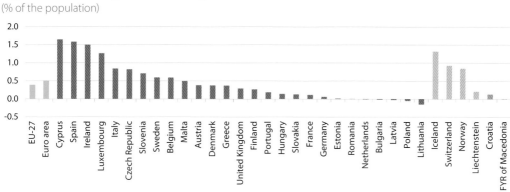

(1) EU-27, euro area, Germany, Ireland, Greece, Spain, France, Italy, Cyprus, Hungary, Malta, Portugal, Slovenia, the United Kingdom, the former Yugoslav Republic of Macedonia and Liechtenstein, provisional.

Source: Eurostat (tsdde230 and tps00001)

Figure 3.21: Immigration by age, 2006 (1)

(%)

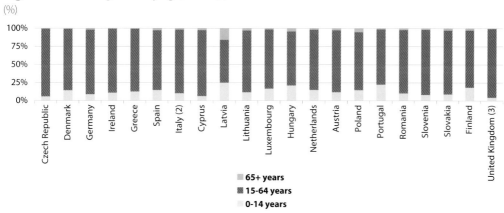

- 65+ years
- 15-64 years
- 0-14 years

(1) Belgium, Bulgaria, Estonia, France and Malta, not available.
(2) 2003.
(3) 2005.

Source: Eurostat (migr_immictz)

Table 3.17: Immigration by age, 2006

	Total immigrants (persons)	Immigration by age (% of total immigration)										
		<15	15-24	25-29	30-34	35-39	40-44	45-49	50-54	55-59	60-64	65+
Belgium (1)	81 913	:	:	:	:	:	:	:	:	:	:	:
Bulgaria	:	:	:	:	:	:	:	:	:	:	:	:
Czech Republic	68 183	5.5	26.0	18.1	14.5	11.3	9.6	7.5	4.1	2.0	0.6	0.7
Denmark	56 750	14.0	36.0	18.2	10.7	7.0	4.8	3.2	2.1	1.6	1.3	1.1
Germany	661 855	8.5	25.3	17.5	13.2	10.2	8.1	6.6	4.6	2.6	1.3	2.1
Estonia	:	:	:	:	:	:	:	:	:	:	:	:
Ireland	103 260	:	:	:	:	:	:	:	:	:	:	:
Greece (2)	86 693	12.3	19.4	17.5	14.7	11.1	8.3	7.0	5.0	2.9	1.1	0.8
Spain	840 844	14.4	23.1	17.3	12.9	9.5	6.6	4.8	3.4	2.7	2.2	2.9
France (3)	182 390	:	:	:	:	:	:	:	:	:	:	:
Italy (1)	440 301	10.0	19.1	20.5	16.2	11.2	8.3	6.0	3.7	1.8	1.3	2.0
Cyprus	15 545	6.0	19.8	19.4	13.7	11.3	9.1	5.9	4.0	3.8	3.6	2.6
Latvia	2 801	24.8	12.4	9.2	8.5	7.5	5.4	5.5	3.0	4.4	3.2	16.0
Lithuania	7 745	11.3	21.5	19.4	12.9	8.9	8.1	7.1	3.5	2.7	1.4	3.2
Luxembourg	14 352	16.4	17.8	18.3	14.8	10.9	8.2	5.2	3.3	2.2	1.1	1.7
Hungary	21 520	21.0	20.8	15.3	10.2	7.7	5.3	4.8	3.6	3.5	3.4	4.4
Malta	1 829	:	:	:	:	:	:	:	:	:	:	:
Netherlands	101 150	14.7	24.9	18.9	13.1	9.6	6.5	4.3	2.8	2.0	1.2	2.0
Austria	100 972	11.5	26.4	17.2	12.1	9.5	7.1	5.3	3.7	2.7	2.0	2.7
Poland (4)	10 802	14.4	15.3	15.0	10.3	7.1	6.9	8.2	7.9	6.3	3.4	5.3
Portugal (2)	27 703	22.4	18.6	14.3	13.6	10.3	7.9	5.6	3.0	1.9	1.1	1.5
Romania (2)	7 714	10.0	13.1	11.9	14.9	15.4	11.4	8.4	6.5	4.2	1.9	2.3
Slovenia	20 016	7.9	25.0	16.6	12.9	11.2	9.4	7.3	4.4	2.2	1.2	2.0
Slovakia	12 611	8.7	22.1	14.1	13.1	11.4	8.7	6.7	5.6	4.2	2.4	3.1
Finland	22 451	18.1	20.6	17.5	13.0	8.9	6.5	4.4	3.5	2.7	1.9	2.9
Sweden	95 750	20.0	20.5	17.5	13.7	9.4	6.5	4.3	2.7	1.9	1.5	2.0
United Kingdom (5)	529 008	4.1	39.5	24.4	12.5	7.8	4.7	3.0	1.9	0.4	0.7	0.8

(1) 2003.
(2) Excluding nationals.
(3) Excluding nationals and EU-15 foreigners.
(4) Immigrants for permanent stay only.
(5) Excluding flows from Ireland; data by age, 2005.

Source: Eurostat (migr_immictz)

Figure 3.22: Immigration by broad group of citizenship, 2006 (1)

(% of total immigrants)

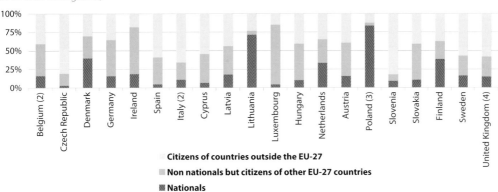

- Citizens of countries outside the EU-27
- Non nationals but citizens of other EU-27 countries
- Nationals

(1) Bulgaria, Estonia, Greece, France, Malta, Portugal and Romania, not available.
(2) 2003.
(3) Immigrants for permanent stay only.
(4) Excluding immigrants from Ireland, whatever their citizenship.

Source: Eurostat (migr_immictz)

Figure 3.23: Asylum applications, 2007 (1)

(persons)

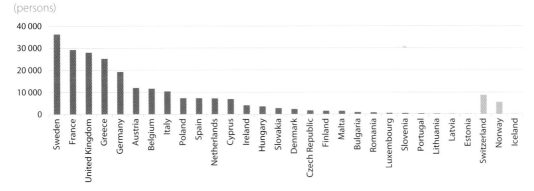

(1) Provisional figures for EU-27, 218 935 asylum applications in 2007; euro area, 136 100 asylum applications in 2007; Italy, Iceland, Norway and Switzerland, 2006.

Source: Eurostat (tps00021)

Table 3.18: Asylum applications

(persons)

	1997	1998	1999	2000	2001	2002	2003	2004	2005	2006	2007
EU-27	:	313 645	380 450	406 585	424 180	421 470	344 800	276 675	234 675	197 410	218 935
Euro area	:	231 670	265 105	273 400	271 355	245 335	215 480	181 720	168 720	129 855	136 100
Belgium	11 790	21 965	35 780	42 690	24 505	18 800	13 585	12 400	12 575	8 870	11 575
Bulgaria	370	835	1 350	1 755	2 430	2 890	1 320	985	700	500	815
Czech Republic	2 110	4 085	7 355	8 790	18 095	8 485	11 400	5 300	3 590	2 730	1 585
Denmark	5 100	5 700	6 530	10 345	12 510	5 945	4 390	3 235	2 280	1 960	2 225
Germany	104 355	98 645	94 775	78 565	88 285	71 125	50 565	35 605	28 915	21 030	19 165
Estonia	0	25	25	5	10	10	15	10	10	5	15
Ireland	3 880	4 625	7 725	10 940	10 325	11 635	7 485	4 265	4 305	4 240	3 935
Greece	4 375	2 950	1 530	3 085	5 500	5 665	8 180	4 470	9 050	12 265	25 115
Spain	4 975	4 935	8 405	7 925	9 490	6 310	5 765	5 365	5 050	5 295	7 195
France	21 415	22 375	30 905	38 745	47 290	51 085	59 770	58 545	49 735	30 750	29 160
Italy	1 890	13 100	18 450	15 195	17 400	16 015	13 705	9 630	9 345	10 350	:
Cyprus	:	225	790	650	1 620	950	4 405	9 675	7 715	4 540	6 780
Latvia	:	35	20	5	15	25	5	5	20	10	35
Lithuania	240	160	145	305	425	365	395	165	100	145	125
Luxembourg	435	1 710	2 930	625	685	1 040	1 550	1 575	800	525	425
Hungary	:	7 120	11 500	7 800	9 555	6 410	2 400	1 600	1 610	2 115	3 420
Malta	70	160	255	160	155	350	455	995	1 165	1 270	1 380
Netherlands	34 445	45 215	39 275	43 895	32 580	18 665	13 400	9 780	12 345	14 465	7 100
Austria	6 720	13 805	20 130	18 285	30 125	39 355	32 360	24 635	22 460	13 350	11 920
Poland	3 580	3 425	3 060	4 660	4 480	5 170	6 810	7 925	5 240	4 225	7 205
Portugal	250	355	305	225	235	245	115	115	115	130	225
Romania	1 425	1 235	1 665	1 365	2 280	1 000	885	545	485	380	660
Slovenia	70	335	745	9 245	1 510	650	1 050	1 090	1 550	500	370
Slovakia	645	505	1 320	1 555	8 150	9 745	10 300	11 395	3 550	2 850	2 640
Finland	970	1 270	3 105	3 170	1 650	3 445	3 090	3 575	3 595	2 275	1 405
Sweden	9 680	12 840	11 220	16 285	23 500	33 015	31 355	23 160	17 530	24 320	36 205
United Kingdom	32 500	46 015	71 160	80 315	71 365	103 080	60 045	40 625	30 840	28 320	27 905
Iceland	:	:	:	:	:	:	:	:	85	40	:
Norway	2 270	8 375	10 160	10 845	14 770	17 480	16 020	7 950	5 400	5 320	:
Switzerland	23 185	39 735	43 935	15 780	18 720	24 255	18 920	12 730	8 650	8 580	:

Source: Eurostat (tps00021)

Table 3.19: Acquisition of citizenship and asylum applications
(persons)

| | Acquisition of citizenship | | Asylum applications | | Asylum decisions | | | | | |
| | | | | | Number of decisions | | of which, rejections (%) | | Number of positive decisions | |
	2005	2006	2006	2007	2006	2007	2006	2007	2006	2007
EU-27	:	:	197 410	218 935	237 970	:	57.8	:	55 135	:
Euro area	:	:	129 855	136 100	146 205	:	66.9	:	23 490	:
Belgium	:	:	8 870	11 575	8 345	:	70.8	:	2 440	:
Bulgaria	:	6 738	500	815	695	770	30.9	31.8	95	335
Czech Republic	2 626	2 346	2 730	1 585	3 020	2 280	72.7	68.9	365	390
Denmark	10 197	7 961	1 960	2 225	925	850	81.6	44.1	170	475
Germany	117 241	124 566	21 030	19 165	30 760	28 570	57.8	44.6	1 950	7 870
Estonia	7 072	4 781	5	15	5	15	100.0	66.7	0	5
Ireland	4 073	5 763	4 240	3 935	4 245	3 810	90.6	90.0	395	375
Greece	:	1 962	12 265	25 115	11 180	20 990	85.9	98.5	195	165
Spain	42 860	62 375	5 295	7 195	4 065	5 400	95.0	95.5	205	245
France	154 827	147 868	30 750	29 160	37 495	29 150	92.4	88.5	2 855	3 350
Italy	:	35 266	10 350	:	9 260	:	39.7	:	5 215	:
Cyprus	3 952	:	4 540	6 780	5 585	7 170	31.9	32.3	170	210
Latvia	20 106	18 964	10	35	15	20	0.0	50.0	10	10
Lithuania	435	467	145	125	130	145	19.2	34.5	95	60
Luxembourg	954	1 128	525	425	890	1 035	55.6	41.5	370	540
Hungary	:	6 101	2 115	3 420	2 020	2 805	60.1	49.0	200	250
Malta	:	474	1 270	1 380	1 185	955	53.6	34.6	550	625
Netherlands	28 488	29 089	14 465	7 100	14 180	:	53.0	:	4 345	:
Austria	34 876	25 746	13 350	11 920	15 490	16 045	37.9	41.4	4 065	5 195
Poland	2 866	989	4 225	7 205	7 280	6 185	12.8	29.7	2 465	3 035
Portugal	:	3 627	130	225	105	110	71.4	77.3	30	25
Romania	767	29	380	660	365	590	74.0	57.6	55	135
Slovenia	2 684	3 204	500	370	900	540	63.3	50.0	10	10
Slovakia	1 393	1 125	2 850	2 640	2 815	2 970	30.6	39.7	10	95
Finland	5 683	4 433	2 275	1 405	2 520	2 020	61.1	51.7	695	840
Sweden	39 573	51 239	24 320	36 205	46 395	32 470	27.3	37.5	22 745	15 640
United Kingdom	161 755	154 015	28 320	27 905	27 520	27 630	74.2	70.5	5 045	6 805
Croatia	:	12 292	:	:	:	:	:	:	:	:
FYR of Macedonia	2 660	2 147	:	:	:	:	:	:	:	:
Turkey	6 901	5 072	:	:	:	:	:	:	:	:
Iceland	:	:	40	:	30	:	66.7	:	0	:
Norway	12 655	11 955	5 320	:	4 215	:	48.0	:	1 685	:
Switzerland	38 437	46 711	8 580	:	:	:	:	:	:	:

Source: Eurostat (tps00024, tps00021, tps00163 and tps00164)

Education

Education, vocational training and more generally lifelong learning play a vital role in both an economic and social context. The opportunities which the EU offers its citizens for living, studying and working in other countries make a major contribution to cross-cultural understanding, personal development and the realisation of the EU's full economic potential. Each year, well over a million EU citizens of all ages benefit from EU-funded educational, vocational and citizenship-building programmes.

The Treaty establishing the European Community[1] acknowledged the importance of these areas by stating that 'the Community shall contribute to the development of quality education by encouraging cooperation between Member States and, if necessary, by supporting and supplementing their action ... The Community shall implement a vocational training policy which shall support and supplement the action of the Member States'. As such, the European Commission follows up on policy cooperation and work with the Member States, while funding programmes, such as the Lifelong Learning Programme (LLP).

The European Council adopted in 2001 a set of goals and objectives for education and training systems that are to be attained by 2010[2], with education ministers agreeing on three goals:

- to improve the quality and effectiveness of education and training systems;
- to ensure that they are accessible to all;
- to open up education and training to the wider world.

These ambitious goals were subsequently subdivided into specific objectives covering the various types and levels of education and training, including areas such as: teacher training; basic skills; the integration of information and communication technologies (ICTs); efficiency of investments; language learning; lifelong guidance; flexibility to make learning accessible to all; mobility; and citizenship education.

---

(1) Consolidated version of the Treaty establishing the European Community, Chapter 3, Articles 149(1) and 150(1) (OJ C 352, 24.12.2002, p. 33); http://eur-lex.europa.eu/en/treaties/dat/12002E/pdf/12002E_EN.pdf.

(2) http://ec.europa.eu/education/policies/2010/doc/repfutobjen.pdf.

Under the principle of subsidiarity every Member State retains responsibility for organising their education system and deciding its content. The EU does however promote cooperation in this field through a variety of funding and action programmes. Indeed, political cooperation has been strengthened through the Education and Training 2010 work programme which integrates previous actions in the fields of education and training at a European level. Five EU benchmarks were set for 2010:

- to limit the rate of early school leavers to no more than 10 %;
- to increase to at least 15 % the total number of graduates in maths, science and technology, while at the same time, reducing the gender imbalance in these subjects;
- to aim for 85 % of 22 year olds to have completed an upper secondary education;
- to halve the number of low-achieving 15 year olds in reading, maths and science, and;
- to increase the EU average level of participation in lifelong learning to at least 12.5 % of the adult working-age population (25 to 64 years old).

As of 2007, the Lifelong Learning Programme become the flagship programme in the field of education and training, covering all learning opportunities from childhood to old age. Over the period 2007 to 2013, this programme has a budget of EUR 7 000 million in order to support projects that foster interchange, cooperation and mobility between education and training systems within the EU. It is made-up of four sub-programmes that focus on the different stages of education and training:

- Comenius for schools;
- Erasmus for higher education;
- Leonardo da Vinci for vocational education and training, and;
- Grundtvig for adult education.

Quantified targets have been set for each of the sub programmes:

- Comenius should involve at least three million pupils in joint educational activities, over the period of the programme;
- Erasmus should reach a total of three million individual participants in student mobility actions;
- Leonardo da Vinci should increase placements in enterprises to 80 000 persons per year by the end of the programme, and;
- Grundtvig should support the mobility of 7 000 individuals involved in adult education each year by 2013

The measurement of progress towards these objectives within the field of education policy requires a range of comparable statistics on enrolment in education and training, numbers of graduates and teachers, language learning, student and researcher mobility, educational expenditure, as well as data on educational attainment and adult learning.

4.1 School enrolment and levels of education

The standards on international statistics on education coming from administrative sources are set by three international organisations, jointly managing data collection:

- the United Nations Educational, scientific, and Cultural Organisation institute for statistics (UNESCO-UIS);
- the Organisation for Economic Co-operation and Development (OECD), and;
- the Statistical Office of the European Union (Eurostat).

The UNESCO / OECD / Eurostat (UOE) questionnaire on education statistics constitutes the main source of information and is the basis for the core components of the Eurostat database on education statistics; Eurostat also collects data on regional enrolments and foreign language learning. The definitions and methodological requirements for the joint UOE data collection and for the Eurostat data collection are available on the Eurostat website[3]. Data on educational attainment and adult learning are mainly provided by household surveys, i.e. the EU Labour Force Survey, which will soon be complemented by an adult education survey[4], while the continuous vocational training survey (CVTS) provides information on training participation, volume and costs for enterprises.

Introduction

School helps young people acquire basic life skills and competences necessary for their personal development. Besides their own personal development, the quality of a pupil's school experience affects their place in society, educational attainment, and employment opportunities too. The quality of the education experienced by pupils is linked directly to the quality of teaching, which in turn is linked to the demands placed upon teachers, the training they receive and the roles they are asked to fill. With this in mind, several Member States are in the process of revising their school curricula in line with the changing needs of society and the economy, as well as reflecting on how to improve teacher training and evaluation.

Demographic trends in the last three decades reflect reductions in birth rates, that have resulted in the structure of the EU's population ageing and the proportion of those aged under 30 decreasing in the majority of Member States. These changes can have a significant impact on human and material resources required for the sound functioning of education systems – such as average class sizes or teacher recruitment strategies.

Most Europeans spend significantly longer in education than the legal minimum requirement. This reflects the choice to enrol in higher education, as well as increased enrolment in pre-primary education and wider participation in lifelong learning initiatives, such as mature (adult) students returning to education – often in order to retrain or equip themselves for a career change.

(3) http://circa.europa.eu/Public/irc/dsis/edtcs/library?l=/public/unesco_collection.
(4) http://epp.eurostat.ec.europa.eu/cache/ITY_OFFPUB/KS-CC-05-005/EN/KS-CC-05-005-EN.PDF.

At the age of 4, a high proportion of children in the EU are already enrolled in pre-primary educational institutions. The general objectives for pre-primary education are fairly similar across countries, focusing on the development of children's independence, well-being, self-confidence, citizenship, and preparation for life and learning at school.

On average, compulsory education lasts 9 or 10 years in most of the EU: lasting longest in Hungary, the Netherlands and the United Kingdom. Age is the sole criterion for admission to compulsory primary education, which starts at the age of 5 or 6 in most countries, although the Nordic countries, as well as Bulgaria and Estonia have a compulsory starting age of 7.

While national curricula include broadly the same subjects across the Member States, the amount of time allocated to each subject varies considerably. In addition, there are wide-ranging differences in the freedoms that teachers have to shape the content of their classes or follow a strict curriculum. The most significant differences between countries tend to relate to the degree of instruction given in foreign languages, information and communication technology, or religion. In contrast, all countries allocate a considerable amount of time to teach their mother tongue and mathematics.

Teaching time tends to be more evenly spread across subjects in compulsory secondary education, with more emphasis given to natural and social sciences, as well as foreign languages. Pupils from a particular country follow the same common curriculum throughout their full-time compulsory education in most Member States, although in Germany, Luxembourg, the Netherlands and Austria parents have to choose a particular type of education for their child at the end of primary school.

The Comenius programme addresses developments in education and school policy and has the following goals:

- to improve and increase the mobility of pupils and educational staff;
- to enhance and increase partnerships between schools in different Member States, with at least three million pupils taking part in joint educational activities by 2010;
- to encourage language learning, innovative ICT-based content, services and better teaching techniques and practices;
- to enhance the quality and European dimension of teacher training, and;
- to improve pedagogical approaches and school management.

Member States have themselves set a number of other benchmarks for improving education. These include benchmarks for, among others, reading proficiency, attainment in mathematics, science and technology, early school leaving, and the completion of secondary school.

Definitions and data availability

The **International Standard Classification of Education (ISCED)** is the basis for international education statistics, describing different levels of education, as well as fields of education and training[5]. The current version, ISCED 97 distinguishes seven levels of education:

- ISCED level 0: **pre-primary education** – defined as the initial stage of organised instruction; it is school- or centre-based and is designed for children aged at least 3 years;
- ISCED level 1: **primary education** – begins between 5 and 7 years of age, is compulsory in all countries and generally lasts from four to six years;
- ISCED level 2: **lower secondary education** – continues the basic programmes of the primary level, although teaching is typically more subject-focused; usually, the end of this level coincides with the end of compulsory education;
- ISCED level 3: **upper secondary education** – generally begins at the end of compulsory education; the entrance age is typically 15 or 16 years and entrance qualifications and other minimum entry requirements are usually needed; instruction is often more subject-oriented and typical duration varies from two to five years;
- ISCED level 4: **post-secondary non-tertiary education** – straddles the boundary between upper secondary and tertiary education; typical examples are programmes designed to prepare pupils for studies at level 5 or programmes designed to prepare pupils for direct labour market entry;

- ISCED level 5: **tertiary education (first stage)** – entry normally requires the successful completion of level 3 or 4; includes tertiary programmes with academic orientation which are largely theoretically based and occupation orientation which are typically shorter and geared for entry into the labour market;
- ISCED level 6: **tertiary education (second stage)** – leads to an advanced research qualification (Ph.D. or doctorate).

The indicator for **four-year-olds in education** presents the percentage of four-year-olds who are enrolled in education-oriented pre-primary institutions. These institutions provide education-oriented care for young children. They must recruit staff with specialised qualifications in education. Day nurseries, playgroups and day care centres, where the staff are not required to hold a qualification in education, are not included. The indicator for **18-year-olds** who are still in any kind of school (all ISCED levels) provides an indication of the number of young people who have not abandoned their efforts to improve their skills through initial education and it includes both those who had a regular education career without any delays as well as those who are continuing even if they had to repeat some steps in the past.

(5) http://www.unesco.org/education/information/nfsunesco/doc/isced_1997.htm.

Pupil-teacher ratios are calculated by dividing the number of full-time-equivalent pupils and students in each level of education by the number of full-time-equivalent teachers at the same level; all institutions, both public and private, are included. This ratio should not be confused with average class-size, as: there can be a difference between the number of hours of teaching provided by individual teachers and the number of hours of instruction prescribed for pupils; more than one teacher can be teaching in a class at the same time; or teachers for special education needs can work with small groups or on a one-to-one basis.

The indicator **youth education attainment level** is defined as the proportion of the population aged 20 to 24 having completed at least an upper secondary education, i.e. with an education level ISCED 3a, 3b or 3c long minimum (numerator). The denominator consists of the total population of the same age group, excluding non-response.

The indicator for **early school leavers** is defined as the proportion of the population aged 18 to 24 with at most a lower secondary level of education, who are no longer in further education or training (respondents declared not having received any education or training in the four weeks preceding the survey). The denominator consists of the total population of the same age group, excluding non-response.

Main findings

There were about 93.9 million pupils and students enrolled in educational establishments in the EU-27 in 2006. The highest share of pupils and students in the EU-27 total was accounted for by Germany, where 14.4 million pupils and students attended education establishments in 2006; this figure was 1.7 million higher than the next largest student population that was registered in the United Kingdom, and 2.1 million higher than in France.

The proportion of students found in each level of education varied considerably between the Member States and reflects, to some degree, the demographic structure of each population. The high proportion of pupils in primary education in Luxembourg (46.0 % in 2006) reflects the lack of a developed tertiary education sector in this country, whereas Ireland, Cyprus and Portugal also reported a relatively high proportion of students within primary education (upwards of 40 %) – reflecting relatively high birth rates. At the other end of the spectrum, Greece, Slovenia, the Baltic Member States, Poland and Finland all had relatively high proportions (around one quarter or more) of their student populations within the tertiary education sector.

The figures above exclude pre-primary education – where 86.8 % of all four-year olds attended establishments in the EU-27 in 2006. Enrolment rates in pre-primary education ranged from 100 % in Belgium, France and Italy, to less than one child in two across Finland, Ireland and Poland.

More than three quarters (77.4 %) of all 18-year olds within the EU-27 remained within the education system in 2006. There was a considerable variation in this proportion between the Member States: as six countries reported more than nine out of ten people of this age remaining in education, while less than half of all 18-year-olds were still attending an educational establishment in three of the Member States (Cyprus, Malta and the United Kingdom); note these figures may reflect a number of factors, in particular, the need for students to go abroad to continue their (tertiary) education, or the practise of making students re-take a whole year if their performance at the end of each academic year is not deemed to be satisfactory.

Pupil/teacher ratios within primary education ranged from an average of less than 11 pupils per teacher in Greece, Italy, Lithuania, Luxembourg (2004), Hungary and Portugal in 2006, to almost double that rate in the Ireland, France (2005) and the United Kingdom (all above 19 pupils per teacher). Between 2001 and 2006 there was a general reduction in the average number of pupils per teacher in most of the Member States.

The average number of pupils per teacher was generally lower for secondary education than for primary education, with an average of less than ten pupils for every teacher in Greece, Spain, Luxembourg (2004) and Portugal within upper secondary education. Germany had by far the highest average number of pupils per teacher within the upper secondary education sector (19.5) in 2006, rising from 13.7 pupils per teacher in 2001.

Data on educational attainment show that, in 2007, just over three quarters (78.1 %) of the EU-27's population aged 20 to 24 had completed at least an upper secondary level of education. However, 14.8 % of those aged 18 to 24 (16.9 % of men and 12.7 % of women) were early school leavers, with at most a lower secondary education.

Table 4.1: Pupils and students (excluding pre-primary education) (1)

	Total (ISCED 1-6) (1 000)		Breakdown of total number of pupils and students (% of total)							
			Primary level of education (ISCED 1)		Lower secondary level of education (ISCED 2)		Upper and post-secondary non-tertiary education (ISCED 3-4)		Tertiary education (ISCED 5-6)	
	2001	2006	2001	2006	2001	2006	2001	2006	2001	2006
EU-27	96 001	93 901	31.2	30.4	24.4	24.4	25.7	25.1	17.2	20.0
Euro area (2)	56 630	57 796	31.0	30.4	27.5	26.3	21.7	23.5	18.2	19.3
Belgium	2 304	2 410	33.5	30.4	17.1	18.0	33.8	35.2	15.6	16.4
Bulgaria	1 322	1 193	28.3	22.9	27.7	25.2	25.3	31.5	18.7	20.4
Czech Republic	1 932	1 869	32.6	25.3	26.8	26.1	27.1	30.5	13.5	18.0
Denmark	1 029	1 142	38.5	36.4	20.0	20.6	23.0	22.9	18.5	20.0
Germany	14 515	14 394	24.2	23.1	38.9	36.7	22.1	23.7	14.4	15.9
Estonia	306	278	38.3	28.6	20.7	21.3	22.1	25.6	18.9	24.5
Ireland	987	1 036	45.0	44.6	18.6	17.1	19.6	20.4	16.9	18.0
Greece	1 906	2 042	33.4	31.6	18.9	16.6	22.6	19.8	25.1	32.0
Spain	7 597	7 529	33.0	35.2	26.2	26.3	16.6	14.8	24.1	23.8
France	11 849	12 321	32.4	32.9	27.9	26.7	21.9	22.4	17.1	17.9
Italy	9 144	9 464	30.9	29.7	19.9	19.1	29.4	29.8	19.8	21.4
Cyprus	140	146	45.6	40.9	23.4	22.3	22.5	22.7	8.5	14.1
Latvia	510	472	24.6	16.7	33.7	31.8	21.5	23.8	20.2	27.8
Lithuania	787	784	26.9	19.2	42.2	39.2	13.7	16.2	17.3	25.4
Luxembourg	70	77	47.3	46.0	22.9	23.7	26.1	26.8	3.6	3.5
Hungary	1 924	1 952	25.5	21.3	26.3	24.5	31.1	31.8	17.2	22.5
Malta	78	78	43.0	37.9	37.2	35.6	10.3	15.0	9.5	11.4
Netherlands	3 217	3 318	39.8	38.5	24.1	23.7	20.3	20.3	15.7	17.5
Austria	1 464	1 471	26.8	24.2	26.1	26.8	29.0	31.8	18.1	17.2
Poland	9 153	8 663	35.2	30.0	13.1	18.6	32.4	26.6	19.4	24.8
Portugal	2 002	1 862	40.0	40.4	20.6	21.1	20.0	18.8	19.4	19.7
Romania	3 954	3 831	27.6	24.5	33.4	25.1	25.5	28.6	13.5	21.8
Slovenia	403	403	21.4	23.2	24.7	19.3	31.2	29.1	22.7	28.5
Slovakia	1 114	1 089	26.9	21.6	35.8	31.7	24.3	28.5	12.9	18.2
Finland	1 172	1 246	33.5	29.9	16.4	16.4	26.2	29.0	23.9	24.8
Sweden	2 085	2 096	37.3	33.0	17.1	20.1	27.5	26.7	17.0	20.2
United Kingdom	15 038	12 736	30.6	35.5	15.4	17.9	40.3	28.2	13.7	18.3
Croatia	:	733	:	26.6	:	28.2	:	26.6	:	18.7
FYR of Macedonia	387	366	32.0	28.7	33.2	31.6	24.4	26.4	10.4	13.2
Turkey	14 893	16 275	70.2	65.6	:	:	:	:	10.8	14.4
Iceland	74	84	42.7	36.1	15.9	16.5	27.7	28.7	13.7	18.6
Liechtenstein	:	6	:	36.2	:	26.1	:	27.5	:	10.3
Norway	993	1 068	42.9	40.2	16.3	17.9	21.6	21.8	19.1	20.1
Switzerland	:	1 340	:	38.6	:	22.4	:	23.0	:	15.3
Japan	20 254	19 095	36.5	37.9	20.4	19.1	22.2	20.5	19.6	21.4
United States	63 653	66 793	39.7	36.4	19.7	19.5	19.2	17.9	21.4	26.2

(1) Refer to the Internet metadata file (http://epp.eurostat.ec.europa.eu/cache/ITY_SDDS/en/educ_esms.htm).
(2) EA-13 instead of EA-15 for 2001.

Source: Eurostat (tps00051 and educ_enrl1tl)

Figure 4.1: Four-year-olds in education, 2006 (1)

(% of all four-year-olds)

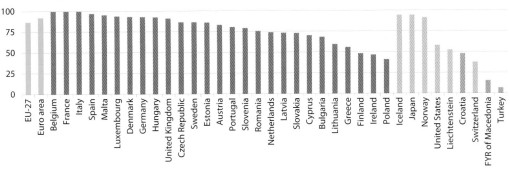

(1) Refer to the Internet metadata file (http://epp.eurostat.ec.europa.eu/cache/ITY_SDDS/en/educ_esms.htm).

Source: Eurostat (tps00053)

Figure 4.2: 18-year-olds in education, 2006 (1)

(% of all 18-year-olds)

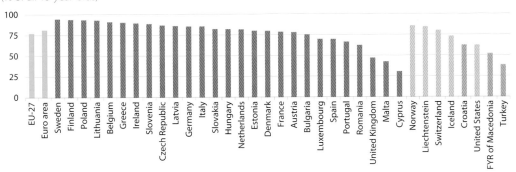

(1) Refer to the Internet metadata file (http://epp.eurostat.ec.europa.eu/cache/ITY_SDDS/en/educ_esms.htm).

Source: Eurostat (tps00060)

Table 4.2: Pupil/teacher ratio in primary, lower and upper secondary education (1)
(average number of pupils per teacher)

	Primary education (ISCED 1)		Lower secondary/second stage of basic education (ISCED 2)		Upper secondary education (ISCED 3)	
	2001	2006	2001	2006	2001	2006
Belgium	13.4	12.6	:	9.4	9.8	10.2
Bulgaria	17.7	15.8	13.0	12.3	11.3	11.7
Czech Republic	19.4	17.3	14.5	12.3	13.1	11.9
Denmark	10.2	:	10.3	11.4	13.3	:
Germany	19.4	18.7	15.7	15.5	13.7	19.5
Estonia	14.7	14.1	11.2	12.3	10.3	13.3
Ireland	20.3	19.4	15.1	:	15.1	14.6
Greece	12.7	10.6	9.8	8.0	11.3	8.3
Spain	14.7	14.2	:	12.5	11.0	7.8
France (2)	19.5	19.4	13.9	14.2	10.9	10.3
Italy	10.8	10.7	9.9	10.3	10.4	11.0
Cyprus	21.1	16.8	15.1	11.6	13.6	12.7
Latvia	17.6	11.8	13.2	10.5	13.2	11.7
Lithuania	16.9	10.7	12.0	8.5	:	:
Luxembourg (3)	11.0	10.7	9.1	:	9.1	9.0
Hungary	11.3	10.4	11.2	10.2	12.5	12.3
Malta	19.0	13.7	9.9	9.3	18.1	14.3
Netherlands	17.2	15.3	:	:	17.1	15.8
Austria	14.3	13.9	9.8	10.4	9.9	11.3
Poland	12.5	11.4	13.1	12.6	16.8	12.7
Portugal	11.6	10.6	9.9	8.3	8.0	7.5
Romania	:	17.1	14.8	12.2	13.3	15.7
Slovenia	13.1	14.9	13.3	10.2	13.8	14.0
Slovakia	20.7	18.6	14.5	13.7	12.9	14.2
Finland	16.1	15.0	10.9	9.7	17.0	15.8
Sweden	12.4	12.1	12.4	11.4	16.6	13.8
United Kingdom	20.8	19.8	17.5	16.7	18.9	11.4
Croatia	:	17.7	:	12.8	:	11.8
FYR of Macedonia	21.2	:	11.4	:	18.9	17.3
Turkey	29.8	26.7	:	:	17.2	15.8
Iceland	12.6	:	:	10.6	10.9	10.8
Liechtenstein	:	10.5	:	7.3	:	11.4
Norway	:	10.9	10.9	10.2	9.2	9.7
Japan	20.6	19.2	16.6	14.9	14.0	12.7
United States	:	14.6	:	14.7	:	15.7

(1) Refer to the Internet metadata file (http://epp.eurostat.ec.europa.eu/cache/ITY_SDDS/en/educ_esms.htm).
(2) 2005 instead of 2006.
(3) 2004 instead of 2006.

Source: Eurostat (tps00054 and educ_iste)

Table 4.3: Youth education attainment level and early school leavers (1)

	Youth education attainment level (%)		Early school leavers (%)					
			Total		Male		Female	
	2002	2007	2002	2007	2002	2007	2002	2007
EU-27	76.7	78.1	17.1	14.8	19.3	16.9	14.9	12.7
Euro area	72.7	74.5	19.3	17.1	22.0	19.6	16.6	14.5
Belgium	81.6	82.6	12.4	12.3	14.9	13.9	9.9	10.7
Bulgaria	77.4	83.3	21.0	16.6	22.5	16.3	19.6	16.9
Czech Republic (2)	92.2	91.8	5.5	5.5	5.3	5.7	5.7	5.4
Denmark	78.6	70.8	8.6	12.4	10.3	15.7	6.9	8.9
Germany	73.3	72.5	12.6	12.7	12.6	13.4	12.6	11.9
Estonia	81.4	80.9	12.6	14.3	15.6	21.0	9.6	:
Ireland	84.0	86.7	14.7	11.5	18.4	14.2	10.9	8.7
Greece	81.1	82.1	16.7	14.7	20.7	18.6	12.6	10.7
Spain	63.7	61.1	29.9	31.0	36.4	36.1	23.1	25.6
France	81.7	82.4	13.4	12.7	14.9	14.6	11.9	10.9
Italy	69.6	76.3	24.3	19.3	27.9	22.6	20.7	15.9
Cyprus	83.5	85.8	15.9	12.6	22.3	19.5	11.0	6.8
Latvia	77.1	80.2	19.5	16.0	26.7	19.7	12.2	12.3
Lithuania	81.3	89.0	14.3	8.7	15.1	11.4	13.4	5.9
Luxembourg	69.8	70.9	17.0	15.1	14.4	19.2	19.6	11.1
Hungary	85.9	84.0	12.2	10.9	12.5	12.5	11.8	9.3
Malta	39.0	54.7	53.2	37.6	56.5	41.5	49.7	33.3
Netherlands	73.1	76.2	15.0	12.0	15.7	14.4	14.3	9.6
Austria	85.3	84.1	9.5	10.9	8.7	11.6	10.2	10.2
Poland	89.2	91.6	7.6	5.0	9.5	6.4	5.6	3.6
Portugal	44.4	53.4	45.1	36.3	52.6	42.0	37.5	30.4
Romania	76.3	77.4	23.2	19.2	24.3	19.2	22.1	19.1
Slovenia	90.7	91.5	4.8	4.3	6.2	5.7	3.3	2.7
Slovakia	94.5	91.3	5.6	7.2	6.7	8.1	4.6	6.3
Finland	85.8	86.5	9.9	7.9	12.6	9.7	7.3	6.3
Sweden (2)	86.7	87.2	10.4	12.0	11.4	13.3	9.3	10.7
United Kingdom (2)	77.1	78.1	17.8	13.0	18.8	14.6	16.7	11.4
Croatia (3)	90.6	94.6	8.3	3.9	9.1	5.2	7.4	5.3
Turkey	42.8	46.4	54.8	47.6	45.4	39.4	63.5	55.0
Iceland (2, 3)	48.5	49.3	28.8	28.1	32.7	31.5	24.8	24.6
Norway (2, 3)	94.8	93.3	14.0	5.9	14.9	7.4	13.1	4.3
Switzerland (3)	79.4	78.1	6.7	7.6	6.3	8.5	7.1	6.7

(1) Refer to the Internet metadata file (http://epp.eurostat.ec.europa.eu/cache/ITY_SDDS/en/educ_esms.htm).
(2) 2006 instead of 2007 for early school leavers.
(3) 2006 instead of 2007 for youth education attainment level.

Source: Eurostat (tsiir110 and tsisc060)

4.2 Foreign language learning

Introduction

The EU recognises 23 official languages, in addition to which there are regional, minority languages, and languages spoken by migrant populations. School is the main opportunity for the vast majority of people to learn these languages – as linguistic diversity is actively encouraged within schools, universities, adult education centres and the workplace.

For several decades it has been mandatory for most European children to learn at least one foreign language during their compulsory education, with the time devoted to foreign language instruction generally increasing in recent years. In 2002, the Barcelona European Council recommended that at least two foreign languages should be learnt from a very early age by each pupil. This recommendation has been implemented to varying degrees, usually for compulsory secondary education, either by making it mandatory to learn a second language, or ensuring that pupils have the possibility to study a second foreign language as part of their curriculum. In November 2005, the European Commission published a Communication (COM(2005) 596) titled 'A New Framework Strategy for Multilingualism'[6]. The EU promotes multilingualism and aims for a situation in which every EU citizen can speak at least two foreign languages in addition to their own mother tongue, based on the premise that multilingual citizens are better equipped to take advantage of educational opportunities and employment opportunities.

This Communication complements an action plan for 2004-2006 for the promotion of language learning and linguistic diversity[7], which focused on: extending the benefits of language learning to all citizens as a lifelong activity; improving the quality of language teaching, and; building an environment favourable to languages.

Definitions and data availability

Data on the number of pupils studying foreign languages are related to the corresponding numbers of students enrolled; mentally handicapped students enrolled in special schools are excluded.

The **average number of foreign languages learned per pupil** is collected for different ISCED levels. The data refer to all pupils, even if teaching languages does not start in the first years of instruction for the particular ISCED level considered. This indicator is defined as the sum of language students divided by the total number of students enrolled in the educational level considered. Each student studying a foreign language is counted once for each language he or she is studying, i.e. students studying more than one language are counted as many times as the number of languages studied. Irish, Luxembourgish and regional languages are excluded, although provision may be made for them in certain Member States. Allowing for exceptions, when one of the national languages is taught in schools where it is not the teaching language, it is not considered as a foreign language.

(6) http://eur-lex.europa.eu/LexUriServ/LexUriServ.do?uri=COM:2005:0596:FIN:EN:PDF.
(7) http://ec.europa.eu/education/doc/official/keydoc/actlang/act_lang_en.pdf.

Main findings

Within primary education establishments, there is a clear pre-eminence in terms of the proportion of pupils that (choose to) study English. Learning English is mandatory in a number of countries within secondary education establishments, and a number of Member States witnessed (near) 100 % shares of pupils learning this language in primary education. The highest shares of primary education pupils studying English were recorded in Greece, Spain, Italy, Malta and Austria, where upwards of nine out of every ten children was studying English. The relative importance of English as a foreign language may be further magnified because pupils tend to receive more tuition in their first foreign language than they do for any subsequent languages they may choose to study.

The 12 Member States that joined the EU since 2004 are in a particular position with respect to language teaching, as many of them used to make it compulsory

to study Russian. This situation has since changed and now most pupils have a free choice as to the language(s) they (wish to) study. In these countries too there has been a marked increase in the proportion of pupils learning English (often above 50 % of all students). Luxembourg is also of particular interest, insofar as this country has three official languages, with most pupils receiving tuition in Luxembourgish, German and French at a primary level, while English is introduced as a foreign language at secondary school.

Turning to language learning within upper secondary education, some 84.1 % of all EU-27 students at ISCED level 3 were studying English in 2006, compared with less than a quarter studying French (24.3 %) or German (22.2 %).

Luxembourg and Estonia stood out as the two countries with the highest average number of foreign languages learnt per pupil; note this indicator includes other languages (such as Russian), besides English, French and German.

Figure 4.3: Proportion of pupils learning foreign languages in primary education, by language, 2006 (1)

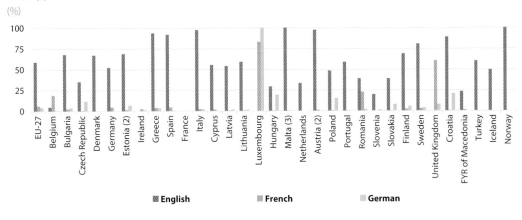

(1) Refer to the Internet metadata file (http://epp.eurostat.ec.europa.eu/cache/ITY_SDDS/en/educ_esms.htm); France, not available; Luxembourg, not available for English; the Netherlands and Norway, not available for French and German; Slovenia and Iceland, not available for French.
(2) Estimates.
(3) 2005 for French and German.

Source: Eurostat (educ_ilang), Unesco, OECD

Table 4.4: Foreign languages learnt per pupil in upper secondary education (ISCED level 3) (1)

	Average number of foreign languages learnt per pupil (number)		Pupils learning English in general programmes (%)		Pupils learning French in general programmes (%)		Pupils learning German in general programmes (%)	
	2001	2006	2001	2006	2001	2006	2001	2006
EU-27	1.3	1.3	71.0	84.1	18.1	22.2	19.4	24.3
Belgium	1.8	1.7	94.1	94.4	48.3	48.1	30.3	28.4
Bulgaria	1.4	1.5	79.0	86.1	20.8	15.3	38.6	40.3
Czech Republic	1.3	1.4	96.6	100.0	14.7	25.0	75.7	72.2
Denmark	1.5	1.5	91.0	99.9	22.9	22.6	69.6	71.9
Germany	0.7	0.9	92.0	94.3	29.4	28.7	-	-
Estonia	2.2	2.2	90.9	92.6	4.3	6.1	46.3	44.1
Ireland	0.9	0.9	-	-	66.2	60.5	19.1	18.2
Greece	1.0	1.0	94.3	94.0	14.0	8.6	3.1	2.9
Spain	1.2	1.2	95.5	94.6	23.9	27.1	0.9	1.1
France	1.7	1.7	99.3	99.4	-	-	31.2	22.8
Italy	1.2	1.4	81.0	96.9	27.0	21.4	7.8	7.7
Cyprus	1.6	1.6	89.8	88.1	68.7	38.3	1.3	2.4
Latvia	:	1.2	89.2	94.9	4.0	4.1	51.8	35.1
Lithuania	1.6	1.4	73.7	82.3	7.8	5.4	37.0	27.2
Luxembourg	2.3	2.3	93.1	97.0	89.4	97.0	87.6	97.0
Hungary	1.2	1.2	60.6	73.3	6.1	6.2	47.8	49.9
Malta (2)	0.7	0.6	80.7	63.5	8.1	7.9	0.8	1.7
Netherlands	1.6	:	98.2	100.0	26.7	70.1	32.0	86.2
Austria	:	1.4	:	96.9	:	54.1	-	-
Poland	1.4	1.7	90.1	90.0	15.2	10.0	62.4	64.0
Portugal	:	0.8	:	50.7	:	15.1	:	1.6
Romania	1.4	1.6	86.1	94.8	84.8	83.6	10.8	11.6
Slovenia	1.4	1.6	95.6	98.9	7.8	10.2	83.3	77.0
Slovakia	1.4	1.5	95.9	97.7	13.1	16.0	78.8	72.6
Finland	:	:	99.5	99.5	22.2	19.7	43.3	35.4
Sweden	1.7	1.6	99.8	99.9	25.6	22.4	53.5	32.4
United Kingdom	:	0.6	-	-	:	34.8	:	13.1
Croatia	:	1.4	:	98.3	:	3.4	:	65.6
FYR of Macedonia	1.3	1.5	:	:	:	:	:	:
Turkey	:	0.8	:	67.3	:	0.7	:	6.5
Iceland	1.3	1.5	65.9	76.1	16.4	17.1	32.8	30.7
Norway	:	0.8	:	:	:	:	:	:

(1) Refer to the Internet metadata file (http://epp.eurostat.ec.europa.eu/cache/ITY_SDDS/en/educ_esms.htm).
(2) 2005 instead of 2006 for average number of foreign languages learnt per pupil.

Source: Eurostat (tps00056, tps00057, tps00058 and tps00059), Unesco, OECD

4.3 Tertiary education

Introduction

Europe has around 4 000 higher education institutions, with over 17 million students and 1.5 million staff; some European universities are among the most well-respected in the world. Higher education plays a central role in the development of human beings and modern societies, enhancing social, cultural and economic development, as well as active citizenship and ethical values.

The European Commission has published a modernisation agenda for universities as part of the Lisbon strategy for growth and jobs. The main fields for reform were identified as:

- Curricular reform: a three cycle system (bachelor-master-doctorate), competence based learning, flexible learning paths, recognition, mobility;
- Governance reform: university autonomy, strategic partnerships, including with enterprises, quality assurance;
- Funding reform: diversified sources of university income better linked to performance, promoting equity, access and efficiency, including the possible role of tuition fees, grants and loans.

Curricular reforms are also promoted through the Bologna Process[8], which sets out plans to create a European area for higher education by 2010, facilitating student mobility, the transparency and recognition of qualifications, while promoting a European dimension within higher education and the attractiveness of European institutions to non-Community students. This initiative has been extended to cover 46 countries within the wider Europe.

The Erasmus programme is one of the most well-known European initiatives. Around 90 % of European universities take part in it and some 1.9 million students have already participated in exchanges since it started in 1987. Erasmus became part of the EU's lifelong learning programme in 2007 and was expanded to cover student placements in enterprises, university staff training and teaching for enterprise staff. The programme seeks to expand its mobility actions in the coming years, with a target of 3 million Erasmus students by 2012.

Some of the most recent policy initiatives in this area include efforts to instigate a dialogue between universities and business to develop links between universities and businesses in areas such as, curriculum development, governance, entrepreneurship, continuing education and knowledge transfer. Otherwise, a Council Resolution on modernising universities for Europe's competitiveness in a global knowledge economy was adopted on 23 November 2007[9].

---

(8) http://ec.europa.eu/education/policies/educ/bologna/bologna_en.html.

(9) http://register.consilium.europa.eu/pdf/en/07/st16/st16096-re01.en07.pdf.

Definitions and data availability

ISCED is used to define the levels of education: **tertiary education** includes both programmes which are largely theoretically-based and designed to provide qualifications for entry to advanced research programmes and professions with high skill requirements, as well as programmes which are classified at the same level of competencies but are more occupationally-oriented and lead to direct labour market access. Persons who are enrolled in tertiary education (including university and non-university studies) in the regular education system in each country correspond to the target population for policy in higher education. It provides an indication of the number of persons who had access to tertiary education and are expected to complete their studies, contributing to an increase of the educational attainment level of the population in the country in case they continue to live and work in the country at the end of their studies.

Student and teacher mobility are both seen as important tools for increasing innovation, productivity and competitiveness. Historically, it has been rare for countries to have precise details concerning the number of students that study abroad in third countries. Instead, these statistics have usually been collected by summing the numbers of students studying in receiving countries. This method has a downside; as a lack of information on the distribution of students according to their nationality is likely to lead to underestimation (for example, the number of students studying abroad may be a count of students enrolled on a certain day, whereas the actual number of foreign students could be higher as many students stay abroad for just a few months).

The number of foreign students may be defined as all students with a foreign nationality – however, this means that permanent residents with a foreign nationality are been included in the numerator, even though they have not changed country for their studies. The statistics in this edition of the Yearbook present, for the first time, information on student mobility that is based on the **actual number of foreign students studying in the host country** and excludes foreigners who are resident.

Main findings

There were almost 19 million students active within tertiary education in the EU-27 in 2006. Proportionally more young men than women opt for a vocational education, while women outnumber men within tertiary education. This may reflect the desire of some young men to enter a vocational profession as rapidly as possible, as well as changing social attitudes and professional activity concerning the position of women. As the emphasis placed on qualifications grows in relation to entering further education or obtaining a job, it is important to note that the participation rate of young women in education after the completion of compulsory education is higher than that for young men in most Member States, and that young women obtain more upper secondary education qualifications than young men.

The highest number of students in tertiary education was recorded in Germany and the United Kingdom – around 2.3 million in each country, equivalent to more than 12 % of the EU-27 total, while there were 2.2 million in France, 2.1 million in Poland and 2 million in Italy.

Gender disparities in educational enrolment and attainment at a tertiary level have been reversed in many Member States during the last couple of decades, with women accounting for 55.1 % of the total number of tertiary students in 2006 in the EU-27; Germany was the only country where the proportion of male tertiary students (50.3 % of the total) was higher than the share accounted for by women.

Educational policies have increasingly shifted to promote particular subject areas, where take-up among female students remains relatively low (for example, science, mathematics and computing, or engineering, manufacturing and construction-related studies). Instead, women appear to have a higher propensity to study health and welfare, humanities and arts, social sciences, business and law, while a higher proportion of men chose to study science and technology related subjects, as well as agriculture and veterinary related subjects. Some 39.7 % of tertiary students in science, mathematics and computing disciplines in the EU-27 were female in 2006, while the proportion of female students among those studying engineering, manufacturing and construction-related studies was 25.1 %, both these values marked an increase compared with the year before.

Some 9.0 % of the tertiary education student population in the EU-27 in 2006 was found to be studying in another country. Some of the most popular destinations for foreign students include countries where English, French or German are spoken, such as the United Kingdom, Austria, Belgium, Germany or France.

Table 4.5: Students in tertiary education, 2006 (1)

	Total number of students in tertiary education (1 000)	of which, studying (%)						
		Human-ities & arts	Social sciences, business & law	Science, math. & com-puting	Engin., manuf. & con-struction	Agricul. & vet-erinary	Health & welfare	Services
EU-27	18 783	12.6	32.6	10.1	13.9	1.8	12.3	3.5
Euro area	11 199	13.1	30.4	10.5	14.8	1.8	12.7	3.5
Belgium	394	10.5	27.5	6.9	10.6	2.5	22.1	1.5
Bulgaria	244	7.9	42.5	5.0	21.0	2.5	6.4	7.6
Czech Republic	337	8.5	27.6	8.5	14.4	3.7	12.1	5.3
Denmark	229	15.0	29.5	8.0	10.1	1.5	22.2	2.3
Germany	2 290	15.6	27.4	15.2	15.7	1.4	14.7	2.5
Estonia	68	11.6	39.0	10.0	12.3	2.5	8.5	8.5
Ireland	186	15.7	23.1	11.6	10.4	1.2	12.8	4.5
Greece (2)	653	11.6	31.9	15.7	16.5	5.9	6.9	5.0
Spain	1 789	10.4	31.9	11.4	17.8	3.4	9.9	5.6
France	2 201	16.5	34.5	12.3	11.5	1.0	14.2	3.5
Italy	2 029	15.5	36.5	7.9	15.6	2.3	12.5	2.6
Cyprus	21	8.5	47.4	12.7	6.1	0.1	6.6	9.2
Latvia	131	7.0	54.2	5.2	10.0	1.2	5.2	4.9
Lithuania	199	7.0	41.8	6.1	18.0	2.3	9.2	3.4
Luxembourg	3	8.2	45.2	8.4	15.0	0.0	0.4	0.0
Hungary	439	8.0	41.6	5.2	12.4	2.9	8.2	8.3
Malta	9	14.0	37.4	8.4	7.6	0.2	20.3	2.2
Netherlands	580	8.4	38.0	6.7	8.3	1.2	16.4	5.9
Austria	253	14.9	35.0	12.4	11.8	1.6	9.4	2.1
Poland	2 146	9.2	40.9	9.7	12.6	2.2	5.7	5.4
Portugal	367	8.6	31.5	7.3	21.9	1.9	16.0	5.6
Romania	835	10.5	50.0	4.7	18.2	2.9	5.7	3.0
Slovenia	115	7.5	43.5	5.4	15.6	3.1	7.4	8.7
Slovakia	198	6.0	28.3	9.0	16.4	2.8	15.2	5.8
Finland	309	14.5	22.5	11.4	25.9	2.2	13.3	4.8
Sweden	423	12.6	26.2	9.7	16.3	0.9	17.2	1.8
United Kingdom	2 336	17.0	27.0	13.7	8.2	0.9	18.8	0.7
Croatia	137	9.9	40.5	7.4	16.3	3.8	7.5	10.2
FYR of Macedonia	48	10.7	32.6	7.2	18.3	3.6	10.2	4.5
Turkey	2 343	6.9	47.4	7.5	13.3	3.5	5.6	3.5
Iceland	16	14.8	38.0	8.0	7.3	0.5	12.4	1.5
Liechtenstein	1	1.4	71.4	0.0	25.0	0.0	2.2	0.0
Norway	215	12.1	32.2	8.9	6.7	0.8	19.3	4.3
Switzerland	205	13.0	37.1	10.7	13.4	1.2	10.2	3.8
Japan	4 085	15.8	29.3	2.9	16.1	2.1	12.2	5.7
United States	17 488	10.6	27.3	8.9	6.7	0.6	13.9	5.1

(1) Refer to the Internet metadata file (http://epp.eurostat.ec.europa.eu/cache/ITY_SDDS/en/educ_esms.htm).
(2) Breakdown by subject is for 2005.

Source: Eurostat (tps00062 and educ_enrl5)

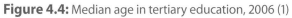
Figure 4.4: Median age in tertiary education, 2006 (1)

(years)

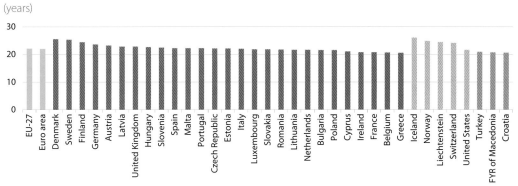

(1) Refer to the Internet metadata file (http://epp.eurostat.ec.europa.eu/cache/ITY_SDDS/en/educ_esms.htm).

Source: Eurostat (tps00061)

Figure 4.5: Gender breakdown of tertiary students, 2006 (1)

(% of total number of tertiary students)

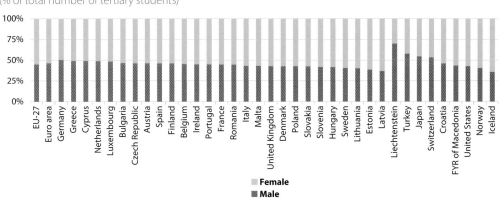

(1) Refer to the Internet metadata file (http://epp.eurostat.ec.europa.eu/cache/ITY_SDDS/en/educ_esms.htm).

Source: Eurostat (tps00063)

Table 4.6: Graduates from tertiary education, by field of education, 2006 (1)

	Total number of graduates from tertiary education (1 000)	of which, studying (%)						
		Human- ities & arts	Social sciences, business & law	Science, math. & com- puting	Engin., manuf. & con- struction	Agricul. & vet- erinary	Health & welfare	Services
EU-27	3 846	12.2	35.3	9.9	12.5	1.7	14.4	3.8
Euro area	2 113	12.9	33.8	10.2	14.3	1.8	15.2	4.3
Belgium	82	9.8	28.3	7.7	9.3	2.3	18.9	2.1
Bulgaria	45	8.4	47.8	5.3	15.6	2.0	6.2	7.7
Czech Republic	69	7.5	28.7	7.6	15.0	3.6	12.4	5.6
Denmark	48	13.8	30.4	7.2	10.9	2.1	23.8	3.3
Germany	415	15.9	23.7	11.4	13.5	1.8	20.4	3.1
Estonia	12	11.4	36.6	9.4	9.9	2.2	11.6	8.6
Ireland	59	19.1	34.7	13.8	12.1	0.6	11.0	2.4
Greece (2)	60	13.1	28.0	15.0	12.3	3.6	9.7	8.5
Spain	286	9.2	28.3	10.0	16.5	1.8	14.2	7.6
France	644	12.1	41.6	11.1	14.7	1.5	13.0	3.9
Italy	279	17.0	38.7	6.8	15.9	1.7	12.4	2.6
Cyprus	4	10.0	43.7	9.7	4.2	0.2	6.7	14.3
Latvia	26	6.2	56.0	4.6	6.8	1.0	5.2	4.9
Lithuania	43	6.7	40.9	5.9	15.9	1.8	9.0	3.5
Luxembourg	:	:	:	:	:	:	:	:
Hungary	70	7.6	43.8	5.8	6.7	2.6	8.8	8.8
Malta	3	15.5	44.2	6.3	4.8	1.0	13.0	3.1
Netherlands	117	8.2	38.2	6.8	8.3	1.5	16.5	4.5
Austria	35	8.7	29.7	12.6	19.8	2.1	9.9	3.7
Poland	504	8.7	42.6	8.5	8.4	1.6	7.8	5.0
Portugal	72	10.3	32.2	11.3	15.1	1.8	24.2	7.2
Romania	175	11.9	48.2	4.5	15.8	2.7	9.6	2.1
Slovenia	17	5.1	49.6	3.5	12.6	2.4	9.9	7.7
Slovakia	40	6.3	27.4	8.6	15.0	2.9	17.1	6.7
Finland	40	13.5	23.4	8.7	20.7	2.3	19.1	6.0
Sweden	61	6.1	24.8	8.1	18.4	1.0	25.3	2.2
United Kingdom	640	15.4	30.5	13.4	8.2	0.9	18.3	0.8
Croatia	21	9.4	39.4	6.3	11.5	3.6	8.9	13.5
FYR of Macedonia	7	13.4	26.9	7.4	13.8	4.0	12.3	5.4
Turkey	373	6.4	37.7	7.8	14.3	4.0	5.7	6.2
Iceland	3	11.2	34.1	8.0	6.4	0.7	11.7	1.4
Liechtenstein	0	3.0	54.5	0.0	34.8	0.0	7.6	0.0
Norway	34	8.8	27.0	8.2	7.5	1.1	24.5	4.8
Switzerland	69	6.5	39.4	10.3	12.1	1.6	11.0	6.7
Japan	1 068	15.2	27.0	3.0	18.2	2.2	12.8	9.7
United States	2 639	13.2	38.1	8.9	7.2	1.1	13.5	6.5

(1) Refer to the Internet metadata file (http://epp.eurostat.ec.europa.eu/cache/ITY_SDDS/en/educ_esms.htm).
(2) 2005.

Source: Eurostat (educ_grad5)

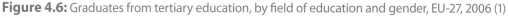

Figure 4.6: Graduates from tertiary education, by field of education and gender, EU-27, 2006 (1)
(1 000)

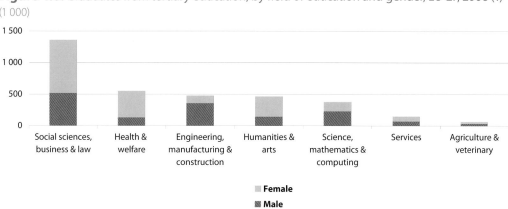

Female

Male

(1) Estimates.

Source: Eurostat (educ_grad5)

Figure 4.7: Student mobility in tertiary education (ISCED 5-6), 2006 (1)
(foreign students as a % of all students in tertiary education)

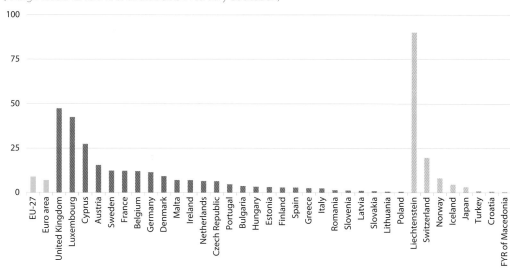

(1) Refer to the Internet metadata file (http://epp.eurostat.ec.europa.eu/cache/ITY_SDDS/en/educ_esms.htm).

Source: Eurostat (educ_enrl8 and educ_enrl1tl)

4.4 Lifelong learning and vocational training

Introduction

The European Commission has integrated its various educational and training initiatives under a single umbrella, the Lifelong Learning Programme (LLP). This new programme replaces previous education, vocational training and e-Learning programmes, which ended in 2006.

Lifelong learning is defined as encompassing learning for personal, civic and social purposes, as well as for employment-related purposes. It can take place in a variety of environments, both inside and outside formal education and training systems. Lifelong learning implies raising investment in people and knowledge; promoting the acquisition of basic skills, including digital literacy and broadening opportunities for innovative, more flexible forms of learning. The aim is to provide people of all ages with equal and open access to high-quality learning opportunities, and to a variety of learning experiences throughout Europe.

The EC Treaty recognised the importance of vocational training in Article 150 by stating that 'Community action shall aim to … facilitate access to vocational training …; stimulate cooperation on training between educational or training establishments and firms' [10].

A European Commission communication of November 2001 entitled 'Making a European area of lifelong learning a reality' [11] underlines in paragraph 1.1 that the 'Lisbon European Council confirmed lifelong learning as a basic component of the European social model'. As such, learning is no longer given weight only in the area of education; it is also seen as a critical factor in the areas of employment and social security, economic performance and competitiveness.

The European employment strategy (EES) [12], agreed on 22 July 2003, introduced two guidelines to tackle the need for improved skills levels through lifelong learning. These guidelines called upon the Member States to address labour shortages and skills bottlenecks and also encourage them to implement comprehensive lifelong learning strategies in order to equip all individuals with the skills required of a modern workforce. The guidelines stated that policies should aim to increase investment in human resources, in particular through the training of adults by enterprises. At the beginning of 2005, the European Commission made a proposal for a revision of the Lisbon strategy, revising the EES by publishing employment guidelines in conjunction with macro-economic and micro-economic guidelines.

The Leonardo da Vinci programme in the field of vocational education and training (VET) is designed to encourage projects which give individuals the chance to improve their competences, knowledge and skills through a period spent abroad, as well as to encourage Europe-wide cooperation between training organisations.

(10) Consolidated version of the Treaty establishing the European Community, Chapter 3, Article 150(2) (OJ C 352, 24.12.2002, p. 33); http://eur-lex.europa.eu/en/treaties/dat/12002E/pdf/12002E_EN.pdf.

(11) 'Making a European area of lifelong learning a reality', COM(2001) 678 final of 21 November 2001; http://ec.europa.eu/education/policies/lll/life/communication/com_en.pdf.

(12) http://ec.europa.eu/social/main.jsp?catId=101&langId=en.

The Gruntvig programme was launched in 2000 and now forms part of the Lifelong Learning Programme. It aims to provide adults with ways of improving their knowledge and skills. It not only covers learners in adult education, but also the teachers, trainers, education staff and facilities that provide these services.

Definitions and data availability

Lifelong learning encompasses all purposeful learning activity, whether formal, non-formal or informal, undertaken on an ongoing basis with the aim of improving knowledge, skills and competence. The intention or aim to learn is the critical point that distinguishes these learning activities from non-learning activities such as cultural activities or sports activities.

Within the domain of lifelong learning statistics, formal education corresponds to education and training in the regular system of schools, universities and colleges. Non-formal education and training includes all types of taught learning activities which are not part of a formal education programme. Note that the statistics presented do not, therefore, cover informal learning, which corresponds to self-learning (through the use of printed material, computer-based learning/training, online Internet-based web education, visiting libraries, etc).

The target population for lifelong learning statistics refers to all persons in private households aged between 25 and 64 years old. Data are collected through the EU Labour Force Survey (LFS). The denominator used in this subchapter consists of the total population of the same age group, excluding those who did not answer to the question participation to education and training. From 27 October 2006, this indicator is based on annual averages of quarterly data instead of one unique reference quarter in spring.

Additional information is available from two other surveys:

- the third European survey of continuing vocational training in enterprises (CVTS3) which was implemented with 2005 as reference year in the EU-27 Member States and Norway, and;
- an adult education survey which was carried out by EU, EFTA and candidate countries between 2005 and 2008; at the time of writing, the results of this survey are not yet available.

Continuing Vocational Training (CVT) concerns persons employed by enterprises; the qualifying criteria are: the training must be planned in advance; the training must be organised or supported with the specific goal of learning; the training must be financed at least partly by the enterprise.

Main findings

In 2007, the proportion of persons aged 25 to 64 receiving some form of lifelong learning in the four weeks preceding the survey was 9.7 % within the EU-27. This figure was 1.2 points higher than the corresponding share for 2003. The proportion of the population who had participated in lifelong learning activities was higher among women (10.6 % in 2007) than among men (8.8 %). Sweden, Denmark, the United Kingdom and Finland stood out as they reported considerably higher proportions of their respective populations participating in lifelong learning (between 32 % and 23 %); in contrast, Bulgaria and Romania reported lifelong learning participation rates of less than 2 %.

As regards vocational training, the proportion of all enterprises that provided training to their employees in 2005 ranged from 21 %, in Greece, to 90 % in the United Kingdom, and averaged 60 % across the EU.

The preliminary EU results of the survey reflect, on average, a slight decrease in the proportion of enterprises offering training to their employees in comparison with the results of the previous survey (conducted in 1999). The northern countries and especially the Scandinavian countries, where considerable efforts were made in previous years, experienced a decrease in participation rates for vocational training, while the proportion rose considerably in most of the Member States that joined the EU since 2004.

The rate of participation of employees in continuous vocational training (CVT) activities was generally highest in the EU-15 Member States. On average, one in three employees (33 %) participated in CVT courses, with this proportion ranging from 11 %, in Latvia, to nearly 60 % in the Czech Republic.

The intensity of continual vocational training, as measured by the average hours of training per employee was similar between the EU-15 Member States and those that joined the EU since 2004. However, three groups of countries could be clearly distinguished: those with high proportions of training enterprises and high intensity in CVT courses, those with high rates of training enterprises and relatively low intensity in CVT courses, and those with low rates of training enterprises and relatively high intensity in CVT courses.

The third vocational training survey included, for the first time, information regarding initial vocational training within enterprises (for example, apprentices). Germany, the United Kingdom, Austria, Denmark, the Netherlands, Italy and France had the highest proportion of enterprises providing initial vocational training in 2005. In these countries the shares were often close to 50 %, while in the majority of the other Member States it did not exceed 10 %.

Table 4.7: Lifelong learning (1)

(% of the population aged 25 to 64 participating in education and training)

	Total		Male		Female	
	2003	2007	2003	2007	2003	2007
EU-27 (2)	8.5	9.7	7.9	8.8	9.1	10.6
Euro area (2)	6.5	8.4	6.4	8.0	6.6	8.8
Belgium	7.0	7.2	7.0	7.0	6.9	7.4
Bulgaria	1.3	1.3	1.1	1.4	1.4	1.3
Czech Republic	5.1	5.7	4.8	5.5	5.4	5.9
Denmark (2)	24.2	29.2	21.0	24.2	27.4	34.2
Germany	6.0	7.8	6.4	8.0	5.6	7.6
Estonia	6.7	7.0	5.0	4.6	8.2	9.3
Ireland (2)	5.9	7.6	5.1	6.2	6.8	9.0
Greece (2)	2.6	2.1	2.6	2.2	2.7	2.1
Spain	4.7	10.4	4.3	9.3	5.1	11.5
France (2)	7.1	7.4	7.0	7.0	7.2	7.9
Italy	4.5	6.2	4.2	5.9	4.8	6.6
Cyprus (2)	7.9	8.4	7.1	8.1	8.5	8.6
Latvia	7.8	7.1	5.4	4.6	10.0	9.3
Lithuania	3.8	5.3	2.8	3.6	4.7	6.8
Luxembourg (2)	6.5	7.0	6.8	6.5	6.1	7.4
Hungary (2)	4.5	3.6	4.0	3.0	4.9	4.1
Malta	4.2	6.0	4.7	6.4	3.6	5.7
Netherlands (2)	16.4	16.6	16.1	16.1	16.8	17.0
Austria (2)	8.6	12.8	8.6	11.6	8.6	14.0
Poland	4.4	5.1	3.9	4.7	4.9	5.5
Portugal	3.2	4.4	3.0	4.4	3.4	4.5
Romania	1.1	1.3	1.1	1.2	1.2	1.4
Slovenia (2)	13.3	14.8	12.0	13.5	14.7	16.1
Slovakia (2)	3.7	3.9	3.5	3.4	3.9	4.3
Finland (2)	22.4	23.4	18.6	19.4	26.2	27.5
Sweden (2)	31.8	32.0	28.4	26.0	35.4	38.3
United Kingdom (3)	27.2	26.6	22.7	22.0	30.9	31.2
Croatia	1.8	2.9	1.8	3.1	1.9	2.8
Turkey	1.2	1.5	1.7	1.8	0.7	1.2
Iceland (2)	29.5	27.9	25.0	22.4	34.1	33.7
Norway (2)	17.1	18.0	16.2	17.1	18.0	18.9
Switzerland (2)	24.7	22.5	25.3	21.7	24.0	23.4

(1) Refer to the Internet metadata file (http://epp.eurostat.ec.europa.eu/cache/ITY_SDDS/en/educ_esms.htm).
(2) Break in series, 2003.
(3) Break in series, 2003 and 2007.

Source: Eurostat (tsiem080)

Table 4.8: Continuous vocational training, 2005

	Training enterprises (% of all enterprises)	Employees participating in CVT courses (%)	Cost of CVT courses (% of total labour cost)	Average time spent in CVT courses per employee (hours)	Share of enterprises providing IVT (% of all enterprises)
EU (1)	60	33	1.6	9	30
Belgium	63	40	1.6	12	9
Bulgaria	29	15	1.1	4	4
Czech Republic	72	59	1.9	14	3
Denmark	85	35	2.7	10	45
Germany	69	30	1.3	9	55
Estonia	67	24	1.6	7	1
Ireland	:	:	:	:	:
Greece	21	14	0.6	3	3
Spain	47	33	1.2	9	14
France	74	46	2.3	13	37
Italy	32	29	1.3	7	40
Cyprus	51	30	1.3	7	2
Latvia	36	11	0.8	3	5
Lithuania	46	15	1.2	5	17
Luxembourg	72	49	2.0	16	28
Hungary	49	16	2.6	6	6
Malta	46	32	1.8	11	12
Netherlands	75	34	2.0	12	41
Austria	81	33	1.4	9	49
Poland	35	21	1.3	6	9
Portugal	44	28	1.1	7	5
Romania	40	17	1.1	5	2
Slovenia	72	50	2.0	14	9
Slovakia	60	38	1.8	12	1
Finland	77	39	1.5	10	17
Sweden	78	46	2.1	15	7
United Kingdom	90	33	1.3	7	51
Norway	86	29	1.3	9	23

(1) EU averages calculated on the basis of the available country data (i.e. excluding Ireland).

Source: Eurostat (trng_cvts3_01, trng_cvts3_41, trng_cvts3_53, trng_cvts3_71 and trng_cvts3_85)

4.5 Educational expenditure

Introduction

Expenditure on education is an investment that may help foster economic growth, enhance productivity, contribute to personal and social development, and reduce social inequalities. The proportion of total financial resources devoted to education is one of the key choices made in each country by governments, enterprises and individual students and their families.

There is an ongoing debate in many Member States as to how to increase education funding, improve efficiency and promote equity. Possible approaches include charging tuition fees, administrative or examination charges, the introduction of grants, or income-contingent loans to try to stimulate enrolment rates in higher education, in particular among the less well-off members of society. Another possible area for raising funds is through promoting partnerships between business and higher educational establishments.

Education accounts for a significant proportion of public expenditure in all of the Member States – the most important budget item being expenditure on staff. The cost of teaching increases significantly as a child moves through the education system, with expenditure per pupil/student considerably higher in universities than primary schools. Although tertiary education costs more per head, the highest proportion of total education spending is devoted to secondary education systems, as these teach a larger share of the total number of pupils/students.

Definitions and data availability

Indicators on education expenditure cover schools, universities and other public and private institutions involved in delivering or supporting educational services. Expenditure on institutions is not limited to expenditure on instructional services but also includes public and private expenditure on ancillary services for students and families, where these services are provided through educational institutions. At the tertiary level, spending on research and development can also be significant and is included, to the extent that the research is performed by educational institutions.

Total public expenditure on education includes direct public funding for educational institutions and transfers to households and enterprises. In general, the public sector finances educational expenditure by assuming direct responsibility for the current and capital expenditure of schools (direct public financing of schools), or by offering financial support to pupils/students and their families (public-sector grants and loans) and by subsidising the education or training activities of the private business sector or non-profit organisations (transfers to households and enterprises). **Expenditure on educational institutions from private sources** comprises school fees; materials (such as textbooks and teaching equipment); transport to school (if organised by the school); meals (if provided by the school); boarding fees; and expenditure by employers on initial vocational training. **Expenditure per pupil/student in public and private institutions** measures how much central, regional and local government, private households, religious institutions and enterprises spend per pupil/student. It includes expenditure for personnel, as well as other current and capital expenditure. **Public schools/institutions** are defined as those which are directly or indirectly administered by a public education authority. **Private schools/institutions** are directly or indirectly administered by a non-governmental organisation (such as a church, trade union, a private business concern or another body) and are considered to be independent if they get less than 50 % of their funding from any level of government (local, regional or national).

Main findings

Public expenditure on education in the EU-27 in 2005 was equivalent to 5.0 % of GDP, while the expenditure of both public and private sources of funds on educational institutions amounted to 5.4 % of GDP.

The highest public spending on education was observed in Denmark (8.3 %

of GDP), while Sweden (7.0 %), Cyprus (6.9 %), Malta (6.8 %) and Finland (6.3 %) also recorded relatively high rates. Most Member States reported that public expenditure on education accounted for between 4 and 6 % of their GDP, although the proportion of public expenditure on education fell to below 4 % of GDP in Greece, Slovakia, Luxembourg and Romania; note that the tertiary education system in Luxembourg is underdeveloped and that the majority of tertiary students attend courses in another Member State.

It should be noted that GDP growth can mask significant increases that have been made in terms of education spending over the last decade within the majority of Member States. Note also that declining birth rates will result in reduced school age populations, which will have an effect on ratios such as the average expenditure per pupil (given that expenditure is held constant). Annual expenditure on public and private educational institutions per pupil/student shows that an average of PPS 5 650 was spent per pupil/student in 2005 in the EU-27.

Figure 4.8: Total public expenditure on education, 2005 (1)
(% of GDP)

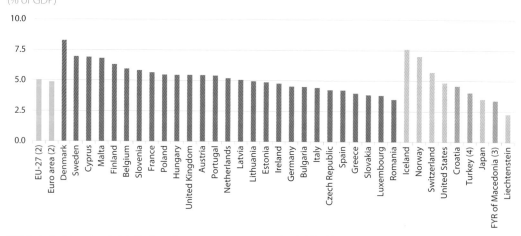

(1) Refer to the Internet metadata file (http://epp.eurostat.ec.europa.eu/cache/ITY_SDDS/en/educ_esms.htm).
(2) Estimate. (3) 2003. (4) 2004.

Source: Eurostat (tsiir010)

Table 4.9: Expenditure on educational institutions (1)

	Public expenditure (% of GDP) (2)	Private expenditure (% of GDP) (3)	Annual expenditure on public and private educational institutions per pupil/student (PPS for full-time equivalents)	
	2005	2005	2000	2005
EU-27	4.7	0.7	:	5 650
Euro area	4.6	0.6	:	6 190
Belgium	5.7	0.4	5 314	6 501
Bulgaria	3.8	0.6	1 277	1 993
Czech Republic	4.1	0.6	2 574	3 809
Denmark	6.8	0.6	7 108	8 244
Germany	4.2	0.9	5 677	6 503
Estonia	4.6	0.4	:	2 868
Ireland	4.3	0.3	4 481	6 012
Greece	4.0	0.3	:	4 606
Spain	4.1	0.5	4 304	5 718
France	5.4	0.6	5 712	6 364
Italy	4.2	0.4	:	5 908
Cyprus	6.0	1.2	4 879	6 684
Latvia	4.7	0.8	1 818	2 746
Lithuania	4.5	0.5	1 716	2 475
Luxembourg	3.7	:	:	:
Hungary	5.1	0.5	:	3 842
Malta	6.8	0.4	3 189	5 882
Netherlands	4.6	0.4	5 211	6 703
Austria	5.0	0.5	7 144	8 293
Poland	5.4	0.6	1 971	3 051
Portugal	5.3	0.4	3 943	4 704
Romania	3.3	0.4	:	1 454
Slovenia	5.3	0.8	:	6 056
Slovakia	3.7	0.7	1 681	2 699
Finland	5.8	0.1	5 455	6 225
Sweden	6.2	0.2	6 185	7 204
United Kingdom	5.0	1.3	4 799	7 084
Croatia	4.6	:	:	:
FYR of Macedonia	3.3	:	:	:
Turkey	3.8	0.1	:	:
Iceland	7.2	0.7	6 501	7 897
Liechtenstein	2.1	:	:	7 389
Norway	5.7	0.1	7 812	9 133
Switzerland	5.5	0.6	:	:
Japan	3.4	1.5	6 091	7 148
United States	4.9	2.4	9 200	10 661

(1) Refer to the Internet metadata file (http://epp.eurostat.ec.europa.eu/cache/ITY_SDDS/en/educ_esms.htm).
(2) Turkey, 2004; the former Yugoslav Republic of Macedonia, 2003.
(3) Turkey and Norway, 2004.

Source: Eurostat (educ_figdp, tps00068 and tps00067), Unesco, OECD

Health

5

Health is an important priority for Europeans, who expect to be protected against illness and disease – at home, in the workplace and when travelling across the EU. Health issues cut across a range of topics – including consumer protection (food safety issues), workplace safety, environmental or social policies – and thus have a considerable impact on the EU's revised Lisbon strategy. The vast majority of policy areas covered within this chapter are under the remit of the Directorate-General for Health and Consumers.

However, the competence for the organisation and delivery of health services and healthcare is largely held by the Member States, while the EU has the responsibility to give added value through launching actions such as those in relation to cross-border health threats and patient mobility, as well as reducing health inequalities and addressing key health determinants. Gathering and assessing accurate, detailed information on health issues is vital for the EU to effectively design policies and target future actions.

A first programme for Community action in the field of public health [1] for the period 2003 to 2008 focused on three main areas, namely:

* to improve health information and knowledge for the development of public health;
* to enhance the capability of responding rapidly and in a coordinated fashion to threats to health, and;
* to promote health and prevent disease through addressing health determinants across all policies and activities.

---

(1) Decision No 1786/2002/EC of the European Parliament and of the Council of 23 September 2002 adopting a programme of Community action in the field of public health (2003-2008) (OJ L 271, 9.10.2002, p. 1); http://europa.eu/eur-lex/pri/en/oj/dat/2002/l_271/l_27120021009en00010011.pdf.

5.1 Healthy life years

On 23 October 2007 – the European Commission adopted a new strategy 'Together for Health: A Strategic Approach for the EU 2008-2013' [2]. In order to bring about the changes sought within the sector and identified within the new strategy, the second programme of Community Action in the Field of Health [3] came into force from 1 January 2008. It puts in place an overarching, strategic framework for work on health at the EU level in the coming years and encompasses work not only in the health sector but across all policy areas. It has four main principles and three strategic themes for improving health in the EU. The principles include taking a value-driven approach, recognising the links between health and economic prosperity, integrating health in all policies, and strengthening the EU's voice in global health issues. The strategic themes include fostering good health in an ageing Europe, protecting citizens from health threats, and dynamic health systems and new technologies. The programme is valued at EUR 321.5 million and will be implemented by means of annual work plans which will set out priority areas and funding criteria.

Introduction

Life expectancy at birth remains one of the most frequently quoted indicators of health status and economic development. While most people are aware that successive generations are living longer, less is known about the condition of health of Europe's ageing population. Life expectancy at birth has risen rapidly in the last century due to a number of important factors, including reductions in infant mortality, rising living standards, improved lifestyles and better education, as well as advances in healthcare and medicine.

The health status of a population is difficult to measure because it is hard to define among individuals, populations, cultures, or even across time periods. As a result, the demographic measure of life expectancy has often been used as a measure of a nation's health status because it is based on a simple and easy to understand characteristic – namely, that of death. However, the use of life expectancy is limited insofar as it does not provide any information on a population's health status.

Indicators on healthy life years (HLY) introduce the concept of the quality of life, by focusing on those years that may be enjoyed by individuals free from the limitations of illness or disability. Chronic disease, frailty, mental disorders and physical disability tend to become more prevalent in older age, and the burden of these conditions may impact on healthcare and pension provisions, while resulting in a low quality of life for those who suffer from such conditions.

(2) http://ec.europa.eu/health/ph_overview/Documents/strategy_wp_en.pdf.
(3) Decision No 1350/2007/EC of the European Parliament and of the Council of 23 October 2007 establishing a second programme of Community action in the field of health (2008-2013) (OJ L 301/3, 20.11.2007); http://eur-lex.europa.eu/LexUriServ/LexUriServ.do?uri=OJ:L:2007:301:0003:0013:EN:PDF.

HLY also monitor health as a productive or economic factor: these indicators form part of the structural indicators that are used to analyse progress being made in the EU with respect to the revised Lisbon criteria. An increase in HLY is one of the main goals for European health policy, given that this would not only improve the situation of individuals (as good health and a long life are fundamental objectives of human activity) but would also result in lower levels of public healthcare expenditure. If HLY are increasing more rapidly than life expectancy, then not only are people living longer, but they are also living a greater proportion of their lives free from health problems. Any loss in health will, nonetheless, have important effects. These will include an altered pattern of resource allocation within the healthcare system, as well as wider ranging effects on consumption and production throughout the economy.

Definitions and data availability

The structural indicator on **healthy life years (HLY)** (also called **disability-free life expectancy (DFLE)**) measures the number of remaining years that a person of a certain age can be expected to live without disability; in other words, this is a health expectancy indicator. The indicator is calculated separately for males and females.

There are two components to the calculation of HLY, namely, mortality statistics and data on self-perceived disability. Mortality data comes from Eurostat's demographic database, while self-perceived disability data has come from the EU's survey of statistics on income and living conditions (EU-SILC). The way this question was implemented by the Member States in EU-SILC hampers cross-country comparisons for the data up to 2008. The EU-SILC question is:

For at least the past 6 months, to what extent have you been limited because of a health problem in activities people usually do? Would you say you have been:

- strongly limited?
- limited?
- not limited at all?

Life expectancy at birth is defined as the mean number of years still to be lived by a person at birth, if subjected throughout the rest of his or her life to the current mortality conditions.

Main findings

While life expectancy rises, political attention has been re-focused on healthy life years (HLY). One measure that can be used to study the relative health of Europe's population is the relationship between healthy life years and total life expectancy, in other words, what percentage of each person's life is lived free from disability and disease. Men were likely to spend the largest proportion of their lives free from disability. Women could expect to live a slightly lower proportion of their lives free from disability; although their overall life expectancy at birth was higher than for men. Indeed, the male population consistently reported a higher proportion of healthy life years in total life expectancy when compared with rates for women, with differences of 8 percentage points or more in Portugal, Lithuania and Latvia.

The HLY indicator is calculated at two ages: birth and the age of 65. Healthy life years at age 65 is of particular interest in relation to the possible future demand for healthcare and social services, or the potential for older persons to remain within the workforce. For both men and women, Estonia, Latvia, Lithuania, Hungary and Slovakia were the countries where people could expect to spend the shortest period

after the age of 65 without a disability. The data for Estonia, Luxembourg, Hungary, Austria and Iceland showed almost identical figures for men and women in terms of additional healthy life years they may expect to live at the age of 65. The highest differences between the sexes were recorded in Poland and Cyprus. In Poland, women aged 65 were expected to have 1.8 years of healthy life more than men, while in Cyprus the opposite situation was found, as men could expect to have 1.9 additional years of healthy life than women.

Figure 5.1: Healthy life years at birth, 2005 (1)

(% of total life expectancy)

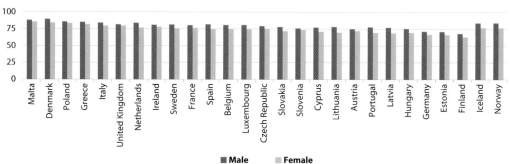

(1) Provisional data; Italy, life expectancy data is for 2004; Bulgaria and Romania, not available; the figure is ranked on the average of male and female.

Source: Eurostat (tsdph100 and tps00025)

Figure 5.2: Healthy life years at age 65, 2005 (1)

(years)

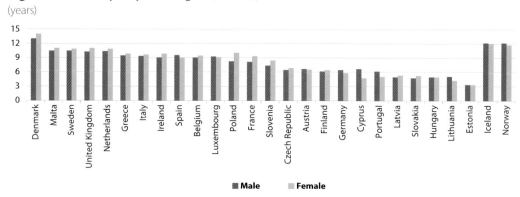

(1) Provisional data; Bulgaria and Romania, not available; the figure is ranked on the average of male and female.

Source: Eurostat (tsdph220)

5.2 Health problems

Introduction

According to the Directorate-General for Health and Consumers [4], the promotion of health and lifestyle choices can play an important role in reducing disease and death. On average, Europeans with better jobs, more education or higher incomes have better health and longer life expectancy. Actions to reduce health inequalities aim:

- to improve everyone's level of health closer to that of the most advantaged;
- to ensure that the health needs of the most disadvantaged are fully addressed;
- to help the health of people in countries and regions with lower levels of health to improve faster.

Health problems linked to lifestyle related health determinants can be age specific (in childhood or in old age), as well as resulting from socio-economic factors. Health promotion in various settings, such as schools, workplaces, families or local communities has proven to be efficient in addressing health issues across communities, focusing on specific diseases or target groups.

Six out of the seven most important risk factors for premature death in the EU (blood pressure, cholesterol, body mass index, inadequate fruit and vegetable intake, physical inactivity, excessive alcohol consumption) relate to how people eat, drink and move (the only exception being tobacco). As such, a balanced diet and regular physical activity, along with restraining from smoking and drinking to excess, are important factors in the promotion and maintenance of good health.

Nevertheless, smoking is the single largest cause of avoidable death in the EU accounting for over half a million deaths each year. The Directorate-General for Health and Consumers estimates that 25 % of all cancer deaths and 15 % of all deaths in the EU can be attributed to smoking. Smoking legislation has been adopted by an increasing number of Member States, restricting or forbidding smoking in public places and/or workplaces, as well as offering protection to passive smokers. The European Commission is developing a tobacco control policy, focused on:

- legislative measures;
- support for Europe-wide smoking prevention and cessation activities;
- mainstreaming tobacco control into a range of other Community policies (such as agricultural, taxation or development policy);
- making sure that the pioneering role played by the European Community in many tobacco control areas has an impact at a global level.

Overweightness and obesity are increasing at an alarming rate in Europe, especially among children. Obesity is a serious public health problem, as it increases significantly the risk of chronic diseases such as cardiovascular disease, type 2 diabetes and certain cancers. Lifestyle factors, including diet, eating habits and levels of physical activity (and inactivity) are often adopted during the early years of life. As such, childhood obesity is strongly linked to adult obesity. However, maintaining a 'normal weight' can be a challenging exercise, given the abundance of energy-rich foods, and lifestyle pressures that decrease

(4) http://ec.europa.eu/health/ph_determinants/healthdeterminants_en.htm.

opportunities for physical activity both at work and during leisure time.

Definitions and data availability

Health Interview Surveys (HIS) are the source of information for describing the health status and the health-related behaviours of the European population. The following topics are usually covered in a HIS:

- height and weight which form the basis for the calculation of the body mass index (BMI);
- self-perceived health;
- activities that have been reduced because of health problems;
- long-standing illnesses or health problems;
- smoking behaviour;
- alcohol consumption.

Many health-related indicators are expressed as percentages within different population cohorts on the basis of background variables covering gender, age, activity status, and educational level. Note that the information comes from non-harmonised national surveys and that the Member States were asked to post-harmonise the data according to a set of common guidelines. Member States have joined efforts on a harmonised EU survey (EHIS) which is, at the time of writing, being implemented.

The **body mass index (BMI)** is a measure of a person's weight relative to his or her height that correlates fairly well with body fat. The BMI is accepted as the most useful measure of obesity for adults when only weight and height data are available.

It is calculated as the result of dividing body weight (in kilograms) by body height (in metres) squared. The following subdivisions are used to categorise the BMI into four categories:

- < 18.5: underweight;
- ≥ 18.5 and < 25: normal weight;
- ≥ 25 and < 30: overweight;
- ≥ 30: obese.

Note that the BMI is not calculated for children. Note that data for Germany and for England relate to valid height and weight measurements, while for the other countries the data correspond to self-declared height and weight.

Main findings

Obesity is a serious public health problem that increases the risk of death and disability; it may be associated primarily with poor dietary habits and a lack of physical activity. Obesity rates have increased considerably in most Member States during the last decade. Approximately half of the EU's population was overweight or obese, a share that rose to as high as 61.0 % in England and 59.7 % in Germany, while Italy and France were the only Member States to report that less than 40 % of their population were either overweight or obese.

The proportion of daily smokers was close to 50 % of the male population in Latvia and Estonia; Sweden (16.5 %) and Finland (21.6 %) reported the lowest proportions of men smoking. Daily smoking rates were lower among women (compared with men) in each of the Member States, with the exception of Sweden

where there was a slightly higher proportion of female daily smokers. Austria and Denmark recorded the highest incidence of daily smoking among women, at just over 30 % of the female population, while Portugal (6.8 %) was the only Member State where the proportion of female daily smokers was in single figures. The largest absolute differences in smoking habits between the sexes were reported for the Baltic States, where the proportion of men smoking daily was upwards of 30 points more than the corresponding share for women. In relative terms, four times as many men (as women) smoked on a daily basis in Portugal, while between three and four times as many men smoked on daily basis in Cyprus, Lithuania, Romania and Latvia.

There would appear to be a shift in smoking patterns across Europe between the sexes. There was a much smaller difference between the proportion of men and women smoking when studying the population aged between 15 and 24. Young females in Sweden and the United Kingdom were more likely to smoke than young males. Furthermore, in the majority of Member States the proportion of young women smoking was often above the corresponding average for women of all ages; this was particularly the case in the United Kingdom, Spain, Ireland and Germany.

Information from the EU's survey on income and living conditions (EU-SILC) provides data on difficulties faced by Europeans in their daily lives and their potential need for assistance; note that the data represents the perceived views of the population and does not specifically measure disability levels. Within the EU-25, some 6.9 % of men and 8.7 % of women (aged 15 or more) reported that they were severely hampered in activities people usually do because of health problems for at least the six months prior to the survey (conducted in 2006).

The proportion of women that were severely hampered in everyday activities due to health problems was higher across each of the Member States than the corresponding share for men (except in Ireland, where the share among men was 0.1 points higher than for women). The difference in rates between the sexes rose to almost 4 percentage points in Portugal, where 13.4 % of women were severely hampered, and was above 3 percentage points in Slovakia, Finland, Lithuania and Latvia; each of these countries reported that in excess of 10 % of their female population was severely hampered in everyday activities because of health problems.

Figure 5.3: Overweight people, 2003 (1)

(% of total population)

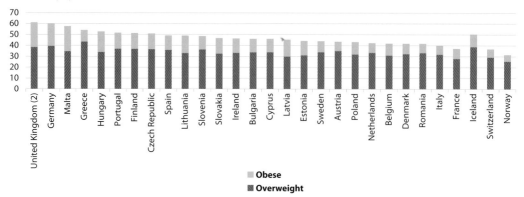

(1) National health interview survey (HIS) data, 1996-2003 depending on the country; note that data for Germany and for England relate to valid height and weight measurements, while for the other countries the data correspond to self-declared height and weight. Luxembourg, not available.
(2) Only England.

Source: Eurostat (hlth_ls_bmia)

Figure 5.4: Daily smokers, 2003 (1)

(% of male / female population)

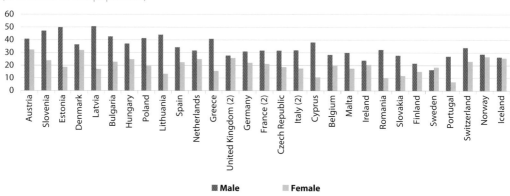

(1) National health interview survey (HIS) data, 1996-2003 depending on the country; Luxembourg, not available; the figure is ranked on the average of male and female.
(2) No distinction between daily and occasional smoking.

Source: Eurostat (tps00169)

Figure 5.5: Daily smokers among the population aged 15-24, 2003 (1)

(% of male/female population aged 15-24)

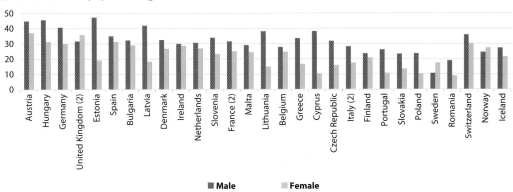

■ **Male**   ■ **Female**

(1) National health interview survey (HIS) data, 1996-2003 depending on the country; Luxembourg, not available; the figure is ranked on the average of male and female.
(2) No distinction between daily and occasional smoking.

Source: Eurostat (tps00170)

Figure 5.6: Persons severely hampered in activities people usually do because of health problems for at least the past 6 months, 2006 (1)

(% of male/female population aged 15 years and over)

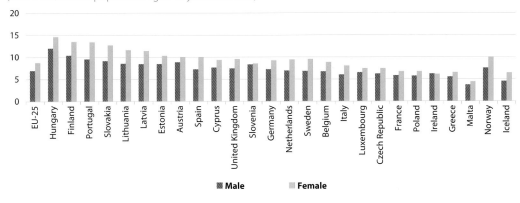

■ **Male**   ■ **Female**

(1) Bulgaria, Denmark and Romania, not available; the figure is ranked on the average of male and female.

Source: Eurostat (hlth_silc_06)

5.3 Healthcare

Introduction

Most Europeans agree that there is a basic need for universal access to healthcare, as the cost of many modern-day health treatments can often be prohibitive to the average person. The provision of healthcare systems varies considerably between the Member States, although widespread use is made of public provision (national or regional health services) and comprehensive healthcare insurance. Healthcare schemes generally cover their entire resident population; nevertheless, an increasing proportion of individuals choose to adhere to private insurance schemes (usually on top of the national provision for care).

Public regulation of the healthcare sector is a complex task, as the healthcare market is characterised by numerous market imperfections. Member States generally aim to balance the efficient use of resources with ensuring that healthcare provisions are available to all. There is no simple answer to the question of how much a country should spend on healthcare, as each of the Member States faces a different burden of disease, while populations have different expectations of what services their national healthcare systems should offer. Indeed, the amount of money needed to fund a healthcare system is a function of a large number of variables, the most obvious being the burden of disease requiring treatment – although there is no simple linear relationship between the burden of disease and the need for resources, as some conditions can be treated simply and at low cost while others may require a complex and expensive care.

The main consumers of healthcare are older people – a section of the European population that is growing rapidly, partly as a result of the baby-boom cohort reaching older age, but also because of continued increases in life expectancy. The likely increase in numbers of elderly persons will probably drive demand for more healthcare provision in the future, while medical advances are also likely to result in more and better treatments being available. Demand for healthcare is also likely to rise in the coming years in relation to long-term care provision (nursing and convalescence homes).

In addition, more patients are travelling across borders to receive treatment, to avoid waiting lists or to seek specialist treatment that may only be available abroad. The EU works towards ensuring that people who move across borders have access to healthcare anywhere within the Union. Indeed, healthcare systems and health policies across the EU are becoming more interconnected. This is not only a result of the movement of patients and professionals between countries, but may also be attributed to a set of common public expectations of health services across Europe, as well as more rapid dissemination of new medical technologies and techniques. On 2 July 2008, as part of a Renewed Social Agenda, the European Commission adopted a draft Directive on the application of patients' rights to cross-border healthcare [5].

(5) http://ec.europa.eu/health/ph_overview/co_operation/healthcare/docs/COM_en.pdf.

Definitions and data availability

Information on healthcare can be divided into two broad groups of data: resource-related healthcare data on human and technical resources; and output-related data that focuses on hospital patients and the treatment(s) they receive. Healthcare data are largely based on administrative data sources, and, to a large degree, they reflect country-specific ways of organising healthcare; as such, the information collected may not always be completely comparable.

Hospitals are defined according to the classification of healthcare providers of the System of Health Accounts (SHA); all public and private hospitals should be covered.

Data on **healthcare staff,** in the form of human resources available for providing healthcare services, is provided irrespective of the sector of employment (i.e. whether the personnel are independent, employed by a hospital, or any other healthcare provider). These statistics cover healthcare professionals such as physicians, dentists, nurses, pharmacists and physiotherapists. In the context of comparing healthcare services across Member States, Eurostat gives preference to the concept of '**practising professionals**', as this best describes the availability of healthcare resources. By way of example, physicians may be counted as licensed, economically active or practising. Data for two or more concepts are available in the majority of Member States. The preference, however, is for **practising**

physicians who are defined as those seeing patients either in a hospital, practice or elsewhere. Practising physicians' tasks include: conducting medical examination and making diagnosis, prescribing medication and giving treatment for diagnosed illnesses, disorders or injuries, giving specialised medical or surgical treatment for particular types of illnesses, disorders or injuries, giving advice on and applying preventive medicine methods and treatments.

Hospital bed numbers provide information on healthcare capacities, i.e. on the maximum number of patients who can be treated by hospitals. Hospital beds are those which are regularly maintained and staffed and immediately available for the care of admitted patients. These include: beds in all hospitals, including general hospitals, mental health and substance abuse hospitals, and other specialty hospitals: occupied and unoccupied beds. The statistics exclude surgical tables, recovery trolleys, emergency stretchers, beds for same-day care, cots for healthy infants, beds in wards which were closed for any reason, provisional and temporary beds, or beds in nursing and residential care facilities. They cover beds accommodating patients who are formally admitted (or hospitalised) to an institution for treatment and/or care and who stay for a minimum of one night in the hospital or other institution providing in-patient care. **Curative care** (or acute care) beds in hospitals are beds that are available for curative care; these form a subgroup of total hospital beds.

Output-related indicators focus on hospital patients and covers the interaction between patients and healthcare systems, namely in the form of the treatment received. Data in this domain are available for a range of indicators including **hospital discharges** of in-patients and day cases by age, sex, and selected (groups of) diseases; the average length of stay of in-patients; or the medical procedures performed in hospitals; the number of hospital discharges is the most commonly used measure of the utilisation of hospital services. Discharges, rather than admissions, are used because hospital abstracts for in-patient care are based on information gathered at the time of discharge. A hospital discharge is defined as the formal release of a patient from a hospital after a procedure or course of treatment. A discharge occurs whenever a patient leaves because of finalisation of treatment, signs out against medical advice, transfers to another healthcare institution or on death; healthy newborn babies should be included; transfers to another department within the same institution are excluded.

Main findings

The highest number of physicians per 100 000 inhabitants was recorded in Greece (almost 500 professionally active physicians in 2005), followed by Belgium (405 practising physicians in 2007) and Austria (376 practising physicians in 2007); note the methodological differences between the various types of physicians reported in each country.

In 2005 there was an average of 590 hospital beds per 100 000 inhabitants within the EU-27, compared with 695 beds in 1997 (an overall reduction of 15 %); Austria was the only Member State to report an increase in hospital bed numbers, rising by 24.6 beds per 100 000 inhabitants over the period 1996 to 2005. A more detailed breakdown shows that reductions in bed numbers were spread across different categories, with an average of 406.3 curative care beds available per 100 000 inhabitants in the EU-27 in 2005, while there were 60.4 psychiatric beds in hospitals per 100 000 inhabitants; compared with 1997 these latest figures represented overall reductions of 16.6 % and 22.6 % respectively.

The general reduction in hospital bed numbers may result from a more efficient use of resources, with an increasing number of operations being dealt with in out-patient treatment, and shorter periods being spent in hospital following an operation. Nevertheless, the output of each National Health Service, as measured by the number of in-patient discharges, will usually (at least to some degree), reflect the number of physicians and hospital beds available. The highest number of hospital discharges in 2006 was recorded in Austria (more than 27 000 per 100 000 inhabitants), which was almost 25 % more than the next highest figure, 21 866 discharges in Lithuania. At the other end of the range, the number of hospital discharges of in-patients was relatively low in both Malta (2004) and Cyprus (below 7 000 per 100 000 inhabitants).

Diseases of the circulatory system accounted for the highest number of hospital discharges in 2006 in the vast majority of countries for which data are available, often with upwards of 3 000 discharges per 100 000 inhabitants. In Bulgaria and Romania (both 2005), higher numbers of discharges were recorded for diseases of the respiratory system. In Ireland, Spain (2005) and Malta (2005) there were more discharges from pregnancies, while in Cyprus the highest number of discharges resulted from injury or poisoning. Ireland, Spain, Cyprus and Malta were characterised by relatively low levels of hospital discharges, which may, at least in some cases, be due to patients travelling abroad in order to receive specialist treatment.

The average length of stay in hospital was generally longest for those patients suffering from cancer or from circulatory system problems. The average time spent in hospital is a function of hospital efficiency, as well as the type of treatments that are on offer; France, Cyprus, Malta and Poland reported the shortest average stays in hospital. At the other end of the range, some of the longest average stays were registered in Finland, the Czech Republic, Germany and Lithuania, with lengthy average stays for diseases of the circulatory system a common feature.

Table 5.1: Healthcare indicators
(per 100 000 inhabitants)

	Practising physicians (1)		Hospital beds		Hospital discharges of in-patients (excluding healthy new born babies)	
	1996	2006 (2)	1996 (3)	2006 (4)	2001	2006 (5)
EU-27	:	:	694.8	590.4	:	:
Belgium	360.3	404.7	798.3	672.3	16 162	16 084
Bulgaria	354.8	366.1	1 049.6	621.4	:	20 217
Czech Republic	298.6	355.7	886.9	817.0	:	20 799
Denmark	252.3	308.4	459.8	:	16 326	:
Germany	310.8	345.5	957.8	829.1	20 060	21 481
Estonia	317.0	328.9	795.5	565.3	:	:
Ireland	208.5	282.4	673.7	524.7	14 025	13 656
Greece	386.3	499.4	517.3	473.8	:	:
Spain	290.2	368.3	389.1	334.1	10 904	10 780
France	324.4	338.2	853.8	707.5	17 937	16 445
Italy	409.9	366.6	655.0	395.2	:	:
Cyprus	246.9	250.4	498.7	373.7	7 031	6 536
Latvia	282.1	286.1	1 038.3	755.4	:	19 970
Lithuania	373.2	364.8	1 092.0	801.0	23 454	21 866
Luxembourg	212.6	327.7	1 079.9	:	18 172	17 242
Hungary	304.3	303.7	903.0	792.1	:	:
Malta	:	332.8	576.8	237.8	:	6 871
Netherlands	189.9	:	522.2	438.2	:	10 135
Austria	280.6	375.7	746.3	770.9	:	27 119
Poland	235.1	218.0	766.3	647.5	:	17 955
Portugal	262.3	267.8	399.3	365.1	:	9 127
Romania	:	215.8	757.0	658.6	:	:
Slovenia	:	235.8	566.6	477.5	:	16 045
Slovakia	257.1	315.9	832.7	671.4	20 534	19 124
Finland	213.7	244.5	803.0	695.6	:	19 620
Sweden	289.0	356.6	559.8	287.7	14 997	:
United Kingdom	:	235.6	433.4	388.7	:	:
Croatia	219.9	:	618.5	545.0	12 268	13 307
FYR of Macedonia	226.4	245.2	523.0	470.2	:	:
Turkey	:	:	248.5	241.2	:	:
Iceland	310.9	364.0	:	:	16 789	16 084
Norway	283.1	377.7	400.6	402.7	15 999	17 424
Switzerland	180.0	:	665.9	555.6	:	15 656

(1) Greece, France, Italy and the former Yugoslav Republic of Macedonia, professionally active physicians; Ireland and Malta, licensed physicians.
(2) Belgium, Spain, Latvia, Malta and Austria, 2007; Denmark, Greece, Finland, the United Kingdom and the former Yugoslav Republic of Macedonia, 2005; Luxembourg and Portugal, 2004.
(3) EU-27, Denmark and the United Kingdom,1997.
(4) France, Latvia and Malta, 2007; EU-27, Greece, Austria, the United Kingdom, Croatia, the former Yugoslav Republic of Macedonia and Switzerland, 2005; Portugal and Turkey, 2004.
(5) Belgium, Bulgaria, Spain, Latvia, Luxembourg, the Netherlands, Poland, Portugal, Slovakia, Croatia, Iceland, Norway and Switzerland, 2005; Malta, 2004.
Source: Eurostat (tps00044, hlth_rs_prs, tps00046 and hlth_co_disch2)

Table 5.2: Hospital beds
(per 100 000 inhabitants)

	Curative care beds in hospitals			Psychiatric care beds in hospitals		
	1996 (1)	2001 (2)	2006 (3)	1996 (1)	2001 (2)	2006 (4)
EU-27	487.2	450.7	406.3	78.0	66.0	60.4
Belgium	503.3	472.6	441.1	257.9	252.8	182.8
Bulgaria	:	583.1	469.0	88.0	71.1	67.1
Czech Republic	728.7	609.6	568.6	100.2	99.3	94.9
Denmark	380.2	349.5	327.8	79.6	75.1	:
Germany	744.5	680.3	634.9	:	:	:
Estonia	638.8	528.1	382.2	100.5	70.6	55.3
Ireland	306.3	281.1	279.8	168.8	126.9	90.3
Greece	389.7	387.3	:	107.1	93.5	86.9
Spain	303.9	287.2	259.9	58.5	51.0	46.2
France	460.8	416.0	372.1	123.6	104.5	91.2
Italy	552.6	407.0	331.7	54.9	14.4	13.1
Cyprus	366.4	370.4	349.1	87.8	38.1	26.9
Latvia	903.9	609.0	531.8	177.0	153.0	136.7
Lithuania	871.4	625.0	529.9	134.0	122.6	102.6
Luxembourg	618.8	572.2	549.4	128.0	83.8	:
Hungary	627.3	563.7	552.0	105.3	42.4	38.3
Malta	387.7	372.7	280.4	47.8	41.4	51.6
Netherlands	331.7	306.5	287.6	172.2	155.9	130.8
Austria	665.4	628.7	606.6	75.2	53.2	61.7
Poland	576.4	509.9	463.2	83.5	73.3	68.0
Portugal	:	:	:	:	:	:
Romania	569.2	551.5	456.3	88.8	83.9	79.7
Slovenia	475.4	446.1	388.2	80.3	75.2	71.4
Slovakia	620.5	566.5	501.1	90.6	93.0	83.8
Finland	295.8	241.2	223.7	120.5	101.1	92.1
Sweden	304.5	245.2	:	82.3	58.6	49.1
United Kingdom	321.0	315.0	309.7	103.0	85.9	73.7
Croatia	390.0	378.1	340.2	106.6	102.7	94.4
FYR of Macedonia	354.2	329.8	312.6	75.6	68.2	60.7
Turkey	190.6	218.0	231.1	12.8	12.5	12.1
Iceland	375.7	:	:	:	:	:
Norway	334.2	311.4	292.4	71.2	72.9	102.3
Switzerland	551.4	412.3	365.9	128.8	113.2	106.1

(1) EU-27, Denmark, Malta and the United Kingdom, 1997.
(2) Hungary and Sweden, break in series.
(3) France, Latvia and Malta, 2007; EU-27, Greece, Austria, the United Kingdom, Croatia, the former Yugoslav Republic of Macedonia and Switzerland, 2005; Luxembourg and Turkey, 2004.
(4) France, Latvia and Malta, 2007; EU-27, Greece, Austria, the United Kingdom, Croatia, the former Yugoslav Republic of Macedonia and Switzerland, 2005; Turkey, 2004.

Source: Eurostat (tps00168 and tps00047)

Table 5.3: Hospital discharges of in-patients by diagnosis (ISHMT - international shortlist for hospital morbidity tabulation), 2006
(per 100 000 inhabitants)

	Neoplasms (cancers)	Diseases of the circulatory system	Diseases of the respiratory system	Diseases of the digestive system	Pregnancy, childbirth & the puerperium	Injury, poisoning & certain other consequences of external causes
Belgium (1)	1 243.6	2 135.3	1 440.6	1 698.0	1 361.8	1 633.9
Bulgaria (1)	1 715.0	3 002.9	3 180.3	1 636.5	1 948.8	1 317.1
Czech Republic	1 760.7	3 225.3	1 367.5	1 837.7	1 520.3	1 730.8
Denmark	:	:	:	:	:	:
Germany	2 359.9	3 322.2	1 322.6	2 077.5	1 071.0	2 127.8
Estonia (1)	1 571.8	3 243.1	2 024.7	1 624.4	1 832.3	1 191.0
Ireland	860.6	1 234.3	1 399.1	1 238.8	2 482.7	1 347.2
Greece	:	:	:	:	:	:
Spain (1)	916.1	1 338.9	1 146.7	1 270.4	1 386.3	898.3
France (1)	1 277.0	1 972.7	1 005.3	1 696.7	1 566.6	1 460.7
Italy (2)	1 330.5	2 480.7	1 144.3	1 461.5	1 336.1	1 323.5
Cyprus	411.8	721.0	656.0	689.7	405.0	842.8
Latvia (1)	1 799.7	3 538.9	2 221.7	1 831.8	1 619.2	2 243.1
Lithuania	1 664.4	4 441.5	2 063.8	1 852.3	1 636.1	1 963.9
Luxembourg (1)	1 743.7	2 275.1	1 436.2	1 664.5	1 329.9	1 262.8
Hungary	:	:	:	:	:	:
Malta (2)	183.4	694.3	540.8	591.9	971.7	580.2
Netherlands (1)	997.4	1 527.5	731.2	915.8	857.5	848.3
Austria	2 809.2	3 720.3	1 685.7	2 502.8	1 331.9	2 909.3
Poland (1)	1 908.4	3 024.1	1 557.4	1 765.5	1 577.4	1 615.1
Portugal (1)	920.3	1 206.2	955.9	1 061.9	1 089.3	684.7
Romania (1)	1 274.6	2 588.1	2 785.3	2 070.8	1 697.3	1 279.2
Slovenia	1 836.4	1 971.8	1 221.7	1 419.5	1 248.7	1 529.9
Slovakia (1)	1 764.1	3 054.4	1 660.4	1 889.0	1 630.9	1 586.2
Finland	1 769.3	3 032.6	1 411.9	1 414.9	1 316.9	1 932.3
Sweden	:	:	:	:	:	:
United Kingdom	:	:	:	:	:	:
Croatia (1)	1 828.4	1 849.4	1 147.3	1 179.1	223.4	1 041.9
FYR of Macedonia (1)	1 164.0	1 553.7	1 424.1	1 038.9	753.5	579.2
Iceland (1)	1 393.8	1 824.9	980.3	1 346.7	2 113.7	1 020.4
Norway (1)	1 794.8	2 467.0	1 531.0	1 237.9	1 487.3	1 854.1
Switzerland (1)	1 123.6	1 735.1	869.4	1 353.3	1 181.9	1 846.2

(1) 2005.
(2) 2004.

Source: Eurostat (hlth_co_disch2)

Table 5.4: Hospital discharges of in-patients by diagnosis (ISHMT - international shortlist for hospital morbidity tabulation), average length of stay, 2006
(days)

	Neoplasms (cancers)	Diseases of the circulatory system	Diseases of the respiratory system	Diseases of the digestive system	Pregnancy, childbirth & the puerperium	Injury, poisoning & certain other consequences of external causes
Belgium (1)	9.4	8.4	8.4	6.1	5.0	8.5
Bulgaria (1)	7.9	7.6	8.5	6.4	4.8	6.6
Czech Republic	10.2	13.6	9.2	7.7	5.5	10.3
Denmark	:	:	:	:	:	:
Germany	10.4	10.5	8.9	7.6	4.9	9.3
Estonia (1)	8.0	10.6	5.0	5.2	3.1	8.8
Ireland	11.5	10.2	6.9	6.4	2.9	5.8
Greece	:	:	:	:	:	:
Spain	9.6	8.4	7.1	5.9	3.2	8.5
France	7.7	7.0	6.9	5.3	4.9	5.7
Italy (2)	9.7	8.7	8.1	6.8	4.0	7.8
Cyprus	8.5	5.9	5.0	4.8	5.5	4.9
Latvia (1)	9.1	9.2	7.9	6.2	5.6	7.5
Lithuania	10.5	13.0	7.9	6.7	4.7	8.5
Luxembourg (1)	8.9	7.9	6.0	5.9	4.8	7.7
Hungary	:	:	:	:	:	:
Malta (3)	7.5	6.5	4.9	3.9	3.5	5.9
Netherlands (1)	8.5	7.8	7.6	6.8	3.8	7.7
Austria	7.8	11.0	8.2	6.8	5.5	8.7
Poland (1)	6.6	7.9	8.1	5.8	5.1	5.3
Portugal (1)	8.7	7.9	8.2	5.9	3.3	9.3
Romania (1)	7.7	8.5	7.5	6.9	5.4	6.5
Slovenia	7.9	8.4	7.5	6.1	4.6	7.0
Slovakia (1)	9.1	9.0	8.2	6.5	5.8	7.1
Finland	9.0	16.3	13.4	6.0	3.7	11.1
Sweden	:	:	:	:	:	:
United Kingdom	:	:	:	:	:	:
Croatia	10.0	10.3	8.9	8.6	8.5	8.7
FYR of Macedonia (1)	8.5	10.9	8.2	6.3	4.4	9.1
Iceland (1)	7.2	6.4	6.2	4.0	2.4	6.4
Norway (1)	7.2	5.4	6.1	4.9	3.7	4.8
Switzerland (1)	10.6	9.3	8.8	7.4	6.1	8.0

(1) 2005.
(2) 2004.
(3) 2007.

Source: Eurostat (hlth_co_inpst)

5.4 Causes of death and infant mortality

Introduction

Broadly speaking, the EU has witnessed a very significant reduction in mortality during the last century or so – both in terms of reduced infant mortality and as a result of declines in infectious and degenerative diseases. Non-communicable diseases – a group of conditions that includes cardiovascular disease, cancer, mental health problems, diabetes mellitus, chronic respiratory disease, and musculoskeletal conditions – cause more than 85 % of deaths in Europe. These disorders are largely preventable and are linked by common risk factors, underlying determinants and opportunities for intervention. Among these, cancer and cardiovascular diseases are currently by far the most important causes of death in the EU for both men and women.

Mortality during the first year of life has decreased considerably in all Member States, such that current levels are among the lowest in the world. There however remain persistent differences in rates across different social groups or across geographical regions.

Definitions and data availability

The **infant mortality rate** represents the ratio between deaths of children under one year and the number of live births in a given year; the value is expressed per 1 000 live births. Note that some countries use different definitions for spontaneous abortion, early foetal death and late foetal death (or stillbirth).

Eurostat began collecting and disseminating **mortality data** in 1994, broken down by:

- a shortlist of 65 causes of death based on the International Statistical Classification of Diseases and Related Health Problems (ICD), that is developed and maintained by the World Health Organisation (WHO);
- gender;
- age;
- geographical region (NUTS level 2).

Causes of death (COD) statistics are based on information derived from medical certificates; the medical certification of death is an obligation in all Member States. They target the underlying cause of death, in other words, 'the disease or injury which initiated the train of morbid events leading directly to death, or the circumstances of the accident or violence which produced the fatal injury' (a definition adopted by the World Health Assembly). Although definitions are harmonised, the statistics may not be fully comparable as classifications may vary when the cause of death is multiple or difficult to evaluate and because of different notification procedures. Annual data are provided in absolute numbers, as crude death rates and as standardised death rates.

The **standardised death rate (SDR)** is a weighted average of the age-specific mortality rates. The weights are the age distribution of the population whose mortality experience is being observed. Since most

causes of death vary significantly by age and sex, the use of standardised death rates improves comparability over time and between countries.

Main findings

The progress made in medical health-care services is reflected in a decreasing infant mortality rate. In the course of the last four decades the infant mortality rate in the EU fell from almost 28 deaths per 1 000 live births in 1965 to 4.7 deaths in 2006. Indeed, as a result of declining infant mortality rates, most of the Member States are now among a group of countries with the lowest infant mortality rates in the world, for example, 1.8 deaths per 1 000 live births in Luxembourg or less than 3 deaths per 1 000 live births in Slovenia, Finland or Sweden. Infant mortality rates have levelled-off in some countries in recent years; this may, in part, be due to factors such as: an increasing number of women deferring childbirth; or a higher number of multiple births as a result of the more common use of fertility treatments.

By far the most important causes of death among men and women in the EU-27 in 2006 were cancer (malignant neoplasm) and ischaemic heart diseases; there were, however, large differences between standardised death rates for men and women.

Deaths from cancer among men had an incidence of 233 per 100 000, while the corresponding rate for women was 134. The difference in the incidence of death from cancer between the sexes was often particularly high among those Member States that joined the EU since 2004, although France and Spain also recorded considerable disparities.

Standardised death rates for ischaemic heart diseases were about twice as high for men (at 132 per 100 000) as for women (68). Heart disease was particularly prevalent among men and women in the Baltic Member States, Slovakia, Hungary and Romania. Indeed, there was a higher incidence of death from heart disease than from cancer in each of these countries across both genders, other than for deaths from cancer among men in Hungary). Those countries reporting the lowest incidence of death from heart disease included France, Spain, Portugal and the Netherlands.

Men reported higher standardised death rates (than women) for all of the main causes of death, with rates as much as four or five times as high as those recorded for women for drug dependence and alcohol abuse, and between three and four times as high for AIDS (HIV) and suicide and intentional self-harm.

Figure 5.7: Infant mortality (1)

(per 1 000 live births)

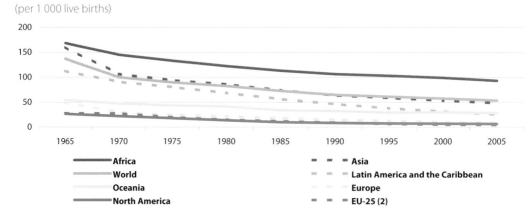

(1) All data (excluding EU-25) are averages of the five-year period up to and including the reference period referred to in the figure.
(2) EU-27 for latest period; 2007 instead of 2005.

Source: Eurostat (demo_minfind), United Nations, Population Division of the Department of Economic and Social Affairs

Figure 5.8: Causes of death - standardised death rate, EU-27, 2006 (1)

(per 100 000 inhabitants)

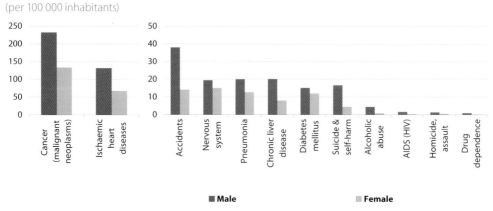

(1) Note the differences in the scales employed between the two parts of the figure; the figure is ranked on the average of male and female; EU-27 averages calculated on the basis of the latest year available for each Member State.

Source: Eurostat (tps00116, tps00119, tps00125, tps00134, tps00128, tps00131, tps00137, tps00122, tps00140, tps00143, tps00146 and tps00149)

Table 5.5: Infant mortality

(per 1 000 live births)

	1965	1970	1975	1980	1985	1990	1995	2000	2005	2007
EU-27 (1)	28.6	25.5	20.8	15.8	12.8	10.3	7.5	5.9	4.9	4.7
Euro area (1)	28.5	23.8	18.9	12.8	9.7	7.6	5.6	4.6	3.9	3.7
Belgium	23.7	21.1	16.1	12.1	9.8	8.0	6.0	4.8	3.7	4.0
Bulgaria	30.8	27.3	23.1	20.2	15.4	14.8	14.8	13.3	10.4	9.2
Czech Republic	23.7	20.2	19.4	16.9	12.5	10.8	7.7	4.1	3.4	3.1
Denmark	18.7	14.2	10.4	8.4	7.9	7.5	5.1	5.3	4.4	4.0
Germany	24.1	22.5	18.9	12.4	9.1	7.0	5.3	4.4	3.9	3.9
Estonia	20.3	17.7	18.2	17.1	14.1	12.3	14.9	8.4	5.4	5.0
Ireland	25.2	19.5	17.5	11.1	8.8	8.2	6.4	6.2	4.0	3.1
Greece	34.3	29.6	24.0	17.9	14.1	9.7	8.1	5.9	3.8	3.5
Spain	29.4	20.7	18.9	12.3	8.9	7.6	5.5	4.4	3.8	3.7
France (1)	22.4	18.2	13.8	10.0	8.3	7.3	4.9	4.5	3.8	3.8
Italy	35.0	:	20.8	14.6	10.5	8.2	6.2	4.5	:	3.7
Cyprus	32.0	26.0	18.2	14.4	14.4	12.9	9.7	5.6	4.6	3.7
Latvia	18.9	17.7	20.3	15.3	13.0	13.7	18.8	:	7.8	8.7
Lithuania	24.7	19.3	19.6	14.5	14.2	10.2	12.5	8.6	6.8	5.9
Luxembourg	24.0	24.9	14.8	11.5	9.0	7.3	5.5	5.1	2.6	1.8
Hungary	38.8	35.9	32.8	23.2	20.4	14.8	10.7	9.2	6.2	5.9
Malta	34.8	27.9	18.3	15.2	14.5	9.1	8.9	5.9	6.0	6.5
Netherlands	14.4	12.7	10.6	8.6	8.0	7.1	5.5	:	4.9	4.1
Austria	28.3	25.9	20.5	14.3	11.2	7.8	5.4	4.8	4.2	3.7
Poland	41.6	36.4	24.8	25.4	22.1	19.4	13.6	8.1	6.4	6.0
Portugal	64.9	55.5	38.9	24.2	17.8	11.0	7.5	5.5	3.5	3.4
Romania	44.1	49.4	34.7	29.3	25.6	26.9	21.2	18.6	15.0	12.0
Slovenia	29.6	24.5	17.3	15.3	13.0	8.4	5.5	4.9	4.1	2.8
Slovakia	28.5	25.7	23.7	20.9	16.3	12.0	11.0	8.6	7.2	6.1
Finland	17.6	13.2	9.6	7.6	6.3	5.6	3.9	3.8	3.0	2.7
Sweden	13.3	11.0	8.6	6.9	6.8	6.0	4.1	3.4	2.4	2.5
United Kingdom (2)	19.6	18.5	18.9	13.9	11.1	7.9	6.2	5.6	5.1	4.9
Croatia	49.5	34.2	23.0	20.6	16.6	10.7	8.9	7.4	5.7	5.6
FYR of Macedonia	105.8	87.9	65.1	54.2	43.4	31.6	22.7	11.8	12.8	10.3
Turkey	:	:	:	:	:	:	:	28.9	23.6	21.7
Iceland	15.0	13.2	12.5	7.7	5.7	5.9	6.1	3.0	2.3	2.0
Liechtenstein	22.8	11.8	6.5	7.6	10.7	:	:	:	2.6	0.0
Norway	14.6	11.3	9.5	8.1	8.5	6.9	4.0	3.8	3.1	3.1
Switzerland	17.8	15.1	10.7	9.1	6.9	6.8	5.0	4.9	4.2	3.9

(1) 2006 instead of 2007. France: including overseas departments starting with 2000.
(2) 2006 instead of 2007.

Source: Eurostat (demo_minfind)

Table 5.6: Causes of death - standardised death rate, 2006 (1)

(per 100 000 inhabitants)

	Cancer (2)	Heart disease (3)	Nervous system	Pneu- monia	Chronic liver disease	Diabetes mellitus	Acci- dents	Sui- cide (4)	Alc. abuse	Homi- cide, assault	AIDS (HIV)	Drug depen- dence
EU-27 (5)	175.6	96.2	17.1	15.7	13.8	13.6	25.8	10.4	2.7	1.0	1.1	0.6
Belgium	:	:	:	:	:	:	:	:	:	:	:	:
Bulgaria	168.3	147.9	8.8	16.5	15.9	18.7	30.2	10.5	0.5	1.7	0.0	0.0
Czech Republic	212.5	168.8	15.7	22.7	15.9	10.7	32.5	12.2	1.8	1.0	0.0	0.0
Denmark	:	:	:	:	:	:	:	:	:	:	:	:
Germany	165.0	97.9	14.2	13.3	14.2	15.1	17.1	9.8	4.7	0.6	0.6	0.8
Estonia	198.9	253.3	17.4	10.7	22.0	12.8	75.5	16.2	9.9	7.1	3.6	0.1
Ireland	180.2	103.4	15.0	38.0	5.8	10.9	17.8	9.1	2.1	0.8	0.1	2.0
Greece	154.7	76.3	7.5	4.9	5.4	7.2	26.7	3.1	0.2	0.8	0.2	0.0
Spain	158.3	51.9	20.6	9.9	9.0	12.5	21.7	6.2	0.6	0.8	2.7	0.2
France	176.1	40.4	25.4	10.2	11.2	11.7	29.6	15.8	4.7	0.8	1.4	0.3
Italy	:	:	:	:	:	:	:	:	:	:	:	:
Cyprus	116.4	79.4	14.0	10.4	4.7	36.5	28.4	2.4	0.4	1.7	0.2	0.7
Latvia	199.7	279.4	13.5	20.4	17.8	8.9	94.9	19.3	3.4	9.1	1.3	0.0
Lithuania	195.4	347.2	14.9	17.3	35.1	8.0	99.4	28.9	0.9	7.3	0.2	0.5
Luxembourg	162.2	67.1	22.8	14.0	11.3	7.6	29.0	9.9	4.5	1.5	0.2	0.4
Hungary	239.9	240.7	12.5	5.1	44.7	21.9	39.9	21.8	4.5	1.9	0.0	0.0
Malta	145.3	149.5	18.1	14.7	6.4	22.1	19.9	4.2	0.4	0.5	0.3	:
Netherlands	186.5	54.3	16.8	22.1	4.2	15.0	15.2	8.7	1.1	0.8	0.3	0.1
Austria	161.9	107.7	15.5	9.3	14.7	26.9	23.4	13.4	3.6	0.8	0.5	2.5
Poland	210.1	111.2	10.9	19.6	15.4	13.1	38.1	14.3	4.6	1.4	0.3	0.0
Portugal	156.0	53.4	15.9	27.5	12.2	27.2	19.9	7.2	0.8	1.3	7.8	0.1
Romania	179.8	213.2	7.9	24.8	39.7	7.9	40.8	11.9	2.2	2.1	0.9	0.0
Slovenia	197.8	68.0	8.8	23.4	23.9	13.4	36.7	22.8	3.0	0.6	0.1	0.1
Slovakia	203.5	248.4	11.9	31.8	25.8	12.3	37.6	9.4	:	1.5	0.0	0.0
Finland	140.5	136.7	36.6	7.2	17.2	6.3	46.1	19.0	2.9	1.9	0.2	0.1
Sweden	152.3	98.4	17.8	10.1	5.6	11.9	20.7	12.0	2.8	0.9	0.2	0.2
United Kingdom	185.2	128.6	18.1	33.5	10.0	7.7	16.5	6.6	1.5	0.4	0.3	1.9
Croatia	209.8	159.6	11.2	18.8	21.7	17.2	35.2	15.5	3.9	1.7	0.2	0.4
FYR of Macedonia	169.5	107.0	7.1	4.5	7.5	36.3	22.3	8.3	0.6	2.5	0.1	0.1
Iceland	159.3	92.3	36.0	14.5	4.0	5.6	19.9	11.5	1.2	1.0	0.3	0.3
Norway	161.9	75.4	19.1	19.1	3.2	10.7	28.6	11.2	3.7	1.0	0.3	0.5
Switzerland	146.1	72.4	21.8	11.3	7.0	11.3	19.2	15.0	2.4	0.9	0.9	3.0

(1) France, Luxembourg, Malta, Portugal, the United Kingdom and Switzerland, 2005; Iceland, 2005 except for AIDS (HIV), 2004; Slovenia, 2005 for AIDS (HIV); Estonia and Romania, 2005 for drug dependence; Slovakia, 2004 for drug dependence.
(2) Malignant neoplasms.
(3) Ischaemic heart diseases.
(4) Suicide and intentional self-harm.
(5) Average calculated on the basis of the latest year available for each Member State.

Source: Eurostat (tps00116, tps00119, tps00134, tps00128, tps00131, tps00137, tps00125, tps00122, tps00140, tps00146, tps00143 and tps00149)

Figure 5.9: Deaths from cancer (malignant neoplasms) - standardised death rate, 2006 (1)

(per 100 000 inhabitants)

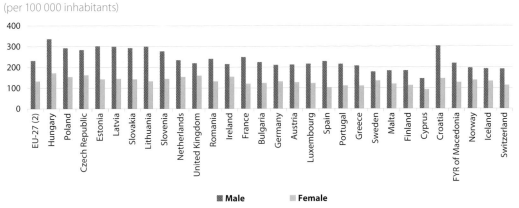

■ Male   ■ Female

(1) France, Luxembourg, Malta, Portugal, the United Kingdom, Iceland and Switzerland, 2005; Belgium, Denmark and Italy, not available; the figure is ranked on the average of male and female.
(2) Average calculated on the basis of the latest year available for each Member State.

Source: Eurostat (tps00116)

Figure 5.10: Deaths from ischaemic heart diseases - standardised death rate, 2006 (1)

(per 100 000 inhabitants)

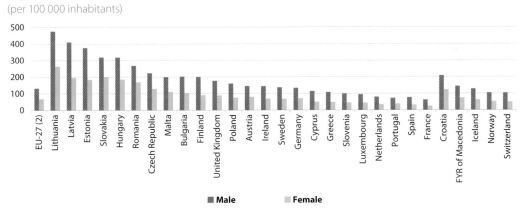

■ Male   ■ Female

(1) France, Luxembourg, Malta, Portugal, the United Kingdom, Iceland and Switzerland, 2005; Belgium, Denmark and Italy, not available; the figure is ranked on the average of male and female.
(2) Average calculated on the basis of the latest year available for each Member State.

Source: Eurostat (tps00119)

Figure 5.11: Deaths from suicide - standardised death rate, 2006 (1)

(per 100 000 inhabitants)

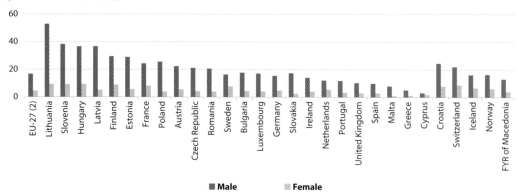

■ **Male**　　■ **Female**

(1) France, Luxembourg, Malta, Portugal, the United Kingdom, Iceland and Switzerland, 2005; Belgium, Denmark and Italy, not available; the figure is ranked on the average of male and female.
(2) Average calculated on the basis of the latest year available for each Member State.

Source: Eurostat (tps00122)

Figure 5.12: Deaths from accidents - standardised death rate, 2006 (1)

(per 100 000 inhabitants)

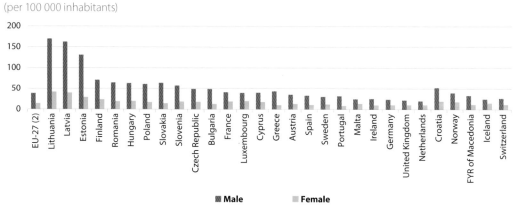

■ **Male**　　■ **Female**

(1) France, Luxembourg, Malta, Portugal, the United Kingdom, Iceland and Switzerland, 2005; Belgium, Denmark and Italy, not available; the figure is ranked on the average of male and female.
(2) Average calculated on the basis of the latest year available for each Member State.

Source: Eurostat (tps00125)

5.5 Safety at work

Introduction

Working conditions change over time. A high proportion of people spend 8 hours a day, 5 days a week at work. While there have been many studies concerning the benefits of work as a source of wealth (for both the individual and the enterprise), there has, until recently, been less interest in the negative effects that work can have on human and public health. Many aspects of work have the potential to bring about illness (or death) and these are not restricted to safety issues and accidents. Rather, health and safety in the workplace has been redefined in order to take account of the move from traditional, industrial, heavy industries, to focus on the modern-day world of work, which is characterised more by issues such as stress and psychological risks, musculoskeletal disorders, noise, or the abuse of tobacco, alcohol, or dangerous substances related to work.

Health at work also involves physical, moral and social well-being (issues such as intimidation and violence in the workplace), which are considered especially important determinants regarding the quality of work and the productivity of the workforce. A strategic health and safety policy is therefore not just crucial to ensuring the well-being of Europe's workers; it is also a key issue in competitiveness.

Definitions and data availability

European statistics on **accidents at work** and occupational diseases respond to the requirements of the Community strategy on health and safety at work 2002-06, as well as the new strategy for the period 2007-2012[6]. The adoption and application in recent decades of a large body of Community laws has improved working conditions in the Member States and reduced the incidence of work-related accidents and illnesses. The new strategy for 2007-2012 aims for a 25 % reduction in the total incidence rate of accidents at work by 2012 in the EU-27, which as well as having direct effects on employees, will also play a role in contributing towards the success of the Growth and Jobs Strategy.

Harmonised data on accidents at work are collected in the framework of the European Statistics on Accidents at Work (ESAW). The ESAW methodology is in accordance with the International Labour Office (ILO) Resolution of 1998 concerning 'Statistics of Occupational Injuries: resulting from Occupational Accidents'. National sources are typically declarations of accidents at work, either to the public (social security) or private insurance systems, or to other relevant national authorities. Data are presented in numbers or as incidence rates. **Incidence rates** are calculated as follows: (number of persons involved in (fatal) accidents at work / number of persons in employment in the reference population) x 100 000.

---

(6) Council Resolution 2002/C 161/01 of 3 June 2002 on a new Community strategy on health and safety at work (2002-06) (OJ C 161, 5.7.2002, p. 1); http://eur-lex.europa.eu/LexUriServ/site/en/oj/2002/c_161/c_16120020705en00010004.pdf.
Council Resolution 2007/C 145/01 of 25 June 2007 on a new Community strategy on health and safety at work (2007-2012) (OJ C 145, 30.6.2007, p. 1); http://eur-lex.europa.eu/LexUriServ/site/en/oj/2007/c_145/c_14520070630en00010004.pdf.

The data on **serious accidents at work** refer to accidents that result in more than three days absence from work. An **accident at work** is a discrete occurrence during the course of work which leads to physical or mental harm. This includes accidents in the course of work outside the premises of his business, even if caused by a third party (on clients' premises, on another company's premises, in a public place or during transport, including road traffic accidents) and cases of acute poisoning. The information presented excludes accidents on the way to or from work (commuting accidents), occurrences having only a medical origin (such as a heart attack at work) and occupational diseases.

A **fatal accident at work** is defined as an accident which leads to the death of a victim generally within one year of the accident. In practice the notification of an accident as fatal ranges from national registration procedures where the accident is registered as fatal when the victim died the same day (the Netherlands) to cases where no time limits are laid down (Belgium, Greece, France, Italy, Luxembourg, Austria, Sweden and Norway).

Main findings

The European Agency for Safety and Health at Work[7] is located in Bilbao, Spain. It claims that every three and a half minutes, somebody in the EU dies from work-related causes, which equates to more than 150 000 deaths a year.

In recent years the incidence rate of serious accidents at work has fallen, such that by 2005 it had decreased by 22 % in relation to 1998 for the EU-27. During the same period there was a 24 % reduction in fatal accidents at work in the EU-27.

Note that these figures may in part reflect the structural shift of the European economy towards services, where the risks of accident and death at work are usually less than within agriculture, industry or construction.

There were only three Member States that reported a higher incidence of serious accidents at work in 2005 when compared with 1998: Estonia (26 % higher), Lithuania (4 % higher) and Ireland (1 % higher). At the other end of the scale, the incidence of serious accidents in Bulgaria, Greece and Romania was almost halved between 1998 and 2004.

The majority of the Member States also reported a reduction in the incidence of fatal accidents at work, although this was not the case in Lithuania (33 % increase), Sweden (31 % increase), Slovenia (28 % increase) and Ireland (17 % increase). Greece, Malta and France each reduced their incidence of fatal accidents at work by at least half over the period considered.

In absolute terms the highest incidence of serious and fatal accidents at work was recorded within the construction sector, with agriculture and transport also recording relatively high values. Men are considerably more likely to have an accident or to die at work. This is due, at least in part, to a higher proportion of men working in 'higher risk' sectors and occupations, while men are also more likely to work on a full-time basis; these characteristics may also explain why the incidence of accidents has tended to fall at a more rapid pace for men than for women. For example, the incidence of serious accidents for men fell by 19 % between 1998 and 2005, while the corresponding reduction for women was 15 %.

---

(7) http://osha.europa.eu/en.

Figure 5.13: Incidence of accidents at work, 2005

(1998=100, based on the number of accidents per 100 000 persons employed)

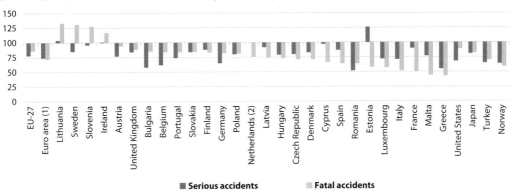

■ Serious accidents   ■ Fatal accidents

(1) EA-12 instead of EA-15.
(2) Break in series for serious accidents (re-based, 2005=100).

Source: Eurostat (tsiem090 and tsiem100)

Figure 5.14: Incidence of serious accidents at work, by gender, 2005 (1)

(1998=100, based on the number of serious accidents per 100 000 persons employed)

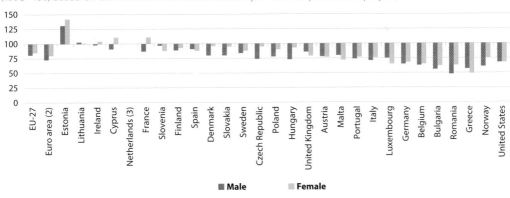

■ Male   ■ Female

(1) Latvia, not available; the figure is ranked on the average of male and female.
(2) EA-12 instead of EA-15, estimates.
(3) Break in series for serious accidents (re-based, 2005=100).

Source: Eurostat (tsiem090)

Living conditions and welfare

6

Eurostat data on living conditions and welfare aims to show a comprehensive picture of the current living conditions in the EU, covering variables related to income, poverty, social exclusion and other living conditions – all social exclusion and housing condition information is collected at the household level.

The demand for information on living conditions and welfare received a new impetus following the social chapter of the Amsterdam Treaty (1997) which became the driving force for EU social statistics. This impetus was reinforced by successive European Councils that have kept the social dimension high on the political agenda.

This data is supplemented by additional information from household budget surveys that detail the breakdown of consumption expenditure, while the third subchapter focuses on housing (status of tenure and average numbers of people living per household).

Income, poverty and social exclusion are multidimensional problems. To monitor them effectively at a European level, a subset of so-called 'social cohesion indicators' has been developed within the structural indicators. Additionally, a broader portfolio of social inclusion indicators are calculated under the Open Method of Coordination for Social Protection and Social Inclusion [1].

The chapter concludes with a snapshot of indicators relating to good governance, in other words, whether political/public institutions allocate resources effectively and take decisions in an efficient and responsible manner. The public's perception of such ideals may be gauged through indicators such as voter turnout or measures of the public's confidence in institutions.

(1) http://ec.europa.eu/employment_social/soc-prot/soc-incl/indicator_en.htm.

6.1 Living conditions

Introduction

Favourable living conditions depend on a wide range of factors, which may be divided into two broad groups – those that are income-related and those that are not. The second group includes factors such as: quality healthcare services, education and training opportunities or good transport facilities – aspects that affect everyday lives and work. Analysis of the distribution of incomes within a country provides a picture of inequalities. On the one hand inequalities may create incentives for people to improve their situation through work, innovation or acquiring new skills, while on the other, crime, poverty and social exclusion are often seen as linked to inequalities in the distribution of incomes.

Definitions and data availability

Eurostat statistical indicators within the ILC (Income and Living Conditions) domain cover a range of topics relating to income poverty and social exclusion. One group of indicators relate to monetary poverty analysed in various ways (for example, by age, gender and activity status), across space and over time. Another set relates to income distribution and income inequalities, while there are also indicators relating to non-monetary poverty and social exclusion (for example, material deprivation, social participation) across space and over time. A newly developed set of child-care arrangement indicators complements the information in this domain.

To calculate living condition indicators, Eurostat initially used micro-data [2] from the European Community Household Panel (ECHP) survey which was launched in 1994. However, after eight years of using this source, a new instrument was introduced in 2003, namely, data collection under a framework regulation on **Community statistics on income and living conditions (EU-SILC)**. One of the main reasons for this change was the need to adapt the content and timeliness of data production to reflect current political and research needs. EU-SILC is now Eurostat's main reference source for comparative income distribution and social exclusion statistics. It comprises both a cross-sectional dimension and a longitudinal dimension. From 2005, EU-SILC covered the EU-25 Member States, as well as Norway and Iceland. Bulgaria, Romania, Turkey and Switzerland launched EU-SILC in 2007. Note that for 2006 Bulgaria and Romania provided indicators from national Household Budget Surveys and that as such, these indicators are not fully harmonised.

While comparisons between countries of standards of living are frequently based on GDP per capita, such figures say little about the distribution of income within a country. In this section, indicators measuring the distribution of income and relative poverty are presented. **Household disposable income** is established by summing up all monetary incomes received from any source by each member of the household (including income from work, investments and social benefits)

---

(2) Data gathered at the micro level, for example, from individuals, households or enterprises, rather than aggregate data compiled at the level of the economy.

plus income received at household level and deducting taxes and social contributions paid and certain unavoidable expenditures. In order to reflect differences in household size and composition, this total is divided by the number of **'equivalent adults'** using a standard (equivalence) scale (the so-called 'modified OECD' scale, which attributes a weight of 1 to the first adult in the household, a weight of 0.5 to each subsequent member of the household aged 14 and over and a weight of 0.3 to household members ages less than 14). The resulting figure is called **equivalised disposable income** and is attributed to each member of the household. For the purpose of poverty indicators, the equivalised disposable income is calculated from the total disposable income of each household divided by the equivalised household size. Consequently, each person in the household is considered to have the same equivalised income.

The **S80/S20 income quintile share ratio** is a measure of the inequality of income distribution and is calculated as the ratio of total income received by the 20 % of the population with the highest income (the top quintile) to that received by the 20 % of the population with the lowest income (the bottom quintile); where all incomes are compiled as equivalised disposable income. Note that the final chapter at the end of this publication presents regional data for the disposable income per habitant.

The **relative median income ratio** is defined as the ratio of the median equivalised disposable income of persons aged above 65 to the median equivalised disposable income of persons aged below 65.

The **at-risk-of-poverty rate** is defined as the share of persons with an equivalised disposable income that is below the at-risk-of-poverty threshold, set at 60 % of the national median equivalised disposable income. This rate may be expressed before or after social transfers, with the difference measuring the hypothetical impact of national social transfers in reducing poverty risk. Retirement and survivor's pensions are counted as income before transfers and not as social transfers. Various breakdowns of this indicator are calculated: by age, gender, activity status, household type, education level, etc. It should be noted that this indicator does not measure wealth but low current income (in comparison with other persons in the same country) which does not necessarily imply a low standard of living.

The **relative median at-risk-of-poverty gap** is calculated as the difference between the median equivalised disposable income of persons below the at-risk-of-poverty threshold and the at-risk-of-poverty threshold, expressed as a percentage of the at-risk-of-poverty threshold (cut-off point: 60 % of national median equivalised income). The EU aggregate is a population weighted average of individual national figures.

In line with decisions of the European Council, the at-risk-of-poverty rate is measured relative to the situation in each country rather than applying a common threshold to all countries.

The indicators related to **jobless households** (the share of children aged 0-17 and the share of persons aged 18-59 who are living in households where no one works) are calculated as the proportion

of persons of the specified age who live in households where no one is working. Students aged 18 to 24 who live in households composed solely of students of the same age class are counted neither in the numerator nor the denominator of the ratio; the data comes from the EU Labour Force Survey (LFS).

Main findings

In 2006, the 20 % of the EU-25 population with the highest equivalised disposable income received almost five times as much income as the 20 % of the population with the lowest equivalised disposable income. Within the Member States, the widest inequalities were recorded in Latvia (a ratio of 7.9) and Portugal (6.8). In contrast, the narrowest income inequalities were in the Nordic Member States, Bulgaria, the Czech Republic and Slovenia, with S80/S20 income quintile share ratios of between 3.4 and 3.6.

A comparison between the number of people on low incomes before social benefits other than pensions and those on low incomes after social benefits (in other words, old age pensions and survivors' benefits are included in income both 'before' and 'after' social benefits), illustrates one of the main purposes of such benefits: their redistributive effect and, in particular, their ability to alleviate the risk of poverty and reduce the percentage of population having to manage with a low income. In 2006, social transfers reduced the at-risk-of-poverty rate from 26 % before transfers for the EU-25 population to 16 % after transfers in 2006; as such, social transfers lifted 38 % of those in poverty above the poverty risk threshold. Social benefits other than pensions reduced the percentage of people at-risk-of-

poverty in all countries, but to very disparate degrees. The proportion of persons who were removed from being at-risk-of-poverty by social transfers was smallest in some of the Mediterranean Member States (Greece, Spain, and Italy), as well as Latvia and Bulgaria. Those countries whose social protection and support systems removed the highest proportion of persons out of being threatened by poverty (over half) included Sweden, Denmark, Finland, the Czech Republic, the Netherlands, Slovenia and Germany.

With a growing proportion of the EU's population aged over 65 years and persistently low fertility rates (see Chapter 3 for more details), there are increasing concerns both about how Member States will be able to pay for the pension and healthcare costs linked to ageing, as well as increased poverty risks for the elderly. By comparing the relative median equivalised disposable income of persons aged above 65 to the median equivalised disposable income of persons aged below 65, the relative standard of living among the elderly can be gauged. With the exception of Poland, those aged over 65 years had an average disposable income in 2006 that was less than those aged below 65 years. In Luxembourg, Hungary, Austria and Germany, the difference in incomes between these two age groups was less than 10 %. In 2006, in the majority of Member States, the difference between the equivalised disposable incomes of those aged 65 and over and those aged between 0 and 64 was between 10°% and 30°%. However, this widened to between 30 % and 35 % in Estonia, Ireland and Latvia, while in Cyprus the median equivalised disposable income of those aged over 65 years was only 57 % of that for persons aged less than 65 years.

This relatively low level of income among pensioners in Cyprus was highlighted as a majority (52 %) of persons aged over 65 in Cyprus were at-risk-of-poverty in 2006. Some 31 % of persons aged over 65 in Spain and 30 % in Latvia were at-risk-of-poverty, which was in contrast to shares of less than 10 % in Hungary, Luxembourg, Poland, Slovakia, the Czech Republic and the Netherlands.

The elderly and retired were not the only group at-risk-of-poverty in 2006. Across the population of the EU-25, an estimated 15 % of persons aged 18 years or over were at-risk-of-poverty after social transfers. The most vulnerable group were the unemployed (self-assessed most frequent activity status), about two fifths (41 %) of whom were at-risk-of poverty, a share that rose to around 60 % in each of the Baltic Member States. Nearly one third (32 %) of single parent households with dependent children were at-risk-of-poverty across the EU-25 in 2006, which

was the highest proportion of any type of household covered by the survey. In contrast, multi-adult households without dependent children tended to be the households with the least risk of poverty [3].

In 2007, some 9.3 % of the EU-27's population aged between 18 and 59 years lived in a jobless household; the proportion of children (up to 17 years) living in jobless households was almost at the same level (9.4 %). The highest proportion of children living in jobless households was recorded in the United Kingdom (16.7 %), followed by Hungary (14.0 %) and Belgium (13.5 %); these two Member States also recorded the highest shares of adults aged 18 to 59 years old living in jobless households, along with Poland. Note that these statistics may be affected by a number of factors, including differences in average numbers of children and inactivity rates between different socio-economic groups.

(3) Please note that the at-risk-of-poverty rate emphasises a relative concept of income poverty, relative to the level of income in one country and does not take into account wealth or actual purchasing power; it also assumes that household members share their resources. Additionally, it is influenced by the equivalence scale chosen. In the future, the at-risk-of-poverty rate will be complemented by other poverty indicators.

Figure 6.1: Inequality of income distribution, 2006
(S80/S20 income quintile share ratio)

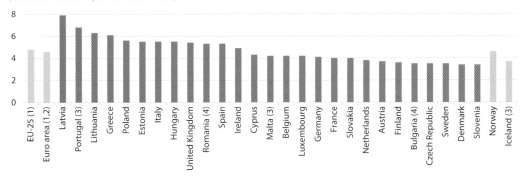

(1) Eurostat estimates based on population-weighted averages of national data.
(2) EA-13 instead of EA-15.
(3) Provisional.
(4) National HBS.

Source: Eurostat (tsisc010)

Figure 6.2: Relative median income ratio, 2006 (1)

(ratio)

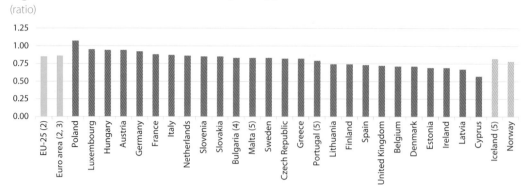

(1) Romania, not available.
(2) Eurostat estimates based on population-weighted averages of national data.
(3) EA-13 instead of EA-15.
(4) National HBS.
(5) Provisional.

Source: Eurostat (ilc_ov7a)

Figure 6.3: Relative median at-risk-of-poverty gap, 2006

(%)

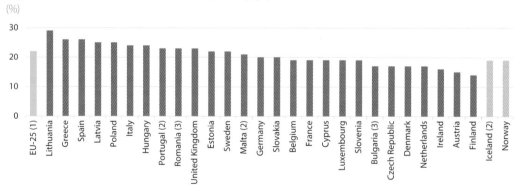

(1) Eurostat estimates based on population-weighted averages of national data.
(2) Provisional.
(3) National HBS.

Source: Eurostat (tsdsc250)

Table 6.1: At-risk-of-poverty rate by most frequent activity status, 2006 (1)

(%)

	Total population	Persons employed	Not employed	Unemployed	Retired	Inactive population, others
EU-25 (2)	15	8	23	41	16	26
Euro area (2, 3)	15	7	22	38	15	25
Belgium	15	4	24	31	20	25
Bulgaria (4)	14	6	20	36	17	16
Czech Republic	8	3	14	44	7	15
Denmark	12	4	22	25	16	28
Germany	12	5	19	43	13	18
Estonia	18	8	32	59	29	29
Ireland	18	6	31	50	26	31
Greece	20	14	26	33	24	26
Spain	19	10	29	38	24	30
France	13	6	19	31	13	25
Italy	19	10	26	44	16	30
Cyprus	17	7	30	31	51	16
Latvia	22	11	37	64	35	29
Lithuania	20	10	30	61	23	28
Luxembourg	13	10	15	48	7	17
Hungary	14	7	20	53	12	25
Malta	13	5	20	40	22	18
Netherlands	9	4	14	27	6	19
Austria	12	6	18	43	13	21
Poland	18	13	22	46	7	23
Portugal	18	11	26	31	23	29
Romania	:	:	:	:	:	:
Slovenia	11	5	18	33	17	17
Slovakia	11	6	15	41	8	17
Finland	13	4	24	42	20	24
Sweden	11	7	18	24	12	29
United Kingdom	18	8	32	57	28	34
Iceland	9	7	15	14	10	21
Norway	10	6	18	31	18	16

(1) Persons aged 18 years and over.
(2) Eurostat estimates based on population-weighted averages of national data.
(3) EA-13 instead of EA-15.
(4) National HBS.

Source: Eurostat (ilc_li04)

Figure 6.4: At-risk-of-poverty rate, 2006

(%)

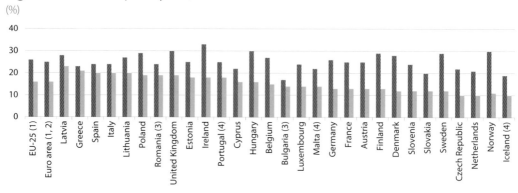

■ **At-risk-of-poverty rate before social transfers**　　　■ **At-risk-of-poverty rate after social transfers**

(1) Eurostat estimates based on population-weighted averages of national data.
(2) EA-13 instead of EA-15.
(3) National HBS.
(4) Provisional.

Source: Eurostat (tsisc020 and tsisc030)

Figure 6.5: At-risk-of-poverty rate after social transfers, by household type, EU-25, 2006 (1)

(%)

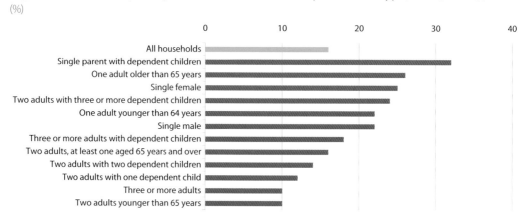

(1) Eurostat estimates based on population-weighted averages of national data.

Source: Eurostat (tsdsc240)

Figure 6.6: At-risk-of-poverty rate after social transfers, persons aged 65 years and over, 2006

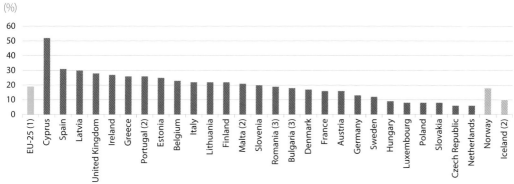

(%)

(1) Eurostat estimate based on population-weighted averages of national data.
(2) Provisional.
(3) National HBS.

Source: Eurostat (tsdsc230)

Figure 6.7: Persons living in jobless households, by age, 2007 (1)

(% of respective age group living in households where no-one works)

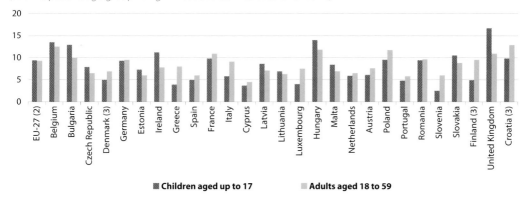

■ **Children aged up to 17**　　　■ **Adults aged 18 to 59**

(1) Sweden, not available.
(2) Estimates.
(3) 2006.

Source: Eurostat (tsdsc310)

Figure 6.8: Persons living in jobless households, by gender, 2007 (1)

(% of respective gender aged 18-59 who are living in households where no-one works)

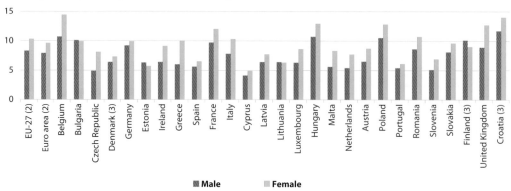

(1) Sweden, not available.
(2) Estimates.
(3) 2006.

Source: Eurostat (tsisc090)

6.2 Household consumption expenditure

Introduction

The final consumption expenditure of households is the biggest component of the expenditure approach of GDP. Its evolution allows an assessment of purchases made by households, reflecting changes in wages and other incomes, but also in employment and in the behaviour towards savings. Therefore, the growth of household consumption can be somewhat different from the growth of wages and incomes.

Definitions and data availability

Final consumption expenditure of households refers to expenditure incurred on the domestic territory (by residents and non-residents) on goods and services used for the direct satisfaction of individual needs. It covers the purchase of goods and services, the consumption of own production (such as garden produce) and the imputed rent of owner-occupied dwellings. The Council regulation for the European system of accounts 1995 [4] provides the underlying basis for the collection of data on household consumption expenditure with respect to data provided by Eurostat's national accounts statistics. Note that the data from national accounts should include institutional households.

The household budget survey (HBS) describes the level and the structure of household expenditure. HBS are national surveys that focus on consumption expenditure, and nationally are used to calculate weights for consumer price indices; they may also be used in the compilation of national accounts. HBS are sample surveys conducted in all of the Member States, as well as Croatia, the former Yugoslav Republic of Macedonia, Turkey, Norway and Switzerland, on a periodic basis (about every five to six years).

HBS provide a picture of the total consumption expenditure of private households, analysed by a variety of socio-economic household characteristics such as the employment status of the main reference person, their income, their age, the number of active persons living in the household, the type of household, the location of the household (rural or urban), or the main source of income. Information is available at a detailed level using the classification of individual consumption by purpose (COICOP), with over 230 headings for different goods and services (including aggregates).

HBS data are confined to the population residing in private households. In other words, the survey excludes collective or institutional households (such as hospitals, old persons' homes, prisons, or military barracks), as well as persons without a fixed place of residence – in contrast to the data collected for national accounts. The basic unit for the collection of information is the household (defined as a social unit which shares household expenses or daily needs, in addition to having a common residence) – in other words, the household is seen as a housekeeping unit. Nevertheless, it is also important to identify the head of the household, as their personal characteristics are often used as the basis to classify information on socio-economic characteristics. The head of the

---

(4) Council Regulation (EC) No 2223/96 (see http://forum.europa.eu.int/irc/dsis/nfaccount/info/data/esa95/esa95-new.htm for a consolidated version that takes account of subsequent changes).

household is defined, for the purpose of the HBS, as the person who contributes the most to the income of the household (the main earner). To take economies of scale into account, household expenditures can be expressed per adult equivalent (see previous subchapter for more details).

For the HBS, **household consumption expenditure** is defined as the value of goods and services used for directly meeting human needs. Household consumption covers expenditure on purchases of goods and services, own consumption, and the imputed rent of owner-occupied dwellings (the rent that the household would pay if it were a tenant). The expenditure effected by households to acquire goods and services is recorded at the price actually paid, which includes indirect taxes (VAT and excise duties) borne by the purchaser. Eurostat guidelines encourage non-monetary components of consumption to be included within the survey results, with internal production valued at retail prices, as if the product had been bought in a shop. Examples of internal production include own production of food (either by a farming household or by a family that has a different professional activity but grows their own food in a kitchen/vegetable garden or allotment), or withdrawals from stocks for own-use in the case of tradesmen or retailers. HBS data should also reflect benefits in kind provided by employers in exchange for work done. Notional rents are imputed to owner-occupiers and households accommodated free of charge.

Main findings

The consumption habits of households vary substantially among the 27 Member States. Factors such as culture, income, weather, household composition, economic structure and degree of urbanisation can influence habits in each country.

According to national accounts, the final consumption expenditure of households was the equivalent of at least one half of GDP in the majority of Member States; the share was highest in Cyprus (75.3 %), Bulgaria and Greece (both 73.9 %) in 2006 and only less than 50 % in Finland, Denmark, the Netherlands, Sweden, Ireland and Luxembourg. Average household consumption expenditure per capita was by far the highest in Luxembourg (PPS 25 800), followed by Greece (PPS 17 900) and Austria (PPS 16 900). Average household expenditure tended to be lowest in those countries that joined the EU since 2004, the principal exceptions being Cyprus and Malta.

National accounts data also reveals that a little over one fifth (21.9 %) of total household consumption expenditure in the EU-27 in 2006 was devoted to housing, water, electricity, gas and other housing fuels. Transport expenditure (13.6 %) and expenditure on food and non-alcoholic beverages (12.7 %), together accounted for a little more than a quarter of total households consumption expenditure, making these the next two most important categories in the EU-27.

Both the household budget survey (HBS) and national accounts provide a far more detailed breakdown of these aggregated consumption expenditure statistics. Switching to HBS data, the proportion of household expenditure devoted to each of the consumption categories varied greatly between the Member States in 2005. The highest proportion of the mean consumption expenditure of households (in PPS) spent on housing, water, electricity, gas and other fuels in 2005 was recorded in Sweden (32.2 %), which was about three times as high as in Malta (9.1 %). The proportion of household consumption spent on food and non-alcoholic beverages tended to be highest in those Member States where household incomes were lowest; in Romania such items accounted for 44.2 % of the mean consumption expenditure of households, which could be compared with an average of 9.3 % in Luxembourg.

Household consumption expenditure was also reflected in certain broad socio-demographic patterns. The mean consumption expenditure of households whose head was aged 30 to 59 years old tended to be much higher than the equivalent expenditure of households whose head was either aged under 30 or over 60. In a number of the Member States that joined the EU since 2004, average household consumption expenditure of those households headed by a person aged under 30 was generally much closer to the expenditure of households headed by someone of an older working age (30 to 59), and in Latvia and Romania was higher.

Households headed by the self-employed or non-manual workers in industry and services in the EU-27 had, on average, the highest mean consumption expenditure of about PPS 32 500 in 2005, with that of households headed by manual workers about 25 % lower.

As may be expected, there was a strong link between household income and expenditure across the EU-27; the 20 % of households with the highest incomes spent an average of about two and three quarters times as much as the poorest 20 % of households in 2005. There was also a strong correlation between average household consumption expenditure, the size of households and the number of active persons in the household. Household consumption expenditure was highest in households with three or more adults with dependent children and lowest within single person households, while households with three or more active persons spent more than households with no active persons. Nevertheless, in both cases the relationship was not linear: economies of scale (for example, sharing a flat or a car, heating a room, etc.) may, at least to some degree, explain why the expenditure of a single person is generally considerably more than half the expenditure of a couple.

Table 6.2: Total consumption expenditure of households (domestic concept)

	As a proportion of GDP (%)			Per capita (PPS)		
	1996	2001	2006 (1)	1996	2001	2006 (1)
EU-27	57.0	57.4	56.3	8 800	11 400	13 300
Euro area	56.8	56.9	56.0	:	12 700	14 600
Belgium	52.5	52.3	50.5	10 200	12 800	14 200
Bulgaria	76.1	73.8	73.9	3 300	4 300	5 800
Czech Republic	53.2	54.0	50.8	6 200	7 500	9 400
Denmark	50.0	46.7	47.5	10 200	11 800	12 900
Germany	55.4	56.5	53.9	10 800	13 000	15 100
Estonia	64.8	59.5	56.2	3 800	5 400	8 900
Ireland	52.1	45.3	43.2	8 700	11 900	14 800
Greece	:	75.8	73.9	:	13 000	17 900
Spain	62.7	62.4	59.5	8 900	12 100	14 700
France	56.2	55.5	56.0	9 900	12 700	15 400
Italy	59.0	60.1	59.7	10 900	14 000	15 000
Cyprus	81.8	82.8	75.3	11 000	14 900	16 300
Latvia	65.1	60.8	63.2	3 300	4 700	8 000
Lithuania	66.6	66.2	65.6	3 700	5 400	8 700
Luxembourg	47.5	46.6	39.3	16 200	21 600	25 800
Hungary	55.9	56.5	53.9	4 300	6 600	8 200
Malta	78.8	77.3	68.9	9 600	11 900	13 200
Netherlands	49.1	48.8	45.7	9 400	12 900	15 000
Austria	58.5	58.1	56.3	12 100	14 400	16 900
Poland	61.3	64.5	61.5	4 200	6 100	7 600
Portugal	65.4	64.2	65.9	7 600	9 800	11 600
Romania	:	69.0	67.8	:	3 800	6 200
Slovenia	61.3	57.8	55.5	7 100	9 000	11 500
Slovakia	53.9	58.8	56.2	4 100	6 100	8 400
Finland	50.6	47.4	48.4	8 300	10 900	14 000
Sweden	47.7	46.6	45.4	9 200	11 200	12 600
United Kingdom	61.4	62.1	59.9	10 700	14 400	16 600
Turkey	67.3	74.9	73.9	3 200	5 300	7 800
Iceland	54.7	52.2	52.5	11 200	13 700	16 100
Norway	47.0	41.7	39.8	10 400	13 300	18 200
Switzerland	59.1	59.5	57.3	13 800	16 600	18 500

(1) Germany, Greece, France, Italy, Malta, the Netherlands, Finland, Turkey and Norway, 2007; Bulgaria and Sweden, 2005; Denmark, 2004.

Source: Eurostat (nama_fcs_c)

Table 6.3: Mean consumption expenditure of households, 2005
(PPS)

| | COICOP code (1) | | | | | | | | | | | |
	01	02	03	04	05	06	07	08	09	10	11	12
EU-27	3 594	560	1 412	6 936	1 416	796	3 078	738	2 187	238	1 417	2 291
Euro area (2)	4 027	602	1 679	7 869	1 588	1 016	3 531	804	2 309	248	1 585	2 845
Belgium	4 043	669	1 425	7 610	1 687	1 400	3 863	878	2 868	136	1 894	3 576
Bulgaria	2 238	269	218	2 461	213	305	355	325	204	34	255	220
Czech Republic	2 503	347	679	2 444	815	239	1 351	555	1 289	66	619	1 234
Denmark	2 872	785	1 168	7 194	1 459	639	3 331	583	2 738	100	960	2 233
Germany	3 185	489	1 355	8 445	1 543	1 024	3 790	828	3 168	236	1 212	3 226
Estonia	2 440	300	601	3 240	568	282	1 087	596	691	145	339	559
Ireland	4 491	2 032	1 851	8 520	2 613	904	4 203	1 255	3 670	687	2 190	3 956
Greece	4 801	1 045	2 154	7 442	1 929	1 824	3 222	1 174	1 285	738	2 661	2 701
Spain	4 685	586	1 786	7 874	1 211	577	2 743	701	1 659	292	2 414	1 499
France	3 733	650	1 853	7 339	1 693	1 167	3 777	914	1 926	165	1 277	3 392
Italy	5 359	506	2 013	8 512	1 670	1 132	3 420	621	1 680	202	1 428	2 242
Cyprus	5 158	646	2 649	7 381	2 008	1 624	4 980	1 164	2 044	1 354	2 830	2 370
Latvia	3 091	329	778	1 810	546	394	1 155	610	667	145	557	508
Lithuania	3 166	332	743	1 776	392	445	762	435	402	102	429	393
Luxembourg	4 851	865	3 343	15 611	3 702	1 351	8 403	1 139	3 869	223	4 098	4 478
Hungary	2 413	380	537	2 073	498	440	1 511	696	909	90	343	803
Malta	6 082	786	2 387	2 596	3 070	869	4 758	837	2 879	352	2 030	1 960
Netherlands	3 089	625	1 694	7 513	1 888	371	3 196	903	3 193	306	1 647	4 945
Austria	3 933	847	1 682	6 732	1 868	946	4 863	793	3 809	242	1 660	2 792
Poland	2 704	262	489	3 341	478	485	862	512	662	138	180	571
Portugal	3 243	477	861	5 560	994	1 264	2 693	616	1 182	356	2 263	1 359
Romania	2 355	307	333	832	201	205	344	259	224	45	58	162
Slovenia	3 966	575	1 678	5 483	1 389	356	3 717	950	2 234	202	1 035	2 220
Slovakia	2 910	333	661	2 517	494	330	986	506	712	92	520	713
Finland	3 086	588	934	6 614	1 238	852	3 818	693	2 731	51	1 021	2 733
Sweden	2 913	531	1 270	8 250	1 640	638	3 623	791	3 398	8	981	1 569
United Kingdom	3 159	753	1 585	9 458	2 092	383	4 305	852	3 943	457	2 558	2 415
Croatia	4 564	548	1 059	4 983	697	315	1 484	729	853	105	465	1 039
Norway	3 402	898	1 618	7 633	1 892	872	5 270	770	3 593	95	1 111	1 951

(1) COICOP codes - 01: food and non-alcoholic beverages; 02: alcoholic beverages and tobacco; 03: clothing and footwear; 04: housing, water, electricity, gas and other fuels; 05: furnishings, household equipment and routine maintenance of the house; 06: health; 07: transport; 08: communications; 09: recreation and culture; 10: education; 11: restaurants and hotels; 12: miscellaneous goods and services.
(2) EA-13 instead of EA-15.

Source: Eurostat (hbs_exp_t121)

Table 6.4: Mean consumption expenditure of households by age of the head of household, 2005
(PPS)

	Less than 30	Aged 30-49	Aged 45-59	60 or more
EU-27	20 882	27 467	29 018	19 606
Euro area (1)	22 904	31 055	33 375	22 787
Belgium	27 820	33 971	32 513	23 965
Bulgaria	8 435	8 922	8 145	5 212
Czech Republic	11 962	14 551	13 812	8 293
Denmark	18 549	27 912	28 828	18 685
Germany	19 121	30 218	34 207	25 428
Estonia	10 422	14 039	11 630	7 630
Ireland	38 889	42 513	43 039	22 634
Greece	25 747	37 247	39 564	21 543
Spain	23 095	27 928	31 830	20 464
France	23 632	31 728	32 181	22 041
Italy	24 955	31 594	34 558	23 405
Cyprus	38 327	38 559	43 721	19 153
Latvia	13 206	12 902	11 723	6 313
Lithuania	10 537	11 608	10 256	6 193
Luxembourg	44 541	53 941	59 954	43 792
Hungary	11 827	12 905	12 680	7 022
Malta	33 060	31 315	34 051	19 483
Netherlands	22 177	33 447	33 445	22 849
Austria	26 197	33 404	35 516	23 603
Poland	10 627	12 424	11 152	8 270
Portugal	20 688	23 750	25 159	14 838
Romania	6 261	5 919	3 685	2 841
Slovenia	25 230	27 486	26 912	16 322
Slovakia	11 504	12 589	11 929	6 956
Finland	19 735	30 868	28 184	17 853
Sweden	18 665	28 669	28 677	22 985
United Kingdom	28 918	35 742	38 198	24 334
Croatia	13 988	21 215	20 691	12 487
Norway	20 637	33 500	32 373	24 566

(1) EA-13 instead of EA-15.

Source: Eurostat (hbs_exp_t135)

Figure 6.9: Consumption expenditure of households on goods and services, EU-27, 2006 (1)
(% of total household consumption expenditure)

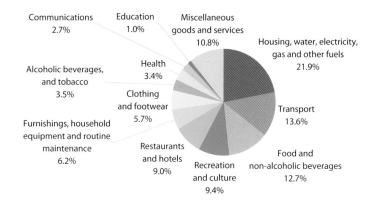

Communications 2.7%
Education 1.0%
Miscellaneous goods and services 10.8%
Housing, water, electricity, gas and other fuels 21.9%
Alcoholic beverages, and tobacco 3.5%
Health 3.4%
Clothing and footwear 5.7%
Furnishings, household equipment and routine maintenance 6.2%
Restaurants and hotels 9.0%
Recreation and culture 9.4%
Transport 13.6%
Food and non-alcoholic beverages 12.7%

(1) Figures do not sum to 100 % due to rounding.

Source: Eurostat (nama_co2_c)

Figure 6.10: Mean consumption expenditure of households by income, EU-27, 2005 (1)
(PPS)

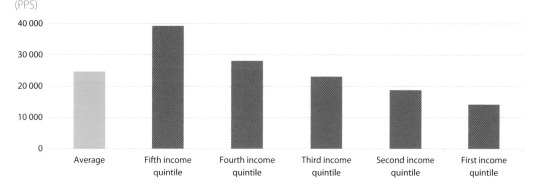

(1) Estimates.

Source: Eurostat (hbs_exp_t133)

Table 6.5: Mean consumption expenditure of households by employment status, 2005
(PPS)

	Manual workers in industry and services	Non-manual workers in industry and services	Self-employed	Unemployed	Retired	Inactive population - other
EU-27	25 442	32 263	32 621	17 968	20 120	18 336
Euro area	28 055	34 943	36 319	19 833	22 933	19 422
Belgium	28 499	36 508	:	16 741	24 012	32 622
Bulgaria	8 102	10 205	8 729	5 135	5 051	5 923
Czech Republic	13 090	14 359	14 790	:	7 198	:
Denmark	26 414	30 050	26 282	:	:	20 861
Germany	27 655	34 122	41 554	17 943	24 397	15 255
Estonia	10 675	16 045	15 378	6 986	6 657	7 241
Ireland	39 927	47 206	41 326	25 837	25 316	25 707
Greece	31 449	44 510	39 691	23 926	23 375	18 179
Spain	26 525	33 942	29 325	20 128	20 644	23 309
France	27 287	35 524	35 038	20 078	22 686	17 520
Italy	28 766	35 298	36 685	22 135	24 411	21 106
Cyprus	33 701	46 544	37 139	32 342	17 600	21 959
Latvia	10 589	15 905	13 537	5 735	5 239	6 163
Lithuania	10 143	13 874	9 504	5 596	5 638	7 041
Luxembourg	47 073·	59 758	66 495	35 441	45 674	38 342
Hungary	10 942	15 175	15 724	7 440	7 169	8 534
Malta	30 198	39 245	34 275	15 156	19 570	:
Netherlands	31 269	34 335	41 961	21 112	22 811	22 348
Austria	30 627	36 156	39 283	20 025	23 716	27 240
Poland	10 271	15 186	12 401	6 504	8 138	7 367
Portugal	23 991	23 991	25 448	17 124	14 441	13 255
Romania	:	:	:	:	:	:
Slovenia	22 820	32 299	32 113	12 570	16 331	20 190
Slovakia	11 633	13 924	14 215	6 766	6 741	7 037
Finland	25 245	33 075	34 285	13 899	16 961	17 550
Sweden	25 545	31 083	:	15 233	20 754	15 823
United Kingdom	30 938	41 664	41 524	21 575	22 148	25 344
Croatia	19 742	25 545	18 496	14 578	13 405	10 584
Norway	:	:	29 222	19 214	22 121	30 606

Source: Eurostat (hbs_exp_t131)

Figure 6.11: Mean consumption expenditure of households by type of household, EU-27, 2005 (1)

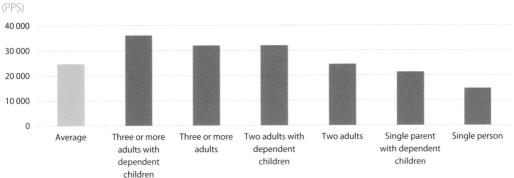

(1) Estimates.

Source: Eurostat (hbs_exp_t134)

Figure 6.12: Mean consumption expenditure of households by number of active persons, EU-27, 2005 (1)

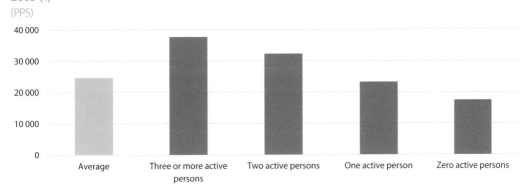

(1) Estimates.

Source: Eurostat (hbs_exp_t132)

6.3 Housing

Introduction

As seen in the previous subchapter, housing, water, electricity, gas and other fuels form the main expenditure item of household budgets in the EU. Questions of social housing, homelessness or integration play an important role within the social policy agenda. The Charter of Fundamental Rights stipulates in Article 34 (3) that 'in order to combat social exclusion and poverty, the Union recognises and respects the right to social and housing assistance so as to ensure a decent existence for all those who lack sufficient resources, in accordance with Community law and national laws and practices'.

However, the EU does not have any responsibilities in respect of housing; rather, national governments have the responsibility for developing their own housing policies. Many countries face similar challenges: for example, how to renew housing stocks, how to plan and combat urban sprawl and promote sustainable development, how to help young and disadvantaged groups to get on the housing ladder, or how to promote energy efficiency among house-owners. The social and economic cost of the absence of decent housing is generally accepted to compromise the efficiency of a country or region. Indeed, decent housing, at an affordable price in a safe environment is likely to alleviate poverty and social exclusion.

Definitions and data availability

From 2005 onwards, EU-SILC covers the EU-25 Member States as well as Norway and Iceland. Bulgaria, Romania, Turkey and Switzerland launched EU-SILC in 2007. The reference population of EU-SILC is all private households and their current members residing in the territory of the Member State at the time of data collection. Persons living in collective households and in institutions are generally excluded from the target population.

Main findings

The average number of persons living in a household in the EU-27 was 2.4 in 2007. The highest average in 2007 was recorded for Malta (3.0), the equivalent of almost one additional person per household when compared with the average in Germany (2.1), where the lowest value was recorded. Generally speaking, the northern Member States tended to report the lowest average number of persons per household, while there were higher figures among the Mediterranean countries and those countries which joined the EU since 2004.

There were wide ranging differences across the Member States as regards housing ownership status in 2006: in the Baltic Member States, Slovakia, Hungary, Slovenia and Spain more than 80 % of households owned their own house/flat, while there was a tendency for lower levels of ownership (and therefore a higher propensity to rent) in Germany, Austria, the Netherlands and Poland. It is difficult to pinpoint the reasons for such differences, as the distribution of households may be related to a range of factors including the degree of urbanisation, the quality of accommodation, or the supply of new or renovated housing.

Figure 6.13: Average number of persons per private household, 2007 (1)

(persons)

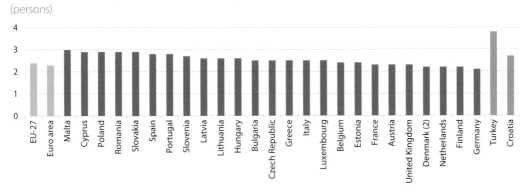

(1) Ireland and Sweden, not available.
(2) 2006.

Source: Eurostat (lfst_hhantych)

Figure 6.14: Tenure status of households, 2006 (1)

(%)

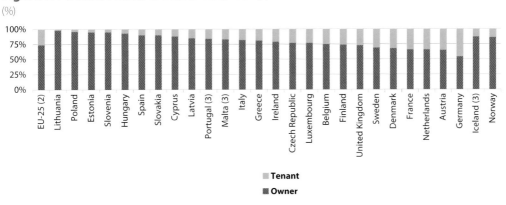

(1) Bulgaria and Romania, not available.
(2) Eurostat estimates based on population-weighted averages of national data.
(3) Provisional.

Source: Eurostat (EU-SILC)

6.4 Social protection

Introduction

Social protection systems are highly developed in the EU: they are designed to protect people against the risks associated with unemployment, parental responsibilities, ill health and invalidity, the loss of a spouse or parent, old age, housing and social exclusion. The organisation and financing of social protection systems is under the responsibility of each of the Member States. The model used in each Member State is therefore somewhat different, while the EU plays a coordinating role to ensure that people who move across borders continue to receive adequate protection. This role also promotes actions among the Member States to combat poverty and social exclusion, and to reform social protection systems on the basis of policy exchanges and mutual learning: this policy is known as the social protection and social inclusion process. The process underpins the revised Lisbon objectives for 2010, promoting a more inclusive Europe that, it is argued, will be vital to achieve the EU's goals of sustained economic growth, more and better jobs and greater social cohesion. The social inclusion process was established in 2000 with the aim of eradicating poverty by 2010, it has also led to general consensus on the following challenges:

- to eradicate child poverty by breaking the vicious circle of intergenerational inheritance;
- to make labour markets truly inclusive;
- to ensure decent housing for everyone;

- to overcome discrimination and increase the integration of people with disabilities, ethnic minorities and immigrants;
- to tackle financial exclusion and over-indebtedness.

Definitions and data availability

Data on expenditure and receipts of social protection are drawn up according to the **European System of integrated Social Protection Statistics (ESSPROS)** methodology; this system has been designed to allow a comparison of social protection flows between Member States. In April 2007 a legal basis was established for the provision of ESSPROS data (with data delivery due to start in 2008 with reference to 2006 data); this basis is provided for by Regulation (EC) No 458/2007 of the European Parliament and of the Council [5].

Social protection encompasses all interventions from public or private bodies intended to relieve households and individuals of the burden of a defined set of risks or needs, associated with old age, sickness and/or healthcare, childbearing and family, disability, unemployment, etc. **Expenditure on social protection** includes: social benefits, which consist of transfers, in cash or in kind, to households and individuals to relieve them of the burden of a defined set of risks or needs; administration costs, which represent the costs charged to the scheme for its management and administration; and other expenditure, which consists of miscellaneous expenditure by social protection schemes (payment of property income and other).

---

(5) http://eur-lex.europa.eu/LexUriServ/LexUriServ.do?uri=OJ:L:2007:113:0003:0008:EN:PDF.

Social protection benefits are direct transfers, in cash or in kind, by social protection schemes to households and individuals to relieve them of the burden of one or more of the defined distinct risks or needs; benefits via the fiscal system are excluded. Social benefits are paid to households by social security funds, other government units, NPISHs (non-profit institutions serving households), employers administering unfunded social insurance schemes, insurance enterprises or other institutional units administering privately funded social insurance schemes. Benefits are classified according to eight social protection functions (which represent a set of risks or needs):

- sickness/healthcare benefits – including paid sick leave, medical care and provision of pharmaceutical products;
- disability benefits – including disability pensions and the provision of goods and services (other than medical care) to the disabled;
- old age benefits – including old age pensions and the provision of goods and services (other than medical care) to the elderly;
- survivors' benefits – including income maintenance and support in connection with the death of a family member, such as survivors' pensions;
- family/children benefits – including support (except healthcare) in connection with the costs of pregnancy, childbirth, childbearing and caring for other family members;
- unemployment benefits – including vocational training financed by public agencies;
- housing benefits – including interventions by public authorities to help households meet the cost of housing;

- social exclusion benefits – including income support, rehabilitation of alcohol and drug abusers and other miscellaneous benefits (except healthcare).

The **pensions aggregate** comprises part of periodic cash benefits under the disability, old age, survivors and unemployment functions. It is defined as the sum of the following social benefits: disability pension, early-retirement benefit due to reduced capacity to work, old age pension, anticipated old age pension, partial pension, survivors' pension, early-retirement benefit for labour market reasons. **Expenditure on care for the elderly** is defined as the percentage of social protection expenditure devoted to old age care in GDP. These expenditures cover care allowance, accommodation, and assistance in carrying out daily tasks. The **aggregate replacement ratio** is defined as the median individual gross pensions of those aged 65-74 relative to median individual gross earnings of those aged 50-59, excluding other social benefits; it is expressed in percentage terms.

The units responsible for providing social protection are financed in different ways, their **social protection receipts** comprise social security contributions paid by employers and protected persons, contributions by general government, and other receipts from a variety of sources (for example, interest, dividends, rent and claims against third parties). **Social contributions by employers** are all costs incurred by employers to secure entitlement to social benefits for their employees, former employees and their dependants. They can be paid by resident or non-resident employers. They include all payments by employers to social protection

institutions (actual contributions) and social benefits paid directly by employers to employees (imputed contributions). **Social contributions made by protected persons** comprise contributions paid by employees, by the self-employed and by pensioners and other persons.

Main findings

Social protection expenditure in the EU-27 represented 27.2 % of GDP in 2005. The largest proportion of expenditure on social expenditure was recorded in Sweden, with slightly less than one third (32 %) of GDP in 2005, closely followed by France (31.5 %). At the other end of the spectrum, the Baltic Member States dedicated the lowest proportion of their GDP to social protection (between 12.4 % and 13.2 %).

The use of a purchasing power standard (PPS) allows an unbiased comparison of social protection expenditure per capita between countries, taking account of differences in price levels. The highest level of expenditure on social protection per capita in 2005 was registered for Luxembourg [6] (PPS 12 946 per capita), while Sweden, Denmark, the Netherlands, Austria, Belgium and France all accounted for between PPS 8 000 and PPS 8 500 per capita. In contrast, average expenditure in the Baltic Member States, Bulgaria and Romania was less than PPS 1 800 per capita. These disparities between countries are partly related to differing levels of wealth and also reflect differences in social protection systems, demographic trends, unemployment rates and other social, institutional and economic factors.

Old age represented the largest social benefit function, accounting for a little more than two fifths (41.4 %) of total social benefits in the EU-27 in 2005, followed by sickness and healthcare (28.6 %). The relative importance of family/child benefit, disability benefit and unemployment benefit was quite similar, accounting for between 6.1 % and 8.0 % of the total in the EU-27, while survivors, housing and social exclusion benefits together accounted for the remaining 7.9 %.

In relation to GDP, expenditure on pensions was equivalent to 12.2 % within the EU-27 in 2005, ranging from a high of 14.8 % in Italy to a low of 4.9 % in Ireland. Expenditure on care for elderly in the EU-27 accounted for some 0.5 % of GDP in the same year, a proportion that rose to 2.5 % in Sweden, but fell to less than 0.1 % of GDP in Greece, Estonia, Belgium, Bulgaria and Romania. The aggregate replacement ratio measures the difference between retirement benefits for pensioners (aged 65 to 74 years old) and salaries received by those aged 50 to 64. This ratio was highest in 2006 in Luxembourg and Austria (where pensioners received on average 65 % of the salary received by those aged 50 to 64). The majority of the remaining Member States were within the range of 40 % to 60 %, with Denmark (37 %), Ireland (35 %) and Cyprus (28 %) below.

The main contributors to EU-27 social protection receipts in 2005 were employers' social contribution (38.3 %) and general government contributions (37.6 %); social contributions paid by protected persons accounted for a further 20.8 % of the total.

---

(6) Luxembourg is a special case insofar as a significant proportion of benefits (primarily expenditure on healthcare, pensions and family benefits) are paid to persons living outside the country.

Table 6.6: Total expenditure on social protection
(% of GDP)

	1995	1996	1997	1998	1999	2000	2001	2002	2003	2004	2005
EU (1)	27.7	27.9	27.5	27.1	27.0	26.6	26.8	27.1	27.4	27.3	27.2
Euro area (2)	27.2	27.6	27.3	26.9	27.0	26.8	26.9	27.4	27.8	27.8	27.8
Belgium	27.4	28.0	27.4	27.1	27.0	26.5	27.3	28.0	29.1	29.3	29.7
Bulgaria	:	:	:	:	:	:	:	:	:	:	16.1
Czech Republic	17.5	17.6	18.6	18.5	19.2	19.5	19.5	20.2	20.2	19.3	19.1
Denmark	31.9	31.2	30.1	30.0	29.8	28.9	29.2	29.7	30.9	30.9	30.1
Germany	28.2	29.3	28.9	28.8	29.2	29.3	29.4	30.0	30.3	29.6	29.4
Estonia	:	:	:	:	:	14.0	13.1	12.7	12.6	13.1	12.5
Ireland	14.8	13.9	12.9	12.0	14.6	14.1	15.0	17.3	17.8	18.2	18.2
Greece	19.9	20.5	20.8	21.7	22.7	23.5	24.1	23.8	23.6	23.6	24.2
Spain	21.6	21.5	20.8	20.2	19.8	20.3	20.0	20.3	20.4	20.6	20.8
France	30.3	30.6	30.4	30.1	29.9	29.5	29.6	30.4	30.9	31.3	31.5
Italy	24.2	24.3	24.9	24.6	24.8	24.7	24.9	25.3	25.8	26.0	26.4
Cyprus	:	:	:	:	:	14.8	14.9	16.2	18.4	17.8	18.2
Latvia	:	:	15.3	16.1	17.2	15.3	14.3	13.9	13.8	12.9	12.4
Lithuania	:	13.4	13.8	15.2	16.4	15.8	14.7	14.1	13.6	13.3	13.2
Luxembourg	20.7	21.2	21.5	21.2	20.5	19.6	20.9	21.6	22.2	22.3	21.9
Hungary	:	:	:	:	20.7	19.3	19.3	20.4	21.1	20.7	21.9
Malta	15.7	17.1	17.5	17.5	17.3	16.5	17.4	17.5	17.9	18.4	18.3
Netherlands	30.6	29.6	28.7	27.8	27.1	26.4	26.5	27.6	28.3	28.3	28.2
Austria	28.8	28.7	28.6	28.3	28.7	28.1	28.4	29.0	29.3	29.0	28.8
Poland	:	:	:	:	:	19.7	21.0	21.1	21.0	20.1	19.6
Portugal	21.0	20.2	20.3	20.9	21.4	21.7	22.7	23.7	24.1	24.7	:
Romania	:	:	:	:	:	13.2	13.2	13.4	12.6	15.1	14.2
Slovenia	:	24.1	24.5	24.8	24.8	24.6	24.8	24.8	24.1	23.7	23.4
Slovakia	18.4	19.3	19.6	20.0	20.0	19.3	18.9	19.0	18.2	17.3	16.9
Finland	31.5	31.4	29.1	27.0	26.2	25.1	24.9	25.6	26.5	26.6	26.7
Sweden	34.3	33.6	32.7	32.0	31.7	30.7	31.2	32.2	33.2	32.7	32.0
United Kingdom	28.0	27.8	27.3	26.7	26.2	26.9	27.3	26.2	26.2	26.3	26.8
Iceland	18.9	18.7	18.5	18.3	18.8	19.2	19.4	21.2	23.0	22.6	21.7
Norway	26.5	25.8	25.1	26.9	26.9	24.4	25.4	26.0	27.2	25.9	23.9
Switzerland	25.6	26.4	27.3	27.3	27.3	26.9	27.6	28.5	29.1	29.3	29.2

(1) EU-15 for 1995-1999; EU-25 for 2000-2004; EU-27 for 2005.
(2) EA-13 instead of EA-15.

Source: Eurostat (tps00098)

Figure 6.15: Total expenditure on social protection per capita, 2005 (1)
(PPS)

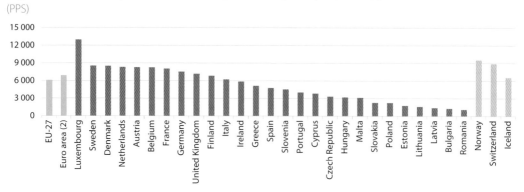

(1) EU-27, euro area and the United Kingdom, estimates; Bulgaria, the Czech Republic, Germany, Spain, France, Italy, Latvia, Lithuania, the Netherlands, Poland, Portugal, Romania, Slovenia, Slovakia and Sweden, provisional; Portugal, 2004.
(2) EA-13 instead of EA-15.

Source: Eurostat (tps00100)

Figure 6.16: Social benefits, EU-27, 2005 (1)
(%, based on PPS)

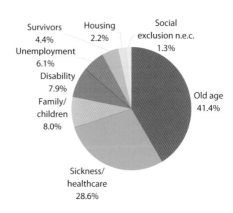

(1) Estimates; figures do not sum to 100 % due to rounding.

Source: Eurostat (tps00107)

Figure 6.17: Expenditure on pensions, 2005 (1)

(% of GDP)

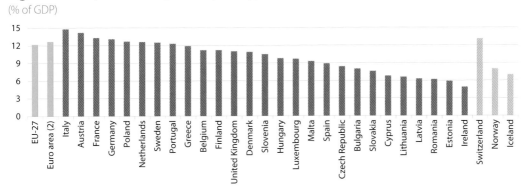

(1) EU-27, euro area and the United Kingdom, estimates; Bulgaria, the Czech Republic, Germany, Spain, France, Italy, Latvia, Lithuania, the Netherlands, Poland, Portugal, Romania, Slovenia, Slovakia and Sweden, provisional; Portugal, 2004.
(2) EA-13 instead of EA-15.

Source: Eurostat (tps00103)

Figure 6.18: Expenditure on care for elderly, 2005 (1)

(% of GDP)

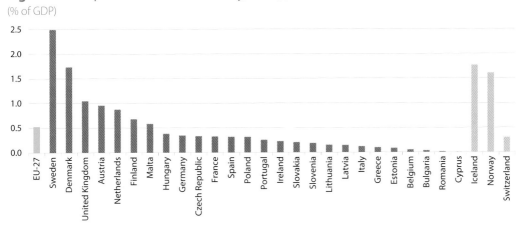

(1) EU-27 and the United Kingdom, estimates; Bulgaria, the Czech Republic, Germany, Spain, France, Italy, Cyprus, Latvia, Lithuania, the Netherlands, Poland, Portugal, Romania, Slovenia, Slovakia and Sweden, provisional; Portugal, 2004; Luxembourg, not available.

Source: Eurostat (tsdde530)

Figure 6.19: Aggregate replacement ratio, 2006 (1)

(%)

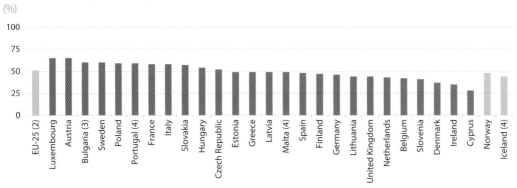

(1) Romania, not available.
(2) Eurostat calculation based on population-weighted averages of national data.
(3) National HBS.
(4) Provisional.

Source: Eurostat (tsdde310)

Figure 6.20: Social protection receipts, EU-27, 2005 (1)

(% of total receipts)

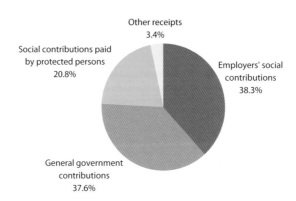

Other receipts
3.4%

Social contributions paid
by protected persons
20.8%

Employers' social
contributions
38.3%

General government
contributions
37.6%

(1) Estimates; figures do not sum to 100 % due to rounding.

Source: Eurostat (tps00108)

6.5 Good governance

Introduction

The term 'governance' covers a wide range of concepts. Indeed, it is used in connection with several contemporary social sciences, especially economics and political science. It originates from the need of economics (enterprise governance, for instance) and political science (State governance). The term 'governance', in both corporate and State contexts, embraces action by executive bodies, assemblies (such as national parliaments) and judicial bodies (national courts and tribunals for example).

In July 2001, the European Commission adopted a White Paper on European Governance. This White Paper contained a series of recommendations on how to enhance democracy in Europe and boost the legitimacy of its institutions. It defined governance in a European context as the rules, processes and behaviour that affect the way in which powers are exercised at European level, particularly as regards openness, participation, accountability, effectiveness and coherence (the five principles of good governance). The White Paper aims to modernise European public action in order to increase the accountability of European executive bodies to the elected assemblies and open up the EU's decision-making procedures to allow citizens to participate in making decisions which concern them. Ultimately, it is hoped that these new forms of governance will bring the EU closer to

its citizens, making it more effective, reinforcing democracy and consolidating the legitimacy of its institutions, while improving the quality of European legislation and making it clearer and more effective.

Definitions and data availability

Voter turnout is the percentage of persons who cast a vote or 'turn out' at an election as a share of the total population entitled to vote. It includes those who cast blank or invalid votes. In Belgium, Luxembourg and Greece, voting is compulsory. In Italy, voting is a civic obligation (no penalty).

The **level of citizens' confidence in each EU institution** (Council of the European Union, European Parliament and European Commission) is expressed as the share of positive opinions (people who declare that they 'tend to trust') about each institution. Trust is not precisely defined and could leave some room for interpretation to the interviewees. The data are based on a twice-yearly Eurobarometer survey which has been used, since 1973, to monitor the evolution of public opinion in the Member States and since 2004 in the candidate countries. The remaining categories, not shown in the table, include the percentage of negative opinions (people who declare that they 'tend not to trust'), as well as 'don't know' and/or 'no answer'.

Main findings

Voter turnout at EU parliamentary elections in June 2004 ranged from 90.8 % in Belgium (where voting is compulsory) to 17.0 % in Slovakia. Voter turnout in Bulgaria and Romania for their first elections to the European Parliament in 2007 was a little less than 30 %, at the lower end of the range among Member States. The next parliamentary elections are planned for 2009.

According to the latest survey of public opinion in 2007, somewhat more than half (55 %) of all citizens declared that they tended to trust the European Parliament, while exactly half (50 %) tended to trust the European Commission. Less than half (44 %) of respondents tended to trust the Council of the European Union, the relative proportions in Denmark, Italy, Luxembourg and Sweden falling relatively sharply when compared with results from 2000.

Figure 6.21: Voter turnout

(%)

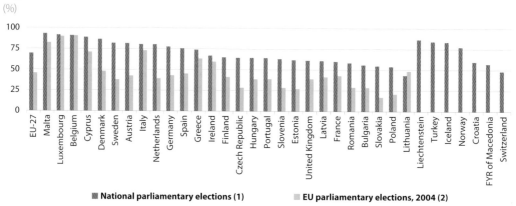

(1) Latest elections: Spain, Italy, Lithuania, Malta, Austria, Slovenia and the former Yugoslav Republic of Macedonia, 2008; Belgium, Denmark, Estonia, Ireland, Greece, France, Poland, Finland, Croatia, Turkey, Iceland and Switzerland, 2007; the Czech Republic, Cyprus, Latvia, Hungary, the Netherlands, Slovakia and Sweden, 2006; Bulgaria, Denmark, Germany, Portugal, the United Kingdom, Liechtenstein and Norway, 2005; Luxembourg and Romania, 2004; EU-27, average estimated by Eurostat on the basis of the trends observed in each of the Member States for national parliamentary elections.
(2) Bulgaria and Romania, 2007; non-EU Member States, not applicable; EU-25 instead of EU-27.

Source: Eurostat (tsdgo310), International Institute for Democracy and Electoral Assistance

Table 6.7: Level of citizens' confidence in EU institutions

(%)

	European Parliament		Council of the European Union		Commission of the European Communities	
	2002	2007	2002	2007	2002	2007
EU-27	:	55	:	44	:	50
Belgium	69	68	54	56	64	67
Bulgaria	:	58	:	40	:	46
Czech Republic	:	61	:	53	:	57
Denmark	59	70	55	48	65	61
Germany	58	52	41	43	47	46
Estonia	:	61	:	52	:	57
Ireland	71	63	60	50	67	60
Greece	61	77	53	68	56	69
Spain	64	62	57	49	59	53
France	62	58	47	46	58	54
Italy	74	53	57	45	65	50
Cyprus	:	59	:	57	:	57
Latvia	:	44	:	37	:	39
Lithuania	:	57	:	47	:	53
Luxembourg	75	65	67	52	74	55
Hungary	:	67	:	54	:	61
Malta	:	63	:	57	:	60
Netherlands	65	61	49	47	60	59
Austria	58	51	47	41	51	48
Poland	:	60	:	55	:	61
Portugal	59	63	54	53	58	59
Romania	:	72	:	53	:	60
Slovenia	:	63	:	59	:	61
Slovakia	:	70	:	59	:	62
Finland	57	53	49	49	55	53
Sweden	51	57	46	30	45	49
United Kingdom	34	25	20	17	31	22
Croatia	:	40	:	41	:	39
FYR of Macedonia	:	57	:	52	:	53
Turkey	:	20	:	17	:	17

Source: Eurostat (tsdgo510), European Commission, Eurobarometer survey

Labour market

7

Labour market statistics are at the heart of many EU policies following the introduction of an employment chapter into the Amsterdam Treaty in 1997. The extraordinary European Council of Luxembourg in November 1997 endorsed an ambitious European employment strategy (EES) aimed at reducing unemployment and the gender gap, while promoting sustainable increases of employment rates. The Lisbon summit in the spring of 2000 put full employment with more and better jobs on the European agenda, setting ambitious EU targets for the year 2010, namely:

- 70 % for the total employment rate;
- 60 % for the female employment rate.

The Stockholm Council in the spring of 2001 subsequently added an employment rate target for persons aged between 55 and 64 years to reach 50 % in the EU by 2010.

In its mid-term review of the EES in 2005, the European Commission made a set of new proposals concerning employment guidelines for the period 2005-08, reflecting a switch of emphasis in favour of growth and employment, with the aim of:

- attracting and retaining more people in employment, increasing labour supply and modernising social protection systems;
- improving the adaptability of the workforce and the business sector;
- increasing investment in human capital through better education and skills.

A Council Decision on 7 July 2008 on guidelines for the employment policies of the Member States [1] introduced a follow-on set of integrated guidelines for the period 2008-2010. These are based on three pillars: macroeconomic policies, microeconomic reforms and employment policies. The Decision introduces a range of guidelines and benchmarks designed to set priorities for the Member States employment policies, such that these reflect the revised Lisbon strategy and take account of common social objectives, including the goals of full employment, improving quality and productivity at work and strengthening economic, social and territorial cohesion.

---

(1) http://register.consilium.europa.eu/pdf/en/08/st10/st10614-re02.en08.pdf.

7.1 People in the labour market – employment

Introduction

EU citizens have the right to work in any Member State without the need for work permits. Although some temporary restrictions apply for workers from countries that joined the EU since 2004, this freedom of movement is designed to help create a single market for jobs and could potentially provide a boost to the economy while helping thousands of people to achieve their career and lifestyle aspirations.

All EU citizens that move to work in another Member State must be treated in the same way as nationals in terms of employment rights that cover work-related issues like pay and dismissal. It is also possible for job hunters to get their unemployment benefits paid in another EU country for a period of time while they try to secure employment.

Flexible working conditions – for example, part-time work or work from home – are thought to stimulate employment and activity rates, by encouraging more persons into the labour force. Other initiatives that may encourage a higher proportion of persons into the labour market include improvements in the availability of childcare facilities, or providing opportunities for lifelong learning. Nevertheless, job mobility within the EU remains relatively low, as just 2 % of the working age population of the EU currently lives and works in another Member State.

Central to this theme is the issue of 'flexicurity': policies that simultaneously address the flexibility of labour markets, work organisation and labour relations, while also taking into account the reconciliation of work and private life, employment security and social protection. It is often argued that if individuals and couples are unable to achieve their desired work/family life balance, not only is their welfare lower but economic development is also curtailed through a reduction in the supply of labour. In this way, flexible working arrangements can be viewed as encouraging more people into work, while liberating individuals to make family choices such as whether to try to have a family or spend more time with children. In contrast, an inflexible labour market can be seen as one reason behind a reduction in birth rates, which has clear repercussions for future labour supply, as well as the knock-on effects regarding the financial sustainability of social protection systems.

Definitions and data availability

Given the considerable interest in labour market policies post-Lisbon, the European Labour Force Survey (LFS) has grown in importance and has become a key tool for observing labour market developments. The LFS is a quarterly household sample survey carried out in the Member States of the European Union, candidate countries and EFTA countries (except

Liechtenstein). It is the main source of information concerning the situation and trends within the labour market of the EU. The LFS primarily reports on the EU's population of working age (15 years and more) which is composed of persons in employment, unemployed persons and economically inactive persons. It provides comprehensive information on these three categories, describing the employment situation of employed persons by reporting on, for example, their education level, the branches in which they work, their occupations, as well as their propensity to engage in part-time work, the duration of their work contracts, and their search for new jobs. Note that coverage in terms of labour force status is restricted to those aged 16 and over in Spain and the United Kingdom. In Denmark, Estonia, Latvia, Hungary, Finland, Sweden (from 2001 onwards) and Norway, the coverage relates to those aged 15 to 74, while in Sweden (prior to 2001) and Iceland, coverage refers to those aged 16 to 74. The sample size amounts approximately to 1.5 million individuals each quarter, with quarterly sampling rates of between 0.2 % and 3.3 % in each country. During the period from 1998 to 2005, the survey underwent a transition towards a continuous quarterly survey. All EU Member States now provide quarterly results.

The economically **active population** (labour force) comprises employed and unemployed persons. **Employment/activity rates** represent employed/active persons as a percentage of same age total population.

Employed persons are defined as persons aged 15 and over who during the reference week performed some work, even for just one hour per week, for pay, profit or family gain or were not at work but had a job or business from which they were temporarily absent because of, for example, illness, holidays, industrial dispute and education or training. **Self-employed persons** work in their own business, farm or professional practice. A self-employed person is considered to be working if she/he meets one of the following criteria: works for the purpose of earning profit; spends time on the operation of a business, or; is in the process of setting-up a business. **Employees** are defined as persons who work for a public or private employer and who receive compensation in the form of wages, salaries, payment by results or payment in kind; non-conscript members of the armed forces are also included.

Annual employment growth gives the change in percentage terms from one year to another of the total number of employed persons on the economic territory of the country or the geographical area.

A **full-time/part-time** distinction in the main job is declared by the respondent, except in Germany, Ireland and the Netherlands, where thresholds for usual hours worked are used.

The indicator for **employed persons with a second job** refers to persons with more than one job at the same time. Persons having changed job during the reference week are not counted as having two jobs.

A job is considered as **temporary** if employer and employee agree that its end is determined by objective conditions, such as a specific date, the completion of an assignment or return of the employee who was temporarily replaced. Typical cases include: persons with seasonal employment; persons engaged by an agency or employment exchange and hired to a third party to perform a specific task (unless there is a written work contract of unlimited duration); persons with specific training contracts.

The **dispersion of regional (NUTS level 2) employment rates** shows regional differences in employment within countries and groups of countries (EU-27, euro area). It is zero when the employment rates in all regions are identical, and will rise if there is an increase in the differences between employment rates among regions. The indicator is not applicable for several countries as these comprise only one or a handful of NUTS level 2 regions. However, the employment rates of these countries are used to compute the indicator at a European level.

Main findings

The employment rate among the EU-27's population aged between 15 and 64 years old was 65.4 % in 2007. Although this represented a further rise in the employment rate since the relative low of 60.7 % recorded in 1997, it remains below the target of 70 % that the Lisbon European Council set for 2010. Employment rates above 70 % were achieved in seven of the Member States (Denmark, the Netherlands, Sweden, Austria, the United Kingdom, Cyprus and Finland). In contrast, employment rates below 60 % were recorded in Romania, Italy, Hungary, Poland and Malta.

Employment rates within the Member States often varied considerably according to regional patterns, with a relatively high dispersion (16.3 %) observed across Italy (as measured by the coefficient of variation for regions at NUTS 2 level). In contrast, there was relatively little divergence in employment rates across the regions of Austria, Greece, Portugal or Sweden (all below 4 %). The dispersion of regional employment across the whole of the EU-27 was seen to be converging, as the coefficient of variation declined from 13.2 % to 11.1 % between 2002 and 2007.

The Lisbon European Council of 2000 set a target employment rate for women of 60 % across the EU. In 2007, the employment rate for women was 58.3 % in the EU-27, a significantly higher rate than that recorded in 2001 (54.3 %), although considerably lower than the corresponding rate for men (72.5 %). Some 15 of the Member States recorded employment rates for women above the target of 60 % in 2007, with the rates in Denmark and Sweden exceeding 70 %.

The Stockholm European Council of 2001 set a target employment rate for older workers (aged between 55 and 64 years) of 50 % by 2010. The employment rate for older workers across the EU-27 was 44.7 % in 2007, much higher than the corresponding rate (37.7 %) recorded in 2001. The employment rate for older workers was higher than 50 % in 12 of the Member States, with the highest rates recorded in Sweden (70.0 %); note there is no official retirement age in this country.

There were considerable differences between employment rates, according to the level of educational attainment. The employment rate of those aged 25 to 64 [2] who had completed tertiary education

(2) For statistics on education level attainment, the age group 25 to 64 is used instead of 15 to 64.

was 85.3 % across the EU-27 in 2007, much higher than the rate (57.2 %) for those who had only attained a low educational level (primary or lower secondary education).

The proportion of the workforce working part-time in the EU-27 increased steadily from 15.9 % in 1997 to 18.2 % by 2007. The highest proportion of people working part-time was found in the Netherlands (46.8 % in 2007), followed by Germany, the United Kingdom, Sweden and Denmark, where part-time work accounted in each case for about a quarter of those in employment. In contrast, part-time employment was relatively uncommon in Bulgaria (1.7 % of those in employment), Slovakia (2.6 %) and Hungary (4.1 %). A little less than one third (31.2 %) of the women employed in the EU-27 did so on a part-time basis in 2007, a much higher proportion than the corresponding share

(7.7 %) for men. Three quarters (75.0 %) of all women employed in the Netherlands worked on a part-time basis in 2007, by far the highest rate among the Member States[3].

Slightly less than one third (31.7 %) of employees in Spain were employed on a temporary basis in 2007, and this share was more than a quarter (28.2 %) of employees in Poland. There was a considerable range in the propensity to use limited duration contracts between Member States that may, at least to some degree, reflect national practices, the supply and demand of labour and the ease with which employers can hire or fire. Among the remaining Member States, the proportion of employees working on a contract of limited duration ranged from 22.4 % in Portugal down to just 1.6 % in Romania.

(3)   Anyone working fewer than 35 hours a week is considered as working part-time in the Netherlands.

Figure 7.1: Employment rate, 2007

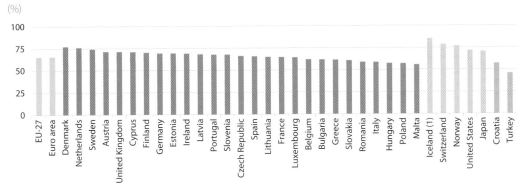

(1) Provisional.

Source: Eurostat (tsiem010)

Table 7.1: Employment rate

(%)

	1997	1998	1999	2000	2001	2002	2003	2004	2005	2006	2007
EU-27	60.7	61.2	61.8	62.2	62.5	62.3	62.6	62.9	63.5	64.5	65.4
Euro area	58.5	59.2	60.4	61.5	62.2	62.4	62.7	63.2	63.8	64.8	65.7
Belgium	56.8	57.4	59.3	60.5	59.9	59.9	59.6	60.3	61.1	61.0	62.0
Bulgaria	:	:	:	50.4	49.7	50.6	52.5	54.2	55.8	58.6	61.7
Czech Republic	:	67.3	65.6	65.0	65.0	65.4	64.7	64.2	64.8	65.3	66.1
Denmark	74.9	75.1	76.0	76.3	76.2	75.9	75.1	75.7	75.9	77.4	77.1
Germany (1)	63.7	63.9	65.2	65.6	65.8	65.4	65.0	65.0	66.0	67.5	69.4
Estonia	:	64.6	61.5	60.4	61.0	62.0	62.9	63.0	64.4	68.1	69.4
Ireland	57.6	60.6	63.3	65.2	65.8	65.5	65.5	66.3	67.6	68.6	69.1
Greece	55.1	56.0	55.9	56.5	56.3	57.5	58.7	59.4	60.1	61.0	61.4
Spain (1)	49.5	51.3	53.8	56.3	57.8	58.5	59.8	61.1	63.3	64.8	65.6
France	59.6	60.2	60.9	62.1	62.8	63.0	64.0	63.7	63.9	63.8	64.6
Italy (2)	51.3	51.9	52.7	53.7	54.8	55.5	56.1	57.6	57.6	58.4	58.7
Cyprus	:	:	:	65.7	67.8	68.6	69.2	68.9	68.5	69.6	71.0
Latvia	:	59.9	58.8	57.5	58.6	60.4	61.8	62.3	63.3	66.3	68.3
Lithuania	:	62.3	61.7	59.1	57.5	59.9	61.1	61.2	62.6	63.6	64.9
Luxembourg	59.9	60.5	61.7	62.7	63.1	63.4	62.2	62.5	63.6	63.6	64.2
Hungary	52.4	53.7	55.6	56.3	56.2	56.2	57.0	56.8	56.9	57.3	57.3
Malta	:	:	:	54.2	54.3	54.4	54.2	54.0	53.9	54.8	55.7
Netherlands	68.5	70.2	71.7	72.9	74.1	74.4	73.6	73.1	73.2	74.3	76.0
Austria (2)	67.8	67.9	68.6	68.5	68.5	68.7	68.9	67.8	68.6	70.2	71.4
Poland	58.9	59.0	57.6	55.0	53.4	51.5	51.2	51.7	52.8	54.5	57.0
Portugal (3)	65.7	66.8	67.4	68.4	69.0	68.8	68.1	67.8	67.5	67.9	67.8
Romania (4)	65.4	64.2	63.2	63.0	62.4	57.6	57.6	57.7	57.6	58.8	58.8
Slovenia	62.6	62.9	62.2	62.8	63.8	63.4	62.6	65.3	66.0	66.6	67.8
Slovakia	:	60.6	58.1	56.8	56.8	56.8	57.7	57.0	57.7	59.4	60.7
Finland	63.3	64.6	66.4	67.2	68.1	68.1	67.7	67.6	68.4	69.3	70.3
Sweden (1)	69.5	70.3	71.7	73.0	74.0	73.6	72.9	72.1	72.5	73.1	74.2
United Kingdom (5)	69.9	70.5	71.0	71.2	71.4	71.3	71.5	71.6	71.7	71.5	71.3
Croatia	:	:	:	:	:	53.4	53.4	54.7	55.0	55.6	57.1
Turkey	:	:	:	48.8	47.8	46.9	45.8	46.1	46.0	45.9	45.8
Iceland	:	:	:	:	:	:	83.3	82.3	83.8	84.6	85.1
Norway	:	:	:	77.5	77.2	76.8	75.5	75.1	74.8	75.4	76.8
Switzerland	76.9	78.0	78.4	78.3	79.1	78.9	77.9	77.4	77.2	77.9	78.6
Japan	70.0	69.5	68.8	68.8	68.7	68.2	68.3	68.6	69.2	69.9	70.6
United States	73.5	73.8	73.9	74.0	73.1	71.9	71.2	71.2	71.5	71.9	71.7

(1) Break in series, 2005.
(2) Break in series, 2004.
(3) Break in series, 1998.
(4) Break in series, 2002.
(5) Break in series, 2000.

Source: Eurostat (tsiem010)

Figure 7.2: Dispersion of regional employment rates (1)

(coefficient of variation of employment rates (of the age group 15-64) across regions (NUTS 2 level))

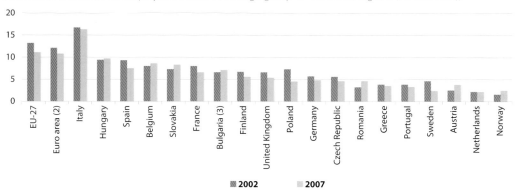

(1) At the NUTS 2 level: Denmark, Estonia, Cyprus, Latvia, Lithuania, Luxembourg, Malta, Slovenia and Iceland are treated as one region; Ireland has two regions.
(2) EA-13 instead of EA-15.
(3) 2003 instead of 2002.

Source: Eurostat (tsisc050)

Figure 7.3: Employment rate by gender, 2007 (1)

(%)

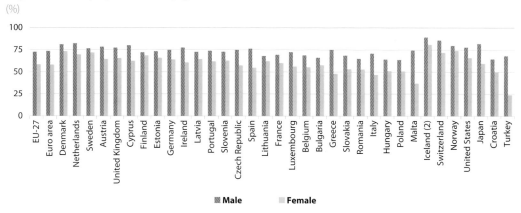

(1) The figure is ranked on the average of male and female.
(2) Provisional.

Source: Eurostat (tsiem010)

 Labour market

Table 7.2: Employment rates for selected population groups
(%)

	Male		Female		Older workers	
	2002	2007	2002	2007	2002	2007
EU-27	70.3	72.5	54.4	58.3	38.5	44.7
Euro area	71.7	73.4	53.1	58.0	36.4	43.3
Belgium	68.3	68.7	51.4	55.3	26.6	34.4
Bulgaria	53.7	66.0	47.5	57.6	27.0	42.6
Czech Republic	73.9	74.8	57.0	57.3	40.8	46.0
Denmark	80.0	81.0	71.7	73.2	57.9	58.6
Germany	71.8	74.7	58.9	64.0	38.9	51.5
Estonia	66.5	73.2	57.9	65.9	51.6	60.0
Ireland	75.4	77.4	55.4	60.6	48.0	53.8
Greece	72.2	74.9	42.9	47.9	39.2	42.4
Spain	72.6	76.2	44.4	54.7	39.6	44.6
France	69.5	69.3	56.7	60.0	34.7	38.3
Italy	69.1	70.7	42.0	46.6	28.9	33.8
Cyprus	78.9	80.0	59.1	62.4	49.4	55.9
Latvia	64.3	72.5	56.8	64.4	41.7	57.7
Lithuania	62.7	67.9	57.2	62.2	41.6	53.4
Luxembourg	75.1	72.3	51.6	56.1	28.1	32.0
Hungary	62.9	64.0	49.8	50.9	25.6	33.1
Malta	74.7	74.2	33.9	36.9	30.1	28.3
Netherlands	82.4	82.2	66.2	69.6	42.3	50.9
Austria	76.4	78.4	61.3	64.4	29.1	38.6
Poland	56.9	63.6	46.2	50.6	26.1	29.7
Portugal	76.5	73.8	61.4	61.9	51.4	50.9
Romania	63.6	64.8	51.8	52.8	37.3	41.4
Slovenia	68.2	72.7	58.6	62.6	24.5	33.5
Slovakia	62.4	68.4	51.4	53.0	22.8	35.6
Finland	70.0	72.1	66.2	68.5	47.8	55.0
Sweden	74.9	76.5	72.2	71.8	68.0	70.0
United Kingdom	77.6	77.3	65.2	65.5	53.4	57.4
Croatia	60.5	64.4	46.7	50.0	24.8	35.8
Turkey	66.9	68.0	27.0	23.8	35.7	29.5
Iceland	:	89.1	:	80.8	:	84.7
Norway	79.9	79.5	73.7	74.0	66.2	69.0
Switzerland	86.2	85.6	71.5	71.6	64.6	67.2
Japan	79.8	81.7	56.5	59.4	61.6	66.1
United States	77.9	77.7	66.0	65.9	59.4	61.8

Source: Eurostat (tsiem010 and tsiem020)

Table 7.3: Total employment rate, by highest level of education, 2007
(% of age group 25-64 years)

	Pre-primary, primary & lower secondary - ISCED levels 0-2	Upper secondary & post-secondary non-tertiary - ISCED levels 3-4	Tertiary - ISCED levels 5-6
EU-27	57.2	74.6	85.3
Belgium	49.8	74.2	84.9
Bulgaria	44.5	75.7	85.1
Czech Republic	45.7	76.1	85.2
Denmark	66.6	82.5	87.8
Germany	54.9	74.9	86.1
Estonia	56.7	79.4	87.4
Ireland	58.7	77.1	86.7
Greece	59.9	69.5	83.0
Spain	60.6	76.3	84.4
France	58.0	75.8	83.5
Italy	52.8	74.5	80.2
Cyprus	66.1	79.3	87.6
Latvia	59.7	77.7	87.3
Lithuania	49.1	75.8	89.4
Luxembourg	62.3	73.9	84.5
Hungary	38.5	70.2	80.4
Malta	47.1	81.4	86.6
Netherlands	61.9	80.3	87.7
Austria	57.9	76.9	86.8
Poland	41.0	65.2	84.5
Portugal	71.6	79.8	85.9
Romania	53.8	70.1	86.9
Slovenia	56.2	75.1	87.7
Slovakia	29.1	73.2	84.2
Finland	58.6	76.2	85.2
Sweden	66.6	83.1	88.5
United Kingdom	64.3	81.2	88.0
Croatia	44.6	67.8	82.2
Turkey	45.3	62.3	75.6
Iceland	84.1	88.6	92.2
Norway	65.8	83.2	90.5
Switzerland	66.3	81.4	90.1

Source: Eurostat (tsdec430)

Figure 7.4: Employment rate by age group, 2007

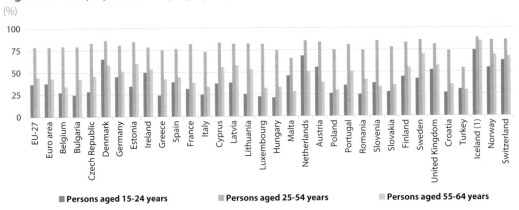

(1) Provisional.

Source: Eurostat (lfsi_emp_a)

Figure 7.5: Annual employment growth

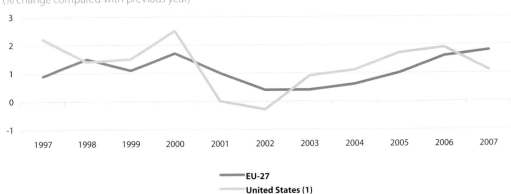

(1) Estimate, 2007.

Source: Eurostat (tsieb050)

Table 7.4: Annual employment growth
(% change compared with previous year)

	1997	1998	1999	2000	2001	2002	2003	2004	2005	2006	2007
EU-27	0.9	1.5	1.1	1.7	1.0	0.4	0.4	0.6	1.0	1.6	1.8
Euro area	0.9	1.9	1.9	2.4	1.5	0.7	0.5	0.7	1.0	1.6	1.8
Belgium	0.5	1.6	1.3	2.0	1.4	-0.1	0.0	0.7	1.2	1.2	1.7
Bulgaria	-3.9	-0.2	-2.1	4.9	-0.8	0.2	3.0	2.6	2.7	3.3	2.8
Czech Republic	0.2	-1.5	-3.4	-0.2	0.5	0.6	-1.3	0.3	1.0	1.6	1.8
Denmark	1.4	1.4	0.8	0.5	0.9	0.0	-1.1	-0.6	0.9	1.6	1.6
Germany	-0.1	1.2	1.4	1.9	0.4	-0.6	-0.9	0.4	-0.1	0.6	1.7
Estonia	0.0	-1.9	-4.4	-1.5	0.9	1.3	1.4	0.0	2.0	5.4	0.7
Ireland	5.6	8.6	6.2	4.6	3.0	1.8	2.0	3.1	4.7	4.3	3.6
Greece	-0.5	2.9	0.3	0.5	0.2	2.0	1.9	0.9	1.5	2.5	1.2
Spain	3.6	4.5	4.6	5.1	3.2	2.4	3.1	3.5	4.1	3.7	3.1
France	0.4	1.5	2.0	2.7	1.8	0.6	0.1	0.1	0.6	1.0	1.3
Italy	0.3	1.0	1.1	1.9	2.0	1.7	1.5	0.4	0.5	2.0	1.1
Cyprus	0.6	1.6	1.9	1.7	2.2	2.1	3.8	3.8	3.6	1.8	3.2
Latvia	4.4	-0.3	-1.8	-2.9	2.2	2.3	1.0	1.1	1.5	4.8	3.5
Lithuania	0.6	-0.8	-2.2	-4.0	-3.8	3.6	2.2	0.0	2.5	1.7	2.9
Luxembourg	3.1	4.5	5.0	5.5	5.6	3.2	1.8	2.2	2.9	3.7	4.2
Hungary	0.2	1.8	3.4	1.3	0.3	0.0	1.3	-0.7	0.0	0.7	-0.1
Malta	:	:	:	8.4	1.8	0.6	1.0	-0.6	1.3	1.3	2.6
Netherlands	3.1	2.6	2.6	2.2	2.1	0.5	-0.5	-0.9	0.5	1.8	2.4
Austria	0.9	1.3	1.6	1.0	0.6	-0.1	0.0	0.2	0.8	1.2	2.2
Poland (1)	2.6	1.3	-0.9	-2.4	-3.2	-1.9	-12.5	-0.3	1.0	1.9	4.5
Portugal	2.6	2.8	1.4	2.1	1.8	0.6	-0.6	-0.1	-0.3	0.5	0.0
Romania	:	:	:	:	:	:	0.0	-1.7	-1.5	2.8	1.3
Slovenia	-1.9	-0.2	1.4	1.9	0.5	1.5	-0.4	0.3	0.2	1.2	2.7
Slovakia	-1.0	-0.5	-2.5	-2.0	0.6	0.1	1.1	-0.2	1.4	2.3	2.1
Finland	3.3	2.0	2.5	2.2	1.5	1.0	0.1	0.4	1.4	1.8	2.2
Sweden	-1.3	1.7	2.1	2.5	2.1	0.0	-0.6	-0.7	0.3	1.7	2.3
United Kingdom	1.7	0.9	1.2	1.4	1.0	0.6	1.0	1.0	1.3	0.7	0.7
Croatia	3.2	-3.0	-3.3	4.0	-5.4	4.2	0.6	1.7	0.8	0.8	2.0
Turkey	-2.5	2.8	2.1	-0.4	-1.0	-1.8	-1.0	3.0	1.4	1.3	1.1
Norway	2.9	2.7	0.9	0.6	0.4	0.4	-1.0	0.5	1.2	3.4	4.0
United States	2.2	1.4	1.5	2.5	0.0	-0.3	0.9	1.1	1.7	1.9	1.1

(1) 2003, break in series.

Source: Eurostat (tsieb050)

Table 7.5: Persons working part-time and persons with a second job
(% of total employment)

	Persons employed working part-time			Persons in employment with second job		
	1997 (1)	2002	2007 (2)	1997 (3)	2002	2007 (4)
EU-27	15.9	16.2	18.2	:	3.6	3.9
Euro area	14.7	16.3	19.6	:	2.8	3.4
Belgium	15.2	19.1	22.1	2.7	3.4	3.9
Bulgaria	:	2.5	1.7	:	0.8	0.8
Czech Republic	5.7	4.9	5.0	3.9	2.4	1.7
Denmark	22.5	20.0	24.1	7.3	10.6	9.9
Germany (5)	17.6	20.8	26.0	2.6	2.2	3.8
Estonia	8.6	7.7	8.2	9.2	4.4	3.6
Ireland	13.6	16.5	16.8	2.1	2.0	2.7
Greece	4.8	4.4	5.6	3.8	3.2	3.2
Spain (6)	7.9	8.0	11.8	1.6	1.7	2.6
France	17.0	16.4	17.2	3.3	3.4	3.1
Italy (7)	6.8	8.6	13.6	1.5	1.3	1.8
Cyprus	:	7.2	7.3	:	5.0	4.4
Latvia	12.8	9.7	6.4	5.1	7.1	6.2
Lithuania	:	10.8	8.6	6.1	6.7	6.1
Luxembourg	8.2	10.7	17.8	1.2	1.1	2.0
Hungary	3.7	3.6	4.1	2.1	1.7	1.6
Malta	:	8.3	11.1	:	4.7	5.3
Netherlands	37.9	43.9	46.8	5.4	5.9	7.2
Austria (7)	14.7	19.0	22.6	4.1	3.7	4.3
Poland	10.6	10.8	9.2	9.5	8.2	7.7
Portugal (8)	10.6	11.2	12.1	6.5	6.8	6.7
Romania (9)	14.9	11.8	9.7	8.3	4.6	3.9
Slovenia	:	6.1	9.3	2.6	2.2	3.8
Slovakia	2.3	1.9	2.6	1.1	0.8	1.1
Finland	10.9	12.8	14.1	4.2	3.9	4.3
Sweden (6)	20.2	21.5	25.0	7.9	9.6	8.1
United Kingdom (10)	24.6	25.4	25.5	4.8	4.2	3.7
Croatia	:	8.3	8.6	:	3.6	3.1
Turkey	:	6.9	8.8	:	:	2.7
Iceland	:	:	21.7	16.6	17.7	11.8
Norway	:	26.4	28.2	8.1	8.8	7.9
Switzerland	29.4	31.7	33.5	5.3	6.3	7.4

(1) The Czech Republic, Estonia, Latvia and Slovakia, 1998.
(2) Ireland, 2004.
(3) Latvia, Lithuania and Slovakia, 1998.
(4) Iceland, 2006.
(5) 2005, break in series for part-time.
(6) 2005, break in series.
(7) 2004, break in series.
(8) 1998, break in series.
(9) 2002, break in series.
(10) 1999, break in series for part-time.

Source: Eurostat (tps00159, tps00074 and lfsi_emp_a)

Figure 7.6: Persons employed part-time, 2007
(% of total employment)

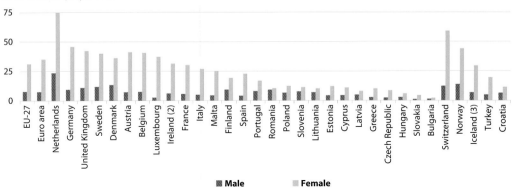

■ Male   **■ Female**

(1) The figure is ranked on the average of male and female.
(2) 2004.
(3) Provisional.

Source: Eurostat (tps00159)

Figure 7.7: Proportion of employees with a contract of limited duration, 2007
(% of total employees)

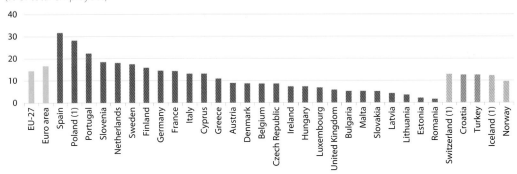

(1) Provisional.

Source: Eurostat (tps00073)

7.2 People in the labour market – unemployment

Introduction

Youth and long-term unemployment rates appear to be more susceptible to cyclical economic changes than the overall unemployment rate. Indeed, social policymakers are often challenged to remedy these situations by designing ways to increase the employment opportunities open to various (disadvantaged) groups of society, those working in particular economic activities, or those living in specific regions.

Globalisation and technological progress have an ever-increasing effect on many daily lives, and the demand for different types of labour and skills is evolving at a rapid pace. While enterprises need to be increasingly innovative and productive, some of their risk may be passed on to the labour force, as increased flexibility is demanded both from those in employment and from those searching for a new job.

Within the context of the European Employment Strategy, there are a number of measures that are designed to help encourage people to remain in work or find a new job, including: the promotion of a lifecycle approach to work, encouraging lifelong learning, improving support to those seeking a job, as well as ensuring equal opportunities.

The integrated employment guidelines for 2008-2010 encouraged Member States to:

- work with renewed endeavour to build employment pathways for young people and reduce youth unemployment, in particular, through adapting education and training systems in order to raise quality, broaden supply, diversify access, ensure flexibility, respond to new occupational needs and skills requirements;
- take action to increase female participation and reduce gender gaps in employment, unemployment and pay, through better reconciliation of work and private life and the provision of accessible and affordable childcare facilities and care for other dependants;
- give support to active ageing, including initiatives for appropriate working conditions, improved health and incentives to work and discouragement of early retirement;
- develop modern social protection systems, including pensions and healthcare, ensuring their social adequacy, financial sustainability and responsiveness to changing needs, so as to support participation, better retention in employment and longer working lives.

The guidelines also set a number of additional benchmarks, whereby Member States were encouraged:

- to ensure that by 2010 every unemployed person was offered a job, apprenticeship, additional training or another employability measure (for young persons leaving school within 4 months, and for adults within no more than 12 months);
- to work towards 25 % of the long-term unemployed participating in training, retraining, work practice, or other employability measures by 2010;
- to guarantee that job seekers throughout the EU are able to consult all job vacancies advertised in the national employment services of each Member State.

Definitions and data availability

Unemployed persons are defined as those persons aged 15-74 [4] who were without work during the reference week, were currently available for work and were either actively seeking work in the past four weeks or had already found a job to start within the next three months. For the purposes of this final point, the following are considered as specific steps in the search for a job: having been in contact with a public employment office to find work, whoever took the initiative (renewing registration for administrative reasons only is not an active step); having been in contact with a private agency (temporary work agency, firm specialising in recruitment, etc.) to find work; applying to employers directly; asking among friends, relatives, unions, etc., to find work; placing or answering job advertisements; studying job advertisements; taking a recruitment test or examination or being interviewed; looking for land, premises or equipment; applying for permits, licences or financial resources. This definition is in accordance with the International Labour Organisation (ILO) standards and Commission Regulation (EC) No 1897/2000.

Unemployment data are generally presented as rates. The **unemployment rate** is the share of unemployed persons over the total number of active persons in the labour market; active persons are those who are either employed or unemployed.

This rate can then be broken down into a number of more detailed groups – for example, **unemployment according to educational attainment**, where the indicator provides a measure of the difficulties that people with different levels of education face in the labour market, offering some information on the impact of education in reducing the chances of being unemployed. The unemployment rate is also available according to the duration of unemployment, namely: the **long-term unemployment rate** defined as the number of persons who have been unemployed for at least 12 months, expressed as a share of the total number of active persons in the labour market; the **very long-term unemployment rate** representing the number of persons who have been unemployed for at least 24 months, again expressed as a share of the total number of active persons in the labour market.

(4)　In Spain and the United Kingdom this is restricted to persons aged 16 to 74 years old.

Main findings

The average unemployment rate across the EU-27 in 2007 was 7.1 %, which represented a further improvement from the relative peak of 9.0 % that was recorded in 2003 and 2004. This latest figure marked a reduction of 1.1 percentage points in comparison with 2006, which was the largest change in unemployment (in either a positive or negative direction) since the series for the EU-27 was established in 2000.

There remain considerable differences in unemployment rates between Member States: the highest rates of 11.1 % and 9.6 % being recorded in Slovakia and Poland; and the lowest (less than 4 %) in Cyprus, Denmark and the Netherlands. Nevertheless, the distribution of unemployment rates across the EU narrowed considerably, as the gap between the highest and the lowest unemployment rates peaked in 2001 at 17.6 percentage points, falling in every subsequent year (and most rapidly in 2006 and 2007), such that it stood at 7.9 percentage points in 2007.

Long-term unemployment is one of the main concerns of governments and social planners/policy-makers. Besides its effects on personal life, long-term unemployment limits social cohesion and, ultimately, hinders economic growth. Some 3.1 % of those actively seeking work in the EU-27 in 2007 had been unemployed for more than one year and 1.8 % were unemployed for more than two years.

The unemployment rate for women (7.8 %) in the EU-27 in 2007 remained higher than that for men (6.6 %); this pattern was reflected in the majority of Member States, with exceptions limited to the Baltic Member States, Romania, Ireland, the United Kingdom and Germany. The difference in unemployment rates between the sexes was particularly marked in the Mediterranean Member States.

Unemployment rates by age group show that persons under the age of 25 tend to face the most difficulty in securing a job. The average unemployment rate among 15 to 24 year olds who were actively seeking employment was 15.3 % across the EU-27 in 2007. The highest youth unemployment rate was in Greece (22.9 %) and the same country reported the largest difference between unemployment rates for those aged 25 or more and those aged less than 25 (15.8 percentage points). This measure of the relative difficulty facing young job seekers was also particularly high in Italy (15.4 percentage points difference), Romania (15.2 percentage points difference) and Sweden (14.8 percentage points difference). In contrast, youth unemployment rates were closest to (but never lower than) the overall unemployment rate in Germany, the Netherlands, Lithuania and Denmark – all less than 5 percentage points difference.

A lack of qualifications can be another discriminating factor for job seekers, as unemployment rates tend to decrease according to the level of education attained. This was a characteristic noted in almost every Member State in 2007, as the average unemployment rate in the EU-27 for those having attained at most a lower secondary education was 9.2 % in 2007, almost three times the rate of unemployment (3.6 %) for those that had a tertiary education.

Table 7.6: Unemployment rate
(%)

	1997	1998	1999	2000	2001	2002	2003	2004	2005	2006	2007
EU-27	:	:	:	8.7	8.5	8.9	9.0	9.0	8.9	8.2	7.1
Euro area	10.5	10.0	9.2	8.3	7.8	8.2	8.6	8.8	8.9	8.3	7.4
Belgium	9.2	9.3	8.5	6.9	6.6	7.5	8.2	8.4	8.5	8.3	7.5
Bulgaria	:	:	:	16.4	19.5	18.2	13.7	12.1	10.1	9.0	6.9
Czech Republic	:	6.4	8.6	8.7	8.0	7.3	7.8	8.3	7.9	7.2	5.3
Denmark	5.2	4.9	5.2	4.3	4.5	4.6	5.4	5.5	4.8	3.9	3.8
Germany	9.4	9.1	8.2	7.5	7.6	8.4	9.3	9.8	10.7	9.8	8.4
Estonia	9.6	9.2	11.3	12.8	12.4	10.3	10.0	9.7	7.9	5.9	4.7
Ireland	9.9	7.5	5.7	4.3	4.0	4.5	4.7	4.5	4.4	4.5	4.6
Greece	9.8	10.8	12.0	11.2	10.7	10.3	9.7	10.5	9.9	8.9	8.3
Spain	16.7	15.0	12.5	11.1	10.3	11.1	11.1	10.6	9.2	8.5	8.3
France	11.5	11.0	10.4	9.0	8.3	8.6	9.0	9.3	9.2	9.2	8.3
Italy	11.3	11.4	11.0	10.1	9.1	8.6	8.5	8.1	7.7	6.8	6.1
Cyprus	:	:	:	4.9	3.8	3.6	4.1	4.7	5.3	4.6	3.9
Latvia	:	14.3	14.0	13.7	12.9	12.2	10.5	10.4	8.9	6.8	6.0
Lithuania	:	13.2	13.7	16.4	16.5	13.5	12.5	11.4	8.3	5.6	4.3
Luxembourg	2.7	2.7	2.4	2.2	1.9	2.6	3.8	5.0	4.6	4.6	4.1
Hungary	9.0	8.4	6.9	6.4	5.7	5.8	5.9	6.1	7.2	7.5	7.4
Malta	:	:	:	6.7	7.6	7.5	7.6	7.4	7.2	7.1	6.4
Netherlands	4.9	3.8	3.2	2.8	2.2	2.8	3.7	4.6	4.7	3.9	3.2
Austria	4.4	4.5	3.9	3.6	3.6	4.2	4.3	4.8	5.2	4.8	4.4
Poland	10.9	10.2	13.4	16.2	18.3	20.0	19.7	19.0	17.8	13.9	9.6
Portugal	6.7	5.0	4.5	4.0	4.1	5.1	6.4	6.7	7.7	7.8	8.1
Romania	:	:	7.1	7.3	6.8	8.6	7.0	8.1	7.2	7.3	6.4
Slovenia	6.9	7.4	7.3	6.7	6.2	6.3	6.7	6.3	6.5	6.0	4.9
Slovakia	:	12.6	16.4	18.8	19.3	18.7	17.6	18.2	16.3	13.4	11.1
Finland	12.7	11.4	10.2	9.8	9.1	9.1	9.0	8.8	8.4	7.7	6.9
Sweden (1)	9.9	8.2	6.7	5.6	4.9	4.9	5.6	6.3	7.4	7.0	6.1
United Kingdom	6.8	6.1	5.9	5.4	5.0	5.1	5.0	4.7	4.8	5.4	5.3
Croatia	:	:	:	:	:	14.8	14.2	13.7	12.7	11.2	9.6
Turkey	:	:	:	:	:	:	:	:	:	8.4	8.5
Norway	4.0	3.2	3.2	3.4	3.6	3.9	4.5	4.4	4.6	3.5	2.6
Japan	3.4	4.1	4.7	4.7	5.0	5.4	5.3	4.7	4.4	4.1	3.9
United States	4.9	4.5	4.2	4.0	4.8	5.8	6.0	5.5	5.1	4.6	4.6

(1) Break in series, 2005.

Source: Eurostat (tsiem110)

Figure 7.8: Unemployment rates, 2007 (1)

(%)

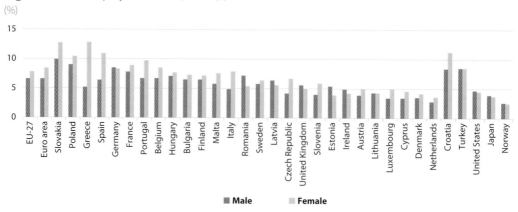

(1) The figure is ranked on the average of male and female.

Source: Eurostat (tsiem110)

Figure 7.9: Unemployment rates by duration, 2007

(%)

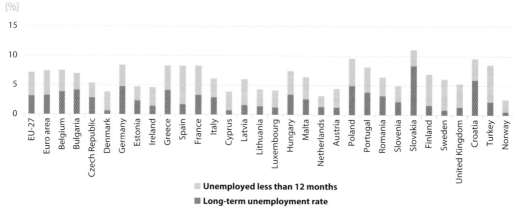

Source: Eurostat (tsiem110 and tsisc070)

Table 7.7: Unemployment rates by age and gender, 2007

(%)

	Gender		Age	
	Male	**Female**	**< 25 years**	**> 25 years**
EU-27	6.6	7.8	15.3	6.1
Euro area	6.6	8.4	14.8	6.5
Belgium	6.7	8.5	18.8	6.3
Bulgaria	6.5	7.3	15.1	6.1
Czech Republic	4.2	6.7	10.7	4.8
Denmark	3.5	4.2	7.9	3.1
Germany	8.5	8.3	11.1	8.0
Estonia	5.4	3.9	10.0	4.0
Ireland	4.9	4.2	9.1	3.8
Greece	5.2	12.8	22.9	7.1
Spain	6.4	10.9	18.2	7.0
France	7.8	8.9	19.4	7.0
Italy	4.9	7.9	20.3	4.9
Cyprus	3.4	4.6	10.0	3.3
Latvia	6.4	5.6	10.7	5.3
Lithuania	4.3	4.3	8.2	3.9
Luxembourg	3.4	5.0	15.3	3.3
Hungary	7.1	7.7	18.0	6.5
Malta	5.8	7.6	13.8	4.7
Netherlands	2.8	3.6	5.9	2.6
Austria	3.9	5.0	8.7	3.7
Poland	9.0	10.4	21.7	8.1
Portugal	6.7	9.7	16.6	7.2
Romania	7.2	5.4	20.1	4.9
Slovenia	4.0	5.9	10.1	4.2
Slovakia	9.9	12.7	20.3	10.0
Finland	6.5	7.2	16.5	5.4
Sweden	5.8	6.4	19.1	4.3
United Kingdom	5.6	5.0	14.3	3.6
Croatia	8.4	11.2	24.0	8.0
Turkey	8.5	8.5	16.8	6.7
Norway	2.6	2.5	7.3	1.8

Source: Eurostat (tsiem110 and une_rt_a)

Table 7.8: Unemployment rates, EU-27

(%)

	2001	2002	2003	2004	2005	2006	2007
Male	7.7	8.3	8.4	8.4	8.3	7.6	6.6
Female	9.4	9.7	9.7	9.8	9.6	8.9	7.8
< 25 years	17.3	17.9	18.0	18.4	18.3	17.1	15.3
> 25 years	7.2	7.6	7.7	7.7	7.6	7.0	6.1
Long-term unemployment rate	3.9	4.0	4.1	4.2	4.1	3.7	3.1
Male	3.5	3.6	3.8	3.8	3.8	3.5	2.8
Female	4.4	4.5	4.5	4.6	4.4	4.0	3.3
Very long-term unemployment rate	1.9	1.9	1.9	2.0	2.3	2.2	1.8

Source: Eurostat (tsiem110, une_rt_a, tsisc070 and une_ltu_a)

Figure 7.10: Unemployment rates (among persons aged 25-64 years) by level of educational attainment, 2007

(%)

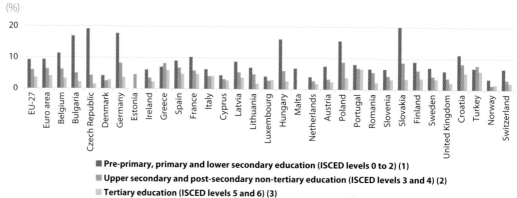

■ **Pre-primary, primary and lower secondary education (ISCED levels 0 to 2) (1)**
■ **Upper secondary and post-secondary non-tertiary education (ISCED levels 3 and 4) (2)**
■ **Tertiary education (ISCED levels 5 and 6) (3)**

(1) Estonia, not available; Lithuania, Luxembourg, Slovenia and Croatia, unreliable data; Slovakia, y-axis has been cut, 41.5 %.
(2) Malta, not available; Estonia and Luxembourg, unreliable data.
(3) Estonia and Malta, not available; Lithuania, Luxembourg, Slovenia and Croatia, unreliable data.

Source: Eurostat (tps00066)

7.3 Job vacancies

Introduction

Policy developments in this area have principally focused on trying to improve the labour market by more closely matching supply and demand, through: the modernisation and strengthening of labour market institutions, notably employment services; removing obstacles to mobility for workers across Europe; better anticipating skill needs, labour market shortages and bottlenecks; providing appropriate management of economic migration; improving the adaptability of workers and enterprises so that there is a greater capacity to anticipate, trigger and absorb economic and social change.

The EU believes that job seekers throughout the EU should be able to consult all job vacancies advertised in each of the Member States' employment services. With this goal in mind, the EU set up EURES, the European jobs and mobility portal, which can be found at: www. eures.europa.eu. This website provides access to a range of job vacancies for 31 European countries (each of the Member States, as well as Iceland, Liechtenstein, Norway and Switzerland). At the time of writing (autumn 2008) there were more than 1.2 million job vacancies advertised by over 18 000 registered employers on the website, while 314 thousand people had posted their CVs.

The 2008 European Job Days marked the third annual edition of another EU initiative in this domain. During September and October 2008, a wide range of events (around 500) took place all over Europe with the aim of raising awareness about the opportunities and practicalities of living and working in another European country. The events typically included job fairs, seminars, lectures, workshops and cultural events, all aimed at improving labour mobility.

Definitions and data availability

A **job vacancy** is defined as a post (newly created, unoccupied or about to become vacant), which the employer:

- is taking active steps to find a suitable candidate from outside the enterprise concerned and is prepared to take more steps; and
- intends to fill either immediately or in the near future.

Under this definition, a job vacancy should be open to candidates from outside the enterprise. However, this does not exclude the possibility of the employer appointing an internal candidate to the post. A vacant post that is open only to internal candidates is not treated as a job vacancy.

The **job vacancy rate (JVR)** measures the percentage of total posts that are vacant, in line with the definition of a job vacancy above, expressed as follows: JVR = number of job vacancies/(number of occupied posts + number of job vacancies) * 100. An occupied post is a post within an organisation to which an employee has been assigned.

Data on job vacancies and occupied posts are broken down by economic activity, occupation, size of enterprise and region. The national institutions responsible for compiling job vacancy statistics send aggregated statistics to Eurostat. These national data are then used to compile the job vacancy rate at EU-27 and euro area levels. At present, job vacancy statistics at the level of the Member States do not provide complete coverage and as a result there are currently no EU totals for the number of job vacancies or occupied posts. The EU job vacancy rate is calculated simply on the basis of the information available; no estimates are made for any country not participating in the collection. As a result, it is also not possible to provide EU-27 job vacancy rates broken down by economic activity, occupation or size of enterprise.

Main findings

The job vacancy rate, in part, reflects the unmet demand for labour, as well as a potential mismatch between the skills and availability of those who are unemployed and those sought by employers.

Job vacancy statistics are used by the European Commission and the European Central Bank to analyse and monitor the evolution of the labour market at national and European level. These statistics are also a key indicator used for the assessment of the business cycle and for structural analysis.

There was a broad upward development in the job vacancy rate in the EU-27, reaching 2.2 % in 2007. Among the Member States for which data are available, the job vacancy rate in 2007 was highest in Cyprus (4.6 %), Germany (3.5 %) and Estonia (3.3 %), and lowest in Spain, Luxembourg and Portugal (2006), where rates were below 1.0 %.

Figure 7.11: Job vacancy rate (1)

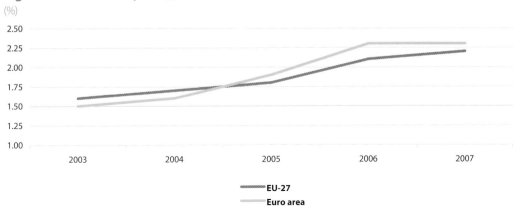

(1) Provisional.

Source: Eurostat (jvs_a)

Figure 7.12: Job vacancy rate, 2007 (1)

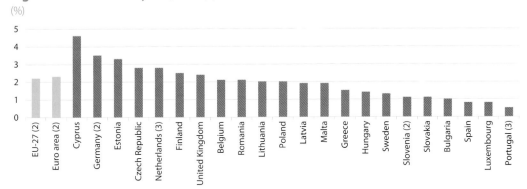

(1) Denmark, Ireland, France, Italy and Austria, not available.
(2) Provisional.
(3) 2006.

Source: Eurostat (jvs_a)

7.4 Labour market policy interventions

Introduction

Labour market policy (LMP) interventions are generally targeted at providing assistance to the unemployed and other groups of people with particular difficulties to enter the labour market. The primary target groups in most countries remain those people that are registered as unemployed by national public employment services (PES). However, public expenditure on labour market policies should not be interpreted exclusively as demonstrating the strength of the political will to combat unemployment. Indeed, policy objectives are increasingly focused on a broader range of inactive persons within society. As such, LMP interventions are increasingly being targeted at women, the young, the elderly, or other groups of society that may face disadvantages and barriers that prevent them from joining the labour force.

Definitions and data availability

The **LMP methodology** provides guidelines for the collection of data on labour market policy interventions: which interventions to cover and how to classify interventions by type of action, how to measure expenditure associated with each intervention and how to calculate the numbers of participants in these interventions (stocks, entrants and exits).

LMP statistics cover all labour market interventions which can be described as 'public interventions in the labour market aimed at reaching its efficient functioning and correcting disequilibria and which can be distinguished from other general employment policy interventions in that they act selectively to favour particular groups in the labour market'.

The scope of LMP statistics is limited to public interventions which are explicitly targeted at groups of persons with difficulties in the labour market: the unemployed, persons employed but at risk of involuntary job loss and inactive persons who would like to enter the labour market.

LMP interventions are classified into three main types:

* **LMP services** refer to labour market interventions where the main activity of participants is job-search related and where participation usually does not result in a change of labour market status.
* **LMP measures** refer to labour market interventions where the main activity of participants is other than job-search related and where participation usually results in a change in labour market status. An activity that does not result in a change of labour market status may still be considered as a measure if the intervention fulfils the following criteria: 1) the activities undertaken are not job-search related, are supervised and constitute a full-time or significant part-time activity of participants during a significant period of time, and 2) the aim is to improve the vocational qualifications of participants, or 3) the intervention provides incentives to take-up or to provide employment (including self-employment).

- **LMP supports** refer to interventions that provide financial assistance, directly or indirectly, to individuals for labour market reasons, or which compensate individuals for disadvantage caused by labour market circumstances.

These main types are further broken down into nine detailed categories according to the type of action:

LMP services
1. Labour market services;

LMP measures
2. Training;
3. Job rotation and job sharing;
4. Employment incentives;
5. Supported employment and rehabilitation;
6. Direct job creation;
7. Start-up incentives;

LMP supports
8. Out-of-work income maintenance and support;
9. Early retirement.

Main findings

The breakdown of expenditure and participants for different labour market policy interventions across the Member States was extremely varied, reflecting the different characteristics and problems faced within individual labour markets, as well as the political convictions of different governments. Within the EU-27,

the highest level of relative expenditure on labour market policy interventions in 2006 was reported in Germany and Belgium (almost 3 % of GDP); this share was lowest in the Czech Republic, Romania, Lithuania and Estonia (all below 0.5 % of GDP). There was also a wide range of expenditure patterns in terms of spending on labour market policy services, with the Netherlands and the United Kingdom reporting the highest relative expenditure (around twice the EU-27 average).

The largest share of expenditure on active labour market policy measures in the EU-27 went on training (41.1 %) to improve the employability of the unemployed and other target groups. Almost one quarter (24.2 %) of EU-27 expenditure was accounted for by employment incentives, with roughly another quarter (26.3 %) being relatively equally shared between programmes developed to promote labour market integration among persons with reduced working capacity and programmes to create additional jobs.

An estimate of the participation in labour market policy initiatives suggests that some 11.4 million persons were engaged in the different types of action across the EU-27 in 2006. Of these, the most common types of action were employment incentives (4.6 million) and training (3.8 million).

Table 7.9: Labour market policy measures, participants by type of action, 2006 (1)
(annual average stock in 1 000)

	Training	Job rotation & job sharing	Employment incentives	Supported employment & rehabilitation	Direct job creation	Start-up incentives
EU-27	3 816.1	106.9	4 606.3	773.6	1 336.9	712.2
Belgium	96.0	-	116.1	38.6	108.9	1.0
Bulgaria	11.6	-	14.3	1.8	74.3	4.6
Czech Republic	7.4	-	16.6	21.0	9.5	4.2
Denmark	:	:	:	:	:	:
Germany	1 585.4	0.4	126.8	23.2	372.9	407.8
Estonia	1.1	-	0.7	0.1	0.0	0.0
Ireland	26.8	-	4.3	1.6	23.8	4.4
Greece	:	:	:	:	:	:
Spain	262.9	68.7	2 591.1	42.9	222.8	158.7
France	553.8	-	556.2	129.5	279.3	76.4
Italy	:	17.4	579.4	-	35.1	8.2
Cyprus	0.1	-	1.1	:	-	0.1
Latvia	5.0	-	2.6	0.5	1.5	-
Lithuania	7.1	0.0	:	:	6.5	0.2
Luxembourg	2.3	-	:	0.1	1.1	-
Hungary	13.9	-	35.4	-	17.0	3.3
Malta	1.5	-	0.4	-	0.0	:
Netherlands	178.5	-	46.7	144.4	-	-
Austria	90.1	0.0	61.0	:	7.6	2.2
Poland	98.8	:	98.0	:	8.2	3.4
Portugal	48.0	:	79.1	5.7	21.2	4.3
Romania	15.1	-	51.4	-	17.4	:
Slovenia	12.0	-	2.4	-	3.3	3.3
Slovakia	2.3	-	13.1	1.9	104.6	20.6
Finland (2)	50.2	7.8	16.1	8.4	13.8	4.5
Sweden	52.0	13.0	118.8	36.9	-	5.4
United Kingdom	39.0	-	30.0	7.2	8.3	-
Norway	34.5	-	4.6	12.6	7.6	0.5

(1) A large number of the cells are unreliable.
(2) 2007.

Source: Eurostat (lmp_partsumm)

Figure 7.13: Public expenditure on labour market policy interventions, 2006 (1)

(% of GDP)

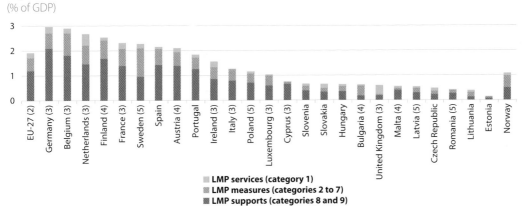

■ LMP services (category 1)
▨ LMP measures (categories 2 to 7)
▨ LMP supports (categories 8 and 9)

(1) Denmark and Greece, not available.
(2) Estimates.
(3) Categories 1 to 7, estimates.
(4) Categories 2 to 7, estimates.
(5) Category 1, estimate.

Source: Eurostat (lmp_expsumm)

Figure 7.14: Public expenditure on labour market policy measures, EU-27, 2006 (1)

(% of total)

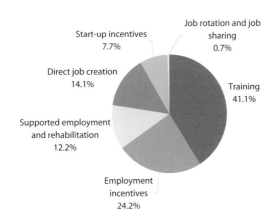

Start-up incentives
7.7%

Job rotation and job
sharing
0.7%

Direct job creation
14.1%

Training
41.1%

Supported employment
and rehabilitation
12.2%

Employment
incentives
24.2%

(1) Estimates.

Source: Eurostat (tps00077)

Industry and services

8

The European Commission's enterprise policy aims to create a favourable environment for enterprises and businesses to thrive within Europe, thus creating the productivity growth, jobs and wealth that are necessary to achieve the objectives set by the revised strategy for growth and jobs that has superseded the Lisbon objectives.

While competitiveness as a macro-economic concept is understood to mean increased standards of living and employment opportunities for those who wish to work, at the level of individual enterprises or industrial sectors, competitiveness is more concerned with the issue of productivity growth. Enterprises have a variety of options to improve their performance, such as tangible investment or spending on human capital, research and development, or other intangible assets. This latter category covers non-monetary assets created over time in the form of legal assets (such as patents or copyrights, which protect intellectual property) and competitive assets (such as collaboration), which can play an important role in determining the effectiveness and productivity of an enterprise. Human capital is generally regarded as the primary source of competitiveness in relation to intangibles, re-enforcing the belief that enterprises need to constantly invest in their workforces, attracting qualified staff, improving their skills, and maintaining their motivation. Innovation is seen as a key element towards the competitiveness of enterprises, and the Competitiveness and Innovation Framework Programme (CIP) aims to support innovation including eco-innovation, see Chapter 1 for more details.

8.1 Business structures

The legal basis for the European Commission's activities with respect to enterprise policy is Article 157 of the EC Treaty, which ensures that the conditions necessary for industrial competitiveness exist. It also provides for conditions to encourage entrepreneurial initiatives, particularly among small and medium-sized enterprises (SMEs). The EU seeks to:

- reduce administrative burden;
- facilitate the rapid start-up of new enterprises, and;
- create an environment more supportive of business.

In October 2007, the European Commission adopted a communication 'Small and medium-sized enterprises — Key for delivering more growth and jobs: a midterm review of modern SME policy'[1], which outlines progress since 2005 in SME policy and notes encouraging results in the mainstreaming of SMEs' interests in policymaking at both national and Community level.

The business environment in which European enterprises operate plays a significant role in their potential success through factors such as access to capital markets (in particular for venture capital), or the openness of markets. Ensuring that businesses can compete openly and fairly is also important with respect to making Europe an attractive place to invest and work in. Creating a positive climate in which entrepreneurs and businesses can flourish is considered by many as the key to generating the growth and jobs that Europe needs. This is all the more important in the globalised economy, where some businesses have considerable leeway to select where they wish to operate.

Introduction

Despite the changing face of the business economy, manufacturing still plays a key role in Europe's prosperity. The European Commission adopted a Communication on fostering structural change: an industrial policy for an enlarged Europe[2] which rejected the claim that Europe was experiencing a widespread process of deindustrialisation. However, the combination of a decline in the competitiveness of European industry, and increased international competition, were identified as threats that could impede the process of structural change in Europe. The Communication also examined how structural change could be brought about and fostered through better regulation, synergies between various Community policies, and strengthening the sectoral dimension of industrial policy.

Small and medium-sized enterprises (SMEs) are often referred to as the backbone of the European economy, providing a potential source for jobs and economic growth. The European Commission's new strategy for SMEs aims to apply the 'think small first' principle to make the business environment easier for SMEs. Policy is concentrated in five priority areas, covering the promotion of entrepreneurship and skills, the improvement of SMEs' access to markets, cutting red tape, the improvement of SMEs' growth potential, and strengthening dialogue and consultation with SME stakeholders. A special SME envoy has been set-up in the European Commission Directorate-General for Enterprise and Industry with

---

(1) COM(2007) 592; http://ec.europa.eu/enterprise/entrepreneurship/docs/com_2007_0592_en.pdf.

(2) COM(2004) 274 final; http://eur-lex.europa.eu/LexUriServ/site/en/com/2004/com2004_0274en01.pdf.

the objective of better integrating the SME dimension into EU policies. Via the European charter for small enterprises, Member States have also committed themselves to develop an SME-friendly business environment, in particular through learning from each other's experience in designing and implementing policies, so each can apply the best practice to their own situations.

Eurostat's structural business statistics (SBS) describe the structure, conduct and performance of economic activities, down to the most detailed activity level (several hundred sectors). SBS with a breakdown by size-class is the main source of data for an analysis of SMEs. SBS may be used to answer questions, such as: how much wealth and how many jobs are created in an activity?; is there a shift from the industrial sector to the services sector and in which specific activities is this trend most notable?; which countries are relatively specialised in the manufacture of aerospace equipment?; what is the average wage of an employee within the hotels and restaurants sector?; how productive is chemicals manufacturing and how does it fare in terms of profitability? Without this structural information, short-term data on the economic cycle would lack background and be hard to interpret.

Definitions and data availability

SBS covers the 'business economy', which includes industry, construction and many services (NACE Sections C to K). Note that financial services (NACE Section J) are treated separately because of their specific nature and the limited availability of most types of standard

business statistics in this area. As such, the term 'non-financial business economy' is generally used within business statistics to refer to economic activities covered by Sections C to I and K of NACE Rev. 1.1 and the units that carry out those activities. Note that SBS do not cover agriculture, forestry and fishing, nor public administration and (largely) non-market services such as education and health.

SBS describe the business economy through the observation of units engaged in an economic activity; the unit in SBS is generally the enterprise. An **enterprise** carries out one or more activities at one or more locations and may comprise one or more legal units. Note that enterprises that are active in more than one economic activity (and the value added and turnover they generate and the persons they employ, etc.) are classified under the NACE heading (Statistical Classification of Economic Activities in the European Community) which is their principal activity, normally the one that generates the largest amount of value added. An abbreviated list of the NACE Rev. 1.1 classification is provided in an annex at the end of the publication. Note that a revised classification (NACE Rev. 2) was adopted at the end of 2006, and its implementation has since begun – however, the first reference year for data using this new classification will be 2008.

SBS are collected within the framework of a Council Regulation on Structural Business Statistics (EC, EURATOM) No. 58/97 of December 1996 (and later amendments); according to the definitions, breakdowns, deadlines for data delivery, and various quality aspects

specified in the Commission Regulations implementing it. Note that the breakdown of economic activities is very detailed and that the data included in the SBS domain of Eurostat's dissemination database goes into much more detail than the short set of information which can (given space constraints) be presented in this yearbook.

SBS contain a comprehensive set of basic variables describing business demographic and employment characteristics, as well as monetary variables (mainly concerning operating income and expenditure or investment). In addition, a set of derived indicators are compiled: for example, in the form of ratios of monetary characteristics or per head values. The variables presented in this section are defined as follows:

- The **number of enterprises** is a count of the number of enterprises active during at least a part of the reference period; the enterprise is the smallest combination of legal units that is an organisational unit producing goods or services, which benefits from a certain degree of autonomy in decision-making, especially for the allocation of its current resources. An enterprise carries out one or more activities at one or more locations. An enterprise may be a sole legal unit.
- **Value added** represents the difference between the value of what is produced and intermediate consumption entering the production, less subsidies on production and costs, taxes and levies.

Value added at factor costs is defined as the gross income from operating activities after adjusting for operating subsidies and indirect taxes; value adjustments (such as depreciation) are not subtracted. It can be calculated from turnover, plus capitalised production, plus other operating income, plus or minus the changes in stocks, minus the purchases of goods and services, minus other taxes on products which are linked to turnover but not deductible, minus the duties and taxes linked to production. Alternatively it can be calculated from gross operating surplus by adding personnel costs.

- The **number of persons employed** is defined as the total number of persons who work in the observation unit (inclusive of working proprietors, partners working regularly in the unit and unpaid family workers), as well as persons who work outside the unit who belong to it and are paid by it (for example, sales representatives, delivery personnel, repair and maintenance teams); it excludes manpower supplied to the unit by other enterprises, persons carrying out repair and maintenance work in the enquiry unit on behalf of other enterprises, as well as those on compulsory military service.
- **Average personnel costs** (or unit labour costs) equal personnel costs divided by the number of employees (paid persons with an employment contract). Personnel costs are defined

as the total remuneration, in cash or in kind, payable by an employer to an employee (regular and temporary employees as well as home workers) in return for work done by the latter during the reference period; personnel costs also include taxes and employees' social security contributions retained by the unit as well as the employer's compulsory and voluntary social contributions.

- **Apparent labour productivity** equals value added divided by the number of persons employed.

The SBS data collection consists of a common module (Annex 1), including a set of basic statistics for all activities, as well as six sector-specific annexes covering a more extended list of characteristics. The sector-specific annexes are: industry (Annex 2), distributive trades (Annex 3), construction (Annex 4), insurance services (Annex 5), credit institutions (Annex 6) and pension funds (Annex 7). A detailed overview of the availability of characteristics by sector is found in Commission Regulation No 2701/98 [3].

SBS are also available broken down by region or by **enterprise size class**. In SBS, size classes are defined based on the number of persons employed, except for specific series within retail trade activities where turnover size classes can also be used. A limited set of the standard SBS variables (number of enterprises, turnover, persons employed, value added, etc.) is available mostly down to the 3-digit (group) level of the NACE Rev. 1.1 classification divided by size class. According to Commission Recommendation 2003/361/EC adopted on 6 May 2003, small and medium-sized enterprises are classified with regard to their number of employees, annual turnover, and their independence. For statistical purposes, small and medium-sized enterprises are generally defined as those enterprises employing fewer than 250 people. The number of size classes available varies according to the activity under consideration. However, the main groups used in this publication for presenting the results are:

- small and medium-sized enterprises (SMEs): with 1-249 persons employed, further divided into
  - micro enterprises: with less than 10 persons employed;
  - small enterprises: with 10 to 49 persons employed;
  - medium-sized enterprises: with 50 to 249 persons employed;
- large enterprises: with 250 or more persons employed.

---

(3) http://eur-lex.europa.eu/LexUriServ/LexUriServ.do?uri=CONSLEG:1998R2701:20031019:EN:PDF.

Structural business statistics also provide information on a number of special topics, of which **business demography** is one. Business demography statistics present data on the active population of enterprises, their birth, survival (followed up to five years after birth) and death. Special attention is paid to the impact of these demographic events on employment levels. Business demography variables presented in this section are defined as follows:

- an **enterprise birth** amounts to the creation of a combination of production factors with the restriction that no other enterprises are involved in the event. Births do not include entries into the population due to mergers, break-ups, split-off or restructuring of a set of enterprises, nor do the statistics include entries into a sub-population resulting only from a change of activity.
- an **enterprise death** amounts to the dissolution of a combination of production factors with the restriction that no other enterprises are involved in the event. An enterprise is included in the count of deaths only if it is not reactivated within two years. Equally, a reactivation within two years is not counted as a birth.
- **survival** occurs if an enterprise is active in terms of employment and/or turnover in the year of birth and the following year(s). Two types of survival can be distinguished: an enterprise born in year x is considered to have survived in year $x+1$ if it is active

in terms of turnover and/or employment in any part of year $x+1$ (survival without change); an enterprise is also considered to have survived if the linked legal unit(s) have ceased to be active, but their activity has been taken over by a new legal unit set up specifically to take over the factors of production of that enterprise (survival by take-over). The information presented in this publication focuses on the two-year survival rate.

Main findings

There were just over 19.6 million active enterprises within the EU-27's non-financial business economy (defined as industry, construction, distributive trades and services, and therefore excluding financial services) in 2005. More than three in every ten (31.9 %) of these enterprises were active in the distributive trades sector (composed of motor trades, wholesale trade, and retail trade and repair), which were also relatively labour-intensive activities, accounting for almost one quarter of the EU-27's non-financial business economy workforce in 2005. It should be noted, though, that the employment data presented here are head counts and not, for example, full-time equivalents, and there may be a significant proportion of persons working part-time in distributive trades. In terms of wealth creation, the manufacturing sector generated the largest proportion of the non-financial business economy's value added (30.4 %), followed by real estate, renting and business activities (21.9 %).

Average personnel costs reached EUR 41 000 per employee in the EU-27's electricity, gas and water supply sector, a level that was almost 2.7 times that for hotels and restaurants and 1.8 times that for the distributive trades in 2005, reflecting in large part the high rates of part-time employment in many service sectors. The variation in wages and salaries was more marked between countries. For example, in manufacturing, average personnel costs were highest in Germany at EUR 55 000 per employee, over 20 times the value recorded in the Member State with the lowest average, Bulgaria (EUR 2 400 per employee).

SBS broken down by enterprise size class (defined in terms of the number of persons employed) show that large enterprises were particularly dominant within mining and quarrying; electricity, gas and water supply; and transport, storage

and communication. These activities are characterised by relatively high minimum efficient scales of production and/ or by (transmission) networks that are rarely duplicated due to their high fixed investment cost. On the other hand, small and medium-sized enterprises (SMEs) were relatively important within the activities of construction and hotels and restaurants, where enterprises with less than 250 persons employed accounted for more than three quarters of the wealth created (value added) and the workforce.

There are significant changes in the stock of enterprises within the business economy from one year to the next, reflecting the level of competition and entrepreneurial spirit. Newly born enterprises accounted for at least one out of every 10 active enterprises in Romania, the United Kingdom, Portugal, Bulgaria, Latvia, Luxembourg, Estonia and Spain in 2005.

Figure 8.1: Breakdown of number of enterprises in the non-financial business economy, EU-27, 2005
(%)

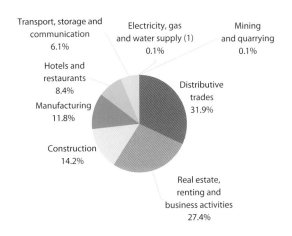

(1) Estimate.

Source: Eurostat (tin00050)

Table 8.1: Value added for non-financial business economy sectors, 2005
(EUR million)

	Mining & quarrying	Manu-facturing	Elec., gas & water supply	Con-struction	Distrib. trades	Hotels & restaur.	Trans., storage & commun-ication	Real estate, renting & business activities
EU-27	83 059	1 629 914	190 000	465 771	1 022 427	167 792	629 936	1 171 191
Belgium	310	48 132	5 358	10 249	29 140	3 673	20 107	26 459
Bulgaria	378	3 209	972	732	1 714	282	1 876	683
Czech Republic (1)	1 468	26 490	4 880	5 288	11 423	1 259	7 566	9 233
Denmark	6 099	25 717	2 890	8 782	21 829	2 128	14 599	28 116
Germany	5 981	429 471	41 633	55 527	187 228	20 803	113 369	226 967
Estonia	88	1 592	336	547	1 317	136	901	949
Ireland	657	34 121	:	5 828	14 745	3 308	10 408	22 567
Greece	865	14 270	3 228	5 844	19 265	3 186	9 631	8 346
Spain	2 341	125 049	13 951	83 431	99 707	23 300	54 068	92 760
France	3 943	214 014	23 763	62 977	144 972	26 866	94 525	188 929
Italy	7 411	208 907	18 917	57 953	108 783	18 984	71 508	99 684
Cyprus	41	1 089	268	1 072	1 579	847	1 034	:
Latvia	33	1 481	319	587	1 970	154	1 402	874
Lithuania	87	2 535	591	883	1 781	133	1 325	983
Luxembourg	28	2 662	240	1 457	2 272	469	2 568	3 361
Hungary	168	16 791	2 309	2 329	6 636	681	5 563	5 818
Malta	:	:	:	:	:	:	:	:
Netherlands	5 701	57 637	:	22 766	54 743	6 343	32 177	58 102
Austria	914	41 601	4 842	11 552	25 182	5 952	15 044	23 544
Poland	5 745	48 298	8 810	7 242	24 132	1 361	13 473	12 924
Portugal	549	18 510	3 153	8 417	16 157	2 846	8 987	10 308
Romania	2 303	9 130	2 060	1 984	5 272	424	3 990	3 024
Slovenia	116	5 803	627	1 192	2 909	448	1 492	1 721
Slovakia	188	5 868	2 238	811	2 488	145	1 854	1 518
Finland	306	30 078	2 915	6 541	13 004	1 675	8 694	12 199
Sweden	1 354	49 948	6 456	10 959	26 622	3 110	15 991	35 329
United Kingdom	36 144	210 720	31 044	91 621	198 626	39 125	117 615	296 525
Norway	57 995	19 774	4 304	8 797	18 524	2 211	16 138	20 345

(1) 2006.

Source: Eurostat (tin00002)

Table 8.2: Number of persons employed for non-financial business economy sectors, 2005
(1 000)

	Mining & quarrying	Manu-facturing	Elec., gas & water supply	Con-struction	Distrib. trades	Hotels & restaur.	Trans., storage & commun-ication	Real estate, renting & business activities
EU-27	772	34 644	1 600	13 548	30 964	8 846	11 824	24 500
Belgium	3	615	24	252	606	159	273	474
Bulgaria	30	645	58	158	449	111	215	150
Czech Republic (1)	44	1 354	57	393	694	158	337	501
Denmark	3	410	17	189	448	100	188	359
Germany	90	7 171	278	1 515	4 411	1 176	1 900	4 131
Estonia	6	131	9	41	94	17	44	56
Ireland	6	217	:	50	286	136	89	191
Greece	13	390	25	310	942	280	247	286
Spain	40	2 599	66	2 658	3 286	1 199	1 028	2 512
France	34	3 737	196	1 538	3 245	888	1 547	3 203
Italy	42	4 610	118	1 810	3 391	1 083	1 220	2 712
Cyprus	1	37	2	37	59	34	24	:
Latvia	3	167	16	62	178	29	80	88
Lithuania	3	266	27	106	255	35	96	87
Luxembourg	0	37	1	34	42	15	23	53
Hungary	6	794	57	235	586	126	269	447
Malta	:	:	:	:	:	:	:	:
Netherlands	9	768	27	471	1 320	302	452	1 330
Austria	6	620	32	250	601	231	241	387
Poland	189	2 473	206	648	2 187	224	723	926
Portugal	15	869	23	481	868	270	192	558
Romania	134	1 621	149	388	904	113	362	367
Slovenia	4	233	12	66	108	30	52	67
Slovakia	9	405	40	69	180	20	102	104
Finland	4	407	15	130	260	52	158	206
Sweden	9	797	30	253	582	120	313	534
United Kingdom	68	3 246	131	1 392	4 948	1 916	1 634	4 776
Norway	38	254	14	146	350	81	164	236

(1) 2006.

Source: Eurostat (tin00004)

Table 8.3: Average personnel costs for non-financial business economy sectors, 2005
(EUR 1 000 per employee)

	Mining & quarrying	Manufacturing	Elec., gas & water supply	Construction	Distrib. trades	Hotels & restaur.	Trans., storage & communication	Real estate, renting & business activities
EU-27	30.2	33.9	41.0	26.9	23.3	15.3	32.4	30.5
Belgium	44.9	49.4	89.3	36.3	38.1	19.2	47.8	42.6
Bulgaria	5.0	2.4	5.8	2.2	1.9	1.5	4.2	2.8
Czech Republic (1)	14.8	11.1	16.1	11.0	10.9	6.7	12.6	13.4
Denmark	59.0	44.5	39.6	38.4	33.8	16.5	42.1	38.3
Germany	62.3	55.0	80.3	32.3	26.9	12.7	33.8	30.5
Estonia	9.0	7.6	10.0	10.3	7.6	5.1	8.9	8.3
Ireland	48.5	41.9	:	47.1	26.9	17.3	40.1	37.6
Greece	40.2	24.3	44.7	16.0	18.0	13.9	35.6	29.7
Spain	33.0	29.7	50.5	25.3	22.3	17.1	31.1	22.8
France	49.5	42.8	61.6	36.5	34.3	26.1	41.9	43.2
Italy	47.0	33.1	49.9	26.3	28.6	18.0	37.2	27.5
Cyprus	28.1	19.4	39.2	21.3	19.3	17.8	29.2	:
Latvia	4.8	4.2	8.0	3.8	3.6	2.5	5.5	4.9
Lithuania	7.8	5.0	8.4	5.6	4.5	2.8	6.1	5.7
Luxembourg	41.9	47.6	74.8	34.6	37.7	24.0	53.2	38.8
Hungary	12.8	10.4	16.5	6.7	7.9	5.0	12.2	10.2
Malta	:	:	:	:	:	:	:	:
Netherlands	60.6	46.1	:	44.7	27.3	15.2	39.7	29.5
Austria	52.5	42.8	69.6	35.9	31.0	21.1	40.4	36.8
Poland	16.6	7.6	13.0	6.6	5.9	4.3	9.3	7.5
Portugal	15.8	13.6	37.5	11.7	12.1	8.6	23.6	12.1
Romania	7.9	3.4	6.3	3.2	2.6	2.3	4.9	3.6
Slovenia	26.2	17.2	24.7	17.7	18.0	12.6	20.1	22.7
Slovakia	8.1	7.7	11.0	6.8	7.5	4.8	8.6	9.0
Finland	38.3	43.0	49.2	37.9	33.3	26.2	38.3	39.0
Sweden	53.6	46.2	56.2	39.8	39.2	24.8	41.6	47.7
United Kingdom	70.0	39.5	51.1	36.8	24.0	13.4	40.8	35.2
Norway	110.9	54.9	64.4	51.0	37.7	23.7	48.7	52.2

(1) 2006.

Source: Eurostat (tin00049)

Figure 8.2: Value added by enterprise size class, EU-27, 2005 (1)
(% of sectoral total)

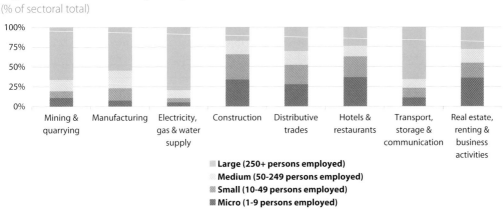

(1) Estimates.

Source: Eurostat (tin00053)

Figure 8.3: Employment by enterprise size class, EU-27, 2005 (1)
(% of sectoral total)

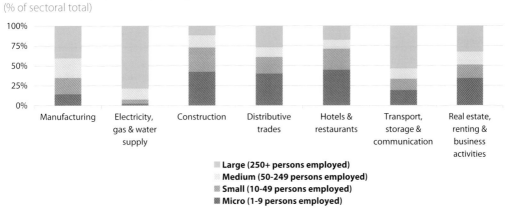

(1) Estimates; mining and quarrying: not available due to incomplete data.

Source: Eurostat (tin00052)

Table 8.4: Value added by enterprise size class, non-financial business economy, 2005

	Value added (EUR million)	Share in total value added (%)			
		Micro (1-9 persons employed)	Small (10-49 persons employed)	Medium-sized (50-249 persons employed)	Large (250+ persons employed)
EU-27 (1)	5 360 072	:	18.9	17.8	42.3
Belgium	143 426	:	:	:	:
Bulgaria	9 845	14.3	17.4	21.5	46.8
Czech Republic	58 084	19.2	16.5	19.7	44.6
Denmark	110 161	26.5	:	:	:
Germany	1 080 980	15.4	:	:	:
Estonia	5 865	20.2	24.9	:	:
Ireland	:	:	:	:	:
Greece	64 634	36.2	:	:	:
Spain	494 607	27.6	24.2	16.8	31.5
France	759 988	20.2	18.5	15.6	45.8
Italy	592 147	31.8	23.2	16.0	29.1
Cyprus	6 960	:	:	:	:
Latvia	6 819	17.2	:	27.9	:
Lithuania	8 318	12.1	:	:	:
Luxembourg	12 871	23.8	:	:	:
Hungary	40 295	15.7	16.3	:	:
Malta	:	:	:	:	:
Netherlands	:	:	:	:	:
Austria	128 631	18.6	:	:	:
Poland	121 985	16.8	11.5	20.1	51.6
Portugal	68 926	24.4	22.0	:	:
Romania	28 188	:	15.0	19.3	:
Slovenia	14 267	19.7	:	:	:
Slovakia	15 109	10.7	15.3	18.5	55.5
Finland	:	:	:	:	:
Sweden	149 766	20.2	17.4	17.9	44.4
United Kingdom	1 021 418	18.9	15.9	16.8	48.4

(1) Rounded estimates based on non-confidential data.

Source: Eurostat (sbs_sc_1b_se02, sbs_sc_3ce_tr02, sbs_sc_4d_co02, sbs_sc_2d_mi02, sbs_sc_2d_dade02, sbs_sc_2d_dfdn02, sbs_sc_2d_el02)

Table 8.5: Number of persons employed by enterprise size class, non-financial business economy, 2005

	Number of persons employed (1 000)	Share in total employment (%)			
		Micro (1-9 persons employed)	Small (10-49 persons employed)	Medium-sized (50-249 persons employed)	Large (250+ persons employed)
EU-27 (1)	126 698	:	:	16.8	32.9
Belgium	2 407	:	:	:	:
Bulgaria	1 816	28.4	22.0	22.2	27.4
Czech Republic	3 502	29.6	19.1	19.5	31.8
Denmark	1 714	20.1	:	:	:
Germany	20 672	18.9	22.1	19.2	39.8
Estonia	397	23.2	27.7	:	:
Ireland	:	:	:	:	:
Greece	2 492	56.2	:	:	:
Spain	13 387	38.6	25.7	14.5	21.3
France	14 388	23.9	21.0	16.5	38.6
Italy	14 987	47.1	21.7	12.4	18.7
Cyprus	211	:	:	:	:
Latvia	623	24.0	26.2	25.4	24.3
Lithuania	875	21.8	:	:	:
Luxembourg	205	19.9	:	:	:
Hungary	2 520	35.8	18.9	16.2	:
Malta	:	:	:	:	:
Netherlands	4 679	29.2	21.1	17.0	32.7
Austria	2 367	25.2	:	:	:
Poland	7 576	39.2	12.0	18.7	30.2
Portugal	3 276	42.6	23.1	:	:
Romania	4 038	20.1	18.5	22.3	39.0
Slovenia	572	27.5	:	:	:
Slovakia	929	13.0	17.5	23.4	46.0
Finland	:	:	:	:	:
Sweden	2 638	24.9	20.4	17.9	36.8
United Kingdom	18 111	21.4	17.5	15.2	46.0

(1) Rounded estimates based on non-confidential data.

Source: Eurostat (sbs_sc_1b_se02, sbs_sc_3ce_tr02, sbs_sc_4d_co02, sbs_sc_2d_mi02, sbs_sc_2d_dade02, sbs_sc_2d_dfdn02, sbs_sc_2d_el02)

Table 8.6: Enterprise demography, business economy, 2005

	Enterprise birth rates (% of enterprise births among active enterprises)	Enterprise death rates (% of enterprise deaths among active enterprises)	Enterprise survival (% of enterprise births of year n-2 which are still active in year n)
Belgium	:	:	:
Bulgaria	11.9	:	:
Czech Republic	8.7	:	61.1
Denmark	:	:	:
Germany	:	:	:
Estonia	11.0		
Ireland	:	10.7	65.6
Greece	:	:	:
Spain	10.4	6.9	71.9
France	:	:	:
Italy	7.8	:	75.4
Cyprus	7.1	:	:
Latvia	11.5	3.9	69.4
Lithuania	:	:	:
Luxembourg	11.1	:	73.9
Hungary	9.0	:	66.2
Malta	:	:	:
Netherlands	9.8	:	73.1
Austria	:	:	:
Poland	:	:	:
Portugal	13.3	:	:
Romania	18.3	9.6	78.6
Slovenia	8.8	4.4	82.5
Slovakia	7.3	:	72.8
Finland	8.3	:	66.7
Sweden	7.0	5.6	85.8
United Kingdom	13.7	10.9	81.2
Norway (1)	9.8	:	:
Switzerland (2)	3.6	3.5	70.7

(1) 2002.
(2) Birth rate and death rate, 2004.

Source: Eurostat (tsier150)

8.2 Industry and construction

Introduction

In its mid-term review of industrial policy [4], the European Commission identified globalisation and technological change as key challenges for European industry. Industrial policy within the EU is designed to complement measures taken by the Member States. Whether or not a business succeeds depends ultimately on the vitality and strength of the business itself, but the environment in which it operates can help or harm its prospects, in particular when faced with the challenges of globalisation and intense international competition.

A Communication on industrial policy in 2005 was based for the first time on an integrated approach: addressing sector-specific as well as common issues. Since this date, the overall performance of European industry continued to develop favourably against a background of an increasingly integrated world and the accelerating pace of technological change. The Commission's new industrial policy includes seven new initiatives on competitiveness, energy and the environment, intellectual property rights, better regulation, industrial research and innovation, market access, skills, and managing structural change. Seven additional initiatives are targeted at key strategic sectors, including pharmaceuticals, defence-related industries, and information and communication technologies.

Definitions and data availability

For background information relating to structural business statistics (SBS), including definitions of value added and persons employed, refer to the section titled 'definitions and data availability' in the previous section (8.1 Business structures). Additional variables presented in this section are defined as follows:

- The **wage adjusted labour productivity ratio** is defined as: (value added at factor cost/personnel costs) * (number of employees/number of persons employed); expressed as a percentage.
- The **gross operating rate** is defined as: the size of the gross operating surplus relative to turnover, and is one measure of profitability; the gross operating surplus is the surplus generated by operating activities after the labour factor input has been recompensed (it can be calculated from value added at factor cost less personnel costs); turnover is often referred to as sales; capital-intensive activities will tend to report higher shares of the gross operating surplus in turnover.

PRODCOM (PRODuction COMmunautaire) is a system for the collection and dissemination of statistics on the production of industrial (mainly manufactured) goods, both in value and quantity terms. It is based on a list of products called the Prodcom List which consists of about 4 500 headings relating to industrial

---

(4) COM(2007) 374; http://ec.europa.eu/enterprise/enterprise_policy/industry/doc/mtr_in_pol_en.pdf.

products. These products are detailed at an 8-digit level, with the first four digits referring to the equivalent NACE class, and the next two digits referring to sub-categories within the statistical classification of products by activity in the European Economic Community (CPA). Most headings correspond to one or more combined nomenclature (CN) codes.

Aside from SBS and PRODCOM, a large proportion of the statistics presented in this section are derived from **short-term business statistics (STS)**. Among these, some of the most important indicators are a set of principal European economic indicators (PEEIs) that are essential to the European Central Bank (ECB) for reviewing monetary policy within the euro area. These short-term statistics give information on a wide range of economic activities according to the NACE Rev. 1.1 classification; they are based on surveys and administrative sources. The Member States are encouraged to transmit seasonally adjusted data and trend-cycle indices. If they do not, Eurostat calculates the seasonal adjustment. The national statistical institutes are responsible for data collection and the calculation of national indices, in accordance with EC Regulations. Eurostat is responsible for euro area and EU aggregations.

The presentation of short-term statistics may take a variety of different forms:

- the adjustment of **working days** takes account of the calendar nature of a given month in order to adjust the index. The adjustment of working days is intended to adjust calendar effects, whatever their nature. The number of working days for a given month depends on the timing of certain public holidays (Easter can fall in March or in April depending on the year), the possible overlap of certain public holidays and non-working days (1 May can fall on a Sunday), the fact that a year is a leap year or not and other reasons

- **seasonal adjustment**, or the adjustment of seasonal variations, aims, after adjusting for calendar effects, to take account of the impact of the known seasonal factors that have been observed in the past. For example, in the case of the production index, annual summer holidays have a negative impact on industrial production. Where necessary, Eurostat calculates the seasonal adjustment using the methods TRAMO (time-series regression with ARIMA noise, missing observations, and outliers) and SEATS (signal extraction in ARIMA time series), referred to as TRAMO/SEATS.

- the trend is a slow variation over a long period of years, generally associated with the structural causes of the phenomenon in question. The cycle is a quasi periodic oscillation characterised by alternating periods of higher and lower rates of change possibly, but not always, involving expansion and contraction. If the irregular component of the time-series is relatively important, the **trend-cycle** series generally offers a better series for analysis of longer-term past developments. However, this advantage is less clear when analysing very recent developments. Trend-cycle values for recent periods may be subject to greater revisions than the equivalent seasonally adjusted values and hence the latter may be more appropriate for the analysis of very recent developments; this is particularly true around turning points.

Short-term business statistics are collected within the scope of the STS regulation [5]. Despite major changes brought in by the STS regulation, and improvements in the availability and timeliness of indicators that followed its implementation, strong demands for further development were voiced even as the STS regulation was being adopted. The emergence of the ECB fundamentally changed expectations as regards STS. As a result, the STS regulation was amended (Regulation (EC) No 1158/2005) on 6 July 2005. Among the main changes introduced were:

- new indicators for the purpose of analysis, namely the introduction of industrial import prices, services output prices, and the division of non-domestic turnover, new orders and industrial output prices between euro area and non-euro area markets;
- more timely data, by shortening deadlines for the delivery of the industrial and construction production indices, the retail trade and services turnover (and volume of sales) indices, and employment indices for all activities;
- more frequent data, increasing the frequency of the index of production for construction to monthly from quarterly.

The **production index** aims to provide a measure of the volume trend in value added at factor cost over a given reference period. The index of production should take account of:

- variations in type and quality of the commodities and of the input materials;
- changes in stocks of finished goods and services and work in progress;
- changes in technical input-output relations (processing techniques);
- services such as the assembling of production units, mounting, installations, repairs, planning, engineering, creation of software.

The data necessary for the compilation of such an index are generally not available on a sub-annual basis. In practice, suitable proxy values for the compilation of the indices are needed. Within industry these may include gross production values (deflated), production quantity data, turnover (deflated), work input, raw material input, or energy input, while within construction they may include input data (consumption of typical raw materials, energy or labour) or output data (production quantities, deflated production values, or deflated sales values).

The **building construction production index** and the **civil engineering production index** is a split of construction production between building construction and civil engineering according to the Classification of types of Construction (CC); the aim of the indices is to show the development of value added for each of the two main parts of construction.

The **output price index** (sometimes referred to as the **producer price index**) shows monthly price changes in industrial output, which can be an indicator of inflationary pressure before it reaches the consumer. The appropriate price is the basic price that excludes VAT and similar deductible taxes directly linked

(5) Council Regulation (EC) No 1165/98 of 19 May 1998 concerning short-term statistics.

to turnover, as well as all duties and taxes on the goods and services invoiced by the unit, whereas subsidies on products received by the producer, if there are any, should be added. The price should refer to the moment when the order is made, not the moment when the commodities leave the factory gates. Output price indices are compiled for the total, domestic and non-domestic markets, with the latter further split between euro area and non-euro area markets (the information presented in this publication refers only to price developments within the domestic market). All price-determining characteristics should be taken into account, including the quantity of units sold, transport provided, rebates, service conditions, guarantee conditions and destination.

Main findings

The EU-27's construction sector generated almost 20 % of the combined industrial and construction sectors' value added in 2005, while food products, beverages and tobacco was the largest of the manufacturing sectors (at the NACE division level) with around 8 % of the total. The construction sector's share of employment was even higher, more than one quarter of the total. A few sectors recorded a notably lower share of employment than value added, and these were concentrated in energy-related activities and chemicals.

Based on PRODCOM data, transport equipment products dominated the list of the most sold manufacturing products in value terms in the EU-27 in 2007, occupying the first two places, with a further three products among the top 20.

Domestic output prices and the volume of industrial production both followed an upward path during most of the last 10 years, although there was a decline in activity evident for the EU-27's index of production during 2001, which was apparent again since February 2008. Otherwise, there was a marked increase in prices from 2004 onwards, largely resulting from increases in the price of oil and associated energy-related and intermediate products. The highest industrial price increases in 2007 were recorded in Lithuania, Romania and Bulgaria, although in Romania the increase of 8.7 % in 2007 was considerably lower than in 2006 and continued a downward trend in the rate of price increases.

Figure 8.4: Breakdown of industrial and construction value added and employment, EU-27, 2005 (1)

(% of industrial and construction value added and employment)

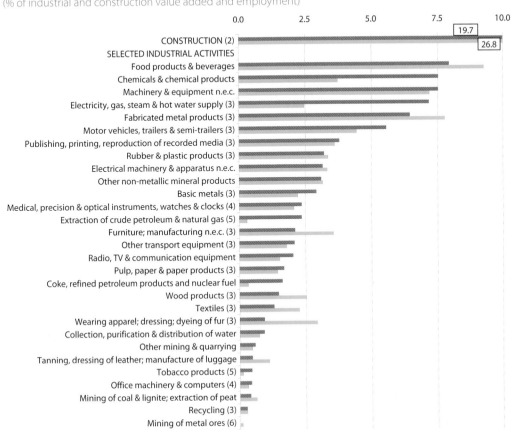

Value added
Employment

(1) Mining of uranium and thorium ores, not available
(2) Note: the axis is cut.
(3) Estimates.
(4) Value added, estimate.
(5) Employment, estimate.
(6) Value added, not available.

Source: Eurostat (ebd_all)

Figure 8.5: Wage adjusted labour productivity ratio for construction and selected industrial activities, EU-27, 2005 (1)

(%)

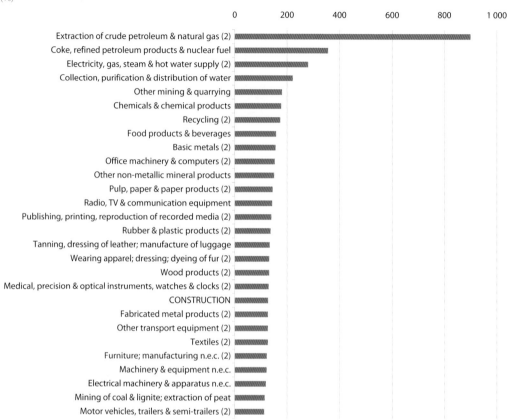

(1) Mining of uranium and thorium ores, mining of metal ores and tobacco products, not available.
(2) Estimate.

Source: Eurostat (ebd_all)

Figure 8.6: Gross operating rate for construction and selected industrial activities, EU-27, 2005 (1)
(%)

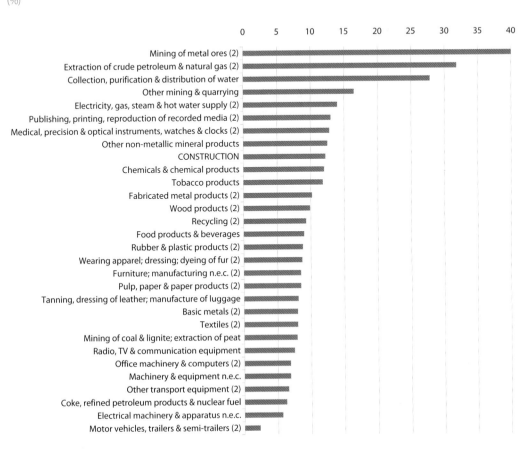

(1) Mining of uranium and thorium ores, not available.
(2) Estimate.

Source: Eurostat (ebd_all)

Figure 8.7: Value added by enterprise size class, mining and quarrying and manufacturing activities, EU-27, 2005 (1)

(% of sectoral total)

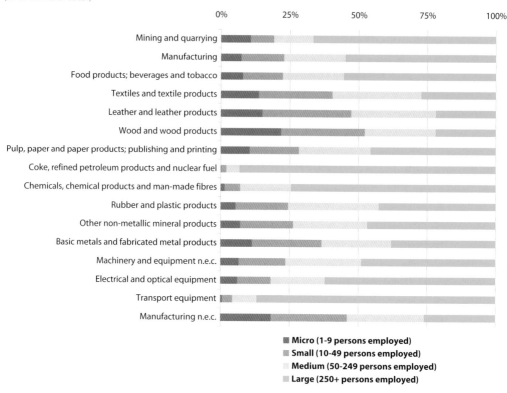

(1) Includes rounded estimates based on non-confidential data.

Source: Eurostat (tin00053)

Table 8.7: Production sold in value terms, selected products, EU-27, 2007

PRODCOM code	Product	Value (EUR million)	Rounding base (million) (1)
34.10.22.30	Motor vehicles with a petrol engine > 1 500 cm³ (including motor caravans of a capacity > 3 000 cm³) (excluding vehicles for transporting >= 10 persons, snowmobiles, golf cars and similar vehicles)	126 510	
34.10.23.30	Motor vehicles with a diesel or semi-diesel engine > 1 500cm³ but <= 2 500cm³ (excluding vehicles for transporting >= 10 persons, motor caravans, snowmobiles, golf cars and similar vehicles)	106 824	
27.41.30.30	Platinum, palladium, rhodium, iridium, osmium and ruthenium, unwrought or in powder form	103 435	
29.42.91.00	Installation services of metalworking machine tools	98 959	
22.13.11.00	Newspapers; journals and periodicals; appearing less than four times a week published by you; or printed and published by you (including advertising revenue)	35 500	500
15.70.10.Z3	Preparations for animal feeds (excluding dog or cat food, p.r.s.)	34 500	500
22.12.11.00	Newspapers; journals and periodicals; appearing at least four times a week published by you; or printed and published by you (including advertising revenue)	32 000	8000
15.96.10.00	Beer made from malt (excluding non-alcoholic beer, beer containing <= 0.5% by volume of alcohol, alcohol duty)	29 992	
26.63.10.00	Ready-mixed concrete	26 015	
15.81.11.00	Fresh bread containing by weight in the dry matter state <= 5% of sugars and <= 5% of fat (excluding with added honey; eggs; cheese or fruit)	24 821	
15.51.40.50	Grated, powdered, blue-veined and other non-processed cheese (excluding fresh cheese, whey cheese and curd)	24 179	
21.21.13.00	Cartons, boxes and cases, of corrugated paper or paperboard	20 443	
34.10.41.10	Goods vehicles with a diesel or semi-diesel engine, of a gross vehicle weight <= 5 tonnes (excluding dumpers for off-highway use)	20 233	
15.81.12.00	Cake and pastry products; other baker's wares with added sweetening matter	19 594	
15.13.12.15	Sausages not of liver	18 247	
15.98.12.30	Waters, with added sugar, other sweetening matter or flavoured, i.e. soft drinks (including mineral and aerated)	18 000	900
26.51.12.30	Grey Portland cement (including blended cement)	17 302	
34.10.13.00	Vehicle compression-ignition internal combustion piston engines (diesel or semi-diesel) (excluding for railway or tramway rolling stock)	16 927	
34.10.23.10	Motor vehicles with a diesel or semi-diesel engine <= 1 500 cm³ (excluding vehicles for transporting >= 10 persons, snowmobiles, golf cars and similar vehicles)	16 642	
22.33.10.70	Reproduction of computer supports bearing data or instructions of a kind used in automatic data-processing machines (excluding magnetic tapes, sound or vision recordings)	16 000	500

(1) Indicates the magnitude of the rounding employed to protect confidential cell (in the case of PRODCOM code 22.13.11.00, the confidential value lies within the range +/- EUR 500 million of the reported value).

Source: Eurostat (http://epp.eurostat.ec.europa.eu/newxtweb/)

Table 8.8: Production sold in volume terms, selected products, EU-27, 2007

PRODCOM code	Product	Quantity (1 000)	Rounding base (1 000) (1)	Unit
27.10.32.10	Flat semi-finished products (slabs) (of stainless steel)	179 689		kg
26.51.12.30	Grey Portland cement (including blended cement)	228 698 020		kg
15.93.11.30	Champagne (excluding alcohol duty)	254 200	50	litres
24.52.11.50	Perfumes	9 763		litres
24.11.11.70	Oxygen	28 018 317		m³
20.10.10.34	Coniferous wood; sawn or chipped lengthwise; sliced or peeled; of a thickness > 6mm; planed (excluding end-jointed or sanded)	18 044		m³
16.00.11.50	Cigarettes containing tobacco or mixtures of tobacco and tobacco substitutes (excluding tobacco duty)	769 304 498		units
32.30.20.60	Flat panel colour TV receivers, LCD/plasma, etc. excluding television projection equipment, apparatus with video recorder/player, video monitors, television receivers with integral tube	27 246		units

(1) Indicates the magnitude of the rounding employed to protect confidential cell (in the case of PRODCOM code 15.93.11.30, the confidential value lies within the range +/- 50 000 litres of the reported value).

Source: Eurostat (http://epp.eurostat.ec.europa.eu/newxtweb/)

Figure 8.8: Production and domestic output price indices for industry, EU-27
(2000=100)

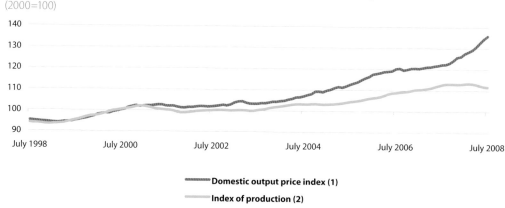

■■■■■■**Domestic output price index (1)**
──────**Index of production (2)**

(1) Gross series.
(2) Trend cycle.

Source: Eurostat (sts_inpr_m and sts_inppd_m)

Table 8.9: Annual growth rates for industry
(%)

	Index of production (1)					Domestic output price index (2)				
	2003	2004	2005	2006	2007	2003	2004	2005	2006	2007
EU-27	0.7	2.4	1.3	3.9	3.3	1.7	3.0	5.3	5.9	2.7
Euro area	0.3	2.1	1.4	4.0	3.4	1.4	2.3	4.1	5.1	2.8
Belgium	0.7	3.2	-0.3	5.1	2.6	0.6	4.5	2.2	4.8	3.0
Bulgaria	13.7	17.3	6.9	5.9	9.1	4.9	6.0	6.9	9.2	8.6
Czech Republic	5.6	9.2	6.7	11.4	8.8	-0.3	5.7	3.0	1.6	4.0
Denmark	0.2	-0.2	1.8	3.5	0.4	3.0	3.0	9.4	7.6	0.3
Germany	0.4	3.0	3.3	5.9	6.1	1.7	1.6	4.6	5.5	2.0
Estonia	11.4	9.7	11.1	10.1	6.7	:	:	:	:	:
Ireland	4.7	0.3	3.0	5.1	7.2	0.9	0.5	2.1	1.8	1.6
Greece	0.3	1.2	-0.9	0.5	2.2	2.3	3.5	5.9	6.9	3.3
Spain	1.4	1.6	0.7	3.9	1.9	1.4	3.4	4.9	5.3	3.3
France	-0.2	1.8	0.3	0.9	1.3	0.9	2.0	3.0	3.4	2.5
Italy	-0.6	-0.3	-0.8	2.4	-0.2	1.6	2.7	4.0	5.6	3.5
Cyprus	0.4	1.4	0.9	0.7	3.1	3.8	5.9	5.1	3.9	4.3
Latvia	6.7	6.4	6.0	5.5	1.0	:	:	:	:	:
Lithuania	16.1	10.8	7.1	7.3	4.0	-0.7	2.4	5.9	6.7	9.2
Luxembourg	3.7	3.8	1.0	2.4	0.3	3.6	9.0	3.9	13.1	6.8
Hungary	5.9	6.6	7.3	10.6	8.4	5.0	8.4	8.3	8.4	6.4
Malta	:	:	:	:	:	:	:	:	:	:
Netherlands	-1.4	4.1	0.4	1.4	2.3	2.2	2.6	7.1	8.2	4.6
Austria	2.1	6.3	4.2	7.3	4.9	0.4	1.8	3.3	2.1	4.4
Poland	8.4	12.3	4.5	12.2	9.5	1.6	7.6	2.1	2.5	3.6
Portugal	0.1	-2.7	0.3	2.8	1.8	0.8	2.7	4.1	4.7	3.2
Romania	3.3	4.5	2.4	7.7	5.0	19.6	18.5	12.5	12.0	8.7
Slovenia	1.0	4.5	4.0	6.5	6.2	2.6	4.3	2.7	2.4	5.3
Slovakia	5.0	4.1	3.3	10.1	12.7	8.3	3.4	4.7	8.4	2.1
Finland	1.2	5.0	0.3	9.8	4.4	0.2	-0.5	1.8	5.2	3.0
Sweden	1.5	4.1	2.4	3.5	4.1	2.7	2.0	3.8	5.9	3.8
United Kingdom	-0.1	0.9	-1.1	0.8	0.3	1.6	4.3	10.9	9.0	1.1
Croatia	4.0	3.0	5.4	4.6	5.6	2.0	3.5	3.0	2.9	3.4
Turkey	8.7	9.8	5.7	5.8	4.4	:	:	:	:	:
Norway	-4.0	2.1	-0.7	-2.4	-0.9	5.9	3.6	6.0	8.8	-0.6
Switzerland	0.1	4.4	2.7	7.8	9.5	:	:	:	:	:
Japan	3.3	4.8	1.4	4.3	2.8	:	:	:	:	:
United States	1.2	2.5	3.3	2.2	1.7	:	:	:	:	:

(1) Working day adjusted.
(2) Gross series.

Source: Eurostat (sts_inprgr_a and sts_inppdgr_a)

Figure 8.9: Average annual growth rate for the industrial index of production, EU-27, 2002-07 (1)
(%)

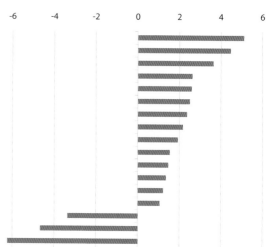

(1) Working day adjusted.

Source: Eurostat (sts_inppd_a)

Figure 8.10: Index of production, construction, EU-27 (1)
(2000=100)

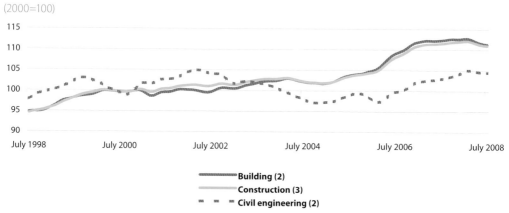

(1) Trend cycle.
(2) Estimates, May 1998 to December 1999 and April 2008 to July 2008.
(3) Estimates, May 1998 to December 1999 and July 2007.

Source: Eurostat (sts_copr_m)

8.3 Services

Introduction

Services accounted for 71.6 % of gross value added in the EU-27 in 2007, and a similar (and rising) proportion of overall employment. The relative importance of services in total value added ranged from almost 56 % of the economy in Romania to upwards of 75 % in Belgium, Greece, France, Cyprus, Malta and the United Kingdom, rising to a high of 84 % in Luxembourg.

The internal market is one of the EU's most important and continuing priorities. The central principles governing the internal market for services are set out in the EC Treaty, which guarantees EU companies the freedom to establish themselves in other Member States, and the freedom to provide services on the territory of another Member State other than the one in which they are established. The objective of the Services Directive [6] is to eliminate obstacles to trade in services, thus allowing the development of cross-border operations. It is intended to improve competitiveness, not just of service enterprises, but also of European industry as a whole. The directive was adopted by the European Parliament and the Council in December 2006 and will have to be transposed by the Member States by the end of 2009. It is hoped that the directive will help achieve potential economic growth and job creation, and it is for this reason that the directive is seen as a central element of the renewed Lisbon strategy for growth and jobs. Moreover, by providing for administrative simplification, it also supports the better regulation agenda.

Definitions and data availability

For background information relating to structural business statistics (SBS), refer to the section titled 'definitions and data availability' in section 8.1 (Business structures), which includes definitions of value added and persons employed, while definitions of wage adjusted labour productivity and gross operating rate are available in section 8.2 (Industry and construction). Equally, a great deal of background information relating to short-term business statistics (STS) is provided in the section titled 'definitions and data availability' in section 8.2 on industry and construction.

The term '**non-financial business economy**' is generally used within business statistics to refer to economic activities covered by Sections C to I and K of NACE Rev. 1.1 and the units that carry out those activities.

For STS, turnover comprises the totals invoiced by the observation unit during the reference period, and this corresponds to market sales of goods or services supplied to third parties. Turnover also includes all other charges (transport, packaging, etc.) passed on to the customer, even if these charges are listed separately in the invoice. Turnover excludes VAT and other similar deductible taxes directly linked to turnover as well as all duties and taxes on the goods or services invoiced by the unit. Reductions in prices, rebates and discounts as well as the value of returned packing must be deducted. Price reductions, rebates and bonuses conceded later to clients, for example at the end of the year, are not taken into account.

---

(6)   Directive 2006/123/EC of the European Parliament and of the Council of 12 December 2006 on services in the internal market.

Retail trade turnover indices are business cycle indicators which show the monthly activity of the retail sector in value and volume terms. The volume measure of the retail trade turnover index is more commonly referred to as the **index of the volume of (retail) sales.** Retail trade turnover indices are short-term indicators for final domestic demand. In order to eliminate the price effect on turnover in retail trade a deflator of sales is used. The deflator of sales is an index with a similar methodology to that of an output price index adapted to the particularities of retail trade but reflecting price changes in the goods retailed rather than the retail service provided. These indices may be split between food and non food products. Food products are sold, either in non-specialised stores (hypermarkets, supermarkets) or in specialised stores (e.g. fruit and vegetable grocers). A greater proportion of sales in specialised stores is a sign of a more traditional pattern of retail trade.

Main findings

Business services play a particularly important role in the services economy. Many of the activities covered by this sector of the economy (computer services, real estate, research and development, and other business activities such as legal, accounting, market research, advertising, industrial cleaning and security services) have taken advantage of the outsourcing phenomenon, which may explain their rapid growth.

Within the non-financial services, other business activities (as defined by NACE Division 74) contributed more than one fifth of the wealth generated (value added) in the EU-27 in 2005; wholesale trade and retail trade and repair contributed respectively another 16 % and 13 %. However, retail trade and other business activities accounted for similar proportions of the EU-27's total workforce in the non-financial services (22.5 % and 23.8 % respectively) in 2005, the large difference in the share for retail trade and repair being explained to some extent by the high incidence of part-time employment.

Over the five years from 2002 to 2007, water, air and land transport services had the fastest growing turnover among the non-financial services activities (in terms of NACE divisions), with average growth rates of 7.3 % or more per annum.

Figure 8.11: Breakdown of non-financial services value added and employment, EU-27, 2005
(% of non-financial services value added and employment)

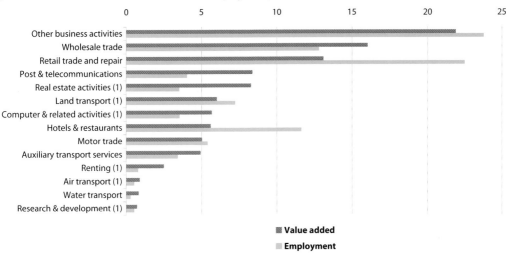

(1) Estimates.

Source: Eurostat (ebd_all)

Figure 8.12: Wage adjusted labour productivity for non-financial services, EU-27, 2005
(%)

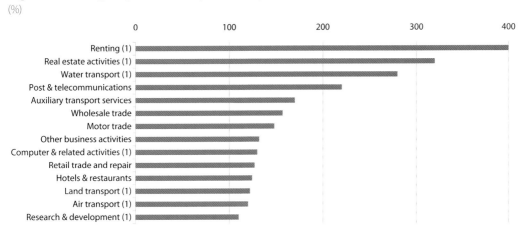

(1) Estimate.

Source: Eurostat (ebd_all)

Figure 8.13: Gross operating rate for non-financial service activities, EU-27, 2005
(%)

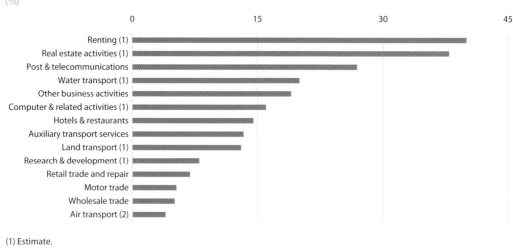

(1) Estimate.
(2) Estimate, 2004.

Source: Eurostat (ebd_all)

Figure 8.14: Non-financial services value added by enterprise size class, EU-27, 2005 (1)
(% of sectoral total)

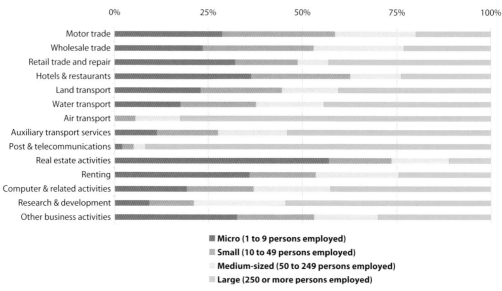

- Micro (1 to 9 persons employed)
- Small (10 to 49 persons employed)
- Medium-sized (50 to 249 persons employed)
- Large (250 or more persons employed)

(1) Includes rounded estimates based on non-confidential data.

Source: Eurostat (tin00053)

Figure 8.15: Average annual growth rate of turnover, selected service activities, EU-27, 2002-2007 (1)
(%)

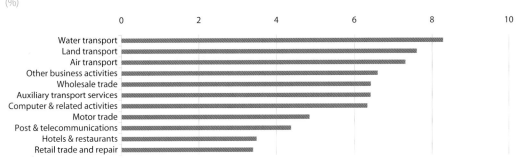

(1) Working day adjusted; real estate activities, renting and research and development, not available.

Source: Eurostat (sts_trtu_a and ebt_setu_a)

Figure 8.16: Index of turnover, selected service activities, EU-27 (1)
(2000=100)

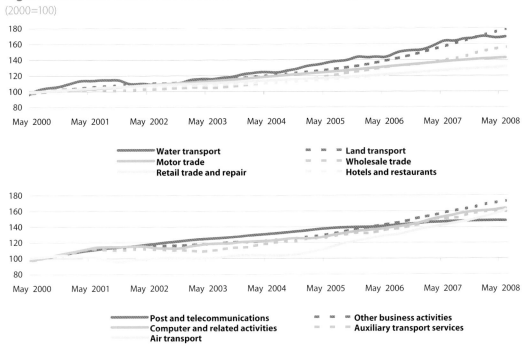

(1) Trend cycle; estimates, 2000 to 2002 and April to June 2008.

Source: Eurostat (ebt_setu_m and sts_trtu_m)

8 Industry and services

Figure 8.17: Breakdown of turnover, retail sales of food, beverages and tobacco, 2005
(% of total turnover)

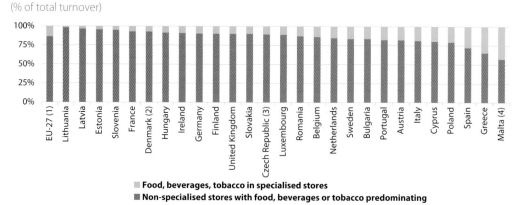

■ Food, beverages, tobacco in specialised stores
▨ Non-specialised stores with food, beverages or tobacco predominating

(1) Non-specialised stores, estimate.
(2) 2004.
(3) 2006.
(4) 2002.

Source: Eurostat (tin00007)

Figure 8.18: Volume of sales index, selected retail trade activities, EU-27 (1)
(2000=100)

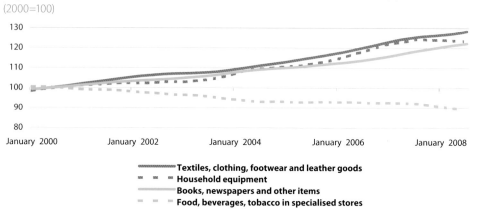

January 2000   January 2002   January 2004   January 2006   January 2008

▧▧▧ Textiles, clothing, footwear and leather goods
▪ ▪ ▪ Household equipment
─── Books, newspapers and other items
▪ ▪ ▪ Food, beverages, tobacco in specialised stores

(1) Trend cycle; estimates, June and July 2008.

Source: Eurostat (sts_trtu_m)

8.4 Tourism

Introduction

The demand for hotel services is split between that from businesses and that from households (for leisure, for example). Business demand tends to fluctuate with the economic cycle, as during periods of recession businesses try to reduce their expenditure. In a similar way, individuals are also more likely to curb their spending on tourism-related activities during periods of low consumer confidence.

Europe remains a major tourist destination and six of the Member States are among the world's top ten destinations for holiday-makers. As a result, tourism plays an important role in terms of its economic and employment potential, while presenting social and environmental implications; these twin characteristics drive the demand for reliable and harmonised statistics within this field.

Tourism can also be a significant factor in the development of European regions. Infrastructure created for tourism purposes contributes to local development, while jobs that are created or maintained can help counteract industrial or rural decline. 'Sustainable tourism' involves the preservation and enhancement of cultural and natural heritage, ranging from the arts, to local gastronomy, or the preservation of biodiversity.

A new policy approach for tourism is in the process of being developed. The European Commission adopted in 2006 a Communication titled, 'a renewed EU tourism policy: towards a stronger partnership for European tourism' [7]. The document addressed a range of challenges that will shape tourism in the coming years, including: Europe's ageing population; growing external competition; consumer demand for more specialised tourism; and the need to develop more sustainable and environmentally-friendly tourism practices. The document argued that a more competitive tourism industry and sustainable destinations would contribute further to the success of the renewed Lisbon strategy, tourist satisfaction, and securing the position of Europe as the world's leading tourist destination. This was followed by a Communication from the European Commission in October 2007 – 'Agenda for a sustainable and competitive European tourism' – which outlined the future steps for promoting the sustainability of European tourism and further contributes to the implementation of the renewed Lisbon strategy for growth and jobs and of the renewed sustainable development strategy, through addressing stakeholders playing a role in European tourism. The sustainable management of destinations, the integration of sustainability concerns by businesses, and sustainability awareness of tourists form the framework of the actions proposed [8].

(7) http://ec.europa.eu/enterprise/services/tourism/communications_2006.htm.
(8) http://ec.europa.eu/enterprise/services/tourism/doc/communications/com2007_0621en01.pdf.

Definitions and data availability

Tourism can be defined as the activities serving persons travelling to and staying in places outside their usual environment for not more than one consecutive year, for leisure or business purposes. A **tourist** is any visitor who stays at least one night in collective or private accommodation. A **night spent** is defined as each night that a guest is registered to stay in a hotel or similar establishment (his/her physical presence there is not necessary). A breakdown of nights spent is provided for **residents and non-residents**, the former are identified as having lived for most of the past year in a country/place, or having lived in that country/place for a shorter period and intending to return within a year to live there; note that a significant proportion of tourism, using the definitions above, is accounted for by business customers. **Tourism intensity** and **international tourism receipts relative to GDP** both give an indication of the importance of the size of tourism. Tourism intensity shows the number of nights spent by tourists relative to the population of the host country.

On the supply side, tourism relies on enterprises from a variety of sectors, which can be summarised as the provision of accommodation, food and drink, transport facilities and services, and entertainment. The term **tourist accommodation** refers to all types of collective accommodation – thus, excluding privately rented tourist accommodation. This may be broken down to cover **hotels and similar establishments** which include the provision of lodging in hotels, motels, inns and similar establishments combined with typical hotel services like bed-making and cleaning of the room and sanitary facilities, and **other collective accommodation establishments** which consist of holiday dwellings, tourist campsites and other short-stay accommodation, like youth hostels, tourist dormitories and holiday homes. The **number of bed places** in an establishment relates to the number of persons who can stay overnight in the beds set up in the establishment, ignoring any extra beds that may have been set up on customer request. One 'bed place' applies to a single bed, while a double bed is counted as two bed places. **Travel services** carried out by enterprises that are engaged in arranging transport, accommodation and catering on behalf of travellers, are classified within NACE Group 63.3, which encompasses the following activities: furnishing travel information, advice and planning; arranging custom-made tours, accommodation and transportation for travellers and tourists; furnishing tickets; selling package tours; tour operating; and organising tourist guides.

Main findings

Although the demand for tourism grew rapidly during the latter part of the last century, this trend was reversed from 2001 until 2003 as an economic slowdown, coupled with concerns over terrorist acts, health epidemics, and a series of natural disasters, contributed to a period of reduced demand. This evolution was counter-balanced by the rapid growth in low-cost airlines and an increase in the number of short breaks taken by Europeans.

There were 201 168 hotels and similar establishments in the EU-27 in 2006 and 221 483 other collective accommodation establishments. While the number of hotels has been in decline there has been an increase in their capacity, as measured by the number of bed places available, which rose to 11.5 million by 2006.

Occupancy rates for hotels and similar establishments vary considerably in the main tourist destinations, largely as a function of the season, whereas in business centres demand is more evenly spread across the whole year (although it may be concentrated during the working week and limited during weekends). There were just over 1 500 million nights

spent in EU-27 hotels and similar establishments during 2006 by residents and non-residents.

In terms of tourism intensity (the ratio of nights spent relative to population size) the most popular holiday destinations in the EU-27 in 2007 included the Mediterranean island destinations of Cyprus and Malta (2006), as well as the alpine destination of Austria. An alternative measure of the importance of tourism is provided by the ratio of international tourism receipts relative to GDP: in 2007, this was highest in Cyprus (12.5 %) and Malta (12.2 %), confirming the importance of tourism to these island nations.

Figure 8.19: Tourism destinations, 2007
(1 000 nights spent in all collective accommodation in the country by non-residents)

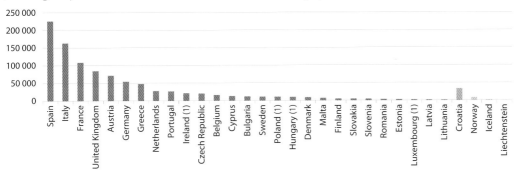

(1) 2006.

Source: Eurostat (tour_occ_ni)

Table 8.10: Leading tourism indicators

	Hotels & similar establishments (units)		Other collective accommodation establishments (units)		Bed places in hotels & similar establishments (1 000)		Nights spent in hotels & similar establishments (1 000) (1)		Share of population (aged 15+) taking part in tourism	
	2002	2007 (2)	2002	2007 (2)	2002	2007 (2)	2002	2007 (2)	2002	2007 (3)
EU-27	204 675	201 168	189 359	221 483	10 686	11 541	:	1 525 008	:	:
Euro area	143 420	142 374	137 571	166 208	8 160	8 717	:	1 209 656	:	:
Belgium	2 010	2 013	1 638	1 503	123	125	14 500	16 197	0.41	0.45
Bulgaria	755	1 526	159	492	133	231	9 980	16 736		:
Czech Republic	4 335	4 559	3 534	3 286	223	248	23 803	27 044	:	0.52
Denmark	482	477	622	598	67	73	9 250	11 080	0.61	0.62
Germany	38 129	35 941	17 508	17 817	1 608	1 644	189 970	214 675	0.67	0.81
Estonia	193	346	227	638	16	29	2 337	3 843	0.26	0.23
Ireland	5 009	4 087	2 803	4 890	145	157	24 716	28 282	:	:
Greece	8 329	9 207	337	324	606	701	53 478	64 086	0.42	0.42
Spain	16 732	18 426	13 748	19 032	1 394	1 639	222 555	272 733	0.51	0.44
France	18 768	18 135	10 492	10 643	1 235	1 254	192 056	204 269	:	0.61
Italy	33 411	34037	80 304	96957	1 930	2142	231 132	254076	0.50	0.49
Cyprus	813	735	133	167	90	88	16 103	14 298	0.77	:
Latvia	223	318	74	82	14	21	1 527	2 759	:	0.19
Lithuania	247	348	229	181	12	22	1 050	2 591	:	0.27
Luxembourg	316	273	284	235	15	15	1 244	1 438	0.62	0.64
Hungary	2 167	2 032	1 220	1 024	155	159	13 834	15 808	:	0.35
Malta	194	173	2	6	40	40	:	7 307	:	:
Netherlands	2 933	3 196	3 729	4 072	177	200	28 515	34 159	0.68	0.68
Austria	14 914	14 204	5 971	6 526	569	574	73 523	79 153	0.46	0.58
Poland	1 478	2 443	5 572	4 275	128	190	13 381	24 307	:	0.34
Portugal	1 898	:	273	:	240	:	34 209	:	0.33	0.27
Romania	2 765	4 163	573	531	197	228	:	19 756	:	0.28
Slovenia	393	396	457	423	28	33	4 763	5 546	:	0.62
Slovakia	816	1 249	1 216	1 426	54	67	7 526	7 233	:	:
Finland	971	909	484	449	118	119	13 273	15 817	0.54	0.60
Sweden	1 737	1 893	2 043	2 083	181	207	21 011	25 416	:	:
United Kingdom	44 657	40 130	35 727	40878	1 188	1 251	178 937	169440	0.44	0.60
Croatia	788	800	485	1 011	188	163	19 596	20 940	:	:
FYR of Macedonia	150	:	175	:	16	:	:	:	:	:
Iceland	273	294	399	286	14	18	1 261	1 917	:	:
Liechtenstein	50	47	120	113	1	1	108	129	:	:
Norway	1 124	1 112	1 151	1 153	144	154	16 188	18 510	0.70	0.72
Switzerland	5 643	5 635	94 100	:	259	270	31 963	36 365	:	:

(1) Nights spent by residents and non-residents.
(2) EU-27, euro area, Hungary and Malta, 2006.
(3) Czech Republic, Germany, Estonia, Italy, Hungary and Portugal, 2006.

Source: Eurostat (tin00039, tin00040, tin00041, tin00043, tin00045 and tps00001)

Figure 8.20: Country of origin for outbound holidays, 2007 (1)

(average number of nights spent abroad per inhabitant)

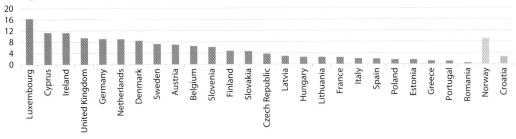

(1) Bulgaria and Malta, not available.

Source: Eurostat (tour_dem_tnw and tps00001)

Figure 8.21: Tourism intensity, 2007

(ratio of nights spent by residents and non-residents in hotels and similar establishments and other collective accommodation establishments per inhabitant)

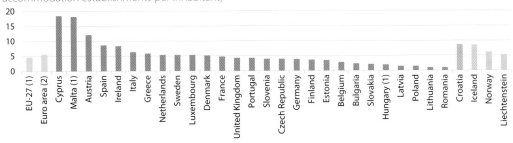

(1) 2006.
(2) EA-12 instead of EA-15; 2006.

Source: Eurostat (tour_occ_ni and tps00001)

Figure 8.22: Proportion of the population aged 15+ going on holiday abroad for at least four nights, 2007 (1)

(%)

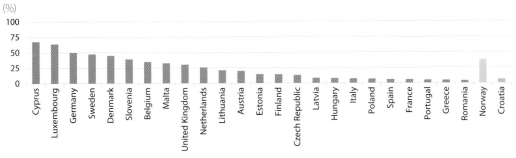

(1) Bulgaria, Ireland and Slovakia, not available.

Source: Eurostat (tour_dem_toage, tps00001 and tps00010)

Table 8.11: Holiday trips of EU residents (aged 15 or more), 2007

	Number of trips (1 000)			Breakdown of all trips by destination and duration (%)			
	All trips	Short trips (1-3 nights)	Long trips (4+ nights)	Short domestic trips (1-3 nights)	Long domestic trips (4+ nights)	Short outbound trips (1-3 nights)	Long outbound trips (4+ nights)
Belgium	10 458	3 453	7 005	16.1	11.7	16.9	55.3
Bulgaria	:	:	:	:	:	:	:
Czech Republic (1)	26 754	17 821	8 933	62.7	18.6	3.9	14.8
Denmark	10 368	4 377	5 991	32.5	15.2	9.7	42.6
Germany	202 409	102 877	99 533	44.3	20.9	6.5	28.3
Estonia	1 245	835	410	53.2	8.7	13.9	24.1
Ireland	11 407	5 551	5 856	36.3	11.9	12.4	39.4
Greece	14 630	6 107	8 522	41.0	51.7	0.8	6.5
Spain	111 903	71 723	40 180	62.2	30.8	1.9	5.1
France	190 381	105 049	85 331	52.2	37.5	3.0	7.3
Italy (1)	188 156	147 022	41 134	18.0	16.5	1.7	5.4
Cyprus	1 663	846	817	45.3	12.3	5.6	36.9
Latvia	4 197	3 330	867	71.2	7.3	8.2	13.3
Lithuania	3 576	2 381	1 196	53.9	13.6	12.6	19.9
Luxembourg (1)	1 099	419	680	1.2	0.2	37.0	61.6
Hungary	25 224	17 481	7 742	64.0	19.9	5.3	10.8
Malta	:	:	:	:	:	:	:
Netherlands (1)	28 574	10 189	18 385	24.9	24.4	10.8	39.9
Austria	15 682	6 997	8 685	31.9	19.9	12.7	35.5
Poland	33 948	16 584	17 364	46.1	40.7	2.7	10.4
Portugal (1)	10 265	6 423	3 842	60.5	29.6	2.1	7.9
Romania (1)	6 892	1 490	5 402	64.1	67.4	0.4	11.0
Slovenia	3 654	1 989	1 665	33.7	11.0	20.8	34.6
Slovakia	6 969	2 083	4 886	24.1	34.5	5.7	35.6
Finland	29 467	22 885	6 582	69.4	15.1	8.3	7.2
Sweden (1)	38 399	25 618	12 781	58.3	19.1	8.5	14.2
United Kingdom (1)	112 695	40 080	72 615	35.7	25.3	9.5	29.5
Croatia	5 434	2 467	2 967	31.8	36.6	13.6	18.0
Norway	15 770	8 840	6 930	42.7	20.7	13.4	23.3

(1) 2006.

Source: Eurostat (tour_dem_ttmd)

Table 8.12: Tourism receipts and expenditure

	Receipts				Expenditure			
	(EUR million)			Relative to GDP, 2007 (%)	(EUR million)			Relative to GDP, 2007 (%)
	1997	2002	2007		1997	2002	2007	
EU-27 (1)	:	:	76 612	0.6	:	:	94 005	0.8
Euro area (2)	:	:	100 437	1.1	:	:	88 860	1.0
Belgium	:	7 317	7 655	2.3	:	10 736	12 044	3.6
Bulgaria	963	1 207	2 287	7.9	339	563	1 331	4.6
Czech Republic	3 220	3 126	4 820	3.8	2 101	1 673	2 648	2.1
Denmark	2 809	5 047	4 495	2.0	3 712	6 193	6 210	2.7
Germany	15 782	20 350	26 289	1.1	42 619	55 504	60 467	2.5
Estonia	420	585	749	4.9	107	243	472	3.1
Ireland	2 290	3 256	4 470	2.4	1 960	3 942	6 318	3.4
Greece (3)	4 904	10 285	11 357	5.0	1 169	2 549	2 383	1.0
Spain	23 739	33 557	42 170	4.0	3 985	7 687	14 360	1.4
France	24 724	34 190	39 643	2.1	14 632	20 580	26 430	1.4
Italy	26 355	28 193	31 038	2.0	14 764	17 801	19 673	1.3
Cyprus	1 461	2 048	1 961	12.5	340	537	1 070	6.8
Latvia	170	170	488	2.4	287	243	677	3.4
Lithuania	317	538	840	3.0	245	360	835	3.0
Luxembourg	:	2 542	2 919	8.1	:	2 042	2 593	7.2
Hungary	3 074	3 452	3 451	3.4	819	1 820	2 147	2.1
Malta	571	645	663	12.2	168	162	272	5.0
Netherlands	5 580	8 150	9 798	1.7	9 107	13 665	13 910	2.5
Austria	9 699	11 887	13 781	5.1	8 915	9 923	7 703	2.8
Poland	2 026	4 554	7 721	2.5	519	3 388	6 205	2.0
Portugal	4 063	6 094	7 393	4.5	1 818	2 247	2 858	1.8
Romania	465	354	1 068	0.9	602	419	1 114	0.9
Slovenia	1 044	1 145	1 618	4.8	461	636	803	2.4
Slovakia	481	769	1 493	2.7	387	470	1 206	2.2
Finland	1 684	1 664	2 060	1.1	1 939	2 118	2 907	1.6
Sweden	3 291	4 979	8 743	2.6	6 138	7 740	10 242	3.1
United Kingdom	19 941	21 620	28 175	1.4	25 196	44 045	53 059	2.6
Croatia (3)	:	:	6 264	16.7	:	:	584	1.6
Turkey (3)	6 174	8 967	13 422	2.8	1 513	1 988	2 185	0.5
Norway (3)	1 896	2 296	2 866	1.0	3 955	5 358	9 197	3.2
Switzerland (3)	:	:	8 477	2.7	:	:	7 873	2.5
Japan (3)	3 823	3 711	6 745	0.2	29 101	28 171	21 407	0.7
United States	75 989	89 628	86 696	0.9	47 332	65 290	59 538	0.6

(1) Extra-EU-27.
(2) EA-13 instead of EA-15; extra-EA-13.
(3) 2006 instead of 2007.

Source: Eurostat (bop_its_deth, bop_its_det and nama_gdp_c), Economic and Social Research Institute, Bureau of Economic Analysis

Agriculture, forestry and fisheries

9

Agriculture was one of the first sectors of the economy (following coal and steel) to receive the attention of European policymakers. Article 39 of the Treaty of Rome on the EEC (1957) set out the objectives for the first common agricultural policy (CAP); these were focused on increasing agricultural productivity as a way to ensure a fair standard of living for the agricultural community, stabilising markets and ensuring security of supply at affordable prices to consumers.

As the primary objective of producing more food was realised, food surpluses accrued, distorting trade and raising environmental concerns. These were the principal drivers for changes in the CAP, a process that started in the early 1990s and has resulted in a change from support for production towards a market-oriented and a more environment-friendly and sustainable form of agriculture. These reforms have focused mainly on increasing the competitiveness of agriculture by reducing support prices and compensating farmers by the introduction of direct aid payments. A decisive step came in the 2003/04 CAP reforms with the decoupling of direct aids from production and a move to try to realign the CAP with consumer concerns. The scope of this latest reform of the CAP was widened with the introduction of a comprehensive rural development policy. Together these policies aim to encourage entrepreneurial behaviour so that farm managers can respond better to market signals, introduce new techniques and promote diversified activities such as rural crafts, food processing facilities on farms, tourism, or afforestation, as well as promoting sustainable farming practices and various other rural development measures.

In November 2007, the European Commission adopted a Communication 'Preparing the Health Check of the CAP reform' with the objective of assessing the implementation of the 2003 CAP reforms, and to introduce those adjustments to the reform process that were deemed necessary. Notably, these proposals included a shift in funding from direct payments to greater rural development support.

Contrary to what is happening in some other parts of the world, forest cover in the EU is slowly increasing. Forests are present in a huge variety of climatic, geographic, ecological and socioeconomic conditions. Ecologically, EU forests belong to numerous vegetation zones, ranging from the coastal plains to the Alpine zone, while socioeconomic management conditions vary from small family holdings to large estates belonging to vertically integrated enterprises.

Fish are a natural, biological, mobile (sometimes over wide distances) and renewable resource. Aside from fish farming, fish can not be owned until they have been caught. For this reason, fish stocks continue to be regarded as a common resource, which therefore need to be managed collectively. This has led to policies that regulate the amount of fishing, as well as the types of fishing techniques and gear used in fish capture.

9.1 Agriculture – farm structure and land use

Introduction

The structure of agriculture in the Member States varies considerably. Among other factors, this reflects differences in geology, topography, climate and natural resources, as well as the diversity in regional activities, infrastructure and social customs. The survey on the Structure of Agricultural Holdings (also known as the Farm Structure Survey – FSS) helps assess the agricultural situation across the EU, monitoring trends and transitions in the structure of holdings, while modelling the impact of external developments or policy proposals.

Rural development policy aims to improve competitiveness in agriculture and forestry, improve the environment and countryside, improve the quality of life in rural areas and encourage the diversification of rural economies. As agriculture modernised and the importance of industry and services within the economy increased, agriculture became much less important as a source of jobs. Consequently, more and more emphasis is placed on the role farmers can play in rural development, including forestry, biodiversity, diversification of the rural economy to create alternative jobs and environmental protection in rural areas. The FSS continues to be adapted to try to provide the necessary data to help analyse and follow these types of developments.

Definitions and data availability

The basic **Farm Structure Survey (FSS)** is carried out by Member States every 10 years (the full scope being the agricultural census) and intermediate sample surveys are carried out three times between these basic surveys. The Member States collect information from individual agricultural holdings and, observing strict rules of confidentiality, data are forwarded to Eurostat. The information collected covers land use, livestock numbers, rural development, management and farm labour input (including age, gender and relationship to the holder). The survey data can then be aggregated to different geographic levels (Member States, regions, and for basic surveys also districts) and can be arranged by size class, area status, legal status of holding, objective zone and farm type.

The basic unit underlying the FSS is the **agricultural holding**. A holding is a technical-economic unit under single management engaged in agricultural production. The FSS covers all agricultural holdings with a utilised agricultural area (UAA) of at least one hectare (ha) and those holdings with a UAA of less than 1 ha if their market production exceeds certain natural thresholds.

The **utilised agricultural area (UAA)** is the sum of arable land, permanent pasture and meadow, land used for permanent crops and kitchen gardens. The UAA excludes unutilised agricultural land, woodland and land occupied by buildings, farmyards, tracks, ponds, etc. **Permanent crops** are those not grown in rotation, other than permanent grassland, which occupy the soil for a long period and yield crops over several years. **Permanent grassland and meadow** is land used permanently (for five years or more) to grow herbaceous forage crops, through cultivation (sown) or naturally (self-seeded) and that is not included in the crop rotation on the holding; the land can be used for grazing or mowed for silage or hay. **Arable land** is land worked (ploughed or tilled) regularly, generally under a system of crop rotation. **Wooded area** is land area covered with trees or forest shrubs, including poplar plantations inside or outside woods and forest-tree nurseries grown in woodland for the holding's own requirements, as well as forest facilities (forest roads, storage depots for timber, etc.). **Built -up and related land** comprises residential land, industrial land, quarries, pits and mines, commercial land, land used by public services, land of mixed use, land used for transport and communications, for technical infrastructure, recreational and other open land. Scattered farm buildings, yards and annexes are excluded. Some figures may refer to the closest year for which data is available (limit +/- 1 or 2 years before or after).

Other gainful activity is any activity other than one relating to farm work, including activities carried out on the holding itself (camping sites, accommodations for tourists, etc.) or that use its resources (machinery, etc.) or products (such as processing farm products, renewable energy production), and which have an economic impact on the holding. Other gainful activity is carried out by the holder, his/her family members, or one or more partners on a group holding.

The **farm labour force** is made-up of all persons having completed their compulsory education (having reached school-leaving age) who carried out farm work on the holding under survey during the 12 months up to the survey day. The figures include the holders, even when not working on the holding, whereas their spouses are counted only if they carry out farm work on the holding.. The **holder** is the natural person (sole holder or group of individuals) or the legal person (e.g. a co-operative, an institution) on whose account and in whose name the holding is operated and who is legally and economically responsible for the holding, i.e. who takes the economic risks of the holding. For group holdings, only the main holder (one person) is counted. The **regular labour force** covers the family labour force (even those who were working accidentally on the holding) and permanently employed (regular) non-family workers. The **family labour force** includes the holder and the members of his/her family who carried out farm work (including all persons of retiring age who continue to work on the holding). One **annual work unit** (AWU) corresponds to the work performed by one person who is occupied on an agricultural holding on a full-time basis. **Full-time** means the minimum hours required by the national provisions governing contracts of employment. If these do not indicate the number of hours, then 1 800 hours are taken to be the minimum (225 working days of eight hours each).

Main findings

According to the FSS, there were 14.5 million agricultural holdings in the EU-27 in 2005. Among the Member States that joined the EU in 2004 and 2007, there was a period of land restitution in the run-up to accession. This led to large State farms being divided up and handed back to private individuals, leading to a substantial rise in numbers of farms and workers. Over a quarter of agricultural holdings (29.4 %) in the EU-27 were located in Romania.

The total EU-27 farm labour force was the equivalent of 12.7 million full-time workers in 2005. Just over one third (35 %) of the regular agricultural labour force in the EU-27 was female, although in the Baltic Member States this share was closer to a half, reaching 50 % in Latvia. Farm holders and their family members make up the vast majority of the labour force, 81 % in the EU-27, with only the Czech Republic and Slovakia recording a significantly lower share, reflecting the different structure of holding ownership in these countries. There are relatively few (6.7 %) agricultural holders in the EU-27 under the age of 35 years, but a relatively large proportion (33.2 %) over the age of 65 years.

The UAA in the EU accounted for 40 % of total land area in 2005; in addition, wooded areas on farm holdings accounted for a further 7.3 % of the total land area. Arable land made up three fifths of the UAA and permanent grassland one third, while land for permanent crops accounted for around 6 % of the UAA.

Table 9.1: Agricultural holdings

	Number of agricultural holdings (1 000)			Holdings with dairy cows (1 000)			Holdings with irrigable area (% of UAA)	
	2003	2005	2007	2003	2005	2007	2005	2007
EU-27	15 021.0	14 478.6	:	:	:	:	:	:
Euro area	5 975.2	5 565.6	:	:	:	:	:	:
Belgium	54.9	51.5	48.0	16.6	15.2	:	4.2	4.7
Bulgaria	665.6	534.6	:	195.0	152.6	:	14.5	:
Czech Republic	45.8	42.3	39.4	8.5	6.8	5.6	4.7	5.2
Denmark	48.6	51.7	44.6	8.0	6.6	5.4	17.9	15.1
Germany	412.3	389.9	:	121.8	110.4	:	:	:
Estonia	36.9	27.8	23.3	12.4	9.2	6.1	:	:
Ireland	135.6	132.7	128.2	28.1	23.8	:	0.0	0.0
Greece	824.5	833.6	:	:	:	:	65.2	:
Spain	1 140.7	1 079.4	:	51.0	42.4	:	46.4	:
France	614.0	567.1	:	113.9	103.9	:	18.0	:
Italy	1 963.8	1 728.5	:	67.5	61.0	:	37.6	:
Cyprus	45.2	45.2	:	0.3	0.2	:	77.3	:
Latvia	126.6	128.7	107.8	63.7	50.9	43.7	0.3	0.2
Lithuania	272.1	253.0	230.3	193.4	170.8	123.2	0.1	0.0
Luxembourg	2.5	2.5	2.3	1.0	1.0	:	:	0.0
Hungary	773.4	714.8	626.3	22.0	16.3	:	2.5	0.2
Malta	11.0	11.1	11.0	0.2	0.2	0.2	27.8	25.5
Netherlands	85.5	81.8	76.7	25.0	23.5	24.5	23.6	26.1
Austria	173.8	170.6	:	65.1	54.6	:	4.4	:
Poland	2 172.2	2 476.5	2 391.0	873.8	727.1	651.1	1.0	1.1
Portugal	359.3	323.9	:	27.1	15.9	:	62.2	:
Romania	4 484.9	4 256.2	:	1 204.9	1 134.4	:	3.5	:
Slovenia	77.2	77.2	75.3	17.2	19.7	19.2	2.3	2.3
Slovakia	71.7	68.5	:	14.2	13.5	:	10.5	:
Finland	75.0	70.6	68.2	19.4	16.9	:	8.1	8.5
Sweden	67.9	75.8	72.6	9.7	8.6	7.1	6.0	5.2
United Kingdom	280.6	286.8	:	28.2	26.3	:	1.4	:
Norway	58.2	53.0	:	17.5	15.9	:	16.8	:
Switzerland	:	63.6	:	:	:	:	0.0	:

Source: Eurostat (tag00001, ef_r_nuts and ef_ov_lusum)

Table 9.2: Farm labour force, 2007 (1)

	Total farm labour force (1 000 AWU) (2)	Regular farm labour force (% of total)	Full-time regular farm labour force (% of total)	Female regular farm labour force (% of total)	Family farm labour force (% of total)	Agric. holders being a natural person (1 000)	Agric. holders <35 years old (1 000)	Agric. holders >=65 years old (1 000)
EU-27	12 714	92	33	35	81	14 222	956	4 722
Euro area	5 642	89	44	28	73	5 366	300	1 774
Belgium	66	95	71	29	79	44	3	9
Bulgaria	625	96	41	39	87	531	22	222
Czech Republic	137	98	68	32	27	36	4	7
Denmark	56	96	70	23	61	44	3	9
Germany	643	92	51	29	70	385	35	28
Estonia	32	98	46	46	61	22	1	7
Ireland	148	98	60	21	93	128	9	32
Greece	601	85	21	30	82	833	57	307
Spain	993	81	41	20	65	1 028	54	359
France	855	89	66	25	49	474	42	75
Italy	1 374	90	37	29	82	1 699	56	735
Cyprus	29	89	30	31	73	45	1	12
Latvia	105	99	30	50	84	108	8	32
Lithuania	180	98	14	48	85	230	10	93
Luxembourg	4	98	63	27	85	2	0	0
Hungary	403	97	25	37	77	619	47	172
Malta	4	99	41	14	88	11	0	3
Netherlands	165	91	56	26	61	73	3	13
Austria	166	97	51	41	89	167	18	19
Poland	2 263	97	34	42	95	2 387	294	388
Portugal	398	93	33	41	83	317	7	150
Romania	2 596	93	3	43	91	4 238	218	1 849
Slovenia	84	96	21	41	92	75	3	26
Slovakia	99	97	43	33	43	67	3	20
Finland	72	94	56	30	83	67	6	4
Sweden	65	97	42	26	76	68	4	15
United Kingdom	339	94	55	24	69	274	9	84
Norway	59	95	35	25	83	53	5	4
Switzerland	:	:	:	:	:	63	:	:

(1) EU-27, euro area, Bulgaria, Germany, Greece, Spain, France, Italy, Cyprus, Austria, Portugal, Romania, Slovakia, the United Kingdom, Norway and Switzerland, 2005.
(2) AWU: annual work unit.

Source: Eurostat (tag00020, ef_ov_lfft, ef_so_lfwtime, ef_so_lfaa, tag00028, tag00029 and tag00030)

Figure 9.1: Agricultural holdings with another gainful activity, 2007 (1)

(%)

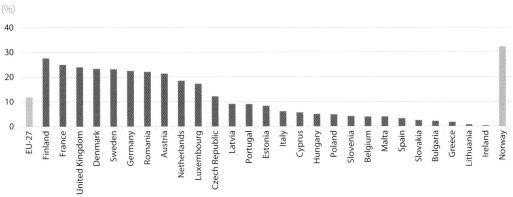

(1) EU-27, Bulgaria, Germany, Greece, Spain, France, Italy, Cyprus, Austria, Portugal, Romania, Slovakia, the United Kingdom and Norway, 2005.

Source: Eurostat (tag00096)

Figure 9.2: Agricultural area by land use, EU (1)

(% of land area)

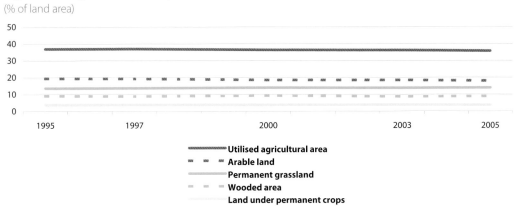

(1) Data available for the years shown in the figure; EU total based on data for Belgium, Denmark, Ireland, Greece, Spain, Italy, Luxembourg, the Netherlands, Austria, Portugal, Finland, Sweden and the United Kingdom.

Source: Eurostat (ef_lu_ovcropesu and reg_d3area)

Table 9.3: Area by land use

	Land area, 2005 (1 000 ha) (1)	Share of land area, 2007 (%) (2)					Built-up area, 2000 (%) (3)
		Utilised agricultural area (total)	of which:			Wooded area (not UAA)	
			Land under permanent crops	Permanent grassland	Arable land		
EU-27	430 296	40.0	2.5	13.0	24.3	7.3	:
Euro area	256 562	40.4	3.8	13.3	23.2	7.2	:
Belgium	3 033	45.3	0.7	16.9	27.8	0.2	18.6
Bulgaria	11 100	24.6	0.7	1.0	22.7	10.1	:
Czech Republic	7 726	45.5	0.5	11.8	33.3	18.9	10.5
Denmark	4 310	61.8	0.2	4.7	56.9	4.8	16.9
Germany	35 709	47.7	0.6	13.8	33.3	3.9	12.8
Estonia	4 343	20.9	0.1	6.3	14.4	5.3	:
Ireland	6 839	60.5	0.0	45.8	14.7	3.6	:
Greece	13 071	30.5	8.3	6.3	15.7	0.4	:
Spain	50 600	49.1	8.4	17.1	23.6	9.6	:
France	63 283	43.6	1.7	12.8	29.0	1.6	6.7
Italy	29 511	43.1	7.7	11.3	23.9	12.8	:
Cyprus	925	16.4	4.4	0.0	11.9	0.3	2.2
Latvia	6 229	28.5	0.3	10.3	17.8	11.4	4.2
Lithuania	6 268	42.3	0.3	13.1	28.9	2.6	3.2
Luxembourg	259	50.6	0.6	26.4	23.6	2.5	8.5
Hungary	9 303	45.5	1.7	5.4	38.2	14.6	:
Malta	32	32.7	4.2	0.0	25.4	0.0	:
Netherlands	3 376	56.7	1.0	24.3	31.4	0.3	17.0
Austria	8 248	39.6	0.8	21.7	17.0	32.1	4.6
Poland	31 269	49.5	1.2	10.5	37.6	3.8	6.6
Portugal	9 212	39.9	7.0	19.2	13.5	9.2	17.8
Romania	23 000	60.5	1.5	19.7	38.6	4.3	4.4
Slovenia	2 014	24.3	1.3	14.3	8.6	18.8	3.9
Slovakia	4 903	38.3	0.5	10.8	26.9	23.6	7.5
Finland	30 409	7.5	0.0	0.1	7.4	10.4	2.5
Sweden	41 034	7.6	0.0	1.2	6.4	9.1	:
United Kingdom	24 250	65.8	0.1	40.4	25.2	2.3	:
Croatia	:	:	:	:	:	:	8.6
Iceland	:	:	:	:	:	:	1.4
Norway	30 428	3.4	0.0	1.3	2.0	8.0	:
Switzerland	4 000	26.5	0.6	15.8	10.2	2.8	7.0

(1) Estonia, Ireland, Latvia, Lithuania, the Netherlands, Slovenia, Finland and Sweden, 2007.
(2) EU-27, euro area, Bulgaria, Germany, Greece, Spain, France, Italy, Cyprus, Austria, Portugal, Romania, Slovakia, the United Kingdom, Norway and Switzerland, 2005.
(3) Latvia and Luxembourg, 1990; Finland and Switzerland, 1995.

Source: Eurostat (ef_lu_ovcropesu, reg_d3area and tsdnr510)

9.2 Agricultural output, price indices and income

Introduction

One of the principal objectives of the Common Agricultural Policy (CAP) remains the aim of providing farmers with a reasonable standard of living. Although this concept is not defined explicitly, one of the measures tracked is the development of incomes from farming activities. Economic Accounts for Agriculture (EAA) are one of the data sources that provide such income measures (see definitions below). This macro-economic set of data is used to analyse the production process of the agricultural activity and the primary income generated by it. The EAA provide key insights into the economic viability of agriculture, its contribution to a Member State's wealth, the structure and composition of agricultural production and inputs, the remuneration of factors of production, relationships between prices and quantities of both inputs and outputs, and responds to the need to have internationally comparable information.

Eurostat also collects annual agricultural prices (in principle net of VAT) to compare agricultural price levels between Member States and study sales channels. Price indices for agricultural products and the means of agricultural production, on the other hand, are used principally to analyse price developments and their effect on agricultural income.

Definitions and data availability

The EAA comprise a production account, a generation of income account, an entrepreneurial income account and some elements of a capital account. For the output items of agricultural, hunting and related service activities, Member States transmit to Eurostat values at basic prices, as well as their components (the value at producer prices, subsidies on products and taxes on products). For the items of intermediate consumption, values at purchaser prices are transmitted. The data for the production account and for gross fixed capital formation are transmitted in both current prices and the prices of the previous year.

Agricultural income indicators (in the EAA) are presented in the form of an index of real income of factors in agricultural activity per annual work unit (indicator A); the index of real net agricultural entrepreneurial income, per unpaid annual work unit (indicator B), and; net entrepreneurial income of agriculture (indicator C).

The concept of output, for **animal and crop output**, comprises sales, changes in stocks, and products used for processing and own final use by producers. EU **agricultural price indices** are obtained by a base-weighted Laspeyres calculation (2000=100), and are expressed both in nominal terms, and deflated using an implicit HICP deflator.

Main findings

Agricultural gross value added in the EU-27 increased by 7.4 % in 2007 (compared with 2006) and as a result was at its highest level in the last ten years. In 2006 and 2007 both crop and animal output increased, with the growth in crop output particularly strong.

Deflated agricultural producer (output) prices rose on average by 0.8 % per annum in the EU-27 between 2002 and 2007. An analysis of (nominal) producer price indices over the same period shows that price increases averaged 3.4 % per annum, with crop output prices rising more than twice as fast as animal output prices (4.5 % per annum compared with 2.0 % per annum). Several cereal products recorded double-digit annual average price increases over this five year period – for example, rye, barley and wheat – due almost entirely to extremely high price increases in 2007. Only a few agricultural products recorded a fall in prices, most notably sugar beet, for which prices fell by 27 % in total between 2004 (the latest peak in prices) and 2007, while there was almost no change in the price of the output of pigs or sheep and goats over the period considered (2002-2007).

Alongside an increase in gross value added, there was an average 5.8 % rise in income from agricultural activity (indicator A) across the EU-27 in 2007 (when compared with the year before). There were large differences between Member States: Romania recorded a fall of 16.7 % in income from agricultural activity in 2007, with Malta, Portugal and Italy recording reductions of at least 3 %; in Lithuania this indicator rose by 46.0 % in 2007, while Belgium, Poland, the Czech Republic and Germany all recorded increases in excess of 20 %.

Table 9.4: Agricultural output and value added

(EUR million)

	Gross value added at producer prices of agricultural industry			Crop output at producer prices			Animal output at producer prices		
	2000	2005	2007	2000	2005	2007	2000	2005	2007
EU-27	130 634	129 933	142 726	149 884	157 679	185 220	126 095	128 459	137 791
Euro area (1)	105 665	102 056	111 621	119 965	123 537	141 725	91 785	91 003	97 495
Belgium	2 484	2 135	2 346	2 931	2 903	3 479	3 841	3 556	3 772
Bulgaria	1 634	1 544	1 243	1 305	1 627	1 511	1 448	1 129	1 242
Czech Republic	831	886	1 068	1 396	1 674	2 389	1 399	1 574	1 670
Denmark	2 496	2 297	2 487	2 603	2 474	3 635	4 767	4 867	4 942
Germany	13 571	13 000	14 565	18 425	18 167	23 293	19 344	19 042	20 382
Estonia	137	186	254	141	201	309	183	265	293
Ireland	1 617	1 642	1 933	1 229	1 380	1 598	3 655	3 652	4 105
Greece	6 240	6 581	6 062	6 525	7 024	6 650	2 499	2 711	2 754
Spain	19 225	20 345	22 571	19 539	21 234	23 700	11 692	12 641	13 958
France	23 890	21 252	25 544	30 337	29 864	36 780	22 242	21 663	22 299
Italy	24 527	24 404	24 088	24 234	25 434	25 784	13 438	13 178	14 310
Cyprus	:	330	338	:	281	300	:	292	299
Latvia	182	222	343	192	308	500	220	282	377
Lithuania	394	407	521	626	657	881	481	693	836
Luxembourg	103	102	124	76	81	99	148	155	165
Hungary	1 814	1 887	2 083	2 343	3 020	3 704	2 073	2 117	2 211
Malta	64	45	45	48	40	44	77	63	63
Netherlands	9 053	7 829	8 786	9 480	10 131	11 645	8 548	7 906	8 906
Austria	2 127	2 167	2 689	2 159	2 262	3 008	2 513	2 540	2 788
Poland	4 598	5 161	7 186	5 992	6 043	9 463	5 886	7 585	8 930
Portugal	2 160	1 998	2 212	3 597	3 584	3 783	2 178	2 241	2 333
Romania	4 121	6 083	5 822	4 887	7 687	8 603	2 984	4 051	4 083
Slovenia	399	397	388	444	496	585	493	468	499
Slovakia	311	382	515	459	691	891	742	759	889
Finland	670	602	702	1 434	1 473	1 908	1 689	1 718	1 724
Sweden	1 094	1 060	1 323	1 805	1 634	2 218	2 303	2 047	2 101
United Kingdom	7 147	6 975	8 120	7 677	7 309	8 461	11 252	11 262	12 160
Norway	856	831	926	1 199	1 229	1 237	1 620	1 800	1 959
Switzerland	3 053	2 582	2 334	3 118	2 855	2 824	3 359	3 171	3 042

(1) EA-12 instead of EA-15.

Source: Eurostat (aact_eaa01)

Figure 9.3: Agricultural output and gross value added (nominal), EU-27
(2000=100)

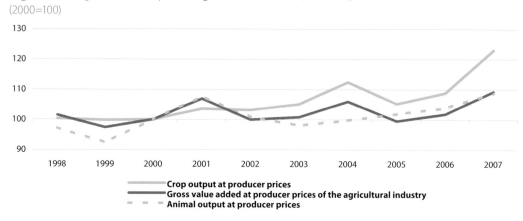

Source: Eurostat (aact_eaa01)

Figure 9.4: Evolution of deflated price indices of agricultural output and means of agricultural production, 2002-07
(average annual growth rate, %)

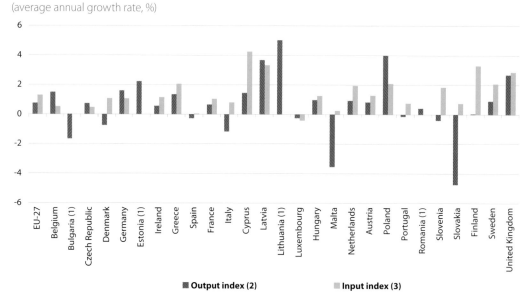

(1) Input index, not available.
(2) Estonia and Cyprus, 2004-07.
(3) Cyprus and Slovakia, 2004-07; EU-27, provisional.

Source: Eurostat (tag00046 and tag00052)

Table 9.5: Price indices of agricultural output (nominal), EU-27

(2000=100)

	2000	2001	2002	2003	2004	2005	2006	2007
CROP OUTPUT (including fruit and vegetables)	100.0	105.7	106.7	114.7	113.0	107.7	116.5	133.1
Cereals (including seeds)	100.0	101.2	93.9	101.0	108.2	90.7	102.6	158.4
Industrial crops	100.0	108.2	106.2	111.4	113.3	105.9	104.1	113.1
Forage plants	100.0	113.7	113.8	116.5	125.6	105.8	103.1	118.6
Vegetables and horticultural products	100.0	105.0	109.3	116.3	107.6	115.1	117.4	121.9
Potatoes (including seeds)	100.0	125.2	126.0	145.7	141.1	128.8	201.4	198.1
Fruits	100.0	109.8	115.3	129.3	124.4	120.4	122.3	134.2
Wine	100.0	95.7	96.6	100.2	102.2	92.3	92.5	98.7
Olive oil	100.0	96.9	105.4	114.3	124.7	146.1	162.9	135.2
Other crop products	100.0	103.2	101.7	106.2	103.9	104.8	107.8	125.1
ANIMAL OUTPUT	100.0	107.4	101.5	101.2	104.1	105.3	107.7	111.9
Animals	100.0	106.1	97.8	97.0	103.5	106.5	110.9	108.2
Cattle	100.0	88.5	94.2	96.6	101.4	108.5	116.7	113.8
Cattle (excluding calves)	100.0	88.6	95.8	97.0	100.4	109.3	116.8	113
Calves	100.0	95.2	96.2	103.4	107.1	103.7	115.4	117.5
Pigs	100.0	119.9	98.4	91.3	102.6	103.7	107.4	98.5
Equines	100.0	111.6	109.6	104.3	102.4	104.5	115.7	117.4
Sheep and goats	100.0	117.4	116.9	119.9	119.6	120.0	122.5	116.1
Poultry	100.0	107.4	101.5	104.4	104.7	103.6	104.0	117.4
Other animals	100.0	109.5	91.4	102.5	102.8	102.5	106.8	96.3
Animal products	100.0	105.8	101.6	102.0	104.8	103.7	103.2	117.2
Milk	100.0	107.8	103.6	103.1	103.7	103.4	101.6	115.3
Eggs	100.0	101.7	102.7	119.4	108.7	102.4	110.9	129.5
Other animal products	100.0	113.2	114.0	105.4	124.0	121.5	129.9	123.2
AGRICULTURAL GOODS (CROP & ANIMAL OUTPUT)	100.0	106.4	103.9	107.9	108.6	106.5	112.2	122.6

Source: Eurostat (apri_pi00_outa)

Table 9.6: Index of income from agricultural activity (indicator A)
(2000=100)

	1997	1998	1999	2000	2001	2002	2003	2004	2005	2006	2007
EU-27	:	:	:	100.0	109.8	104.9	106.6	116.1	105.8	109.6	116.0
Euro area (1)	100.8	98.3	97.2	100.0	103.7	96.6	97.9	99.5	92.4	95.2	103.2
Belgium	99.7	95.2	88.8	100.0	91.7	81.1	89.6	91.1	68.0	70.5	89.5
Bulgaria	:	:	:	100.0	111.8	89.9	84.6	91.9	97.9	94.3	97.0
Czech Republic	:	97.8	82.3	100.0	127.2	99.6	87.3	137.5	152.1	153.9	186.2
Denmark	112.2	81.1	78.5	100.0	119.8	85.3	83.3	93.8	95.3	102.5	107.5
Germany	87.5	78.6	77.8	100.0	124.5	91.9	84.6	122.5	110.9	116.1	139.5
Estonia	76.6	115.0	76.0	100.0	134.2	128.7	136.9	233.3	250.3	236.4	335.3
Ireland	85.3	82.1	76.5	100.0	94.6	82.6	79.1	83.6	99.4	88.5	98.6
Greece	104.9	103.7	102.1	100.0	101.0	97.7	90.1	84.9	86.1	85.3	86.0
Spain	106.5	102.1	95.8	100.0	107.9	104.5	118.1	108.6	96.0	95.4	105.3
France	101.4	105.7	101.3	100.0	100.8	97.7	95.8	94.4	90.0	99.5	110.9
Italy	102.0	99.7	105.5	100.0	98.1	96.4	96.7	97.0	84.6	81.5	79.1
Cyprus	:	:	102.7	100.0	111.9	113.3	108.3	96.8	95.2	99.3	100.3
Latvia	:	132.0	94.8	100.0	129.8	127.7	140.0	233.2	243.0	314.3	336.7
Lithuania	122.8	130.0	105.3	100.0	92.6	86.0	96.6	152.6	191.8	179.4	262.0
Luxembourg	101.6	114.9	105.7	100.0	101.1	101.2	96.0	95.9	97.0	93.1	110.7
Hungary	169.9	135.1	105.1	100.0	107.1	91.0	91.7	144.7	145.6	162.9	174.6
Malta	:	116.5	111.9	100.0	113.0	112.1	106.4	110.9	107.7	107.6	101.8
Netherlands	119.3	106.9	99.1	100.0	93.4	79.6	85.5	79.5	79.0	94.1	92.4
Austria	93.2	91.5	92.7	100.0	117.3	108.4	107.4	112.2	109.7	119.0	132.2
Poland	:	113.7	98.5	100.0	115.0	103.9	96.0	180.8	164.1	181.3	227.7
Portugal	105.6	95.4	117.8	100.0	107.3	102.4	103.5	114.4	104.8	109.4	104.9
Romania	:	158.2	120.9	100.0	174.6	159.7	192.1	278.9	161.0	148.4	123.5
Slovenia	93.3	91.3	89.8	100.0	86.8	114.6	90.3	139.2	139.9	136.4	150.6
Slovakia	111.1	98.5	104.1	100.0	113.6	106.7	100.3	129.7	120.9	147.9	154.0
Finland	80.6	65.8	82.2	100.0	97.0	97.6	103.8	101.5	114.9	110.6	125.0
Sweden	101.1	104.5	91.1	100.0	107.8	119.0	117.5	106.5	105.9	105.6	123.1
United Kingdom	120.2	103.3	100.5	100.0	105.1	117.0	133.3	125.3	119.2	126.7	134.3
Norway	115.4	127.8	115.3	100.0	97.5	102.1	99.3	98.1	80.6	76.2	85.8
Switzerland	98.4	100.9	97.0	100.0	93.0	99.1	92.1	102.8	96.9	94.5	101.3

(1) EA-12 instead of EA-15.

Source: Eurostat (tag00057)

9.3 Agricultural products

Introduction

In October 2007 the Council adopted legislation to establish a single Common Market Organisation (CMO) for agricultural products. This is designed to reduce the volume of legislation in the farming sector, improve legislative transparency, and make agricultural policy more easily accessible. During the course of 2008, the single CMO has replaced 21 CMOs for different products such as bananas, eggs, sugar or wine.

Collecting data on agricultural products is important to understand developments in the markets across Member States, both current (estimated production levels for the current year) and historical (to help distinguish between cycles and changing production patterns for example), and also to analyse the response to policy actions or testing policy scenarios. As predominantly supply side information, agricultural product data are important to understand corresponding price developments (which are of particular interest to agricultural commodity traders and policy analysts) but can also illustrate the consequences of policy decisions taken within agriculture.

Definitions and data availability

Annual statistics on the production of 200 specific crops are mostly covered by Council regulations, although the data for fresh fruit and vegetables are collected under gentlemen's agreements from Member States.

Crop production figures relate to harvested production. **Agricultural production of crops** is harvested production (excluding losses to the harvest). The **harvested production** includes marketed quantities, as well as quantities consumed directly on the farm, losses and waste on the holding, and losses during transport, storage and packaging. **Cereals** include wheat (common wheat and spelt and durum wheat), rye, meslin, barley, oats, mixed grain other than meslin, grain maize, sorghum, triticale, other cereals, and rice. **Vegetables** include brassicas (for example, cabbage, cauliflower and broccoli), other leafy or stalked vegetables (for example, celery, leeks, lettuce, spinach and asparagus), vegetables cultivated for fruit (for example, tomatoes, cucumbers, gherkins, melons, egg plant (aubergine), pumpkins and red pepper), root and tuber vegetables (for example, turnips, carrots, onions, garlic, beetroot and radishes), pulses (for example, peas and beans), cultivated mushrooms, wild products and other fresh vegetables. **Fruit** includes apples, pears, stoned fruits (for example, peaches or apricots), nuts (for example, walnuts or hazelnuts), other top fruits (for example, figs or kiwi), berries, citrus fruits, grapes, olives and wild fruits.

Statistics on milk, eggs and meat products are also compiled according to Community legislation. Milk production covers production on the farm of milk from cows, ewes, goats and buffaloes. A distinction should be made between **milk collected by dairies** and **milk production**

on the farm. Milk collection is only a part of the total use of milk production on the farm, the remainder generally includes domestic consumption, direct sale and cattle feed. **Dairy cows** are female bovines that have calved (including any aged less than 2 years). They are cows kept exclusively or principally for the production of milk for human consumption and/or dairy produce, including cows for slaughter (fattened or not between last lactation and slaughter.

Meat production is based on the **carcass weight** of meat fit for human consumption. The concept of carcass weight varies according to the animal under consideration. For **pigs** (the species Sus), it is the weight of the slaughtered pig's cold body, either whole or divided in half along the mid-line, after being bled and eviscerated and after removal of the tongue, bristles, hooves, genitalia, flare fat, kidneys and diaphragm. Regarding **cattle** (the species Bos taurus), it is the weight of the slaughtered animal's cold body after being skinned, bled and eviscerated, and after removal of the external genitalia, the limbs, the head, the tail, the kidneys and kidney fats, and the udder. For **sheep and goats**, the carcass weight is the slaughtered animal's cold body after having been bled, skinned and eviscerated, and after removal of the head, feet, tail and genital organs; kidneys and kidney fats are included. For **poultry** (defined as hens, chicken, ducks, turkey, guinea fowl and geese), the weight is the cold body of slaughtered farmyard poultry after being bled, plucked and eviscerated; the value includes poultry offal, with the exception of foie gras. For all other animal species, the carcass weight is considered to be the weight of the animal's cold body.

Main findings

The EU-27 produced 258.4 million tonnes of cereals in 2007, of which a little under half (46.0 %) was wheat, more than one fifth (22.1 %) barley, and less than one fifth grain maize (18.4 %). France and Germany were by far the largest cereal, sugar beet and rape producing Member States, together accounting for nearly 40 % of the EU-27's cereal production, over 50 % of its sugar beet production, and over 60 % of its rape production in 2007. While EU-27 production of cereals fluctuated between 2000 and 2007, potatoes and sugar beet production decreased through to 2006, while rape production increased significantly (also to 2006).

In the EU-27, the most important vegetables in terms of production were tomatoes, carrots and onions, while the most important fruits were apples, oranges and peaches. Spain and Italy had the largest vegetables and fruit production, both exceeding 13.5 million tonnes of vegetables and around 20 million tonnes of fruit production. Indeed, together these two Member States produced more fruit than all of the other Member States put together.

The principal meat product in the EU is pig meat (22.9 million tonnes for the EU-27 in 2007), significantly more than other types of meat, such as beef/veal (8.2 million tonnes). A little over one fifth (21.8 %) of pig meat production in the EU-27 came from Germany, the next highest contributions coming from Spain (15.4 %) and France (10.0 %): the 7.9 % share of Denmark is also notable. A little under one fifth (18.7 %) of beef/veal in the EU-27 was produced in France in 2007, with further significant production coming from Germany, Italy, the United Kingdom, Spain and Ireland.

Dairy production is structured quite differently among Member States, both as a result of varying farm and dairy herd sizes as well as yields. However, milk production has been controlled under a system of milk quotas since 1984 that effectively puts a limit on the amount of milk produced. Germany and France have by far the largest quotas, and the 27.3 million tonnes of milk collected in Germany in 2007 was double the third highest level that was collected, in the United Kingdom. One third (32.6 %) of the milk collected in the EU-27 in 2007 was converted into cheese, with butter accounting for the next highest proportion (24.4 %). Only one tenth (10.1 %) of the milk collected was used as drinking milk in 2007.

Figure 9.5: Indices of the agricultural production of crops, EU-27
(2000=100)

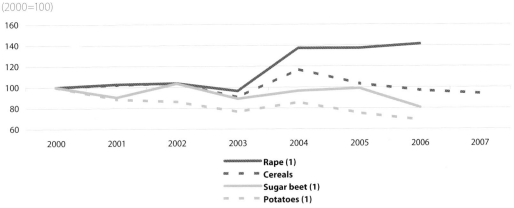

(1) 2007, not available.

Source: Eurostat (tag00104, tag00031, tag00106 and tag00108)

Table 9.7: Agricultural production of crops, 2007
(1 000 tonnes)

	Cereals (1)	Potatoes (2)	Sugar beet (3)	Rape (4)	Vegetables (5)	Fruit (6)
EU-27	258 394	56 769	110 410	15 903	:	:
Euro area	162 521	32 890	:	:	:	:
Belgium	2 787	3 190	5 731	41	1 531	572
Bulgaria	3 171	299	16	93	490	487
Czech Republic	7 153	821	2 890	1 032	296	397
Denmark	8 220	1 626	2 255	596	245	72
Germany	40 632	11 644	25 139	5 321	3 012	2 425
Estonia	860	143	0	109	72	7
Ireland	1 980	455	45	12	274	18
Greece	3 622	830	862	:	3 575	5 423
Spain	23 305	2 518	5 297	35	13 575	19 810
France	59 248	7 206	33 213	4 684	5 654	10 141
Italy	18 756	1 782	4 630	15	13 550	20 722
Cyprus	44	143	:	:	144	226
Latvia	1 535	630	11	212	141	37
Lithuania	3 017	572	800	312	239	57
Luxembourg	148	20	0	18	2	23
Hungary	9 659	536	1 676	494	1 760	900
Malta	:	19	:	:	67	9
Netherlands	1 623	6 870	5 512	12	4 356	708
Austria	4 758	669	2 656	145	549	1 180
Poland	27 143	11 791	12 682	2 130	4 420	1 694
Portugal	948	639	320	:	1 671	2 159
Romania	7 910	3 708	753	349	2 145	2 124
Slovenia	532	131	262	15	65	277
Slovakia	2 793	288	847	321	99	95
Finland	4 137	702	673	114	245	16
Sweden	5 058	790	2 189	223	227	32
United Kingdom	19 354	5 684	7 150	1 896	2 503	398
Croatia	2 534	296	1 583	39	191	269
FYR of Macedonia	453	181	8	0	696	:
Turkey	30 427	4 246	12 415	29	24 671	14 399
Iceland	3	9	:	:	:	:
Norway	1 229	317	:	11	:	33
Switzerland	1 049	490	1 584	68	:	:

(1) Norway, 2006; Turkey, 2003; Iceland, 1997.
(2) EU-27, euro area, Malta and the United Kingdom, 2006; Norway, 2005; Iceland, 1998.
(3) EU-27, Slovenia, Sweden and the United Kingdom, 2006.
(4) Ireland, 2008; EU-27, 2006; Norway, 2005.
(5) Denmark and France, 2006; Spain, 2005; Belgium, the Czech Republic, Poland and Portugal, 2003; Sweden, 2002; the former Yugoslav Republic of Macedonia, 2001; Germany and Ireland, 2000.
(6) Denmark, Greece, France and Norway, 2006; Spain and Romania, 2005; Germany and Portugal, 2003; Belgium and Sweden, 2002; the Czech Republic, 2001; Ireland and the Netherlands, 2000.

Source: Eurostat (tag00031, tag00108, tag00106, tag00104, tag00097 and tag00112)

Figure 9.6: Production of cereals (including rice), EU-27, 2007 (1)
(%)

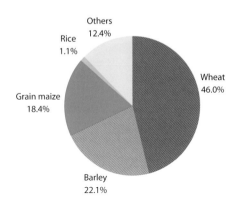

(1) Provisional.

Source: Eurostat (apro_cpp_crop)

Figure 9.7: Breakdown of production of vegetables, EU, 2007 (1)
(% of total, based on tonnes)

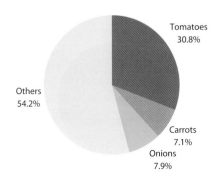

(1) EU based on available data: Denmark and France, 2006; Spain, 2005; excluding Belgium, the Czech Republic, Germany, Ireland, Poland and Portugal.

Source: Eurostat (tag00035, tag00110, tag00111 and tag00097)

Figure 9.8: Breakdown of production of fruit, EU, 2007 (1)

(% of total, based on tonnes)

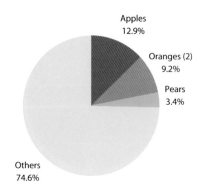

(1) EU based on available data: Denmark, Greece and France, 2006; Spain and Romania, 2005; excluding Belgium, Bulgaria, the Czech Republic, Germany, Estonia, Ireland, the Netherlands, Portugal, Finland and Sweden.
(2) Member States not reporting any production are assumed to have negligible or no production of oranges.

Source: Eurostat (tag00036, tag00114, tag00113 and tag00112)

Figure 9.9: Utilisation of milk, EU, 2007 (1)

(%)

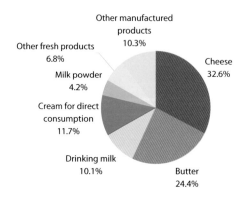

(1) Figures do not sum to 100 % due to rounding; EU excluding Bulgaria, Ireland, Greece, Italy, Luxembourg, Austria, Slovenia and the United Kingdom; Sweden, 2006.

Source: Eurostat (apro_mk_pobta)

Table 9.8: Agricultural production related to animals, 2007

(1 000 tonnes)

	Collection of cows' milk (1)	Butter (2)	Cheese (3)	Meat: cattle (4)	Meat: pigs (4)	Meat: sheep & goats (5)
EU-27	132 641	43 846	8 539	8 203	22 858	:
Euro area	93 003	1 621	6 580	6 245	16 278	:
Belgium	2 879	102	70	273	1 063	1
Bulgaria	746	2	78	6	41	:
Czech Republic	2 446	37	116	79	360	2
Denmark	4 484	109	351	130	1 802	2
Germany	27 321	445	1 927	1 185	4 985	44
Estonia	593	7	32	15	38	:
Ireland	5 241	223	:	581	205	70
Greece	670	2	154	58	122	114
Spain	5 729	39	309	658	3 513	238
France	22 967	396	1 884	1 532	2 281	129
Italy	10 090	117	1 154	1 127	1 603	66
Cyprus	144	0	11	4	55	7
Latvia	631	7	35	23	40	0
Lithuania	1 347	14	90	56	99	1
Luxembourg	259	:	:	9	10	0
Hungary	1 448	8	72	35	499	1
Malta	41	0	3	1	8	0
Netherlands	10 799	174	732	386	1 290	5
Austria	2 661	33	145	216	531	0
Poland	8 744	162	594	365	2 091	1
Portugal	1 837	28	69	91	364	13
Romania	1 136	8	69	211	491	:
Slovenia	530	3	20	36	33	0
Slovakia	964	10	44	23	114	1
Finland	2 293	55	102	89	213	1
Sweden	3 130	41 752	119	134	265	4
United Kingdom	13 647	121	339	882	739	330
Croatia	673	:	:	55	156	1
FYR of Macedonia	42	:	:	23	21	1
Iceland	113	2	4	:	:	4
Norway	1 686	:	83	:	:	330

(1) EU-27, euro area, Greece and Sweden, 2006; Iceland, 2005; the former Yugoslav Republic of Macedonia, 1996.
(2) EU-27, euro area, excluding Luxembourg and Malta; EU-27, euro area, Greece, Slovenia and Sweden, 2006; Iceland, 2005.
(3) EU-27, euro area, excluding Ireland and Luxembourg; EU-27, euro area, Greece, Italy, Slovenia and Sweden, 2006; Iceland, 2005; Norway, 1996.
(4) The former Yugoslav Republic of Macedonia, 1999.
(5) Croatia, 2006.

Source: Eurostat (tag00037, tag00038, tag00040, tag00044, tag00042 and tag00045)

9.4 Agriculture and the environment

Introduction

Around 40 % of the EU's land area is farmed. This fact alone highlights the importance of farming for the EU's natural environment. The links between the two, however, are complex. On the one hand, farming has contributed over the centuries to creating and maintaining a variety of valuable semi-natural habitats and agricultural landscapes. While many of these are maintained by different farming practices and a wide range of wild species rely on this for their survival, agriculture can also have an adverse impact on natural resources. Pollution of soil, water and air, fragmentation of habitats, and a loss of wildlife can result from agricultural practices and land use. This complex relationship has necessitated the integration of environmental concerns and safeguards into the Common Agricultural Policy (CAP), with particular attention paid to reducing the risks of environmental degradation through cross-compliance criteria (as a condition for benefiting from direct payments, farmers must comply with certain requirements, some related to environmental protection), incentives and targeted environmental measures, while encouraging farmers to continue to play a positive role to enhance the sustainability of agro-ecosystems.

The importance attached to assessing the interaction between agriculture and the environment is underlined by the fact that the Commission adopted a list of 28 agri-environmental indicators [1] in 2006.

Definitions and data availability

Organic farming can be defined as a method of production which places the highest emphasis on environmental protection and animal welfare considerations. In the EU, farming is only considered to be organic if it complies with Council Regulation (EEC) No 2092/91. Organic farming involves holistic production management systems for crops and livestock, emphasising the use of management practices in preference to the use of off-farm inputs. This is accomplished by using, where possible, cultural, biological and mechanical methods in preference to synthetic chemical units such as fertilisers, pesticides (fungicides, herbicides and insecticides), additives and medicinal products

The **irrigable area** is that which is equipped for irrigation – the actual amount of land irrigated varies depending, for example, on meteorological conditions or the choice of crop. Over-exploitation of water can lead to the drying-out of natural areas, and to salt-water intrusion in coastal aquifers.

The **livestock density index** measures the stock of animals per hectare. It is the ratio of the livestock units (converted from the number of animals using standard coefficients) per hectare of utilised agricultural area. A **livestock unit (LSU)** is a reference unit which facilitates the aggregation of livestock from various species and ages. Eurofarm LSU coefficients are established by convention (originally,

(1) COM(2006) 508 final.

they were related to the animals' feed requirements, the reference being a dairy cow with an annual yield of 3 000 kg of milk, without additional concentrated feedingstuffs). In the interpretation of the livestock density index, the limits of this theoretical unit are to be taken into account. The livestock species aggregated in the LSU total, for the purpose of the indicator in this publication are: equidae, cattle, sheep, goats, pigs, poultry and rabbits.

Main findings

There is increasing consumer awareness and interest in food production and distribution, for example, concerning where and how food is produced, and how it moves from the farm to the fork. As an example of a sustainable farming system, many agricultural holdings have converted to certified organic production methods. Just over 4.3 % of the utilised agricultural area in the EU-27 was classified as organic agricultural production in 2005, ranging from 11.0 % in Austria and 8.4 % in Italy to below 1 % in Ireland, Poland and Malta.

The proportion of agricultural area that is irrigable is, unsurprisingly, particularly high in the southern Member States, notably Greece, Italy, Cyprus and Malta, where irrigation is essential for many types of agriculture. Supplementary irrigation is also used to improve production elsewhere, and large irrigable areas are also found in the Netherlands.

Plant and animal protection products are important in agriculture to preserve crops and maintain healthy livestock, but their intensive use can have negative environmental impacts, and this depends to some extent on whether or not such products are used properly. Total sales of pesticides vary greatly across the Member States, from particularly high levels in Malta and to a lesser extent in Italy and Belgium (above 6 kg per hectare of utilised agricultural area) to relatively low levels in Sweden and Estonia (0.5 kg per hectare or less). To some degree, these differences reflect the climatic conditions, the types of farming that are practised, and varying price of pesticides.

Figure 9.10: Area occupied by organic farming, 2005 (1)
(% of UAA)

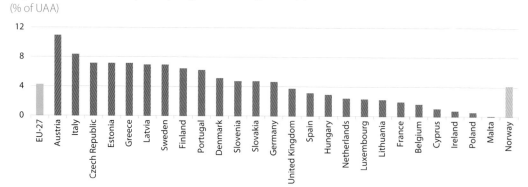

(1) EU-27, Luxembourg and Poland, estimates; Bulgaria and Romania, not available.

Source: Eurostat (food_in_porg1)

Figure 9.11: Sales of pesticides (1)
(kg of active ingredient per hectare of utilised agricultural area)

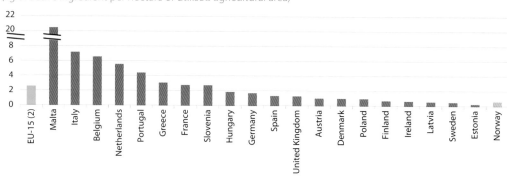

(1) Finland, Sweden, the United Kingdom and Norway, 2006; Germany, Austria, Portugal and Slovenia, 2005; Estonia, 2004; Ireland and Malta, 2003; Belgium, Denmark, Italy and Hungary, 2002; EU-15, Greece and Spain, 2001; remaining Member States, not available; for some Member States the UAA of a different reference year has been used as the denominator.
(2) Excluding Luxembourg.

Source: Eurostat (tag00084 and ef_lu_ovcropesu)

Table 9.9: Environmental and agricultural indicators, 2005

	Utilised agricultural area (UAA) (1 000 hectares)	Organic crop area (fully converted) (% UAA)	Total organic area (% UAA) (1)	Irrigable area (% UAA)	Livestock density index (livestock units per km²)
EU-27	156 039	:	:	:	0.8
Euro area	103 722	:	4.2	:	:
Belgium	1 386	1.4	1.7	1.6	2.8
Bulgaria	2 729	:	:	4.1	0.5
Czech Republic	3 558	6.4	7.2	1.3	0.6
Denmark	2 708	4.9	5.0	16.6	1.7
Germany	17 035	:	4.7	:	1.1
Estonia	829	4.4	7.2	:	0.4
Ireland	4 219	0.6	0.8	0.0	1.5
Greece	3 984	5.2	7.2	40.0	0.6
Spain	24 855	1.9	3.2	15.1	0.6
France	27 591	:	2.0	9.8	0.8
Italy	12 708	5.8	8.4	31.3	0.8
Cyprus	152	0.2	1.1	30.3	1.6
Latvia	1 702	1.2	7.0	0.0	0.3
Lithuania	2 792	0.5	2.3	0.2	0.5
Luxembourg	129	:	:	0.0	1.2
Hungary	4 267	2.0	3.0	3.6	0.6
Malta	10	0.0	0.1	29.5	4.5
Netherlands	1 958	2.4	2.5	20.8	3.3
Austria	3 266	:	11.0	3.7	0.8
Poland	14 755	:	:	0.8	0.7
Portugal	3 680	3.0	6.3	16.8	0.6
Romania	13 907	:	:	5.8	0.5
Slovenia	485	3.3	4.8	0.9	1.1
Slovakia	1 879	1.4	4.8	9.6	0.4
Finland	2 264	6.0	6.5	3.1	0.5
Sweden	3 192	6.3	7.0	5.2	0.6
United Kingdom	15 957	3.3	3.8	1.3	0.9
Norway	1 035	3.5	4.2	11.3	1.2
Switzerland	1 062	:	:	0.0	1.7

(1) Euro area, excluding Luxembourg; data for total organic area, fully converted area and area under conversion.

Source: Eurostat (ef_lu_ovcropesu, food_in_porg1, tag00095 and tsdpc450)

9.5 Forestry

Introduction

In 2006 the Commission underpinned its support for enhancing sustainable forest management and the multifunctional role of forests by adopting an EU forest action plan. The action plan provides a framework for forest-related actions and will serve as an instrument of coordination between Community actions and the forest policies of the Member States, with 18 key actions proposed by the Commission to be implemented jointly with the Member States during the period 2007-2011. The Action Plan focuses on four main objectives:

- improving long-term competitiveness;
- improving and protecting the environment;
- contributing to the quality of life;
- fostering coordination and communication.

Definitions and data availability

An Intersecretariat Working Group (IWG) brings together Eurostat, the United Nations Economic Commission for Europe (UNECE), the Food and Agriculture Organisation of the United Nations (FAO) and the International Tropical Timber Organisation (ITTO) in collecting forest sector statistics; other Directorates-General of the European Commission are also represented. Within this context, the primary tool for statistical cooperation is the joint Eurostat/UNECE/FAO/ITTO forest sector questionnaire (JFSQ), which is used by all organisations; each agency collects data from the countries for which it is responsible. Eurostat is responsible for data from the EU Member States and EFTA countries.

Forest is defined as land with tree crown cover (or equivalent stocking level) of more than 10 % and area of more than 0.5 ha. The trees should be able to reach a minimum height of 5 m at maturity in situ.

Roundwood production is a synonym for **removals**; it comprises all quantities of wood removed from the forest and other wooded land or other felling site during a given time period; it is reported in cubic metres underbark (i.e. excluding bark). **Sawnwood production** is wood that has been produced either by sawing lengthways or by a profile-chipping process and that exceeds 6 mm in thickness; it includes planks, beams, joists, boards, rafters, scantlings, laths, boxboards and lumber, etc., in the following forms: unplaned, planed, end-jointed, etc; it is reported in cubic metres solid volume (m³).

Paper and paperboard is the sum of: graphic papers; newsprint; sanitary and household papers; packaging materials and other paper and paperboard; it excludes manufactured paper products such as boxes, cartons, books and magazines, etc.

The **degree of defoliation** is the extent of visually assessed defoliation of trees is based on a method developed by the International Cooperative Programme of the Executive Committee for the Convention on Long-range Transboundary Air Pollution in Europe. Damage is classed on a scale from 0 to 4. No defoliation (class 0) – covers up to and including 10 % needle/leaf loss. Slight (warning stage) defoliation (class 1) – covers more than 10 % and up to 25 % needle/leaf loss. Moderate defoliation (class 2) – covers more than 25 % and up to 60 % needle/leaf loss. Severe defoliation (class 3) – covers more than 60 % and up to 100 % needle/leaf loss. Dead (class 4) – covers 100 % defoliation.

Main findings

The EU-27 had a total area of forests and other wooded land of 176.7 million hectares in 2005, equivalent to approximately 42 % of its land area. The largest forest and wooded land areas were in Sweden, Spain and Finland, and in all three of these Member States, as well as in Estonia, Greece and Slovenia, forest and wooded land areas made up more than half of the total land area, with Latvia and Austria recording shares just below 50 %.

After strong growth in the volume of EU-27 roundwood production in 2005, it dropped in 2006 to 425 million cubic metres. Sweden, Germany, France and Finland each recorded volumes in excess of 50 million cubic metres in all of the years from 2005 to 2007, and were clearly the largest producers. In terms of roundwood production per capita, Finland and Sweden were the most specialised Member States, followed by Latvia, Estonia and Austria.

Roundwood production can be divided into coniferous and non-coniferous species, with the former generally referred to as softwood, and the latter as broadleaved or hardwood. Almost 80 % of roundwood production in the EU-27 in 2006 was from coniferous species. There has also been growth in the volume of EU-27 sawnwood production in recent years, reaching 112 million cubic metres by 2006, almost 10 % more than in 2003.

The production of paper and paperboard in the EU-27 reached 102 million tonnes in 2006, 4.3 % higher than the previous year, continuing an upward trend in output that started in 2002. Relative to its size (in population terms), Finland had by far the highest output of paper and paperboard in 2007, some 2.7 tonnes per capita, more than double the level in Sweden, and more than four times the level of the third most specialised producer, Austria.

Between one fifth and one quarter of forest and woodland trees suffered from moderate or worse defoliation in the EU in 2006. More than one third of trees suffered from such defoliation in France and Bulgaria, with this proportion above 40 % in Luxembourg and just over 50 % in the Czech Republic.

Table 9.10: Wood production
(1 000 m³)

	Roundwood production					Sawnwood production				
	2003	2004	2005	2006	2007	2003	2004	2005	2006	2007
EU-27	387 181	393 668	454 120	425 448	:	102 074	105 864	108 072	111 962	:
Euro area	202 327	207 858	237 029	242 152	:	61 286	63 647	64 683	67 497	:
Belgium	4 765	4 850	4 950	4 230	4 100	1 215	1 235	1 285	1 520	1 555
Bulgaria	4 833	5 986	5 862	5 992	599	332	569	569	569	569
Czech Republic	15 140	15 601	15 510	17 678	18 508	3 805	3 940	4 003	5 080	5 454
Denmark	1 627	1 516	2 962	2 358	:	248	196	196	196	:
Germany	51 182	54 504	56 946	62 290	76 728	17 596	19 538	21 931	24 420	25 170
Estonia	10 500	6 800	5 500	5 400	5 900	1 954	2 029	2 063	1 923	1 800
Ireland	2 683	2 562	2 648	2 672	2 710	1 005	939	1 015	1 094	985
Greece	1 673	1 694	1 523	1 523	:	191	191	191	191	:
Spain	16 105	16 290	15 531	15 716	14 528	3 630	3 730	3 660	3 806	3 332
France	32 828	33 647	63 171	61 790	62 759	9 539	9 774	9 715	9 992	10 190
Italy	8 219	8 697	8 691	8 618	8 125	1 590	1 580	1 590	1 748	1 700
Cyprus	12	10	10	7	20	6	5	4	4	9
Latvia	12 916	12 754	12 843	12 845	12 173	3 951	3 988	4 227	4 320	3 459
Lithuania	6 275	6 120	6 045	5 870	6 195	1 400	1 450	1 445	1 466	1 380
Luxembourg	257	277	249	268	:	133	133	133	133	:
Hungary	5 785	5 660	5 940	5 913	5 640	299	205	215	186	235
Malta	0	0	0	0	0	0	0	0	0	0
Netherlands	1 044	1 026	1 110	1 107	1 022	269	273	279	265	271
Austria	17 055	16 483	16 471	19 135	21 317	10 473	11 133	11 074	10 507	11 262
Poland	30 836	32 733	31 945	32 384	35 653	3 360	3 743	3 360	3 607	4 100
Portugal	9 673	10 869	10 746	10 805	:	1 383	1 060	1 010	1 010	:
Romania	15 440	15 809	14 501	13 970	15 341	4 246	4 588	4 321	3 476	4 050
Slovenia	2 591	2 551	2 733	3 179	2 882	511	512	527	580	580
Slovakia	6 355	7 240	9 302	7 869	8 131	1 651	1 837	2 621	2 440	2 781
Finland	54 240	54 398	52 250	50 812	56 870	13 745	13 544	12 269	12 227	12 477
Sweden	67 100	67 300	98 200	64 600	77 200	16 800	16 900	17 600	18 300	18 600
United Kingdom	8 046	8 291	8 482	8 417	8 962	2 742	2 772	2 770	2 902	3 142
Croatia	3 847	3 841	4 018	4 452	:	585	582	624	669	:
Turkey	15 810	16 503	16 185	16 813	:	5 615	6 215	6 445	7 079	:
Iceland	0	0	0	0	0	0	0	0	0	0
Norway	8 298	8 782	9 667	8 594	10 514	2 186	2 230	2 326	2 389	2 339
Switzerland	5 120	5 132	5 285	5 702	:	1 345	1 505	1 591	1 668	:
Canada	179 642	208 406	211 501	205 893	:	56 892	60 952	60 187	58 709	:
Russia	174 000	178 400	185 000	190 600	:	20 155	21 380	22 033	22 500	:
United States	448 513	461 739	467 347	472 618	:	86 159	93 067	97 020	93 016	:

Source: Eurostat (tag00072 and tag00073), UNECE

Table 9.11: Wood production (1)

	Roundwood						Sawnwood production per capita (m³)	
	Production per capita (m³)		Coniferous production (million m³ under bark)		Non-coniferous production (million m³ under bark)			
	2002	2007	2002	2007	2002	2007	2002	2007
EU-27	0.8	0.9	248.8	263.1	73.6	74.1	0.2	0.2
Euro area	0.6	0.8	125.6	138.6	39.8	42.0	0.2	0.2
Belgium	0.4	0.4	3.0	3.2	1.0	1.0	0.1	0.1
Bulgaria	0.6	0.8	1.3	1.9	1.4	1.3	0.0	0.1
Czech Republic	1.4	1.8	12.4	15.9	1.2	0.9	0.4	0.5
Denmark	0.3	0.4	0.6	1.1	0.2	0.1	0.0	0.0
Germany	0.5	0.9	30.0	59.2	7.8	8.9	0.2	0.3
Estonia	7.7	4.4	5.9	3.2	2.7	1.5	1.3	1.3
Ireland	0.7	0.6	2.6	2.7	0.0	0.0	0.2	0.2
Greece	0.1	0.1	0.3	0.3	0.2	0.2	0.0	0.0
Spain	0.4	0.3	8.6	6.6	5.3	5.9	0.1	0.1
France	0.6	1.0	21.8	19.8	10.9	9.6	0.2	0.2
Italy	0.1	0.1	1.0	1.4	1.6	1.6	0.0	0.0
Cyprus	0.0	0.0	0.0	0.0	0.0	0.0	0.0	0.0
Latvia	5.7	5.3	7.9	7.1	4.4	4.0	1.7	1.5
Lithuania	1.8	1.8	2.8	2.8	2.1	2.1	0.4	0.4
Luxembourg	0.6	0.6	0.1	0.1	0.1	0.1	0.3	0.3
Hungary	0.6	0.6	0.6	0.6	2.9	2.1	0.0	0.0
Malta	0.0	0.0	0.0	0.0	0.0	0.0	0.0	0.0
Netherlands	0.1	0.1	0.5	0.5	0.2	0.2	0.0	0.0
Austria	1.8	2.6	10.9	15.6	0.9	1.0	1.3	1.4
Poland	0.7	0.9	18.7	25.2	6.3	7.0	0.1	0.1
Portugal	0.8	1.0	3.1	3.5	5.1	6.7	0.1	0.1
Romania	0.7	0.7	6.0	5.9	6.1	5.7	0.2	0.2
Slovenia	1.1	1.4	1.3	1.7	0.7	0.4	0.3	0.3
Slovakia	1.1	1.5	2.8	4.8	2.8	2.9	0.2	0.5
Finland	10.3	10.8	42.5	44.9	6.1	6.8	2.6	2.4
Sweden	7.5	8.5	57.2	66.5	3.5	4.8	1.8	2.0
United Kingdom	0.1	0.1	7.1	8.4	0.4	0.1	0.0	0.1
Croatia	0.8	1.0	0.5	0.7	2.4	2.8	0.1	0.2
Turkey	0.2	0.2	6.3	7.0	4.9	5.3	0.1	0.1
Iceland	0.0	0.0	0.0	0.0	0.0	0.0	0.0	0.0
Norway	1.9	2.2	7.4	8.1	0.1	0.1	0.5	0.5
Switzerland	0.6	0.8	3.1	3.7	0.5	0.5	0.2	0.2
Canada	6.3	6.3	161.5	160.4	33.7	42.7	1.9	1.8
Russia	1.1	1.3	81.2	107.8	37.4	36.8	0.1	0.2
United States	1.6	1.6	275.4	303.6	129.6	124.2	0.3	0.3

(1) EU-27, euro area, Denmark, Greece, Luxembourg, Portugal, Croatia, Turkey, Switzerland, Canada, Russia and the United States, 2006 instead of 2007.

Source: Eurostat (tag00072, for_rdw51, tag00073 and tps00001); UNECE

Table 9.12: Total paper and paperboard production
(1 000 tonnes)

	1997	1998	1999	2000	2001	2002	2003	2004	2005	2006	2007
EU-27	80 286	82 151	84 782	89 698	88 028	90 545	92 646	97 289	97 584	101 788	:
Euro area	:	:	63 333	67 276	65 739	68 053	69 562	73 129	73 304	77 139	:
Belgium (1)	1 618	1 831	1 666	1 727	1 662	1 704	1 919	1 957	1 897	1 897	:
Bulgaria	153	153	126	136	171	171	171	326	326	326	330
Czech Republic	750	768	770	804	864	870	920	934	969	1 042	1 023
Denmark	390	393	397	263	389	384	388	402	423	423	:
Germany	15 911	16 311	16 742	18 182	17 879	18 526	19 310	20 391	21 679	22 656	23 172
Estonia	38	43	48	54	70	75	64	66	64	73	68
Ireland	42	42	42	43	43	44	45	45	45	45	45
Greece	604	622	352	496	495	493	493	510	510	510	:
Spain	3 668	3 545	4 436	4 765	5 131	5 365	5 437	5 526	5 697	6 893	6 714
France	8 867	9 161	9 603	10 006	9 625	9 809	9 939	10 255	10 332	10 006	9 871
Italy	7 929	8 254	8 568	9 129	8 926	9 317	9 491	9 667	9 999	10 008	10 112
Cyprus	0	0	0	0	0	0	0	0	0	0	0
Latvia	21	18	19	16	24	33	38	38	39	57	60
Lithuania	42	37	37	53	68	78	92	99	113	119	124
Luxembourg (2)	:	:	0	0	0	0	0	0	0	0	:
Hungary	410	482	473	506	495	517	546	579	571	553	552
Malta	0	0	0	0	0	0	0	0	0	0	0
Netherlands	3 130	3 180	3 256	3 333	3 174	3 346	3 339	3 459	3 471	3 367	3 219
Austria	3 884	4 009	4 141	4 385	4 250	4 419	4 565	4 852	4 950	5 213	5 199
Poland	1 660	1 718	1 839	1 934	2 086	2 342	2 461	2 635	2 732	2 857	2 947
Portugal	1 114	1 136	1 163	1 290	1 419	1 537	1 530	1 664	1 570	1 644	:
Romania	298	301	289	340	395	370	443	454	371	432	558
Slovenia	430	491	417	411	633	704	436	767	763	760	765
Slovakia	674	597	803	925	988	710	674	798	858	888	915
Finland	12 519	12 703	12 947	13 509	12 502	12 789	13 058	14 036	12 391	14 140	14 334
Sweden	9 654	9 879	10 071	10 786	10 534	10 724	11 061	11 589	11 775	12 066	11 902
United Kingdom	6 481	6 477	6 576	6 605	6 204	6 218	6 226	6 240	6 039	5 813	5 463
Croatia	395	403	417	406	451	467	463	464	592	564	:
Turkey	1 282	1 357	1 349	1 567	1 513	1 643	1 643	1 643	1 643	1 643	:
Iceland	0	0	:	:	:	:	:	:	:	0	0
Norway	2 162	2 260	2 241	2 300	2 220	2 114	2 186	2 294	2 223	2 109	2 010
Switzerland	1 462	1 592	1 755	1 616	1 750	1 805	1 818	1 777	1 751	1 685	:
Canada	18 730	18 875	20 280	20 921	19 834	20 073	19 964	20 462	19 498	18 176	:
Russian Federation	2 960	3 595	4 535	5 310	5 625	5 978	6 377	6 830	7 126	7 451	:
United States	86 916	86 469	88 670	86 252	81 249	81 879	80 712	82 084	83 697	84 317	:

(1) 1997-98, including Luxembourg.
(2) 1997-98, included within Belgium.

Source: Eurostat (tag00074), UNECE

Figure 9.12: Paper and paperboard production per capita, 2007 (1)

(tonnes)

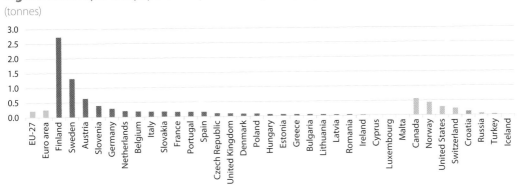

(1) EU-27, euro area, Denmark, Greece, Luxembourg, Portugal, Croatia, Turkey, Switzerland, Canada, Russia and the United States, 2006; includes estimates and provisional data.

Source: Eurostat (tag00074 and tps00001), UNECE

Figure 9.13: Forest trees damaged by defoliation, 2006 (1)

(%)

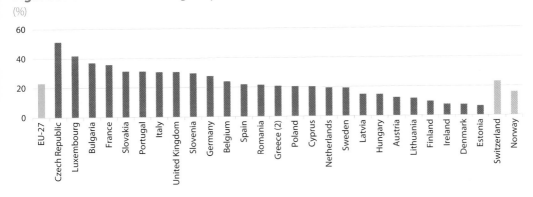

(1) Malta, not available.
(2) 2005.

Source: Eurostat (tsdnr530)

9.6 Fisheries

Introduction

The first common European policy measures in the fishing sector date from 1970. They set rules for access to fishing grounds, markets and structures. All these measures became more significant when, in 1976, Member States followed an international movement and agreed to extend their rights to marine resources from 12 to 200 miles from their coasts. After years of difficult negotiations, the common fisheries policy (CFP), the EU's instrument for the management of fisheries and aquaculture, was born in 1983.

The EU has a common fisheries policy in order to manage fisheries for the benefit of both fishing communities and consumers, and for the protection of resources. Common measures are agreed in four main areas:

- conservation – to protect fish resources by regulating the amount of fish taken from the sea, by allowing young fish to reproduce, and by ensuring that measures are respected;
- structures – to help the fishing and aquaculture sectors adapt their equipment and organisations to the constraints imposed by scarce resources and the market;
- markets – to maintain a common organisation of the market in fish products and to match supply and demand for the benefit of both producers and consumers;

- relations with the outside world – to set-up fisheries agreements and to negotiate at an international level within regional and international fisheries organisations for common conservation measures in deep-sea fisheries.

The CFP sets maximum quantities of fish that can be safely caught every year: the total allowable catch (TAC). Each country's share is called a national quota.

The 2002 reform of the CFP identified the need to limit fishing efforts, the level of catches, and to enforce certain technical measures. The European Fisheries Fund (EFF) has a budget of around EUR 3.8 billion and covers the period 2007-13. It aims to support the objectives of the (CFP) by:

- supporting sustainable exploitation of fisheries resources and a stable balance between these resources and the capacity of Community fishing fleet;
- strengthening the competitiveness and the viability of operators in the sector;
- promoting environmentally-friendly fishing and production methods;
- providing adequate support to people employed in the sector;
- fostering the sustainable development of fisheries areas.

Definitions and data availability

Fishery statistics are derived from official national sources either directly by Eurostat for the members of the European Economic Area (EEA) or indirectly through other international organisations for other countries. The data are collected using internationally agreed concepts and definitions developed by the Coordinating Working Party on Fishery Statistics, comprising Eurostat and several other international organisations with responsibilities in fishery statistics. The flag of the fishing vessel is used as the primary indication of the nationality of the catch, though this concept may be varied in certain circumstances.

In general, the data refer to the **fishing fleet** size on 31 December of the reference year. The data are derived from the national registers of fishing vessels which are maintained pursuant to Council Regulation (EC) No 26/2004 which contains information on the vessel characteristics to be recorded on the registers - the administrative file of fishing vessels maintained by the European Commission's Directorate-General for Maritime Affairs and Fisheries. There has been a transition in measuring the tonnage of the fishing fleet from gross registered tonnage (GRT) to that of gross tonnage (GT). This change, which has taken place at different speeds within the national administrations, gives rise to the possibility of non-comparability of data over time and of non-comparability between countries.

Catches of fishery products (fish, molluscs, crustaceans and other aquatic animals, residues and aquatic plants) includes items taken for all purposes (commercial, industrial, recreational and subsistence) by all types and classes of fishing units (fishermen, vessels, gear, etc.) operating both in inland, fresh and brackish water areas, and in inshore, offshore and high-seas fishing areas. The catch is normally expressed in **live weight** and derived by the application of conversion factors to the landed or product weight. As such, catch statistics exclude quantities which are caught and taken from the water (that is, before processing) but which, for a variety of reasons, are not landed. The production from aquaculture (see below) is excluded.

Geographical **fishing areas** are defined for a number of specific areas of water, including: the north-east Atlantic, which is roughly the area to the east of 42°W longitude and north of 36°N latitude, including the waters of the Baltic Sea; the north-west Atlantic, which is the region that is roughly the area to the west of 42°W longitude and north of 35°N latitude; the eastern central Atlantic, which is the region to the east of 40°W longitude between latitudes 36°N and 6°S; the Mediterranean, which is also known as FAO Major Fishing Area 37, comprises the Mediterranean Sea and the adjacent Black Sea.

Aquaculture is the farming of aquatic organisms including fish, molluscs, crustaceans and aquatic plants. Farming implies some form of intervention in the rearing process to enhance production, such as regular stocking, feeding and protection from predators. Farming also implies individual or corporate ownership of, or rights resulting from contractual arrangements to, the stock being cultivated.

Main findings

In terms of power, Italy had the largest fishing fleet among the EU-27 Member States, but only slightly larger than France and Spain. In terms of gross tonnage, Spain had by far the largest fleet, more than double the size of the fleets in the United Kingdom, France and Italy.

Collectively Denmark, Spain, the United Kingdom, France and the Netherlands accounted for three fifths of the EU-27's catch in 2006. This combined share has

fallen recently, as it was around two thirds in 2000, and the fall is mainly because of a reduction in the share of the Danish and Spanish catches. Since 1997, the total EU-27 catch has fallen every year except in 2001, with the catch in 2006 nearly 30 % lower than in 1997. Three quarters of the catches made by the EU-27 in 2006 were in the North-East Atlantic, with the Mediterranean the second largest fishing area.

The level of aquaculture production in the EU remained relatively stable between 1.2 million tonnes and 1.4 million tonnes during the period 1996 to 2005. France, Spain, Italy, the United Kingdom and Greece together accounted for nearly three quarters of the EU-27's aquaculture production in 2005. Between 1996 and 2006 Greece recorded a particularly large increase in aquaculture production, nearly trebling, while the opposite trend was observed in Germany and the Netherlands, with output more than halving.

Figure 9.14: Fishing fleet, 2007 (1)

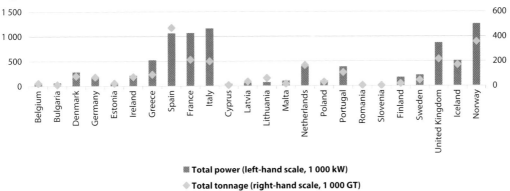

■ Total power (left-hand scale, 1 000 kW)

◆ Total tonnage (right-hand scale, 1 000 GT)

(1) In 2007, EU-27 total power was 7 011 719 kW and total tonnage was 1 920 654 GT; the Czech Republic, Luxembourg, Hungary, Austria and Slovakia are landlocked countries without a marine fishing fleet.

Source: Eurostat (tsdnr420 and tag00083), Directorate-General for Maritime Affairs and Fisheries

Figure 9.15: Catches by fishing region, EU-27, 2006

(%, based on tonnes)

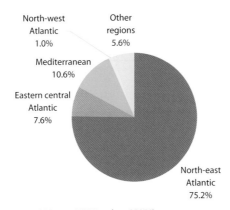

Source: Eurostat (tag00078, tag00080, tag00081, tag00079 and tag00076)

Table 9.13: Total catches in all fishing regions
(1 000 tonnes live weight)

	1996	1997	1998	1999	2000	2001	2002	2003	2004	2005	2006
EU-27	7 427	7 525	7 285	6 880	6 794	6 933	6 339	5 901	5 874	5 631	5 312
Euro area	3 795	3 795	3 824	3 707	3 598	3 734	3 287	3 379	3 264	3 223	3 028
Belgium	31	31	31	30	30	30	29	27	27	25	23
Bulgaria	9	11	19	11	7	7	15	12	8	5	8
Czech Republic	4	3	4	4	5	5	5	5	5	4	5
Denmark	1 681	1 827	1 557	1 405	1 534	1 511	1 442	1 031	1 090	911	868
Germany	237	259	267	239	205	211	224	261	262	286	279
Estonia	109	124	119	112	113	105	101	79	88	100	87
Ireland	333	293	325	284	276	356	282	266	280	262	211
Greece	151	157	110	121	99	94	96	93	93	92	97
Spain	1 174	1 204	1 243	1 170	1 070	1 107	865	866	770	768	711
France	641	638	599	664	703	681	704	709	671	595	583
Italy	366	344	306	283	302	310	270	296	279	298	312
Cyprus	13	25	19	40	67	81	2	2	2	2	2
Latvia	143	106	102	125	136	128	114	115	125	151	140
Lithuania	89	44	67	73	79	151	150	157	162	140	153
Luxembourg	0	0	0	0	0	0	0	0	0	0	0
Hungary	8	7	7	8	7	7	7	7	7	8	8
Malta	9	1	1	1	1	1	1	1	1	1	1
Netherlands	411	452	537	515	496	518	464	526	522	549	433
Austria	0	0	0	0	0	0	0	0	0	0	0
Poland	343	348	242	236	218	225	223	180	192	156	123
Portugal	263	224	228	213	191	193	202	209	221	212	229
Romania	18	8	9	8	7	8	7	10	5	6	7
Slovenia	2	2	2	2	2	2	2	1	1	1	1
Slovakia	1	1	1	1	1	2	2	2	2	2	2
Finland	164	165	156	145	156	150	146	122	135	132	146
Sweden	371	357	411	351	339	312	295	287	270	256	269
United Kingdom	868	892	923	841	748	740	690	637	655	669	616
Croatia	18	17	22	19	21	18	21	20	30	35	:
FYR of Macedonia	0	0	0	0	0	0	0	0	0	0	:
Turkey	528	459	487	574	503	528	567	508	550	426	:
Iceland	2 074	2 225	1 700	1 754	2 000	2 001	2 145	2 002	1 750	1 661	1 345
Liechtenstein	0	0	0	0	0	0	0	0	0	0	:
Norway	2 650	2 863	2 861	2 628	2 700	2 687	2 740	2 549	2 525	2 393	2 245
Switzerland	2	2	2	2	2	2	2	2	2	1	:
Canada	923	999	1 037	1 059	1 039	1 093	1 099	1 082	:	:	:
Japan	6 086	6 067	5 419	5 305	5 105	4 825	4 489	4 784	4 427	4 178	:
United States	4 995	4 972	4 751	4 822	4 807	5 020	5 006	4 989	5 144	4 846	:

Source: Eurostat (tag00076), FAO

Table 9.14: Total aquaculture production

(1 000 tonnes live weight)

	1996	1997	1998	1999	2000	2001	2002	2003	2004	2005	2006
EU-27	1 230	1 254	1 378	1 432	1 402	1 389	1 277	1 347	1 332	1 272	:
Euro area	996	1 002	1 119	1 143	1 116	1 084	981	1 038	994	968	:
Belgium	1	1	1	2	2	2	2	1	1	1	:
Bulgaria	5	5	4	8	4	3	2	4	2	3	3
Czech Republic	18	18	17	19	19	20	19	20	19	20	20
Denmark	42	40	42	43	44	42	32	38	43	39	28
Germany	83	65	73	80	66	53	50	74	57	45	38
Estonia	0	0	0	0	0	0	0	0	0	1	1
Ireland	35	37	42	44	51	61	63	63	58	60	53
Greece	40	49	60	84	95	98	88	101	97	106	113
Spain	232	239	315	321	312	313	259	273	299	222	295
France	286	287	268	265	267	252	252	240	261	258	:
Italy	189	196	209	210	217	218	184	192	118	181	174
Cyprus	1	1	1	1	2	2	2	2	2	2	4
Latvia	0	0	0	0	0	0	0	1	1	1	1
Lithuania	2	2	2	2	2	2	2	2	3	2	2
Luxembourg	0	0	0	0	0	0	0	0	0	0	0
Hungary	8	9	10	12	13	13	12	12	13	14	15
Malta	2	2	2	2	2	1	1	1	1	1	7
Netherlands	100	98	120	109	75	57	54	67	76	68	41
Austria	3	3	3	3	3	2	2	2	2	2	3
Poland	28	29	30	34	36	35	33	35	35	37	36
Portugal	5	7	8	6	8	8	8	8	7	6	7
Romania	14	11	10	9	10	11	9	9	8	7	9
Slovenia	1	1	1	1	1	1	1	1	2	2	1
Slovakia	1	1	1	1	1	1	1	1	1	1	1
Finland	18	16	16	15	15	16	15	13	13	14	13
Sweden	8	7	5	6	5	7	6	6	6	6	8
United Kingdom	110	130	137	155	152	171	179	182	207	173	172
Croatia	3	4	6	6	7	10	8	8	13	14	:
FYR of Macedonia	1	1	1	2	2	1	1	1	1	1	:
Turkey	33	45	57	63	79	67	61	80	94	119	:
Iceland	4	4	4	4	4	4	4	6	9	8	:
Norway	322	368	411	476	491	511	551	584	637	657	709
Switzerland	1	1	1	1	1	1	1	1	1	1	:
Canada	72	82	91	113	128	153	171	151	145	154	:
Japan	1 349	1 340	1 290	1 315	1 292	1 311	1 385	1 302	1 261	1 254	:
United States	393	438	445	479	456	479	497	544	607	472	:

Source: Eurostat (tag00075), FAO

External trade

The EU has a common trade policy whereby the European Commission negotiates trade agreements and represents the EU's interests on behalf of its 27 Member States. The European Commission consults Member States through an advisory committee which discusses the full range of trade policy issues affecting the Community including multilateral, bilateral and unilateral instruments.

Multilateral trade issues are dealt with under the auspices of the World Trade Organisation (WTO). Its membership covers 153 countries (as of July 2008), with several candidate members in the process of joining. The WTO sets the global rules for trade, provides a forum for trade negotiations, and for settling disputes between members. The European Commission negotiates with its WTO partners on behalf of the EU Member States, and has participated in the latest round of WTO multilateral trade negotiations, known as the Doha Development Agenda (DDA). However, having missed deadlines to conclude the talks in 2005 and again in 2006, the Doha round of talks broke down again at a WTO meeting in July 2008[1] and at the time of writing the future of these multilateral trade negotiations remains uncertain.

(1)   http://ec.europa.eu/trade and http://www.wto.org.

10.1 Share in world trade

Introduction

External trade statistics are used extensively by public body decision makers at an international, EU and national level, as well as by the private sector. In the case of Community authorities, external trade statistics help in the preparation of multilateral and bilateral trade negotiations, in defining and implementing anti-dumping policies, for the purposes of macroeconomic and monetary policies and in evaluating the progress of the Single Market, or the integration of European economies. In the private sector, businesses can use external trade data to carry out market research and define their commercial strategy.

Definitions and data availability

Within the EU, there are two main sources for statistics on external trade. **External trade statistics (ETS)** provide information on trade in goods, collected predominantly on the basis of customs and Intrastat[2] declarations. ETS provide information on the value and volumes (quantity) of external trade in goods with great detail concerning the type of commodity. The second source is the **balance of payments statistics (BoP)** that register all the transactions of an economy with the rest of the world. The current account of the BoP provides information not only on external trade in goods (generally the largest category), but also on external transactions in services, income (from employment and investment) and current transfers. For all these transactions, the BoP registers the value of exports (credits) and imports (debits), the difference of which is usually referred to as the balance (surplus or deficit).

Trade integration of goods and services is measured as the average value of debits and credits (summed together and divided by two) expressed relative to GDP. This indicator is calculated for both goods and services, based on BoP data; higher values indicate higher integration within the international economy. It is normal that smaller countries will display a higher recourse to external trade, as they are more likely to import a range of goods and services that are not produced within the domestic market.

Main findings

The economy of the EU-27 was more integrated with the international economy in 2007 (in terms of the credits and debits relative to GDP) than at any time in the previous five years. The average value of EU-27 trade flows of goods corresponded to 10.7 % of GDP in 2006, a much higher ratio than the relative low of 8.8 % in 2003 (for the EU-25), reflecting a broad upturn in economic activity. Although the volume of external trade in services is less than that for goods, the trade integration of services also rose, reaching the equivalent of 3.7 % of GDP in 2007.

The EU-27 had a trade deficit with the rest of the world in goods that equated to -1.2 % of GDP in 2007, in contrast to

(2) Paper or electronic declarations of intra-EU trade addressed by the traders to the competent national administration.

a surplus in services that corresponded to 0.7 % of GDP. There were stark contrasts among the Member States, reflecting among other factors, the relative size of the country and differences in respective economic structures. Trade deficits in goods were equivalent to one fifth or more of GDP in Cyprus, Bulgaria and Latvia. In contrast, the trade surpluses in goods recorded in Ireland, Germany and the Netherlands were equivalent to 12.3 %, 8.4 % and 6.8 % of GDP respectively in 2007, the highest relative levels among the Member States. Relative to GDP, there were large trade surpluses in services recorded in Luxembourg, Cyprus and Malta in 2007.

Figure 10.1: Trade integration, EU-27 (1)
(% of GDP)

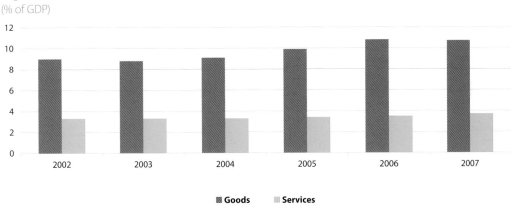

(1) 2002 and 2003, EU-25.

Source: Eurostat (tsier120)

Table 10.1: Share of goods and services in GDP, 2007 (1)

(% of GDP)

	Goods			Services		
	Exports	Imports	Balance	Exports	Imports	Balance
EU-27	10.1	11.3	-1.2	4.1	3.4	0.7
Euro area (2)	17.0	16.3	-1.4	5.5	5.0	0.5
Belgium	71.2	71.0	0.2	17.1	15.6	1.5
Bulgaria	46.7	72.0	-25.6	15.9	12.1	3.8
Czech Republic	69.9	66.7	3.1	9.6	8.1	1.6
Denmark	32.4	32.7	-0.4	19.8	17.4	2.4
Germany	40.7	32.4	8.4	6.5	7.8	-1.3
Estonia	53.0	70.1	-17.0	21.0	14.4	6.5
Ireland	45.4	33.1	12.3	34.9	37.0	-2.2
Greece	7.1	21.0	-13.8	13.9	6.0	7.9
Spain	17.8	26.4	-8.5	9.0	6.9	2.1
France	21.1	23.2	-2.0	5.3	4.8	0.5
Italy	23.9	23.7	0.1	5.4	5.8	-0.4
Cyprus	7.0	36.5	-29.4	40.9	17.3	23.7
Latvia	30.1	54.7	-24.6	13.5	10.0	3.5
Lithuania	44.6	59.2	-14.6	10.7	8.6	2.1
Luxembourg	37.4	46.8	-9.4	126.5	72.8	53.7
Hungary	68.0	66.5	1.4	12.1	11.0	1.1
Malta	42.5	60.9	-16.6	42.5	27.7	14.8
Netherlands	58.9	52.1	6.8	11.5	11.3	0.3
Austria	45.4	44.9	0.5	15.0	10.5	4.5
Poland	34.1	37.8	-3.7	6.8	5.8	0.9
Portugal	23.1	33.7	-10.7	10.0	6.2	3.8
Romania	24.2	38.8	-14.6	6.3	6.1	0.2
Slovenia	59.0	63.8	-5.1	12.2	9.2	3.0
Slovakia	77.0	78.4	-1.5	9.3	8.8	0.7
Finland	36.5	31.7	4.8	8.4	8.5	-0.1
Sweden	37.4	33.3	4.1	13.7	10.5	3.1
United Kingdom	16.0	22.3	-6.3	10.0	7.2	2.8
Turkey	17.2	24.4	-7.2	4.4	2.2	2.1
Norway	36.0	19.8	16.2	10.5	10.1	0.4
Japan	14.1	12.2	1.9	2.7	3.1	-0.4
United States	7.8	14.1	-6.3	3.2	2.6	0.6

(1) Japan and the United States, 2006; Greece, 2005.
(2) EA-13 instead of EA-15.

Source: Eurostat (tec00039, tec00040 and tec00001)

10.2 External trade in services

Introduction

Services cover a heterogeneous range of products and activities that are difficult to encapsulate within a simple definition. Services are also often difficult to separate from goods with which they may be associated or bundled in varying degrees, and trade in goods may indistinguishably include service charges such as insurance, maintenance contracts, transport charges, or royalty/licence payments.

Services differ from goods in a number of ways, most commonly in the immediacy of the relationship between supplier and consumer. Many services are non-transportable, in other words, they require the physical proximity of service provider and consumer – for example, the provision of a hotel service requires that the hotel is where the customer wishes to stay, a cleaning service for a business must be provided at the site of the business, and a haircut requires both hairstylist and client to be present. This proximity requirement implies that many services transactions involve factor mobility. Thus, an important feature of services is that they are provided via various modes of supply.

Following the General Agreement on Trade in Services (GATS), the four-part typology of external services transactions that constitutes the generally accepted framework for services analysis encompasses:

- cross border supply (mode 1) of a service from one jurisdiction to another;
- consumption abroad (mode 2) requires the presence of consumers in the supplier's country of residence;

- commercial presence (mode 3), in which a service supplier establishes a foreign based corporation, joint venture, partnership, or other establishment in the consumer's country of residence to supply services to persons in the host country; and,
- presence of natural persons (mode 4), which involves an individual, functioning alone or as an employee of a service provider, temporarily travelling abroad to deliver a service in the consumer's country of residence.

Services tend not to be homogenous or mass produced, many being tailored according to the client's needs and tastes. For external trade in such non-transportable services to take place, either the consumer must go to the service provider or the service provider must go to the consumer.

Definitions and data availability

The main methodological references for the production of statistics on external trade in services are the International Monetary Fund's fifth balance of payments manual (BPM5) and the United Nations' manual on statistics of international trade in services. The breakdown of Eurostat **statistics on trade in services** includes three main sub-items – transportation, travel, and other services.

- **Transportation** covers services provided by all modes of transportation – sea, air, and other, which includes space, rail, road, inland waterway and pipeline. The different types of services offered include the transport of passengers, the transport of freight, and other supporting and auxiliary services (such as storage and warehousing).

- The debit side of **travel** consists of goods and services which are acquired by residents who stay abroad for less than one year. The credit side includes purchases of the same type made by foreign travellers on the national territory. The travel item contains two main categories, namely business travel and personal travel (leisure, study, health-related purposes, etc.). Note that international transportation costs of the traveller to a destination are recorded under the heading transportation, but all movements within the country, including cruises, are entered under travel.

- **Other services** comprise those external transactions not covered under transportation or travel (such as communication services, construction services, insurance services, financial services, computer and information services, royalties and licence fees, other business services, personal, cultural and recreational services, and government services).

In the balance of payments (BoP) statistics, the EU current account is geographically allocated according to the residence of the trading partner. Eurostat provides detailed information on the geographical breakdown of the external trade in services of the EU, distinguishing between:

- **intra-EU transactions**, corresponding to the sum of the transactions declared by EU Member States with other EU Member States, and;

- **extra-EU transactions**, corresponding to the transactions declared by EU Member States with countries outside the EU. Extra-EU transactions are further broken down into detailed partner zones, for example, for individual countries (such as the United States or Japan), for economic zones (such as the OECD, ACP or NAFTA countries), and for geographical zones or continents (such as Africa, Asia or North America);

- **world transactions** are equal to the sum of intra-EU transactions and extra-EU transactions.

Finally, it is worth noting that the classification of external trade in services following BPM5 is not consistent with the four-type GATS classification of trade in services. BoP statistics presented in this chapter generally refer to services traded externally, mainly by the first and second mode, and, to a limited extent, to trade via the movement of natural persons (part of computer and information services, of other business services, and of personal, cultural and recreational services) and via commercial presence (part of construction services). Therefore, given the limited modal coverage of BoP statistics, additional sources of information need to be consulted with respect to the other modes of supply in order to give a more complete picture of trade in services [3].

---

(3) See the Manual on Statistics of International Trade in Services, developed jointly by the IMF, the OECD, Eurostat, WTO, UN and UNCTAD for more details on additional sources.

Within the BoP the terms credits and debits are used which, to the extent that they concern the trading of goods and services, can roughly be considered to be equivalent to exports and imports.

Main findings

The importance of services within EU economies continues to grow and in 2007 services contributed 71.7 % of the gross value added within the EU-27. However, this importance is scarcely reflected in terms of external trade. Indeed, the share of services in total trade (goods and services) has remained fairly stable at around 25 % to 27 % since 2001.

The EU-27 reported a surplus in service transactions of EUR 88 400 million with the rest of the world in 2007, reflecting credits of EUR 501 400 million and debits of EUR 413 000 million. This represented strong growth when compared with the surplus of EUR 69 500 million that was recorded for 2006, itself a big increase over 2005.

The United Kingdom recorded a net credit (extra and intra-EU combined) of EUR 56 100 million in service transactions in 2007, the highest net credit among the Member States and considerably more than the next highest that was recorded by Spain (EUR 22 100 million). In contrast, Germany recorded a net deficit in service transactions of EUR 30 400 million in 2007, the largest deficit by far among the Member States.

North America represented the EU-27's principal external trading partner in service transactions, accounting for 32.8 % of the EU-27's debits and 35.0 % of its credits (when intra-EU trade is not included). It is important to underline that most (59 %) of EU-27 trade in services was between EU Member States (intra-EU transactions).

More than two thirds of the EU-27's credits (68.4 %) and debits (73.5 %) in the external trade of services were accounted for by transportation, travel and the category of other business services in 2007. The surplus of EUR 40 100 million for other business services was the highest among services for the EU-27 in 2007, closely followed by the surplus of EUR 33 100 million for financial services. In contrast, there were large deficits of EUR 10 600 million for royalties and license fees and EUR 17 400 million for travel.

Table 10.2: External trade in services (1)

(EUR 1 000 million)

	Credits			Debits			Net	
	2006	2007	2006-07 growth rate (%)	2006	2007	2006-07 growth rate (%)	2006	2007
EU-27	450.0	501.4	11.4	380.4	413.0	8.6	69.5	88.4
Euro area (2)	433.7	491.1	13.2	395.9	443.9	12.1	37.8	47.3
Belgium	47.4	56.5	19.2	42.3	51.6	22.0	5.1	4.9
Bulgaria	4.2	4.6	9.5	3.3	3.5	6.1	0.9	1.1
Czech Republic	10.9	12.3	12.8	9.4	10.3	9.6	1.5	2.0
Denmark	41.7	45.0	7.9	36.4	39.5	8.5	5.3	5.4
Germany	149.6	158.2	5.7	178.6	188.6	5.6	-29.0	-30.4
Estonia	2.8	3.2	14.3	2.0	2.2	10.0	0.8	1.0
Ireland	55.1	64.8	17.6	62.5	68.7	9.9	-7.4	-4.0
Greece	:	:	:	:	:	:	:	:
Spain	84.7	94.1	11.1	62.4	72.0	15.4	22.3	22.1
France	94.2	100.3	6.5	86.0	91.4	6.3	8.3	8.9
Italy	78.4	83.3	6.2	79.9	89.5	12.0	-1.5	-6.2
Cyprus	5.8	6.4	10.3	2.4	2.7	12.5	3.4	3.7
Latvia	2.1	2.7	28.6	1.6	2.0	25.0	0.5	0.7
Lithuania	2.9	3.0	3.4	2.0	2.4	20.0	0.9	0.6
Luxembourg	40.5	45.7	12.8	24.0	26.3	9.6	16.5	19.4
Hungary	10.5	12.2	16.2	9.3	11.1	19.4	1.3	1.1
Malta	2.1	2.3	9.5	1.3	1.5	15.4	0.8	0.8
Netherlands	65.5	65.4	-0.2	63.3	63.8	0.8	2.2	1.7
Austria	36.8	40.7	10.6	26.6	28.4	6.8	10.2	12.3
Poland	16.3	20.9	28.2	15.8	18.0	13.9	0.6	2.9
Portugal	14.2	16.3	14.8	9.4	10.1	7.4	4.8	6.2
Romania	5.6	7.6	35.7	5.6	7.4	32.1	0.0	0.2
Slovenia	3.5	4.1	17.1	2.6	3.1	19.2	0.9	1.0
Slovakia	4.3	5.1	18.6	3.8	4.8	26.3	0.5	0.4
Finland	13.9	15.1	8.6	14.8	15.2	2.7	-0.9	-0.1
Sweden	39.6	45.4	14.6	31.6	35.0	10.8	7.9	10.4
United Kingdom	186.6	202.3	8.4	141.0	146.2	3.7	45.5	56.1
Turkey	20.0	20.9	4.5	9.1	10.7	17.6	10.9	10.2
Norway	26.2	29.8	13.7	25.1	28.7	14.3	1.2	1.1
Japan	93.5	:	:	107.9	:	:	-14.4	:
United States	333.4	:	:	272.9	:	:	60.5	:

(1) Transactions are registered vis-à-vis the rest of the world; EU-27 partner is extra EU-27, euro area partner is extra euro area, Member States partner is the rest of the world.
(2) EA-13 instead of EA-15.

Source: Eurostat (tec00040)

Table 10.3: Contribution to extra EU-27 trade in services, 2006

	Credits		Debits		Net
	(EUR 1 000 million)	Share of EU-27 credits (%)	(EUR 1 000 million)	Share of EU-27 debits (%)	(EUR 1 000 million)
EU-27	441.6	100.0	373.1	100.0	68.5
Euro area	425.6	96.4	390.5	104.7	35.1
Belgium	11.9	2.7	10.7	2.9	1.2
Bulgaria	1.3	0.3	0.9	0.2	0.5
Czech Republic	3.2	0.7	3.0	0.8	0.2
Denmark	21.4	4.8	17.0	4.6	4.4
Germany	63.9	14.5	71.3	19.1	-7.3
Estonia	0.8	0.2	0.5	0.1	0.3
Ireland	24.6	5.6	32.5	8.7	-7.8
Greece	13.3	3.0	6.0	1.6	7.3
Spain	21.5	4.9	21.1	5.6	0.4
France	44.8	10.1	42.1	11.3	2.6
Italy	30.0	6.8	30.1	8.1	-0.1
Cyprus	1.7	0.4	0.8	0.2	0.9
Latvia	1.0	0.2	0.7	0.2	0.4
Lithuania	1.3	0.3	0.8	0.2	0.5
Luxembourg	10.4	2.4	5.9	1.6	4.5
Hungary	3.3	0.7	3.0	0.8	0.2
Malta	0.5	0.1	0.4	0.1	0.1
Netherlands	32.9	7.4	29.1	7.8	3.7
Austria	8.9	2.0	7.2	1.9	1.7
Poland	4.1	0.9	3.8	1.0	0.4
Portugal	3.1	0.7	2.5	0.7	0.6
Romania	1.6	0.4	1.4	0.4	0.1
Slovenia	0.9	0.2	1.0	0.3	-0.1
Slovakia	1.1	0.2	0.6	0.2	0.4
Finland	7.1	1.6	4.7	1.3	2.4
Sweden	19.2	4.4	10.6	2.8	8.6
United Kingdom	107.7	24.4	64.9	17.4	42.8

Source: Eurostat (bop_its_det)

Table 10.4: Contribution to intra EU-27 trade in services, 2006

	Credits		Debits		Net
	(EUR 1 000 million)	Share of EU-27 credits (%)	(EUR 1 000 million)	Share of EU-27 debits (%)	(EUR 1 000 million)
EU-27	599.9	100.0	566.6	100.0	33.4
Belgium	35.5	5.9	31.5	5.6	3.9
Bulgaria	2.8	0.5	2.3	0.4	0.5
Czech Republic	7.4	1.2	6.4	1.1	1.0
Denmark	20.5	3.4	19.7	3.5	0.8
Germany	75.1	12.5	103.7	18.3	-28.5
Estonia	2.0	0.3	1.5	0.3	0.5
Ireland	30.4	5.1	30.0	5.3	0.4
Greece	15.1	2.5	7.1	1.2	8.0
Spain	63.0	10.5	41.3	7.3	21.7
France	49.5	8.2	43.8	7.7	5.7
Italy	48.4	8.1	49.8	8.8	-1.4
Cyprus	4.1	0.7	1.6	0.3	2.5
Latvia	1.1	0.2	0.9	0.2	0.2
Lithuania	1.5	0.3	1.2	0.2	0.4
Luxembourg	30.2	5.0	18.1	3.2	12.0
Hungary	7.3	1.2	6.3	1.1	1.1
Malta	1.5	0.3	0.9	0.2	0.6
Netherlands	42.2	7.0	43.3	7.6	-1.2
Austria	28.1	4.7	18.7	3.3	9.4
Poland	12.2	2.0	10.8	1.9	1.4
Portugal	11.0	1.8	6.8	1.2	4.3
Romania	3.9	0.7	4.1	0.7	-0.1
Slovenia	2.5	0.4	1.6	0.3	0.9
Slovakia	3.2	0.5	3.2	0.6	0.1
Finland	5.7	1.0	7.7	1.4	-2.0
Sweden	20.1	3.4	18.4	3.2	1.7
United Kingdom	75.0	12.5	75.1	13.2	0.0

Source: Eurostat (bop_its_det)

Figure 10.2: Trade in services, EU-27, 2006

(% share of extra EU-27 transactions)

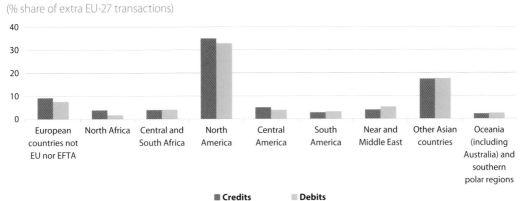

Credits ■ Debits

Source: Eurostat (tec00082 and bop_its_det)

Table 10.5: EU-27 credits for services

(%)

	2003	2004	2005	2006	2007
All countries of the world	100.0	100.0	100.0	100.0	100.0
Extra-EU	42.6	41.4	41.8	42.4	43.2
European Free Trade Association	7.1	6.9	6.8	6.8	:
Switzerland	5.5	5.3	5.1	5.1	5.2
European countries not EU nor EFTA	5.2	2.5	3.0	3.2	:
Central and Eastern Europe	2.9	0.4	0.4	0.4	:
Community of Independent States	1.4	1.6	1.8	2.0	:
Russian Federation	1.0	1.1	1.3	1.4	1.6
Africa	2.6	2.5	2.5	2.5	:
America	17.3	16.8	16.7	16.9	:
Canada	0.9	0.9	0.9	1.0	1.0
United States	14.0	13.3	12.8	12.9	12.0
Brazil	0.4	0.4	0.5	0.5	0.6
Asia	8.7	9.3	9.7	9.7	:
China (excl. Hong Kong)	0.9	1.0	1.3	1.2	1.5
Hong Kong	0.8	0.8	0.9	0.7	0.7
India	0.4	0.4	0.6	0.7	0.8
Japan	2.1	2.1	2.0	1.8	1.7
Oceania (including Australia) and southern polar regions	0.9	1.1	1.1	1.1	:
	2003	2004	2005	2006	2007
OECD countries	82.8	83.0	81.9	81.2	:
North American Free Trade Association member countries	15.3	14.7	14.1	14.3	:
Petroleum Exporting Countries (OPEC)	2.3	2.2	2.3	2.6	:
African, Caribbean and Pacific countries, signatories of the Partnership Agreement (Cotonou agreement)	1.9	1.9	1.9	2.0	:
Association of South-East Asian Nations	1.6	1.6	1.6	1.7	:
Southern Common Market	0.5	0.6	0.7	0.8	:

Source: Eurostat (tec00080)

Table 10.6: EU-27 debits for services
(%)

	2003	2004	2005	2006	2007
All countries of the world	100.0	100.0	100.0	100.0	100.0
Extra-EU	39.8	39.6	39.6	39.7	40.0
European Free Trade Association	5.6	5.5	5.6	5.3	:
Switzerland	4.3	4.2	4.3	4.0	4.0
European countries not EU nor EFTA	7.0	3.4	3.6	3.7	:
Central and Eastern Europe	3.9	0.7	0.7	0.7	:
Community of Independent States	1.2	1.5	1.7	1.9	:
Russian Federation	0.8	0.9	1.0	1.1	1.1
Africa	2.9	3.1	3.1	3.1	:
America	17.7	17.4	17.3	17.0	:
Canada	0.9	0.9	0.9	0.9	0.9
United States	13.7	13.5	13.4	13.0	12.4
Brazil	0.5	0.4	0.5	0.5	0.5
Asia	7.1	7.8	7.9	8.4	:
China (excl. Hong Kong)	0.6	0.9	1.1	1.2	1.3
Hong Kong	0.6	0.6	0.6	0.7	0.8
India	0.4	0.5	0.5	0.6	0.6
Japan	1.3	1.4	1.4	1.4	1.3
Oceania (including Australia) and southern polar regions	0.8	0.8	0.9	0.9	:

	2003	2004	2005	2006	2007
OECD countries	83.1	82.6	82.4	81.4	:
North American Free Trade Association member countries	15.0	14.7	14.6	14.1	:
Petroleum Exporting Countries (OPEC)	1.5	1.5	1.5	1.6	:
African, Caribbean and Pacific countries, signatories of the Partnership Agreement (Cotonou agreement)	2.1	2.1	2.2	2.0	:
Association of South-East Asian Nations	1.6	1.6	1.6	1.7	:
Southern Common Market	0.7	0.6	0.6	0.7	:

Source: Eurostat (tec00081)

Table 10.7: Development of trade in services, by selected partner, EU-27
(EUR 1 000 million)

	2005			2006			2007		
	Credits	Debits	Net	Credits	Debits	Net	Credits	Debits	Net
Total	402.9	350.0	52.9	441.6	373.1	68.5	501.4	413.0	88.4
United States	123.2	118.2	4.9	134.7	122.1	12.6	139.0	127.9	11.2
EFTA	65.4	49.0	16.4	70.4	49.4	21.1	:	:	:
Japan	19.6	12.3	7.3	18.9	12.9	6.0	19.4	13.4	6.0
Russia	12.3	9.1	3.2	14.2	10.8	3.4	18.2	11.5	6.6
China	12.3	9.6	2.7	12.8	11.3	1.4	17.7	13.1	4.6
Canada	9.0	7.6	1.3	10.2	8.2	2.0	11.2	9.5	1.8
India	5.4	4.8	0.6	7.0	5.5	1.4	9.0	6.6	2.4
Hong Kong	8.3	5.6	2.6	6.9	6.7	0.2	8.4	7.8	0.6
Brazil	4.6	4.0	0.6	5.2	4.6	0.5	6.6	4.8	1.8
Other countries	142.8	129.6	13.2	161.3	141.5	19.8	:	:	:

Source: Eurostat (bop_its_det)

Figure 10.3: Trade by main service categories, EU-27, 2007 (1)
(EUR 1 000 million)

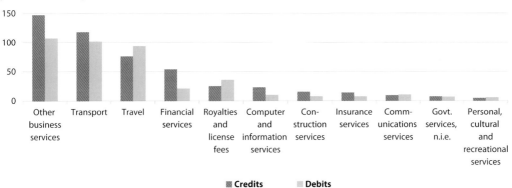

(1) Provisional.

Source: Eurostat (tec00063, tec00058, tec00062, tec00069, tec00071, tec00070, tec00067, tec00068, tec00066, tec00065 and tec00064)

10.3 External trade in goods

Introduction

The value of external trade in goods significantly exceeds that of services. This reflects, among other things, that in most cases goods are by their nature commodities which can be traded and transported across borders, whereas many services are non-transportable items for which it is not possible to separate the place of consumption from the place of production.

Definitions and data availability

In broad terms, the aim of **external trade statistics on goods (ETS)** is to record all flows of goods that add to or subtract from the stock of material resources of a country by entering or leaving its territory. The most important component of external trade statistics is related to transactions involving actual or intended transfer of ownership against compensation. Nevertheless, external trade statistics also cover movements of goods without a transfer of ownership, such as operations following, or with a view to, processing under contract (for example, processing textiles).

The nomenclature of countries and territories for ETS of the Community and statistics of trade between Member States is an essential element in compiling statistics – this nomenclature is called the **geonomenclature**. In particular, it makes it possible to identify those involved in trade, in other words, the reporting country and the partner country. If necessary the geonomenclature is subject to annual revision in order to incorporate the adjustments needed for statistical purposes and to take into account any geopolitical change that may have occurred.

Exports are recorded at their 'free on board' (fob) value and **imports** at their 'cost, insurance and freight' (cif) value. Therefore, and contrary to balance of payments statistics (see the previous subchapter), import values for external trade statistics include charges, such as transport and insurance, relating to that part of the journey which takes place outside the statistical territory of the importing country. In contrast, export values correspond to the value of goods at the place and time where they leave the statistical territory of the exporting country.

Information on external trade for the European Union and the euro area are calculated as the sum of trade with countries outside these areas. In other words, each of these geographical areas is considered as a single trading entity and trade flows are measured into and out of the area, but not within it. On the other hand, external trade flows for individual Member States and other countries are generally presented with the rest of the world as the trading partner, including trade with other Member States (intra-EU trade). For **intra-EU trade**, the terms dispatches and arrivals are used; these are equivalent to the terms exports and imports used for **extra-EU trade** flows.

External trade statistics report export and import values and volumes (quantities) for goods using a product classification. One of the most common classifications for studying aggregate product statistics is the **Standard International Trade Classification of the United Nations** (SITC Rev. 4); this classification allows a comparison to be made on a worldwide basis. The commodity groupings of SITC reflect: a) the materials used in production; b) the processing stage; c) market practices and uses of the products; d) the importance of the commodities in terms of world trade, and; e) technological changes. Agrifood products are food products obtained from agriculture. They are classified according to Sections 0 and 1 of the SITC. Trade in raw materials refers to Sections 2 and 4 of the SITC. Trade in fuel products refers to products classified according to Section 3 of the SITC. Trade in chemicals refers to products classified according to Section 5 of the SITC. Trade in machinery and transport equipment refers to products classified according to Section 7 of the SITC and trade in other manufactured goods to products classified according to Sections 6 and 8. The statistics presented are based on the fourth revision of the classification; an abbreviated list of the SITC is provided in an annex at the end of the publication. SITC Revision 4 was accepted by the United Nations Statistical Commission at its 37th session in 2006 and its implementation is underway.

Main findings

The EU-27 accounts for a little less than one fifth of the world's imports and exports of goods. The EU-27 exported goods to non-member countries to the value of EUR 1 240 000 million in 2007 and imported goods from them to the value of EUR 1 426 000 million. The EU-27 exported EUR 392 000 million more goods than the United States in 2007, but imported EUR 46 000 million less. Note that the EU-27 imports and exports less goods than does the EU-15, reflecting the fact that part of the EU-15's trade came from the countries that joined the EU in 2004 and 2007, and these transactions are not included in the external trade of the EU-27.

Since 1999 (the period since when trade data for the EU-27 are available), the EU-27 has recorded consecutive annual trade deficits for goods as a whole, although the level of these deficits has fluctuated strongly. The EU-27 trade deficits for goods have tended to reduce strongly during periods of stagnant or falling economic activity, whilst growing during periods of economic expansion. The EU-27's trade deficit for goods in 2007 was EUR 186 000 million, a slight reduction compared with 2006, but higher than any other year for which data are available.

The trade in goods between Member States (the EU's internal market) was by far the most important market for goods produced within the EU-27; intra-EU dispatches of goods were worth EUR 2 646 000 million in 2007, more than double the value of exports to non-member countries. Indeed, in each of the Member States the majority of the trade in goods in 2007 was with other Member States (intra-EU trade) as opposed to with non-member countries (extra-EU trade). The proportion of the total trade in goods accounted for by these two flows varied considerably among the Member States, reflecting to some degree historical ties and geographical location. The highest levels of trade integration within the EU were recorded for the Czech Republic, Slovakia and Luxembourg; each of these countries reported that intra-EU trade in goods accounted for about 80 % or more of their total trade in goods. In contrast, about 60 % or less of the external trade in goods of the United Kingdom, Italy, Bulgaria, Greece and Finland were accounted for by intra-EU trade.

In a reverse of the situation for trade in services, in 2007 Germany recorded the highest trade surplus (extra and intra-EU combined) for goods, valued at EUR 195 000 million, with the United Kingdom recording the largest trade deficit in goods of EUR 135 000 million. Italy, Hungary and Slovakia recorded a narrowing of their trade deficits for goods between 2006 and 2007, while Austria moved from a deficit to a surplus.

The United States was by far most the important market for EU-27 exports of goods in 2007, accounting for 21.1 % of all exports to non-member countries, a much higher proportion than that for Switzerland (7.5 %), which was the next most important market. However, as in 2006, China was the principal source of imports of goods in 2007, its share of extra-EU-27 imports reaching 16.2 % in 2007 compared with 12.7 % for the United States and 10.1 % for Russia.

Machinery and transport equipment was the largest category of exports of goods from the EU-27 to non-member countries in 2007 with a share of 43.8 %, and this category also accounted for the largest share of imports (29.1 %). Compared with five years earlier, the most notable change in the structure of EU-27 extra-EU exports and imports was the increased shares accounted for by mineral fuels, lubricants and related materials in both trade flows. It should be noted that these shares are calculated on the basis of the value of transactions, and as such comparisons over time reflect changes in quantity and price levels. Alongside this change, the other main difference was the reduced share of machinery and transport equipment, particularly concerning imports.

Table 10.8: Main players for external trade

(EUR 1 000 million)

	Exports			Imports			Trade balance		
	1997	2002	2007	1997	2002	2007	1997	2002	2007
EU-27 (1)	:	892	1 240	:	937	1 426	:	-45	-186
EU-15 (2)	721	997	1 414	673	989	1 516	49	8	-102
Norway	42	64	99	31	37	58	11	27	41
Switzerland	67	93	126	67	89	118	0	4	8
Canada	191	267	306	174	235	277	17	32	29
China (excluding Hong Kong)	161	344	889	126	312	698	36	32	191
Japan	371	441	521	299	357	454	72	84	67
United States	606	733	848	792	1 271	1 472	-186	-538	-624

(1) External trade flows with extra EU-27.
(2) External trade flows with extra EU-15.

Source: Eurostat (ext_lt_intertrd)

Figure 10.4: Main players for external trade, 2007

(EUR 1 000 million)

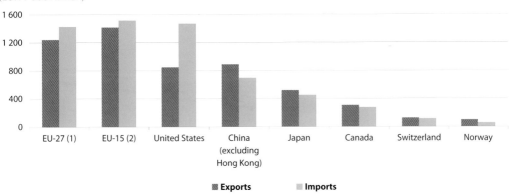

(1) External trade flows with extra EU-27.
(2) External trade flows with extra EU-15.

Source: Eurostat (ext_lt_intertrd)

Figure 10.5: Shares in the world market for exports, 2006
(% share of world exports)

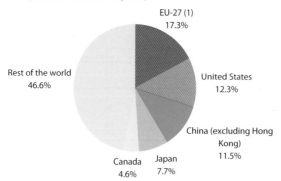

Figure 10.6: Shares in the world market for imports, 2006
(% share of world imports)

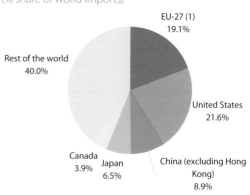

(1) External trade flows with extra EU-27.

Source: Eurostat (tet00018)

(1) External trade flows with extra EU-27.

Source: Eurostat (tet00018)

Figure 10.7: Development of external trade, EU-27 (1)
(EUR 1 000 million)

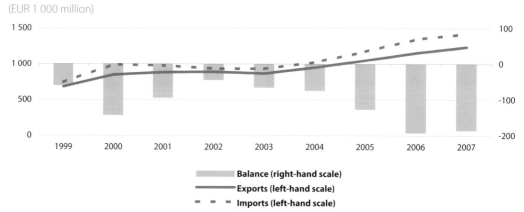

(1) External trade flows with extra EU-27.

Source: Eurostat (ext_lt_intertrd)

Table 10.9: External trade

(EUR 1 000 million)

	Exports			Imports			Balance	
	2006	2007	2006-07 growth rate (%)	2006	2007	2006-07 growth rate (%)	2006	2007
EU-27 (1)	1 159.3	1 239.9	7.0	1 351.7	1 426.0	5.5	-192.5	-186.1
Euro area (2)	1 383.6	1 500.0	8.4	1 392.2	1 471.8	5.7	-8.6	28.2
Belgium	292.2	315.3	7.9	280.3	301.7	7.6	11.9	13.6
Bulgaria	11.8	13.5	14.6	15.4	21.9	41.9	-3.7	-8.4
Czech Republic	75.6	89.3	18.2	74.2	86.0	15.9	1.4	3.3
Denmark	73.7	75.5	2.4	68.1	72.9	7.0	5.6	2.6
Germany	882.5	967.8	9.7	722.1	772.4	7.0	160.4	195.4
Estonia	7.7	8.0	3.9	10.7	11.3	5.8	-3.0	-3.3
Ireland	86.6	88.5	2.2	58.2	60.5	3.9	28.4	28.0
Greece	16.5	17.2	4.1	50.7	55.6	9.8	-34.1	-38.4
Spain	170.2	175.9	3.3	261.8	271.9	3.8	-91.6	-96.0
France	394.9	403.8	2.2	431.6	448.9	4.0	-36.7	-45.1
Italy	332.0	358.6	8.0	352.5	368.1	4.4	-20.5	-9.5
Cyprus	1.1	1.0	-3.8	5.5	6.3	13.9	-4.5	-5.3
Latvia	4.9	6.1	23.7	9.2	11.2	21.7	-4.3	-5.1
Lithuania	11.3	12.5	11.1	15.4	17.8	15.4	-4.2	-5.3
Luxembourg	18.2	16.4	-10.3	21.2	20.0	-5.4	-2.9	-3.7
Hungary	59.9	69.6	16.1	62.3	69.7	11.9	-2.4	-0.1
Malta	2.1	2.1	0.5	3.2	3.2	0.3	-1.0	-1.1
Netherlands	369.3	401.9	8.8	332.0	359.4	8.3	37.3	42.5
Austria	108.9	119.4	9.6	109.3	119.0	8.9	-0.4	0.4
Poland	88.2	102.3	15.9	101.1	120.9	19.5	-12.9	-18.7
Portugal	34.5	37.5	8.8	53.1	57.0	7.4	-18.6	-19.5
Romania	25.9	29.4	13.7	40.8	51.0	25.1	-14.9	-21.6
Slovenia	18.5	22.0	18.7	19.2	23.0	19.8	-0.7	-1.1
Slovakia	33.3	42.5	27.4	35.7	43.9	23.1	-2.4	-1.5
Finland	61.5	65.7	6.8	55.3	59.6	7.9	6.2	6.1
Sweden	117.7	123.4	4.8	101.6	110.4	8.7	16.1	13.0
United Kingdom	357.3	320.3	-10.4	479.0	454.8	-5.0	-121.7	-134.6
Iceland	2.8	3.5	26.1	4.8	4.9	1.9	-2.0	-1.4
Norway	96.9	99.3	2.5	51.1	58.5	14.5	45.8	40.8
Switzerland	117.5	125.5	6.8	112.7	117.6	4.4	4.9	7.9
Canada	309.0	306.4	-0.8	278.7	277.4	-0.5	30.4	29.1
China	771.7	888.6	15.1	630.3	697.5	10.7	141.4	191.0
Japan	515.1	521.2	1.2	461.2	454.0	-1.6	53.9	67.2
United States	825.9	848.3	2.7	1 528.4	1 471.8	-3.7	-702.4	-623.6

(1) External trade flows with extra EU-27.
(2) EA-13 instead of EA-15; external trade flows with extra EA-13.

Source: Eurostat (tet00002)

Table 10.10: Contribution to extra EU-27 external trade, 2007

	Imports		Exports		Trade balance
	(EUR 1 000 million)	Share of EU-27 imports (%)	(EUR 1 000 million)	Share of EU-27 exports (%)	(EUR 1 000 million)
EU-27	1 426.0	100.0	1 239.9	100.0	-186.1
Euro area	1 052.5	73.8	958.5	77.3	-93.9
Belgium	87.7	6.2	74.7	6.0	-13.1
Bulgaria	9.1	0.6	5.3	0.4	-3.8
Czech Republic	16.9	1.2	13.2	1.1	-3.7
Denmark	19.4	1.4	22.5	1.8	3.1
Germany	267.7	18.8	340.3	27.4	72.6
Estonia	2.4	0.2	2.4	0.2	-0.1
Ireland	18.3	1.3	32.4	2.6	14.1
Greece	23.5	1.6	6.0	0.5	-17.4
Spain	105.3	7.4	52.9	4.3	-52.5
France	138.0	9.7	141.1	11.4	3.1
Italy	158.4	11.1	143.2	11.6	-15.2
Cyprus	2.0	0.1	0.3	0.0	-1.7
Latvia	2.5	0.2	1.7	0.1	-0.9
Lithuania	5.6	0.4	4.4	0.4	-1.2
Luxembourg	5.3	0.4	1.9	0.2	-3.4
Hungary	21.3	1.5	14.7	1.2	-6.6
Malta	0.9	0.1	1.1	0.1	0.2
Netherlands	179.3	12.6	88.1	7.1	-91.2
Austria	24.6	1.7	32.7	2.6	8.1
Poland	32.3	2.3	21.6	1.7	-10.7
Portugal	14.0	1.0	8.7	0.7	-5.3
Romania	14.7	1.0	8.3	0.7	-6.5
Slovenia	6.1	0.4	6.7	0.5	0.7
Slovakia	11.3	0.8	5.6	0.5	-5.7
Finland	21.4	1.5	28.4	2.3	6.9
Sweden	32.2	2.3	47.8	3.9	15.5
United Kingdom	205.7	14.4	134.0	10.8	-71.7

Source: Eurostat (ext_lt_intratrd)

Table 10.11: Contribution to intra EU-27 external trade, 2007

	Arrivals		Dispatches		Trade balance
	(EUR 1 000 million)	Share of EU-27 arrivals (%)	(EUR 1 000 million)	Share of EU-27 dispatches (%)	(EUR 1 000 million)
EU-27	2 572.5	100.0	2 645.5	100.0	-
Euro area	1 874.2	72.9	2 034.6	76.9	160.5
Belgium	214.0	8.3	240.7	9.1	26.7
Bulgaria	12.8	0.5	8.2	0.3	-4.6
Czech Republic	69.1	2.7	76.2	2.9	7.1
Denmark	53.5	2.1	53.0	2.0	-0.5
Germany	504.7	19.6	627.5	23.7	122.8
Estonia	8.9	0.3	5.6	0.2	-3.3
Ireland	42.2	1.6	56.1	2.1	13.9
Greece	32.2	1.3	11.2	0.4	-21.0
Spain	166.5	6.5	123.0	4.6	-43.5
France	310.9	12.1	262.7	9.9	-48.2
Italy	209.7	8.1	215.4	8.1	5.8
Cyprus	4.3	0.2	0.7	0.0	-3.6
Latvia	8.7	0.3	4.4	0.2	-4.3
Lithuania	12.2	0.5	8.1	0.3	-4.1
Luxembourg	14.7	0.6	14.5	0.5	-0.2
Hungary	48.5	1.9	55.0	2.1	6.5
Malta	2.3	0.1	1.1	0.0	-1.3
Netherlands	180.2	7.0	313.8	11.9	133.6
Austria	94.4	3.7	86.7	3.3	-7.7
Poland	88.6	3.4	80.7	3.0	-8.0
Portugal	43.0	1.7	28.8	1.1	-14.2
Romania	36.3	1.4	21.1	0.8	-15.1
Slovenia	17.0	0.7	15.2	0.6	-1.8
Slovakia	32.6	1.3	36.8	1.4	4.2
Finland	38.2	1.5	37.3	1.4	-0.9
Sweden	78.2	3.0	75.6	2.9	-2.6
United Kingdom	249.2	9.7	186.3	7.0	-62.9

Source: Eurostat (ext_lt_intratrd)

Figure 10.8: Intra and extra EU-27 external trade, 2007
(% share of total trade)

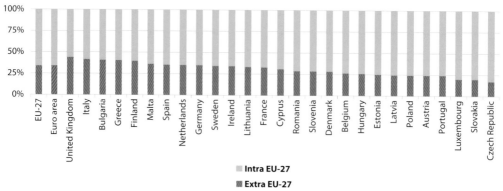

Source: Eurostat (ext_lt_intratrd)

Figure 10.9: Main trading partners for exports, EU-27, 2007
(% share of extra EU-27 exports)

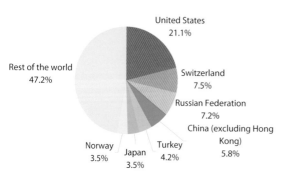

United States
21.1%

Switzerland
7.5%

Russian Federation
7.2%

China (excluding Hong Kong)
5.8%

Rest of the world
47.2%

Norway
3.5%

Japan
3.5%

Turkey
4.2%

Source: Eurostat (ext_lt_maineu)

Figure 10.10: Main trading partners for imports, EU-27, 2007
(% share of extra EU-27 imports)

China (excluding Hong Kong)
16.2%

United States
12.7%

Russian Federation
10.1%

Japan
5.5%

Norway
5.4%

Switzerland
5.4%

Turkey
3.3%

Rest of the world
41.4%

Source: Eurostat (ext_lt_maineu)

Figure 10.11: Main exports, EU-27
(% share of extra EU-27 exports)

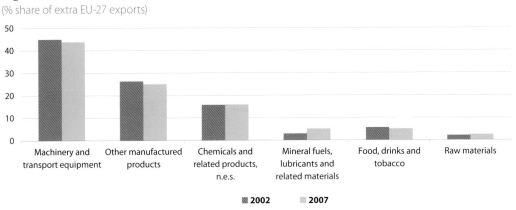

Source: Eurostat (ext_lt_intertrd)

Figure 10.12: Main imports, EU-27
(% share of extra EU-27 imports)

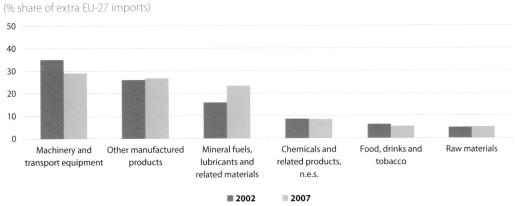

Source: Eurostat (ext_lt_intertrd)

Transport

Transport plays a crucial role in an economy, transferring goods between the place of production and consumption, as well as transporting passengers for work or pleasure. However, key problems of congestion, quality of services (such as punctuality and connectivity), affordability and environmental impact put economic development at risk. Measures to address these concerns, among others, whilst maintaining the EU's competitiveness, are at the heart of the EU transport policy White paper titled 'European transport policy for 2010: time to decide' [1], which was adopted in 2001. This policy document remains the bedrock of the current EU sustainable transport policy and was supplemented in June 2006 by a mid-term review communication [2] 'Keep Europe moving – sustainable mobility for our continent'. Some of the key conclusions of this communication were that each transport mode must be optimised to help ensure competitiveness and prosperity; all modes must become more environmentally friendly, safe and energy efficient; each mode should be used efficiently on its own and in combination to achieve an optimal and sustainable utilisation of resources. The communication proposed a wide range of implementing measures that were largely driven by evolving issues:

- environmental commitments – such as those under the Kyoto Protocol, as well as air quality, noise pollution, and land use;
- a greater focus on technology – this included the encouragement of further research and development into areas such as intelligent transport systems (such as Galileo, SESAR, ERTMS) involving communication, navigation and automation, engine technology that could improve fuel efficiency, and the promotion of alternative fuels. Other activities cited included the modernisation of air traffic systems, improvements in safety and security, urban mobility and the decongestion of transport corridors, as well as the efficient use of different modes on their own and in combination;

(1)   COM(2001) 370 final; http://ec.europa.eu/transport/white_paper/index_en.htm.
(2)   COM(2006) 314 final; http://ec.europa.eu/transport/transport_policy_review/index_en.htm.

11.1 Modal breakdown

- consolidation within the transport sector – especially in aviation and maritime transport, but also with the creation of large logistics enterprises with worldwide operations;
- enlargement – allowing the possibility to expand trans-European networks to corridors that are particularly suitable for rail and waterborne transport;
- changes in the international context – such as the threat of terrorism, or globalisation that has affected trade flows and increased demand for international transport services.

The European Commission has already started the launch of a range of action plans on key transport policy issues, such as a Green paper on urban transport, a road charging Directive [3], and a Logistics Action plan [4].

Eurostat's transport statistics describe the most important features of transport, not only in terms of the quantities of freight and numbers of passengers that are moved each year, or the number of vehicles and infrastructure that are used, but also the contribution of transport services to the economy as a whole. Data collection is supported by several legal acts obliging the Member States to report statistical data, as well as voluntary agreements to supply additional data.

Introduction

The demand for increased mobility from individuals and increased flexibility and timeliness of delivery from enterprises has led to road transport becoming the dominant mode of transport in the EU. The growth in road transport has had a significant impact on road congestion, road safety, pollution and land use.

One of the main challenges identified by the 2001 White paper was to address this imbalance in the development of the different modes of transport. Specific actions looking to boost rail and maritime connections were foreseen and then established (the Marco Polo programmes).

The Commission's Intermodal Freight Transport policy was established to support the efficient 'door to door' movement of goods, using two or more modes of transport, in an integrated transport chain. This policy recognises that each mode of transport has its own advantages either in terms of potential capacity, levels of safety, flexibility, energy consumption, or environmental impact and, as such intermodal transport allows each mode to play its role in building transport chains which overall are more efficient, cost effective and sustainable.

The White paper also proposed the development of 'Motorways of the Sea' as a real competitive alternative to land transport and a legal framework for funding this work was secured in 2004.

(3) Directive 2006/38/EC; http://ec.europa.eu/transport/road/policy/road_charging/charging_tolls_en.htm.
(4) COM(2007) 606; http://ec.europa.eu/transport/logistics/freight_logistics_action_plan/index_en.htm.

Definitions and data availability

Definitions of terms used within transport statistics are available in the 'Glossary for Transport statistics – Third Edition'. Key definitions include:

- a **passenger-kilometre** is the unit of measure representing the transport of one passenger by a given mode of transport over one kilometre;
- a **tonne-kilometre** is the unit of measure representing the transport of one tonne of goods by a given mode of transport over one kilometre;
- **rail and inland waterways movements** are recorded in each reporting country on national territory ('territoriality principle'), regardless of the nationality of the vehicle or vessel; road statistics are based on all movements, in the registration country or abroad, of the vehicles registered in the reporting country ('nationality principle');
- **inland passenger transport** corresponds to road (buses and passenger cars) and rail (including inter-city and urban rail transport), thus excluding air and water transport;
- **inland freight transport** corresponds to road, rail, inland waterways and pipeline transport, thus excluding air and sea transport.

The **modal split** (of transport) indicates the share of each mode of transport based on passenger-kilometres (p-km) for passenger transport and tonne-kilometres (t-km) for goods (freight) transport, based on movements on national territory, regardless of the nationality of the vehicle. It should be noted that the data collection methodology is not harmonised at the EU level. As statistics on road and other inland modes are based on different principles, the figures of the smallest reporting countries (for example, Luxembourg and Slovenia) may be misleading. Data on the relative shares of inland freight transport are annual and generally available for every year since the early 1990s. Modes of transport include train, sea, inland waterways and air (for goods and passengers), as well as passenger cars, powered two-wheelers, buses, coaches, trams and metros for passengers and pipelines for goods. In practice, an analysis of the modal split may exclude certain modes, for example, it may be limited to inland transport and therefore exclude sea transport.

Passenger cars are road motor vehicles, other than motor cycles, intended for the carriage of passengers and designed to seat no more than nine persons (including the driver). The term passenger car therefore covers microcars (which need no permit to be driven), taxis, and hired passenger cars, provided that they have fewer than 10 seats; this category may also include pick-ups.

Railways are lines of communication made up by rail exclusively for the use of railway vehicles.

Inland waterways (navigable) are stretches of water, not part of the sea, over which vessels of a carrying capacity of not less than 50 tonnes can navigate when normally loaded. This term covers both navigable rivers and lakes and navigable canals. The length of rivers and canals is measured in mid channel. The length of lakes and lagoons is measured along the shortest navigable route between the most distant points to and from which transport operations are performed. A waterway forming a common frontier between two countries is reported by both.

Main findings

A little over three quarters (76.7 %) of inland freight transport (excluding pipelines) in the EU-27 was accounted for by road transport in 2006. Less than one fifth (17.7 %) of inland freight transport was by rail, with the rest (5.6 %) accounted for by inland waterways. The dominance of freight transport by road was reflected in the data for the majority of Member States, the exceptions being Estonia and Latvia where more than three fifths of inland freight was transported by rail in 2006. Inland waterways transport accounted for one tenth of inland freight transport in Romania, Germany and Belgium, while in the Netherlands its share was closer to one third.

The main measure of the volume of passenger transport is the number of passenger-kilometres travelled within the national territory, which can be analysed by mode of transport. Some caution must be applied in making comparisons because of the coverage of national data. Nonetheless, car transport accounted for a sizable majority of inland passenger transport (excluding motorbikes and other powered two-wheelers) among all the Member States for which data are available [5]. The reliance on the car for inland passenger transport was particularly strong in Lithuania, the Netherlands and the United Kingdom, where it accounted for upwards of 87 % of all inland passenger-kilometres. In Bulgaria around 30 % of inland passenger-kilometres were by bus, with shares over 20 % also recorded in Hungary, Estonia, Greece and Slovakia. Hungary, Romania and Austria reported the highest modal shares for railways (including also trams and underground railways/metros), all over 10 %.

It should be noted that the above analysis refers only to inland transport: significant proportions of international freight and passenger travel are accounted for by maritime and air transport, and in some countries national (domestic) maritime and air transport may also be important.

(5) Cyprus and Malta, not available.

Table 11.1: Modal split of inland passenger and freight transport, 2006

	(% of total inland passenger-km) (1)			(% of total inland freight transport in tonne-km) (2)		
	Passenger cars	Buses	Railways, trams and metros	Railways	Roads	Inland waterways
EU-27	83.4	9.5	7.1	17.7	76.7	5.6
Belgium	79.9	13.1	7.0	14.0	71.2	14.7
Bulgaria	64.3	30.4	5.3	27.1	69.0	3.9
Czech Republic	75.6	16.9	7.5	23.8	76.1	0.1
Denmark	79.8	11.2	9.1	8.2	91.8	-
Germany	85.7	6.5	7.8	21.4	65.9	12.8
Estonia	76.0	22.0	2.0	65.3	34.7	0.0
Ireland	76.1	18.8	5.1	1.2	98.8	-
Greece	76.3	21.9	1.8	1.9	98.1	-
Spain	82.6	12.0	5.4	4.6	95.4	-
France	85.3	5.3	9.4	15.7	80.9	3.4
Italy	81.9	12.1	5.9	9.9	90.1	0.0
Cyprus	:	:	0.0	-	100.0	-
Latvia	76.2	18.2	5.6	61.0	39.0	0.0
Lithuania	90.5	8.5	1.0	41.6	58.4	0.0
Luxembourg	85.3	10.8	3.9	4.6	91.5	4.0
Hungary	63.2	23.8	13.0	23.9	71.6	4.5
Malta	:	:	0.0	-	100.0	-
Netherlands	87.5	3.8	8.7	4.1	63.6	32.3
Austria	79.4	10.3	10.3	33.8	63.2	3.0
Poland	82.5	10.6	6.9	29.4	70.4	0.2
Portugal	82.8	12.8	4.5	5.1	94.9	-
Romania	74.0	15.6	10.5	19.4	70.5	10.0
Slovenia	85.6	11.4	3.0	21.8	78.2	-
Slovakia	72.7	21.2	6.1	30.9	68.8	0.3
Finland	84.9	10.3	4.8	27.1	72.7	0.2
Sweden	84.1	7.5	8.4	35.5	64.5	-
United Kingdom	87.4	6.5	6.1	11.8	88.1	0.1
Croatia	83.7	11.8	4.5	24.3	74.8	0.9
FYR of Macedonia	:	:	:	8.4	91.6	-
Turkey	53.2	43.9	2.9	5.1	94.9	-
Iceland	87.2	12.8	0.0	-	100.0	-
Norway	88.0	7.3	4.8	14.7	85.3	-

(1) Excluding powered two-wheelers; Bulgaria, Latvia and Romania, 2005; Turkey, 2004.
(2) Excluding pipelines; Iceland, 2005.

Source: Eurostat (tsdtr210 and tsdtr220)

11.2 Passenger transport

Introduction

EU transport policies have been designed both for households and the business community, regardless of location, whether urban or rural. The recent midterm review of the 2001 White paper shed a spotlight on urban travel, reflecting the fact that 'eighty per cent of Europeans live in an urban environment'. The review points to picking up on the best-practice initiatives used by a number of cities regarding 'transport infrastructure, norm-setting, congestion and traffic management, public transport services, infrastructure charging, urban planning, safety, security and cooperation with the surrounding region'. The Commission published a Green paper [6] on a new culture for urban mobility in September 2007 that looks to stimulate the adoption of these best practices.

Intra-urban transport is only one element of passenger transport policy. Enlargement of the EU has opened up further opportunities for inter-urban passenger travel by rail, road or airplane, which has been and continues to be strengthened by improvements to the infrastructure (such as extensions of the high-speed rail links or raising of airport capacity), by more competition and greater co-ordination (such as the 'single sky' policy). The strengthening of passenger rights has also made passengers more secure to enjoy the freedom to travel and work throughout the EU. The recent mid-term review underlined the point that rail and sea passengers should benefit from similar rights, and this was achieved for rail passengers with the adoption of the third railway package in October 2007 [7].

Definitions and data availability

The **volume of inland passenger transport** is defined as the ratio between passenger-km (inland modes) and GDP (gross domestic product, chain-linked values, at 2000 exchange rates), and within this subchapter is indexed on 2000. It is based on transport movements by passenger cars, buses and coaches, and trains on national territory, regardless of the nationality of the vehicle.

Rail transport statistics are reported on the basis of the '**territoriality principle**'. This means that each reporting country reports the loading / embarkation, unloading / disembarkation and movements of goods and passengers that take place in their national territory. For this reason, indicators that use tonne-kilometres and passenger-kilometre as units are generally considered as the best measure for comparisons between transport modes and countries, because the use of tonnes or passengers entails a high risk of double counting, particularly in international transport. A **rail passenger** is any person, excluding members of the train crew, who makes a journey by rail. A **rail passenger-kilometre** is a unit of measure representing the transport of one rail passenger by rail over a distance of one kilometre. Rail passenger data are not available for Malta and Cyprus as they do not have railways. Annual passenger transport statistics (international and national breakdown) cover railway undertakings subject to detailed reporting only, while total annual passenger statistics may include the undertakings under simplified reporting as well. Some countries apply detailed reporting to all railway undertakings and

(6) COM(2007) 551 final; http://ec.europa.eu/transport/clean/green_paper_urban_transport/index_en.htm.

(7) http://ec.europa.eu/transport/rail/packages/2007_en.htm.

in the case of these countries the total passenger transport is equal to the sum of international and national passenger transport.

Maritime transport data are available for most of the period from 2001 onwards, although some Member States have provided data for the period since 1997. Maritime transport data are not transmitted to Eurostat by the Czech Republic, Luxembourg, Hungary, Austria and Slovakia as they have no maritime traffic. A **merchant ship** is a ship designed for the carriage of goods, transport of passengers or specially fitted out for a specific commercial duty. A **sea passenger** is any person that makes a sea journey on a merchant ship. Service staff assigned to merchant ships are not regarded as passengers. Non-fare paying crew members travelling but not assigned and infants in arms are excluded.

Air transport statistics concern national and international transport. Passenger transport is measured by the number of passengers on board, passengers carried and passenger commercial air flights, in all cases separating arrivals and departures. Statistics on individual routes provide information on seats available, again separating arrivals from departures. The data are presented with monthly, quarterly and annual frequencies. Annual data are available for the EU-27 Member States for most of the period from 2003 onwards. **Air passengers carried** relate to all passengers on a particular flight (with one flight number) counted once only and not repeatedly on each individual stage of that flight. This includes all revenue and non-revenue passengers whose journey begins or terminates at the reporting airport and transfer passengers joining or leaving the flight at the reporting airport; but excludes direct transit passengers.

Fatalities caused by road accidents include drivers and passengers of motorised vehicles and pedal cycles as well as pedestrians, killed within 30 days from the day of the accident. For Member States not using this definition, corrective factors were applied.

Main findings

In the vast majority of Member States, GDP grew faster between 1996 and 2006 than the volume of inland passenger transport. The most notable exception was Lithuania which, relative to GDP, recorded considerable growth in inland passenger transport volumes in 2004 and 2005, and to a lesser extent in 2006. Slovakia and Hungary both recorded GDP growing considerably faster than the volume of inland passenger transport between 1996 and 2006.

The average distance travelled on railways (national and international travel) per inhabitant, was higher in France, Denmark, Sweden and Austria than elsewhere in the EU-27 in 2006, averaging 1 000 kilometres or more per year per person in each of these Member States. In terms of international travel, the average distance travelled on railways per inhabitant was highest in Luxembourg and Austria, reflecting, for example, the number of international borders, the importance of international commuters within the workforce, the relative proximity of capitals or other cities to international borders, the access to high-speed network rail links, or their position on major international transport corridors.

Almost 800 million passengers were carried by air in 2007 in the EU-27. The largest number of passengers carried was reported by the United Kingdom, over 217 million, equivalent to 3.6 passengers carried per inhabitant. Relative to the size of the population the largest numbers of air passengers carried were reported by the islands of Cyprus and Malta, closely followed by Ireland.

In 2007, London's Heathrow airport remained the busiest in terms of passenger numbers (about 68 million), followed by Paris' Charles de Gaulle airport, Frankfurt and Madrid's Barajas airport – all with over 50 million passengers. Madrid's Barajas airport stands out from other leading airports in that national (domestic) flights accounted for a large proportion of the passengers carried, some 44 % in comparison to around 10 % for the others. Relatively large proportions of passengers were also on national flights to and from Barcelona, Roma's Fiumicino airport, and Paris' Orly airport.

Ports in the EU-27 handled 398 million[8] maritime passengers in 2006: a short time-series for the EU-25 shows that passenger numbers increased by 2.8 % in 2006 compared with the year before, partially recouping the 4.9 % fall in 2005. Greek and Italian ports handled more passengers than the ports in any other Member State, followed by Danish and Swedish ports. Relative to the size of population, the largest numbers of maritime passengers were recorded in Denmark and Greece, both over 8 passengers per inhabitant, followed by Estonia, Sweden, Finland and Italy.

Road fatalities in the EU-27 fell sharply between 1996 and 2006, from 59 357 deaths to 42 955 deaths, a fall of over 25 %. In 2006 the road fatality rate, expressed as the number of deaths per million inhabitants averaged 87 in the EU-27. There were nevertheless stark differences between countries, with the highest rates in the Baltic Member States, all exceeding 150 deaths per million inhabitants, and Greece marginally below this level. In contrast, Sweden and the Netherlands recorded fewer than 50 deaths in road accidents per million inhabitants, with only Malta recording a lower rate (27).

Around 2 600 people were victims (seriously injured or killed) of railway accidents in the EU-27 in 2007, with slightly more persons killed than seriously injured. There was an increase of around 2 % in the number of victims between 2006 and 2007, following on from falls of 23 % the previous year, and 6 % the year before that; it should be noted that the number of victims in any particular year can be greatly influenced by a small number of major incidents. Of the total number of victims seriously injured or killed in railway accidents in the EU-27 in 2007, less than one fifth (18 %) were either train passengers or railway employees, and when restricted to victims that were killed, just 7 % were passengers or railway employees. Approximately two thirds (64 %) of the lives lost in rail accidents were from incidents involving rolling stock in motion, with just over a quarter (28 %) from incidents at level-crossings. The highest numbers of rail fatalities within the EU-27 in 2007 occurred in Poland (350) and Germany (200).

(8) The total number of maritime passengers includes passengers who have been double-counted, once when embarking and then when disembarking. The double counting arises when both ports of embarkation and disembarkation report data to Eurostat. This is quite common for the maritime transport of passengers, which is a short distance activity, compared with the seaborne transport of goods. Indeed, there is no significant difference between the number of passengers embarking and disembarking at an aggregated level, as most transport corresponds to main national and intra-EEA ferry connections.

Table 11.2: Volume of inland passenger transport (1)

(index of inland passenger transport volume relative to GDP (2000=100))

	1996	1997	1998	1999	2000	2001	2002	2003	2004	2005	2006
EU-27	:	:	:	:	100.0	:	99.8	:	:	96.5	94.9
Belgium	104.8	102.6	104.3	102.6	100.0	101.3	101.9	102.5	101.6	98.0	96.8
Bulgaria	:	:	:	:	100.0	98.2	99.8	92.6	86.9	84.9	:
Czech Republic	97.9	98.2	100.0	100.6	100.0	98.6	96.9	95.5	90.5	87.4	82.2
Denmark	108.1	106.7	105.5	104.2	100.0	98.0	97.7	98.0	98.2	96.8	95.3
Germany	107.2	105.4	104.6	104.7	100.0	100.9	101.4	101.1	101.4	99.7	98.2
Estonia	:	:	:	:	:	:	:	:	:	:	:
Ireland	117.7	113.9	110.7	105.0	100.0	98.5	96.1	95.4	94.3	92.6	93.4
Greece	89.5	91.3	92.8	95.6	100.0	100.7	102.0	100.2	99.9	100.8	100.8
Spain	102.4	101.5	101.6	102.3	100.0	98.4	97.2	95.8	96.0	94.5	91.1
France	105.1	104.4	103.8	103.3	100.0	101.6	101.6	101.0	98.8	96.2	94.2
Italy	95.4	95.0	96.4	95.5	100.0	97.4	96.4	96.4	96.1	92.8	91.7
Cyprus	:	:	:	:	:	:	:	:	:	:	:
Latvia	:	:	:	:	100.0	:	99.8	:	:	133.0	:
Lithuania	:	:	:	:	100.0	:	93.3	98.8	120.2	145.4	151.3
Luxembourg	114.1	110.0	105.3	97.5	100.0	101.3	99.8	98.1	95.1	93.7	91.3
Hungary	116.6	111.1	106.1	103.6	100.0	96.3	93.2	89.5	85.1	79.9	77.0
Malta	:	:	:	:	:	:	:	:	:	:	:
Netherlands	110.5	109.4	106.0	103.8	100.0	98.5	99.8	99.5	100.5	97.6	94.7
Austria	109.8	106.6	104.1	102.3	100.0	100.0	99.6	100.0	98.5	96.9	95.4
Poland	104.5	103.0	103.8	100.3	100.0	101.5	103.1	101.3	99.6	102.2	104.5
Portugal	95.7	97.7	97.9	99.5	100.0	99.8	102.1	105.4	107.3	110.7	112.0
Romania	:	:	:	:	100.0	95.6	91.6	93.0	88.3	89.1	87.1
Slovenia	110.3	111.2	105.1	105.4	100.0	98.5	96.8	94.8	92.4	89.9	86.7
Slovakia	102.9	95.0	89.9	93.1	100.0	96.4	94.1	88.3	81.9	79.3	74.4
Finland	112.4	108.7	105.3	103.6	100.0	99.1	99.5	99.5	97.7	96.4	92.7
Sweden	109.6	107.4	104.4	102.8	100.0	99.6	99.6	99.5	95.8	93.1	89.7
United Kingdom	98.1	108.4	105.8	104.0	100.0	99.7	100.8	97.7	95.7	93.7	91.7
Croatia	:	:	:	:	100.0	101.2	99.7	96.9	95.4	93.3	96.8
FYR of Macedonia	:	:	:	:	100.0	100.0	103.6	107.8	:	104.8	:
Turkey	102.5	:	:	108.1	100.0	100.6	:	93.5	89.9	:	:
Iceland	89.2	90.2	89.9	89.8	100.0	103.7	106.5	107.0	102.5	101.9	102.7
Norway	109.5	103.8	102.9	102.1	100.0	99.8	100.2	101.1	98.4	97.2	95.5

(1) Break in series: Hungary and the United Kingdom, 1996; Italy, 2000, the Netherlands, 2003.

Source: Eurostat (tsien070)

Table 11.3: Rail passenger transport

	Rail passenger transport (million passenger-km)				Rail passenger transport (passenger-km per inhabitant)				Rail accidents (number of persons)			
	National		International		National		International		Killed		Seriously injured	
	2005	2006	2005	2006	2005	2006	2005	2006	2006	2007	2006	2007
EU-27	:	361 305	:	21 149	:	733	:	43	1 324	1 374	1 236	1 193
Euro area	244 626	254 062	16 652	16 962	782	807	53	54	626	652	607	555
Belgium	7 771	8 190	740	774	744	779	71	74	20	37	28	48
Bulgaria	:	2 366	:	45	:	307	:	6	68	27	55	33
Czech Republic	6 285	6 564	381	358	615	640	37	35	52	25	89	101
Denmark	5 433	5 531	322	359	1 004	1 019	60	66	14	10	10	12
Germany	71 643	75 263	3 300	3 472	868	913	40	42	186	200	196	199
Estonia	224	231	25	26	166	172	19	19	16	14	21	19
Ireland	1 654	1 872	127	0	403	445	31	0	0	6	0	1
Greece	1 804	1 748	50	63	163	157	5	6	39	18	51	38
Spain	19 075	20 260	734	714	443	463	17	16	65	75	47	34
France	69 066	72 359	7 821	7 476	1 103	1 149	125	119	88	80	52	46
Italy	43 889	43 712	2 255	2 726	751	744	39	46	83	71	85	49
Cyprus	-	-	-	-	-	-	-	-	-	-	-	-
Latvia	800	893	89	93	347	389	39	41	30	28	33	17
Lithuania	259	246	21	22	76	72	6	6	49	34	23	11
Luxembourg	203	219	64	79	440	467	139	168	2	0	15	0
Hungary	9 340	9 190	374	334	925	912	37	33	65	59	98	92
Malta	-	-	-	-	-	-	-	-	-	-	-	-
Netherlands	14 752	15 445	231	251	905	946	14	15	16	20	15	10
Austria	6 948	7 051	1 147	1 211	847	853	140	147	43	52	61	63
Poland	17 331	17 675	552	565	454	463	14	15	277	350	225	271
Portugal	3 753	3 821	57	55	356	362	5	5	53	58	33	34
Romania	7 816	7 902	144	164	361	366	7	8	12	36	2	0
Slovenia	666	675	50	48	333	337	25	24	9	17	11	30
Slovakia	2 039	2 043	143	170	379	379	27	32	63	57	32	36
Finland	3 402	3 447	76	93	650	656	15	18	22	18	13	3
Sweden	8 339	9 037	571	580	925	999	63	64	19	25	16	15
United Kingdom	42 981	45 565	1 434	1 472	716	754	24	24	33	57	25	31
Croatia	1 161	1 257	66	65	261	283	15	15	36	27	45	25
Turkey	4 977	5 201	59	76	70	72	1	1	111	108	96	204
Liechtenstein	:	:	:	:	:	:	:	:	0	0	0	0
Norway	2 671	2 779	39	41	580	599	8	9	1	2	4	3

Source: Eurostat (rail_pa_typepkm, tps00001 and rail_ac_catvict)

Figure 11.1: Rail passenger transport, 2006 (1)

(passenger-km per inhabitant)

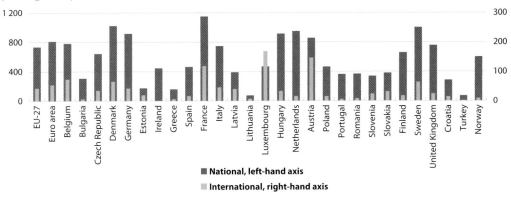

■ National, left-hand axis

■ International, right-hand axis

(1) Cyprus, Malta and Liechtenstein, not applicable.

Source: Eurostat (rail_pa_typepkm and tps00001)

Figure 11.2: Top 15 airports, passengers carried (embarked and disembarked), EU-27, 2007

(million passengers)

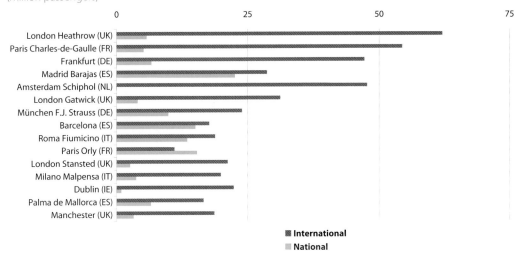

■ International

■ National

Source: Eurostat (avia_paoa)

Table 11.4: Air and sea passenger transport (1)

	Air passengers, 2007 (2)		Maritime passengers, 2006	
	(1 000)	(passengers per inhabitant)	(1 000)	(passengers per inhabitant)
EU-27 (2)	792 636	1.6	397 550	0.8
Belgium	20 805	2.0	891	0.1
Bulgaria	6 071	0.8	15	0.0
Czech Republic	13 098	1.3	-	-
Denmark	24 042	4.4	48 145	8.9
Germany	163 844	2.0	29 256	0.4
Estonia	1 723	1.3	6 691	5.0
Ireland	29 840	6.9	3 207	0.8
Greece	34 786	3.1	90 402	8.1
Spain	163 523	3.7	22 167	0.5
France	120 034	1.9	26 402	0.4
Italy	106 294	1.8	85 984	1.5
Cyprus	7 004	9.0	182	0.2
Latvia	3 156	1.4	217	0.1
Lithuania	2 196	0.6	190	0.1
Luxembourg	1 634	3.4	-	-
Hungary	8 580	0.9	-	-
Malta	2 971	7.3	218	0.5
Netherlands	50 501	3.1	2 127	0.1
Austria	22 926	2.8	-	-
Poland	17 120	0.4	1 737	0.0
Portugal	24 324	2.3	686	0.1
Romania	6 909	0.3	:	:
Slovenia	1 504	0.7	30	0.0
Slovakia	2 232	0.4	-	-
Finland	14 465	2.7	16 739	3.2
Sweden	26 967	3.0	32 334	3.6
United Kingdom	217 288	3.6	29 930	0.5
Croatia	:	:	23 061	5.2
Iceland	2 278	7.6	433	1.4
Norway	26 386	5.6	6 280	1.4
Switzerland	34 538	4.6	-	-

(1) For air: aggregates exclude the double-counting impact of passengers flying between countries belonging to the same aggregate. For maritime: figures refer to the number of passengers 'handled in ports' (i.e. the sum of passengers embarked and then disembarked in ports); if both the port of embarkation and disembarkation report data to Eurostat, then these passengers are counted twice.
(2) Total passengers carried (arrivals and departures for national and international); Iceland, 2006.

Source: Eurostat (ttr00012 and mar_pa_aa)

Figure 11.3: People killed in road accidents, 2006

(persons killed per million inhabitants)

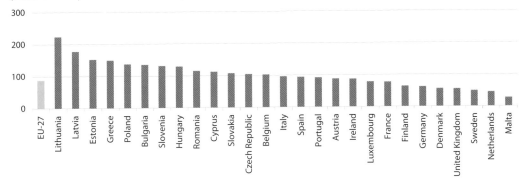

Source: Eurostat (tsdtr420), European Commission CARE database (Community Database on Road Accidents)

Table 11.5: Rail accidents by type of victim and accident, EU-27, 2007 (1)

(number of persons)

	Total		Passengers		Railway employees		Others	
	Killed	Seriously injured	Killed	Seriously injured	Killed	Seriously injured	Killed	Seriously injured
Total	1 374	1 193	65	262	38	99	1 271	832
Collisions (excluding level-crossing accidents)	81	115	2	20	5	29	74	66
Derailments	5	18	2	14	3	4	0	0
Accidents involving level-crossings	381	403	6	32	2	12	373	359
Accidents to persons caused by rolling stock in motion	882	532	45	105	27	37	810	390
Fire in rolling stock	0	0	0	0	0	0	0	0
Others	25	117	10	91	1	12	14	14

(1) Slightly injured persons are not included in rail accident statistics; Cyprus and Malta, not applicable.

Source: Eurostat (rail_ac_catvict)

11.3 Freight transport

Introduction

The ability to move goods safely, quickly and cost-efficiently to market is important for international trade, national distributive trades, and economic development. Strains on infrastructure, demonstrated by congestion and delays, as well as the constraints of disparate standards, technical barriers, poor interoperability and governance all impact on economic development.

The EU has already taken a number of steps to improve freight transport throughout the EU, but the mid-term review of the 2001 White paper specified further actions. The package of measures being proposed by the European Commission concern:

- a freight transport logistics action plan: this covers, among other ideas, e-freight and intelligent transport systems, the promotion of interoperability across modes, single transport documents and the removal of regulatory obstacles;
- a rail network giving priority to freight [9]: ideas being proposed include the creation of freight corridor structures to measure service quality, improvement of the infrastructure of existing freight corridors, the introduction of harmonised rules for the allocation of train paths, the development of priority rules in the case of traffic disturbance, and the improvement of terminal and marshalling yard capacities;

- a ports policy: ideas being proposed include several that might be grouped under 'modernisation', such as the simplification of procedures for short-sea shipping, an e-maritime approach to administration, and improved port equipment, as well as the expansion of capacity whilst respecting the environment;
- a maritime and short-sea shipping policy [10]: challenges faced include reducing bureaucracy, improving promotion and marketing, ensuring the availability of suitable vessels, providing adequate training, the availability of good quality hinterland connections, and establishing integrated information systems.

Definitions and data availability

Weight transported by rail and inland waterways is the gross-gross weight of goods. This includes the total weight of the goods, all packaging, and tare-weight of the container, swap-body and pallets containing goods. In the case of rail, it also includes road goods vehicles carried by rail. The tare-weight is the weight of a transport unit before any cargo is loaded; when the tare-weight is excluded, the weight is the gross weight. The weight measured for sea and road freight transport is the gross weight.

(9) COM(2007) 608.

(10) Commission Staff Working Document SEC(2007) 1367.

Goods loaded are those goods placed on a road vehicle/railway vehicle/merchant ship and dispatched by road/rail/sea. Unlike in road and inland waterway transport, transhipments from one railway vehicle directly to another and change of tractive vehicle are not regarded as unloading/loading; however, if the goods are unloaded from one railway vehicle to another railway vehicle, this is considered as a break of the journey. **Goods unloaded** are those goods taken off a road vehicle/railway vehicle/merchant ship.

Road freight transport statistics are reported by Member States for vehicles registered in their country. On the basis of information on the reporting country, country of loading and country of unloading of a journey, five types of operations are derived:

- national transport;
- international transport – goods loaded in the reporting country;
- international transport – goods unloaded in the reporting country;
- international transport – cross-trade (transport between two countries by a vehicle registered in a third country);
- international transport – cabotage (transport inside one country by a vehicle registered in another country).

Rail freight data are provided to Eurostat in line with Regulation 91/2003; this Regulation has been implemented from 2004. Whereas the quarterly data concern railway enterprises under detailed reporting (usually large ones[11]), annual data cover all enterprises. Rail freight data are not

available for Malta and Cyprus as they do not have railways. Switzerland will provide railway statistics starting from 2008 as a reference year, while Iceland has no railways.

Maritime transport data are available for most of the period from 2001 onwards, although some Member States have provided data for the period since 1997. Maritime transport data are not transmitted to Eurostat by the Czech Republic, Luxembourg, Hungary, Austria and Slovakia as they have no maritime ports.

Air freight and mail transport statistics are broken down by freight and mail on board (arrivals, departures and total), freight and mail loaded and unloaded and all-freight and mail commercial air flights (arrivals, departures and total). The data are presented with monthly, quarterly and annual frequencies. Annual data are available for most of the EU-27 Member States for the period from 2003, with a majority also providing data for 2001 and 2002, while some Member States have provided data back to 1993.

The volume of inland freight transport is defined as the ratio between tonne-km (inland modes) and GDP (gross domestic product, chain-linked values, at 2000 exchange rates), and within this subchapter is indexed on 2000. Rail and inland waterways transport are based on movements on national territory, regardless of the nationality of the vehicle or vessel. Road transport is based on all movements of vehicles registered in the reporting country.

---

(11) Countries may cover all railway undertakings operating on their national territory with detailed reporting only (irrespective of the undertaking's transport performance). In this case, quarterly data are comparable with annual ones.

Main findings

The volume of inland freight transport in the EU-27 has changed roughly in line with the change in GDP since 1996. Relative to growth in GDP, Portugal recorded the most dramatic growth in the volume of inland freight transport during this period, followed by Spain, Bulgaria, Estonia and Ireland, while Romania recorded even stronger growth during the period from 1999 to 2006. In contrast, the change in GDP exceeded the change in the volume of inland freight transport by the greatest extent in Slovakia, followed by Cyprus and Denmark.

Estonia and Latvia were the only Member States where a greater volume of freight was transported by rail than by road, while Belgium and the Netherlands were the only Member States where a greater volume of freight was transported by inland waterways than by rail. Relative to the size of the population, the greatest volume of road freight transport was reported by Luxembourg, over 18 000 tonne-km per inhabitant, more than three times the next highest volume which was recorded by Slovenia. In both cases, the majority of road freight was performed outside the borders of these countries but by vehicles registered in them.

Less than 5 % of air freight and mail transport is national, totalling 579 470 tonnes in 2007 in the EU-27, with France accounting for the largest share. In total, including national and international transport, 3.4 million tonnes of air freight was carried through German airports in 2007. Some of the smaller Member States are relatively specialised in air freight, notably all of the Benelux Member States, particularly Luxembourg.

In 2006, 3 834 million tonnes of goods were handled in EU-27 maritime ports (3.2 % higher than in 2005). With 584 million tonnes, the United Kingdom had the highest share (15 %) of goods handled in EU-27 ports, followed by Italy (14 %). Among the smaller Member States, the weight of goods handled in maritime ports was particularly high in Estonia, the Netherlands, Latvia, Finland, Belgium and Sweden.

Table 11.6: Volume of inland freight transport (1)

(index of inland freight transport volume relative to GDP, 2000=100)

	1996	1997	1998	1999	2000	2001	2002	2003	2004	2005	2006
EU-27	99.7	101.3	101.0	100.0	100.0	99.1	100.1	99.4	105.4	105.5	107.5
Belgium	93.8	94.2	89.0	80.3	100.0	102.2	101.2	97.0	91.2	84.9	82.3
Bulgaria	81.3	82.0	63.6	49.9	100.0	104.8	105.0	109.9	119.7	128.0	118.3
Czech Republic	99.2	117.3	100.9	101.5	100.0	99.6	103.9	105.2	98.6	88.5	94.0
Denmark	99.0	97.7	95.6	100.1	100.0	91.9	92.7	94.5	93.9	91.0	80.2
Germany	93.6	95.4	97.0	100.4	100.0	99.9	98.9	100.0	104.7	106.2	110.1
Estonia	60.2	65.4	76.4	91.3	100.0	89.4	92.5	84.7	89.3	85.7	74.7
Ireland	78.4	76.8	82.0	91.9	100.0	94.8	101.9	106.5	111.5	109.2	100.1
Greece	:	:	:	:	:	:	:	:	:	:	:
Spain	84.2	87.5	93.6	95.5	100.0	104.0	95.0	116.1	128.1	130.1	129.6
France	99.6	100.3	100.3	103.2	100.0	97.1	95.0	92.5	92.8	87.4	87.8
Italy	102.9	101.1	105.1	99.4	100.0	98.8	100.4	91.6	101.7	108.3	110.8
Cyprus	106.9	106.3	104.8	101.6	100.0	99.3	101.2	105.3	80.7	96.6	77.6
Latvia	101.2	110.7	104.3	96.7	100.0	99.9	101.9	111.0	107.2	105.0	91.6
Lithuania	88.1	91.0	85.3	97.2	100.0	90.0	107.6	109.2	106.2	116.7	118.5
Luxembourg	67.3	77.5	80.9	91.6	100.0	109.2	109.4	111.0	106.3	91.6	87.2
Hungary	99.9	100.0	110.7	102.2	100.0	94.0	89.5	87.3	93.8	104.8	118.0
Malta	:	:	:	:	:	:	:	:	:	:	:
Netherlands	101.6	103.7	106.7	106.9	100.0	97.4	95.5	96.2	105.6	99.3	96.0
Austria	90.4	91.9	93.4	98.1	100.0	104.7	105.7	105.2	104.3	98.1	101.9
Poland	119.5	118.3	112.0	103.0	100.0	97.6	98.4	98.4	108.2	108.9	115.2
Portugal	101.8	105.5	101.6	101.2	100.0	108.4	107.0	99.7	143.5	148.6	153.8
Romania	:	:	:	95.0	100.0	106.3	119.5	127.0	145.0	174.1	171.3
Slovenia	106.8	106.1	106.2	102.1	100.0	101.0	95.5	98.9	114.5	129.1	132.4
Slovakia	120.6	114.9	116.3	112.9	100.0	92.4	86.9	88.1	88.0	93.6	86.7
Finland	97.8	97.0	98.6	98.4	100.0	93.4	94.8	91.7	91.5	87.1	81.5
Sweden	108.8	110.4	102.9	98.0	100.0	95.4	96.9	96.7	94.4	95.3	94.5
United Kingdom	112.4	111.9	110.2	104.2	100.0	97.1	95.2	94.2	92.7	91.5	91.4
FYR of Macedonia	:	:	:	:	100.0	93.4	111.7	146.0	138.9	141.4	198.4
Turkey	96.6	92.8	96.7	99.2	100.0	98.4	92.2	89.1	84.2	82.2	81.7
Iceland	101.4	102.4	102.1	103.8	100.0	105.5	108.3	108.8	109.7	113.2	119.2
Norway	96.0	101.8	102.6	101.5	100.0	97.8	96.6	101.4	103.1	105.7	109.6

(1) Break in series: Sweden, 1995; Estonia, 1997; Bulgaria, Hungary and Slovakia, 2000; Bulgaria, 2001; EU-27, Spain, Portugal and Romania, 2004.

Source: Eurostat (tsien060)

Table 11.7: Inland freight transport, 2007

	(million t-km)			(t-km per inhabitant)			National air freight and mail transport (tonnes) (4)
	Road (1)	Rail (2)	Inland water-ways (3)	Road (1)	Rail (2)	Inland water-ways (3)	
EU-27	1 852 614	450 769	137 711	3 721	910	279	579 470
Belgium	43 017	8 235	8 908	4 064	778	848	658
Bulgaria	13 765	5 241	1 011	1 792	682	132	23
Czech Republic	50 376	16 304	36	4 897	1 585	4	3 142
Denmark	21 254	1 779	-	3 902	327	-	1 496
Germany	330 016	114 615	64 685	4 009	1 392	786	116 384
Estonia	5 548	8 430	:	4 133	6 280	:	0
Ireland	17 454	129	-	4 047	30	-	13 111
Greece	34 002	835	-	3 044	75	-	13 487
Spain	241 788	11 064	-	5 437	249	-	110 576
France	211 445	41 190	9 208	3 336	654	145	157 559
Italy	191 900	25 285	:	3 605	428	:	72 761
Cyprus	1 165	-	-	1 496	-	-	685
Latvia	10 753	18 313	:	4 714	8 027	:	0
Lithuania	18 134	14 373	:	5 357	4 246	:	0
Luxembourg	8 807	427	345	18 495	897	724	157
Hungary	30 479	10 048	2 212	3 028	998	220	1
Malta	:	-	-	:	-	-	0
Netherlands	83 193	7 216	42 310	5 086	441	2 590	1
Austria	39 187	21 371	2 597	4 722	2 575	313	838
Poland	128 315	54 253	277	3 366	1 423	7	7 471
Portugal	44 835	2 586	-	4 230	244	-	20 867
Romania	57 288	15 757	8 195	2 657	731	380	501
Slovenia	12 112	3 603	:	6 025	1 792	:	12
Slovakia	22 212	9 647	1 004	4 118	1 789	186	0
Finland	29 715	10 434	:	5 631	1 977	:	4 531
Sweden	39 918	23 250	-	4 380	2 551	-	:
United Kingdom	165 936	26 384	:	2 831	434	:	127 970
Croatia	:	3 574	:	:	805	:	:
Turkey	:	9 755	-	:	140	-	:
Iceland	:	-	-	:	-	-	4
Liechtenstein	339	18	:	9 639	512	:	:
Norway	19 387	3 456	-	4 142	738	-	18 068
Switzerland	:	:	:	:	:	:	5 026

(1) All data refer to 2006; road transport is based on movements all over the world of vehicles registered in the reporting country; EU-25 instead of EU-27.
(2) France, 2006.
(3) EU-27, Belgium and the Netherlands, 2006.
(4) Italy and Malta, 2006; Iceland, 2005; Denmark does not include data for Copenhagen/Kastrup airport; France underestimated as freight transport at Paris Charles-de-Gaulle and Paris Orly is incomplete.

Source: Eurostat (road_go_ta_tott, rail_go_typeall, ttr00007, tps00001 and avia_gooc) and Directorate-General for Energy and Transport

Figure 11.4: Air freight transport, 2007 (1)

(1 000 tonnes)

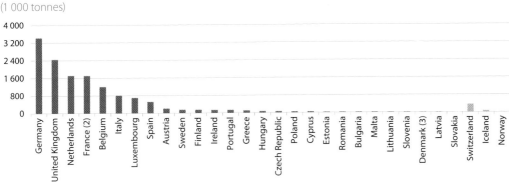

(1) Italy and Iceland, 2006; Sweden, 2004.
(2) Underestimated: freight transport at Paris Charles-de-Gaulle and Paris Orly is incomplete.
(3) Excluding freight transport at Copenhagen/Kastrup airport.

Source: Eurostat (ttr00011) and Directorate-General for Energy and Transport

Figure 11.5: Gross weight of seaborne goods handled in ports, 2006 (1)

(million tonnes)

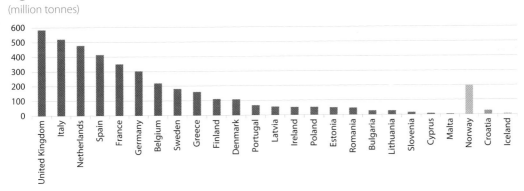

(1) The Czech Republic, Luxembourg, Hungary, Austria and Slovakia, not applicable.

Source: Eurostat (mar_go_aa)

Environment

12

The sixth environment action programme (sixth EAP) [1], adopted in 2002, is the EU's ten-year (2002-2012) policy programme for the environment. It identifies four key priorities:

- tackling climate change: to achieve the EU's target of reducing greenhouse gas emissions by 8 % by 2008-2012;
- nature and biodiversity: to avert the loss of species and their habitats in Europe by completion of the Natura 2000 network and by developing new sectoral biodiversity action plans, and to pay greater attention to protecting landscapes, the marine environment and soils, and to establish measures to prevent industrial and mining accidents;
- environment and health: to completely overhaul the EU's risk-management system for chemicals, to develop a strategy for reducing risks from pesticides, protection of water quality in the EU, noise abatement and a thematic strategy for air quality;
- sustainable use of natural resources and the management of waste: to increase resource efficiency and decouple resource use from economic growth, to increase recycling and waste prevention with the aid of an integrated product policy and measures targeting specific waste streams such as hazardous waste, sludges and biodegradable waste.

In order to implement the sixth EAP, the European Commission adopted seven thematic strategies; these are air pollution (adopted in September 2005), marine environment (October 2005), the prevention and recycling of waste (December 2005), the sustainable use of natural resources (December 2005), urban environment (January 2006), soil (September 2006) and the sustainable use of pesticides (July 2006).

---

(1) Decision No 1600/2002/EC of the European Parliament and of the Council of 22 July 2002 laying down the Sixth Community Environment Action Programme; http://europa.eu/eur-lex/pri/en/oj/dat/2002/l_242/l_24220020910en00010015.pdf.

12.1 Climate change

Each strategy follows an in-depth review of existing policy and wide-ranging stakeholder consultation. The aim is to create positive synergies between the seven strategies, as well as to integrate them with existing sectoral policies, the revised Lisbon strategy and the sustainable development strategy.

A 2007 mid-term review of the sixth EAP[2] was held and results adopted by the European Commission in April 2007: this confirmed the programme as the framework for Community action in the field of the environment up to 2012. The EU also set a target for more radical global emission cuts in the order of 20 % by 2020.

Eurostat, in close partnership with the European Environment Agency (EEA), provides statistics, indicators and meta-information on environmental pressures and the state of the environment to support the implementation and monitoring of the sixth EAP.

Introduction

The fourth assessment report from the International Panel on Climate Change (IPCCC) confirmed that climate change exists and is projected to continue; the emission of greenhouse gases from human activities, such as the burning of coal, oil and gas, is causing an overall warming of the earth's atmosphere, and climate change is the most likely result with potentially major economic and social consequences[3].

Data on greenhouse gas emissions are officially reported under the United Nations Framework Convention on Climate Change – UNFCCC[4] – and the Kyoto Protocol. The so-called Kyoto basket includes six greenhouse gases (GHG): carbon dioxide (CO_2), methane (CH_4), nitrous oxide (N_2O), hydrofluorocarbons (HFCs), perfluorocarbons (PFCs) and sulphur hexafluoride (SF_6).

Under the Kyoto Protocol, the European Community has agreed to an 8 % reduction in its greenhouse gas emissions by 2008-2012, compared with a base year which in general terms is 1990. The reductions for each of the EU-15 Member States have been agreed under the so-called EU burden sharing agreement, which allows some countries to increase emissions, provided these are offset by reductions in other Member States. The ten Member States that joined the EU in 2004, as well as Bulgaria and Romania, have chosen other reduction targets and other base years as allowed under the protocol. Emissions of the six greenhouse gases

(2) Commission Communication on the mid-term review of the Sixth Community Environment Action Programme, http://eur-lex.europa.eu/LexUriServ/LexUriServ.do?uri=CELEX:52007SC0547:EN:HTML.

(3) 'Winning the battle against global climate change', COM(2005) 35; http://ec.europa.eu/environment/climat/pdf/comm_en_050209.pdf.

(4) http://unfccc.int.

covered by the protocol are weighted by their global warming potentials (GWPs) and aggregated to give total emissions in CO_2 equivalents.

In February 2006, the European Commission adopted the fourth national communication [5] from the European Community under the UNFCCC, in which it describes the wide range of policies on climate change, provides projections for greenhouse gas emissions, and outlines the effect of European Community policies and measures on such gases. In August 2006, the European Commission adopted a communication implementing a Community strategy to reduce CO_2 emissions from cars [6].

In January 2007, the European Commission set out proposals and options for an ambitious global agreement in its Communication 'Limiting Global Climate Change to 2 degrees Celsius: The way ahead for 2020 and beyond', proposing a number of EU targets for 2020:

- greenhouse gas emissions should be cut by 20 % compared with 1990 levels;
- renewable energy sources (such as hydro, solar and wind energy) should provide 20 % of all energy used;
- biofuels should account for 10 % of all transport fuels; and
- total energy consumption should be cut by 20 % through increased energy efficiency.

At their spring European Council in March 2007, EU Heads of State and Government pledged that the EU would reduce its emissions in the order of 30 % below 1990 levels by 2020 provided that

other developed countries agreed to make similar efforts. EU leaders endorsed the package of climate and energy measures put forward by the Commission as the basis for achieving this goal.

In January 2008, the Commission proposed a major package [7] of climate and energy-related legislative proposals to implement these commitments and targets, which (at the time of writing) are being discussed by the European Parliament and the Council.

Definitions and data availability

The European Environment Agency, assisted by its European Topic Centre on Air and Climate Change, compiles the annual European Community greenhouse gas inventory report for submission to the UNFCCC Secretariat.

Emissions data for the six greenhouse gases (GHG): CO_2, CH_4, N_2O, HFC, PFC and SF_6 are weighted by their global warming potentials (GWPs) and aggregated to give total emissions in CO_2-equivalents. To obtain emissions in CO_2-equivalents using their global warming potential, the following weighting factors are used: carbon dioxide=1, methane=21, nitrous oxide=310 and sulphur hexafluoride=23 900. Hydrofluorocarbons and perfluorocarbons comprise a large number of different gases that have different GWPs.

Land use changes and forestry are excluded from the calculations of GHG emissions. The base quantity is defined by the GHG emissions in the base year, which is 1990 for the non-fluorinated gases (CO_2, CH_4 and N_2O) and 1995 for

(5) COM(2006) 40; http://unfccc.int/resource/docs/natc/eunce4.pdf.
(6) COM(2006) 463; http://eur-lex.europa.eu/LexUriServ/site/en/com/2006/com2006_0463 en01.pdf.
(7) COM(2008) 30 final on '20 20 by 2020 – Europe's climate change opportunity'; http://eur-lex.europa.eu/LexUriServ/LexUriServ.do?uri=CELEX:52008DC0030:EN:NOT.

the fluorinated gases (HFC, PFC and SF$_6$), with exceptions for some countries. Greenhouse gas emission reduction targets for 2008-2012 are those agreed upon in Council Decision 2002/358/EC (for the Member States) or in the Kyoto Protocol (all other countries).

Main findings

Total greenhouse gas (GHG) emissions across the EU-27 declined by 7.7 % between 1990 and 2006, although most of this decline took place in the period before 1998. Indeed, the EU-27's GHG emission levels for 2006 remained 1.5 % higher than the relative low recorded in 2000.

Developments among Member States varied considerably: of the twelve Member States where GHG emission levels in 2006 were higher than in 1990, by far the strongest rises (45 % to 70 % higher) were recorded for Cyprus, Spain and Malta. In comparison to the Kyoto targets set for the 2008-2012 period (note that targets were not set for Cyprus and Malta), GHG emission levels in 2006 were relatively high in Spain, Luxembourg, Austria and Denmark –where emissions also remained above 1990 levels.

In contrast, GHG emissions in 2006 were lower than 1990 levels in 15 of the Member States, with some of the largest reductions being recorded among the three Baltic Member States, where emissions fell by more than 50 % to be well within their respective Kyoto targets.

Greenhouse gas emissions rose by the equivalent of 77.6 million tonnes of CO$_2$ between 2000 and 2006 in the EU-27. In absolute terms, the largest rises in GHG emissions in this period came from Spain (48 million tonnes), Romania (18 million tonnes) and Italy (16 million tonnes). In contrast, there were notable falls recorded in the United Kingdom (18 million tonnes), Germany (15 million tonnes), France (14 million tonnes, which was almost entirely in 2006) and Belgium (9 million tonnes).

A majority (60.4 %) of the EU-27's GHG emissions in 2006 came from energy (excluding transport). Compared with the situation in 1990, however, a much greater proportion (19.3 % compared with 14.0 %) of GHGs came from transport. The relative shares of GHG emissions from other sectors decreased; in the case of energy this was in part explained by a reduction in the use of coal, and in the case of agriculture by a lower use of fertilisers and pesticides.

The latest projections suggest that in order for the EU to reach its intended targets for 2020, it will have to put emissions on a much steeper reduction path after 2012.

Figure 12.1: Total greenhouse gas emissions (1)

(base year=100; for EU-27, Cyprus and Malta, 1990=100)

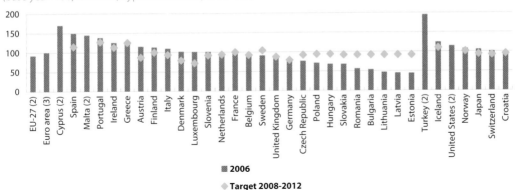

■ **2006**

◆ **Target 2008-2012**

(1) Generally index based on 1990=100.
(2) No target under the Kyoto Protocol.
(3) EA-12 instead of EA-15; no target under the Kyoto Protocol.

Source: Eurostat (tsien010), European Environment Agency, European Topic Center on Air and Climate Change

Figure 12.2: Greenhouse gas emissions, EU-27 (1)

(1990=100)

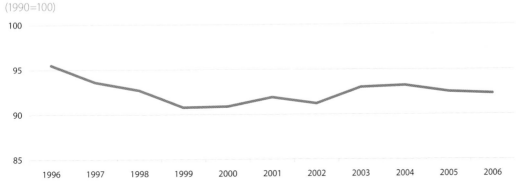

(1) Weighted emissions of greenhouse gases represented 5 320 million tonnes of CO_2 equivalent in 1996 and 5 143 million tonnes in 2006.

Source: Eurostat (tsien010 and ten00072), European Environment Agency, European Topic Center on Air and Climate Change

Table 12.1: Greenhouse gas emissions

	Total greenhouse gas emissions (1990=100) (1)				Weighted emissions of greenhouse gases (million tonnes of CO_2 equivalent)			
	1996	2001	2006	Target 2008 2012	1996	2001	2006	Share in EU-27 (%)
EU-27	95.5	91.9	92.3	:	5 319.5	5 121.2	5 142.8	-
Euro area	99.3	100.3	100.6	:	3 325.5	3 356.4	3 367.3	65.5
Belgium	106.0	99.6	94.0	92.5	154.5	145.2	137.0	2.7
Bulgaria	65.0	52.0	53.8	92.0	86.2	69.0	71.3	1.4
Czech Republic	82.2	76.7	76.3	92.0	159.6	149.0	148.2	2.9
Denmark	129.1	100.2	101.7	79.0	89.5	69.4	70.5	1.4
Germany	90.4	84.1	81.5	79.0	1 114.7	1 036.3	1 004.8	19.5
Estonia	50.8	42.9	44.3	92.0	21.7	18.3	18.9	0.4
Ireland	110.4	127.2	125.5	113.0	61.4	70.7	69.8	1.4
Greece	106.5	121.1	124.4	125.0	113.9	129.6	133.1	2.6
Spain	107.4	133.0	149.5	115.0	311.3	385.5	433.3	8.4
France	101.3	98.9	96.0	100.0	571.3	557.6	541.3	10.5
Italy	101.3	108.0	109.9	93.5	523.4	558.0	567.9	11.0
Cyprus	125.3	142.1	170.1	:	7.4	8.4	10.0	0.2
Latvia	48.5	41.1	44.9	92.0	12.6	10.7	11.6	0.2
Lithuania	47.1	41.2	47.0	92.0	23.3	20.3	23.2	0.5
Luxembourg	79.2	79.6	101.2	72.0	10.4	10.5	13.3	0.3
Hungary	70.6	68.8	68.1	94.0	81.5	79.4	78.6	1.5
Malta	119.7	129.3	145.0	:	2.6	2.8	3.2	0.1
Netherlands	108.9	101.1	97.4	94.0	232.0	215.3	207.5	4.0
Austria	105.9	107.9	115.2	87.0	83.7	85.3	91.1	1.8
Poland	79.6	68.4	71.1	94.0	448.4	385.5	400.5	7.8
Portugal	112.8	138.7	138.3	127.0	67.8	83.4	83.2	1.6
Romania	68.3	51.7	56.3	92.0	190.0	143.7	156.7	3.0
Slovenia	95.0	97.4	101.2	92.0	19.4	19.8	20.6	0.4
Slovakia	71.1	69.7	67.9	92.0	51.2	50.2	48.9	1.0
Finland	108.8	105.6	113.1	100.0	77.3	75.0	80.3	1.6
Sweden	107.2	95.6	91.1	104.0	77.3	69.0	65.8	1.3
United Kingdom	93.7	86.7	84.0	87.5	727.2	673.3	652.3	12.7
Croatia	72.4	84.2	94.8	95.0	23.5	27.4	30.8	-
Turkey	142.4	154.1	195.1	:	0.2	0.3	0.3	-
Iceland	96.3	109.1	124.2	110.0	3.3	3.7	4.2	-
Liechtenstein	86.8	86.8	:	92.0	0.0	0.0	0.0	-
Norway	106.2	110.1	107.7	101.0	52.8	54.7	53.5	-
Switzerland	98.1	99.6	100.8	92.0	51.8	52.6	53.2	-
Japan	106.8	104.0	105.3	94.0	1 358.2	1 322.7	1 340.8	-
United States	109.3	112.5	114.4	:	6 706.6	6 901.4	7 107.3	-

(1) Generally index based on 1990=100; EU-27, Cyprus, Malta, Turkey and the United States, no target under the Kyoto Protocol.

Source: Eurostat (tsien010 and ten00072), European Environment Agency, European Topic Center on Air and Climate Change

Figure 12.3: Greenhouse gas emissions by sector, EU-27, 2006 (1)

(%, based on data in million tonnes CO_2 equivalent)

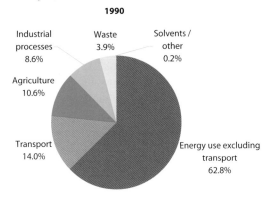

1990

Industrial processes 8.6%

Waste 3.9%

Solvents / other 0.2%

Agriculture 10.6%

Transport 14.0%

Energy use excluding transport 62.8%

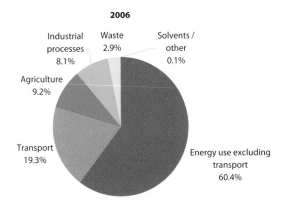

2006

Industrial processes 8.1%

Waste 2.9%

Solvents / other 0.1%

Agriculture 9.2%

Transport 19.3%

Energy use excluding transport 60.4%

(1) Total emissions were 5 143 million tonnes of CO_2 equivalent for the EU-27; figures do not sum to 100 % due to rounding.

Source: Eurostat (env_air_emis), European Environment Agency

12.2 Air pollution

Introduction

Data on air pollution is officially reported under the Convention on Long-range Transboundary Air Pollution – CLRTAP – to the EMEP project; EMEP stands for Co-operative Programme for Monitoring and Evaluation of the Long-range Transmission of Air pollutants in Europe. The air pollutants that are reported are ammonia (NH_3), sulphur oxides (SO_2 and SO_3 as SOx), nitrogen oxides (NO and NO_2 as NOx), non-methane volatile organic compounds (NMVOC), carbon monoxide (CO), and particulate matter (PM10, particles defined as having aerodynamic diameter of 10 μm or less). Where PM10 data are not reported by countries to EMEP/CLRTAP, emission estimates can be obtained from the Regional Air Pollution Information and Simulation (RAINS) model.

Air pollution caused by human activities, the rise of industrial and energy production, the burning of fossil fuels and increased transport can lead to serious health problems. Air pollution damages the health of hundreds of thousands of Europeans every year. A 2004 WHO evaluation found that air pollution contributed to 100 000 premature deaths and 725 000 working days lost annually in Europe.

Since the early 1970s, the EU has been working to improve air quality by controlling emissions of harmful substances into the atmosphere, improving fuel quality, and by integrating environmental protection requirements into the transport and energy sectors. In 2008, a new Directive[8] of the European Parliament and of the Council regarding ambient air quality and cleaner air for Europe was adopted and came in to force. There was also a 2008 Directive[9] of the Council concerning integrated pollution prevention and control of stationary source emissions.

Although ozone (O_3) is present in small concentrations throughout the atmosphere, most ozone (about 90 %) exists in the stratosphere, a layer between 10 and 50 km above the surface of the earth. This ozone layer performs the essential task of filtering out most of the sun's biologically harmful ultraviolet (UV-B) radiation. At ground level, ozone is harmful. It is formed by atmospheric pollutants and is often associated with human activities, such as the burning of fossil fuels and biomass, traffic emissions, or the use of aerosols, while natural events, such as volcanic eruptions, can also have an impact. Areas with heavy traffic are particularly susceptible to the formation of ground level ozone; this problem is exacerbated by particular climatic conditions. Ground level ozone is a secondary pollutant caused by nitrogen oxide and volatile organic compounds reacting in sunlight; it harms human health, nature and biological diversity, crops and materials. People living in urban areas are therefore most at risk from ground level ozone. Higher concentrations of ground level ozone can have harmful effects on the respiratory tract, can cause breathing difficulties, damage lungs and can trigger asthma attacks.

---

(8) Directive 2008/50/EC of the European Parliament and of the Council of 21 May 2008; http://eur-lex.europa.eu/LexUriServ/LexUriServ.do?uri=CELEX:32008L0050:EN:NOT.

(9) Directive 2008/1/EC of the Council of 15 January 2008; http://eur-lex.europa.eu/LexUriServ/LexUriServ.do?uri=CELEX:32008L0001:EN:NOT.

Indeed, human health is also at risk from high concentrations of particles, particularly those smaller than 10 μm, which penetrate deeply into the lungs, increasing the death rate in members of the population suffering from heart and lung diseases. Particles smaller than 2.5 μm are mostly soot, especially wood smoke and diesel-engine exhaust. These can persist in the air for long periods and can be transported over long distances. Coarser particles (soil and mineral ash) originate mainly from mechanical processes such as mining, quarrying and other industrial processes, as well as wear and tear of tyres and brakes in road traffic.

Definitions and data availability

The European Environment Agency (EEA) and its European Topic Centre on Air and Climate Change compile data on emissions of air pollutants and on air quality for the Member States and the candidate countries. A near to real-time ozone information system is available on the EEA website [10].

Emissions of key air pollutants are available in EPER, a web-based register, which enables the public to view data from large industrial point sources in the EU [11].

Urban population exposure to air pollution shows the population weighted annual mean concentration of particulate matter and yearly sum of maximum daily 8-hour mean ozone concentrations above a threshold (70 microgram ozone per m³) at urban background stations in agglomerations and the . **Fine particulates** (PM10), i.e. particulates whose diameter

is less than 10 micrometers, can be carried deep into the lungs where they can cause inflammation and a worsening of the condition of people with heart and lung diseases. In 1996, the Environment Council adopted Framework Directive 96/62/EC on ambient air quality assessment and management. The first Daughter Directive (1999/30/EC) relating to limit values for PM10 and other pollutants in ambient air fixed an annual limit value of 40 microgram of PM10 per m³. Annual reporting must follow Commission Decision 2004/224/EC of 20 February 2004 laying down arrangements for the submission of information under Council Directive 96/62/EC in relation to limit values for certain pollutants in ambient air. **Ozone** is a strong photochemical oxidant, which causes serious health problems and damage to the ecosystem, agricultural crops and materials. Human exposure to elevated ozone concentrations can give rise to inflammatory responses and decreases in lung function. In 1996, the Environment Council adopted Framework Directive 96/62/EC on ambient air quality assessment and management. The third Daughter Directive (2002/3/EC) relating to ozone was adopted on 12 February 2002 with a long-term objective of 120 microgram ozone per m³ as a maximum daily 8-hour mean within a calendar year. The annual reporting must follow the Commission Decision 2004/224/CE of 20 February 2004 laying down arrangements for the submission of information under Council Directive 96/62/EC in relation to limit values for certain pollutants in ambient air.

(10) Ozone today – European status; http://www.eea.europa.eu/maps/ozone/welcome.

(11) http://ec.europa.eu/environment/ippc/eper/index.htm.

Weighted emissions of acidifying substances tracks trends in anthropogenic atmospheric emissions of acidifying substances (sulphur dioxide, nitrogen oxides and ammonia) by source sector. Acidifying substance emissions are combined in terms of their acidifying effects, and expressed in acid equivalents.

Main findings

Although the data is incomplete in terms of country coverage, the highest concentration of particulate matter among people living in urban areas was found in Bulgaria and Romania in 2006, at upwards of 75 % more than the EU-27 average level. Exposure to air pollution by ozone was highest for the urban populations of Italy and Greece, where the mean ozone concentrations registered in 2006 were about 75 % higher than the EU-27 average. These measures of air pollution were relatively low in Finland, Sweden and the United Kingdom in 2006.

Carbon dioxide is by far the most common type of air pollutant, with more 4 258 million tonnes released across the EU-27 in 2006, up slightly on the level in 1996. The developments among the Member States were largely as described for GHGs as a whole, as presented in Subchapter 12.1, with a rise of almost 50 % in carbon dioxide levels in Spain and 40 % in Cyprus being by far the steepest. In contrast, there were relatively large reductions in the amounts of other air pollutants released in the EU-27; the amounts of carbon monoxide released declined by over a third (37.6 %) in the ten years through until 2005, of nitrous oxides and methane by a little over a fifth (down 22.7 % and 21.7 % respectively) and of sulphur oxides by about 8 %. Aside from carbon dioxide, there were declines in the emissions of air pollutants in almost all of the Member States, particularly sharp declines being recorded in the United Kingdom (up to twice the average rate across the EU-27). Among the exceptions, there were higher emission levels of carbon monoxide in Finland and Latvia, and notably higher emissions of methane in Spain, sulphur oxides in Denmark and nitrogen oxides in Austria and Spain.

When related to the size of each Member States' population, carbon dioxide emissions were between 25 % and 45 % higher than the EU-27 average in Finland, the Czech Republic, Estonia, Belgium and Ireland. The particularly high figure for Luxembourg is at least in part explained by the high proportion of the country's workforce that live over the border in neighbouring Belgium, Germany or France. In contrast, carbon dioxide emissions were less than one half of the EU-27 figure per head of population in Lithuania and Latvia.

Emissions of acidifying substances contribute to acid deposition, leading among other things to potential changes in soil and water quality and damage to forests, crops and other vegetation, and to adverse effects on aquatic ecosystems in rivers and lakes. About one quarter (25.7 %) of the emissions of acidifying substances across the EU-27 in 2006 came from agriculture, with another quarter (24.7 %) coming from energy industries (particularly the coal-based energy industry).

Table 12.2: Air pollutants

	Emissions of carbon dioxide (million tonnes)		Emissions of carbon monoxide (million tonnes)		Emissions of methane (million tonnes)		Emissions of sulphur oxides (million tonnes of SO_2 equivalent)		Emissions of nitrogen oxides (million tonnes of NO_2 equivalent)	
	1996	2006	1995	2005	1996	2006	1995	2005	1995	2005
EU-27	4 241.7	4 257.6	51.08	31.89	25.49	19.96	17.16	15.82	14.60	11.29
Belgium	128.0	119.1	1.11	0.88	0.46	0.34	0.26	0.24	0.37	0.29
Bulgaria	65.0	55.1	0.85	0.74	0.73	0.54	1.48	1.42	0.27	0.23
Czech Republic	138.4	127.9	1.00	0.51	0.64	0.57	1.09	0.94	0.37	0.28
Denmark	74.0	57.6	0.71	0.61	0.29	0.26	0.14	0.17	0.26	0.19
Germany	943.3	880.3	6.53	4.03	3.73	2.18	1.73	1.45	2.17	1.44
Estonia	18.7	16.0	0.21	0.16	0.10	0.10	0.12	0.12	0.04	0.03
Ireland	37.1	47.3	0.32	0.23	0.67	0.63	0.16	0.15	0.12	0.12
Greece	89.3	109.7	1.32	0.64	0.44	0.40	0.54	0.52	0.32	0.32
Spain	243.0	359.6	3.22	2.38	1.55	1.79	1.81	1.58	1.33	1.53
France	402.4	404.3	9.57	5.68	3.26	2.67	0.97	0.94	1.65	1.21
Italy	439.3	488.0	7.17	4.21	2.10	1.82	1.32	1.21	1.81	1.17
Cyprus	5.9	8.2	0.10	0.04	0.04	0.04	0.04	0.05	0.02	0.02
Latvia	9.2	8.3	0.32	0.34	0.09	0.08	0.05	0.05	0.04	0.04
Lithuania	15.9	14.5	0.29	0.19	0.17	0.16	0.09	0.09	0.07	0.06
Luxembourg	9.4	12.1	0.11	0.04	0.02	0.02	0.01	0.01	0.02	0.01
Hungary	63.4	60.4	0.76	0.59	0.40	0.37	0.70	0.67	0.19	0.20
Malta	2.3	2.6	:	:	0.01	0.02	0.03	0.03	0.01	0.01
Netherlands	177.7	172.2	0.86	0.60	1.10	0.78	0.13	0.12	0.47	0.34
Austria	67.4	77.3	1.01	0.72	0.40	0.33	0.05	0.04	0.19	0.23
Poland	374.9	330.5	4.55	3.33	2.05	1.77	2.38	2.37	1.12	0.81
Portugal	50.3	64.5	0.85	0.65	0.54	0.56	0.33	0.27	0.27	0.28
Romania	135.4	111.0	2.09	1.41	1.62	1.38	0.89	0.86	0.32	0.31
Slovenia	15.7	16.9	0.09	0.08	0.10	0.10	0.13	0.11	0.07	0.06
Slovakia	42.4	40.0	0.42	0.30	0.22	0.22	0.25	0.23	0.18	0.10
Finland	64.0	68.1	0.44	0.52	0.29	0.22	0.10	0.11	0.26	0.18
Sweden	61.6	51.5	0.90	0.60	0.32	0.26	0.07	0.07	0.28	0.20
United Kingdom	568.0	554.8	6.30	2.42	4.17	2.33	2.32	1.97	2.38	1.63
Croatia (1)	16.9	23.0	0.34	0.31	0.12	0.15	0.08	0.06	0.06	0.07
FYR of Macedonia	:	:	0.02	0.10	:	:	0.02	0.02	0.01	0.03
Turkey (1)	190.7	256.9	3.99	3.78	2.14	2.35	1.01	1.16	0.80	0.95
Iceland (1)	2.4	2.9	0.00	0.00	0.02	0.02	0.00	0.00	0.00	0.00
Liechtenstein (1)	0.2	0.2	0.00	0.00	0.00	0.00	0.00	0.00	0.00	0.00
Norway (1)	40.8	43.2	0.73	0.45	0.24	0.22	0.03	0.03	0.21	0.20
Switzerland (1)	44.1	46.0	0.49	0.33	0.19	0.17	0.03	0.03	0.12	0.09

(1) 2005 instead of 2006 for emissions of carbon dioxide and methane.

Source: Eurostat (ten00073, ten00070, ten00074, ten00067 and ten00068)

Figure 12.4: Urban population exposure to air pollution - population weighted, 2006 (1)

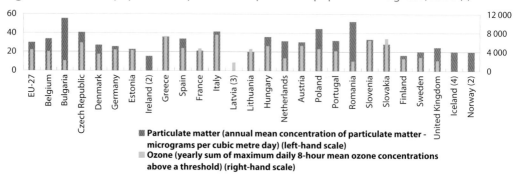

■ **Particulate matter (annual mean concentration of particulate matter - micrograms per cubic metre day) (left-hand scale)**
■ **Ozone (yearly sum of maximum daily 8-hour mean ozone concentrations above a threshold) (right-hand scale)**

(1) Cyprus, Luxembourg and Malta, not available.
(2) Ozone, not available.
(3) Particulate matter, not available.
(4) Ozone, 2005.

Source: Eurostat (tsien110), European Environment Agency, European Topic Center on Air and Climate Change

Figure 12.5: Emissions of carbon dioxide, 2006

(kg per capita)

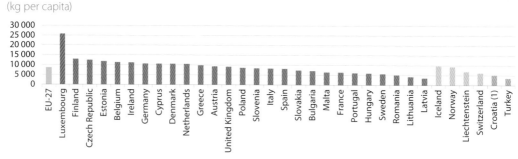

(1) Estimate.

Source: Eurostat (ten00073 and tps00001)

Figure 12.6: Weighted emissions of acidifying substances, by sector, EU-27, 2005 (1)

(%, based on acid equivalents)

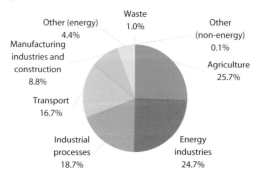

(1) Total emissions were 745 210 tonnes of acid equivalent; figures do not sum to 100 % due to rounding.

Source: Eurostat (tsdpc260), European Environment Agency, Topic Centre on Air and Climate

12.3 Water

Introduction

Water is essential for life, as well as an indispensable resource for the economy, while playing a fundamental role in the climate regulation cycle. The management and the protection of water resources, of fresh and salt water ecosystems, and of the water we drink and bathe in are therefore major concerns all around the world.

A study conducted for the European Commission estimates that water use efficiency could be improved by nearly 40 % through technological improvements alone and that changes in human behaviour or production patterns could increase such savings further. In a scenario without changes in practices it is estimated that water consumption by the public, industry and agriculture would increase by 16 % by 2030. Conversely, the use of water saving technologies and irrigation management in the industrial and agricultural sectors could reduce excesses by as much as 43 %, while water efficiency measures could decrease water wastage by up to a third.

In a Communication on water scarcity and droughts [12] adopted in July 2007, the European Commission identified an initial set of policy options to be taken at European, national and regional levels to address water scarcity within the EU. This set of proposed policies aims to move the EU towards a water-efficient and water-saving economy. Indeed, both the quality and availability of water are major concerns in many regions. While water resources are limited, water quality is affected by human activities such as industrial production, household discharges, or arable farming (the latest report [13] on the protection of waters against pollution by nitrates from agricultural sources being issued in March 2007). The pollution of rivers, lakes and groundwater remains of worldwide concern. Increasingly variable weather patterns and catastrophic floods (such as the those along the Danube and Elbe in 2002) prompted a review of flood risk management, which culminated in a European Commission Directive [14] of November 2007 that aims to reduce and manage the risks that floods pose to human health, the environment, cultural heritage and economic activity.

The majority of the EU's population is connected to public water supplies, with the proportion rising close to 100 % in most Member States. Looking at the 'other end of the pipe', namely the treatment of wastewater, a number of countries reported that less than half of their population was connected to urban wastewater treatment.

(12) COM(2007) 414 final; http://eur-lex.europa.eu/LexUriServ/site/en/com/2007/com2007_0414en01.pdf.

(13) COM(2007) 120 final; http://eur-lex.europa.eu/LexUriServ/LexUriServ.do?uri=CELEX:52007DC0120:EN:NOT.

(14) Directive 2007/60/EC of 26 November 2007: http://eur-lex.europa.eu/LexUriServ/LexUriServ.do?uri=OJ:L:2007:288:0027:0034:EN:PDF.

Definitions and data availability

Water statistics are collected through the inland waters section of a joint OECD/Eurostat questionnaire which is continuously adapted to the EU policy framework. It currently reports on the following:

- **freshwater resources** in groundwater and surface waters – these can be replenished by precipitation and by external inflows (water flowing in from other territories);
- **water abstraction** – a major pressure on resources, although a large part of the water abstracted for domestic, industrial (including energy production), or agricultural use is returned to the environment and its water bodies, but often as wastewater with impaired quality;
- **water use**, analysed by supply category and by industrial activities;
- treatment capacities of **wastewater treatment plants and the share of the population connected to them** – this gives an overview of the development status of the infrastructure, in terms of quantity and quality, that is available for the protection of the environment from pollution by wastewater;
- **sewage sludge production and disposal** – an inevitable product of wastewater treatment processes; its impact on the environment depends on the methods chosen for its processing and disposal;

- **generation and discharge of wastewater** – pollutants present in wastewater have different source profiles, and similarly the efficiency of treatment of any pollutant varies according to the method applied.

Statistics on water resources are usually calculated on the basis of long-term annual averages of at least 20 years, to take account of the fluctuations in rainfall and evaporation/transpiration from one year to the next. **Precipitation** is defined as the total volume of atmospheric wet precipitation (mainly rain, snow and hail) and is usually measured by meteorological or hydrological institutes. **Evapotranspiration** is the volume of water that is transported from the ground (including inland water surfaces – streams, rivers, freshwater lakes and glaciers) into the atmosphere by evaporation or by transpiration of plants. Internal flow is defined as the total volume of river run-off and groundwater generated, in natural conditions, exclusively by precipitation into a territory. The **internal flow** is equal to precipitation less evapotranspiration and can be calculated or measured. If the river run-off and groundwater generation are measured separately, transfers between surface and groundwater should be netted out to avoid double counting. **External inflow** is the volume of inflow derived from rivers and groundwater that originate in a neighbouring territory. Freshwater resources refer to the volume of water resulting from internal flow and external inflow. **Outflow** is the volume of water that flows from rivers and groundwater into the sea and into neighbouring territories. Total additional freshwater resources available are calculated as the sum of internal and external flows.

Fresh surface water is defined as water which flows over, or rests on the surface of a land mass, natural watercourse – such as rivers, streams, brooks and lakes – as well as artificial watercourse – such as irrigation, industrial and navigation canals, drainage systems and artificial reservoirs. **Fresh groundwater** is defined as freshwater which is being held in, and can usually be recovered from, or via, an underground formation. All permanent and temporary deposits of water, both artificially charged and naturally, in the subsoil, of sufficient quality for at least seasonal use. **Total freshwater resources** is the total volume of water that is additionally available due to internal flow and external inflow.

Water abstraction covers **groundwater abstraction** and surface water abstraction. Groundwater abstraction is abstraction of freshwater from underground deposits. These can be permanent or temporary, both artificially charged or naturally. Groundwater includes springs, both concentrated and diffused, which may also be subaqueous. **Surface water abstraction** is water abstracted from natural or artificial surface watercourses holding freshwater, such as lakes, rivers, streams, canals etc.

Public water is that supplied by economic units engaged in the collection, purification and distribution of water (including desalting of sea water to produce water as the principal product of interest, and excluding system operation for agricultural purposes and treatment of wastewater solely in order to prevent pollution); corresponds to NACE Rev. 1.1 Division 41.

Wastewater is defined as water which is of no further immediate value to the purpose for which it was used or in the pursuit of which it was produced because of its quality, quantity or time of occurrence. However, wastewater from one user can be a potential supply to another user elsewhere. Domestic wastewater is defined as wastewater from residential settlements and services which originates predominantly from the human metabolism and from household activities. Urban wastewater is domestic wastewater or the mixture of domestic wastewater with industrial wastewater and/or run-off rain water. **Urban wastewater treatment** is all treatment of wastewater in urban wastewater treatment plants (UWWTPs). UWWTPs are usually operated by public authorities or by private enterprises working by order of public authorities. This includes wastewater delivered to treatment plants by trucks. This approach used in international water statistics is different to the concept applied in the EU Urban Wastewater Treatment Directive (91/271/EC) where only a system of conduits (sewage pipes) is taken into account for connection to the treatment plant. The

population connected to urban waste-water treatment relates to the proportion of persons who are connected to any kind of sewage treatment that is carried out in municipal treatment plants by public authorities or private enterprises on behalf of local authorities. Thereby, urban wastewater is treated by a process generally involving biological treatment with a secondary settlement or other process, resulting in a biochemical oxygen demand (BOD) removal of at least 70 % and a chemical oxygen demand (COD) removal of at least 75 %.

Main findings

Given the natural resources available, geographical characteristics and freshwater management, there are wide differences among the countries in terms of freshwater resources. On the basis of long-term annual averages of at least 20 years among the Member States, an overall picture shows that Finland and Sweden recorded the highest volume of freshwater resources per capita in 2006, while the Czech Republic and Cyprus recorded the lowest averages.

There are considerable differences between Member States in the amount of water that is abstracted from the ground or from surface areas (like lakes and rivers), in part reflecting the resources available on the one hand but also, on the other, abstraction practices for public water supply, industrial purposes, agricultural purposes, land drainage and land sealing. Where time-series are available,

the amount of groundwater extracted by Member States in 2005 was generally lower than in 1995; in Bulgaria, Lithuania, Latvia, and the Czech Republic and Romania, extraction was about one half its level of 1995. The three main exceptions were Spain, Slovenia and Finland, where extraction levels were between 10 % and 15 % higher.

Developments in surface water abstraction levels were even more contrasting. In Slovenia, surface water abstraction levels in 2005 were about three quarters less than in 1995, with strong declines also recorded in Romania, Lithuania, Latvia, Slovakia, the Czech Republic and Belgium. In contrast, surface water abstraction levels in Spain increased by about 15 % to 32 000 million m^3 in 2004, the highest level among those Member States for which information is available.

The population connected to urban wastewater treatment relates to the proportion of persons who are connected to any kind of sewage treatment (on behalf of local authorities). Although the data set is incomplete, only in seven of the 19 Member States with available data did the proportion of households connected to the urban wastewater treatment near or exceed 80 % in 2005, with the proportion almost reaching 100 % in the Netherlands. At the other end of the spectrum, household connection rates were less than 40 % in six of the Member States, with a relatively low proportion in Malta, where the connection rate was around 13 % (but new treatment plants are under construction).

Table 12.3: Groundwater and surface water abstraction

	Groundwater abstraction (million m³)			Surface water abstraction (million m³)		
	1995	2000	2005	1995	2000	2005
Belgium (1)	685	640	640	7 500	6 833	5 936
Bulgaria	907	574	447	5 419	5 558	5 570
Czech Republic	719	555	385	2 024	1 363	1 564
Denmark (2)	887	709	659	:	17	21
Germany	7 623	:	:	35 751	:	:
Estonia (2)	350	255	310	1 430	1 216	:
Ireland	:	:	364	:	:	435
Greece	3 119	:	:	4 614	:	:
Spain (2)	5 408	4 979	6 196	27 880	32 091	31 963
France	:	6 259	:	:	26 456	:
Italy	:	:	:	:	:	:
Cyprus	:	137	141	:	45	81
Latvia	*195*	119	102	*222*	165	136
Lithuania	304	166	157	4 278	3 412	2 208
Luxembourg	29	:	:	28	:	:
Hungary (2)	969	740	708	:	18 138	19 991
Malta	20	19	14	0	0	0
Netherlands	:	:	1 025	:	:	9 301
Austria	1 164	:	:	2 285	:	:
Poland	2 846	:	:	10 078	:	:
Portugal	:	:	400	:	:	687
Romania	1 280	1 107	724	9 020	6 860	4 577
Slovenia	164	136	184	222	168	53
Slovakia (3)	578	448	374	808	723	621
Finland	257	*285*	*285*	2 278	:	:
Sweden (2)	661	635	628	2 064	2 053	2 048
United Kingdom	:	:	:	:	:	:
FYR of Macedonia	33	14	:	2 829	2 258	:
Turkey	8 450	10 350	11 622	*25 032*	*33 300*	:
Iceland	158	158	160	7	5	5
Norway	:	:	:	:	:	:
Switzerland	892	886	811	1 679	1 678	1 696

(1) 2003 instead of 2005.
(2) 2004 instead of 2005.
(3) 2003 instead of 2005 for surface water abstraction.

Source: Eurostat (ten00004 and ten00005)

Figure 12.7: Freshwater resources per capita - long-term average (1)
(1 000 m³ per inhabitant)

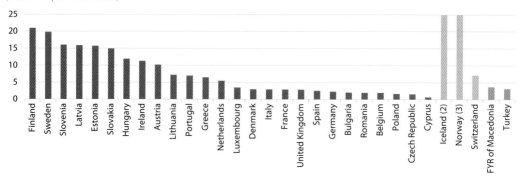

(1) The minimum period taken into account for the calculation of long term annual averages is 20 years; population data are as of 1 January 2006; Luxembourg, estimate; Malta, not available.
(2) Y-axis is cut, 566.9.
(3) Y-axis is cut, 84.2.

Source: Eurostat (ten00001 and tps00001)

Figure 12.8: Population connected to urban wastewater treatment, 2005 (1)
(%)

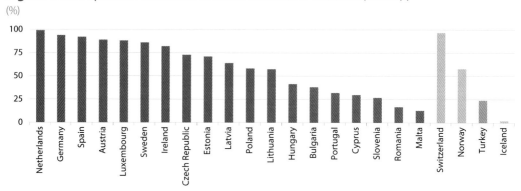

(1) Germany, Estonia, Hungary, Austria and Turkey, 2004; Luxembourg and Portugal, 2003; Belgium, Denmark, Greece, France, Italy, Slovakia, Finland and the United Kingdom, not available.

Source: Eurostat (tsdnr320)

12.4 Waste

Introduction

Waste refers to materials for which the generator has no further use for their own purpose of production, transformation or consumption; these materials are discarded. In some circumstances there may be statutory requirements on a producer to dispose of waste in a certain manner, for example, when waste materials are hazardous.

The EU's sustainable development strategy and the sixth environment action programme, which identifies waste prevention and management as one of four top priorities, underline the relationship between the efficiency of resources and waste generation and management. The objective is to decouple the use of resources and generation of waste from economic growth, while sustainable consumption should not exceed environmental capacity.

The EU's approach to waste management is based on three principles: waste prevention, recycling and reuse, and improving final disposal and monitoring. Waste prevention can be achieved through cleaner technologies, eco-design, or more eco-efficient production and consumption patterns. Waste prevention and recycling, focused on materials technology, can also reduce the environmental impact of resources that are used through limiting raw materials extraction and transformation during production processes. Where possible, waste that cannot be recycled or reused should be safely incinerated, with landfill only used as a last resort. Both these methods need close monitoring because of their potential for causing severe environmental damage.

The European Commission has defined several specific waste streams for priority attention, the aim being to reduce their overall environmental impact; this includes packaging waste, end-of-life vehicles, batteries, electrical and electronic waste. Member States are required to introduce legislation on waste collection, reuse, recycling and disposal of these waste streams. In 2006 the new Waste Framework Directive[15] and the Waste Shipment Regulation[16] were adopted by the European Parliament and the Council, with the aim to strengthen, simplify and clarify the control procedures applicable to waste management.

Definitions and data availability

In order to be able to monitor the implementation of waste policy, in particular compliance with the principles of recovery and safe disposal, reliable **statistics on the production and management of waste** from businesses and private households are needed. In 2002, Regulation No 2150/2002/EC on waste statistics[17] was adopted, creating a framework for harmonised Community statistics on waste.

Starting with the reference year 2004, the Regulation requires the EU Member States to provide data on the generation, recovery and disposal of waste every two years. Thus, the Regulation on waste

(15) Directive 2006/12/EC of the European Parliament and of the Council of 5 April 2006); http://eur-lex.europa.eu/ LexUriServ/site/en/oj/2006/l_114/l_11420060427en00090021.pdf.

(16) Regulation (EC) No 1013/2006 of the European Parliament and of the Council of 14 June 2006; http://eur-lex.europa.eu/ LexUriServ/site/en/oj/2006/l_190/l_19020060712en00010098.pdf.

(17) Regulation (EC) No 2150/2002 of the European Parliament and of the Council of 25 November 2002; http://eur-lex. europa.eu/LexUriServ/LexUriServ.do?uri=OJ:L:2002:332:0001:0036:EN:PDF

statistics replaces the Eurostat/OECD Joint Questionnaire as the main source of European waste data. Whereas reporting by the Joint Questionnaire was voluntary, the provisions of the Regulation are binding by law. The second delivery of data based on the Regulation on waste statistics was in June 2008; and hence, data are now available for the reference years 2004 and 2006.

The concept of 'municipal waste', a central waste category of the Joint Questionnaire is replaced in the new Regulation by the category 'waste generated by households'. The concept of municipal waste has always been disputed as its content is directly linked to different national or regional waste management systems. However, data on municipal waste generation and treatment are still collected annually from the countries, as it is part of the series of structural indicators on the environment.

Municipal waste consists of waste collected by or on behalf of municipal authorities and disposed of through the waste management system. The information presented on municipal waste includes waste generated by various branches of economic activity and households (which accounts for the bulk of this waste stream). The quantity of waste generated is expressed in kg per person per year. Data for **waste recovery and recycling** is not collected from countries but calculated as the difference between municipal waste generation and municipal waste incinerated and landfilled.

Treatment of municipal waste can be classified into three principal categories:

- **landfill**, which is defined as the depositing of waste into or onto land, including specially engineered landfill, and temporary storage of over one year on permanent sites;.the definition covers both landfill in internal sites (i.e. where a generator of waste is carrying out its own waste disposal at the place of generation) and in external sites;

- **incineration**, which refers to the thermal treatment of waste in specifically designed incineration plants as defined in Article 3(4) or co-incineration plants as defined in Article 3(5) of the Directive on the incineration of waste (Directive 2000/76/EC of 4 December 2000), and;

- **recovery**, which refers to any waste management operation that diverts a waste material from the waste stream and which results in a certain product with a potential economic or ecological benefit.

The disposal of waste can have a serious environmental impact: for example, landfill takes up land space, and may cause air, water and soil pollution. Incineration can also result in emissions of dangerous air pollutants, unless properly regulated.

Main findings

On average across the EU-27, each individual generated the equivalent of 517 kg of municipal waste in 2006, some 6.6 % more than in 1996, although slightly lower than in 2001. During this period, the way in which waste was treated changed significantly. About 60 % of municipal waste was put into landfill in 1996, with a further 14 % being incinerated, the rest being treated in other ways, such as recycling and composting. By 2006, the proportion of municipal waste that was put into landfill had declined to 41 %, recycling and composting becoming a much more significant form of treatment in many countries.

Municipal waste per inhabitant in 2006 was between 33 % and 50 % higher than the EU-27 average in Ireland, Cyprus, Denmark and Luxembourg, in each case rising relatively progressively from levels recorded in 1996. In contrast, average waste levels were between 40 % and 50 % lower than the EU-27 average in Poland and the Czech Republic. In the ten years through to 2006, average municipal waste per inhabitant declined by 170 kg in Bulgaria, the highest decline of any Member State, followed closely by Slovenia (158 kg), Germany (76 kg) and Poland (42 kg).

In Germany, the amount of municipal waste going into landfill shrank from 225 kg per head in 1996 to only 4 kg in 2006. There were also significant reductions to below 60 kg per head in Belgium, the Netherlands, Austria and Sweden. In contrast, the amount of municipal waste going into landfill rose sharply in Malta, Romania, Slovakia, Greece and Cyprus.

Those countries that reduced the use of landfill tended to have relatively high levels of waste incineration in 2006. Newly installed waste incinerators are equipped with systems for energy recovery. Energy statistics show that a large proportion of energy recovery from waste took place in France, Germany, Sweden and Spain in 2006.

Under the Waste Statistics Regulation, Member States reported that in 2006 in the EU-27 about 2 950 million tonnes of waste were generated by economic activities and by households, of which some 88 million tonnes involved hazardous waste. It has to be noted that a large share of the total was generated by construction (including demolition) activities and by mining and quarrying industries, while manufacturing industries produced the majority of the hazardous waste.

About 70 million tonnes of metallic waste were recovered across the EU-27 in 2006, with a further 37 million tonnes of paper and cardboard and 12 million tonnes of glass. A majority of these products were recovered in Germany, Spain, France, Italy and the United Kingdom, although a significant amount of metal recovery took place in Poland (11.4 % of the EU-27 total) and of paper and cardboard in the Netherlands (7.1 % of the EU-27 total).

Figure 12.9: Municipal waste, EU-27

(kg per inhabitant)

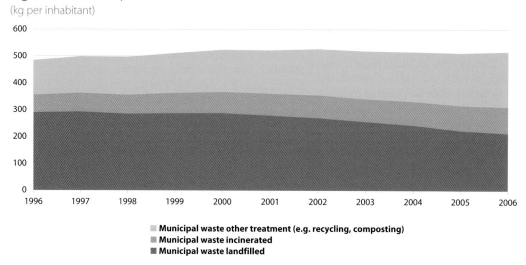

■ **Municipal waste other treatment (e.g. recycling, composting)**
▨ **Municipal waste incinerated**
▨ **Municipal waste landfilled**

Source: Eurostat (tsien120 and tsien130)

Table 12.4: Municipal waste

(kg per capita)

	Municipal waste generated (1)			Municipal waste landfilled (2)			Municipal waste incinerated (3)		
	1996	2001	2006	1996	2001	2006	1996	2001	2006
EU-27	485	522	517	290	279	213	66	82	98
Euro area	525	570	557	265	247	173	86	106	125
Belgium	451	467	475	189	54	24	152	160	155
Bulgaria	616	491	446	477	392	356	0	0	0
Czech Republic	310	273	296	310	214	234	0	35	29
Denmark	619	658	737	82	47	37	308	374	405
Germany	642	633	566	225	160	4	106	135	179
Estonia	396	372	466	396	295	278	0	1	1
Ireland	524	705	804	419	540	471	0	0	0
Greece	337	417	443	322	380	386	0	0	0
Spain	536	658	583	298	364	289	25	37	41
France	486	528	553	225	215	192	170	175	183
Italy	457	516	548	380	346	284	27	45	65
Cyprus	642	703	745	593	634	652	0	0	0
Latvia	263	302	411	247	285	292	0	4	2
Lithuania	400	377	390	400	335	356	0	0	0
Luxembourg	589	650	702	163	131	131	306	275	266
Hungary	468	451	468	367	375	376	32	35	39
Malta	344	542	652	317	494	562	0	0	0
Netherlands	563	615	625	115	50	12	171	199	213
Austria	517	578	617	186	192	59	54	65	181
Poland	301	290	259	295	278	236	0	0	1
Portugal	399	472	435	231	355	274	0	104	95
Romania	333	345	385	235	272	326	0	0	0
Slovenia	590	479	432	465	358	362	0	0	3
Slovakia	275	239	301	172	209	234	28	25	36
Finland	410	466	488	275	284	286	0	41	42
Sweden	385	442	497	126	99	25	147	169	233
United Kingdom	512	592	588	440	474	353	36	43	55
Turkey	471	457	434	345	360	364	0	0	0
Iceland	437	469	534	328	353	370	82	53	47
Norway	632	635	793	425	274	245	81	99	132
Switzerland	602	659	715	69	40	1	282	315	355

(1) Breaks in series for Estonia (2001), Latvia (2006), Lithuania (1999), Hungary (2000), Malta (1999), Portugal (2002), Slovenia (2002),
Slovakia (2002), Turkey (2004) and Switzerland (2004).
(2) Breaks in series for Estonia (2001), Latvia (2006), Lithuania (1999), Hungary (2000), Malta (1999), Portugal (2002) and Turkey (2004).
(3) Break in series for Italy (2002).

Source: Eurostat (tsien120 and tsien130)

Table 12.5: Generation of waste, total arising and by selected economic activities

(1 000 tonnes)

	Total waste from economic activities and households		Manufacturing industry		Mining and quarrying activities		Construction and demolition activities		Other economic activities (services)	
	2004	2006	2004	2006	2004	2006	2004	2006	2004	2006
EU-27	2 918 220	2 946 667	384 676	363 743	862 155	740 743	:	:	146 754	155 807
Belgium	52 809	59 352	18 177	15 308	384	159	11 037	13 090	8 689	7 039
Bulgaria	252 058	242 489	5 611	4 316	222 231	225 338	2 999	1 023	9 181	1 473
Czech Republic	29 276	24 746	8 618	5 932	708	472	8 131	8 380	933	1 025
Denmark	12 814	12 821	1 555	1 179	0	0	4 274	5 802	1 515	1 486
Germany	364 022	363 786	30 163	31 705	55 880	47 222	191 563	196 536	16 343	15 107
Estonia	20 861	18 933	6 288	3 981	5 306	5 961	489	717	1 720	1 601
Ireland	24 513	30 005	5 356	4 067	4 046	4 793	11 287	16 599	1 184	1 327
Greece	34 953	51 325	4 554	5 285	1 902	14 888	3 324	6 829	1 518	1 518
Spain	160 668	160 947	28 377	22 427	21 780	26 015	46 320	47 323	14 194	15 376
France	429 153	445 865	21 434	22 973	166	1 040	:	:	24 158	24 158
Italy	139 806	155 025	39 472	39 997	761	1 005	49 151	52 316	3 860	5 534
Cyprus	2 332	1 870	557	413	119	60	488	307	403	403
Latvia	1 257	1 859	349	570	0	0	8	19	99	239
Lithuania	7 010	7 665	2 632	2 948	4	6	357	349	158	586
Luxembourg	8 322	9 586	725	604	46	56	6 985	6 775	179	243
Hungary	24 661	22 287	5 071	5 528	1 640	27	1 736	3 045	1 965	2 445
Malta	2 482	2 861	10	50	0	0	2 206	2 493	160	173
Netherlands	88 099	93 808	16 086	15 562	296	213	49 612	56 610	5 276	5 349
Austria	53 021	54 287	15 073	11 470	622	1 043	27 935	31 322	2 856	3 458
Poland	251 243	266 741	61 514	61 131	38 311	38 671	1 993	14 141	1 965	3 512
Portugal	29 272	34 077	10 123	14 699	4 761	3 563	2 626	3 607	4 202	10 352
Romania	371 503	331 863	11 156	9 184	326 553	199 138	54	34	3 096	3 841
Slovenia	5 771	6 036	1 960	2 385	129	377	908	995	426	429
Slovakia	10 668	14 502	3 878	5 527	211	332	1 404	916	761	4 859
Finland	74 361	72 205	23 266	17 976	23 819	21 501	20 843	23 146	1 276	1 668
Sweden	109 741	115 583	27 614	30 363	58 600	62 084	10 272	8 943	1 517	1 517
United Kingdom	357 544	346 144	35 056	28 161	93 883	86 779	99 234	109 546	39 120	41 088
Croatia	7 209	:	3 695	:	347	:	646	:	116	:
Turkey	58 820	46 092	16 325	:	:	:	:	:	62	:
Iceland	501	:	61	:	1	:	19	:	6	:
Norway	7 454	9 051	2 956	3 519	116	136	1 101	1 248	865	1 472

Source: Eurostat (env_wasgen)

Table 12.6: Waste treatment (non-hazardous), recovery, 2006

(1 000 tonnes)

	Metallic waste	Glass waste	Paper and cardboard waste	Rubber waste	Plastic waste	Wood waste	Textile waste
EU-27 (1)	69 935	11 816	37 789	1 508	:	:	1 651
Belgium	2 711	282	630	8	130	440	10
Bulgaria	1 148	47	125	2	24	0	3
Czech Republic	1 307	50	201	13	89	120	18
Denmark	942	131	788	54	54	863	:
Germany	7 648	2 024	5 922	192	1 119	2 502	68
Estonia	4	7	6	6	10	398	0
Ireland	31	14	26	9	25	180	7
Greece	644	54	425	31	42	63	9
Spain	5 083	1 412	3 346	352	1 450	573	79
France	10 136	2 174	6 050	230	435	3 727	388
Italy (1)	6 981	1 429	3 335	49	959	4 248	244
Cyprus	18	4	45	1	26	5	0
Latvia	9	1	18	1	8	0	0
Lithuania	15	26	141	11	36	34	1
Luxembourg	:	:	0	0	:	:	0
Hungary	760	21	344	10	49	174	1
Malta	0	1	3	1	0	1	0
Netherlands	1 910	483	2 688	73	265	1 317	92
Austria	1 160	249	1 425	30	164	2 282	34
Poland	8 004	136	212	785	446	419	1 294
Portugal (1)	558	237	345	43	98	1 109	56
Romania	2 319	80	335	9	198	109	4
Slovenia	750	:	373	:	22	:	:
Slovakia	509	11	108	11	29	421	3
Finland	1 266	149	734	24	5	4 122	0
Sweden	1 866	:	1 846	35	:	10 916	0
United Kingdom	10 538	1 198	4 174	25	426	2 747	117
Croatia (1)	16	13	4	1	3	35	0
Turkey	9	7	23	2	13	0	1
Iceland (1)	0	6	8	4	2	23	1
Norway	880	91	670	39	36	348	13

(1) 2004.

Source: Eurostat (env_wastrt)

12.5 Environment and economy

Introduction

Resources are the backbone of every economy. In using resources and transforming them, capital stocks are built up which add to the wealth of present and future generations. However, the dimensions of our current resource use are such that the chances of future generations – and the developing countries – to have access to their fair share of scarce resources are endangered. Moreover, the consequences of our resource use in terms of impacts on the environment may induce serious damages that go beyond the carrying capacity of the environment. These effects risk being aggravated once the developing world has taken up growth and resource use similar to the levels currently experienced in (post-)industrialised countries.

A key component of the EU's environment and health action programme within the sixth EAP is the need for a complete overhaul of EU policy on chemicals management. A European Regulation [18] on the Registration, Evaluation, Authorisation and restriction of Chemicals (REACH) came into force in June 2007. The major objective of REACH is to ensure a high level of protection for human health and the environment, including promotion of alternative methods for the assessment of hazards of substances as well as the free circulation of substances on the internal market while enhancing competitiveness and innovation in the EU chemical industry. Through different types of measures, REACH is expected to lead to a decrease in risks to human health and the environment.

The EU's eco-management and audit scheme (EMAS) is a management tool for enterprises and other organisations to evaluate, report and improve their environmental performance. Enterprises have been able to participate in the scheme since 1995 [19]. It was originally restricted to enterprises within the industrial economy, however, since 2001 EMAS has been open to all economic sectors including public and private services. In addition, EMAS was strengthened by the integration of the ISO 14001 international standard, which is primarily concerned with environmental management and aims to help organisations establish or improve an environmental management system, to minimise harmful effects on the environment caused by its activities, and continually improve their environmental performance [20]. Organisations participating in EMAS are committed to evaluate and improve their own environmental performance, comply with relevant environmental legislation, prevent pollution, and provide relevant information to the public (via verified environmental audits). In July 2008 the European Commission proposed to revise EMAS to increase the participation of companies and reduce the administrative burden and costs, particularly for small and medium-sized enterprises [21].

---

(18) http://ec.europa.eu/environment/chemicals/index.htm.

(19) Council Regulation (EEC) No 1836/93 of 29 June 1993; http://eur-lex.europa.eu/LexUriServ/LexUriServ.do?uri=CELEX:319
      93R1836:EN:HTML.

(20) Commission Regulation (EC) No 196/2006 of 3 February 2006 amending Annex I to Regulation (EC) No 761/2001 of the
      European Parliament and of the Council to take account of the European Standard EN ISO 14001:2004, and repealing
      Decision 97/265/EC; http://eur-lex.europa.eu/LexUriServ/site/en/oj/2006/l_032/l_03220060204en00040012.pdf.

(21) http://ec.europa.eu/environment/emas/pdf/com_2008_402_draft.pdf.

Definitions and data availability

Resource productivity measures the efficiency with which the economy uses energy and materials (the natural resource inputs needed to achieve a given economic output). If the definition of natural resources includes pollution sinks – the capacity of the atmosphere, the land area and the world's oceans and rivers to absorb waste and pollution – resource productivity also measures the economy's ability to produce goods and services relative to its environmental impacts. This wider measure is particularly useful to policy-makers, because there are pressing concerns regarding the way in which pollution sinks are being used up as a resource. Resource productivity is defined as GDP divided by **domestic material consumption** (DMC). DMC is related to the consumption activities of residents of a national economy (DMC = domestic extraction (DE) plus imports minus exports). The three main DMC material categories (biomass, fossil fuels and minerals) can be further disaggregated into different material categories. It is important to note that the term consumption as used in DMC denotes apparent consumption and not final consumption. DMC does not include upstream hidden flows related to imports and exports of raw materials and products.

Eurostat has developed a **production index of toxic chemicals**. This indicator presents the trend in aggregated production volumes of toxic chemicals, broken down into five toxicity classes. The classes are derived from the Risk Phrases assigned to the individual substances in Annex 6 of the Dangerous Substance Directive (Council Directive 67/548/EEC as last amended in 2001). The **toxicity classes**, beginning with the most dangerous, are: carcinogenic, mutagenic and reprotoxic (CMR-chemicals); chronic toxic chemicals; very toxic chemicals; toxic chemicals and chemicals classified as harmful. Production volumes are extracted from Prodcom (statistics on the production of manufactured goods) and are aggregated to the five classes according to their toxicity. EU-15 data covers the years from 1995 to 2007, for 2004 to 2007 data for EU-25 is available.

The **eco-management and audit scheme (EMAS)** is an EU voluntary instrument which acknowledges organisations that improve their environmental performance on a continuous basis. The scheme integrates ISO 14001 (International Standard for Environmental Management System) as its environmental management system element. EMAS registered organisations are legally compliant, run an environment management system and report on their environmental performance through the publication of an independently verified environmental statement. They are recognised by the EMAS logo, which guarantees the reliability of the information provided. To receive EMAS registration an organisation must comply with the following steps:

- conduct an environmental review;
- establish an effective environmental management system;
- carry out an environmental audit and;
- provide a statement of its environmental performance.

The EU **eco-label scheme**, as laid down in a Regulation of the European Commission [22] is now part of a wider approach on integrated product policy (IPP). The Community eco-label is awarded to products and services with reduced environmental impacts. It is administered by the European eco-labelling board (EUEB) and receives the support of the European Commission, all EU Member States and the European Economic Area. The eco-labelling board includes representatives such as industry, environment protection groups and consumer organisations. The scheme has been in operation since 1993.

Main findings

The efficient use of resources (many of which come from outside the EU) can contribute to relatively steady growth, whereas inefficiency and over-exploitation may put long-term growth in jeopardy. Although the wealth of the EU-15, as measured by GDP, increased on average by 2.3 % per annum between 1995 and 2004, the consumption activities of the EU-15's residents (domestic material consumption) remained stable over the same period of time. As a result, resource productivity during the same period rose by a little over one fifth (22.2 %) in the EU-15.

The chemicals industry is one of the largest European manufacturing sectors and it has a pivotal role in providing innovative materials and technological solutions which have a direct impact on Europe's industrial competitiveness. Manufactured chemicals can, however, have an environment impact on soil, water and air quality, and chemicals like hydrofluorocarbons (HFCs), perfluorocarbons (PFCs) and sulphur hexafluoride (SF6) were included in the Kyoto Protocol because they are gases related to global warming. Between 1996 and 2006 the total production of chemicals grew by 22 % (EU-15). The production of chemicals classified as toxic increased by 16 % over this period, with 10 % growth for CMR chemicals, although in both cases falling back slightly from relative highs in 2004.

The EU Eco-Management and Audit Scheme (EMAS) is a management tool for companies and other organisations to evaluate, report and improve their environmental performance. By 2007, by far the highest uptake was in Austria (just under 60 sites per million inhabitants), followed by Denmark and Belgium, with the only other countries to have a ratio in double figures being Spain, Germany and Italy. Denmark and Austria were also at the forefront of eco-label awards in 2007. In a majority of Member States, however, less than one eco-label per million inhabitants was awarded by 2007.

(22) Regulation (EC) No 1980/2000 of the European Parliament and of the Council of 17 July 2000: http://eur-lex.europa.eu/LexUriServ/site/en/oj/2000/l_237/l_23720000921en00010012.pdf.

Figure 12.10: Resource productivity, EU-15
(1995=100)

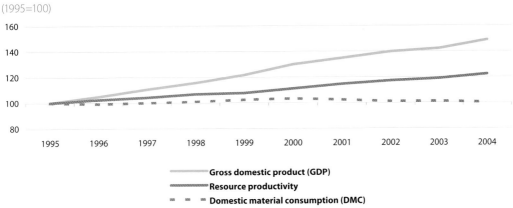

Source: Eurostat (tec00001, tsien140 and tsdpc230)

Figure 12.11: Production volume of toxic chemicals, EU-15 (1)
(1997=100)

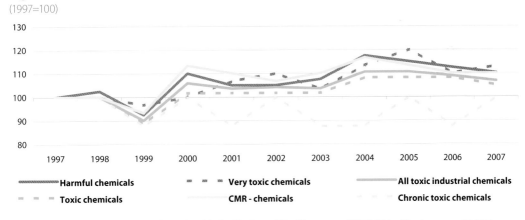

(1) In 2007, the volume of toxic chemicals produced in the EU-15 was: 317 million tonnes (EU-25: 354 million tonnes; an EU-25 time series is only available from 2004 to 2007). The share of substances classified as toxic was 183 million tonnes (EU-25: 206 million tonnes). Of the EU-25 production volume, starting with the most toxic substances, 36 million tonnes were classified as 'CMR-chemicals', 8 million tonnes as 'chronic toxic' chemicals, 39 million tonnes as 'very toxic', 74 million tonnes as 'toxic' and 49 million tonnes as 'harmful' chemicals in 2007.

Source: Eurostat (tsdph320)

Figure 12.12: Number of sites having implemented an eco-management and audit scheme (EMAS), 2007 (1)

(per million inhabitants)

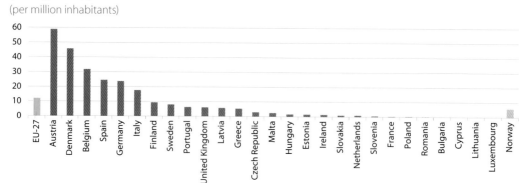

(1) EU-27, Ireland, Greece, Portugal and the United Kingdom, estimates.

Source: Eurostat (tsdpc410 and tps00001), European Commission (EMAS)

Figure 12.13: Eco-label awards, 2007 (1)

(per million inhabitants)

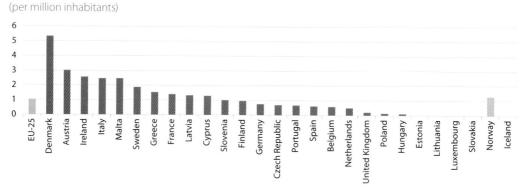

(1) EU-25, Ireland, Greece, Portugal and the United Kingdom, estimates; Bulgaria and Romania, not available.

Source: Eurostat (tsdpc420 and tps00001), Directorate-General Environment

12.6 Biodiversity

Introduction

A contraction of biological diversity, biodiversity reflects the number, variety and variability of living organisms, including mankind. The global scale of the biodiversity issue has led to international action within this domain, with the framework for action being the United Nations (UN) convention on biological diversity (CBD), which the EU ratified in 1993. In 1998, the EU adopted a biodiversity strategy. Four biodiversity action plans were adopted under this strategy in 2001 (conservation of natural resources, agriculture, fisheries, economic and development cooperation).

At the United Nations world summit on sustainable development in Johannesburg in 2002, governments committed themselves to significantly reducing the rate of biodiversity loss by 2010. A number of concrete measures and a programme of funding to help achieve this goal were reached at a UN Conference in Bonn in May 2008.

The EU has also set itself the objective of halting the loss of biodiversity on its own territory by 2010 [23]. Nature and biodiversity is one of four priorities of the EU's sixth environment action programme (2002-12), together with climate change, resource and waste management, and health in relation to the environment.

Definitions and data availability

EU policy on nature conservation is part of the EU's biodiversity strategy. It is essentially based on the implementation of two Directives: Council Directive 92/43/EEC of 21 May 1992 (the habitats Directive) on the conservation of natural habitats and of wild fauna and flora [24]) and Council Directive 79/409/EEC of 2 April 1979 (the birds Directive) on the conservation of wild birds, which includes the setting-up of a coherent European ecological network of sites under the title Natura 2000.

Annual data are available on **protected areas under the habitats Directive** and these are presented as a percentage of total country area. The indicator on protected areas is based on territories proposed by countries to be designated for the protection of natural and semi-natural habitats, wild fauna and flora according to the habitats Directive. The **index of sufficiency** measures the extent to which sites of Community importance proposed by the Member States adequately cover the species and habitats listed in the annexes I and II of the Habitats Directive.

Birds are considered good proxies for biodiversity and the integrity of ecosystems as they tend to be at, or near, the top of the food chain, have large ranges and can migrate and thus reflect changes in

(23) COM(2006) 216 final; http://ec.europa.eu/development/icenter/repository/com2006_0216en01_en.pdf.
(24) Council Directive 79/409/EEC of 2 April 1979 (birds Directive) and Council Directive 92/43/EEC of 21 May 1992 (habitat Directive); http://eur-lex.europa.eu/LexUriServ/LexUriServ.do?uri=CELEX:31979L0409:EN:HTML.

ecosystems rather rapidly. By focusing attention on the population trends of relatively large groups of abundant European species associated with different habitats, these indicators are designed to capture the overall, average changes in population levels of common birds to reflect the health and functioning of ecosystems. The **population index of common birds** is an aggregated index (with base year 1990 or the first year the Member State entered the scheme) of population trend estimates of a selected group of common bird species. Indices are calculated for each species independently and are then combined to create a multi-species EU indicator by averaging the indices with an equal weight using a geometric mean. Indices are averaged rather than bird abundance in order to give each species an equal weight in the resulting indicator. The EU index is based on trend data from 18 Member States, derived from annually operated national breeding bird surveys obtained through the pan-European common bird monitoring scheme (PECBMS). Three different indices are presented, covering: farmland (36 species), forest (29 species) and 'all common birds' (135 species). For the first two categories, the bird species have a high dependence on the habitats in the nesting season and for feeding during most of the year; the aggregate index regroups farmland and forest species together with other common species.

Main findings

Protected areas for biodiversity are based on areas proposed by countries under the Habitats Directive and reflect the share of the total area of a country. About 13 % of the EU-25's territory was considered as a protected area in 2007, but individual Member States can have a much higher share, for example, a little above 30 % in Slovenia.

There was a negative trend in the past 25 years for common bird species, in particular for common farmland birds, which have become more threatened during the period considered. Part of the relatively steep decline in numbers of common farmland bird species may be explained by changes in land use and agricultural practices which affect birds' capacity for nesting or feeding. After a couple of years of limited upturn, the population of farmland species fell relatively sharply again in 2006. In contrast, the index for forest birds showed some improvement compared with its relative low recorded in 2000, despite a contraction between 2004 and 2005.

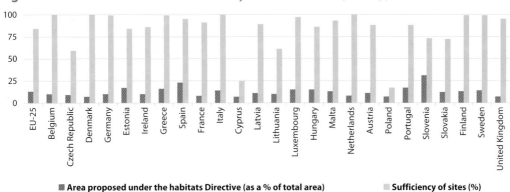

Figure 12.14: Protected areas for biodiversity: habitats Directive, 2007 (1)

■ Area proposed under the habitats Directive (as a % of total area)   ■ Sufficiency of sites (%)

(1) Bulgaria and Romania, not available.

Source: EEA/European Topic Centre on Biodiversity, Eurostat (env_bio1)

Figure 12.15: Common bird indices, EU (1)
(aggregated index of population estimates of a selected group of breeding bird species dependent on agricultural land for nesting or feeding, 1990=100)

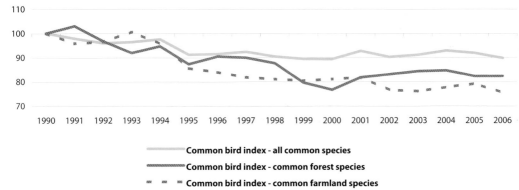

——— Common bird index - all common species
▧▧▧▧▧ Common bird index - common forest species
▬ ▬ ▬ Common bird index - common farmland species

(1) Based on information for Belgium, Bulgaria, the Czech Republic, Denmark, Germany, Estonia, Ireland, Spain, France, Italy, Latvia, Hungary, the Netherlands, Austria, Poland, Portugal, Finland, Sweden and the United Kingdom; 'all common species' covers information on 135 different bird species; 'common farmland species' covers 36 bird species; 'common forest species' covers 29 bird species.

Source: EBCC/RSPB/BirdLife/Statistics Netherlands, Eurostat (env_bio2)

Energy

A competitive, reliable and sustainable energy sector is essential for an economy, and this has been put under the spotlight in recent years by a number of issues, including the volatility in oil prices, interruptions to energy supply from non-member countries, blackouts aggravated by inefficient connections between national electricity networks, the difficulties of market access for suppliers in relation to gas and electricity markets, and increased attention to climate change. These issues have pushed energy towards the top of national and European political agendas.

The use of renewable energy sources is seen as a key element in energy policy, reducing the dependence on fuel from non-member countries, reducing emissions from carbon sources, and decoupling energy costs from oil prices. The second key element is constraining demand, by promoting energy efficiency both within the energy sector itself and at end-use.

In January 2007 the European Commission adopted a communication (COM(2007) 1) proposing an energy policy for Europe [1], with the goal to combat climate change and boost the EU's energy security and competitiveness. This set out the need for the EU to draw up a new energy path towards a more secure, sustainable and low-carbon economy, for the benefit of all users. Based on the European Commission's proposal, in March 2007 the Council endorsed the following targets:

- reducing greenhouse gas emissions by at least 20 % (compared with 1990 levels) by 2020;
- improving energy efficiency by 20 % by 2020;
- raising the share of renewable energy to 20 % by 2020;
- increasing the level of renewables (such as biofuels) in transport fuel to 10 % by 2020.

(1) http://ec.europa.eu/energy/energy_policy/index_en.htm.

13.1 Energy production and imports

Introduction

Energy commodities extracted or captured directly from natural resources are called primary energy sources. All energy commodities which are produced from primary sources in transformation plants are called derived products. Primary energy production covers the national production of primary energy sources. Whenever consumption exceeds primary production the shortfall is accounted for by imports of primary or derived products. The dependency of the EU on imports, particularly for oil and more recently for gas, has formed the backdrop for policy concerns relating to the security of supply.

Definitions and data availability

Any kind of extraction of energy products from natural sources to a usable form is called **primary production**. Primary production takes place when the natural sources are exploited, for example, in coal mines, crude oil fields, hydro power plants or fabrication of biofuels. It is the sum of energy extraction, heat produced in reactors as a result of nuclear fission, and the use of renewable energy sources. Transformation of energy from one form to another, like electricity or heat generation in thermal power plants or coke production in coke ovens is not primary production.

In a Communication in November 2007, the European Commission put forward a strategic energy technology plan (SET-plan) 'Towards a low carbon future'[2]. This aims to support decarbonised energy technologies, such as off-shore wind, solar technology, or second generation biomass, by accelerating their development and implementation. In January 2008 the European Commission proposed a package of measures[3] related to energy and the climate, to supplement the existing measures for achieving the agreed targets. The European Council, on 11 and 12 December 2008[4], reached an agreement on the energy/climate change package which should enable this package to be finalised with the European Parliament by the end of 2008. This decisive breakthrough will enable the EU to honour commitments entered into during 2007 and to maintain its leading role in the search for an ambitious and comprehensive global agreement at Copenhagen in 2009.

In order to meet the increasing requirements of policy-makers for energy monitoring, Eurostat has developed a coherent and harmonised system of energy statistics. Annual data collection covers the 27 Member States of the EU, the candidate countries of Croatia and Turkey, and the European Free Trade Association countries of Iceland, Norway and Switzerland; time-series run back to 1985 for some countries, but are more generally available from 1990. Although not presented in this yearbook, monthly data are also available.

---

(2) http://ec.europa.eu/energy/res/setplan/index_en.htm.

(3) http://ec.europa.eu/commission_barroso/president/focus/energy-package-2008/index_en.htm.

(4) http://www.consilium.europa.eu/ueDocs/cms_Data/docs/pressData/en/ec/104692.pdf.

The heat produced in a reactor as a result of nuclear fission is regarded as **primary production of nuclear heat**, or in other words nuclear energy. It is either the actual heat produced or calculated on the basis of reported gross electricity generation and the thermal efficiency of the nuclear plant. **Primary production of coal and lignite** consists of quantities of fuels extracted or produced, calculated after any operation for removal of inert matter. **Primary production of biomass, hydropower, geothermal energy, wind and solar energy** are included in **renewable energies**:

* biomass (heat content of the produced biofuels or biogas; heat produced after combustion during incineration of renewable wastes);
* hydropower covers potential and kinetic energy of water converted into electricity in hydroelectric plants (the electricity generated in pumped storage plants is not included);
* geothermal energy comprises energy available as heat emitted from within the earth's crust, usually in the form of hot water or steam;
* wind energy covers the kinetic energy of wind converted into electricity in wind turbines;
* solar energy covers the solar radiation exploited for solar heat (hot water) and electricity production.

Net imports are simply calculated as the quantity of imports minus the equivalent quantity of exports. Imports represent all entries into the national territory excluding transit quantities (notably via gas and oil pipelines); electrical energy is an exception and its transit is always recorded under foreign trade. Exports similarly cover all quantities exported from the national territory.

The **energy dependency rate** is defined as net imports divided by gross consumption, expressed as a percentage; gross consumption is equal to gross inland consumption plus the energy (oil) supplied to international marine bunkers.

Gross inland consumption covers consumption by the energy branch itself, distribution and transformation losses, and final non-energy and energy consumption. A negative dependency rate indicates a net exporter of energy. A dependency rate in excess of 100 % indicates that energy products have been stocked. Gross inland consumption is calculated as follows: primary production + recovered products + net imports + variations of stocks – bunkers. It corresponds to the addition of consumption, distribution losses, transformation losses and statistical differences.

Main findings

Production of primary energy in the EU-27 totalled 871 million tonnes of oil equivalent (toe) in 2006. Production was dominated by the United Kingdom with a 21 % share of the EU-27 total, while France and Germany were the only other Member States to report production in excess of 100 million toe.

Primary energy production in the EU-27 in 2006 was concentrated among nuclear energy, solid fuels (mainly coal) and natural gas. However, the pace at which the primary production of renewable energy was growing exceeded that of all the other energy types, with particularly strong growth since 2002. The production of coal and lignite, crude oil, and natural gas fell in recent years: crude oil output peaked in 1999, and natural gas two years later. As a result of these different developments, the production of primary energy from renewable sources in 2006 exceeded that from oil for the first time in the available time-series.

Among renewable energies, the most important source was biomass and waste, representing over 87 million toe of primary production in the EU-27 in 2006. Hydropower was the only other significant contributor to the renewable energy mix (27 million toe). Although production still remains small, there has been a particularly rapid expansion in the production of wind energy, reaching 7 million toe in the EU-27 in 2006.

The EU-27's imports of primary energy exceeded exports by some 1 010 million toe in 2006. The largest net importers of primary energy were usually the largest Member States, with the exception of the United Kingdom and Poland (both of whom have significant primary production, mainly oil, natural gas or coal). Since 2004 the only net exporter among the Member States has been Denmark.

The sources of EU energy imports have changed rapidly in recent years. In 2006 the EU-27's imports of crude oil from Russia were more than double those from Norway, whereas in 2000 Norway's and Russia's deliveries to the EU-27 had been practically the same. For natural gas the same two countries were also the biggest suppliers to the EU-27 market in 2006: although Russia's contribution to EU imports of natural gas has declined in recent years in percentage terms, in 2006 it still supplied two fifths of the total.

Since 2004 the EU-27's net imports of energy have been greater than its primary production of energy, witnessed by its dependency rate exceeding 50 % (meaning that more than half of gross inland consumption was supplied by net imports rather than primary production). In 2005 the dependency rate increased to reach 52.6 % and in 2006 it increased further to 53.8 %. Energy dependency ratios were highest for crude oil and petroleum products (83 %), although the dependency on non-member countries for supplies of solid fuels and natural gas grew at a faster pace in the last decade than the EU's dependency on oil (which was already at a high rate). As it was a net exporter, Denmark was the only Member State in 2006 with a negative dependency rate. Among the other Member States the lowest dependency rates were recorded by Poland and the United Kingdom, while Cyprus, Malta and Luxembourg were all almost entirely dependent on imports.

Table 13.1: Total production of primary energy
(million tonnes of oil equivalent)

	1996	1997	1998	1999	2000	2001	2002	2003	2004	2005	2006	Share in EU-27, 2006 (%)
EU-27	971.4	962.5	940.5	942.8	933.0	933.0	933.2	927.2	923.1	891.4	871.2	100.0
Euro area	459.4	448.6	435.0	436.5	434.9	440.1	442.9	446.1	458.6	448.9	451.7	51.8
Belgium	11.3	12.6	12.0	13.3	13.1	12.7	12.9	13.1	13.2	13.5	13.4	1.5
Bulgaria	10.6	9.8	10.2	9.0	9.8	10.3	10.5	10.1	10.2	10.6	10.9	1.3
Czech Republic	32.2	32.3	30.5	27.7	29.6	30.2	30.4	34.1	32.8	32.4	33.1	3.8
Denmark	17.7	20.2	20.3	23.7	27.7	27.1	28.5	28.4	31.0	31.3	29.5	3.4
Germany	138.8	138.5	131.7	134.6	132.1	133.1	133.9	135.2	137.0	135.7	136.9	15.7
Estonia	3.7	3.6	3.2	3.0	3.2	3.4	3.7	4.2	4.0	4.2	3.9	0.4
Ireland	3.5	2.8	2.4	2.5	2.2	1.8	1.5	1.8	1.8	1.6	1.6	0.2
Greece	10.1	9.9	10.0	9.4	9.9	9.9	10.5	9.9	10.3	10.3	10.1	1.2
Spain	32.0	30.7	32.0	30.3	31.2	32.9	31.6	32.8	32.4	30.1	31.2	3.6
France	131.0	128.1	125.1	127.2	131.1	131.7	133.4	134.8	135.7	135.5	135.6	15.6
Italy	30.1	30.3	30.1	29.0	26.8	25.7	26.3	27.3	28.1	27.7	27.1	3.1
Cyprus	0.0	0.0	0.0	0.0	0.0	0.0	0.0	0.0	0.0	0.0	0.1	0.0
Latvia	1.4	1.6	1.8	1.6	1.4	1.5	1.6	1.7	1.8	1.9	1.8	0.2
Lithuania	4.3	3.9	4.4	3.5	3.2	4.1	4.8	5.1	5.0	3.7	3.2	0.4
Luxembourg	0.0	0.0	0.1	0.0	0.1	0.1	0.1	0.1	0.1	0.1	0.1	0.0
Hungary	13.1	12.8	11.9	11.5	11.2	10.8	11.1	10.7	10.2	10.4	10.3	1.2
Malta	-	-	-	-	-	-	-	-	-	-	-	-
Netherlands	74.0	65.7	62.9	59.4	57.2	60.9	60.4	58.4	67.7	61.9	60.8	7.0
Austria	8.4	8.5	8.7	9.4	9.6	9.6	9.7	9.5	9.7	9.3	9.6	1.1
Poland	97.8	99.1	86.8	82.8	78.4	79.4	79.1	78.7	78.0	77.7	76.8	8.8
Portugal	3.8	3.8	3.7	3.4	3.8	3.9	3.6	4.3	3.9	3.6	4.3	0.5
Romania	33.0	31.6	29.2	28.1	28.7	27.6	28.0	28.3	28.4	27.5	27.4	3.1
Slovenia	3.0	3.0	3.0	2.9	3.1	3.1	3.4	3.2	3.4	3.5	3.4	0.4
Slovakia	4.7	4.6	4.7	5.2	6.0	6.4	6.5	6.3	6.2	6.3	6.3	0.7
Finland	13.4	14.8	13.1	15.2	14.7	14.7	15.6	15.5	15.4	16.2	17.8	2.0
Sweden	31.5	32.0	33.0	32.7	30.0	33.3	31.2	30.4	33.8	34.2	32.3	3.7
United Kingdom	261.9	262.3	269.5	277.6	269.1	258.7	254.9	243.2	223.2	202.5	183.9	21.1
Croatia	4.2	4.1	4.0	3.6	3.6	3.7	3.7	3.7	3.9	3.8	4.1	-
Turkey	27.2	28.0	29.1	27.5	26.8	25.2	24.6	23.9	24.2	23.6	26.5	-
Iceland	1.6	1.7	1.8	2.2	2.3	2.5	2.5	2.5	2.5	2.6	3.3	-
Norway	208.1	212.7	206.6	209.6	225.0	228.9	233.6	236.0	238.5	234.0	223.7	-
Switzerland	10.0	10.5	10.6	11.2	11.1	11.7	11.2	11.4	11.4	10.5	11.8	-

Source: Eurostat (ten00076)

Figure 13.1: Production of primary energy, EU-27, 2006
(% of total, based on tonnes of oil equivalent)

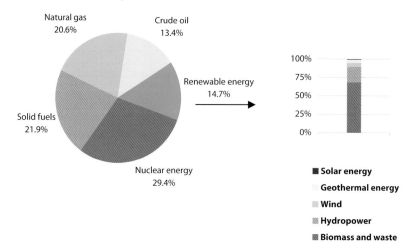

Source: Eurostat (ten00080, ten00077, ten00079, ten00078, ten00081, ten00082 and ten00076)

Figure 13.2: Development of the production of primary energy (by fuel type), EU-27
(1995=100, based on tonnes of oil equivalent)

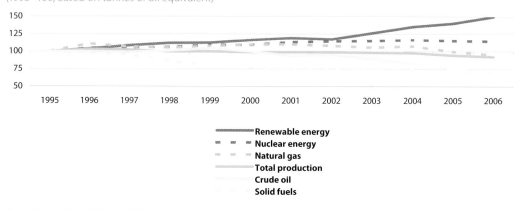

Source: Eurostat (ten00081, ten00080, ten00079, ten00076, ten00078 and ten00077)

Table 13.2: Net imports of primary energy
(million tonnes of oil equivalent)

	1996	1997	1998	1999	2000	2001	2002	2003	2004	2005	2006	Share in EU-27, 2006 (%)
EU-27	774.0	784.7	813.9	790.8	826.3	857.5	858.2	904.5	941.0	986.2	1 010.1	100.0
Euro area	698.8	716.4	752.2	752.7	783.2	792.6	800.5	822.7	834.5	854.4	855.2	84.7
Belgium	49.4	49.3	52.1	49.2	50.8	51.3	49.3	53.2	53.9	53.8	53.5	5.3
Bulgaria	13.2	10.8	10.1	8.9	8.7	9.0	8.9	9.3	9.2	9.5	9.5	0.9
Czech Republic	10.6	10.6	10.6	9.8	9.4	10.7	11.4	11.4	11.7	12.9	12.9	1.3
Denmark	5.5	3.9	1.3	-3.4	-7.3	-5.8	-8.6	-6.9	-9.9	-10.4	-8.1	-0.8
Germany	208.8	209.4	214.0	203.7	205.7	216.7	209.3	213.0	215.5	215.3	215.5	21.3
Estonia	2.0	1.9	2.0	1.9	1.6	1.7	1.5	1.5	1.7	1.5	1.9	0.2
Ireland	8.4	9.5	10.7	11.7	12.3	13.7	13.7	13.6	13.9	13.7	14.2	1.4
Greece	18.9	19.3	21.2	19.8	22.1	22.4	23.3	22.6	24.7	23.4	24.9	2.5
Spain	74.3	80.8	88.4	95.3	99.3	99.8	108.0	109.1	115.3	124.0	123.8	12.3
France	125.0	122.8	132.4	132.8	134.2	136.8	137.5	138.9	141.5	144.3	141.7	14.0
Italy	134.8	134.9	140.7	144.2	153.4	148.3	153.4	156.4	159.5	161.0	164.6	16.3
Cyprus	2.2	2.1	2.2	2.4	2.5	2.5	2.6	2.7	2.4	2.8	3.0	0.3
Latvia	3.5	2.7	2.6	2.2	2.2	2.5	2.5	2.8	3.2	3.0	3.2	0.3
Lithuania	5.1	5.1	4.8	4.4	4.3	3.9	3.7	4.1	4.4	5.1	5.5	0.5
Luxembourg	3.4	3.3	3.3	3.4	3.6	3.7	4.0	4.2	4.5	4.6	4.7	0.5
Hungary	13.9	13.6	14.4	13.9	14.0	13.9	14.8	16.4	16.1	17.5	17.3	1.7
Malta	0.9	1.0	0.9	1.0	0.8	0.7	0.9	0.9	0.9	1.0	0.9	0.1
Netherlands	14.8	23.7	24.5	26.9	35.4	32.6	32.5	36.7	31.4	38.4	37.2	3.7
Austria	20.1	19.4	20.5	19.2	19.1	20.0	21.2	23.1	23.5	24.7	24.9	2.5
Poland	5.6	6.6	8.2	9.7	10.3	9.5	10.2	12.1	13.5	16.9	19.6	1.9
Portugal	16.9	18.6	19.6	22.3	21.9	21.8	22.5	22.4	22.7	24.4	21.6	2.1
Romania	15.0	14.8	11.9	8.0	8.1	9.5	9.1	10.2	11.9	10.8	11.9	1.2
Slovenia	3.5	3.6	3.4	3.6	3.4	3.4	3.5	3.7	3.7	3.8	3.8	0.4
Slovakia	13.3	13.2	12.5	11.7	11.6	12.2	12.6	12.7	13.2	12.5	12.0	1.2
Finland	17.5	18.7	18.5	17.3	18.6	18.9	18.8	22.4	21.0	19.3	20.9	2.1
Sweden	21.3	19.8	19.9	18.2	19.3	19.3	19.9	22.8	20.4	20.2	19.8	2.0
United Kingdom	-33.4	-34.8	-36.6	-47.2	-39.2	-21.6	-28.2	-14.6	11.1	32.3	49.3	4.9
Croatia	3.2	3.7	4.0	4.4	4.2	4.2	5.0	5.0	5.1	5.3	4.9	-
Turkey	41.0	42.9	43.6	43.5	51.1	46.2	51.1	56.8	58.7	62.1	69.3	-
Iceland	0.9	0.9	0.9	1.0	1.0	0.9	1.0	0.9	1.1	1.1	1.1	-
Norway	-182.5	-187.4	-180.6	-182.0	-198.3	-203.3	-208.7	-207.1	-210.0	-200.6	-197.6	-
Switzerland	14.9	14.8	15.3	14.0	14.0	15.2	15.0	14.7	15.1	16.2	16.1	-

Source: Eurostat (ten00083)

Table 13.3: Main origin of primary energy imports, EU-27
(% of extra EU-27 imports)

	Crude oil						
	2000	2001	2002	2003	2004	2005	2006
Russia	20.3	24.8	29.0	30.9	32.8	32.4	32.9
Norway	21.0	19.6	19.3	19.2	18.9	16.8	15.5
Libya	8.2	7.9	7.3	8.3	8.7	8.7	9.3
Saudi Arabia	11.8	10.4	10.0	11.1	11.2	10.5	8.9
Iran	6.4	5.7	4.9	6.3	6.2	6.1	6.3
Kazakhstan	1.8	1.6	2.5	2.9	3.9	4.5	4.7
Nigeria	4.1	4.7	3.5	4.2	2.6	3.2	3.5
Iraq	5.7	3.7	3.0	1.5	2.2	2.1	2.9
Algeria	3.9	3.5	3.4	3.4	3.8	3.9	2.9
Azerbaijan	0.7	0.8	1.0	1.0	0.9	1.2	2.1
Venezuela	1.3	1.6	1.7	0.9	0.8	1.2	1.9
Others	15.0	15.5	14.4	10.2	8.1	9.4	9.2
	Natural gas						
	2000	2001	2002	2003	2004	2005	2006
Russia	49.6	48.8	46.1	46.1	44.5	41.8	40.4
Norway	21.7	23.6	26.3	25.4	25.2	22.5	23.3
Algeria	24.1	21.6	21.6	20.3	18.4	19.0	17.5
Nigeria	1.9	2.4	2.2	3.2	3.7	3.7	4.6
Libya	0.4	0.4	0.3	0.3	0.4	1.8	2.6
Egypt	0.0	0.0	0.0	0.0	0.0	1.7	2.6
Qatar	0.1	0.3	0.9	0.8	1.4	1.7	2.0
Trinidad and Tobago	0.4	0.3	0.2	0.0	0.0	0.3	1.3
Uzbekistan	0.4	0.3	0.0	0.3	0.2	0.5	1.0
Croatia	0.0	0.0	0.0	0.0	0.0	0.0	0.4
Turkmenistan	0.0	0.0	0.0	0.1	0.1	0.7	0.3
Others	1.5	2.0	2.0	3.3	5.6	5.7	3.7

Source: Eurostat (nrg_123a and nrg_124a)

Table 13.4: Energy dependency rate, EU-27

(% of net imports in gross inland consumption and bunkers, based on tonnes of oil equivalent)

	1996	1997	1998	1999	2000	2001	2002	2003	2004	2005	2006
All products	44.1	45.0	46.1	45.2	46.8	47.5	47.6	48.9	50.3	52.6	53.8
Hard coal	31.8	34.8	36.3	38.4	42.7	47.2	47.3	49.0	53.8	55.8	58.5
Crude oil and petroleum	75.6	75.9	77.2	73.1	76.0	77.4	76.1	78.4	79.9	82.4	83.6
Natural gas	43.5	45.2	45.7	47.9	48.9	47.3	51.2	52.5	54.0	57.7	60.8

Source: Eurostat (nrg_100a, nrg_101a, nrg_102a and nrg_103a)

Figure 13.3: Energy dependency rate - all products, 2006 (1)

(% of net imports in gross inland consumption and bunkers, based on tonnes of oil equivalent)

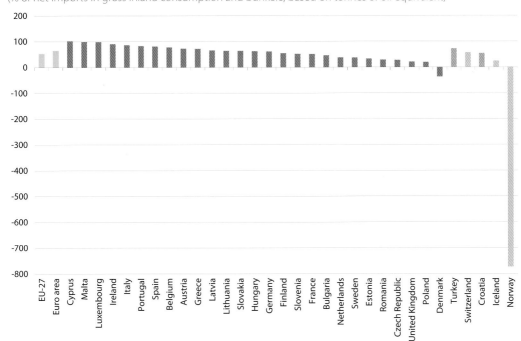

(1) EU-27 and Slovenia, provisional.

Source: Eurostat (tsdcc310)

13.2 Electricity generation

Introduction

One of the reasons for the increased dependency rate for natural gas is the shift in fuels used for electricity generation: among the main sources for generation, natural gas has increased at the expense of coal, lignite and oil, probably as a result of lower emissions from gas. Over the same period there has been an increase in the use of renewables, particularly wind turbines, although their contribution remains relatively small.

The use of nuclear power for electricity generation has received renewed attention against a background of increasing dependency on imported primary energy, rising oil and gas prices, and commitments to reduce greenhouse gas emissions, balanced against long-standing concerns about safety and waste from nuclear power plants. Some Member States have recently started construction or have planned new nuclear reactors.

Renewable energy sources can have an important role to play in reducing CO_2 emissions. A sustainable energy policy is, in part, reliant upon increasing the share of renewable energy, which may at the same time help improve the security of energy supply by reducing the EU's growing dependence on imported energy sources. The European Parliament and Council set indicative targets in 2001 for the promotion of electricity from renewable energy sources, whereby 22 % of the EU-15's gross electricity consumption should be electricity produced from renewables by 2010; the target for the EU-25 is 21 %.

Definitions and data availability

Gross electricity generation at the plant level is defined as the electricity measured at the outlet of the main transformers, in other words, the consumption of electricity in plant auxiliaries and in transformers is included.

The indicator of **electricity from renewable energy sources** is the ratio between electricity produced from renewable energy sources and gross national electricity consumption. It measures the contribution of electricity produced from renewable energy sources to the national electricity consumption. Electricity produced from renewable energy sources comprises the electricity generation from hydropower plants (excluding pumping), wind, solar, geothermal and electricity from biomass/wastes.

The indicator on the **market share of the largest electricity generator** is based on net electricity production, and as such the electricity used by generators for their own consumption is not taken into account. The net production of each generator during the same year is considered in order to calculate the corresponding market shares. Only the largest market share is reported under this indicator.

Main findings

Total gross electricity generation in the EU-27 was 3.4 million GWh in 2006, of which close to 30 % came from nuclear power plants. Natural gas and coal-fired power stations each accounted for around one fifth of the total, and lignite-fired and oil-fired power stations 10 % and 4 % respectively. Among the renewable sources, the largest share was from hydropower providing 10 % of the total, followed by biomass-fired power stations and wind turbines each generating between 2 % and 3 % of the total.

Germany and France were the principal electricity generators in the EU-27, with shares of 19 % and 17 % respectively, while the United Kingdom was the only other Member State to report a share above 10 %.

The EU-27 has recorded average growth of 1.7 % per annum in its level of electricity generation between 1996 and 2006. Luxembourg recorded an exceptional increase in electricity generation in 2002: this aside, the Member States with the largest increase in their respective levels of generation in the ten years to 2006 were Cyprus, Spain and Latvia. Lithuania and Denmark were the only Member States to record a lower level of generation in 2006 than in 1996.

Electricity generated from all renewable sources combined was equivalent to 14.5 % of gross national electricity consumption in the EU-27 in 2006. Several of the Member States had much higher ratios concerning the relative importance of renewables, in particular Austria (56.6 %), Sweden (48.2 %) and Latvia (37.7 %) which all generated large proportions of their electricity from hydropower, as well as (in some cases) from biomass. In contrast, the relatively high share of renewables in Denmark (25.9 %) was mainly due to wind power and to a lesser extent biomass.

One measure that can be used to monitor the success of liberalisation within electricity markets is the market share of the largest generator. The small island nations of Cyprus and Malta continued to report a complete monopoly, with 100 % of their electricity being generated by the largest generator, and three other Member States, namely Latvia, Greece and Estonia, also reported shares over 90 %. Ten of the 25 Member States for which data are available reported that the largest generator provided less than 50 % of the total, with the share below 25 % in Finland, the United Kingdom and Poland.

Figure 13.4: Electricity generation by fuel used in power stations, EU-27, 2006 (1)
(% of total, based on GWh)

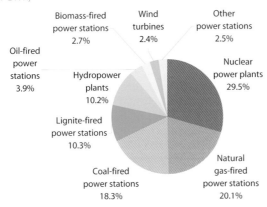

(1) Figures do not sum to 100 % due to rounding.

Source: Eurostat (nrg_105a)

Table 13.5: Total gross electricity generation
(1 000 GWh)

	1996	1997	1998	1999	2000	2001	2002	2003	2004	2005	2006	Share in EU-27, 2006 (%)
EU-27	2 830	2 841	2 910	2 940	3 021	3 108	3 117	3 216	3 288	3 309	3 358	100.0
Euro area	1 887	1 906	1 951	1 990	2 061	2 110	2 127	2 203	2 266	2 276	2 322	69.1
Belgium	76	79	83	85	84	80	82	85	85	87	86	2.5
Bulgaria	43	43	42	38	41	44	43	43	42	44	46	1.4
Czech Republic	64	65	65	65	73	75	76	83	84	83	84	2.5
Denmark	54	44	41	39	36	38	39	46	40	36	46	1.4
Germany	555	552	557	555	572	586	572	599	617	620	637	19.0
Estonia	9	9	9	8	9	8	9	10	10	10	10	0.3
Ireland	19	20	21	22	24	25	25	25	26	25	27	0.8
Greece	43	44	46	50	54	54	55	58	59	60	61	1.8
Spain	174	190	195	209	225	238	246	263	280	294	303	9.0
France	513	505	511	524	541	550	559	567	574	576	574	17.1
Italy	244	251	260	266	277	279	284	294	303	304	314	9.4
Cyprus	3	3	3	3	3	4	4	4	4	4	5	0.1
Latvia	3	5	6	4	4	4	4	4	5	5	5	0.1
Lithuania	17	15	18	14	11	15	18	19	19	15	12	0.4
Luxembourg	1	1	1	1	1	1	4	4	4	4	4	0.1
Hungary	35	35	37	38	35	36	36	34	34	36	36	1.1
Malta	2	2	2	2	2	2	2	2	2	2	2	0.1
Netherlands	85	87	91	87	90	94	96	97	101	100	98	2.9
Austria	55	57	57	61	62	62	62	60	64	66	64	1.9
Poland	143	143	143	142	145	146	144	152	154	157	162	4.8
Portugal	35	34	39	43	44	47	46	47	45	47	49	1.5
Romania	61	57	53	51	52	54	55	57	56	59	63	1.9
Slovenia	13	13	14	13	14	14	15	14	15	15	15	0.5
Slovakia	25	25	25	28	31	32	32	31	31	31	31	0.9
Finland	69	69	70	69	70	74	75	84	86	71	82	2.5
Sweden	141	149	158	155	146	162	147	135	152	158	143	4.3
United Kingdom	347	345	362	368	377	385	387	398	394	398	398	11.9
Croatia	11	10	11	12	11	12	12	13	13	12	12	-
Turkey	95	103	111	116	125	123	129	141	151	162	176	-
Iceland	5	6	6	7	8	8	8	9	9	9	10	-
Norway	105	112	117	123	143	122	131	107	111	138	122	-
Switzerland	57	63	63	70	68	72	67	67	66	60	64	-

Source: Eurostat (ten00087)

Figure 13.5: Proportion of electricity generated from renewable energy sources
(% of gross electricity consumption)

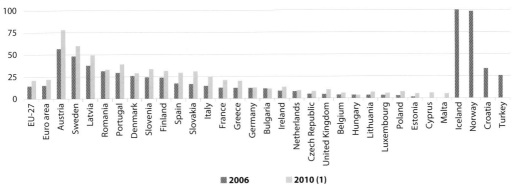

(1) Indicative targets for 2010 are not available for Croatia, Turkey, Iceland and Norway.

Source: Eurostat (tsien050)

Figure 13.6: Market share of the largest generator in the electricity market, 2006 (1)
(% of total generation)

(1) Bulgaria and the Netherlands, not available.
(2) 2004.
(3) 2005.
(4) 2001.

Source: Eurostat (tsier060)

13.3 Consumption of energy

Introduction

As well as supply-side policies, a number of EU initiatives have been aimed at reducing energy demand, in an attempt to decouple it from the growth in economic activity. Several instruments and implementing measures exist in this field, including the promotion of co-generation, the energy performance of buildings (whether private or public buildings), and energy labelling of domestic appliances.

In October 2006 the European Commission adopted an action plan for energy efficiency (COM(2006) 545) [5] which was supported by the Council in November 2006. The plan proposes to cut energy consumption by 20 % by 2020, and in so doing simultaneously address the issues of import dependency, energy-related emissions, and energy costs.

Providing transport for goods and passengers, whether for own-use or for hire and reward, consumes significant amounts of energy. There are many factors that impact on energy use and emissions in transport, for example, overall economic growth, the efficiency of individual transport modes, the combination of different transport modes, alternative fuels, and lifestyle choices.

In 2001, the European Commission adopted a policy to promote biofuels for transport, and a number of targets were set. In March 2007 the Council supported increasing the level of renewables (such as biofuels) in transport fuel to 10 % by 2020.

Definitions and data availability

Gross inland consumption expresses the total energy needs of a country. It covers consumption by the energy branch itself, distribution and transformation losses, and final energy consumption. The share of renewables in gross inland energy consumption is defined as the percentage share of renewables in gross inland energy consumption.

Final energy consumption includes the consumption by all users except the energy branch itself (whether deliveries for transformation and/or own use), and includes, for example, energy consumption by agriculture, industry, services and households, as well as energy consumption for transport. It should be noted that the fuel quantities transformed in the electrical power stations of industrial auto-producers and the quantities of coke transformed into blast-furnace gas are not part of overall industrial consumption but of the transformation sector. Final energy consumption in transport covers the consumption in all types of transportation, i.e., rail, road, air transport and inland navigation. Final energy consumption in households, services, etc. covers quantities consumed by private households, commerce, public administration, services, agriculture and fisheries.

(5) http://ec.europa.eu/energy/action_plan_energy_efficiency/index_en.htm.

Energy intensity is measured as the ratio between gross inland consumption of energy and gross domestic product (GDP) for a given calendar year. It measures the energy consumption of an economy and its overall energy efficiency. The ratio is expressed as kgoe (kilogram of oil equivalent) per EUR 1 000, and to facilitate analysis over time the calculations are based on GDP in constant prices (currently using 1995 prices). If an economy becomes more efficient in its use of energy, and its GDP remains constant, then the ratio for this indicator should fall; this energy intensity ratio is also considered as an indicator of energy efficiency. The GDP figures are taken at constant prices to avoid the impact of the inflation, base year 1995.

Main findings

Gross inland consumption of energy within the EU-27 in 2006 was 1 825 million toe, almost unchanged compared with both 2004 and 2005, and as such was just over double the level of the production of primary energy. The gross inland consumption of each Member State depends on the structure of its energy system and the availability of natural resources. This is true not only for conventional fuels and nuclear power, but also for renewables. For example, although small in absolute levels, the use of solar power is relatively high in the Mediterranean countries such as Cyprus, while the use of biomass is high in countries with large forest areas, for example, Latvia, Finland and Sweden. In the same vein,

hydropower is particularly important in mountainous countries with ample water supplies, such as Austria or Sweden.

Final energy consumption in the EU-27 was equivalent to just under two thirds of gross inland consumption, at 1 176 million toe in 2006. This level was only slightly higher than the previous two years, and over the ten years from 1996 to 2006 final energy consumption increased on average by just 0.5 % per annum. An analysis by main type of energy shows a shift in the energy mix between 1996 and 2006, most notably through a fall in the consumption of solid fuels (-3.8 % per annum) and an increase in the consumption of renewables (2.8 % per annum) and electricity (2.0 %).

An analysis of the end-use of energy shows three dominant categories, namely industry, households and road transport, each with a share of just over one quarter of the total. Combining all forms of transport, including road, air transport and others (such as inland waterways and rail), the transport share reached 31 %: road transport accounted for 82 % of the total energy consumption for transport purposes, and air transport for 14 %. Between 1996 and 2006 energy consumption for inland waterways and for rail transport fell, while consumption for road transport increased by an average of 1.6 % per annum and for air transport it increased, on average, by 3.8 % per annum. The rates of change for 2006 compared with 2005 were broadly in line with these longer term trends, except for inland water transport which recorded an increase of 11.0 % in consumption in 2006, following on from a 4.4 % increase in 2005 bringing consumption for inland waterways to its highest level since 1999.

In 2007 a minimum target was set that renewables (such as biofuels) should account for 10 % of transport petrol and diesel by 2020. Data for 2006 show that biofuels made the biggest contribution to transport consumption of fuels in Germany (5.5 %), Slovakia (2.5 %) and Sweden (2.2 %), and these were the only Member States (for which data are available) where the share of biofuels was above the EU-27 average of 1.5 %.

The lowest level of energy intensity recorded by the EU-27 Member States was in Denmark, while the most energy-intensive countries were Bulgaria and Romania. It should be noted that the economic structure of an economy plays an important role in determining energy intensity, as post-industrial economies with large service sectors will, a priori, display low levels of energy intensity compared with economies that have a considerable proportion of their economic activity within industrial activities.

Table 13.6: Gross inland consumption of energy

(million tonnes of oil equivalent)

	1996	1997	1998	1999	2000	2001	2002	2003	2004	2005	2006	Share in EU-27, 2006 (%)
EU-27	1 719	1 704	1 722	1 710	1 723	1 762	1 758	1 803	1 824	1 826	1 825	100.0
Euro area	1 134	1 135	1 158	1 163	1 178	1 207	1 208	1 238	1 257	1 257	1 253	68.6
Belgium	58	59	60	61	61	60	58	61	61	61	60	3.3
Bulgaria	23	20	20	18	19	19	19	20	19	20	21	1.1
Czech Republic	43	43	41	38	41	42	42	46	46	45	46	2.5
Denmark	23	21	21	20	20	20	20	21	20	20	21	1.1
Germany	350	347	346	340	341	353	346	349	350	347	349	19.1
Estonia	6	6	5	5	5	5	5	5	6	6	5	0.3
Ireland	12	12	13	14	14	15	15	15	16	15	16	0.9
Greece	25	26	27	27	28	29	30	30	31	31	32	1.7
Spain	101	107	113	118	124	127	131	135	141	145	144	7.9
France	255	249	256	256	260	267	267	272	276	276	273	15.0
Italy	162	164	169	172	173	174	174	183	185	187	186	10.2
Cyprus	2	2	2	2	2	2	2	3	2	2	3	0.1
Latvia	5	4	4	4	4	4	4	4	4	4	5	0.3
Lithuania	9	9	9	8	7	8	9	9	9	9	8	0.5
Luxembourg	3	3	3	3	4	4	4	4	5	5	5	0.3
Hungary	26	26	26	25	25	25	26	27	27	28	28	1.5
Malta	1	1	1	1	1	1	1	1	1	1	1	0.0
Netherlands	77	76	76	76	77	79	80	82	84	82	81	4.4
Austria	29	29	29	29	29	31	31	33	33	34	34	1.9
Poland	104	103	96	94	91	91	90	92	92	94	98	5.4
Portugal	20	22	23	25	25	25	26	26	26	27	25	1.4
Romania	48	45	42	37	37	37	38	40	40	39	41	2.2
Slovenia	6	7	6	6	6	7	7	7	7	7	7	0.4
Slovakia	18	18	17	17	18	19	19	19	19	19	19	1.0
Finland	31	33	33	33	33	33	35	37	37	35	38	2.1
Sweden	52	50	51	50	48	51	51	50	53	52	51	2.8
United Kingdom	229	223	231	229	232	233	227	231	233	233	230	12.6
Croatia	7	8	8	8	8	8	8	9	9	9	9	-
Turkey	68	71	73	71	78	72	75	79	82	85	95	-
Iceland	2	3	3	3	3	3	3	3	3	4	4	-
Norway	23	24	26	27	26	27	24	27	28	32	25	-
Switzerland	25	26	26	26	26	27	26	27	27	27	28	-

Source: Eurostat (ten00086)

Table 13.7: Final energy consumption
(million tonnes of oil equivalent)

	1996	1997	1998	1999	2000	2001	2002	2003	2004	2005	2006	Share in EU-27, 2006 (%)
EU-27	1 115	1 104	1 111	1 108	1 114	1 140	1 126	1 158	1 171	1 172	1 176	100.0
Euro area	745	741	756	759	767	789	781	805	813	814	815	69.3
Belgium	38	38	39	39	39	39	38	40	39	38	38	3.2
Bulgaria	12	9	10	9	9	9	9	9	9	10	10	0.9
Czech Republic	26	25	24	24	24	24	24	25	26	26	26	2.2
Denmark	15	15	15	15	15	15	15	15	15	15	16	1.3
Germany	231	225	224	219	218	224	219	222	220	218	223	19.0
Estonia	3	3	3	2	2	3	3	3	3	3	3	0.2
Ireland	8	9	9	10	11	11	11	11	12	12	13	1.1
Greece	17	17	18	18	19	19	20	21	20	21	21	1.8
Spain	65	68	72	74	80	84	86	91	95	97	97	8.2
France	150	148	153	152	152	158	154	157	160	159	158	13.4
Italy	115	116	119	124	123	126	125	130	131	133	131	11.1
Cyprus	1	1	2	2	2	2	2	2	2	2	2	0.2
Latvia	4	4	4	3	3	4	4	4	4	4	4	0.4
Lithuania	4	5	4	4	4	4	4	4	4	4	5	0.4
Luxembourg	3	3	3	3	4	4	4	4	4	4	4	0.4
Hungary	16	16	16	16	16	16	17	18	17	18	18	1.5
Malta	0	1	0	0	0	0	0	0	0	1	0	0.0
Netherlands	52	50	50	49	50	51	51	52	53	52	51	4.3
Austria	23	22	23	23	23	25	25	26	26	27	27	2.3
Poland	66	65	60	58	55	56	54	56	57	57	60	5.1
Portugal	15	15	16	17	18	18	18	18	20	19	19	1.6
Romania	30	29	26	22	22	23	23	24	25	25	25	2.1
Slovenia	4	5	4	4	4	5	5	5	5	5	5	0.4
Slovakia	11	11	10	10	10	11	11	11	11	11	11	0.9
Finland	22	24	24	25	24	24	25	26	26	25	27	2.3
Sweden	35	34	34	34	34	33	34	34	34	34	33	2.8
United Kingdom	150	148	149	152	152	153	149	151	152	152	151	12.8
Croatia	5	5	5	5	5	5	6	6	6	6	6	-
Turkey	49	50	50	49	55	50	55	59	60	63	69	-
Iceland	2	2	2	2	2	2	2	2	2	2	2	-
Norway	18	18	18	19	18	19	18	18	18	18	18	-
Switzerland	20	20	20	21	20	21	20	21	21	22	22	-

Source: Eurostat (ten00095)

Figure 13.7: Share of renewables in gross inland energy consumption, 2006 (1)
(%)

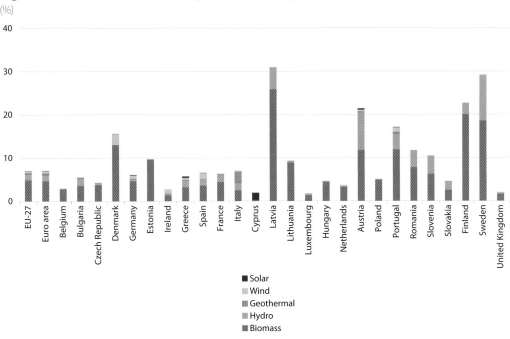

- ■ Solar
- ▨ Wind
- ▨ Geothermal
- ▨ Hydro
- ▨ Biomass

(1) Malta, not available; EU-27, euro area and Slovenia, provisional.

Source: Eurostat (tsdcc110)

Figure 13.8: Final energy consumption, EU-27 (1)
(1996=100)

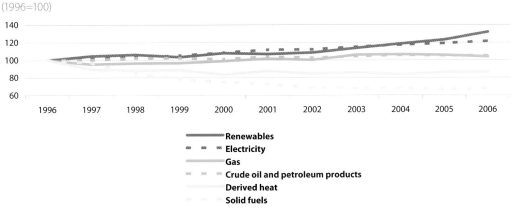

- Renewables
- Electricity
- Gas
- Crude oil and petroleum products
- Derived heat
- Solid fuels

(1) Final energy consumption, 2006 (million toe): renewables 59.1; electricity 241.9; gas 278.7; crude oil and petroleum products 496.7; derived heat 41.3; solid fuels 55.5.

Source: Eurostat (nrg_1071a, nrg_105a, nrg_103a, nrg_102a, nrg_106a and nrg_101a)

Figure 13.9: Share of biofuels in total fuel consumption of transport, 2006 (1)
(%)

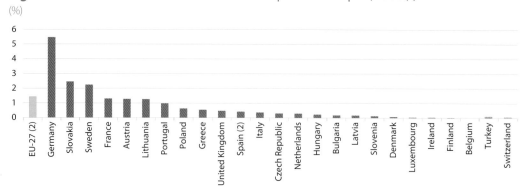

(1) Estonia, Cyprus, Malta and Romania, not available.
(2) Provisional.

Source: Eurostat (nrg_1073a and nrg_100a)

Figure 13.10: Final energy consumption, EU-27, 2006 (1)
(% of total, based on tonnes of oil equivalent)

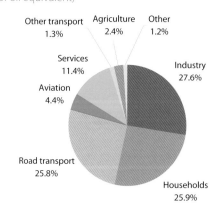

Other transport
1.3%

Agriculture
2.4%

Other
1.2%

Services
11.4%

Industry
27.6%

Aviation
4.4%

Road transport
25.8%

Households
25.9%

(1) Provisional.

Source: Eurostat (tsdpc320 and tsdtr100)

Figure 13.11: Energy consumption by transport mode, EU-27 (1)

(1996=100)

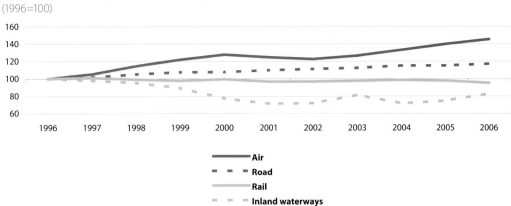

(1) Provisional: 2002 for all modes; provisional: 2005 and 2006 for rail.

Source: Eurostat (tsdtr100)

Figure 13.12: Energy intensity of the economy, 2006

(kgoe per EUR 1 000 of GDP)

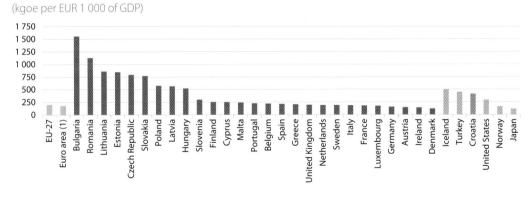

(1) EA-13 instead of EA-15.

Source: Eurostat (tsien020)

13.4 Energy prices

Introduction

Ever increasing energy demand, the global geopolitical situation and severe weather conditions have induced rapid, large changes in energy prices. Crude oil prices increased significantly from 2004 to the middle of 2008, since when they have dropped back sharply, although at the time of writing remain well above their levels at the beginning of 2004. Changes in oil prices have an impact on the price of substitutes, notably natural gas, and also feed into the prices of products from other sectors that are heavy users of energy or of energy products as raw materials.

The price and reliability of energy supplies, and of electricity in particular, is a key element of a country's energy supply, and particularly important with respect to international competitiveness, as electricity usually represents a high proportion of total energy costs to households and businesses. In contrast to the price of fossil fuels, which are usually traded on global markets with relatively uniform prices, there is a particularly wide range of prices within the EU for electricity. The price of electricity is, to some degree, influenced by the price of primary fuels and more recently also by the cost of carbon dioxide (CO_2) emission certificates, and it is possible that resulting higher prices for electricity will provide an incentive for greater energy efficiency and lower levels of carbon emissions.

There have been moves within the EU to liberalise the electricity and gas market since the second half of the 1990s. Directives of the European Parliament and the Council adopted in 2003 established common rules for the internal markets in electricity and natural gas, and set deadlines for market opening, allowing customers to choose their supplier: 1 July 2004 for all business customers and 1 July 2007 for all consumers including households. Certain countries anticipated the liberalisation process, while others were slower in adopting these measures. Significant barriers to entry remain in many electricity and natural gas markets, as witnessed in many Member States which are still dominated by (near) monopoly suppliers. In September 2007, the European Commission adopted a third package of legislative proposals[6] aimed at ensuring a real and effective choice of supplier and benefits for customers; at the time of writing the Council had unanimously reached a political agreement on this package, which was due for a second reading by the European Parliament.

Definitions and data availability

Energy prices are currently collected at a national level, whereas in the past they were collected at a regional level or, in some cases, even for individual cities. Time-series for prices start in 1985, with data for the Member States that joined the EU in 2004 and 2007 generally available from 2004 onwards.

---

(6) http://ec.europa.eu/energy/electricity/package_2007/index_en.htm.

Statistics on **electricity and natural gas prices** are collected on a half-yearly basis – they are shown here as a snapshot as of 1 January of each year. Electricity prices for households are normally shown including taxes and value added tax (VAT), as these are generally the end price paid by the consumer at point of use. For the purposes of comparison industrial gas and electricity prices are also shown here including all taxes, although in practise enterprises can deduct VAT paid.

Automotive fuel prices shown are at the pump prices of premium unleaded gasoline (petrol) 95 RON and automotive diesel oil. The prices are supplied to the Directorate-General for Energy and Transport of the European Commission by the Member States as being the most frequently encountered on the first Monday after the 15th of each month. Eurostat also publishes price information on heating oil and residual fuel oil.

Main findings

Electricity and gas tariffs vary from one supplier to another. They may be the result of negotiated contracts, especially for large industrial consumers. For smaller consumers they are generally set according to the amount of electricity or gas consumed, and a number of other characteristics that vary from one country to another; most tariffs also include some form of fixed charge. Therefore, there is no single price for electricity or gas in any EU Member State. In order to compare prices over time and between countries, two 'standard consumers' are presented, one representing domestic consumers and the other industrial consumers. All electricity price data are given in euro per 100 kWh and correspond to prices applicable on 1 January of the reference year; a similar set of criteria are used for gas prices, except the unit changes to euro per GJ.

Electricity and gas prices have increased strongly in recent years, particularly gas prices. Between 2005 and 2007 prices increased for households and industrial users in nearly all Member States for both types of energy: Latvia recorded significantly lower electricity prices for households, Finland slightly lower electricity prices for industrial users, and Denmark recorded lower prices for industrial users for both types of energy. In percentage terms, price increases for households were particularly high in Romania, the United Kingdom and Ireland, while industrial users faced the largest increases in the United Kingdom, Romania and Slovakia. In 2007, the price of electricity for households was nearly four times higher in the most expensive Member State, Denmark, than in the cheapest Member States, namely Bulgaria and Latvia. The range of household prices for gas was even greater, with the highest prices again in Denmark, more than five times the lowest, in Estonia; household gas prices were also significantly higher in Sweden than in other Member States. A large part of the price differences between the Member States can be attributed to taxes, as the range in prices excluding taxes is less than the range when including taxes.

As with electricity and gas prices, petrol and diesel prices have also risen in recent years. The highest prices for unleaded petrol in the EU during the first half of 2008 were recorded in the Netherlands, Belgium, Portugal and the United Kingdom, while the United Kingdom had by some margin the most expensive pump price for diesel. The lowest prices for petrol and diesel were in Romania and Bulgaria, the Baltic Member States, the islands of Cyprus and Malta, as well as in Slovenia, while Luxembourg and Spain also recorded particularly low diesel prices.

Table 13.8: Electricity and gas prices (including taxes), as of 1 January
(EUR)

	Electricity prices (per 100 kWh)						Gas prices (per GJ)					
	Households (1)			Industry (2)			Households (3)			Industry (4)		
	2005	2006	2007	2005	2006	2007	2005	2006	2007	2005	2006	2007
EU-15	13.82	14.40	15.81	8.94	9.98	10.97	11.81	13.51	15.66	7.84	10.34	11.29
Euro area (5)	14.70	15.10	16.05	9.49	10.27	11.22	13.36	15.33	16.98	7.93	10.28	11.08
Belgium	14.81	14.42	15.81	9.38	11.72	11.73	11.16	13.50	12.89	6.43	8.61	8.47
Bulgaria	6.44	6.60	6.60	5.16	5.52	5.62	6.73	7.70	8.83	4.53	5.40	6.26
Czech Republic	8.68	9.85	10.67	7.13	8.70	9.30	7.49	10.03	9.45	6.08	8.74	7.81
Denmark	22.78	23.62	25.79	10.86	12.06	10.74	28.44	29.82	30.84	8.49	8.58	8.16
Germany	17.85	18.32	19.49	10.47	11.53	12.72	13.56	15.98	18.45	10.29	13.44	15.79
Estonia	6.78	7.31	7.50	5.57	6.02	6.30	4.63	4.63	5.89	3.25	3.36	4.36
Ireland	14.36	14.90	16.62	10.56	11.48	12.77	9.98	12.51	16.73	:	:	:
Greece	6.88	7.01	7.20	6.97	7.28	7.61	:	:	:	:	:	:
Spain	10.97	11.47	12.25	8.36	8.79	9.87	11.90	13.63	14.23	5.43	8.40	8.21
France	11.94	11.94	12.11	6.91	6.91	7.01	10.57	12.72	13.46	7.58	9.78	9.26
Italy	19.70	21.08	23.29	12.02	13.29	15.26	15.34	16.50	18.34	7.30	8.41	9.88
Cyprus	10.74	14.31	13.76	9.27	13.04	12.26	-	-	-	-	-	-
Latvia	8.28	8.29	6.88	4.82	4.82	5.23	4.54	5.34	7.50	4.11	4.77	6.24
Lithuania	7.18	7.18	7.76	5.88	5.88	6.46	5.41	6.24	7.04	4.25	5.26	7.10
Luxembourg	14.78	16.03	16.84	9.02	9.49	10.54	8.14	10.33	11.52	7.36	9.55	10.45
Hungary	10.64	10.75	12.22	8.86	9.13	9.84	5.10	5.28	7.16	6.94	9.40	11.64
Malta	7.64	9.49	9.87	7.41	7.46	9.42	-	-	-	-	-	-
Netherlands	19.55	20.87	21.80	10.70	11.38	12.25	15.17	16.92	18.42	8.90	11.15	11.59
Austria	14.13	13.40	15.45	9.92	10.35	11.43	13.36	15.65	15.99	9.83	12.99	13.27
Poland	10.64	11.90	12.16	6.78	7.27	7.23	7.55	9.46	10.69	6.47	8.25	9.20
Portugal	13.81	14.10	15.00	7.49	8.58	9.03	12.34	14.52	13.88	6.33	8.01	8.15
Romania	7.79	9.43	10.17	9.15	9.20	10.02	4.79	7.66	9.05	4.38	7.42	8.71
Slovenia	10.33	10.49	10.64	7.33	7.81	8.90	10.33	12.99	13.86	7.07	9.55	9.75
Slovakia	13.38	14.48	15.37	8.37	9.20	11.11	8.14	10.88	11.48	6.04	9.12	9.52
Finland	10.57	10.78	11.60	6.99	6.86	6.89	:	:	:	8.43	9.51	9.87
Sweden	13.97	14.35	17.14	4.68	5.93	6.31	22.18	25.95	26.58	9.20	12.26	12.21
United Kingdom	8.77	10.20	13.16	6.96	9.66	11.44	7.26	8.24	11.76	7.17	10.82	12.75
Norway	15.71	15.33	18.56	8.12	8.06	10.58	:	:	:	:	:	:

(1) Annual consumption: 3 500 kWh of which night 1 300.
(2) Annual consumption: 2 000 MWh; maximum demand: 500 kW; annual load: 4 000 hours); special category for Luxembourg.
(3) Annual consumption: 83.70 GJ.
(4) Annual consumption: 41 860 GJ; load factor: 200 days, 1 600 hours); special category for Belgium.
(5) EA-12 instead of EA-15.

Source: Eurostat (nrg_pc_priceind)

Figure 13.13: Price of premium unleaded gasoline and diesel oil, January 2008
(EUR per litre, including taxes)

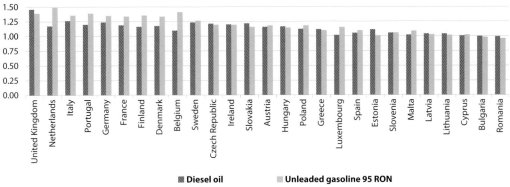

■ **Diesel oil**   ■ **Unleaded gasoline 95 RON**

Source: Eurostat (ten00103 and ten00102) and Directorate-General for Energy and Transport

Science and technology

14

Research and development (R & D) is often considered as a driving force behind economic growth, job creation, innovation, and the subsequent increasing quality of products. The seventh framework programme for research and technological development (FP7) is the EU's main instrument for funding research in Europe[1]; it runs from 2007-2013 and has a total budget of EUR 53 200 million. This money is generally intended to finance grants to research actors all over Europe, usually through co-financing research, technological development and demonstration projects. Grants are determined on the basis of calls for proposals and a peer review process. The main aims of FP7 are to increase Europe's growth, competitiveness and employment. This is done through a number of initiatives and existing programmes including, the competitiveness and innovation framework programme[2], educational and training programmes, as well as regional development through structural and cohesion funds. FP7 is made up of four broad programmes (cooperation, ideas, people and capacities) and a fifth specific programme on nuclear research. The ten thematic areas that are covered by FP7 cooperation include: health, food, agriculture and biotechnology, information and communication technologies, nanosciences, nanotechnologies, materials and new production technologies, energy, environment, transport, socio-economic sciences and humanities, space and security.

In 2000, the EU decided to create the European Research Area (ERA): a unified area all across Europe, which should:

- enable researchers to move and interact seamlessly, benefit from world-class infrastructures and work with excellent networks of research institutions;
- share, teach, value and use knowledge effectively for social, business and policy purposes;
- optimise and open European, national and regional research programmes in order to support the best research throughout Europe and coordinate these programmes to address major challenges together;
- develop strong links with partners around the world so that Europe benefits from the worldwide progress of knowledge, contributes to global development and takes a leading role in international initiatives to solve global issues.

(1) http://cordis.europa.eu/fp7/home_en.html.
(2) http://cordis.europa.eu/innovation/en/policy/cip.htm.

14.1 Personnel

A debate was conducted during 2007 on what should be done to create a more unified and attractive research area to meet the needs of business, the scientific community and citizens. The European Commission published a Green paper on the ERA reviewing progress made. In 2008 a new set of initiatives to develop the ERA were launched, including enhanced political governance of ERA, called the 'Ljubljana Process', as well as specific initiatives for five different areas (researchers' careers and mobility, research infrastructures, knowledge sharing, research programmes and international science and technology cooperation).

Information technology develops on a daily basis, and it may be argued that a society's wealth and growth are, at least to some degree, based on its ability to handle information efficiently. Information technology is not only a technical phenomenon, it is a means of transforming the way in which people communicate, do business, and live their everyday lives. It holds enormous potential and opportunities for Europe's economy and societies. The i2010 initiative [3] is the European Commission's strategic policy framework in this area, laying out broad policy guidelines for the information society and media in the years up to 2010. It is designed to promote an open and competitive digital economy, research into information and communication technologies, as well as their application to improve social inclusion, public services and the quality of life.

Introduction

The European Commission has placed renewed emphasis on the conversion of Europe's scientific expertise into marketable products and services, while also focusing on improving the mobility of European researchers, encouraging networks between researchers from different Member States, and promoting R & D as an occupation for women.

This latter point has been one particular area of concern for policy-makers who consider that women's intellectual potential, and their contribution to society are not being fully capitalised upon. In particular, their participation is low in certain branches of the natural sciences, engineering and technology, which are considered key R & D areas. Furthermore, women are also under-represented in the business enterprise sector where the EU's R & D is most highly concentrated, as well as in senior academic grades and influential positions [4].

In May 2008, the European Commission adopted a communication to launch an initiative for creating a 'European partnership for researchers for mobility and career development' [5]. The goal of this initiative was to improve the mobility of researchers and to enhance the diffusion of knowledge throughout Europe, by: balancing demand and supply for researchers at a European level; helping create centres of excellence, and; improving the skills of researchers in Europe.

(3)   http://ec.europa.eu/information_society/eeurope/i2010/index_en.htm.

(4)   http://ec.europa.eu/research/science-society/index.cfm?fuseaction=public.topic&id=27.

(5)   http://eur-lex.europa.eu/LexUriServ/LexUriServ.do?uri=COM:2008:0317:FIN:EN:HTML.

Definition and data availability

Researchers are professionals engaged in the conception or creation of new knowledge, products, processes, methods and systems, and in the management of the projects concerned.

Data on **R & D personnel** provide indicators for useful international comparisons of human resources devoted to R & D activity. R & D personnel include all persons employed directly on R & D, plus persons supplying direct services to R&D, such as managers, administrative staff and office staff. For statistical purposes, indicators on R & D personnel who are mainly or partly employed on R & D are compiled as head counts (HC) and as full-time equivalents (FTEs), or person-years.

Eurostat also compiles a number of series in relation to stocks of **human resources in science and technology (HRST)** with breakdowns available according to gender, age, region, sector of activity, occupation, educational attainment and fields of education (although it should be noted that not all combinations are possible). This information is derived from the Labour Force Survey (LFS). HRST indicators are presented as absolute figures and as shares of the economically active population in the age group 25 to 64 years old. HRST are defined as persons having either successfully completed tertiary education, or persons who are employed in an occupation where such an education is normally required.

Data on **employment in high-and medium-high technology manufacturing and in high-technology knowledge-intensive service sectors** and related derived indicators are also built-up using data from the LFS; these data are available both at the national and regional level. The definition of high- and medium-high technology manufacturing sectors is based on the OECD definition. **High-technology manufacturing** comprises manufacturing of office machinery and computers, manufacturing of radio, television and communication equipment and apparatus, and manufacturing of medical precision and optical instruments, watches and clocks. **Medium-high-technology manufacturing** includes the manufacture of chemicals and chemical products, manufacture of machinery and equipment n.e.c., manufacture of electrical machinery and apparatus n.e.c., manufacture of motor vehicles, trailers and semi-trailers, and manufacturing of transport equipment. The definition of **high-technology knowledge-intensive services (KIS)** is based on a selection of relevant items of NACE Rev. 1; it comprises water transport, air transport, post and telecommunications, financial intermediation, insurance and pension funding (except compulsory social security), activities auxiliary to financial intermediation, real estate activities, renting of machinery and equipment without operator and of personal and household goods, computer and related activities, research and development, other business activities, education, health and social work, and recreational, cultural and sporting activities.

Education statistics are based on the International Standard Classification of Education (ISCED). The basic unit of classification in ISCED-97 is the educational programme. The number of PhD graduates is measured by graduates from ISCED level 6. Indicators on the number of PhD students provide an idea of the extent to which countries will have researchers at the highest level of education in the future. The data on science and technology graduates relate to the number of new graduates in the reference year, not the total number (stock) available in the labour market that year. The term PhD is defined in terms of general tertiary programmes which lead to the award of an advanced research degree, e.g. a doctorate in economics. The programmes are therefore devoted to advanced study and original research and are not based on course-work alone. They usually require 3-5 years of research and course work, generally after a master's degree.

The indicator of **tertiary graduates in science and technology** includes new graduates from all public and private institutions completing graduate and post graduate studies in science and technology fields, and is calculated as a percentage of all graduates.

Main findings

The number of researchers in the EU-27 regularly increased in recent years. There were approximately 1.3 million researchers in full-time equivalents in the EU-27 in 2006, which marked an 18 % increase on the level from 2000. According to a gender breakdown, men accounted for the majority of researchers in all sectors, and represented slightly less than three quarters (72 %) of the total R & D workforce; there was almost no change in the proportion of male and female researchers during the period 2000-2006.

Turning to a breakdown of the number of researchers by institutional sector, there were different patterns among the Member States. The business sector concentrated more than 60 % of all researchers in Luxembourg, Sweden, Austria, Denmark, Germany and the Netherlands in 2006. Bulgaria was the only country to report a majority of its researchers in the government sector (almost 60 %), while the Baltic Member States, Poland, Slovakia, Greece, Cyprus, Portugal (2005) and Malta, all reported that more than half of all researchers were working in the higher education sector.

The gender split among PhD students in 2006 was generally much more balanced: as a majority of PhD students were female in the Baltic Member States, Portugal, Italy, Finland, Spain and Bulgaria, and women accounted for at least 40 % of PhD students in all of the other Member States for which data are available, with the exception of the Czech Republic and Malta.

Finland reported the highest proportion of R & D personnel (3.0 %) as a share of the total labour force, with more than twice the EU-27 average, which stood at 1.3 % in 2006; the remaining Nordic countries and Luxembourg (all 2005) also reported a relatively high propensity to employ R & D personnel.

An average of 6.6 % of those in employment in the EU-27 worked in high- and medium-high-technology manufacturing sectors in 2006 (a reduction of 0.8 percentage points in relation to the share some five years before). Germany and the Czech Republic had the highest shares of their national workforces employed within high- and medium-high-technology manufacturing sectors, both into double-digits, and in Slovakia this share grew at a rapid pace to reach 9.6 %. Sweden, Denmark, Luxembourg, the United Kingdom, the Netherlands and Finland had the highest shares of total employment in knowledge-intensive services (KIS) in 2006, with upwards of 40 % of their respective workforces employed in this area. Furthermore, the share of the total workforce employed in these activities rose in each of the countries, often quite considerably, between 1996 and 2006.

Table 14.1: Researchers, by institutional sector, 2006 (1)

	Total - all sectors (1 000 FTE)	Business enterprise sector (1 000 FTE)	(% of total)	Government sector (1 000 FTE)	(% of total)	Higher education sector (1 000 FTE)	(% of total)
EU-27	1 301.0	641.3	49.3	180.4	13.9	462.9	35.6
Euro area	895.3	450.3	50.3	124.5	13.9	308.7	34.5
Belgium	33.9	17.1	50.5	2.5	7.4	14.0	41.4
Bulgaria	10.3	1.3	12.6	6.1	59.5	2.8	26.7
Czech Republic	26.3	11.3	43.0	6.6	25.0	8.4	31.8
Denmark	28.7	17.4	60.6	2.2	7.6	8.9	31.0
Germany	282.1	171.1	60.6	40.0	14.2	71.0	25.2
Estonia	3.5	0.9	24.9	0.5	14.6	2.0	58.1
Ireland	12.2	7.0	57.5	0.5	4.1	4.7	38.4
Greece	19.9	5.4	27.1	2.3	11.3	12.1	60.8
Spain	115.8	39.9	34.5	20.1	17.3	55.4	47.9
France (2)	204.5	108.8	53.2	25.9	12.7	66.3	32.4
Italy (3)	82.5	28.8	34.9	14.9	18.0	37.1	44.9
Cyprus	0.8	0.2	23.2	0.1	15.2	0.4	57.0
Latvia	4.0	0.8	19.3	0.6	14.9	2.6	65.8
Lithuania	8.0	0.9	10.9	1.7	21.2	5.5	67.8
Luxembourg	2.3	1.7	73.9	0.4	16.5	0.2	9.6
Hungary	17.5	6.2	35.6	5.2	29.8	6.1	34.6
Malta	0.5	0.2	46.3	0.0	3.6	0.2	50.1
Netherlands	45.9	27.8	60.6	7.1	15.6	:	:
Austria	30.5	19.4	63.6	1.2	4.0	9.7	31.9
Poland	59.6	9.3	15.7	12.4	20.9	37.7	63.2
Portugal (2)	21.1	4.0	19.0	3.3	15.8	11.0	51.9
Romania	20.5	7.7	37.6	5.6	27.2	7.1	34.8
Slovenia	5.8	2.3	38.8	1.8	30.9	1.7	29.8
Slovakia	11.8	1.9	16.1	2.5	21.2	7.4	62.6
Finland	40.4	22.7	56.2	4.5	11.1	12.8	31.8
Sweden	55.7	37.7	67.6	3.0	5.5	14.7	26.4
United Kingdom (4)	180.5	93.8	52.0	8.9	5.0	:	:
Croatia	5.2	0.7	13.8	1.6	31.2	2.9	54.9
Turkey	42.7	11.2	26.4	4.7	11.0	26.7	62.6
Iceland (2)	2.2	1.0	47.0	0.5	23.2	0.6	27.1
Norway (5)	21.7	11.7	53.8	3.4	15.9	7.5	34.7
Switzerland (6)	25.4	12.6	49.8	0.4	1.7	12.3	48.6
Japan (2)	704.9	481.5	68.3	34.0	4.8	180.5	25.6
United States (7)	1 394.7	1 104.5	79.2	:	:	:	:

(1) Shares do not sum to 100 % due to estimates, differences in reference years, the exclusion of private non-profit sector data from the table and the conversion of data to a count in terms of FTE.
(2) 2005.
(3) Total - all sectors and higher education sector, 2005.
(4) Total - all sectors, 2005.
(5) 2005, except for business enterprise sector, 2006.
(6) Total - all sectors, business enterprise sector and higher education sector, 2004.
(7) Total - all sectors and business enterprise sector, 2005.

Source: Eurostat (tsc00004), OECD

Figure 14.1: Gender breakdown of researchers in all institutional sectors, 2006 (1)

(% of total researchers)

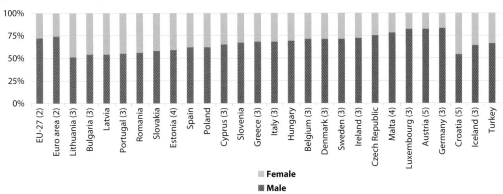

(1) France, the Netherlands, Finland and the United Kingdom, not available.
(2) Estimates.
(3) 2005.
(4) Provisional.
(5) 2004.

Source: Eurostat (tsc00006)

Figure 14.2: Proportion of research and development personnel by sector, 2006

(% of the total labour force)

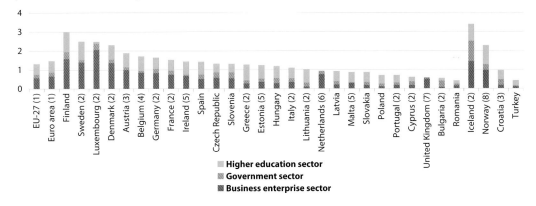

(1) Estimates.
(2) 2005.
(3) 2004.
(4) Business enterprise sector, estimate; government sector and higher education sector, 2005.
(5) Business enterprise sector, estimate.
(6) Business enterprise sector and government sector, 2005; higher education sector, not available.
(7) Business enterprise sector and government sector, estimate; higher education sector, not available.
(8) Government sector and high education sector, 2005.

Source: Eurostat (tsc00002)

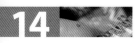

Table 14.2: PhD students (ISCED level 6), 2006
(% of total PhD students)

	Total number of PhD students (1 000)	Male	Female	Social sciences, busi-ness & law	Teacher training & educ.; human-ities & arts	Science, maths & computing; engineering, manuf. & construction	Agri-culture & vet-erinary	Health & welfare; services	Others (1)
EU-27	516.5	52.4	47.6	22.9	21.6	36.9	2.8	13.9	1.9
Belgium	7.5	59.0	41.0	19.6	13.3	46.2	7.1	13.9	0.0
Bulgaria	5.2	49.7	50.3	21.2	22.5	39.7	3.8	12.8	0.0
Czech Republic	22.6	62.1	37.9	16.3	15.3	46.4	4.5	15.8	1.7
Denmark	4.8	54.2	45.8	12.8	14.5	39.3	8.2	25.2	0.0
Germany	:	:	:	:	:	:	:	:	:
Estonia	2.0	46.5	53.5	21.2	21.0	42.3	5.6	9.8	0.0
Ireland	5.1	52.1	47.9	14.7	21.0	49.2	2.0	8.4	4.6
Greece (2)	22.5	55.6	44.4	17.5	22.6	55.9	1.7	2.2	0.0
Spain	77.1	49.0	51.0	23.9	21.8	22.8	2.0	18.5	10.9
France	69.8	53.9	46.1	30.7	27.0	38.9	0.1	3.3	0.0
Italy	38.3	48.3	51.7	19.7	15.0	42.4	6.3	15.6	0.9
Cyprus	0.3	51.0	49.0	21.2	28.8	50.0	0.0	0.0	0.0
Latvia	1.8	39.6	60.4	33.5	24.1	30.1	2.2	10.1	0.0
Lithuania	2.9	43.4	56.6	31.6	13.8	40.8	3.7	10.1	0.0
Luxembourg	:	:	:	:	:	:	:	:	:
Hungary	8.0	53.0	47.0	20.6	24.9	32.2	6.0	16.3	0.0
Malta	0.1	64.1	35.9	20.3	37.5	28.1	0.0	14.1	0.0
Netherlands (3)	7.4	58.6	41.4	:	:	:	:	:	:
Austria	16.8	54.3	45.7	37.9	24.4	29.6	3.3	4.7	0.0
Poland	32.7	50.7	49.3	24.1	30.5	31.2	5.0	9.2	0.0
Portugal	20.5	44.0	56.0	30.2	23.8	29.4	1.8	14.8	0.0
Romania	21.7	51.7	48.3	17.5	15.3	31.6	7.8	27.7	:
Slovenia	1.1	53.5	46.5	15.8	17.2	47.8	3.9	15.3	0.0
Slovakia	10.7	57.1	42.9	19.8	18.4	39.4	3.4	18.9	:
Finland	22.1	48.4	51.6	22.6	24.3	40.2	2.1	10.9	0.0
Sweden	21.4	51.3	48.7	12.4	12.6	41.5	2.0	31.6	0.0
United Kingdom	94.2	55.4	44.6	20.9	21.6	40.5	1.4	15.3	0.3
Croatia	1.3	53.3	46.7	7.2	22.0	46.2	6.5	18.1	0.0
Turkey	32.6	60.6	39.4	24.3	22.5	33.4	8.1	11.7	0.0
Iceland	0.2	41.7	58.3	17.3	28.8	26.9	0.0	26.9	0.0
Norway	5.0	53.6	46.4	17.4	12.7	41.1	4.4	24.4	0.0
Switzerland	17.2	59.7	40.3	26.3	15.6	39.7	2.8	15.3	0.4
Japan	75.0	70.3	29.7	13.2	13.6	33.0	5.8	32.4	2.0
United States	388.7	48.2	51.8	26.9	24.4	30.3	0.8	17.7	0.0

(1) Unknown or not specified.
(2) 2005, except for total number of PhD students, 2006.
(3) Total number of PhD students, 2005.

Source: Eurostat (educ_enrl5)

Table 14.3: Human resources in science and technology (1)

	People working in a S&T occupation					People who have a third level education and work in a S&T occupation				
	(1 000)	(% of total employment)				(1 000)	(% of total employment)			
	2006	2003	2004	2005	2006	2006	2003	2004	2005	2006
EU-27	58 856	27.3	28.0	28.4	29.0	34 455	15.4	16.1	16.6	17.0
Belgium	1 303	29.6	29.9	31.1	31.2	919	21.0	21.4	21.6	22.0
Bulgaria	635	22.0	21.2	22.0	20.6	488	15.6	15.4	16.2	15.9
Czech Republic	1 467	29.0	29.3	31.0	31.3	537	10.1	10.4	11.1	11.5
Denmark	983	36.9	37.3	38.9	40.2	676	24.6	25.4	26.5	27.6
Germany	12 474	32.9	33.0	33.5	34.5	6 416	16.9	17.3	17.8	17.7
Estonia	152	23.2	22.8	26.1	26.0	106	15.5	14.9	17.3	18.2
Ireland	419	24.1	24.7	24.2	24.2	324	17.7	18.3	18.1	18.7
Greece (2)	970	19.6	21.0	20.9	22.0	754	15.0	16.5	16.3	17.1
Spain	4 435	21.3	22.4	23.5	23.4	3 519	16.2	17.3	18.1	18.6
France	7 299	29.4	29.3	29.9	29.9	4 567	17.6	17.5	18.3	18.7
Italy (2)	6 785	27.0	29.1	28.6	30.4	2 633	10.2	11.2	11.1	11.8
Cyprus	85	26.8	25.9	25.3	26.0	65	20.1	19.7	18.8	20.0
Latvia (3)	250	21.8	21.4	23.6	25.6	142	10.5	12.2	13.9	14.5
Lithuania	353	21.1	22.5	25.3	24.8	245	13.5	15.0	17.3	17.2
Luxembourg (4)	74	32.8	38.4	38.2	38.7	45	14.1	23.0	25.7	23.9
Hungary	987	24.8	25.5	24.5	25.4	569	13.4	14.4	14.0	14.6
Malta	35	23.8	24.4	26.5	26.6	17	10.1	12.7	13.3	12.8
Netherlands (3)	2 719	39.0	40.0	39.8	38.3	1 640	21.6	23.4	24.0	23.1
Austria (2)	1 075	25.4	32.5	31.0	30.8	443	11.7	13.5	12.9	12.7
Poland	3 577	22.2	22.4	22.9	24.3	2 194	11.7	12.6	13.5	14.9
Portugal (2)	842	14.8	17.5	17.3	17.9	524	8.8	10.9	10.7	11.1
Romania	1 652	17.7	18.0	18.3	19.3	935	8.7	9.6	9.9	10.9
Slovenia (3)	286	29.2	29.7	31.2	32.0	162	15.2	15.7	16.8	18.2
Slovakia	634	25.1	24.4	25.6	27.0	274	9.5	9.7	10.7	11.7
Finland	789	31.9	32.8	33.5	34.4	550	22.7	23.3	23.4	24.0
Sweden	1 641	39.1	39.3	39.6	40.0	1 005	22.5	22.9	23.9	24.5
United Kingdom	6 935	26.2	26.9	27.3	28.0	4 704	17.7	18.4	18.7	19.0
Turkey	2 422	:	:	:	12.5	1 488	:	:	:	7.7
Iceland	50	34.4	34.1	37.7	36.4	22	22.0	21.6	23.9	16.1
Norway	809	36.7	37.9	39.1	39.3	565	24.5	25.3	26.8	27.4
Switzerland	1 396	37.9	38.4	38.7	39.7	763	19.5	20.1	20.9	21.7

(1) Break in series, 2006, with the exception of Belgium and Luxembourg.
(2) Break in series, 2004.
(3) Break in series, 2003.
(4) Break in series, 2003 and 2004.

Source: Eurostat (hrst_st_nsec)

Table 14.4: Science and technology graduates
(tertiary graduates in science and technology per 1 000 persons aged 20-29 years)

	Total		Male		Female	
	2000	2005	2000	2005	2000	2005
EU-27	10.0	12.9	13.7	17.6	6.2	8.2
Belgium	9.7	10.9	14.4	15.7	4.9	6.0
Bulgaria	6.6	8.6	7.0	9.9	6.1	7.3
Czech Republic	5.5	8.2	7.8	11.7	3.0	4.6
Denmark	11.7	14.7	16.5	19.3	6.8	10.1
Germany	8.2	9.7	12.6	14.5	3.6	4.8
Estonia	7.8	12.1	10.0	13.5	5.7	10.7
Ireland	24.2	24.5	29.8	33.8	18.5	15.0
Greece	:	10.1	:	11.5	:	8.7
Spain	9.9	11.8	13.3	16.2	6.4	7.2
France	19.6	22.5	27.0	32.0	12.1	12.9
Italy	5.7	9.7	7.2	12.2	4.3	7.2
Cyprus	3.4	3.6	4.9	4.3	2.0	2.7
Latvia	7.4	9.8	10.1	13.0	4.7	6.5
Lithuania	13.5	18.9	17.2	24.2	9.7	13.5
Luxembourg	1.8	:	:	:	:	:
Hungary	4.5	5.1	6.8	7.0	2.1	3.1
Malta	3.4	3.4	4.9	4.6	1.9	2.1
Netherlands	5.8	8.6	9.5	13.6	2.1	3.5
Austria	7.2	9.8	11.6	14.8	2.9	4.6
Poland	6.6	11.1	8.3	13.9	4.8	8.3
Portugal	6.3	12.0	7.3	14.3	5.4	9.7
Romania	4.9	10.3	6.2	12.1	3.5	8.5
Slovenia	8.9	9.8	13.3	14.1	4.2	5.3
Slovakia	5.3	10.2	7.3	12.9	3.2	7.3
Finland	16.0	17.7	22.7	24.3	8.9	10.8
Sweden	11.6	14.4	15.5	18.7	7.6	9.9
United Kingdom	18.5	18.4	25.2	25.3	11.9	11.4
Croatia	:	5.7	:	7.5	:	3.8
FYR of Macedonia	3.7	4.0	4.2	4.1	3.1	3.8
Turkey	4.4	5.7	5.9	8.0	2.8	3.3
Iceland	8.4	10.1	10.3	12.5	6.5	7.6
Liechtenstein	:	12.7	:	18.1	:	7.3
Norway	7.9	9.0	11.4	13.1	4.3	4.7
Switzerland	:	16.1	:	26.8	:	5.4
Japan	12.6	13.7	21.5	23.0	3.3	4.1
United States	9.7	10.6	13.0	14.2	6.2	6.8

Source: Eurostat (tsiir050)

Table 14.5: Proportion of persons working in high- and medium-high-technology manufacturing and knowledge-intensive service sectors (1)

(% of total employment)

	Employment in high- and medium-high-technology manufacturing			Employment in knowledge-intensive services		
	1996	2001	2006	1996	2001	2006
EU-27	:	7.4	6.6	:	30.9	32.8
Belgium	7.7	6.9	6.3	34.6	37.8	38.8
Bulgaria	:	5.5	4.9	:	23.1	22.0
Czech Republic	:	9.2	10.4	:	24.1	25.1
Denmark	7.1	7.0	6.0	40.1	42.7	43.5
Germany	11.1	11.2	10.7	27.9	31.0	34.1
Estonia	:	4.9	3.8	:	28.0	28.6
Ireland	7.1	7.3	5.7	30.2	32.0	34.9
Greece	2.3	2.2	2.3	20.5	22.5	25.0
Spain	5.1	5.5	4.5	23.6	24.8	27.9
France	7.0	7.2	5.9	33.6	35.0	36.9
Italy	7.4	7.4	7.6	24.7	27.0	30.4
Cyprus	:	1.0	1.0	:	26.5	28.3
Latvia	:	1.7	1.7	:	24.8	25.5
Lithuania	:	3.1	2.5	:	26.9	25.6
Luxembourg	1.7	1.2	1.3	33.4	35.8	43.5
Hungary	7.6	8.7	8.5	25.3	26.3	28.4
Malta	:	8.0	6.6	:	27.8	31.0
Netherlands	5.1	4.3	3.1	36.4	40.0	42.0
Austria	6.6	6.5	7.0	26.5	29.3	30.4
Poland	:	:	5.1	:	:	24.7
Portugal	4.2	3.6	3.3	22.0	19.7	23.1
Romania	:	5.1	5.5	:	11.3	14.6
Slovenia	9.2	8.8	8.7	20.8	23.1	26.2
Slovakia	:	6.8	9.6	:	25.3	24.9
Finland	7.2	7.4	6.8	37.4	39.1	41.1
Sweden	8.4	7.7	6.3	44.2	46.1	47.7
United Kingdom	7.9	7.1	5.5	37.3	40.5	43.0
Croatia	:	:	4.7	:	:	23.0
Turkey	:	:	3.6	:	:	12.8
Iceland	1.5	1.7	1.7	38.4	40.9	42.5
Norway	5.5	4.2	4.5	40.6	43.6	46.1
Switzerland	7.8	8.1	7.3	34.1	39.0	41.3

(1) Break in series, 2006, with the exception of Belgium and Luxembourg.

Source: Eurostat (tsc00011 and tsc00012)

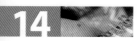

14.2 Expenditure

Introduction

Research and development (R & D) lies at the heart of the EU's strategy to become the most competitive and dynamic knowledge-based economy by 2010; one of the original goals set by the Lisbon strategy was for the EU to increase its R & D expenditure to at least 3 % of GDP by 2010.

One area that has received notable attention in recent years is the structural difference in R & D funding between Europe and its main competitors. Policymakers in Europe have tried to increase R & D business expenditure so that it is more in line with the ratios observed in Japan or the United States. In October 2008, the EU industrial R & D investment scoreboard was released[6]. This presents information on the top 1 000 companies in terms of R & D investors whose registered offices are in the EU. The report shows that R & D investment by the top 1 000 EU companies grew in 2007 at a faster pace than for non-EU competitors from either the United States or Japan; note there was a marked reduction in investment activity in the United States. Nevertheless, the data presented show that R & D investment by EU companies grew for the fifth consecutive year. The regional distribution of companies in the top 50 R & D investors in 2007 was split: 20 in the United States, 18 in the EU and 9 in Japan. Nokia was the EU company with the highest level of R & D investment in 2007, while Volkswagen and Daimler were also among the top 10 in the world, as was Roche (Switzerland).

In January 2006 the European Commission presented to the European Council its 2006 annual report on the revised Lisbon strategy, in the form of a communication – COM(2006) 30 – entitled 'Time to move up a gear – the new partnership for growth and jobs'[7]. One of the four areas for priority actions set out by the European Commission was to invest more in knowledge and innovation, and to increase the proportion of national wealth devoted to research and development through to 2010. The communication also referred to planned spending targets for R & D, stating that if these were met in the 18 countries that had set targets as part of their national plans then R & D expenditure was estimated to rise to 2.6 % of GDP by 2010. The communication also stressed that while all Member States appreciate the importance of the spread and effective use of information and communication technologies and environmental technologies, the link between the identified challenges and the measures proposed to address them in national plans was not always clear.

Definition and data availability

R & D is defined as comprising creative work undertaken on a systematic basis to increase the stock of knowledge (of man, culture and society) and the use of this stock to devise new applications. R & D is an activity where there are significant transfers of resources between units, organisations and sectors.

(6) http://iri.jrc.ec.europa.eu/research/docs/2008/Scoreboard_2008.pdf.
(7) http://eur-lex.europa.eu/LexUriServ/site/en/com/2006/com2006_0030en01.pdf.

R & D expenditure is a basic measure that covers intramural expenditure, in other words, all expenditures for R & D that are performed within a statistical unit or sector of the economy, whatever the source of the funds. Expenditures made outside the statistical unit or sector but in support of intramural R & D (for example, purchase of supplies for R & D) are included; both current and capital expenditures are included.

Gross domestic expenditure on R & D (often referred to as GERD) is composed of four separate sectors of performance: business enterprises, government, higher education, and private non-profit organisations. Expenditure data consider the research spend on the national territory, regardless of the source of funds; data are usually expressed in relation to GDP, otherwise known as R & D intensity.

Government budget appropriations or outlays for research and development (GBAORD) are the amount governments allocate towards R & D activities and include all appropriations allocated to R & D in central (or federal) government budgets. Provincial (or State) government is only included if the contribution is significant, whereas local government funds are excluded. Comparisons of GBAORD across countries give an impression of the relative importance attached to state-funded R & D.

Main findings

Gross domestic expenditure on R & D (GERD) for the EU-27 followed a generally positive evolution in the five years up to 2002. However, in 2003 the share of R & D expenditure in GDP decreased and this pattern was repeated in 2004, although a small gain was recorded in 2005. The latest information available for 2006 showed that GERD was stable, accounting for 1.84 % share of GDP. As noted above, the EU-27's R & D expenditure tends to lag behind that of Japan and the United States. For comparison, Japanese GERD was 3.32 % of GDP in 2005, and the corresponding share in the United States for 2006 was 2.61 % (the Japanese share has followed an upward trend over the last decade for which data are available, while the trend of GERD in the United States was similar to that observed for the EU-27). As noted above, these differences are often explained as a result of the levels of expenditure within the business enterprise sector, where expenditure in the EU-27 was considerably lower (1.17 % of GDP) than in the United States (1.83 %) in 2006.

Among the Member States, the highest R & D intensity was recorded in Sweden and Finland, the only Member States where R & D intensity exceeded the 3 % goal set by the Lisbon strategy. In contrast, there were ten Member States that reported R & D expenditure accounting for less than 1 % of their GDP in 2006.

When focusing on the breakdown of gross domestic expenditure on R & D by source of funds in 2005, slightly more than half of the total (54.6 %) in the EU-27 came from the business enterprise sector, while just over one third (34.2 %) was derived from government, and a further 8.9 % came from abroad; industry-funded R & D accounted for 76.1 % of R & D expenditure in Japan and 64.9 % in the United States (2006).

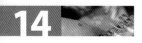

Table 14.6: Gross domestic expenditure on R & D (GERD)

(% of GDP)

	1996	1997	1998	1999	2000	2001	2002	2003	2004	2005	2006
EU-27	1.76	1.78	1.79	1.84	1.86	1.87	1.88	1.87	1.83	1.84	1.84
Euro area	:	:	:	:	1.84	1.86	1.87	1.87	1.85	1.85	1.86
Belgium	1.77	1.83	1.86	1.94	1.97	2.08	1.94	1.88	1.87	1.84	1.83
Bulgaria (1, 2)	0.52	0.51	0.57	0.57	0.52	0.47	0.49	0.50	0.50	0.49	0.48
Czech Republic	0.97	1.08	1.15	1.14	1.21	1.20	1.20	1.25	1.25	1.41	1.54
Denmark	1.84	1.92	2.04	2.18	2.24	2.39	2.51	2.58	2.48	2.45	2.43
Germany	2.19	2.24	2.27	2.40	2.45	2.46	2.49	2.52	2.49	2.48	2.53
Estonia	:	:	0.57	0.69	0.61	0.71	0.72	0.77	0.86	0.93	1.14
Ireland	1.30	1.27	1.24	1.18	1.12	1.10	1.10	1.17	1.24	1.26	1.32
Greece	:	0.45	:	0.60	:	0.58	:	0.57	0.55	0.58	0.57
Spain	0.81	0.80	0.87	0.86	0.91	0.91	0.99	1.05	1.06	1.12	1.20
France (3, 4, 5)	2.27	2.19	2.14	2.16	2.15	2.20	2.23	2.17	2.15	2.12	2.09
Italy (3)	0.99	1.03	1.05	1.02	1.05	1.09	1.13	1.11	1.10	1.09	:
Cyprus	:	:	0.22	0.23	0.24	0.25	0.30	0.35	0.37	0.40	0.42
Latvia	0.42	0.38	0.40	0.36	0.44	0.41	0.42	0.38	0.42	0.56	0.70
Lithuania (1)	0.50	0.54	0.55	0.50	0.59	0.67	0.66	0.67	0.76	0.76	0.80
Luxembourg	:	:	:	:	1.65	:	:	1.66	1.63	1.57	1.47
Hungary (5)	0.65	0.72	0.68	0.69	0.78	0.92	1.00	0.93	0.88	0.94	1.00
Malta (5)	:	:	:	:	:	:	0.26	0.26	0.54	0.54	0.54
Netherlands (1)	1.98	1.99	1.90	1.96	1.82	1.80	1.72	1.76	1.78	1.74	1.67
Austria	1.59	1.69	1.77	1.88	1.91	2.04	2.12	2.23	2.22	2.43	2.49
Poland	0.65	0.65	0.67	0.69	0.64	0.62	0.56	0.54	0.56	0.57	0.56
Portugal	0.57	0.59	0.65	0.71	0.76	0.80	0.76	0.74	0.77	0.81	0.83
Romania	:	:	0.49	0.40	0.37	0.39	0.38	0.39	0.39	0.41	0.45
Slovenia	1.31	1.29	1.36	1.39	1.41	1.52	1.49	1.29	1.42	1.46	1.59
Slovakia (3)	0.91	1.08	0.78	0.66	0.65	0.64	0.57	0.57	0.51	0.51	0.49
Finland	2.52	2.70	2.86	3.16	3.34	3.30	3.36	3.43	3.45	3.48	3.45
Sweden (6)	:	3.47	3.55	3.57	:	4.18	:	3.86	3.62	3.80	3.73
United Kingdom	1.86	1.80	1.79	1.86	1.85	1.82	1.82	1.78	1.71	1.76	1.78
Croatia	:	:	:	:	:	:	1.04	1.05	1.13	1.00	0.87
Turkey	0.45	0.49	0.37	0.47	0.48	0.54	0.53	0.48	0.52	0.59	0.58
Iceland	:	1.83	2.00	2.30	2.67	2.95	2.95	2.82	:	2.77	:
Norway	:	1.63	:	1.64	:	1.59	1.66	1.71	1.59	1.52	1.52
Switzerland	2.65	:	:	:	2.53	:	:	:	:	2.90	:
Japan (1)	2.81	2.87	3.00	3.02	3.04	3.12	3.17	3.20	3.17	3.32	:
United States	2.53	2.56	2.61	2.65	2.73	2.74	2.64	2.67	2.58	2.61	2.61

(1) Break in series, 1996.
(2) Break in series, 1999.
(3) Break in series, 1997.
(4) Break in series, 2000.
(5) Break in series, 2004.
(6) Break in series, 2005.

Source: Eurostat (tsiir020), OECD

Table 14.7: Gross domestic expenditure on R & D by sector

(% of GDP)

	Business enterprise sector		Government sector		Higher education sector	
	2001	2006	2001	2006	2001	2006
EU-27	*1.21*	*1.17*	*0.25*	*0.25*	*0.40*	*0.40*
Euro area	*1.19*	*1.18*	*0.27*	*0.27*	*0.39*	*0.39*
Belgium	1.51	*1.24*	0.13	*0.16*	0.41	*0.41*
Bulgaria	0.10	0.12	0.31	0.31	0.06	0.05
Czech Republic	0.72	1.02	0.29	0.27	0.19	0.25
Denmark (1)	1.64	*1.62*	0.28	*0.16*	0.45	*0.63*
Germany	1.72	1.77	0.34	*0.35*	0.40	*0.41*
Estonia	0.24	*0.51*	0.10	0.15	0.36	0.46
Ireland	0.77	*0.89*	0.09	0.09	0.24	0.34
Greece	0.19	*0.17*	0.13	*0.12*	0.26	*0.27*
Spain (2)	0.48	0.67	0.15	0.20	*0.28*	0.33
France (3, 4, 5)	1.39	*1.32*	0.36	*0.36*	0.42	*0.38*
Italy (6)	0.53	*0.54*	0.20	*0.19*	0.35	:
Cyprus	0.05	*0.09*	0.12	*0.12*	0.07	*0.18*
Latvia	0.15	0.35	0.09	0.11	0.17	0.24
Lithuania	0.20	0.22	0.27	0.18	0.21	0.40
Luxembourg	:	*1.25*	0.14	*0.19*	0.01	*0.04*
Hungary (7)	0.37	0.48	0.24	0.25	0.24	0.24
Malta (4)	:	*0.34*	:	0.03	:	0.18
Netherlands (8)	1.05	*0.96*	0.25	0.24	0.49	:
Austria	:	*1.66*	:	*0.13*	:	*0.65*
Poland	0.22	0.18	0.19	0.21	0.20	0.17
Portugal	0.26	*0.35*	0.17	:	0.29	:
Romania	0.24	0.22	0.11	0.15	0.04	0.08
Slovenia	0.88	0.96	0.37	0.39	0.25	0.24
Slovakia	0.43	0.21	0.15	0.16	0.06	0.12
Finland	2.35	2.46	0.34	0.32	0.60	0.65
Sweden (9)	3.23	2.79	0.12	0.17	0.83	0.76
United Kingdom (3, 10)	1.19	1.10	0.18	0.18	0.41	0.46
Croatia	:	0.32	:	0.23	:	0.32
Turkey	0.18	0.21	0.04	0.07	0.32	0.30
Iceland	1.74	:	0.59	:	0.55	:
Norway	0.95	0.82	0.23	0.24	0.41	0.46
Switzerland	:	:	:	0.02	:	:
Japan	2.30	:	0.30	:	0.45	:
United States	1.99	1.83	0.31	0.29	0.33	0.37

(1) Break in series, government sector and higher education sector, 2002.
(2) Break in series, business enterprise sector, 2002.
(3) Break in series, business enterprise sector, 2001.
(4) Break in series, business enterprise sector, 2004.
(5) Break in series, higher education sector, 2004.
(6) Break in series, higher education sector, 2005.
(7) Break in series, government sector, 2004.
(8) Break in series, government sector, 2003.
(9) Break in series, business enterprise sector, government sector and higher education sector, 2005.
(10) Break in series, government sector, 2001.

Source: Eurostat (tsc00001), OECD

Table 14.8: Gross domestic expenditure on R & D by source of funds
(% of total gross expenditure on R & D)

	Business enterprise		Government		Abroad	
	2001 (1)	2006 (2)	2001 (1)	2006 (2)	2001 (1)	2006 (2)
EU-27	55.9	54.6	33.9	34.2	8.0	8.9
Euro area	57.2	56.7	35.7	35.0	5.8	6.8
Belgium	63.4	59.7	22.0	24.7	12.1	12.4
Bulgaria	27.1	27.8	66.2	63.9	5.7	7.6
Czech Republic	52.5	56.9	43.6	39.0	2.2	3.1
Denmark	61.4	59.5	28.2	27.6	7.8	10.1
Germany	65.7	67.6	31.4	28.4	2.5	3.7
Estonia	32.9	38.1	52.0	44.6	12.5	16.3
Ireland	66.7	59.3	25.6	30.1	6.0	8.9
Greece	33.0	31.1	46.6	46.8	18.4	19.0
Spain	47.2	47.1	39.9	42.5	7.7	5.9
France (3)	54.2	52.2	36.9	38.4	7.2	7.5
Italy	:	39.7	:	50.7	:	8.0
Cyprus	15.3	16.8	65.5	67.0	12.6	10.9
Latvia	18.3	32.7	50.0	58.2	31.7	7.5
Lithuania	37.1	26.2	56.3	53.6	6.6	14.3
Luxembourg	90.7	79.7	7.7	16.6	1.6	3.6
Hungary (4)	34.8	43.3	53.6	44.8	9.2	11.3
Malta	18.6	52.1	59.8	34.4	21.6	13.5
Netherlands	51.9	:	35.8	:	11.0	:
Austria	41.8	45.6	38.3	36.0	19.7	16.4
Poland	30.8	33.1	64.8	57.5	2.4	7.0
Portugal	31.5	36.3	61.0	55.2	5.1	4.7
Romania	47.6	30.4	43.0	64.1	8.2	4.1
Slovenia	54.7	59.3	37.1	34.4	7.2	5.8
Slovakia	56.1	35.0	41.3	55.6	1.9	9.1
Finland (5)	70.8	66.6	25.5	25.1	2.5	7.1
Sweden (6)	71.5	65.7	21.3	23.5	3.4	7.7
United Kingdom	45.5	45.2	28.9	31.9	19.7	17.0
Croatia	45.7	34.6	46.4	55.8	1.5	6.8
Turkey	44.9	46.0	48.0	48.6	0.8	0.5
Iceland	46.2	48.0	34.0	40.5	18.3	11.2
Norway	51.6	46.4	39.8	44.0	7.1	8.0
Switzerland	69.1	69.7	23.2	22.7	4.3	5.2
Japan	73.0	76.1	18.6	16.8	0.4	0.3
United States	66.6	64.9	27.5	29.3	:	:

(1) Malta and Croatia, 2002; Luxembourg and Switzerland, 2000.
(2) EU-27, euro area, Belgium, Bulgaria, Denmark, Germany, Greece, France, Italy, Cyprus, Luxembourg, Portugal, Sweden, Iceland, Norway and Japan, 2005; Switzerland, 2004.
(3) Break in series, 2004.
(4) Break in series for government sector, 2004.
(5) Break in series for abroad, 2005.
(6) Break in series, 2005.

Source: Eurostat (tsiir030), OECD

14.3 Patents

Introduction

Intellectual property rights and in partic-ular patents provide a link between inno-vation, inventions and the marketplace. Applying for a patent makes an invention public, but at the same time gives it pro-tection. A count of patents is one measure that reflects a country's inventive activ-ity and also shows its capacity to exploit knowledge and translate it into potential economic gains. In this context, indica-tors based on patent statistics are widely used to assess the inventive and innova-tive performance of a country.

Patents are generally used to protect R & D results, but they are also signifi-cant as a source of technical informa-tion, which may prevent re-inventing and re-developing ideas because of a lack of information. However, the use of patents is relatively restricted within the EU – this may be for a number of reasons including: their relative cost; the overlap between national and European proce-dures; or the need for translation into for-eign languages.

Most studies in this area show that in-novative enterprises tend to make more use of intellectual property protection than companies that do not innovate. Enterprise size and the economic sector in which an enterprise operates are also likely to play an important role in deter-mining whether an enterprise chooses to protect its intellectual property.

The European Council held in Lisbon in March 2000 called for the creation of a Community patent system to address shortcomings in the legal protection of in-ventions, while providing an incentive for investments in research and development and contributing to the competitiveness of the economy as a whole. In July 2000 the European Commission made a first proposal for the creation of a Commu-nity patent. This was discussed at various levels and despite various proposals and amendments for a Council Regulation on the Community patent during 2003 and 2004 no legal basis was forthcoming. In April 2007 the European Commission released a Communication entitled, 'En-hancing the patent system in Europe' [8]. It highlighted that the European pat-ent system is more expensive, uncertain and unattractive, while underlining that the European Commission believes a more competitive and attractive Com-munity patent system can be achieved, based upon the creation of a unified and specialised patent judiciary, with compe-tence for litigation on European patents and future Community patents.

Definition and data availability

Following changes in the production of patent statistics at Eurostat in 2007, data shown on the Eurostat website are no longer fully comparable with data previ-ously disseminated. From 2007 onwards, Eurostat's production of European Patent

---

(8)   COM(2007) 165 final; http://eur-lex.europa.eu/LexUriServ/LexUriServ.do?uri=COM:2007:0165:FIN:en:PDF.

Office (EPO) and United States Patent and Trademark Office (USPTO) data has been based almost exclusively on the EPO Worldwide Statistical Patent Database. The worldwide statistical patent database, also known as 'PATSTAT', was developed by the EPO in 2005, using their collection and knowledge of patent data.

European patent applications refer to applications filed directly under the European Patent Convention or to applications filed under the Patent Co-operation Treaty (PCT) and designated to the EPO (Euro-PCT), regardless of whether the patents are granted or not. For patent applications to the EPO all direct applications (EPO-direct) are taken into account, but among the PCT applications (applications following the procedure laid down by the PCT) made to the EPO, only those that have entered into the regional phase are counted. Patent applications are counted according to the priority date, i.e. the year in which they were filed anywhere in the world at the EPO and are broken down according to the International Patent Classification (IPC). Applications are assigned to a country according to the inventor's place of residence, using fractional counting if there are multiple inventors to avoid double counting. To normalise the data, the total number of applications at the EPO can be divided by the national population and expressed in terms of patent applications per million inhabitants.

High-technology patents are counted following the criteria established by the trilateral statistical report, where the subsequent technical fields are defined as high technology groups in accordance to the international patent classification (IPC): computer and automated business equipment; micro-organism and genetic engineering; aviation; communication technology; semiconductors; and lasers.

The European Patent Office (EPO) grants European patents for the contracting states to the European Patent Convention (EPC). There are currently 32 of these; the EU-27 Member States, Iceland, Liechtenstein, Switzerland, Monaco and Turkey. The falling trend between 2000 and 2005 is linked to the length of patenting procedures and should not be understood as a real decline in the patenting activity. For this reason the 2005 figures in Eurostat's reference database are flagged as provisional.

In contrast, the **United States Patent and Trademark Office (USPTO)** data refers to patents granted and data are recorded by year of publication as opposed to the year of filing. Patents are allocated to the country of the inventor, using fractional counting in the case of multiple inventor countries. The methodology used is not harmonised with that of Eurostat and therefore the comparison between EPO and USPTO patents data should be interpreted with caution.

Main findings

EU-27 patent applications to the EPO in-creased significantly from 1995 to 2000 to reach 51 158, with the number of applica-tions increasing, on average, by 11.6 % per annum. However, the steady upward trend then stagnated and there was lit-tle change in the number of applications through to another relative peak in 2004 (52 968 patent applications). The latest information available for 2005 showed a contraction in applications of 6.1 %, such that a total of 49 730 applications were made to the EPO.

Among the Member States, Germany had by far the highest number of patent appli-cations to the EPO, some 22 219 in 2005 (which was 44.7 % of the EU-27 total). In relative terms, Germany was also the Member State with the highest number of patent applications per million inhabit-ants (269), followed by Finland (223) and Luxembourg (189).

EU-27 high-tech patent applications to the EPO represented an increasing share of total patent applications up until 2001 (when they accounted for 18.5 % of all applications). Their relative importance declined somewhat after this, as did their absolute number. From a high of 9 337 high-tech patent applications in 2001, there was a relatively slow reduction through to 2004, followed by a collapse in the number of high-tech applications in 2005, falling from 8 484 in 2004 to 3 192 a year later (-62.4 %). This pattern was observed across the majority of the Member States, in particular for the larg-er countries or in those countries with traditionally the highest propensity to make patent applications. Germany and Belgium registered the highest number of high-technology patent applications per million inhabitants in 2005, both just over 15, while Sweden and France were the only other Member States to record a ratio in double-digits. These figures were in stark contrast to those for the majority of the previous decade, when Finland and Sweden were clearly the most specialised countries.

Figure 14.3: Patent applications to the European Patent Office (EPO), EU-27
(number of applications)

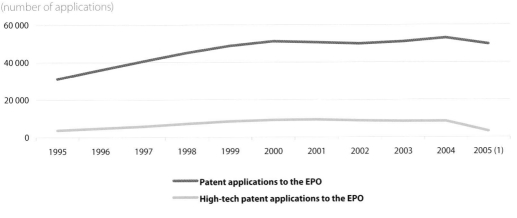

Patent applications to the EPO

High-tech patent applications to the EPO

(1) Estimate.

Source: Eurostat (tsc00009 and pat_ep_ntec), European Patent Office

Table 14.9: Patent applications to the European Patent Office (EPO) and patents granted by the USPTO

	Patent applications to the EPO			High technology patent applications to the EPO			Patents granted by the US Patent & Trademark Office (USPTO)		
	(number of applications)		(per million inhab.)	(number of applications)		(per million inhab.)	(number of patents granted)		(per million inhab.)
	2000	2005 (1)	2005 (1)	2000	2005 (2)	2005 (2)	1997	2002	2002 (3)
EU-27	51 158	49 730	101.3	9 110	3 192	6.5	28 565	20 394	42.1
Euro area	41 768	41 990	:	6 974	2 728	:	22 130	16 485	:
Belgium	1 288	1 302	124.6	198	159	15.2	842	451	43.8
Bulgaria	7	4	0.5	1	2	0.2	6	2	0.3
Czech Republic	67	71	7.0	3	9	0.8	39	44	4.3
Denmark	936	842	155.6	175	39	7.1	481	293	54.6
Germany	22 016	22 219	269.3	3 100	1 272	15.4	11 677	9 204	111.6
Estonia	6	7	5.2	1	1	0.4	4	3	2.2
Ireland	218	237	57.7	56	8	2.1	139	173	44.4
Greece	54	48	4.3	10	7	0.6	27	10	0.9
Spain	790	1 135	26.4	105	44	1.0	302	304	7.4
France	7 250	7 201	115.2	1 401	722	11.6	4 375	2 491	40.6
Italy	3 982	4 197	71.8	369	254	4.3	1 782	1 454	25.5
Cyprus	7	6	8.2	1	3	3.9	1	2	2.8
Latvia	7	12	5.2	1	1	0.3	2	2	0.9
Lithuania	5	2	0.6	1	1	0.2	3	1	0.3
Luxembourg	79	86	189.0	5	3	6.6	34	54	121.6
Hungary	121	64	6.3	26	2	0.2	71	26	2.6
Malta	5	9	22.4	:	1	2.5	1	2	5.1
Netherlands	3 418	2 695	165.3	1 015	133	8.2	1 451	1 156	71.8
Austria	1 175	1 477	180.0	106	55	6.7	582	555	68.8
Poland	43	108	2.8	4	15	0.4	31	39	1.0
Portugal	42	113	10.7	4	24	2.2	15	21	2.0
Romania	7	45	2.1	2	1	0.0	7	12	0.6
Slovenia	51	59	29.5	3	1	0.3	11	19	9.5
Slovakia	11	31	5.8	0	2	0.4	7	1	0.2
Finland	1 393	1 169	223.2	601	46	8.8	891	588	113.2
Sweden	2 270	1 370	152.0	532	107	11.9	1 875	797	89.5
United Kingdom	5 912	5 206	86.7	1 391	287	4.8	3 910	2 690	45.4
Croatia	15	24	5.4	:	1	0.1	11	20	4.5
Turkey	43	211	3.0	5	2	0.0	9	18	0.3
Iceland	36	21	73.0	7	3	9.2	14	7	24.4
Liechtenstein	23	21	606.9	2	1	28.9	17	17	507.1
Norway	395	401	87.1	49	4	1.0	298	141	31.2
Switzerland	2 694	2 929	395.0	339	189	25.5	1 519	1 088	150.0
Japan	21 356	20 099	157.3	5 040	2 515	19.7	35 083	32 942	258.5
United States	30 513	29 538	99.6	8 043	1 530	5.2	99 614	90 870	315.2

(1) Cyprus and Malta, 2004.
(2) Iceland, 2004; Cyprus, Lithuania and Malta, 2003.
(3) Estonia, 2001.

Source: Eurostat (tsc00009, tsiir060, pat_ep_ntec, tsc00010, pat_us_ntot and tsiir070), European Patent Office

14.4 Information society

Introduction

Information and communication technologies (ICT) are considered as critical for improving the competitiveness of European industry and, more generally, to meet the demands of its society and economy. ICT affects many aspects of everyday lives, at both work and in the home, and EU policies in this area range from the regulation of entire industrial sectors to the protection of an individual's privacy.

The policy framework for ICT is the i2010 initiative [9] – 'A European Information Society for Growth and Employment' – which seeks to boost efficiency throughout the European economy by means of wider use of ICT. The initiative is designed to promote an open and competitive digital economy, research into information and communication technologies, as well as their application to improve social inclusion, public services and quality of life. Indeed, at the heart of the policy is a desire to ensure that social and geographical differences are overcome, thus creating a fully-inclusive digital society. The i2010 initiative has three main priorities:

- creating a Single European Information Space, which promotes an open and competitive internal market for information society and media services;
- stimulating the information society – to strengthen investment in innovation and research in ICT;

- exploiting the benefits of ICT – to foster inclusion, better public services and quality of life through the use of ICT.

Digital literacy and e-skills are crucial to increasing participation in the information society. The 2007 results of Eurostat's household survey of information and communication technologies presented in this subchapter include findings on the levels of computer skills of the population. Additional data on Internet skills of the population and demand for e-skilled labour by enterprises can be found in the Eurostat database. According to a Communication from the European Commission on 'e-skills for the 21st century: fostering competitiveness, growth and jobs' [10], there is evidence of skills shortages across Europe, with a lack of up to half a million people with advanced networking technology skills, while enterprises report a skills shortfall for ICT practitioners, particularly in ICT strategy, security and new business solutions. The i2010 benchmarking framework [11] has addressed specific modules on e-skills in the 2007 surveys.

After undergoing a mid-term review, an updated i2010 strategy was presented in April 2008, addressing key challenges for the period 2008-2010. This was followed by a European Commission communication on future networks and the Internet [12] which outlined the full breadth of the social and economic potential of the Internet in the future, based

(9)   http://ec.europa.eu/information_society/eeurope/i2010/index_en.htm.

(10) COM(2007) 496 final, http://ec.europa.eu/enterprise/ict/policy/ict-skills/2007/COMM_PDF_COM_2007_0496_F_EN_ACTE.pdf.

(11) For more information: http://ec.europa.eu/information_society/eeurope/i2010/benchmarking/index_en.htm.

(12) COM(2008) 594 final; http://ec.europa.eu/information_society/eeurope/i2010/docs/future_internet/act_future_networks_internet_en.pdf.

on the premise of a high-speed Internet available to all, internationally open and competitive, secure and safe to use, with transparent and effective governance. These fundamental conditions of accessibility, openness, transparency and security form the basis of the European Commission's short-term agenda for the Internet of the future, as summarised by six actions:

- the construction of high-speed internet infrastructures that are open to competition and give consumers real choices.
- promoting access for all to a good-quality Internet connection at an affordable price.
- keeping the Internet open to competition, innovation and consumer choice
- launching a debate on the design and development of the Internet of the future.
- providing clear guidelines on the implementation of existing rules on data protection and a coherent strategy for a secure Internet of the future.
- taking into account the crucial role played by international policy, regulatory dialogue and research cooperation in all these developments.

Broadband technologies are considered to be of major importance when measuring access and use of the Internet as they offer users the possibility to rapidly transfer large volumes of data and keep their access line open; the take-up of broadband is considered a key indicator within the domain of ICT policy making. Widespread access to the Internet via broadband is seen as essential for the

development of advanced services on the Internet, such as eBusiness, eGovernment or eLearning. Broadband growth has continued in recent years and 42 % of all households in the EU-27 have broadband. Digital Subscriber Lines (DSL) remain the main form of delivery for broadband technology, although alternatives such as cable, satellite, fibre optics and wireless local loops are seeing more widespread use.

Definition and data availability

Statisticians are well aware of the challenges posed by rapid technological change in areas related to the Internet and other new means of ICT. As such, there has been a considerable degree of evolution in this area, with statistical tools being adapted to satisfy new demands for data. Statistics within this domain are re-assessed on an annual basis in order to meet user needs and reflect the rapid pace of technological change.

The data presented within this section are from **Eurostat's surveys on information and communication technologies in households and by individuals, and surveys on information and communication technologies in enterprises and e-commerce.** These annual surveys on ICT usage in enterprises and in households/by individuals are carried out by National Statistical Institutes. Results are used to benchmark ICT-driven developments. While the surveys initially concentrated on access and connectivity issues, their scope has subsequently been extended to cover a variety of subjects (including, for example, e-government, e-skills) and socio-economic breakdowns, such as regional diversity, gender specificity, age, educational differences and the individual's employment situation in the household survey or a breakdown by size (small, medium, large) in the enterprise survey. The scope of the surveys with respect to different technologies is also adapted so as to cover new product groups and means of delivering communication technologies to end-users (enterprises and households).

Households are defined as having at least one member in the age group 16-74 years old. **Internet access of households** refers to the percentage of households with an Internet access, so anyone in the household could use the Internet at home, if desired, even if just to send an e-mail. **Internet users** are defined as all individuals aged 16-74 who had used the Internet in the previous three months. **Regular Internet users** are individuals who used the Internet, on average, at least once a week in the three months prior to the survey (in general, during the first quarter of 2007).

The most commonly used technologies to access the Internet are divided between broadband and dial-up access. **Broadband includes digital subscriber lines (DSL)** and uses technology that transports data at high speeds. **Broadband lines** are defined as having a capacity equal to or higher than 144 kbit/s. A **dial-up access** using a modem can be made over a normal or an ISDN telephone line. Due to its limited bandwidth it is often referred to as narrowband.

A **computer** is defined as a personal computer that is run using one of the main operating systems (Macintosh, Linux or Microsoft); handheld computers or palmtops (PDAs) are also included. Individuals were asked if they have experiences in carrying out selected activities in order to measure their level of **basic computer skills**. Six computer-related items were applied: copied or moved a file or folder; used copy and paste tools to duplicate or move information within a document; used basic arithmetic formulas to add, subtract, multiply or divide figures in a spreadsheet; compressed files; connected and installed new devices, e.g. a printer or a modem; wrote a computer program using a specialised programming language. The level of an individual's skills was determined as: low level: 1 or 2 activities carried out; medium level: 3 or 4 activities carried out; high level: 5 or 6 activities carried out.

The **ordering of goods and services by individuals** includes confirmed reservations for accommodation, purchasing financial investments, participation in lotteries and betting, Internet auctions, as well as information services from the Internet that are directly paid for. Goods and services that are obtained via the Internet for free are excluded. Orders made by manually written e-mails are also excluded. The indicator shows the percentage of individuals aged 16-74 who have used the Internet, in the 12 months prior to the survey, for ordering goods or services.

The survey on ICT usage in enterprises covers enterprises with 10 or more persons employed. Its activity coverage is restricted to those enterprises whose principal activity is within NACE Sections D, F, G, I and K and Groups 55.1, 55.2, 92.1 and 92.2, in other words manufacturing, construction, distributive trades, hotels and accommodation, transport and communication, real estate, renting and business activities, motion picture, video, radio and television activities.

Internet access among enterprises is measured in terms of the proportion of the total number of persons employed having access to the Internet or access via a broadband connection; this indicator is considered as a proxy for productivity within enterprises. The **availability of broadband** is measured by the percentage of enterprises that are connectable to an exchange that has been converted to support xDSL-technology, to a cable network upgraded for Internet traffic, or to other broadband technologies.

The indicator measuring enterprise **turnover from e-commerce** is shown as a percentage of total turnover. The indicator is calculated as the enterprises' receipts from sales through the Internet as percentage of the total turnover. Sales through other networks are not included, leaving out for instance EDI-based sales. The year given relates to the survey year. The e-commerce data relates to the year prior to the survey. **E-commerce** is defined as ordering or selling goods and services over computer mediated networks. Online purchases or orders received exclude those relating to manually typed e-mail

purchases or orders received. The indicator on enterprises having **received orders or made purchases online** covers online selling via Internet and EDI or other networks within the previous year. Only enterprises buying/selling more than 1 % online are included.

Indicators relating to **online access to public services** show the percentage of 20 selected basic services which are fully available online, in other words, for which it is possible to carry out full electronic case handling. For example, if in a country 13 of the 20 services were measured as being 100 % available online and one service was not relevant (e.g. does not exist), the indicator is 13/19 which is 68.4 %. Measurement is based on a sample of URLs of public websites agreed with Member States as relevant for each service.

The indicators concerning the use of **e-government services** are based on usage during the three months prior to the survey for individuals and the year prior to the survey for enterprises. E-government services concern interaction with public authorities in one or more of the following activities: obtaining information from public authority websites, downloading official forms, submitting completed forms and e-procurement (for the enterprise survey).

Data on **information technology (IT) expenditure** covers expenditure for IT hardware, equipment, software and other services.

Main findings

During the last decade, information and communication technologies (ICTs) have become widely available to the general public, in terms of accessibility as well as cost. The increasing use of these technologies is such that in 2007 for the first time, a majority (54 %) of households in the EU-27 had an Internet access. Among the Member States, a high proportion (83 %) of households in the Netherlands had an Internet access in 2007, while Sweden, Denmark and Luxembourg reported shares of at least 75 %.

Widespread and affordable broadband access would appear to be one means of promoting the knowledge-based and informed society. The vast majority of households in the EU-27 accessed the Internet using a broadband connection, some 42 % compared with 14 % of households that had a dial-up or ISDN Internet access. Romania and Greece were the only Member States where a higher proportion of households used a dial-up or ISDN connection to access the Internet. Some 81% of individuals living in a household in the EU-27 with broadband connection accessed the Internet regularly (at least once a week), compared with 63 % of individuals living in households with Internet access but no broadband. Just over four fifths (81 %) of all Internet users aged 16 to 74 in the EU-27 declared they accessed Internet at home in 2007; while 43 % of Internet users accessed the Internet from their place of work.

Results on the supply of e-skills from 2007 show that three quarters or more than three quarters of the population in Denmark, Luxembourg, the Netherlands, Sweden and Germany had basic computer skills. The lowest proportions were registered in Bulgaria (32 %) and Romania

(29 %). The Member States which had the highest proportions of individuals with a high level of computer skills were Denmark and Luxembourg.

The proportion of individuals aged 16-74 in the EU-27 who used the Internet at least once in the last 12 months to buy or order goods or services for private use was 30 % in 2007. Between 2006 and 2007, all EU Member States registered an increase in e-shopping. In 2007, more than half of all individuals in Denmark, Germany, the Netherlands, Sweden and the United Kingdom had bought or ordered goods or services over the Internet in the last 12 months. On the other hand, less than 5 % of individuals had shopped over the Internet in Bulgaria and Romania.

The provision of fully-online e-government services in EU-27 reached a level of 59 % in 2007. Considering the available results from previous years, there has been a considerable increase during the last years. The EU-25 average grew by 11 percentage points from 2006 to 2007. Austria is the only Member State with an online availability of 100 %, i.e. all considered government services can be completely managed via the Internet. Malta, Portugal, Slovenia and the United Kingdom exceed a level of 75 % of the considered government services, whereas Poland and Bulgaria achieve a maximum of 25 % of government services fully available online. It seems that political prioritisation of e-government services together with a moderate size and a more centrally organised administration enable a more rapid progress in e-government online availability.

Almost one third (30 %) of individuals made use of e-government initiatives to access a range of public services online in 2007, mainly for obtaining information, but increasingly for downloading and filling in forms (such as tax returns). The Nordic Member States, the Netherlands and Luxembourg stood out, as a majority of individuals in each of these countries made use of such e-government services.

Almost all (97 %) of the workforce among enterprises with ten or more full-time persons employed in the EU-27 had an Internet connection in 2007 and more than 90 % of these accessed the Internet using a broadband connection. An average of 17 % of enterprises with ten or more full-time persons employed had in 2006 the facility to allow remote persons to connect to their IT systems from home; this figure grew considerably as a function of the average size of an enterprise, rising to a 55 % share among those enterprises employing 250 or more persons. Enterprises in the Nordic Member States, the Netherlands and the United Kingdom reported the highest propensity to make use of remote access to their IT systems, irrespective of the size of enterprise.

Around two thirds (65 %) of enterprises made use of e-government services: a majority using e-government services to obtain information and to download forms (57 % and 58 % respectively), while 45 % of enterprises returned filled in forms using e-government services. The take-up of e-government services among enterprises in 2007 reflected the relatively high levels of take-up among households in countries like Denmark, Luxembourg, the Netherlands or Finland. Several other countries – including Ireland, Greece, Italy, Austria, Slovenia and Slovakia – also recorded relatively high take-up of e-government services by enterprises, in contrast to household take-up. Bulgaria, Latvia and Romania were the only countries to report a minority of enterprises making use of e-government services.

Some 15 % of enterprises in the EU-27 received orders online during 2007, which was roughly half the proportion of enterprises (29 %) that used the Internet to place orders to purchase goods or services. The general pattern across Member States is one where a considerably higher proportion of enterprises have made purchases online when compared with those that have received orders online (probably reflecting the greater complexity of setting up an online selling system compared with making purchases). One third of all enterprises in Denmark received orders online in 2007, while corresponding shares were equal to or above one quarter in the United Kingdom, Ireland, Sweden and the Netherlands. In contrast, a majority of enterprises in Ireland and Germany (55 % and 52 % respectively) made purchases online in 2007, while upwards of 40 % of all enterprises in the United Kingdom, Sweden, Belgium and Austria made purchases online.

The proportion of total turnover accounted for by e-commerce via the Internet equated to 4.2 % in the EU-27 in 2007, with only a handful of countries – Ireland, the United Kingdom, Spain and Lithuania – reporting that e-commerce represented more than 5 % of total turnover.

Compared with its main competitors, the EU has a relatively low share of ICT expenditure when expressed as a share of GDP. Indeed, expenditure on information technology represented 2.7% of GDP in the EU-27 in 2006, compared with 3.4 % in Japan and 3.3 % in the United States.

Figure 14.4: Internet access of households
(% of all households)

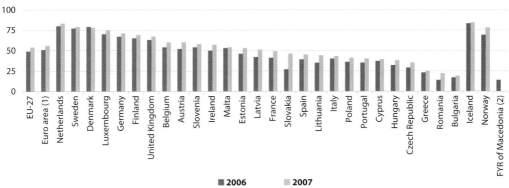

■ 2006 ■ 2007

(1) EA-12 in 2006; EA-13 in 2007.
(2) Not available for 2007.

Source: Eurostat (tsiir040)

Figure 14.5: Internet access of households by type of connection, 2007
(% of all households)

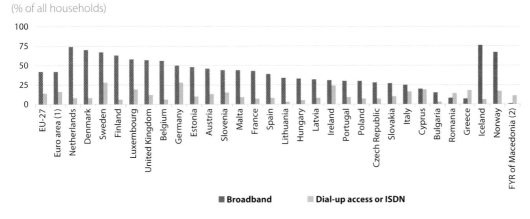

■ Broadband ■ Dial-up access or ISDN

(1) EA-13 instead of EA-15.
(2) 2006.

Source: Eurostat (tin00073)

Table 14.10: Place of Internet use by individuals, 2007

(% of individuals aged 16 to 74 who used the Internet in the last three months)

	Home	Place of work (other than home)	Place of education	Neighbour, friend or relative's house	Other place
EU-27	81	43	13	21	12
Euro area (1)	81	43	11	23	12
Belgium	89	34	10	8	5
Bulgaria	71	38	12	6	16
Czech Republic	76	42	19	15	6
Denmark	95	52	13	17	8
Germany	89	42	10	18	10
Estonia	83	43	18	15	7
Ireland	77	39	11	5	9
Greece	62	44	11	12	17
Spain	74	45	13	25	21
France	72	40	8	36	11
Italy	78	48	13	22	16
Cyprus	72	54	11	15	9
Latvia	77	40	19	15	12
Lithuania	80	40	24	23	13
Luxembourg	92	44	11	11	3
Hungary	74	40	21	23	11
Malta	92	40	9	9	3
Netherlands	97	50	13	16	5
Austria	82	48	10	8	5
Poland	74	33	23	23	13
Portugal	68	43	21	32	20
Romania	67	34	21	12	9
Slovenia	85	53	18	25	16
Slovakia	60	51	21	20	15
Finland	89	49	21	35	20
Sweden	91	52	14	22	12
United Kingdom	87	45	13	19	11
FYR of Macedonia (2)	32	17	19	9	54
Iceland	93	63	30	48	30
Norway	92	56	15	18	13

(1) EA-13 instead of EA-15.
(2) 2006.

Source: Eurostat (isoc_pibi_pai)

Figure 14.6: Individuals regularly using the Internet by type of connection, 2007
(% of all individuals aged 16 to 74)

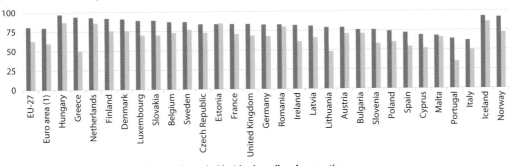

■ **Living in a household with a broadband connection**
■ **Living in a household with Internet access but with no broadband connection**

(1) EA-13 instead of EA-15.

Source: Eurostat (tin00061)

Figure 14.7: Individuals' level of computer skills, 2007
(% of all individuals aged 16 to 74)

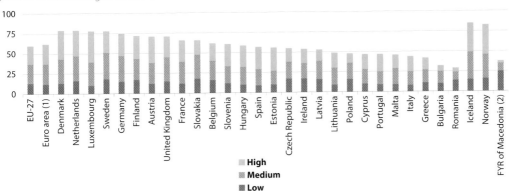

■ **High**
■ **Medium**
■ **Low**

(1) EA-13 instead of EA-15.
(2) 2006.

Source: Eurostat (tsdsc460)

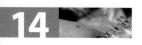

14 Science and technology

Figure 14.8: Individuals who ordered goods or services over the Internet for private use in the last twelve months
(% of all individuals aged 16 to 74)

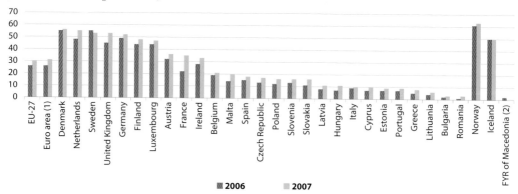

2006   2007

(1) EA-12 in 2006; EA-13 in 2007.
(2) Not available for 2007.

Source: Eurostat (isoc_ec_ibuy)

Figure 14.9: E-government on-line availability, 2007
(% of online availability of 20 basic public services)

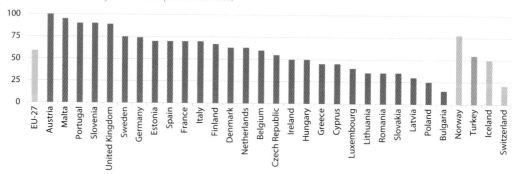

Source: Eurostat (tsiir120), Directorate-General Information Society and Media

Table 14.11: Individuals using the Internet for interacting with public authorities, 2007
(% of all individuals aged 16 to 74)

	E-government usage by individuals			Individuals using the Internet for interacting with public authorities		
	Total	Male	Female	Obtaining information	Downloading official forms	Returning filled in forms
EU-27	30	33	28	27	18	13
Euro area (1)	33	36	30	30	19	13
Belgium	23	26	20	21	11	8
Bulgaria	6	6	7	4	4	3
Czech Republic	16	17	15	14	8	4
Denmark	58	62	55	58	37	33
Germany	43	47	39	39	26	17
Estonia	30	29	32	27	21	20
Ireland	32	34	31	26	22	19
Greece	12	14	9	10	4	5
Spain	26	29	24	25	14	8
France	41	42	40	37	24	18
Italy	17	19	14	15	11	5
Cyprus	20	21	19	18	13	10
Latvia	18	16	20	17	7	6
Lithuania	18	17	19	18	12	11
Luxembourg	52	62	41	44	38	21
Hungary	25	25	25	22	19	14
Malta	25	28	21	22	17	9
Netherlands	55	61	49	49	30	33
Austria	27	32	23	24	19	13
Poland	15	15	15	12	9	4
Portugal	19	22	17	17	13	13
Romania	5	6	5	4	3	2
Slovenia	30	29	31	28	15	6
Slovakia	24	23	24	20	15	8
Finland	50	51	50	43	31	17
Sweden	53	55	50	47	29	24
United Kingdom	38	42	34	33	22	18
FYR of Macedonia (2)	15	19	11	12	5	2
Turkey (3)	6	8	4	5	2	1
Iceland	59	63	54	54	33	19
Norway	60	65	55	55	33	26

(1) EA-13 instead of EA-15.
(2) 2006.
(3) 2005.

Source: Eurostat (tsiir130 and tin00064)

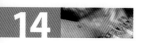

Table 14.12: Proportion of enterprises that have remote employed persons who connect to IT systems from home, 2006 (1)

(% of enterprises)

	Total (10+ persons employed)	Small (10-49 persons employed)	Medium (50-249 persons employed)	Large (250+ persons employed)
EU-27	17	13	30	55
Euro area (2)	15	11	30	57
Belgium	27	21	50	71
Bulgaria	9	9	10	17
Czech Republic	19	15	31	48
Denmark	53	46	81	95
Germany	21	15	39	65
Estonia	22	18	34	53
Ireland	25	20	38	59
Greece	16	14	25	52
Spain	8	5	17	40
France	:	:	:	:
Italy	3	2	7	23
Cyprus	14	10	28	62
Latvia	7	5	12	27
Lithuania	12	11	13	30
Luxembourg	19	16	25	66
Hungary	10	8	16	36
Malta	:	:	:	:
Netherlands	35	29	56	85
Austria	20	16	37	64
Poland	4	3	8	15
Portugal	9	7	21	49
Romania	7	6	9	20
Slovenia	26	23	32	65
Slovakia	13	12	17	34
Finland	32	24	56	77
Sweden	39	34	59	84
United Kingdom	32	26	49	79
Iceland	47	42	67	66
Norway	49	44	78	94

(1) Enterprises with 10 or more full-time persons employed; enterprises that have their main activity in NACE Sections D, F, G, I and K or NACE Groups 55.1, 55.2, 92.1 and 92.2.
(2) EA-12 instead of EA-15.

Source: Eurostat (tin00082 and isoc_ci_tw_e)

Table 14.13: Enterprises using the Internet for interacting with public authorities, 2007 (1)

(% of enterprises)

	E-government usage by enterprises	Obtaining information	Downloading official forms	Returning filled in forms
EU-27	65	57	58	45
Euro area (2)	68	58	60	47
Belgium	51	44	35	37
Bulgaria	45	40	36	29
Czech Republic	73	70	65	34
Denmark	88	83	83	61
Germany	56	44	49	43
Estonia	76	74	71	58
Ireland	89	79	82	69
Greece	82	71	70	77
Spain	58	53	53	38
France	69	61	64	59
Italy	84	74	70	35
Cyprus	54	53	43	14
Latvia	45	42	41	26
Lithuania	76	71	75	60
Luxembourg	85	76	81	35
Hungary	55	51	52	44
Malta	77	74	68	49
Netherlands	81	67	69	73
Austria	81	60	75	54
Poland	64	53	56	56
Portugal	72	66	65	66
Romania	42	39	36	20
Slovenia	83	78	76	61
Slovakia	85	78	80	56
Finland	94	88	91	78
Sweden	79	77	76	55
United Kingdom	54	52	49	40
Croatia	51	45	48	33
Iceland (3)	95	85	79	81
Norway	71	65	66	61

(1) Enterprises with 10 or more full-time persons employed; enterprises that have their main activity in NACE Sections D, F, G, I and K or NACE Groups 55.1, 55.2, 92.1 and 92.2. The year given relates to the survey year. The e-government data relates to the year prior to the survey.
(2) EA-13 instead of EA-15.
(3) 2006.

Source: Eurostat (tsiir140 and tin00065)

Figure 14.10: Internet access and broadband connections among enterprises, 2007 (1)

(% of persons employed)

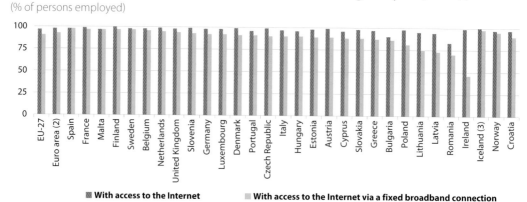

■ **With access to the Internet**   ■ **With access to the Internet via a fixed broadband connection**

(1) Enterprises with 10 or more full-time persons employed; enterprises that have their main activity in NACE Sections D, F, G, I and K or NACE Groups 55.1, 55.2, 92.1 and 92.2.
(2) EA-13 instead of EA-15.
(3) 2006.

Source: Eurostat (isoc_ci_in_p and isoc_ci_it_p)

Figure 14.11: Proportion of enterprises' total turnover from e-commerce via Internet, 2007 (1)

(%)

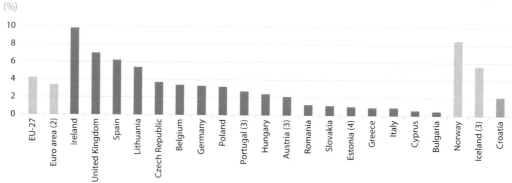

(1) Enterprises with 10 or more full-time persons employed; enterprises that have their main activity in NACE Sections D, G, I and K or NACE Groups 55.1 and 55.2; Denmark, France, Latvia, Luxembourg, Malta, the Netherlands, Slovenia, Finland and Sweden, not available.
(2) EA-13 instead of EA-15.
(3) 2006.
(4) 2005.

Source: Eurostat (tsiir100)

Figure 14.12: Enterprises having received orders/made purchases on-line, 2007 (1)

(% of enterprises)

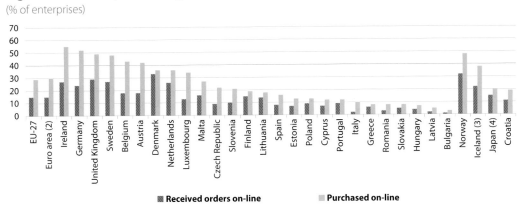

■ **Received orders on-line**   ■ **Purchased on-line**

(1) Enterprises with 10 or more full-time persons employed; enterprises that have their main activity in NACE Sections D, F, G, I and K or NACE Groups 55.1, 55.2, 92.1 and 92.2; France, not available.
(2) EA-13 instead of EA-15.
(3) 2006.
(4) 2005.

Source: Eurostat (tin00068 and isoc_ec_ebuy)

Figure 14.13: Information technology expenditure, 2006 (1)

(% of GDP)

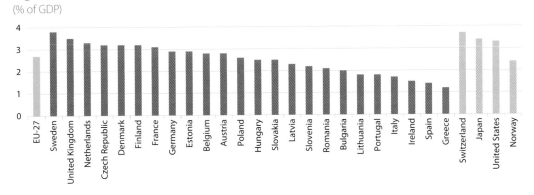

(1) Cyprus, Luxembourg and Malta, not available.

Source: Eurostat (tsiir090), European Information Technology Observatory (EITO)

14.5 Telecommunications

Introduction

Telecommunication networks and services are the backbone of Europe's developing information society. Individuals, enterprises and public organisations alike have come to rely ever more on convenient, reliable networks and services for a variety of services.

The European telecommunications sector was historically characterised by public service, monopoly providers, often run in conjunction with postal services. Liberalisation moves began in the first half of the 1980s and, at first, concerned value added services or business users, while basic services were left in the hands of monopoly providers. By 1998, telecommunications were, in principle, fully liberalised across all of the Member States. The liberalisation of telecommunication markets has led to considerable reductions in prices. This may, in part, reflect the introduction of competition into a number of markets that were previously the domain of incumbent, monopoly suppliers, as well as reflecting technological changes that have increased capacity and made it possible to communicate not only by voice, but also over the Internet. Market regulation has nonetheless continued, and the European Commission oversees this to ensure that consumers benefit. Regulation continues to monitor the significant market power of former monopolies, ensure universal service and protect consumers, especially those social groups that may otherwise face exclusion, through overseeing the correct implementation and enforcement of Directives.

On 30 June 2007, a new set of rules on roaming entered into force. These foresee that people travelling within the EU are able to phone across borders at more affordable and transparent prices. The Roaming Regulation [13] put in place a set of maximum prices for phone calls made and received while abroad (Eurotariff); these maximum prices apply to all consumers unless they opt for special packages offered by operators. The European Commission and national regulators have closely monitored price developments for text messages and data services. On the basis of this monitoring, a review was conducted which came to the conclusion that competition has not encouraged mobile operators to voluntarily reduce very high roaming charges for text messages. The European Commission therefore proposed on 23 September 2008:

* to bring down prices for text messages sent while travelling in another EU country;
* to ensure that consumers are kept informed of the charges that apply for data roaming services;
* to introduce a Euro-SMS Tariff from 1 July 2009 so that sending an SMS from abroad would cost no more than 11 cents (excluding VAT), while receiving an SMS in another EU country would remain free of charge;

(13) Regulation (EC)No 717/2007 of the European Parliament and of the Council of 27 June 2007 on roaming on public mobile telephone networks within the Community and amending Directive 2002/21/EC; http://eur-lex.europa.eu/LexUriServ/LexUriServ.do?uri=OJ:L:2007:171:0032:0040:EN:PDF.

- to improve transparency so that customers travelling to another Member State should receive an automated message of the charges that apply for data roaming services upon arrival; while from 1 July 2010, operators should provide customers with the opportunity to determine in advance how much they want to spend before a data roaming service is 'cut-off';
- to restrict to EUR 1 per megabyte wholesale data roaming fees, so these are more predictable for operators;
- to reduce further the cost of Eurotariff voice calls, with the price for making calls decreasing from 43 cents on 1 July 2009, to 40 cents, 37 cents and 34 cents in each of the subsequent years, while the price of receiving a call would decrease from 19 cents on 1 July 2009 to 16 cents, 13 cents and 10 cents.

Definition and data availability

Eurostat's data collection in relation to **telecommunications statistics** is conducted through the use of a predefined questionnaire (TELECOM), which is sent on annual basis to the national statistical institutes. They collect information from their relevant regulatory authorities and send the completed questionnaires back to Eurostat.

Main telephone lines are the traditional way of connecting to communication networks. They are usually used for voice telephony, but may also be used for accessing the Internet via a modem or dial-up connection. The rapid growth of more powerful means to access the Internet (broadband) and mobile communications has eroded somewhat the market for traditional fixed telecommunication networks.

Indicators presented in relation to market share refer to fixed-line telecommunications and mobile telephony. The market share of the **incumbent** for **fixed-line telephony** is defined as the enterprise active in the market just before liberalisation and is calculated on the basis of retail revenues. Indicators relating to the **mobile market** refer to the number of subscriptions to public cellular mobile telecommunication systems and also include active pre-paid cards. Note that an increasing number of people have multiple mobile subscriptions (for example, for private and work use, or for use in different countries).

Data on **expenditure for telecommunications** covers hardware, equipment, software and other services. The data are not collected by Eurostat; further methodological information is available at: http://www.eito.com/.

Telecommunications prices are based on the price (including VAT) in euro of a 10-minute call at 11 am on a weekday in August, based on normal rates. Three markets are presented, namely a **local call** (3 km), a **national long distance call** (200 km) and an **international call** (to the United States). The data are not collected by Eurostat; further methodological information is available at: http://www.tel-igen.com/.

Main findings

Telecommunications expenditure accounted for 3.0 % of GDP in the EU-27 in 2006, compared with 2.1 % in the United States and 4.2 % in Japan. The highest relative levels of expenditure were generally recorded in those Member State that joined the EU since 2004 (Cyprus and Malta, not available), in particular in the Baltic Member States, Bulgaria and Romania.

Although overall expenditure on telephony has increased, the proportion accounted for by ex-monopoly providers has generally been reduced, as the share of the total telecommunication market accounted for by fixed-line voice operations has shrunk, whereas growth has been concentrated in mobile markets and other data services. The incumbents in fixed telecommunications markets across the EU-25 accounted for 72 % of local calls in 2005, 66 % of national calls and 56 % of international calls. In contrast, the share of incumbents in the mobile market was relatively low at 39 % in 2006.

The average number of mobile subscriptions per 100 inhabitants stood at 106 in the EU-27 in 2006, and surpassed parity in 17 of the Member States, where there were more subscriptions than inhabitants.

The price of telecommunications fell between 2004 and 2006 in a large number of Member States. Price reductions were most apparent for national long distance and international calls (defined here as calls to the United States), as on average in the EU-25 the price of a national long distance call was reduced by almost 20 % overall between 2004 and 2006, while the price of an international call was reduced by almost 16 %. In comparison, there was a modest reduction in the price of a local call, which was reduced by less than 3 %.

The prices of local, national long distance or international calls varied greatly across the Member States in 2006. Local and national distance calls were most expensive in Slovakia, while the price of international calls was highest in Latvia. The cheapest tariff for local calls was found in Spain, for national long distance calls in Cyprus, and for calls to the United States in Germany.

Table 14.14: Market share of incumbents and leading operators in telecommunication markets
(% of total market)

	Fixed telecommunications, 2005			Market share of the leading operator in mobile tele-communications, 2006 (4)
	Local calls (1)	National long distance calls (2)	International calls (3)	
EU-25	72	66	56	39
Belgium	68	68	58	45
Bulgaria	:	:	:	:
Czech Republic	76	63	65	41
Denmark	:	:	:	32
Germany	56	57	39	37
Estonia	:	:	:	46
Ireland	83	63	62	47
Greece	78	73	74	41
Spain	78	75	62	46
France	80	68	67	46
Italy	71	73	47	41
Cyprus	100	100	86	90
Latvia	97	98	72	35
Lithuania	97	88	76	36
Luxembourg	:	:	:	51
Hungary	92	90	87	45
Malta	99	99	98	52
Netherlands	75	75	45	48
Austria	53	59	50	39
Poland	85	70	71	34
Portugal	:	78	80	46
Romania	:	:	:	:
Slovenia	100	100	83	71
Slovakia	99	100	88	56
Finland	95	45	41	45
Sweden	:	:	:	43
United Kingdom	60	52	53	26
Norway	:	73	61	57

(1) Austria and Finland, 2004; Cyprus, 2003.
(2) Finland, 2004; Cyprus, 2003.
(3) Finland, 2004.
(4) Norway, 2005.

Source: Eurostat (tsier070 and tsier080), National Regulatory Authorities

Figure 14.14: Telecommunications expenditure, 2006 (1)

(% of GDP)

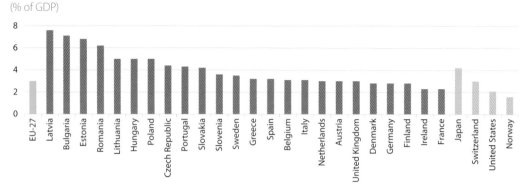

(1) Cyprus, Luxembourg and Malta, not available.

Source: Eurostat (tsiir090), European Information Technology Observatory (EITO)

Figure 14.15: Mobile phone subscriptions, 2006

(average number of subscriptions per 100 inhabitants)

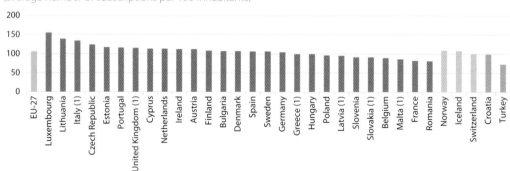

(1) Source: International Telecommunication Union (ITU).

Source: Eurostat (tin00060)

Table 14.15: Price of fixed telecommunications
(EUR per 10-minute call)

	Local calls			National long distance calls			Calls to the United States		
	2004	2005	2006	2004	2005	2006	2004	2005	2006
EU-25	0.37	0.35	0.36	0.92	0.76	0.74	2.13	2.11	1.79
Belgium	0.57	0.57	0.57	0.57	0.57	0.57	1.98	1.98	1.98
Bulgaria	:	:	:	:	:	:	:	:	:
Czech Republic	0.56	0.56	0.56	1.46	1.13	0.56	3.64	2.02	2.02
Denmark	0.37	0.37	0.37	0.37	0.37	0.37	2.38	2.38	2.38
Germany	0.42	0.39	0.39	1.20	0.49	0.49	1.23	1.23	0.46
Estonia	0.23	0.23	0.23	0.23	0.23	0.23	2.26	2.10	2.13
Ireland	0.49	0.49	0.49	0.82	0.82	0.82	1.91	1.91	1.91
Greece	0.31	0.31	0.31	0.73	0.74	0.74	2.91	2.93	3.49
Spain	0.28	0.28	0.19	0.88	0.84	0.85	1.53	1.53	1.53
France	0.39	0.33	0.36	0.96	0.83	0.89	2.24	2.27	2.32
Italy	0.25	0.22	0.22	1.15	1.15	1.15	2.12	2.12	2.12
Cyprus	0.20	0.22	0.22	0.20	0.22	0.22	0.80	0.66	0.66
Latvia	0.36	0.36	0.36	1.03	1.03	1.03	5.94	5.94	5.94
Lithuania	0.39	0.39	0.39	0.79	0.79	0.79	4.07	4.07	4.07
Luxembourg	0.31	0.31	0.31	:	:	:	1.37	1.37	1.37
Hungary	0.41	0.41	0.40	1.09	1.09	1.04	2.43	2.97	2.88
Malta	0.25	0.25	0.25	:	:	:	1.65	1.77	1.64
Netherlands	0.33	0.33	0.33	0.49	0.49	0.49	0.85	0.85	0.85
Austria	0.49	0.49	0.49	0.59	0.59	0.59	1.90	1.90	1.90
Poland	0.35	0.30	0.50	1.22	1.22	1.00	3.67	3.74	1.23
Portugal	0.40	0.37	0.37	0.65	0.65	0.65	3.06	3.11	3.11
Romania	:	:	:	:	:	:	:	:	:
Slovenia	0.26	0.26	0.26	0.26	0.26	0.26	1.75	1.40	1.40
Slovakia	0.60	0.60	0.60	1.29	1.23	1.29	3.02	3.02	1.23
Finland	0.24	0.24	0.24	0.90	0.94	0.94	4.77	4.90	4.90
Sweden	0.29	0.29	0.29	0.29	0.29	0.29	1.06	1.06	1.18
United Kingdom	0.44	0.44	0.44	0.44	0.44	0.44	2.08	2.08	2.23
Norway	0.32	0.34	:	0.32	0.34	:	0.82	0.77	:
Japan	0.25	0.25	0.25	1.02	1.02	1.02	4.39	4.39	4.34
United States	0.07	0.07	0.07	1.03	1.03	1.03	-	-	-

Source: Eurostat (tsier030), Teligen

Europe's regions

Introduction

The EU's regional policy aims to strengthen economic, social and territorial cohesion by reducing disparities in the level of development among regions and Member States. Its three main concerns are:

- convergence, under which the poorest Member States and regions are eligible, accounting for around 82 % of the funds available in the period 2007 to 2013;
- regional competitiveness and employment, accounting for around 16 % of the funds available in the period 2007 to 2013;
- European territorial cooperation, accounting for around 2.5 % of the funds available in the period 2007 to 2013.

The main instruments of regional policy are the structural and cohesion funds.

- The European Regional Development Fund (ERDF) operates in all Member States and co-finances physical investments and, to a limited extent, training for citizens.
- The European Social Fund (ESF) will be implemented in line with the European Employment Strategy.
- The Cohesion Fund co-finances mainly transport and environment projects in Member States whose gross national income per inhabitant is less than 90 % of the EU average.
- The regional development component, as well as the cross-border cooperation component of the new Instrument for Pre-Accession (IPA), helps candidate countries to develop their competitiveness, particularly through the development of transport networks and environmental infrastructure.

The ERDF is concentrated on the poorest regions in terms of gross domestic product (GDP) per inhabitant. It aims to strengthen economic and social cohesion in the EU by correcting imbalances between its regions. The fund can intervene in the three objectives of regional policy. In regions covered by the convergence objective, it focuses its intervention on modernising and diversifying economic structures as well as safeguarding or creating sustainable jobs. Concerning regional competitiveness and employment, the priorities of the ERDF are innovation and the knowledge-based economy, environment and risk prevention, and access to transport and telecommunications services of general economic interest. With respect to European territorial cooperation, the ERDF is concerned with the development of economic and social cross-border activities, the establishment and development of transnational cooperation, and increasing the efficiency of regional policy through interregional promotion and cooperation, as well as the networking and exchange of experiences between regional and local authorities.

The ESF sets out to improve employment and job opportunities in the EU. It intervenes in the framework of the convergence and regional competitiveness and employment objectives. The ESF supports actions in Member States and focuses on four key areas: increasing adaptability of workers and enterprises (lifelong learning schemes, designing and spreading innovative working organisations); enhancing access to employment and participation in the labour market; reinforcing social inclusion by combating discrimination and facilitating access to the labour market for disadvantaged people; and promoting partnership for reform in the fields of employment and inclusion.

The Cohesion Fund is aimed at Member States whose gross national income (GNI) per inhabitant is less than 90 % of the EU average. It serves to reduce their economic and social shortfall, as well as to stabilise their economy. It supports actions in the framework of the convergence objective. For the 2007-2013 period, the Cohesion Fund concerns Bulgaria, the Czech Republic, Estonia, Greece, Cyprus, Hungary, Latvia, Lithuania, Malta, Poland, Portugal, Romania, Slovenia and Slovakia; Spain is eligible to a phase-out fund only. The Cohesion Fund finances activities under two categories: trans-European transport networks, notably priority projects of European interest; and the environment, also supporting projects related to energy or transport, as long as they clearly present a benefit to the environment.

Definitions and data availability

Comparable **regional statistics** form an important part of the European statistical system, and have been collected for several decades. Eurostat's regional statistics cover the principal features of economic and social life within the EU. The concepts and definitions used for these regional statistics are as close as possible to those used for the production of statistics at a national level.

All statistics at a regional level within the EU are based on the nomenclature of territorial units for statistics (NUTS). The NUTS classification has been used for many decades for regional statistics, but it was only in 2003 that NUTS acquired a legal basis (Regulation (EC) No 1059/2003). As new Member States have joined the EU the NUTS Regulation has been amended to include the regional classification in those countries. This was the case in 2004, when the EU took in 10 new Member States, and again in 2007 when Bulgaria and Romania became members. A review of the NUTS classification was conducted in 2006 and a revised version (NUTS 2006 – Regulation (EC) No 105/2007) entered into force on 1 January 2008.

NUTS is a hierarchical classification; it subdivides each Member State into a number of regions at NUTS 1 level. Each of these is then subdivided into regions at NUTS 2 level, and these in turn into regions at NUTS 3 level. The NUTS regions are, in general, administrative units, reflecting the remit of local authorities. These administrative regions are generally adopted by statisticians as the most appropriate units for data collection, processing and dissemination. The current NUTS (version 2006) subdivides the territory of the European Union (EU-27) into 97 NUTS level 1 regions, 271 NUTS level 2 regions and 1 303 NUTS level 3 regions.

Since 2004, Eurostat has also collected and published **urban statistics**, measuring the 'quality of life' through a set of some 338 indicators for 321 cities within the EU, Croatia, Turkey, Norway and Switzerland. Data are available for three levels: the core city; larger urban zones;

and for sub-city districts. The main goal of the **Urban Audit** data collection is to provide information to assess the quality of life in European towns and cities, as measured through a broad range of indicators (covering urban living, such as demography, housing, health, crime, the labour market, income disparity, local administration, educational qualifications, the environment, climate, travel patterns, information society and cultural infrastructure), as well as perception surveys conducted among persons living in these cities.

Main findings

The maps presented here illustrate the diversity of Europe's regions. They show that for many economic and social aspects, quite large variations can also be found within a given country. In most cases, the capital region of a country is economically better off than the more rural areas.

The richest European regions in 2005, as defined by GDP per inhabitant, were concentrated within the major conurbations of the EU-15 Member States, with inner London topping the list (EUR 67 798 per inhabitant). Among the top 20 regions Praha and Bratislavský kraj stood out as the only regions from the countries that have joined the EU since 2004, ranked in 12th and 18th place respectively of the 271 regions within the EU-27 Member States for which data are presented. The ten poorest regions (using this measure) were all in Bulgaria and Romania, with Polish, Romanian and Hungarian regions making up those regions ranked between 10th and 20th poorest. The region at the top of the ranking was more than twelve times as rich as the one at the bottom.

The widest disparities in the distribution of wealth creation between the regions within a country were recorded in the United Kingdom, France, Belgium and Slovakia. In each of these cases the highest GDP per inhabitant was recorded for the region including the capital city, and the exclusion of this region narrows considerably the distribution. The pattern of the highest GDP per inhabitant being recorded in the region with the capital city was not observed in all of the Member States, as for example, Hamburg was the wealthiest region in Germany, Åland the wealthiest in Finland, while the provinces of Bolzano/Bozen and Lombardia were the wealthiest in Italy. Care should be taken with the interpretation of data on GDP per inhabitant as the ratio is influenced by commuters working in one region but living in another: the very high GDP per inhabitant within Inner London, Luxembourg or Bruxelles-Capitale/Brussels Hoofdstedelijk Gewest (the three regions with the highest GDP per inhabitant) can, at least in part, be explained by a large daily influx of commuters from neighbouring regions or, in the case of Luxembourg, from across neighbouring borders.

In stark contrast to the level of GDP per inhabitant, several regions of Bulgaria and Romania as well as the three Baltic Member States (Estonia, Latvia and Lithuania) recorded strong growth in GDP per inhabitant: an analysis of the period 2001-2005 shows that the top 15 regions within the EU-27 for the growth of GDP per inhabitant included eight from Romania, three from Bulgaria, the three Baltic Member States, as well as one region each from the Czech Republic and Slovakia. The highest growth rate was

11.5 % for Estonia, while four Romanian regions (Vest, Sud – Muntenia, Nord-Vest and Sud-Est) reported growth in excess of 10 %. The slowest growing 20 regions in the EU-27 included 18 regions in Italy, Åland in Finland and French Guyane. Of these, seven of the Italian regions, Åland and Guyane all reported a fall in GDP per inhabitant over the period considered, the largest reduction being an average of 1.1 % per annum in Abruzzo.

There were 19 regions in the EU-27 that had a population density of more than 1 000 inhabitants per square kilometre. Out of these, six were in the United Kingdom (including the most densely populous region of Inner London (9 159 inhabitants per km²)), three were in Germany (including Berlin), alongside the capitals of Belgium, Austria, the Czech Republic, Romania and Greece, while the other regions included Malta, Zuid-Holland (the Netherlands) and the two autonomous regions of Melilla and Ceuta (Spain). Eight out of the ten least populous regions for which data are available were in Finland or Sweden, along with Guyane (France) and Castilla-la Mancha (Spain).

Although Guyane reported the lowest population density, it also reported the highest population growth (3.5 % per annum) between January 2001 and January 2006. Seven of the ten fastest growing populations in the EU-27 were in Spain, principally in the islands, easterly coastal regions and the Comunidad de Madrid. The two other regions among the ten fastest growing in the EU-27 were Flevoland (the Netherlands) and Border, Midlands and Western (Ireland). Just over one quarter (27.8 %) of the 263 regions for which data are available reported a decline in their populations over the period considered. Of these, six regions, two in Germany and four in Bulgaria, recorded annual population reductions in excess of 1 % per annum; with only Severozapaden (Bulgaria) reporting a decline in excess of 2 % per annum.

Some of the highest old-age dependency ratios are found in rural, agricultural areas of Italy, France and Portugal, or eastern regions of Germany (Chemnitz, Dresden, Sachsen-Anhalt or Leipzig).

The highest unemployment rates in 2007 were recorded in the four French departments of Réunion, Guadeloupe, Martinique and Guyane, followed by the two Spanish autonomous regions of Ceuta and Melilla. Out of the next 11 regions, seven were in eastern Germany, two were in Slovakia and the other was Bruxelles-Capitale/Brussels Hoofdstedelijk Gewest. Seven of the 15 regions with the lowest unemployment rates were Dutch, including the region with the lowest rate, Zeeland (2.1 %).

Map 15.1: Gross domestic product (GDP) per inhabitant, by NUTS 2 regions, 2005 (1)

(PPS per inhabitant)

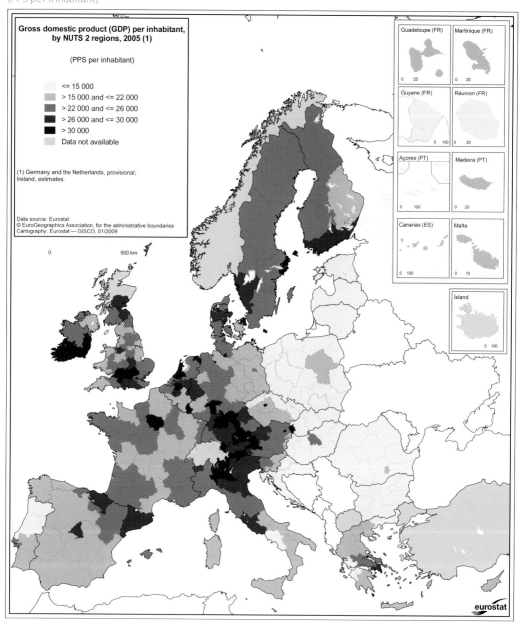

Gross domestic product (GDP) per inhabitant,
by NUTS 2 regions, 2005 (1)

(PPS per inhabitant)

- <= 15 000
- > 15 000 and <= 22 000
- > 22 000 and <= 26 000
- > 26 000 and <= 30 000
- > 30 000
- Data not available

(1) Germany and the Netherlands, provisional;
Ireland, estimates.

Data source: Eurostat
© EuroGeographics Association, for the administrative boundaries
Cartography: Eurostat — GISCO, 01/2009

Source: Eurostat (tgs00005)

Map 15.2: Average annual growth rate of gross domestic product (GDP) per inhabitant, by NUTS 2 regions, 2001-2005 (1)

(% per annum)

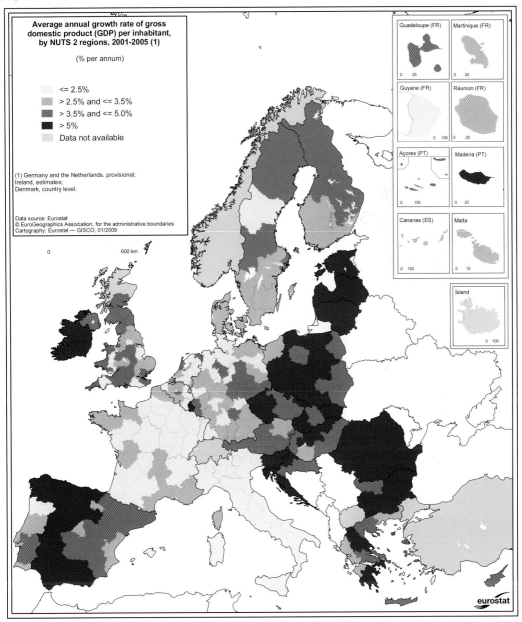

Average annual growth rate of gross domestic product (GDP) per inhabitant, by NUTS 2 regions, 2001-2005 (1)

(% per annum)

- <= 2.5%
- > 2.5% and <= 3.5%
- > 3.5% and <= 5.0%
- > 5%
- Data not available

(1) Germany and the Netherlands, provisional;
Ireland, estimates;
Denmark, country level.

Data source: Eurostat
© EuroGeographics Association, for the administrative boundaries
Cartography: Eurostat — GISCO, 01/2009

0   600 km

Guadeloupe (FR)   Martinique (FR)
0   25   0   20

Guyane (FR)   Réunion (FR)
0   100   0   20

Açores (PT)   Madeira (PT)
0   100   0   20

Canarias (ES)   Malta
0   100   0   10

Ísland
0   100

Source: Eurostat (tgs00005)

Map 15.3: Population density, by NUTS 2 regions, 2006 (1)
(inhabitants per km²)

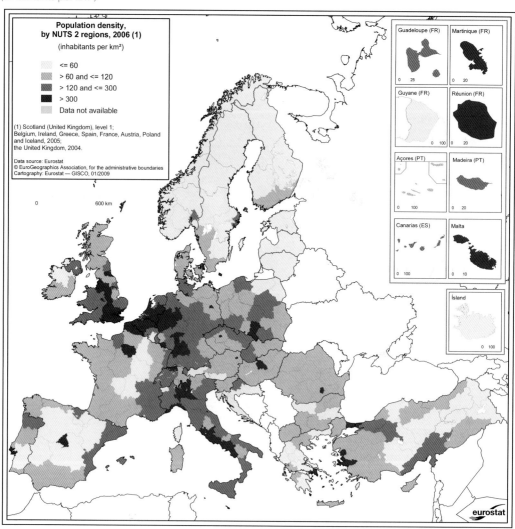

Source: Eurostat (tgs00024)

Map 15.4: Average annual growth rate of population, by NUTS 2 regions, 1 Jan. 2001 - 1 Jan. 2006 (1)
(% per annum)

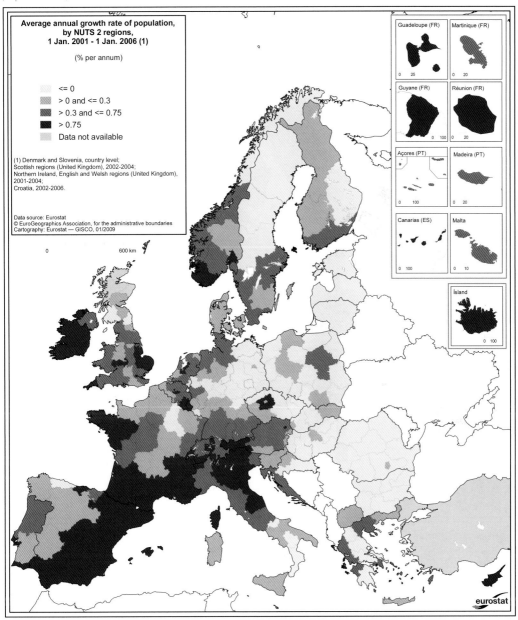

Source: Eurostat (reg_d2jan)

Map 15.5: Old age dependency, population ratio by age: > 64 / 15-64, by NUTS 2 regions, 2007 (1)
(%)

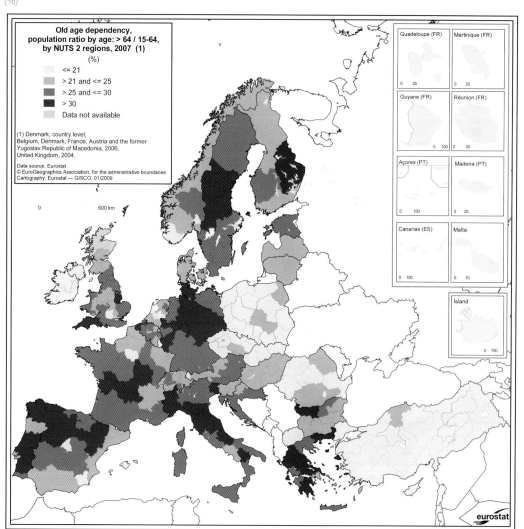

Source: Eurostat (reg_d2jan)

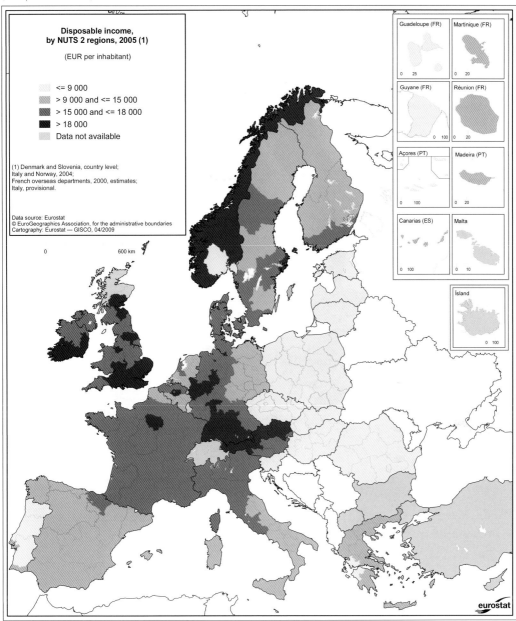

Map 15.6: Disposable income, by NUTS 2 regions, 2005 (1)
(EUR per inhabitant)

Disposable income,
by NUTS 2 regions, 2005 (1)

(EUR per inhabitant)

<= 9 000
> 9 000 and <= 15 000
> 15 000 and <= 18 000
> 18 000
Data not available

(1) Denmark and Slovenia, country level;
Italy and Norway, 2004;
French overseas departments, 2000, estimates;
Italy, provisional.

Data source: Eurostat
© EuroGeographics Association, for the administrative boundaries
Cartography: Eurostat — GISCO, 04/2009

0   600 km

Guadeloupe (FR)   Martinique (FR)
0   25   0   20

Guyane (FR)   Réunion (FR)
            0   100   0   20

Açores (PT)   Madeira (PT)
0   100   0   20

Canarias (ES)   Malta
0   100   0   10

Ísland
                       0   100

Source: Eurostat (tgs00026)

Map 15.7: Employment rate, by NUTS 2 regions, 2007 (1)
(%)

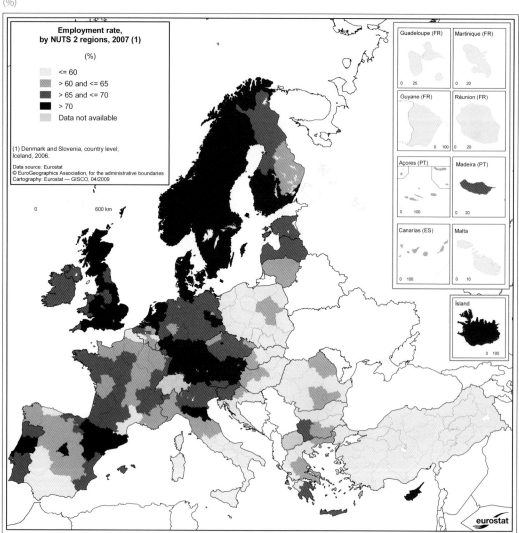

Employment rate,
by NUTS 2 regions, 2007 (1)

(%)

<= 60
> 60 and <= 65
> 65 and <= 70
> 70
Data not available

(1) Denmark and Slovenia, country level;
Iceland, 2006.

Data source: Eurostat
© EuroGeographics Association, for the administrative boundaries
Cartography: Eurostat — GISCO, 04/2009

Guadeloupe (FR)   Martinique (FR)

Guyane (FR)   Réunion (FR)

Açores (PT)   Madeira (PT)

Canarias (ES)   Malta

Ísland

Source: Eurostat (tgs00007)

Map 15.8: Old age employment rate (55-64), by NUTS 2 regions, 2007 (1)
(%)

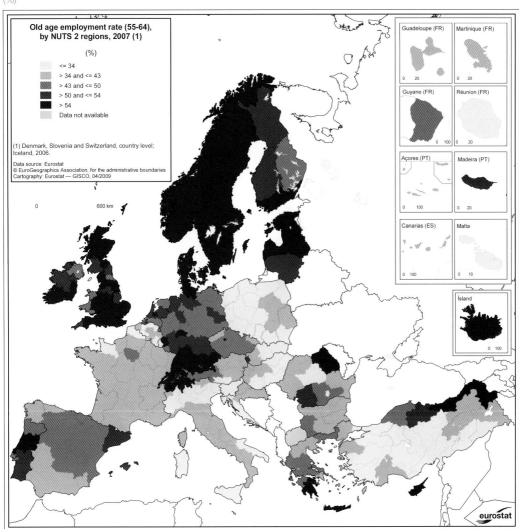

Old age employment rate (55-64),
by NUTS 2 regions, 2007 (1)

(%)

<= 34
> 34 and <= 43
> 43 and <= 50
> 50 and <= 54
> 54
Data not available

(1) Denmark, Slovenia and Switzerland, country level;
Iceland, 2006.

Data source: Eurostat
© EuroGeographics Association, for the administrative boundaries
Cartography: Eurostat — GISCO, 04/2009

0   600 km

Source: Eurostat (reg_lfe2emprt)

Map 15.9: Unemployment rate, by NUTS 2 regions, 2007 (1)

(%)

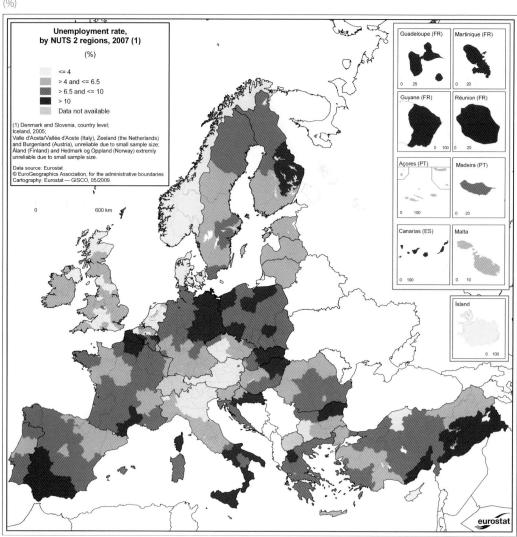

Source: Eurostat (tgs00010)

Table 15.1: Dispersion of regional employment rates (1)

(coefficient of variation)

	1999	2000	2001	2002	2003	2004	2005	2006	2007
EU-27	12.9	13.0	13.2	13.2	12.9	12.1	11.9	11.4	11.1
Euro area	13.3	13.0	12.7	12.1	11.5	10.5	10.6	10.6	10.8
Belgium	8.0	7.9	8.0	8.0	7.7	8.7	8.4	8.7	8.6
Bulgaria	:	:	:	:	6.6	6.9	7.2	7.3	7.1
Czech Republic	5.6	5.8	5.7	5.6	5.8	5.6	5.5	5.2	4.6
Denmark	:	:	:	:	:	:	:	:	:
Germany	5.4	5.4	5.8	5.7	5.9	6.0	5.6	5.2	4.8
Estonia	-	-	-	-	-	-	-	-	-
Ireland	-	-	-	-	-	-	-	-	-
Greece	5.2	5.1	4.3	3.8	3.2	4.1	4.3	3.7	3.5
Spain	10.8	10.7	10.0	9.3	9.0	8.7	8.3	7.8	7.5
France	7.1	6.9	8.3	8.0	7.2	7.1	7.2	7.4	6.6
Italy	17.4	17.5	17.1	16.7	17.0	15.6	16.0	16.0	16.3
Cyprus	-	-	-	-	-	-	-	-	-
Latvia	-	-	-	-	-	-	-	-	-
Lithuania	-	-	-	-	-	-	-	-	-
Luxembourg	-	-	-	-	-	-	-	-	-
Hungary	9.1	9.0	8.8	9.4	8.5	9.4	9.9	9.1	9.7
Malta	-	-	-	-	-	-	-	-	-
Netherlands	2.3	2.2	2.3	2.2	2.3	2.3	2.0	2.2	2.2
Austria	2.3	2.5	2.6	2.5	3.0	3.5	4.1	3.4	3.8
Poland	4.8	6.9	7.2	7.3	7.2	6.4	5.6	5.1	4.5
Portugal	3.6	4.3	3.5	3.8	3.9	3.5	3.3	3.1	3.3
Romania	4.2	4.6	5.6	3.2	3.5	4.9	4.5	3.6	4.6
Slovenia	-	-	-	-	-	-	-	-	-
Slovakia	8.1	9.1	8.3	7.3	7.6	9.0	9.8	8.6	8.3
Finland	6.7	6.8	7.0	6.7	6.1	5.5	5.5	5.4	5.6
Sweden	4.8	4.5	4.2	4.6	4.3	4.4	3.0	2.9	2.4
United Kingdom	7.5	7.1	6.8	6.6	6.1	5.9	5.7	5.5	5.4
Croatia	:	:	:	:	:	:	:	:	7.5
Iceland	-	-	-	-	-	-	-	-	-
Liechtenstein	-	-	-	-	-	-	-	-	-
Norway	2.4	2.4	2.2	1.6	1.6	1.7	1.3	2.3	2.5

(1) Variation of employment rates for the age group 15-64 across regions (NUTS 2 level) and within countries.

Source: Eurostat (tsisc050)

Linking statistics to European policies

16

Effective economic and political decision-making depends on the regular supply of reliable information. Statistics are one of the principle sources of such information, providing essential quantitative support to the elaboration and implementation of policies. Statistics are also a powerful tool for communicating with the general public.

The information needs of politicians require constant interaction between policy-makers and statisticians: the former formulate their needs for data, and the latter attempt to adapt the statistical production system so as to fulfil those needs. In this fashion, new policies lead to improvements in statistical production, both in terms of enhancing the quality of existing indicators and of creating new ones.

Whereas politicians require aggregated indicators which provide a synthetic and clear picture of the different phenomena they are interested in, statisticians tend to deal with less aggregated basic data. Statisticians therefore have to transform, synthesise and model basic data in order to increase data readability and extract signals (i.e. indicators).

Over recent years, three particularly significant policies have substantially influenced Eurostat's priorities and activities:

* economic and monetary union (EMU) and the creation of the euro area (1999);
* the Lisbon strategy (2000, re-focused in 2005);
* the sustainable development strategy (2001, renewed in 2006).

Economic and monetary union and the setting-up of the European Central Bank (ECB) required a broad range of infra-annual short-term statistics to measure economic and monetary developments within the euro area and to assist in the implementation of a common monetary policy. Effective monetary policy depends on timely, reliable and comprehensive economic statistics giving an overview of the economic situation. Such data are also needed for the assessment of the business cycle.

However, measuring economic and monetary developments within the euro area is not the only concern of European policies. Europeans place a high value on their quality of life, including aspects such as a clean environment, social protection, prosperity and equity.

In recent years the European Council has focused on a number of key areas intended to shape the future development of the EU, in particular by adopting two complementary strategies. While the goal of the Lisbon strategy is for the EU to 'become the most competitive and dynamic knowledge-based economy in the world, capable of sustainable economic growth with more and better jobs and greater social cohesion', the sustainable development strategy is concerned with the continuous improvement of quality of life, both for current and future generations, through seeking a balance between economic development, social cohesion and protection of the environment.

Eurostat has responded to politicians needs in these new areas by developing three sets of indicators:

* Euro-Indicators, of which the Principal European Economic Indicators (PEEIs) are the core, for monetary policy purposes;
* structural indicators, for the (revised) Lisbon strategy, used to underpin the Commission's analysis in an annual progress report to the European Council;
* sustainable development indicators, extending across a wide range of issues affecting the quality of life, including environmental, social, economic and governance issues.

These indicators have been developed by experts and agreed at a political level. They are continuously monitored, improved and reviewed in order to be in line with evolving policy requirements.

Eurostat has created three 'special topics' on its website, linked to these three collections of indicators. This chapter briefly presents the main characteristics of these three areas.

Euro-indicators/PEEIS

Since October 2001 the Euro-Indicators/ PEEIs web pages have been a reference point for all users of official statistics dealing with short-term data. They were initially conceived as an independent website, available in parallel to the Eurostat website. However, since October 2004, Euro-Indicators/PEEIs have been integrated into the Eurostat website as a so-called 'special topic'. It is possible to access Euro-Indicators/PEEIs from Eurostat's homepage or directly via the following link: http://ec.europa.eu/eurostat/ euroindicators. It is also possible to e-mail the Euro-Indicators/PEEIs team at: ESTAT-EUROINDICATORS@ec.europa. eu.

Euro-Indicators/PEEIs aims to supply business-cycle analysts, policymakers, media, researchers, students, and other interested users with a comprehensive, well structured and high quality set of information which is useful in their daily activities. The core of Euro-Indicators/ PEEIs comprises a set of statistical indicators giving an accurate and as timely as possible overview of the economic evolution of the euro area, the EU, and the individual Member States. Moreover, Euro-Indicators contains the following additional products and services intended to assist in the understanding and analysis of data:

* Principal European Economic Indicators (PEEIs),
* background,
* data,
* publications,
* news releases,
* methodology.

Euro-indicators/PEEIS data

The data presented in Euro-Indicators/ PEEIs are built around a set of the most relevant statistical indicators, called Principal European Economic Indicators, a complete list of which can be found in the Commission communication COM(2002) 661. Euro-Indicators/ PEEIs includes detailed breakdowns for PEEIs, as well as additional qualitative and quantitative indicators which are useful to give an overall picture of the economic situation in Europe. They are structured in three main parts:

* selected Principal European Economic Indicators (containing 22 selected indicators for the euro area and European Union) directly accessible on the Euro-Indicators/PEEIs homepage;
* key short-term indicators (a subset of pre-defined tables);
* European and national short-term statistics database (Euroind).

Both the key short-term indicators and the Euroind database are divided into the following eight domains:

* balance of payments,
* business and consumer surveys,
* consumer prices,
* external trade,
* industry, commerce and services,
* labour market,
* monetary and financial indicators,
* national accounts.

The new Euro-Indicators/PEEIs home-page launched in October 2007 gives a general overview of the economic situation of the euro area and European Union, bringing together in one single place a set of the most relevant and timely short-term economic indicators for the euro area and the European Union. This webpage provides policy-makers, analysts, academics, the media, and the public with essential information for decision making, economic analysis and research. Key short-term indicators are available from the data page and these provide an easy way to look at the most recent data in tabular or graphical format, including a short explanatory text; a download facility is also provided for the 320 tables that are currently available.

The Euroind database (accessible either from the Euro-Indicators data page or from the data dissemination tree on the Eurostat website as European and national short-term indicators) constitutes a large database of infra-annual macro-economic indicators; about 70 000 series are currently available and these can be selected and downloaded in a variety of formats.

Meta-data

In conformity with Eurostat standards, the Euro-Indicators data are documented in accordance with the International Monetary Fund's (IMF) special data dissemination standard (SDDS). SDDS files are regularly monitored and revised so that they are in line with the published data. The creation of a more user-oriented meta-data set is one of the objectives of the Euro-Indicators team (currently under construction).

Quality reports

Since 2001, the Euroind database has been subject to monthly quality monitoring. The results of this assessment are presented in a detailed online publication called 'State of affairs', accessible from the tab entitled 'Publications' within the Euro-Indicators/PEEIs 'special topic'. A synthesis of this monthly assessment is presented in another online publication, entitled the 'Monitoring report', which is also accessible from the same tab.

Publications and working papers

The main publication produced by the Euro-Indicators team is the monthly 'Eurostatistics'. It presents a synthetic picture of the economic situation together with detailed statistical analysis of the latest economic events for the euro area, EU and the Member States. The current issue of 'Eurostatistics' is accessible from the Euro-Indicators/PEEIs home page as an essential product. Past issues are accessible from the 'Publications' tab within the Euro-Indicators/PEEIs 'special topic'. Moreover, under the same tab users can find a collection of Euro-Indicators selected readings and working papers, containing both methodological and empirical studies on statistical improvements and analyses of European data.

Other products and services

The Euro-Indicators/PEEIs 'special topic' also provides users with access to the European release calendar for infra-annual statistics, which is updated on a weekly basis, as well as access to related press releases – both of these are found within the tab entitled 'news releases'. In addition, a monthly online newsletter is accessible from the 'Publications' tab. The newsletter contains short articles, news from the Member States and Eurostat, announcements, useful links, etc. Note that all papers and proceedings presented in conferences in relation to Euro-Indicators are also available on the Euro-Indicators/PEEIs 'special topic' under the tab for methodology by selecting the final point concerning 'Eurostat seminars and conferences'.

Planned improvements

Euro-Indicators/PEEIs is constantly evolving to meet user needs. The main improvements for 2009 will concern the improvement of the new Euro-Indicators/PEEIs homepage and the methodological pages. Concerning the new Euro-Indicators/PEEIs page, new features and facilities will be added and the list of indicators updated. A new set of methodological pages related to key topics, such as flash estimates, back-recalculation, interpolation and extrapolation, seasonal adjustment, business-cycle analysis, and the construction of coincident and leading indicators will be progressively implemented within the 'Methodology' tab. These pages will cover methodological papers, online bibliographies, software and routines, links to specialised sites and, whenever possible, new indicators or quantitative analyses (documented in SDDS format) produced on the basis of advanced statistical techniques.

Structural indicators

At the Lisbon European Council in the spring of 2000, the EU set itself the following strategic goal for the next decade: 'to become the most competitive and dynamic knowledge-based economy in the world, capable of sustainable economic growth with more and better jobs and greater social cohesion'.

The Council recognised the need to regularly discuss and assess progress made in achieving this goal on the basis of a commonly agreed set of structural indicators and to this end, invited the European Commission to draw up an annual spring report on progress being made. This report was to be based on the evolution of structural indicators in the following areas:

- general economic background,
- employment,
- innovation and research,
- economic reform,
- social cohesion,
- environment (since 2002).

For the first time, in 2004, the European Commission presented a shortlist of 14 structural indicators which were included in the statistical annex to its spring report to the European Council. This shortlist was agreed with the Council; its concise layout makes it easier to present policy messages and the Member States' positions with regard to the key Lisbon targets. The same shortlist indicators were presented in the annexes of subsequent annual progress reports to the European Council.

Shortlist of structural indicators

General economic background

- GDP per capita in PPS
- Labour productivity

Employment

- Employment rate
- Employment rate of older workers

Innovation and research

- Youth educational attainment level by gender
- Gross domestic expenditure on R & D relative to GDP

Economic reform

- Comparative price levels
- Business investment

Social cohesion

- At risk-of-poverty rate after social transfers
- Long-term unemployment rate
- Dispersion of regional employment rates

Environment

- Greenhouse gas emissions
- Energy intensity of the economy
- Volume of freight transport relative to GDP

The Lisbon strategy has entered a new phase since the spring of 2005, with the spotlight on delivering results, focusing on growth and jobs. By submitting national reform programmes, Member States have accepted a new responsibility, setting out detailed commitments for action. At the same time, Community programmes specify what has to be done at an EU level. National reform programmes provide the basis for the reform agenda, prioritising growth and employment.

Time-series are presented for the EU-27, the euro area, the Member States, the candidate countries, the EFTA countries, Japan and the United States (subject to data availability).

More information regarding structural indicators may be found on Eurostat's website at: http://ec.europa.eu/eurostat/ structuralindicators. Alternatively, for further information, contact Eurostat's structural indicators co-ordination team, at: estat-structuralindicators@ec.europa.eu.

Sustainable development indicators

The European Union's Sustainable Development Strategy (SDS), adopted by the European Council in Gothenburg in June 2001, and renewed in June 2006, aims to continuously improve quality of life, both for current and for future generations, through reconciling economic develop-ment, social cohesion and protection of the environment. A set of sustainable de-velopment indicators (SDI) has been de-veloped to monitor progress in the imple-mentation of the strategy. The indicators are organised under ten different themes that reflect different political priorities: socio-economic development, sustain-able consumption and production, social inclusion, demographic changes, public health, climate change and energy, sus-tainable transport, natural resources, global partnership and good governance.

Each theme is further divided into sub-themes to organise the set of indicators in a way that reflects the operational objectives and actions of the sustainable development strategy. In order to facili-tate communication, the set of indicators has been built as a three-level pyramid. This distinction between the three levels

of indicators reflects the structure of the renewed strategy (overall lead objectives, operational priority objectives, actions/explanatory variables) and also responds to different kinds of user needs, with the headline indicators having the highest communication value, as described in the table below.

The three-levels are complemented with contextual indicators, which do not mon-itor directly the strategy's objectives, but provide valuable background informa-tion for analysis. The SDI data set also de-scribes indicators which are not yet fully developed but which will, in the future, be necessary to get a more complete pic-ture of progress, differentiating between indicators that are expected to become available within two years, with sufficient quality ('indicators under development'), and those to be developed in the longer term ('indicators to be developed').

Table 16.1: Framework for sustainable development indicators

Indicator level	Hierarchical framework	Objectives
Level 1	Lead objectives	Headline (or level-1) indicators are at the top of the pyramid. They are intended to monitor the 'overall objectives' of the strategy. They are well-known indicators with a high communication value. They are robust and available for most EU Member States for a period of at least five years.
Level 2	SDS priority objectives	The second level of the pyramid consists of indicators related to the operational objectives of the strategy. They are the lead indicators in their respective subthemes. They are robust and available for most EU Member States for a period of at least three years.
Level 3	Actions/explanatory variables	The third level consists of indicators related to actions outlined in the strategy or to other issues which are useful to analyse progress towards the SDS objectives. Breakdowns of level-1 or -2 indicators are usually also found at level 3.
Contextual indicators	Background	Contextual indicators are part of the SDI set, but they either do not monitor directly any of the strategy's objectives or they are not policy responsive. Generally they are difficult to interpret in a normative way. However, they provide valuable background information on issues having direct relevance for sustainable development policies and are useful for the analysis.

Headline sustainable development indicators

Economic development

- Growth rate of GDP per inhabitant

Production and consumption patterns

- Resource productivity

Poverty and social exclusion

- At-risk-of-poverty rate after social transfers, by gender

Ageing society

- Employment rate of older workers

Public health

- Healthy life years and life expectancy at birth, by gender

Climate change and energy

- Total greenhouse gas emissions
- Renewables in gross inland energy consumption

Transport

- Energy consumption by transport mode

Management of natural resources

- Common bird index
- Fish catches taken from stocks outside safe biological limits

Global partnership

- Official development assistance

More information regarding sustainable development indicators may be found on the Eurostat website: (http://ec.europa.eu/eurostat/sustainabledevelopment).

Alternatively, for further information, contact Eurostat's sustainable development indicators team at: estat-sdi@ec.europa.eu.

Annexes

NUTS (classification of territorial units for statistics)

European Union: NUTS 2 regions

Belgium

BE10	Région de Bruxelles-Capitale/ Brussels Hoofdstedelijk Gewest
BE21	Prov. Antwerpen
BE22	Prov. Limburg (B)
BE23	Prov. Oost-Vlaanderen
BE24	Prov. Vlaams-Brabant
BE25	Prov. West-Vlaanderen
BE31	Prov. Brabant Wallon
BE32	Prov. Hainaut
BE33	Prov. Liège
BE34	Prov. Luxembourg (B)
BE35	Prov. Namur

Bulgaria

BG31	Severozapaden
BG32	Severen tsentralen
BG33	Severoiztochen
BG34	Yugoiztochen
BG41	Yugozapaden
BG42	Yuzhen tsentralen

Czech Republic

CZ01	Praha
CZ02	Střední Čechy
CZ03	Jihozápad
CZ04	Severozápad
CZ05	Severovýchod
CZ06	Jihovýchod
CZ07	Střední Morava
CZ08	Moravskoslezsko

Denmark

DK01	Hovedstaden
DK02	Sjælland
DK03	Syddanmark
DK04	Midtjylland
DK05	Nordjylland

Germany

DE11	Stuttgart
DE12	Karlsruhe
DE13	Freiburg
DE14	Tübingen
DE21	Oberbayern
DE22	Niederbayern
DE23	Oberpfalz
DE24	Oberfranken
DE25	Mittelfranken
DE26	Unterfranken
DE27	Schwaben
DE30	Berlin
DE41	Brandenburg — Nordost
DE42	Brandenburg — Südwest
DE50	Bremen
DE60	Hamburg
DE71	Darmstadt
DE72	Gießen
DE73	Kassel
DE80	Mecklenburg-Vorpommern
DE91	Braunschweig
DE92	Hannover
DE93	Lüneburg
DE94	Weser-Ems
DEA1	Düsseldorf
DEA2	Köln
DEA3	Münster
DEA4	Detmold
DEA5	Arnsberg
DEB1	Koblenz
DEB2	Trier
DEB3	Rheinhessen-Pfalz
DEC0	Saarland
DED1	Chemnitz
DED2	Dresden
DED3	Leipzig
DEE0	Sachsen-Anhalt
DEF0	Schleswig-Holstein
DEG0	Thüringen

Estonia

EE00	Eesti

Ireland

IE01	Border, Midland and Western
IE02	Southern and Eastern

Greece

GR11	Anatoliki Makedonia, Thraki
GR12	Kentriki Makedonia
GR13	Dytiki Makedonia
GR14	Thessalia
GR21	Ipeiros
GR22	Ionia Nisia
GR23	Dytiki Ellada
GR24	Sterea Ellada
GR25	Peloponnisos
GR30	Attiki
GR41	Voreio Aigaio
GR42	Notio Aigaio
GR43	Kriti

Spain

ES11	Galicia
ES12	Principado de Asturias
ES13	Cantabria
ES21	País Vasco
ES22	Comunidad Foral de Navarra
ES23	La Rioja
ES24	Aragón
ES30	Comunidad de Madrid
ES41	Castilla y León
ES42	Castilla-La Mancha
ES43	Extremadura
ES51	Cataluña
ES52	Comunidad Valenciana
ES53	Illes Balears
ES61	Andalucía
ES62	Región de Murcia
ES63	Ciudad Autónoma de Ceuta
ES64	Ciudad Autónoma de Melilla
ES70	Canarias

France

FR10	Île-de-France
FR21	Champagne-Ardenne
FR22	Picardie
FR23	Haute-Normandie
FR24	Centre
FR25	Basse-Normandie
FR26	Bourgogne
FR30	Nord – Pas-de-Calais
FR41	Lorraine
FR42	Alsace
FR43	Franche-Comté
FR51	Pays de la Loire
FR52	Bretagne
FR53	Poitou-Charentes
FR61	Aquitaine
FR62	Midi-Pyrénées
FR63	Limousin
FR71	Rhône-Alpes
FR72	Auvergne
FR81	Languedoc-Roussillon
FR82	Provence-Alpes-Côte d'Azur
FR83	Corse
FR91	Guadeloupe
FR92	Martinique
FR93	Guyane
FR94	Réunion

Italy

ITC1	Piemonte
ITC2	Valle d'Aosta/Vallée d'Aoste
ITC3	Liguria
ITC4	Lombardia
ITD1	Provincia Autonoma Bolzano/Bozen
ITD2	Provincia Autonoma Trento
ITD3	Veneto
ITD4	Friuli-Venezia Giulia
ITD5	Emilia-Romagna
ITE1	Toscana
ITE2	Umbria
ITE3	Marche
ITE4	Lazio
ITF1	Abruzzo
ITF2	Molise

ITF3	Campania
ITF4	Puglia
ITF5	Basilicata
ITF6	Calabria
ITG1	Sicilia
ITG2	Sardegna

Cyprus

CY00	Kypros/Kıbrıs

Latvia

LV00	Latvija

Lithuania

LT00	Lietuva

Luxembourg

LU00	Luxembourg (Grand-Duché)

Hungary

HU10	Közép-Magyarország
HU21	Közép-Dunántúl
HU22	Nyugat-Dunántúl
HU23	Dél-Dunántúl
HU31	Észak-Magyarország
HU32	Észak-Alföld
HU33	Dél-Alföld

Malta

MT00	Malta

Netherlands

NL11	Groningen
NL12	Friesland (NL)
NL13	Drenthe
NL21	Overijssel
NL22	Gelderland
NL23	Flevoland
NL31	Utrecht
NL32	Noord-Holland
NL33	Zuid-Holland
NL34	Zeeland
NL41	Noord-Brabant
NL42	Limburg (NL)

Austria

AT11	Burgenland (A)
AT12	Niederösterreich
AT13	Wien
AT21	Kärnten
AT22	Steiermark
AT31	Oberösterreich
AT32	Salzburg
AT33	Tirol
AT34	Vorarlberg

Poland

PL11	Łódzkie
PL12	Mazowieckie
PL21	Małopolskie
PL22	Śląskie
PL31	Lubelskie
PL32	Podkarpackie
PL33	Świętokrzyskie
PL34	Podlaskie
PL41	Wielkopolskie
PL42	Zachodniopomorskie
PL43	Lubuskie
PL51	Dolnośląskie
PL52	Opolskie
PL61	Kujawsko-Pomorskie
PL62	Warmińsko-Mazurskie
PL63	Pomorskie

Portugal

PT11	Norte
PT15	Algarve
PT16	Centro (P)
PT17	Lisboa
PT18	Alentejo
PT20	Região Autónoma dos Açores
PT30	Região Autónoma da Madeira

Romania

RO11	Nord-Vest
RO12	Centru
RO21	Nord-Est
RO22	Sud-Est
RO31	Sud — Muntenia
RO32	Bucureşti — Ilfov
RO41	Sud-Vest Oltenia
RO42	Vest

Slovenia

SI01	Vzhodna Slovenija
SI02	Zahodna Slovenija

Slovakia

SK01	Bratislavský kraj
SK02	Západné Slovensko
SK03	Stredné Slovensko
SK04	Východné Slovensko

Finland

FI13	Itä-Suomi
FI18	Etelä-Suomi
FI19	Länsi-Suomi
FI1A	Pohjois-Suomi
FI20	Åland

Sweden

SE11	Stockholm
SE12	Östra Mellansverige
SE21	Småland med öarna
SE22	Sydsverige
SE23	Västsverige
SE31	Norra Mellansverige
SE32	Mellersta Norrland
SE33	Övre Norrland

United Kingdom

UKC1	Tees Valley and Durham
UKC2	Northumberland and Tyne and Wear
UKD1	Cumbria
UKD2	Cheshire
UKD3	Greater Manchester
UKD4	Lancashire
UKD5	Merseyside
UKE1	East Yorkshire and Northern Lincolnshire
UKE2	North Yorkshire
UKE3	South Yorkshire
UKE4	West Yorkshire
UKF1	Derbyshire and Nottinghamshire
UKF2	Leicestershire, Rutland and Northamptonshire
UKF3	Lincolnshire
UKG1	Herefordshire, Worcestershire and Warwickshire
UKG2	Shropshire and Staffordshire
UKG3	West Midlands
UKH1	East Anglia
UKH2	Bedfordshire and Hertfordshire
UKH3	Essex
UKI1	Inner London
UKI2	Outer London
UKJ1	Berkshire, Buckinghamshire and Oxfordshire
UKJ2	Surrey, East and West Sussex
UKJ3	Hampshire and Isle of Wight
UKJ4	Kent
UKK1	Gloucestershire, Wiltshire and Bristol/Bath area
UKK2	Dorset and Somerset
UKK3	Cornwall and Isles of Scilly
UKK4	Devon
UKL1	West Wales and the Valleys
UKL2	East Wales
UKM2	Eastern Scotland
UKM3	South Western Scotland
UKM5	North Eastern Scotland
UKM6	Highlands and Islands
UKN0	Northern Ireland

Candidate countries: statistical regions at level 2

Croatia

HR01	Sjeverozapadna Hrvatska
HR02	Središnja i Istočna (Panonska) Hrvatska
HR03	Jadranska Hrvatska

The former Yugoslav Republic of Macedonia

MK00	Poranešna jugoslovenska Republika Makedonija

Turkey

TR10	İstanbul
TR21	Tekirdağ
TR22	Balıkesir
TR31	İzmir
TR32	Aydın
TR33	Manisa
TR41	Bursa
TR42	Kocaeli
TR51	Ankara
TR52	Konya
TR61	Antalya
TR62	Adana
TR63	Hatay
TR71	Kırıkkale
TR72	Kayseri
TR81	Zonguldak
TR82	Kastamonu
TR83	Samsun
TR90	Trabzon
TRA1	Erzurum
TRA2	Ağrı
TRB1	Malatya
TRB2	Van
TRC1	Gaziantep
TRC2	Şanlıurfa
TRC3	Mardin

EFTA countries: statistical regions at level 2

Iceland

IS00	Ísland

Liechtenstein

LI00	Liechtenstein

Norway

NO01	Oslo og Akershus
NO02	Hedmark og Oppland
NO03	Sør-Østlandet
NO04	Agder og Rogaland
NO05	Vestlandet
NO06	Trøndelag
NO07	Nord-Norge

Switzerland

CH01	Région lémanique
CH02	Espace Mittelland
CH03	Nordwestschweiz
CH04	Zürich
CH05	Ostschweiz
CH06	Zentralschweiz
CH07	Ticino

A full listing of the classification is accessible on the Eurostat website (http://ec.europa.eu/eurostat/ramon/nuts/codelist_en.cfm?list=nuts).

NACE Rev. 1.1 (classification of economic activities in the European Community)

A Agriculture, hunting and forestry
B Fishing
C Mining and quarrying
D Manufacturing
E Electricity, gas and water supply
F Construction
G Wholesale and retail trade; repair of motor vehicles, motorcycles and personal and household goods
H Hotels and restaurants
I Transport, storage and communication
J Financial intermediation
K Real estate, renting and business activities
L Public administration and defence; compulsory social security
M Education
N Health and social work
O Other community, social and personal service activities
P Activities of households
Q Extra-territorial organisations and bodies

A full listing of the NACE Rev. 1.1 classification is accessible on the Eurostat website (http://ec.europa.eu/eurostat/ramon/nomenclatures/index.cfm?TargetUrl=ACT_OTH_BUILD_TREE&StrNom=NACE_1_1&StrLanguageCode=EN).

Note that a revised classification (NACE Rev. 2) is in the process of being implemented and that data based on this classification is being collected from reference year 2008 onwards. Given that the vast majority of the data presented in this publication for economic activities is for years prior to 2008, NACE Rev. 1.1 has been used systematically for all sources.

SITC Rev. 4 (standard international trade classification)

0 Food and live animals
1 Beverages and tobacco
2 Crude materials, inedible, except fuels
3 Mineral fuels, lubricants and related materials
4 Animal and vegetable oils, fats and waxes
5 Chemicals and related products, n.e.s.
6 Manufactured goods classified chiefly by material
7 Machinery and transport equipment
8 Miscellaneous manufactured articles
9 Commodities and transactions not classified elsewhere in the SITC

A full listing of the classification is accessible on the UN website (http://unstats.un.org/unsd/trade/sitcrev4.htm).

ISCED (international standard classification of education)

The classification comprises 25 fields of education (at two-digit level) which can be further refined into three-digit level. For the purpose of this publication only the following nine broad groups (at one-digit level) are distinguished, except for the fields dealt with by the Spotlight chapter (where more information is presented for some two-digit codes in relation to science and to engineering, manufacturing and construction):

0   General programmes
1   Education
2   Humanities and arts
3   Social sciences, business and law
4   Science
    42 Life sciences
    44 Physical sciences
    46 Mathematics and statistics
    48 Computing
5   Engineering, manufacturing and construction
    52 Engineering and engineering trades
6   Agriculture
7   Health and welfare
8   Services

Empirically, ISCED assumes that several criteria exist which can help allocate education programmes to levels of education. The following ISCED levels can be distinguished:

0   Pre-primary education
1   Primary education
2   Lower secondary education
3   Upper secondary education
4   Post-secondary non-tertiary education
5   Tertiary education (first stage)
6   Tertiary education (second stage)

A full listing of the classification and more details are accessible on the UNESCO website (http://www.uis.unesco.org/TEMPLATE/pdf/isced/ISCED_A.pdf).

Statistical symbols, abbreviations and acronyms

Statistical symbols

Statistical data are often accompanied by additional information in form of statistical symbols (also called 'flags') to indicate missing information or some other meta-data. In this yearbook, the use of statistical symbols has been restricted to a minimum. The following symbols are included where necessary:

Italic	Value is either a forecast, provisional or an estimate and is therefore likely to change
:	Not available, confidential or unreliable value
–	Not applicable or zero by default
0	Less than half the final digit shown and greater than real zero

Breaks in series are indicated in the footnotes provided with each table and graph.

In the case of the EU Member States, even when data are not available, these countries have been included in tables and graphs systematically (with appropriate footnotes for graphs indicating that data are not available, while in tables use has been made of the colon (:) to indicate that data are not available). For non-member countries outside of the EU, when data are not available for a particular indicator the country has been removed from the table or graph in question.

Geographical aggregates

EU   European Union

EU-27 [1]   European Union of 27 Member States from 1 January 2007 (BE, BG, CZ, DK, DE, EE, IE, EL, ES, FR, IT, CY, LV, LT, LU, HU, MT, NL, AT, PL, PT, RO, SI, SK, FI, SE, UK)

EU-25   European Union of 25 Member States from 1 May 2004 to 31 December 2006 (BE, CZ, DK, DE, EE, IE, EL, ES, FR, IT, CY, LV, LT, LU, HU, MT, NL, AT, PL, PT, SI, SK, FI, SE, UK)

EU-15   European Union of 15 Member States from 1 January 1995 to 30 April 2004 (BE, DK, DE, IE, EL, ES, FR, IT, LU, NL, AT, PT, FI, SE, UK)

Euro area [2] At the time of writing the euro area is composed of BE, DE, IE, EL, ES, FR, IT, CY, LU, MT, NL, AT, PT, SI, FI. The euro area was initially composed of 11 Member States (BE, DE, IE, ES, FR, IT, LU, NL, AT, PT, FI) – as of 1 January 2001 Greece joined; as of 1 January 2007 Slovenia joined; and as of 1 January 2008 Cyprus and Malta joined

EA-15   Euro area of BE, DE, IE, EL, ES, FR, IT, CY, LU, MT, NL, AT, PT, SI, FI

EA-13   Euro area of BE, DE, IE, EL, ES, FR, IT, LU, NL, AT, PT, SI, FI

EA-12   Euro area of BE, DE, IE, EL, ES, FR, IT, LU, NL, AT, PT, FI

EA-11   Euro area of BE, DE, IE, ES, FR, IT, LU, NL, AT, PT, FI

(1) Note that EU aggregates are back-calculated when sufficient information is available – for example, data relating to the EU-27 aggregate is often presented for periods prior to the accession of Bulgaria and Romania in 2007 and the accession of ten new Member States in 2004, as if all 27 Member States had always been members of the EU. A footnote is added when this is not the case and the data for the EU refers to either another aggregate (EU-25 or EU-15) or to a partial total that has been created from an incomplete set of country information (no data for certain Member States).

(2) Note that the euro area aggregate is back-calculated when sufficient information is available – for example, data relating to the euro area is often presented for periods prior to the accession of Cyprus and Malta in 2008, Slovenia in 2007 or Greece in 2001, as if all 15 Member States had always been members of the euro area. A footnote is added when this is not the case and the data for the euro area refers to another aggregate based on either 11 (EA-11), 12 (EA-12) or 13 (EA-13) participating Member States.

Other abbreviations and acronyms

ACP	African, Caribbean and Pacific countries
BOD	biochemical oxygen demand
BoP	balance of payments
BPM5	fifth balance of payments manual
CAP	common agricultural policy
CBD	convention on biological diversity
CC	classification of types of construction
CFP	common fisheries policy
Cif	cost, insurance and freight
CIP	competitiveness and innovation framework programme
CIS5	fifth Community innovation survey
CMO	common market organisation
CMR	carcinogenic, mutagenic and reprotoxic (chemicals)
COD	1. chemical oxygen demand 2. causes of death
COFOG	classification of the functions of government
COICOP	classification of individual consumption by purpose
CVT	continuing vocational training
DAC	development assistance committee
DFLE	disability-free life expectancy
DMC	domestic material consumption
DSL	digital subscriber line
EAA	economic accounts for agriculture
EAP	environmental action programme
ECB	European Central Bank
ECHO	European Commission's Humanitarian Aid Office
ECHP	European Community household panel
EEA	1. European economic area 2. European Environment Agency
EEAICP	European economic area index of consumer prices
EES	European employment strategy
EFF	European fisheries fund
EFTA	European free trade association
EICP	European index of consumer prices
EITO	European Information Technology Observatory
EMAS	eco-management and audit scheme
EMU	economic and monetary union
EPO	European Patent Office
EPC	European patent convention
ERA	European research area
ERDF	European regional development fund
ERM	exchange rate mechanism
ERTMS	European railway traffic management system
ESA	European system of national and regional accounts (ESA 95)
ESAW	European statistics on accidents at work
ESF	European social fund
Esspros	European system of integrated social protection statistics
ETS	external trade statistics
EU	European Union
EU-SILC	Community statistics on income and living conditions

Eurofarm	a project for standardisation of methods for obtaining agricultural statistics; provides an overview of farm structure, agricultural holdings, wine growing and orchard fruit trees.	ISHMT	international shortlist for hospital morbidity tabulation
		IT	information technology
		JVR	job vacancy rate
		KIS	knowledge-intensive services
		LDCs	least developed countries
		LFS	labour force survey
Eurostat	the statistical office of the European Communities	LLP	lifelong learning programme
		LMP	labour market policy
FAO	Food and Agriculture Organisation (UN)	MUICP	monetary union index of consumer prices
Fob	free on board	NACE	statistical classification of economic activities within the European Community
FDI	foreign direct investment		
FP7	seventh framework programme		
		NAFTA	North American free trade agreement (CA, MX, US)
FSS	farm structure survey		
GATS	General Agreement on Trade in Services	n.e.c.	not elsewhere classified
		n.e.s.	not elsewhere specified
GBAORD	government budget appropriation or outlays on R & D	NGO	non-governmental organisation
		NPISH	non-profit institutions serving households
GDP	gross domestic product		
GERD	gross domestic expenditure on R & D	NUTS	classification/nomenclature of territorial units for statistics (Eurostat) (NUTS 1, 2, etc.)
GHG	greenhouse gas		
GNI	gross national income	ODA	overseas development assistance
GUF	general university funds		
GWP	global warming potential	OECD	Organisation for Economic Cooperation and Development
HBS	household budget survey		
HICP	harmonised index of consumer prices		
		OPEC	Organisation of Petroleum Exporting Countries
HRST	human resources in science and technology		
		PCT	Patent co-operation treaty
ICT	information and communication technology	PECBMS	Pan-European common bird monitoring scheme
ILO	International Labour Organisation	PEEI	principal European economic indicator
IMF	International Monetary Fund	PES	public employment service
IPA	instrument for pre-accession	R & D	research and development
IPC	international patent classification	REACH	(European Regulation on the) registration, evaluation, authorisation and restriction of chemicals
ISCED	international standard classification of education		

RON	research octane number
RPP	regional protection programme
S & T	science and technology
SBS	structural business statistics
SEPAR	single euro payments area
SESAR	single European sky ATM research
SGP	stability and growth pact
SHA	system of health accounts
SII	summary innovation index
SITC	standard international trade classification
SME	small and medium-sized enterprise
SNA	system of national accounts (UN)
STS	short-term (business) statistics
UN	United Nations
UNCAT	United Nations convention against torture and other forms of cruel or inhuman treatment
UNECE	United Nations economic commission for Europe
UNESCO	United Nations educational, scientific and cultural organisation
UNFCCC	United Nations framework convention on climate change
UNHCR	United Nations High Commissioner for refugees
UOE	United Nations/OECD/Eurostat
USPTO	United States patent and trademark office
UWWTP	urban wastewater treatment plant
VAT	value added tax
VET	vocational education and training
WHO	World Health Organisation
WTO	World Trade Organisation

Units of measurement

%	percent(age)
AWU	annual work unit
BMI	body mass index
CHF	Swiss franc
EUR	euro
FTE	full-time equivalent
GT	gross tonnage
GWh	gigawatt-hour
ha	hectare (1 ha = 10 000 square metres)
HC	head count
HLY	healthy life years
JPY	Japanese yen
kbit/s	kilobit per second
kg	kilogram
kgoe	kilogram of oil equivalent
km	kilometre
km²	square kilometre
kW	kilowatt
kWh	kilowatt hour
LSU	livestock unit
m	metre
m³	cubic metre
MWh	megawatt-hour
p-km	passenger-kilometre
PPP	purchasing power parity
PPS	purchasing power standard
SDR	standard death rate
t	tonne
t-km	tonne-kilometre
toe	tonne of oil equivalent
UAA	utilised agricultural area
USD	United States dollar

Subject index

Selection of Eurostat publications

For further reading, Eurostat offers various types of publications on a wide range of statistical topics. Below you find some references to some of the most recent Eurostat publications. All publications are made available in PDF format and can be downloaded free of charge from the Eurostat website at http://ec.europa.eu/eurostat. Paper copies of publications can be ordered via the EU Bookshop at http://bookshop.europa.eu. Both websites allow searches to be made using the catalogue number (e.g.: KS-HA-08-001-EN-C) and offer guidance on how paper copies can be ordered.

Statistical books

This collection contains publications which provide in-depth analysis, tables, graphs or maps for one or more statistical domains.

European Economic Statistics

The publication covers key economic indicators available within Eurostat, including: national accounts, government finances, balance of payments, foreign trade, prices, monetary and financial accounts, and the labour market. In addition, editorial and methodological sections provide commentary on topical issues and on the data presented.

Available language: English

KS-30-08-410-EN-C;
paper version: EUR 20

Eurostat regional yearbook 2008

The Eurostat regional yearbook 2008 offers a wealth of information on life across European regions. A broad set of regional data are presented on the following themes: population, urban statistics, gross domestic product, household accounts, structural business statistics, the labour market, sectoral productivity, labour costs, transport, tourism, science, technology and innovation, health and agriculture.

Available languages: German, English, French

KS-HA-08-001-EN-C;
paper version: EUR 30

European business

This publication gives a comprehensive picture of the structure, development and characteristics of European business and its different activities: from energy and the extractive industries to communications, information services and media. It describes for each activity: production and employment; country specialisation and regional distribution; productivity and profitability; the importance of small and medium-sized enterprises (SMEs); employment characteristics; external trade, etc.

Available language: English

KS-BW-07-001-EN-C; paper version: EUR 25

Measuring progress towards a more sustainable Europe

The EU's sustainable development strategy, launched in 2001 and renewed in June 2006, aims for the continuous improvement with respect to the quality of life for current and future generations. Eurostat's monitoring report, to be published every two years, underpins the European Commission's progress report on the implementation of this strategy. It provides an objective, statistical picture of progress, based on an EU set of sustainable development indicators.

Available language: English

KS-77-07-115-EN-C; paper version: EUR 35

Pocketbooks and brochures

Pocketbooks aim to give users a set of basic figures on a specific topic. Available in both PDF and paper versions, all pocketbooks are free of charge. Brochures are also analytical publications that are published in a slightly bigger A5 format; they are available only in English.

Key figures on Europe	*Living conditions in Europe*	*Food: from farm to fork statistics*	*Tourism statistics*	*EU foreign direct investment*	*Agricultural statistics*	*Key figures on European business*

KS-EI-08-001-EN-C	KS-DZ-08-001-EN-C	KS-30-08-339-EN-C	KS-DS-08-001-EN-C	KS-BK-08-001-EN-C	KS-ED-08-001-EN-C	KS-ET-08-001-EN-C

Candidate countries	*Science, technology and innovation*	*Energy, transport and environment*	*EU economic data*	*Statistical portrait 2008: European Year of Intercultural dialogue*	*European Price Statistics*	*Regions of the European Union*

KS-PF-08-001-EN-C	KS-30-08-148-EN-C	KS-DK-07-001-EN-C	KS-CZ-08-002-EN-C	KS-EP-07-001-EN-C	KS-70-07-038-EN-C	KS-EP-08-001-EN-C

News-oriented publications

Three collections are dedicated to the rapid release of key data: news releases, Statistics in focus and Data in focus. They are web-based publications that are freely available on the Eurostat website.

Methodologies and working papers

Statistical manuals, classifications or nomenclatures are published under the collection 'Methodologies and working papers'. Intended for specialists, these publications are also only released through the Internet, they are freely on the Eurostat website.

More information on Eurostat publications may be found at: http://epp.eurostat.ec.europa.eu/portal/page/portal/publications/collections.

European Commission

Europe in figures – Eurostat yearbook 2009

Luxembourg: Office for Official Publications of the European Communities

2009 — 560 pp. — 17.6 x 25 cm

ISBN 978-92-79-11625-4
ISSN 1681-4789

Price (excluding VAT) in Luxembourg: EUR 30

How to obtain EU publications

Publications for sale:

- via EU Bookshop (http://bookshop.europa.eu);
- from your bookseller by quoting the title, publisher and/or ISBN number;
- by contacting one of our sales agents directly. You can obtain their contact details on the Internet (http://bookshop.europa.eu) or by sending a fax to +352 2929-42758.

Free publications:

- via EU Bookshop (http://bookshop.europa.eu);
- at the European Commission's representations or delegations. You can obtain their contact details on the Internet (http://ec.europa.eu) or by sending a fax to +352 2929-42758.